DERIVATIVES MARKETS

Derivatives Markets is a thorough and well-presented textbook that offers readers an introduction to derivatives instruments, with a gentle introduction to mathematical finance, and provides a working knowledge of derivatives to a wide spectrum of market participants.

This new and accessible book provides a lucid, down-to-earth, theoretically rigorous but applied introduction to derivatives. Many insights have been discovered since the seminal work in the 1970s and the text provides a bridge to these insights, and incorporates them. It develops the skill sets needed to both understand and intelligently use derivatives. These skill sets are developed, in part, by using concept checks that test the reader's understanding of the material as it is presented.

The text discusses some fairly sophisticated topics not usually discussed in introductory derivatives texts; for example, real-world electronic market trading platforms such as CME's Globex. On the theory side, there is a much-needed and detailed discussion of what risk-neutral valuation really means in the context of the dynamics of the hedge portfolio.

The text is a balanced, logical presentation of the major derivatives classes including forward and futures contracts in Part 1, swaps in Part 2, and options in Part 3. The material is unified by providing a modern conceptual framework and exploiting the no-arbitrage relationships between the different derivatives classes.

Some of the elements explained in detail in the text are:

- Hedging, Basis Risk, Spreading, and Spread Basis Risk.
- Financial Futures Contracts, their Underlying Instruments, Hedging and Speculating.
- OTC Markets and Swaps.
- Option Strategies: Hedging and Speculating.
- Risk-Neutral Valuation and the Binomial Option Pricing Model.
- Equivalent Martingale Measures: A Modern Approach to Option Pricing.
- Option Pricing in Continuous Time: From Bachelier to Black–Scholes and Beyond.

Professor Goldenberg's clear and concise explanations, running concept checks, and end-of-chapter problems guide the reader through the derivatives markets, developing the reader's skill sets needed in order to incorporate and manage derivatives in a corporate or risk management setting. This textbook is for students, both undergraduate and postgraduate, as well as for those with an interest in how and why these markets work and thrive.

David H. Goldenberg is an independent researcher in New York, USA.

DERIVATIVES MARKETS

David H. Goldenberg

LONDON AND NEW YORK

First published 2016
by Routledge
2 Park Square, Milton Park, Abingdon, Oxon OX14 4RN

by Routledge
711 Third Avenue, New York, NY 10017

Routledge is an imprint of the Taylor & Francis Group, an informa business

© 2016 David H. Goldenberg

The right of David H. Goldenberg to be identified as author of this work has been asserted by him in accordance with the Copyright, Designs and Patent Act 1988.

All rights reserved. No part of this book may be reprinted or reproduced or utilised in any form or by any electronic, mechanical, or other means, now known or hereafter invented, including photocopying and recording, or in any information storage or retrieval system, without permission in writing from the publishers.

Every effort has been made to contact copyright holders for their permission to reprint material in this book. The publishers would be grateful to hear from any copyright holder who is not here acknowledged and will undertake to rectify any errors or omissions in future editions of this book.

Trademark notice: Product or corporate names may be trademarks or registered trademarks, and are used only for identification and explanation without intent to infringe.

British Library Cataloguing in Publication Data
A catalogue record for this book is available from the British Library

Library of Congress Cataloging in Publication Data
Goldenberg, David Harold, 1949–
 Derivatives markets / David H. Goldenberg.
 1. Derivative securities. I. Title.
 HG6024.A3G645 2015
 332.64′57—dc23
 2015000492

ISBN: 978-0-415-59901-6 (hbk)
ISBN: 978-1-315-68924–1 (ebk)

Typeset in Bembo and Univers
by Florence Production Ltd, Stoodleigh, Devon, UK
Printed and bound in Great Britain by
Ashford Colour Press Ltd, Gosport, Hampshire

CONTENTS

List of figures	xxiii
List of tables	xxvii
Preface	xxxi
Acknowledgments	xxxvii

PART 1
Forward Contracts and Futures Contracts   1

1.	**SPOT, FORWARD, AND FUTURES CONTRACTING**	**3**
2.	**HEDGING WITH FORWARD CONTRACTS**	**33**
3.	**VALUATION OF FORWARD CONTRACTS ON ASSETS WITHOUT A DIVIDEND YIELD**	**65**
4.	**VALUATION OF FORWARD CONTRACTS ON ASSETS WITH A DIVIDEND YIELD**	**87**
5.	**FUTURES CONTRACTS: MARKET ORGANIZATION**	**121**
6.	**HEDGING WITH FUTURES CONTRACTS, BASIS RISK, AND SPREADING**	**139**
7.	**INTRODUCTION TO FINANCIAL FUTURES CONTRACTS**	**211**

PART 2
Trading Structures Based on Forward Contracts   271

8.	**STRUCTURED PRODUCTS, INTEREST-RATE SWAPS**	**273**

PART 3
Options 321

9. INTRODUCTION TO OPTIONS MARKETS 323

10. OPTION TRADING STRATEGIES, PART 1 345

11. RATIONAL OPTION PRICING 369

12. OPTION TRADING STRATEGIES, PART 2 415

13. MODEL-BASED OPTION PRICING IN DISCRETE TIME, PART 1: THE BINOMIAL OPTION PRICING MODEL (BOPM, N=1) 435

14. OPTION PRICING IN DISCRETE TIME, PART 2: DYNAMIC HEDGING AND THE MULTI-PERIOD BINOMIAL OPTION PRICING MODEL, N>1 473

15. EQUIVALENT MARTINGALE MEASURES: A MODERN APPROACH TO OPTION PRICING 507

16. OPTION PRICING IN CONTINUOUS TIME 539

17. RISK-NEUTRAL VALUATION, EMMS, THE BOPM, AND BLACK–SCHOLES 595

Index 637

DETAILED CONTENTS

List of figures	xxiii
List of tables	xxvii
Preface	xxxi
Acknowledgments	xxxvii

PART 1
Forward Contracts and Futures Contracts 1

CHAPTER 1   SPOT, FORWARD, AND FUTURES CONTRACTING 3

1.1	Three Ways to Buy and Sell Commodities	5
1.2	Spot Market Contracting (Motivation and Examples)	5
1.3	Forward Market Contracting (Motivation and Examples)	7
1.4	Problems with Forward Markets	11
1.5	Futures Contracts as a Solution to Forward Market Problems (Motivation and Examples)	13
1.6	Futures Market Contracting	17
1.7	Mapping Out Spot, Forward, and Futures Prices	20
	1.7.1 Present and Future Spot Prices	20
	1.7.2 Forward Prices	24
	1.7.3 Futures Prices	25

CHAPTER 2   HEDGING WITH FORWARD CONTRACTS 33

2.1	Motivation for Hedging	33
2.2	Payoff to a Long Forward Position	37
2.3	Payoff to a Short Forward Position	39

viii DETAILED CONTENTS

2.4	Hedging with Forward Contracts	43
2.5	Profits to a Naked (Unhedged) Long Spot Position	45
2.6	Profits to a Fully Hedged Current Long Spot Position	47
2.7	Adding Profit Tables to Determine Profits from a Fully Hedged Position	50
2.8	Combining Charts to See Profits from the Hedged Position	54

CHAPTER 3   VALUATION OF FORWARD CONTRACTS ON ASSETS WITHOUT A DIVIDEND YIELD   **65**

3.1	Comparing the Payoffs from a Naked Long Spot Position to the Payoffs from a Naked Long Forward Position	66
3.2	Pricing Zero-Coupon, Unit Discount Bonds in Continuous Time	69
	3.2.1 Continuous Compounding and Continuous Discounting	69
	3.2.2 Pricing Zero-Coupon Bonds	71
3.3	Price vs. Value for Forward Contracts	73
3.4	Valuing a Forward Contract at Expiration	74
3.5	Valuing a Forward Contract at Initiation	75
3.6	Interpreting Forward Contracts via Synthetic Forward Contracts	78

CHAPTER 4   VALUATION OF FORWARD CONTRACTS ON ASSETS WITH A DIVIDEND YIELD   **87**

4.1	Stock Forwards when the Stock Pays Dividends	88
4.2	Modeling Continuous Yields: An Introduction to Non-Stochastic Differential Equations	90
	4.2.1 Modeling Zero-Coupon Bond Yields	90
	4.2.2 Modeling Continuous Dividend Yields for Stocks	93

DETAILED CONTENTS ix

4.3	How Dividend Payments Affect Stock Prices	94
4.4	How Capital Gains Affect Stock Prices	98
4.5	Pricing Forward Contracts on Stocks with a Dividend Yield Using the Net Interest Model	99
4.6	Pricing a Forward Contract on a Dividend-Paying Stock Using No-Arbitrage	100
4.6.1	Arbitrage Definitions	100
4.6.2	Forward Pricing Using No-Arbitrage	102
4.7	Currency Spot and Currency Forwards	103
4.7.1	Price Quotes in the FX Market	103
4.7.2	Pricing Currency Forwards	105
4.7.3	Pricing FX Forward Contracts Using No-Arbitrage	106
4.7.4	An Example of Pricing FX Forward Contracts	107
4.8	Appendix: Modeling Stock Returns with and without Dividends	109

CHAPTER 5 FUTURES CONTRACTS: MARKET ORGANIZATION 121

5.1	Futures Market Participants	122
5.2	Three Phases of Futures Trading	125
5.3	'Buying' and 'Selling' Futures Contracts	126
5.4	Alternative Types of Orders: Market, Market with Protection, Limit	127
5.4.1	Market Orders and Market Orders with Protection	127
5.4.2	Limit Orders	129
5.4.3	The Limit Order Book (LOB)	130
5.4.4	Depth in the LOB	131
5.5	Globex and the Globex LOB	134
5.6	Pit Trading and the Order Flow Process	136

X DETAILED CONTENTS

5.7	Operations and Functions of the Clearing House	139
	5.7.1 Matching Trades and Guaranteeing Futures Obligations	139
	5.7.2 The Clearing Process and Offsetting Futures Trades	141
	5.7.3 Marking to Market and the Daily Settlement Process	144
	5.7.4 Tracking the Equity in an Investor's Account	151
5.8	The Effective Price and the Invoice Price upon Delivery	153
	5.8.1 Offset vs. Delivery	155
5.9	Cash Settlement vs. Commodity Settlement	157

CHAPTER 6 **HEDGING WITH FUTURES CONTRACTS, BASIS RISK, AND SPREADING** **163**

6.1	Hedging as Portfolio Theory	165
	6.1.1 Hedging as Synthesizing Negative Correlation	165
	6.1.2 Hedging's Objective	167
	6.1.3 Hedging Definitions	168
6.2	Traditional Theories of Hedging	168
	6.2.1 Traditional (One-for-One) Theory with No Basis Risk	168
	6.2.2 Profits in a Traditional Short Hedge and the Basis	171
	6.2.3 When is a Traditional (One-for-One) Hedge with No Basis Risk Consistent with No-Arbitrage?	172
	6.2.4 Traditional (One-for-One) Theory with Basis Risk	174
6.3	Basis Risk vs. Spot Price Risk	178
	6.3.1 When Does Traditional Hedging Reduce Risk?	179
6.4	Non-Traditional (λ-for-One) Hedging Theory	182

DETAILED CONTENTS xi

	6.4.1 When Does λ-for-One Hedging Reduce Risk?	183
	6.4.2 Minimum Variance Hedging	185
6.5	Carrying Charge Hedging	188
	6.5.1 Implications of Convergence	189
	6.5.2 Overall Profits in a Carrying Charge Hedge	189
	6.5.3 Equilibrium (No-Arbitrage) in a Full Carrying Charge Market	190
6.6	Comparing Equilibrium Forward Pricing and Equilibrium Futures Pricing	193
6.7	Storage and the Price (Cost) of Storage	195
6.8	Contango and Backwardation	198
6.9	Spreads as a Speculative Investment	199

CHAPTER 7 INTRODUCTION TO FINANCIAL FUTURES CONTRACTS 211

7.1	Currency Futures	213
	7.1.1 Contract Specifications	213
	7.1.2 The Quote Mechanism: Futures Price Quotes	216
7.2	Risk Management Strategies Using Currency Futures	217
	7.2.1 Exchange Rate Risks and Currency Futures Positions	217
	7.2.2 The Rolling Hedge Strategy	220
	7.2.3 Interpretations of Profits from the Rolling Hedge	221
	7.2.4 Numerical Example of the Roll-Over Hedge Strategy	223
7.3	Hedging	224
	7.3.1 Issues in Hedging, Quantity Uncertainty	224
	7.3.2 Currency Futures Pricing vs. Currency Forward Pricing	225

DETAILED CONTENTS

7.4 Stock Index Futures 225

    7.4.1 The S&P 500 Spot Index 225

    7.4.2 S&P 500 Stock Index Futures Contract Specifications 227

    7.4.3 The Quote Mechanism for S&P 500 Futures Price Quotes 230

7.5 Risk Management Using Stock Index Futures 231

    7.5.1 Pricing and Hedging Preliminaries 231

    7.5.2 Monetizing the S&P 500 Spot Index 231

    7.5.3 Profits from the Traditional Hedge 235

    7.5.4 Risk, Return Analysis of the Traditional Hedge 236

    7.5.5 Risk-Minimizing Hedging 238

    7.5.6 Adjusting the Naive Hedge Ratio to Obtain the Risk-Minimizing Hedge Ratio 239

    7.5.7 Risk Minimizing the Hedge Using Forward vs. Futures Contracts 241

    7.5.8 Cross-Hedging, Adjusting the Hedge for non S&P 500 Portfolios 243

7.6 The Spot Eurodollar Market 245

    7.6.1 Spot 3-month Eurodollar Time Deposits 246

    7.6.2 Spot Eurodollar Market Trading Terminology 248

    7.6.3 $LIBOR_3$, $LIBID_3$, and Fed Funds 250

    7.6.4 How Eurodollar Time Deposits are Created 252

7.7 Eurodollar Futures 254

    7.7.1 Contract Specifications 254

    7.7.2 The Quote Mechanism, Eurodollar Futures 256

    7.7.3 Forced Convergence and Cash Settlement 258

    7.7.4 How Profits and Losses are Calculated on Open ED Futures Positions 262

DETAILED CONTENTS xiii

PART 2
Trading Structures Based on Forward Contracts 271

CHAPTER 8 STRUCTURED PRODUCTS, INTEREST-RATE SWAPS 273

8.1 Swaps as Strips of Forward Contracts 274

8.1.1 Commodity Forward Contracts as Single Period Swaps 275

8.1.2 Strips of Forward Contracts 277

8.2 Basic Terminology for Interest-Rate Swaps: Paying Fixed and Receiving Floating 278

8.2.1 Paying Fixed in an IRD (Making Fixed Payments) 278

8.2.2 Receiving Variable in an IRD (Receiving Floating Payments) 279

8.2.3 Eurodollar Futures Strips 280

8.3 Non-Dealer Intermediated Plain Vanilla Interest-Rate Swaps 281

8.4 Dealer Intermediated Plain Vanilla Interest-Rate Swaps 284

8.4.1 An Example 284

8.4.2 Plain Vanilla Interest-Rate Swaps as Hedge Vehicles 286

8.4.3 Arbitraging the Swaps Market 292

8.5 Swaps: More Terminology and Examples 293

8.6 The Dealer's Problem: Finding the Other Side to the Swap 294

8.7 Are Swaps a Zero Sum Game? 298

8.8 Why Financial Institutions Use Swaps 299

8.9 Swaps Pricing 301

8.9.1 An Example 301

DETAILED CONTENTS

8.9.2	Valuation of the Fixed-Rate Bond	303
8.9.3	Valuation of the Floating-Rate Bond	305
8.9.4	Valuation of the Swap at Initiation	308
8.9.5	Implied Forward Rates (IFRs)	309
8.9.6	Three Interpretations of the Par Swap Rate	311

PART 3
Options

321

CHAPTER 9   INTRODUCTION TO OPTIONS MARKETS

323

9.1	Options and Option Scenarios	323
9.2	A Framework for Learning Options	326
9.3	Definitions and Terminology for Plain Vanilla Put and Call Options	327
9.4	A Basic American Call (Put) Option Pricing Model	332
9.5	Reading Option Price Quotes	334
9.6	Going Beyond the Basic Definitions: Infrastructure to Understand Puts and Calls	337
9.7	Identifying Long and Short Positions in an Underlying	339

CHAPTER 10   OPTION TRADING STRATEGIES, PART 1

345

10.1	Profit Diagrams	346
10.2	Eight Basic (Naked) Strategies Using the Underlying, European Puts and Calls, and Riskless, Zero-Coupon Bonds	347
10.2.1	Strategy 1. Long the Underlying	347
10.2.2	Strategy 2. Short the Underlying	349
10.2.3	Strategy 3. Long a European Call Option on the Underlying	351

DETAILED CONTENTS   XV

10.2.4 Strategy 4. Short a European Call Option on the Underlying   355

10.2.5 Strategy 5. Long a European Put Option on the Underlying   357

10.2.6 Strategy 6. Short a European Put Option on the Underlying   359

10.2.7 Strategy 7. Long a Zero-Coupon Riskless Bond and Hold it to Maturity   360

10.2.8 Strategy 8. Short a Zero-Coupon Riskless Bond and Hold it to Maturity   362

CHAPTER 11 RATIONAL OPTION PRICING   369

11.1 Model-Independent vs. Model-Based Option Pricing   370

11.2 Relative Pricing Trades vs. Directional Trades   371

11.3 The Dominance Principle   373

11.4 Implications of the Dominance Principle, ROP for Puts and Calls   374

11.4.1 Lower Bound for an American Call Option on an Underlying with no Dividends (LBAC)   374

11.4.2 Lower Bound for a European Call Option on an Underlying with no Dividends (LBEC)   375

11.4.3 Lower Bound for an American Put Option on an Underlying with no Dividends (LBAP)   378

11.4.4 Lower Bound for a European Put Option on an Underlying with no Dividends (LBEP)   380

11.4.5 Lower Bound for a European Call Option on an Underlying with Continuous Dividends (LBECD)   382

11.4.6 Lower Bound for an American Call Option on an Underlying with Continuous Dividends (LBACD)   383

11.4.7 Lower Bound for a European Put Option on an Underlying with Continuous Dividends (LBEPD)   386

xvi DETAILED CONTENTS

	11.4.8	Lower Bound for an American Put Option on an Underlying with Continuous Dividends (LBAPD)	387
11.5	Static Replication and European Put-Call Parity (No Dividends)	388
	11.5.1	Partially Replicating a European Call Option (the Embedded Forward Contract)	388
	11.5.2	Fully Replicating a European Call Option (the Embedded Insurance Contract)	391
	11.5.3	From Strategies to Current Costs and Back	393
	11.5.4	Working Backwards from Payoffs to Costs to Derive European Put-Call Parity	393
11.6	Basic Implications of European Put-Call Parity	394
	11.6.1	What is a European Call Option?	394
	11.6.2	The Analogue of the Basic American Option Pricing Model for European Options	396
	11.6.3	What is a European Put Option?	398
11.7	Further Implications of European Put-Call Parity	399
	11.7.1	Synthesizing Forward Contract from Puts and Calls	399
11.8	Financial Innovation using European Put-Call Parity	401
	11.8.1	Generalized Forward Contracts	401
	11.8.2	American Put-Call Parity (No Dividends)	403
11.9	Postscript on ROP	405

CHAPTER 12   OPTION TRADING STRATEGIES, PART 2   **415**

12.1	Generating Synthetic Option Strategies from European Put-Call Parity	416
12.2	The Covered Call Hedging Strategy	419
	12.2.1	Three Types Of Covered Call Writes	420

DETAILED CONTENTS xvii

12.2.2 Economic Interpretation of the Covered Call Strategy — 426

12.3 The Protective Put Hedging Strategy — 427

12.3.1 Puts as Insurance — 427

12.3.2 Economic Interpretation of the Protective Put Strategy — 429

CHAPTER 13 MODEL-BASED OPTION PRICING IN DISCRETE TIME, PART 1: THE BINOMIAL OPTION PRICING MODEL (BOPM, N=1) — 435

13.1 The Objective of Model-Based Option Pricing (MBOP) — 437

13.2 The Binomial Option Pricing Model, Basics — 437

13.2.1 Modeling Time in a Discrete Time Framework — 437

13.2.2 Modeling the Underlying Stock Price Uncertainty — 438

13.3 The Binomial Option Pricing Model, Advanced — 440

13.3.1 Path Structure of the Binomial Process, Total Number of Price Paths — 440

13.3.2 Path Structure of the Binomial Process, Total Number of Price Paths Ending at a Specific Terminal Price — 442

13.3.3 Summary of Stock Price Evolution for the N-Period Binomial Process — 444

13.4 Option Valuation for the BOPM (N=1) — 445

13.4.1 Step 1, Pricing the Option at Expiration — 445

13.4.2 Step 2, Pricing the Option Currently (time t=0) — 446

13.5 Modern Tools for Pricing Options — 448

13.5.1 Tool 1, The Principle of No-Arbitrage — 448

13.5.2 Tool 2, Complete Markets or Replicability, and a Rule of Thumb — 449

13.5.3 Tool 3, Dynamic and Static Replication — 450

xviii DETAILED CONTENTS

13.5.4	Relationships between the Three Tools	450
13.6	Synthesizing a European Call Option	453
13.6.1	Step 1, Parameterization	454
13.6.2	Step 2, Defining the Hedge Ratio and the Dollar Bond Position	455
13.6.3	Step 3, Constructing the Replicating Portfolio	456
13.6.4	Step 4, Implications of Replication	462
13.7	Alternative Option Pricing Techniques	464
13.8	Appendix: Derivation of the BOPM ($N=1$) as a Risk-Neutral Valuation Relationship	467

CHAPTER 14   OPTION PRICING IN DISCRETE TIME, PART 2: DYNAMIC HEDGING AND THE MULTI-PERIOD BINOMIAL OPTION PRICING MODEL, $N>1$ **473**

14.1	Modeling Time and Uncertainty in the BOPM, $N>1$	475
14.1.1	Stock Price Behavior, $N=2$	475
14.1.2	Option Price Behavior, $N=2$	476
14.2	Hedging a European Call Option, $N=2$	477
14.2.1	Step 1, Parameterization	477
14.2.2	Step 2, Defining the Hedge Ratio and the Dollar Bond Position	478
14.2.3	Step 3, Constructing the Replicating Portfolio	478
14.2.4	The Complete Hedging Program for the BOPM, $N=2$	484
14.3	Implementation of the BOPM for $N=2$	485
14.4	The BOPM, $N>1$ as a RNVR Formula	490
14.5	Multi-period BOPM, $N>1$: A Path Integral Approach	493

DETAILED CONTENTS xix

14.5.1 Thinking of the BOPM in Terms of Paths 493

14.5.2 Proof of the BOPM Model for general N 499

CHAPTER 15 EQUIVALENT MARTINGALE MEASURES: A MODERN APPROACH TO OPTION PRICING 507

15.1 Primitive Arrow–Debreu Securities and Option Pricing 508

15.1.1 Exercise 1, Pricing $B(0,1)$ 510

15.1.2 Exercise 2, Pricing $AD_u(\omega)$ and $AD_d(\omega)$ 511

15.2 Contingent Claim Pricing 514

15.2.1 Pricing a European Call Option 514

15.2.2 Pricing any Contingent Claim 515

15.3 Equivalent Martingale Measures (EMMs) 517

15.3.1 Introduction and Examples 517

15.3.2 Definition of a Discrete-Time Martingale 521

15.4 Martingales and Stock Prices 521

15.4.1 The Equivalent Martingale Representation of Stock Prices 524

15.5 The Equivalent Martingale Representation of Option Prices 526

15.5.1 Discounted Option Prices 527

15.5.2 Summary of the EMM Approach 528

15.6 The Efficient Market Hypothesis (EMH), A Guide To Modeling Prices 529

15.7 Appendix: Essential Martingale Properties 533

CHAPTER 16 OPTION PRICING IN CONTINUOUS TIME 539

16.1 Arithmetic Brownian Motion (ABM) 540

16.2 Shifted Arithmetic Brownian Motion 541

16.3 Pricing European Options under Shifted Arithmetic Brownian Motion with No Drift (Bachelier) 542

DETAILED CONTENTS

16.3.1 Theory (FTAP$_1$ and FTAP$_2$)	542
16.3.2 Transition Density Functions	543
16.3.3 Deriving the Bachelier Option Pricing Formula	547
16.4 Defining and Pricing a Standard Numeraire	551
16.5 Geometric Brownian Motion (GBM)	553
16.5.1 GBM (Discrete Version)	553
16.5.2 Geometric Brownian Motion (GBM), Continuous Version	559
16.6 Itô's Lemma	562
16.7 Black–Scholes Option Pricing	566
16.7.1 Reducing GBM to an ABM with Drift	567
16.7.2 Preliminaries on Generating Unknown Risk-Neutral Transition Density Functions from Known Ones	570
16.7.3 Black–Scholes Options Pricing from Bachelier	571
16.7.4 Volatility Estimation in the Black–Scholes Model	582
16.8 Non-Constant Volatility Models	585
16.8.1 Empirical Features of Volatility	585
16.8.2 Economic Reasons for why Volatility is not Constant, the Leverage Effect	586
16.8.3 Modeling Changing Volatility, the Deterministic Volatility Model	586
16.8.4 Modeling Changing Volatility, Stochastic Volatility Models	587
16.9 Why Black–Scholes is Still Important	588

CHAPTER 17 RISK-NEUTRAL VALUATION, EMMS, THE BOPM, AND BLACK–SCHOLES — **595**

17.1 Introduction	596
17.1.1 Preliminaries on FTAP$_1$ and FTAP$_2$ and Navigating the Terminology	596

DETAILED CONTENTS xxi

17.1.2 Pricing by Arbitrage and the $FTAP_2$ 597

17.1.3 Risk-Neutral Valuation without Consensus and with Consensus 598

17.1.4 Risk-Neutral Valuation without Consensus, Pricing Contingent Claims with Unhedgeable Risks 599

17.1.5 Black–Scholes' Contribution 601

17.2 Formal Risk-Neutral Valuation without Replication 601

17.2.1 Constructing EMMs 601

17.2.2 Interpreting Formal Risk-Neutral Probabilities 602

17.3 MPRs and EMMs, Another Version of $FTAP_2$ 605

17.4 Complete Risk-Expected Return Analysis of the Riskless Hedge in the (BOPM, $N=1$) 607

17.4.1 Volatility of the Hedge Portfolio 608

17.4.2 Direct Calculation of σ_S 611

17.4.3 Direct Calculation of σ_C 612

17.4.4 Expected Return of the Hedge Portfolio 616

17.5 Analysis of the Relative Risks of the Hedge Portfolio's Return 618

17.5.1 An Initial Look at Risk Neutrality in the Hedge Portfolio 618

17.5.2 Role of the Risk Premia for a Risk-Averse Investor in the Hedge Portfolio 620

17.6 Option Valuation 624

17.6.1 Some Manipulations 624

17.6.2 Option Valuation Done Directly by a Risk-Averse Investor 626

17.6.3 Option Valuation for the Risk-Neutral Investor 631

Index 637

FIGURES

1.1	Canada/US Foreign Exchange Rate	4
1.2	Intermediation by the Clearing House	15
1.3	Offsetting Trades	15
1.4	Gold Fixing Price in London Bullion Market (USD$)	22
2.1	Graphical Method to Get Hedged Position Profits	55
2.2	Payoff Per Share to a Long Forward Contract	62
2.3	Payoff Per Share to a Short Forward Contract	62
2.4	Profits per bu. for the Unhedged Position	63
3.1	Profits Per Share to a Naked Long Spot Position	67
3.2	Payoffs Per Share to a Naked Long Spot Position	67
3.3	Payoffs (=Profits) Per Share to a Naked Long Forward Position	68
3.4	Payoffs Per Share to a Naked Long Spot Position and to a Naked Long Forward Position	68
5.1	Order Flow Process (Pit Trading)	137
5.2	The Futures Clearing House	142
5.3	Offsetting Trades	143
5.4	Overall Profits for Example 2	150
6.1	Long vs. Short Positions	164
6.2	Synthetic Treasury Bill vs. Actual	165
6.3	Perfectly Negatively Correlated Asset Returns	166
6.4	Synthesizing a Treasury Bill	166
7.1	The Rolling Hedge Bases (4 Periods)	221
7.2	The Rolling Hedge Bases (3 Periods)	223
7.3	Hedging a Cross Hedge	244
7.4	Currency Composition of Foreign Exchange Reserves (Pie Chart)	247
7.5	Currency Composition of Foreign Exchange Reserves (Graph)	248
7.6	$LIBOR_3$ vs. Fed Funds	251
7.7	Eurodollar Deposit Creation	253
7.8	Timing in Eurodollar Futures	257
7.9	Forced Convergence of ED Futures	260

8.1	Paying Fixed, Receiving Floating in a Commodity Forward Contract	276
8.2	Long's Position in a Strip of Forward Contracts	277
8.3	Cash Flows to the Short in an ED Futures Strip	281
8.4	Cash Flows in a Non-Intermediated Swap	282
8.5	Cash Flows to Alfa in the Non-Intermediated Swap	284
8.6	The Bid Side in a Dealer-Intermediated Swap with BBB	285
8.7	The Asked Side in a Dealer-Intermediated Swap with BBB	286
8.8	Synthetic Fixed-Rate Strategy for BBB	290
8.9	Bid Side in a Dealer-Intermediated Swap with AA	295
8.10	Asked Side in a Dealer-Intermediated Swap with AA	295
8.11	Synthetic Floating-Rate Financing for AA	297
8.12	Full Set of Swap Cash Flows for BBB, AA, and the Dealer	298
8.13	Cash Flows for an Annual Rate Swap from the Dealer's Point of View	302
8.14	Decomposing a Swap's Cash Flows into its Implicit Bonds	303
8.15	The Implicit Fixed-Rate Bond in a Swap, Written in Terms of Zero-Coupon Bonds	304
8.16	The Floating-Rate Bond Implicit in the Swap	306
8.17	Floating-Rate Payments as Expected Cash Flows	306
8.18	Valuing the Floating-Rate Bond One Period Prior to Maturity	306
8.19	Valuing the Floating-Rate Bond Two Periods Prior to Maturity	307
8.20	Complete Valuation of the Implicit Floating-Rate Bond in an Interest-Rate Swap	308
8.21	The Two Strategies that Generate Implied Forward Rates	309
8.22	The First Interpretation of the Par Swap Rate in Terms of Implied Forward Rates	311
9.1	Moneyness of a Call (Put) Option	329
9.2	The Options Clearing House (Calls)	331
9.3	The Options Clearing House (Puts)	332
9.4	Long vs. Short Positions	340
9.5	CBOE Equity Option Specifications	343
9.6	CBOE Mini Equity Option Specifications	344
10.1	Merck Stock Price (11/30/2007 through 2/29/2008)	346
10.2	Strategy 1: Profits from a Long Position in an Underlying	348
10.3	Strategy 2: Profits from a Short Position in an Underlying	350
10.4	Strategy 3: Profits from a Long Position in a European Call Option on an Underlying	352

10.5	Strategy 4: Profits from a Short Position in a European Call Option on an Underlying	356
10.6	Strategy 5: Profits from a Long Position in a European Put Option on an Underlying	358
10.7	Strategy 6: Profits from a Short Position in a European Put Option on an Underlying	360
10.8	Strategy 7: Profits from Longing the Risk-Free Bond	361
10.9	Strategy 8: Profits from Shorting the Risk-Free Bond	362
11.1	Optimal Early Exercise for an American Put Option (No Underlying Dividends) Along the Early Exercise Boundary	379
11.2	Payoffs to a Long Position in a European Call Option on an Underlying Stock	389
11.3	Payoffs to a Long Position in a European Put Option on an Underlying Stock	392
11.4	European Call Option Price, $C^E(S_t,\tau,E)$, for a Given Maturity $\tau=T-t$	406
12.1	An In-the-Money Covered Call Write	423
12.2	An Out-of-the-Money Covered Call Write	425
12.3	Out-of-the-Money Protective Put Profits (E_1=$40, $P_{t,1}$=$1, S_t=$45)	428
12.3	(PP-Out) Excel Chart for Out-of-the-Money Protective Put Profits (E_1=$40, $P_{t,1}$=$1, S_t=$45)	432
13.1	Modeling Time in the Binomial Model	438
13.2	Stock Price Uncertainty in the BOPM, any N	439
13.3	The Binomial Process (N=1), Example	439
13.4	Stock Price Evolution for the Binomial Process, (N=2)	440
13.5	Stock Price Evolution, Total Number of Price Paths, BOPM, N=3	441
13.6	Stock Price Evolution, Total Number of Price Paths Ending at a Specific Price, BOPM, N=3	443
13.7	Summary of Stock Price Evolution (N-Period BOPM)	445
13.8	European Call Option Valuation at Expiration (E=100)	446
13.9	The Binomial Process N=1 (E=100)	448
13.10	Option Price Dynamics (BOPM, N=1)	457
13.11	Replicating Portfolio Price Dynamics (BOPM, N=1)	457
14.1	Stock Price Behavior (BOPM, N=2)	475

14.2	Option Price Behavior (BOPM, $N=2$)	476
14.3	The Natural Call Option under Scenario 1	480
14.4	The Replicating Portfolio under Scenario 1	481
14.5	Valuing C_u	486
14.6	Valuing C_d	487
14.7	Stock Price Tree for the BOPM, $N=2$	488
14.8	The BOPM, $N=2$, as a Set of BOPMs, $N=1$	491
14.9	The BOPM for $N=3$	494
14.10	Summary of Stock Price Evolution (N-Period Binomial Process)	499
15.1	Strategy for Example 2	519
16.1	Non Smoothness of Brownian Motion Paths	560

TABLES

1.1	Forward Mortgage Rates (March 7, 2014)	9
1.2	Weekly Average Spot 30-Year Fixed Mortgage Rates	10
1.3	GBP/USD Futures	18
1.4	GBP/USD Futures Price Quote (16:22:56 CT11 Mar 2014)	19
1.5	JYen June 2014 Futures Price Quote (March 12, 2014)	25
1.6	Japanese Yen Exchange Rate (January 30, 2014)	27
1.7	Exchange Rates (March 11, 2014): New York Closing Snapshot	30
2.1	Payoff to a Long Forward Position in IBM Contracted at $F_{t,T}$=$190/share	40
2.2	Payoff to a Short Forward Position in IBM Contracted at $F_{t,T}$=$190/share	43
2.3	Profits to a Naked (Unhedged) Long Spot Position with the Current Spot Price=$5.9875/$bu.$	46
2.4	Profits to a Long Spot Position Sold Forward at $F_{t,T}$	49
2.5	Profits from a Fully Unhedged Spot Position in Wheat	51
2.6	Profits from a Short Forward Position in Wheat	52
2.7	Profit from the Fully Hedged Spot Position	53
2.8	Price Data Summary	53
2.9	Data for End of Chapter 2, Exercise 2	57
2.10	Data for End of Chapter 2, Exercise 3	58
2.11	Data for End of Chapter 2, Exercise 4	59
2.12	Data for End of Chapter 2, Exercise 5	60
3.1	End of Chapter 3, Exercise 5c	85
4.1	Exchange Rates (April 7, 2014): New York Closing Snapshot	104
5.1	Forward Contracts vs. Futures Contracts	122
5.2	Top 5 FCMs Ranked by Segregated Consumer Funds	124
5.3	Simple Limit Order Book (Current Time)	131
5.4	Depth and Height of the LOB (Current Time)	133
5.5	Trading within the Bid–Asked Spread (at a Later Time)	133
5.6	Hypothetical Example 1 of a Globex LOB	134

TABLES

5.7	Hypothetical Example 2 of a Globex LOB	136
5.8	The Daily Settlement Process	149
5.9	Tracking the Equity in an Investor's Account	152
6.1	CME Corn Contract Price Quotes	207
7.1	Selected Financial Futures Contracts	213
7.2	JPY/USD Futures	214
7.3	Daily Settlements for Japanese Yen Future Futures (Final)	216
7.4	Currency Forward Positions vs. Currency Futures Positions	220
7.5	S&P 500 Futures	228
7.6	Daily Settlements for S&P 500 Future Futures (Final)	230
7.7	Eurodollar Futures, CME (by Volume)	245
7.8	Currency Composition of Foreign Exchange Reserves	247
7.9	Buying or Selling Spot Eurodollars	250
7.10	Eurodollar Futures	255
7.11	'Buying' and 'Selling' Eurodollar Futures	256
7.12	Daily Settlements for Eurodollar Future Futures (Final)	259
8.1	Swaps Dealer's Schedule for BBB-Type Firms for 5-year Swaps	285
8.2	Credit Spreads in the Spot Market for BBB-Type Firms	289
8.3	Generic Example: a 5-Year Swap	294
8.4	Dealer Swap Schedule for AA-Type Firms	295
8.5	Credit Spreads in the Spot Market for AA-Type Firms	296
8.6	Credit Spreads for AA and BBB	298
8.7	Bank Of America's Simplified Balance Sheet	299
8.8	LIBOR Yield Curve (Spot Rates)	304
9.1	Exchange-Traded (CBOE) Option Contracts	325
9.2	Merck Options Price Quotes	335
9.3	A Particular Merck Option Price Quote	336
10.1	The Eight Basic Naked Strategies	348
10.2	Profits for Alternative Terminal Stock Prices, S_T	365
10.3	Total Dollar Returns ($10,000 initial investment)	366
10.4	Percentage Rates of Return ($10,000 initial investment)	366
11.1	Classification of Options	374
11.2	Proving LBEC	376
11.3	Interpretation 1 of the Underlying Asset as a European Call Option	377

11.4	Lower Bound for a European Put Option	381
11.5	Lower Bound for a European Call Option with Dividends	383
11.6	Lower Bound for a European Put Option with Dividends on the Underlier	387
11.7	States of the World for a European Call Option (No Dividends)	389
11.8	Partially Replicating the Payoffs to a European Call Option (No Dividends)	390
11.9	Fully Replicating the Payoffs to a European Call Option	392
11.10	Current Costs of the Synthetic Call Option and of the Natural Call Option	393
11.11	Current Costs of the Synthetic Put Option and of the Natural Put Option	399
11.12	Current Costs of a Natural Forward Contract	400
11.13	Current Costs of a Synthetic Forward Contract	400
11.14	Generalized Forward Contracts	402
12.1	The Eight Synthetic Equivalents to the Eight Basic Strategies	417
12.2	Covered Calls and Protective Put Strategies	419
12.3	Profits for the In-the-Money Covered Call Write, $E_1{=}\$40$, $S_t{=}\$45$ and $C_{t,1}{=}\$8$	421
12.4	Profits for the Out-of-the-Money Covered Call Write ($E_2{=}\$50$, $S_t{=}\$45$, and $C_{t,2}{=}\$1$)	424
12.5	Current Costs of the Natural Covered Call Write and of the Synthetic Covered Call Write	426
12.6	Profits for the Out-of-the-Money Protective Put with $E_1{=}\$40$, $S_t{=}\$45$, and $P_{t,1}{=}\$1$	428
12.7	Current Costs of the Natural Protective Put and of the Synthetic Protective Put	430
12.8	Profits for the In-the-Money Protective Put with $E_2{=}\$50$, $S_t{=}45$ and $P_{t,2}{=}\$6$	433
13.1	Binomial Process ($N{=}2$), Price Paths Structure	441
13.2	Logic of the BOPM ($N{=}1$) and its Drivers	463
13.3	Schematic by Level of Complexity	470
14.1	Stock Price Behavior (BOPM, $N{=}2$)	476
14.2	Option Price Behavior (BOPM, $N{=}2$)	476
14.3	The Complete Hedging Program for the BOPM, $N{=}2$	484

14.4	Complete Hedging Strategy for the BOPM ($N=2$) Example	489
14.5	Path Structure of the BOPM, $N=3$	497
14.6	Value Contributions to C_0 made by the Paths of the BOPM, $N=3$	498
15.1	A Fair Game With Equal Probabilities	518
16.1	Price Data for End of Chapter 16, Exercise 1	591

PREFACE

Derivatives Markets offers readers a modern introduction to derivatives instruments and it provides the tools needed in order to develop a *working* knowledge of derivatives. The idea of this text is to present a down-to-earth, yet theoretically rigorous and applied introduction to derivatives. It also presents a gentle introduction to mathematical finance, which is needed in order to understand modern (post-1970s) developments.

In order to understand the approach of this text, a brief discussion of the history of derivatives is useful. Many insights about derivatives have been discovered since the seminal work in the 1970s, and the text provides a bridge to and incorporates those insights. It develops the skill sets needed both to understand and intelligently use derivatives. These skill sets are developed, in part, by using concept checks that test the reader's understanding of the material as it is presented.

The text discusses some fairly sophisticated topics, *not* usually discussed in introductory derivatives texts; for example, real-world electronic market trading platforms such as CME's Globex, an understanding of which is needed in order to understand other worldwide electronic trading systems. On the theory side, a detailed discussion of what risk-neutral valuation really means in the context of the dynamics of the hedge portfolio is provided for the simplest option pricing model.

A balanced, logical presentation of the major derivatives classes is given. This includes: Forward and futures contracts in Part 1; Swaps in Part 2; and Options in Part 3. The material is unified by providing a modern conceptual framework and exploiting the no-arbitrage relationships between the different derivatives classes.

The goals of the text are to guide the reader through the derivatives markets; to develop the reader's skill sets needed in order to incorporate and manage derivatives in a corporate or risk management setting; and to provide a solid foundation for further study. This textbook is for students, both undergraduate and graduate, as well as for those with an interest in how and why these markets work and thrive.

TO THE STUDENT

Concept checks and end-of-chapter exercises are an integral part of this text. I suggest that you do the concept checks as you go along. Selected solutions have been presented at the end of the chapters. Solutions to the other concept checks can be attempted through discussion with your colleagues, and/or with the help of the instructor.

Another feature of the text is its emphasis on '*the quote mechanism*'. Frequent references to the Internet are made so that you can see the world of data that underlies derivatives markets. Most of the websites are fairly stable and therefore should be valid when you read this text. Keep in mind, though, that the Internet changes rapidly. These websites will be updated on the textbook's website (see below).

Finally, there is no royal road to understanding derivatives markets, other than effort on your part. If there were such a royal road, then many more people would understand derivatives than actually do. That would reduce the applied value to you of studying the subject. Some students have gone on to careers in the derivatives field. You don't have to be a rocket scientist in order to learn derivatives. Much more important is that you simply put the required effort into properly learning the material.

STUDENT RESOURCES

The textbook's website is https://www.routledge.com/products/9780415 599016. There you can find useful resources to aid in understanding the material. This includes the websites referred to in the text, (updated) data sources, a list of errata, and other materials which will be added over time.

TO THE INSTRUCTOR

The text is suitable for a one-semester course on derivatives at the undergraduate level or at the graduate level. If time is at a premium, Chapters 8, 15 and 17 can be omitted. Or one could cover swaps in Chapter 8 and omit Chapters 15, 16 and 17. You should be able to cover the remaining 14 chapters in a normal semester. Ancillaries for adopters will be provided on an appropriate password-protected website.

Pedagogical features are included, and these include the Concept Checks. Most of these are straightforward, and the ones for which solutions have not been provided at the end of the chapters can be used as 'talking points'.

Further, I have tried to make the end-of-chapter exercises both relevant and interesting. I also use redundancy as a pedagogical tool to show the reader how the concepts apply in different contexts.

On the issue of starting with forwards vs. starting with options, I have selected the former. Forward contracts seem to be an easier means of entry into the subject matter. Options, on the other hand, are more nuanced financial instruments. As noted above, modern research insights on derivatives have been incorporated. Some of these have already made their way into the pedagogical literature. But some have not because they have been viewed as too mathematical for the student to be able to understand.

I do not share this view, but rather believe that many of the insights of modern finance (including derivatives), if given the appropriate economic intuition and an understanding of ordinary calculus, are well within the grasp of the intelligent reader. Certain topics in derivatives border on rocket science, but many topics do not. Along these lines, I have tried to provide *all* the details necessary to understand the material—because many students, and instructors, know that 'the devil is in the details'.

Some of the highlights of the text are:

1. an emphasis on the *quote mechanism*, and understanding where to find and how to read and interpret the data that underlies this field;
2. an early presentation of the *hedging role of forward contracts* in Chapter 2, with the use of Microsoft Excel charts as visual aids;
3. an early emphasis on FX markets to develop a *global* perspective, as opposed to the usual stock market focus;
4. separating out forward contract valuation in the no-dividend case from the dividend case, as exemplified in Chapters 3 and 4;
5. recognizing the *alternative* derivative valuation problems: at initiation, at expiration, and at an intermediate time;
6. an emphasis on *market microstructure* in Chapter 5 on futures markets, with due attention to the limit order book and Globex;
7. a *portfolio* approach to hedging with futures contracts in Chapter 6, with a discussion of most of the approaches to hedging, including carrying charge hedging;

8. discussion of difficult to explain, yet important concepts such as *storage, the price of storage,* and the all-important *spreads* notion;

9. an extensive Chapter 7 on financial futures contracts, with particular emphasis on Eurodollar spot and futures, since these are the basis for understanding swaps in Chapter 8;

10. a complete discussion of stock index futures in Chapter 8, and their uses in alternative hedging strategies. This includes a discussion of the difference between hedging stock portfolios with forwards and hedging with futures;

11. an entry into understanding swaps, by viewing them as *structured* products, based on the forward concept;

12. the difference between commodity and interest rate swaps, and a detailed explanation of what it means to *pay fixed* and *receive floating* in an interest rate swap;

13. understanding Eurodollar futures strips, notation shifts, and the role of the quote mechanism;

14. discussion of swaps as a zero-sum game, and research challenges to the comparative advantage argument;

15. swaps pricing and alternative interpretations of the par swap rate;

16. a step-by-step approach to options starting in Chapter 9 with the usual emphasis on the quote mechanism, as well as incorporation of real asset options examples;

17. an American option pricing model in Chapter 9, and its extension to European options in Chapter 11;

18. the importance of identifying *short*, not just long, positions in an underlying asset and the hedging demand they create;

19. two chapters on option trading strategies; one basic, one advanced, including the three types of covered calls, the protective put strategy, and their interpretations;

20. a *logical* categorization of rational option pricing results in Chapter 11, and the inclusion of American puts and calls;

21. neither monotonicity nor convexity, which are usually assumed, are rational option results;

22. partial vs. full static replication of European options;

23. working backwards from payoffs to costs as a method for devising and interpreting derivatives strategies;

24. the introduction of *generalized* forward contracts paves the way for the connection between (generalized) forward contracts and options, and the discussion of American put-call parity;

25. the Binomial option pricing model, $N=1$, and why it works—which is *not* simply no-arbitrage;
26. three tools of modern mathematical finance: no-arbitrage, replicability and complete markets, and dynamic and static replication, and a rule of thumb on the number of hedging vehicles required to hedge a given number of independent sources of uncertainty;
27. static replication in the Binomial option pricing model, $N=1$, the hedge ratio can be 1.0 and a preliminary discussion in Chapter 13 on the meaning of risk-neutral valuation;
28. dynamic hedging as the new component of the BOPM, $N>1$, and a path approach to the multi-period Binomial option pricing model;
29. equivalent martingale measures (EMMs) in the representation of option and stock prices;
30. the efficient market hypothesis (EMH) as a guide to modeling prices;
31. arithmetic Brownian motion (ABM) and the Louis Bachelier model of option prices;
32. easy introduction to the tools of continuous time finance, including Itô's lemma;
33. Black–Scholes derived from Bachelier, illustrating the important connection between these two models;
34. modeling non-constant volatility: the deterministic volatility model and stochastic volatility models;
35. why Black–Scholes is still important;
36. and a final synthesis chapter that includes a discussion of the different senses of risk-neutral valuation, their meaning and economic basis, and a complete discussion of the dynamics of the hedge portfolio in the BOPM, $N=1$.

I would like to thank the giants of the derivatives field including: Louis Bachelier, Fischer Black, John Cox, Darrell Duffie, Jonathan Ingersoll, Kiyoshi Itô, Robert Merton, Paul Samuelson, Myron Scholes, Stephen Ross, Mark Rubinstein, and many others. I sincerely hope that the reader enjoys traveling along the path to understanding *Derivatives Markets*.

David Goldenberg
Independent researcher, NY, USA

ACKNOWLEDGMENTS

I would like to thank everyone at Routledge for their hard work on this book. Special thanks go to Laura Johnson, Editorial Assistant, for her care and attention throughout, especially to the text design and overall look of the book. Thanks go to Andy Humphries, Commissioning Editor, for his expertise and support. I wish to thank Josh Goldenberg for consulting on the creative design of the book, and I would also like to thank the production and marketing teams for their care and attention. This book would not have been possible without them. Finally, one of my students, Roopa Subbu, provided helpful comments on some chapters in the text.

PART 1
Forward Contracts and Futures Contracts

CHAPTER 1

SPOT, FORWARD, AND FUTURES CONTRACTING

1.1 Three Ways to Buy and Sell Commodities	5
1.2 Spot Market Contracting (Motivation and Examples)	5
1.3 Forward Market Contracting (Motivation and Examples)	7
1.4 Problems with Forward Markets	11
1.5 Future Contracts as a Solution to Forward Market Problems (Motivation and Examples)	13
1.6 Futures Market Contracting	17
1.7 Mapping Out Spot, Forward, and Futures Prices	20
1.7.1 Present and Future Spot Prices	20
1.7.2 Forward Prices	24
1.7.3 Futures Prices	25

INTRODUCTION AND MOTIVATION

You will be traveling from your home country to Canada in a month and you know that you will need to obtain Canadian dollars to use while in Canada. To get an idea of the risk you face, you decide to look at the Canadian/US dollar exchange rate. Indeed, over the past year it has fluctuated with parity occurring around May 2013. The risk to you is that you may have to pay *more* for Canadian dollars in a month than you would pay today. Of course, it is possible that you could pay less in a month.

The problem is that you do not know today whether your currency will depreciate or appreciate relative to the Canadian dollar. You face currency (foreign exchange=FX) risk. Figure 1.1 indicates how many Canadian dollars were contained in 1 USD$ over the period March 2013–March 2014. This is what is meant by USD/CAD.

4   FORWARD CONTRACTS AND FUTURES CONTRACTS

It is defined as USD$1/(US Dollar Value of 1$CAD), and describes how many Canadian dollars it takes to buy 1 US dollar, or how many Canadian dollars are 'in' 1 US dollar, or the Canadian dollar price of 1 US dollar.

For example, the CAD dollar price of 1 US dollar was approximately 1.1 Canadian dollars in March 2014. By solving USD$1/(US Dollar Value of 1$CAD)=1.1 for the denominator, this translates into the US dollar value of 1CAD$ of USD$ 0.90. You can see from this example that understanding the 'quote mechanism' is important. Are we quoting Canadian dollars in terms of US dollars, or are we quoting US dollars in terms of Canadian dollars? Understanding the quote mechanism is an essential prerequisite for being able to intelligently deal with derivatives and the instruments that underlie them.

One Canadian dollar was worth 0.90 US dollars in March 2014. A move upward (downward) in the USD/CAD ratio indicates that the Canadian dollar is depreciating (appreciating), because there are more (fewer) Canadian dollars in 1 US $. If it takes *more* Canadian dollars to purchase 1 US dollar, then the Canadian dollar is *depreciating* relative to the US dollar. Another way to put

FIGURE 1.1 Canada/US Foreign Exchange Rate

Source: *St.* Louis Fed, reprinted with permission.

this is that if 1 US dollar buys more (fewer) Canadian dollars, then the Canadian currency is weakening (strengthening) relative to the US dollar. Alternatively, more USD in a single CAD dollar means that the CAD is appreciating relative to the USD dollar.

1.1 THREE WAYS TO BUY AND SELL COMMODITIES

What are your alternatives today to try and manage the foreign exchange risk you are certain to experience? To answer this important question we first examine the ways in which you can transact in a foreign currency. There are three main ways. You could transact:

1. In the *spot* (*cash*) market;
2. in the *forward* market, or;
3. in the *futures* market.

1.2 SPOT MARKET CONTRACTING (MOTIVATION AND EXAMPLES)

What does it mean to transact in the spot market? The easiest way to think about this is as a *cash and carry* transaction. You go out and buy something for immediate delivery and you pay the going price in the market. For example, you fill your car's gas tank with gasoline. When you do so, you pay the (posted) spot price of gasoline even though the theoretical spot price determined in the spot market for gasoline keeps changing, based upon demand and supply conditions. Most of our purchases are of this form, but there are some notable exceptions.

Let's formalize the idea of spot markets and spot transactions.

Spot (Cash) refers to the characteristic of being available for immediate or nearly immediate delivery. Other features are:

- No standardized contract;
- no organized exchange in which trading necessarily takes place;
- commodities underlying spot transactions may have different grades (quality levels);
- the terms of a spot agreement are tailor-made to suit the parties to the agreement.

6 FORWARD CONTRACTS AND FUTURES CONTRACTS

These terms include:

a. Grade;
b. time of delivery. Financial instruments sold in the spot market usually have a 0-day to 3-day delivery window;
c. place of delivery;
d. other terms as suit the parties.

A *spot transaction* is one in which two (counter)parties engage in a transaction for immediate or nearly immediate delivery of some commodity.

The *spot market* is the (not necessarily organized) market in which spot transactions take place. It is an abstract entity. The spot market is just the set of all spot transactions.

The *spot price* of a commodity, at a point in time, is the price agreed upon for purchase and sale of the commodity under such terms as the two counterparties agree upon. Delivery is immediate, or nearly immediate.

Price Quotes in Spot Markets

We will look at spot prices in the FX (Foreign Exchange) market. A useful source for data is the *Wall Street Journal*, online.wsj.com. Go to that page and click '*Markets*'. One of the categories listed is '*Market Data*'. Having reached this point, click *FX*. You will see a tab titled '*New York Closing*' under '*Complete Currencies Data*'. This takes you to '*Exchange Rates: New York Closing Snapshot*'. This gives spot and some forward prices for most of the world's major currencies.

Usually, forward '*prices*' are called forward *rates* because they show you how to convert from one currency to another.

As a concrete example, on the quote date March 11, 2014, according to this source, the going spot price of one UK (British) Pound was USD$1.6617. Inverting this, we quickly see that USD1$ would buy 0.601793 British Pounds. We will delve into FX in much more detail in Chapter 4.

■ CONCEPT CHECK 1

(*Solutions for selected Concept Check questions are at the end of the chapters*)

Choose the quote date–March 11, 2014–look at the FX price quotes at online.wsj.com and answer the following questions (you can even download the entire data set into Excel.) Historical data is available from 'Find Historical Data', and it apparently goes back to May 1, 2007.

a. Which currencies have forward price quotes, in addition to spot FX price quotes?
b. Find the euro. How many US dollars does it take to buy one euro in the spot FX market?
c. How many Euros were in 1 US dollar on the quote date?

1.3 FORWARD MARKET CONTRACTING (MOTIVATION AND EXAMPLES)

Consider a potential homeowner who goes to a financial institution to raise part of the capital needed to purchase a home. This is done by borrowing from a financial institution, who therefore acts as the lender. To do so, he *issues (sells)* a fixed-rate mortgage.

Home buyers have to arrange mortgage financing *before* they close on a property. But most of them do not want to assume the interest rate risk associated with long-term fixed-rate mortgages. That is, if home buyers waited the customary 30 or 60 days to lock in the interest rate on their loans, then they might have to pay a *higher* interest rate than the one currently prevailing. To prevent this from happening, home buyers arrange for financing in *advance at a fixed rate*.

This means that they take a *short position* in a forward contract which enables them to fix the long-term mortgage interest rate that they will pay. The homeowner has a short forward position because he wishes to *borrow* by *issuing* (selling) the mortgage bond, but in advance at the forward rate.

Then, when the mortgage is actually issued, he will pay a fixed rate for, say, 30 years. He is in a scenario where, no matter what happens to long-term mortgage interest rates in the 30 to 60 days before closing, he has *locked* in a rate. This rate is called the 30 (60) day forward rate on the long-term mortgage interest rate.

A financial institution, such as Bank of America, that invests in this forward mortgage (lender) is *buying* the forward contract. That is, it is *buying forward* the long-term mortgage bond and thereby receiving the fixed monthly mortgage payments. As such, it assumes the risk that long-term mortgage interest rates will increase over the subsequent period in which the rate is locked in.

The risk to the financial institution arises because, if interest rates actually do rise, then they could have charged the homeowner a higher interest rate. By locking in the forward rate in advance, they lose the present value of the interest that would have been earned over 30 years had they charged the higher spot mortgage interest rate. This is a substantial problem for financial institutions and is one reason they may favor the variable-rate mortgages that played a notorious role in the financial crisis of 2007–2008.

Forward contracts are useful, and were one of the first types of derivatives to be used in ancient times. In the olden days, Japanese rice farmers used forward contracts to lock in the price of their subsequent crops. This helped them to manage the risk of being in the rice production business. The ability to contract in forward markets is the second way that one can purchase a commodity. Its usefulness becomes readily apparent.

Forward refers to the characteristic of being available for delivery at some future time, at a *fixed* price determined today. Features of this mode of contracting include:

- No standardized contract;
- no organized exchange in which trading necessarily takes place;
- commodities underlying forward contracts can have different grades (quality levels) because they are just spot commodities;
- the terms of a forward agreement are tailor-made to suit the parties to the agreement.

These terms include:

a. Grade;
b. time of delivery;
c. place of delivery;
d. other terms as suit the parties.

A *forward transaction* is one in which two (counter)parties agree to purchase and sell a commodity at some future time, under such terms as they mutually agree upon. Basically, a forward transaction shares almost all the characteristics of a spot transaction. As such, it is a *deferred spot market* transaction at the forward price.

The *forward market* is the (not necessarily organized) market in which forward transactions take place. It is an abstract entity. The forward market is just the set of all forward transactions.

The *forward price* of a commodity is the price agreed upon today for purchase and sale of the commodity to be delivered at the specified future date. No monies are initially exchanged at the origination of the forward contract. Delivery and payment are deferred. There is one exception, and that is a *pre-paid* forward contract.

Price Quotes in Forward Markets

We can easily illustrate forward mortgage rates using online.wsj.com once again.

■ CONCEPT CHECK 2

(*Exploring forward rates in the long-term mortgage market*)

Start from the online.wsj.com home page. Go directly to '*Market Data*'. Then to '*Rates*', then to '*Bonds, Rates, and Credit Markets*'. Under '*Complete bonds, rates and credit markets data*' you will find '*Benchmarks and comparisons*'; scroll down until you encounter the link for '*Money Rates*' and click it. Then scroll down to Fannie Mae 30 year mortgage yields and you will see a price quote that looks like that in Table 1.1. The data you will see is the latest when this exercise is done. Included in that data, but not in our Table 1.1, are the 52-week high and low rates.

Look up the historical data for March 7, 2014.

TABLE 1.1 **Forward Mortgage Rates (March 7, 2014)**

Forward 30-year fixed-rate mortgage rates	03/07/2014	02/28/2014
30 days forward	3.96202	3.89237
60 days forward	4.00284	3.93017

Table compiled by the author from data available at www.fanniemae.com/singlefamily/historical-daily-required-net-yields (last accessed May 27, 2015).

a. Do you find the same data as in Table 1.1 there?
b. What were the 52-week high and low rates?
c. Do you see substantial *volatility* in forward mortgage rates over the one-year period?

These are Fannie Mae's 30-day forward rates for 30-year fixed-rate mortgages and the 60-day forward rates for 30-year fixed-rate mortgages. Note what is happening here. The quote date was March 7, 2014. We are in the forward market, because it is locking in mortgage rates for delivery in 30 and in 60 days, no matter what happens in 30 or in 60 days. This is a fantastic thing to be able to do and is precisely what the forward market offers.

Using forward markets in this way, you can manage the interest-rate risk that you would otherwise assume between the time you arrange financing in the mortgage market and you close on the property (typically in 30 or in 60 days). If you did not contract in the forward market, but took your chances in the spot 30-year mortgage market, then in 30 or 60 days you would have to take the going rates. Things could turn out quite badly if 30-year mortgage rates spike in 30 or in 60 days. Of course, rates could *decline* as well. But the average consumer is not in the business of predicting long-term interest rates.

This is something that even professionals have difficulty with, due to the efficiency of interest rate markets, which implies unpredictability. The average consumer probably wants to more or less effectively manage his/her life by locking in a 'reasonable' rate. For reference, anything under 5% is low by historical standards.

It is also important to understand the spot mortgage market. To construct Table 1.2, we will take a direct route to the spot 30-year fixed-rate mortgage market, which are weekly average rates. We will take the week of March 6, 2014 and the week of Feb 27, 2014. The data, available from www.freddie mac.com/pmms/archive.html?year=2014 (accessed May 27, 2015), is given in Table 1.2.

TABLE 1.2 **Weekly Average Spot 30-Year Fixed Mortgage Rates**

	Week of March 6, 2014	Week of Feb 27, 2014
30-year fixed mortgage rate (weekly average)	4.28%	4.37%

Table compiled by the author from Freddie Mac's Mortgage Market Survey Archive, Compilation of Weekly Survey Data for 2014, www.freddiemac.com/pmms/archive.html?year=2014 (last accessed May 27, 2015).

SPOT, FORWARD, AND FUTURES CONTRACTING 11

■ CONCEPT CHECK 3

(*Exploring spot rates in the long-term mortgage market for available data*)

Go back to *Bonds, Rates, and Credit Markets*. Instead of going to '*Money Rates*' simply scan the page for '*Consumer Rates*', which were taken from bankrate.com, the key consumer bank rate quote mechanism. The data there is based on base rates posted by 70% of the nation's largest banks from their source which was SIX Financial Information, WSJ Market Data Group, and Bankrate.com.

a.   Discuss the spot 30-year mortgage rates you find at the site for a specific date you choose. Note that historical data is not available for Consumer Rates on online.wsj.com. That's why we went to the source Freddie Mac in Table 1.2.

Be careful in using online databases, and don't expect to get the same numbers from different databases. One has to look carefully into how price and rate quotes from different sources are determined. For example, bankrate.com uses *overnight* averages and explains them on their site. Do not assume that quotes from different sources are directly comparable to the second decimal place.

Rather, these kind of publicly available quotes are intended to give an idea of the *level* of the market, rather than the *precise* market. In the case of 30-year mortgages, they differ by lending institution and locality. That's why bankrate.com asks for zip codes to offer local borrowing rates in one's area.

1.4 PROBLEMS WITH FORWARD MARKETS

Forward markets serve an important risk management function. But they are not without their flaws. There are two main problems associated with forward contracts and with the structure of forward markets.

Since forward contracts are bilateral contracts directly between individuals, and delivery and payment is deferred, there is *counterparty* risk. This could happen if either party to the forward transaction does not honor his obligation. Note that forward contracts are not options, one is *required* to make (take) delivery of the commodity at the specified date.

12   **FORWARD CONTRACTS AND FUTURES CONTRACTS**

Why would someone default on such an agreement? Generally, default becomes a real possibility when there are *incentives* to default. If I agree to sell a commodity at a *fixed* price three months down the road, then I have *locked in* that price. If the price rises in the meantime, then I suffer an opportunity loss if I honor my commitment.

Case Example: SouthWest Airlines

As an example, suppose that Southwest Airlines is worried about fuel cost containment. The price of jet fuel could precipitously rise in 3 months. If Southwest waits 3 months to buy jet fuel, then it would have to pay the spot price at that time.

Alternatively, Southwest could simply *buy* a 3-month forward contract in the forward market for jet fuel and lock in the 3-month forward jet fuel price today. This would certainly achieve its objective of cost containment, *if* the price of jet fuel rises in 3 months.

But suppose that jet fuel becomes *cheaper* in 3 months. Suppose that the spot price falls below the locked-in forward price. Then Southwest would have to buy jet fuel at a forward price that exceeds the spot price in 3 months. This could cost it massive amounts of money. It clearly has an incentive to default in order to minimize its ultimate cost of jet fuel.

Considerations such as these make companies think twice before they make forward commitments. The downside of thinking too much about these issues is that it biases management to take speculative positions. We will discuss hedging and speculation, and the difficulty of drawing a hard and fast line between them, in this text.

■ CONCEPT CHECK 4

a. Did Southwest lose out by entering into the forward contract in the first place?

A similar argument could be given from the point of view of the *seller* of jet fuel forward contracts. If the spot price *rises* above the agreed upon 3-month forward price, then the seller of the forward contract has an incentive to default.

In case any of this appears to be academic, note that over the counter (OTC) markets tend to have this feature of counterparty risk. The credit default swaps market is a notable example, allegedly playing a role in the 2007–2008 financial crisis.

This suggests that market organization is important. A financial instrument can play an important and useful risk management role, but the way the market is organized can create havoc.

How can counterparty risk be controlled? One way is to *know* the counterparty. For example, in the forward exchange (FX) market the major players are banks with known reputations. Clearly, a bank could default on its forward market commitments if they are likely to put it out of business. Short of this, banks tend to worry about their reputations. This counteracts counterparty risk in the FX market.

Another way to control counterparty risk is to change the very structure of the market while keeping its basic economic functionality intact. The basic problem with forward markets appears to be the lack of an exit mechanism. If market participants could somehow fulfill their financial obligations and exit the market before the delivery date, then they would have the best of both worlds. This is the idea behind futures markets.

Let's summarize the problems with forward market organization. As currently organized, forward markets are delivery markets. Cancellation by one party to the contract may be impossible or involve penalties. Having contracts between individuals allows *customization* but opens the door to counterparty risk.

Forward contracts are typically customized products, and are not standardized. This lack of standardization of forward contracts makes them harder to trade in a liquid, secondary market. Basically, forward contracts are just like spot contracts, except that payment and delivery is deferred. One receives and pays for the commodity only at delivery.

1.5 FUTURES CONTRACTS AS A SOLUTION TO FORWARD MARKET PROBLEMS (MOTIVATION AND EXAMPLES)

Spot and forward contracting occur in markets that are known as OTC (over the counter). This means that transactions are essentially between individuals. What other ways could transactions occur?

The brief answer is that they could be *intermediated*. This means that some third party intervenes. Then, there is an alternative to you being the buyer (seller) to the seller (buyer), as in OTC markets. You could be the buyer (seller) to the intervening third party.

14 **FORWARD CONTRACTS AND FUTURES CONTRACTS**

This third party would then assume two roles. First, it would be seller to the buyer. At the same time, it would be buyer to the seller. In the case of futures markets, the third party is the *Clearing House*.

Why such a complex, seemingly circular market organization? Indeed, according to the popular wisdom, doesn't it pay to 'eliminate the middleman'? It turns out that there are advantages to having a properly defined middleman in the case of forward/futures markets.

Organized futures markets are a clever way to solve the illiquidity and counterparty risk problems of forward markets, while keeping the basic economic function of forward contracting intact. That function is to *lock in* today a forward price at which deferred transactions take place.

Organized futures markets accomplish these goals by first standardizing futures contracts. This is a necessary condition in order to have a liquid secondary market. It is very difficult to trade a financial product that is highly customized for the needs of particular customers. One can initiate trades in them, of course. Otherwise, OTC markets would not exist. The question is how to *exit* a trade once initiated.

Standardization is a big step towards providing liquidity. If the futures contract that all buyers and sellers trade is a homogeneous financial contract, then they could be traded just like US dollar bills or any of the world's currencies. However, the problem of counterparty risk still remains. To move towards resolving this, organized futures markets introduce a *clearing house*. In futures markets, the clearing house has a set of critical economic functions.

The first role of the clearing house in futures markets is to *intermediate* all trades.

Example 1 (Intermediation by the Clearing House)

Suppose that a buyer named Smith submits a buy order for 10 futures contracts. At the same time, a seller named Adams submits a sell order for 10 of the identical contract. These orders are executed through the trading process on the floor of a futures exchange, or electronically.

In normal bilateral transactions, Smith would be buying directly from Adams. This is not so in futures markets, because the clearing house steps in between Smith and Adams. Now Smith is buying from the clearing house, who acts as the seller. Adams is selling to the clearing house, who acts as the buyer. The picture is as follows in Figure 1.2.

FIGURE 1.2 **Intermediation by the Clearing House**

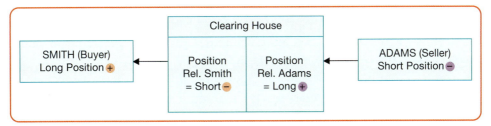

Example 2 (The Exit Mechanism)

This somewhat unfamiliar market structure makes it possible for both Smith and Adams to exit the market by 'reversing' their trades. Suppose that Smith wants to exit the market. Provided that Smith fulfills the financial obligations created by his initial long futures position, there is no reason that he cannot exit. He simply submits a sell order in the identical futures contract. In a liquid market that order will be matched with the buy order of another market participant, let's say named Wilson. After the transaction, the picture is Figure 1.3.

FIGURE 1.3 **Offsetting Trades**

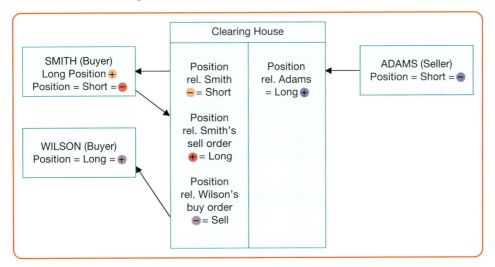

Note that the direction of the arrow indicates the commodity flow. Take Smith's long position. Smith initially is obligating himself to take delivery of the commodity underlying the futures contract. Hence the arrow points towards Smith.

16 FORWARD CONTRACTS AND FUTURES CONTRACTS

■ CONCEPT CHECK 5

a. Why does the arrow point away (towards the clearing house) from Adams?

The rather complicated diagram in Figure 1.3 illustrates the exit mechanism incorporated into futures markets. By making a reversing trade, Smith has essentially exited the market. Smith has two arrows based upon his two trades.

The first points toward him because he went long and incurred the obligation to *take* delivery of the commodity underlying the futures contract.

Later he went short, thereby incurring the obligation to *make* delivery of the underlying commodity. It would be redundant to actually force Smith to take delivery and then to turn around, and make delivery of the commodity. As long as Smith covers the financial implications of his trade, he is out.

What happened to Adams? Did Smith just default on him? Not at all. Note that the contract is *not* between Smith and Adams. It is between Smith and the clearing house. And it is between Adams and the clearing house. So, even if Smith defaulted (which he did not), the clearing house would pick up the slack and honor its obligation to Adams as buyer to the seller.

This, of course, would be a major difficulty for the clearing house, and it is not necessary. Wilson has entered the market as a buyer and Smith's original obligation as the buyer has effectively been *transferred* to Wilson. The clearing house is in the clear as it were; it is long to Adams and short to Wilson. In case of delivery, it could require Adams (as seller) to deliver the commodity and it could redeliver it to Wilson (as buyer). Everyone is happy.

Liquidity has been enabled. Think of it this way: if you buy 100 shares of IBM stock and then sell them you have exited the market. The person who bought your shares is the new owner. Here the commodity is not actually being bought or sold as in a spot transaction. Rather, the *obligations* to buy and sell the commodity at prices fixed today for subsequent delivery are being transferred. This is slightly more abstract but the same concept.

Note that if the contract was directly between Smith and Adams, then this tricky reversing-out transaction would be difficult or impossible. Smith would have to ask Adams for permission to exit his obligation and, if Adams gives such permission, then Smith would have to find someone else to whom to transfer Smith's buy obligation. In practice, due to the potential difficulty of exit, forward markets are less liquid than futures markets.

1.6 FUTURES MARKET CONTRACTING

The following is a key definition and should be committed to memory:

A *Futures Contract* is a standardized agreement between a *buyer* and the clearing house of an organized exchange to *take delivery* of a specified quantity and quality of a commodity and between a *seller* and the clearing house of an organized exchange to *make delivery* of a specified quantity and quality of a commodity. Delivery is deferred and occurs during specified periods (delivery months), according to the rules of the futures exchange in which the specific futures contract is offered for trading.

The main thing to note here is that, unlike OTC forward and spot market transactions, every futures transaction is intermediated by the exchange's clearing house as illustrated in example 1.

Note that there is flexibility built into the contract with regard to quality, time, and place of delivery. These are called *seller's options*. However, all terms of the contractual futures contract are specified in the contract itself, except for the futures price at which people are contracting for delivery of the commodity. This is determined either on the floor of an organized futures exchange or electronically, depending on what trading venue the futures trade was executed.

A *futures transaction* is one in which two parties agree to purchase and sell a commodity at some future time under the terms (*contract specifications*) of the futures contract.

The *futures market* is the organized market in which futures transactions take place. It is not an abstract entity.

The *futures price*, at a given point in time and associated to a futures contract, is the price determined either on the floor of an organized exchange or electronically through the trading process.

Price Quotes in Futures Markets

We will go back to our earlier example of the British Pound. Let's say you want to buy British Pounds forward for delivery in September 2014. The current date we will assume is March 11, 2014. We go to www.cmegroup.com

and hit the button for FX. Then '*View all FX products*' and find '*British pound futures*'.

The first step in understanding futures markets is to remember that a futures contract is a standardized financial instrument. It is the same for everyone. The terms of any futures contract traded on an organized exchange is given in 'contract specifications'.

Hit the contract specifications tab under British Pound futures. You will find something like Table 1.3 (the exchange can change contract specifications as it sees fit).

TABLE 1.3 GBP/USD Futures

Contract Size	62,500 British pounds.
Contract Month Listings	Six months in the March quarterly cycle (Mar, Jun, Sep, Dec).
Settlement Procedure	Physical delivery.
Position Accountability	10,000 contracts.
Ticker Symbol	CME Globex Electronic Markets: 6B.
Open Outcry:	BP.
Minimum Price Increment	$.0001 per British pound increments ($6.25/contract).
OPEN OUTCRY (RTH)	7:20 a.m.–2:00 p.m.
GLOBEX (ETH)	Sundays: 5:00 p.m.–4:00 p.m. Central Time (CT) next day. Monday–Friday: 5:00 p.m.–4:00 p.m. CT the next day, except on Friday–closes at 4:00 p.m. and reopens Sunday at 5:00 p.m. CT.
CME ClearPort	Sunday–Friday 6:00 p.m.–5:15 p.m. (5:00 p.m.–4:15 p.m. Chicago Time/CT) with a 45-minute break each day beginning at 5:15 p.m. (4:15 p.m. CT).
Last Trade Date/Time	9:16 a.m. Central Time (CT) on the second business day immediately preceding the third Wednesday of the contract month (usually Monday).
Exchange Rule	These contracts are listed with, and subject to, the rules and regulations of CME.
Block Trade Eligibility	Yes. View more on Block Trade eligible contracts.
Block Trade Minimum	100 Contracts.
EFP Eligibility	Yes. View more on EFPs.

Source: www.cmegroup.com, reprinted with permission from CME Group Inc., 2014.

SPOT, FORWARD, AND FUTURES CONTRACTING **19**

The main characteristics of this contract for our purposes are first contract size which is 62,500 BP. Contract size refers to the spot commodity underlying the futures contract. The delivery dates are six months in the March quarterly cycle (Mar, Jun, Sep, Dec). Delivery is physical, which we will discuss later.

Under 'Trading Hours', you will see the venues in which these contracts are traded. The first is by open outcry on the floor of the CME Group in Chicago. The second is on the CME Group's electronic trading platform called Globex. Most importantly, the futures price quote is in US dollars and cents.

Hit 'Quotes' and then 'Open Outcry Futures'. A number of headings appear including those in Table 1.4.

TABLE 1.4 **GBP/USD Futures Price Quote**

(16:22:56 CT 11 Mar 2014)

Month	Charts	Last	Change	Prior Settle	Open1/ Open2	High	Low	Close1/ Close2	Updated
Sep 2014		—	—	1.6603	—	1.6610	1.6610	1.6616	16:22:56 CT 11 Mar 2014

Reprinted with permission from CME Group Inc., 2014.

The four prices for which there is data (prior settle, high, low, close1/close2) in our quote are futures prices for the futures contract maturing in September 2014.

You can think of these as *fancy forward prices*. They are all roughly equal to US$1.661 for one BP. On the quote date of March 11, 2014 you could contract to buy or sell 62,500 BP for delivery in September 2014 at the fixed price of USD$1.661, no matter what happens in the FX market by that date.

■ CONCEPT CHECK 6

a. What is the commodity underlying the CME GBP/USD futures contract?
b. If you went long the Sept. 2014 contract on March 11, 2014 what would be the total US$ price at which you would be agreeing to buy the underlying commodity for?

20 FORWARD CONTRACTS AND FUTURES CONTRACTS

1.7 MAPPING OUT SPOT, FORWARD, AND FUTURES PRICES

A useful tool to help us understand the forward delivery characteristic of derivatives in general is the time line. This will also be handy when we discuss hedging with derivatives.

$$t \longrightarrow T = \text{maturity (expiration) date of}$$

current date   the forward or futures contract

t is the current date, sometimes written as $t=0$. It is the point where time starts.

T is the maturity date of the contract. This highlights the fact that derivatives are *finite-lived* instruments. Unlike common stock, they come to an end or expire. At that time, the particular contract in question has matured and it ceases to exist.

1.7.1 Present and Future Spot Prices

For example, suppose we consider the commodity gold. One of the first things to do is to search for the spot price of gold. That seems simple enough, but let's see. We go back to online.wsj.com, hit *expand* which takes you to '*Market Data*', find '*Market Data Center*', then go to '*Commodities and Futures*' and then to '*Cash Commodity Prices*' (under '*Spot Prices*').

Under '*Precious Metals, Gold*' (per Troy Oz.) you will see at least 12 different grades of spot gold, and they have different spot prices! The different grades (as of March 12, 2014) are Engelhard industrial bullion, Engelhard fabricated products, . . . , American Eagle, Troy oz.-E, and Austria Phil. This just illustrates that spot commodities tend to come in different grades.

One of the usual quote standards for Gold is the *London p.m. fixing,* which on the quote date was US\$1366.00 per troy ounce. On our time line, we would call this Gold Price$_t$.

Gold
Price$_t$

$$t \longrightarrow T$$

SPOT, FORWARD, AND FUTURES CONTRACTING   21

■ CONCEPT CHECK 7

a. What would 100 troy ounces cost at the London PM fixing (ignore transactions fees, shipping etc.)?

We are also interested in the spot gold price in 3 months perhaps because we already own gold and anticipate selling it, or we are waiting for a drop in the price of gold and wish to purchase it in 3 months.

Our time T is then 3 months from today which we could write as $T=t+3$ months. Of course, the question on everyone's mind is 'What is the spot price of gold going to be in 3 months?'.

While this is a great question, the answer is that the *future* spot price of gold (or of any volatile commodity) is a matter of speculation. No one really knows. At best, we can assign probabilities to the spot gold price being within certain ranges at the end of 3 months.

If anyone actually knew with complete certainty that the spot price of gold would be above the current price by more than carrying charges (interest, insurance, convenience yield, and storage) in 3 months' time, then they could amass huge amounts of wealth by simply investing in it, holding it for 3 months, and then selling it at the end of that time period.

■ CONCEPT CHECK 8

a. Would you invest everything you have in a bet that the above scenario concerning the price of gold in 3 months would be the likely outcome?

If you believe that past commodity price behavior is a guide to future price behavior, then one piece of interesting information to at least ponder is the behavior of the spot price of gold over the *last* 3 months. Historical spot prices for London Fixing PM gold, the usual standard for the gold spot price, can be found at FRED which is the economic research department of the St. Louis Federal Reserve Bank, http://research.stlouisfed.org/fred2/series/GOLD PMGBD228NLBM (last accessed May 27, 2015). Cut and paste the link into your browser.

At this site you can make your own graphs and even download the underlying data back to April 1, 1968. Click the link and you will find a non-interactive chart in which you can select the first 3 months of data for 2014 by editing the graph.

22 FORWARD CONTRACTS AND FUTURES CONTRACTS

FIGURE 1.4 Gold Fixing Price in London Bullion Market (USD$)

Source: St. Louis Fed, reprinted with permission.

The chart is reproduced above in Figure 1.4, where we took the data up to mid-March. This non-interactive chart for 01/01/2014 to 03/14/2014 shows the ups and downs of spot gold prices.

Basically, you will see that spot gold prices have had a rocky history of ups and downs over the 3-month period. Note the peaks and troughs and unpredictable *turning* points. This suggests that it is going to be very hard to predict spot gold prices over any subsequent 3-month period. That is, future spot gold prices are uncertain.

The uncertainty (volatility) in gold prices is well known to market participants. There is no reason to expect gold prices to continually go upwards or to go in any fixed direction over any period. Gold prices reflect both good (for gold) news and bad (for gold) news.

This uncertainty is partly based upon the fact that gold prices respond to many factors that in themselves are highly uncertain. These include the state of the economy, both domestic and global, and a host of other essentially unpredictable factors. Briefly, spot gold prices respond to and reflect the uncertainties of the 'market'.

■ CONCEPT CHECK 9

On the non-interactive charts on the FRED site look at gold prices over 1 day, 1 month, 3 months, 6 months, 1 year, 3 years, 5 years, and YTD (year to date). Notice the bumps in the longer-term charts.

a. Suppose that you are in a trough and have no further information. How do you know the trough has bottomed out?
b. Suppose that you are on a peak and have no further information. How do you know the peak has peaked?
c. What conclusions do you draw from looking at these spot gold price charts?

Going back to our time line, the gold price at expiration of the forward or futures contract is a random variable, Gold Price$_T(\omega)$. Randomness is notated by the symbol ω which in this context means 'the state of nature'. You can think of the state of nature as the state of the economy and of all the factors that affect spot gold prices.

The time line looks like this at the current date, time t.

Gold Price$_t$ Gold Price$_T(\omega)$

t T

Using the London PM fixing gold price we found on the quote date of $t=03/13/2014$, the gold price at time t was \$1,368.750 and Gold Price$_T(\omega)$ where $T=t+3$ months from 03/13/2014 depends on what happens in the world between now and then.

US\$1,368.750   Gold Price$_T(\omega)$=?

$t=03/13/2014$ T

We can now do this in general. We have some multi-grade commodity in which we are interested. We determine a *standard* for pricing the multi-grade spot commodity, just as we did for London pm fixing gold.

We then find the spot price of the standard spot commodity at the current date, P_t. The spot price at some future date T is a random variable, $P_T(\omega)$. It depends on economic uncertainties that are summarized by the single symbol ω.

P_t $P_T(\omega)$

t T

1.7.2 Forward Prices

We can also represent forward prices using time lines, and this exercise is instructive. Foreign currencies (FX) are the easiest commodities for which to find forward prices. Go to online.wsj.com, '*Market Data*', '*Currencies*', then '*Exchange Rates: New York Closing*'. Forward prices are quoted for several currencies.

For example, on the quote date of 03/13/2014, the 3-month forward price of Japanese Yen was quoted at USD$0.00974. This means that you could engage in a forward transaction today to buy or sell Japanese yen for delivery in 3 months from the quote date for the forward price of USD$0.00974 per 1 Japanese yen.

This forward price is locked in, no matter what happens in the market between now and the delivery date 3 months from today. That is just the definition of the forward price.

There is no uncertainty in the forward price. It is the price at which the forward transaction will ultimately take place. All uncertainty has been completely removed from the forward price. Contrast this with future *spot* prices which typically are volatile. A useful notation for the forward price today would be $F_{t,T}$.

This notation means today's (time=t) forward price for delivery of the underlying commodity at the future date time T. In our example, t=03/13/2014, T=3 months from 03/12/2014, and $F_{t,T}$=USD$0.00974 per 1 Japanese yen.

Now the question is, where does $F_{t,T}$ go on the time line? The answer is today, time t. This is because the forward price is determined in today's forward market. It then applies to the forward transaction at the expiration date of the forward contract.

$F_{t,T}$ ———————————→ Transaction Occurs

t T=expiration date
                          of the forward contract

For our example, this would look like,

USD$0.00974 ———————————→ Transaction Occurs

03/12/2014 T=3 months from 03/12/2014

SPOT, FORWARD, AND FUTURES CONTRACTING 25

Note that a typical forward contract could call for delivery of 12,500,000 Japanese yen at expiration (see cme.com).

■ CONCEPT CHECK 10

a. What price would the long (buyer) pay for the Japanese yen at expiration?

1.7.3 Futures Prices

Mapping out futures prices is basically the same as mapping out forward prices. Remember that futures contracts serve the same basic economic function as forward contracts, but are exchange-traded instruments. Futures prices are just 'fancy' forward prices.

As an example, we will use the JYen traded on the CME (see Table 1.5). Here is a price quote from March 12, 2014, where we have selected the June 2014 delivery contract. The quote date is 03/12/2014.

TABLE 1.5	JYen June 2014 Futures Price Quote (March 12, 2014)							
Month	Open	High	Low	Last	Change	Settle	Estimated Volume	Prior Day Open Interest
JUN 14	9715	9756	9704	9737B	+21	9743	88,449	71,181

Reprinted with permission from CME Group Inc., 2014.

There are a number of prices quoted including open, high, low, last, and prior settlement price. Looking at the June 14 contract, the price quote of open 9715 means USD$0.009715 per 1 JYen. The last was USD$ .009737 (bid) per 1 JYen.

The time line looks exactly like the forward time line for forward prices,

1 J yen=USD$ .009737

03/12/2014 T=expiration date
           of the futures contract
           during the delivery month June, 2014

Note that the exact expiration of the contract is not specified. Only a 'delivery period' is specified. In the case of the JYen futures contract this is currently the entire delivery month of June 2014. This is in accord with 'seller's options'.

■ CONCEPT CHECK 11

a. What price per 12,500,000 JYen for June 2014 delivery is the long (buyer) contracting at, if he initiated a long position at the opening price on 03/12/2014?

We can do this for any futures contract. We denoted the forward price at time t for delivery of the commodity at time T as $F_{t,T}$. A futures contract is not exactly the same thing as a forward contract, and we cannot assume that futures prices are equal to forward prices, so we will call $Fut_{t,T}$ the futures price at time t for delivery of the commodity at time T.

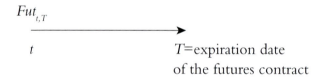

We will delve into the operations of futures markets in Chapter 5. There is a lot to discuss, and a lot of details. Mapping out spot, forward, and futures prices is the first step because it helps us to keep track of timing considerations. It also leads to mapping out the co-movements between derivative prices and spot prices, which is the key to hedging applications.

■ ■ ■

SPOT, FORWARD, AND FUTURES CONTRACTING 27

■ KEY CONCEPTS

1. Three ways to buy (sell) commodities: spot, forward, and futures.
2. Spot transaction, spot market, spot price, spot price quotes.
3. Forward transaction, forward market, forward price, forward price quotes.
4. Forward market problems: counterparty risk, illiquidity.
5. Futures contracts as a solution to forward market problems.
6. Futures transaction, futures market, futures price, futures price quotes.
7. Mapping out spot, forward, and futures prices.

■ END OF CHAPTER EXERCISES FOR CHAPTER 1

1. (*Basic Definitions*)

   Explain the distinctions between spot, forward, and futures transactions.

2. (*Exchange Rate Calculations*)

   The following Table 1.6 gives exchange rate data for the Japanese Yen, US Dollar exchange rate.

   TABLE 1.6 **Japanese Yen Exchange Rate (January 30, 2014)**

Rates in currency units per US dollar	
29-Jan-14	102.2000
30-Jan-14	102.8300

   Source: Board of Governors of the Federal Reserve System, Foreign Exchange Rates–H.10 Country Data.

   a. How much in US dollars would 10,000,000 spot Japanese Yen be worth on Thursday, January 30, 2014?
   b. How much in US dollars would 10,000,000 spot Japanese Yen be worth on Wednesday, January 29, 2014?
   c. Did the spot Japanese Yen appreciate or depreciate relative to the USD$ from Wednesday to Thursday?
   d. Has the US dollar appreciated or depreciated vs. the Japanese Yen from Wednesday to Thursday?

28 FORWARD CONTRACTS AND FUTURES CONTRACTS

3. (*Long and Short in the Forward Mortgage Market*)

Individuals, just like corporations, issue bonds to finance investments in autos, houses, and education. These car, mortgage, and education loans create financial securities called bonds that investors can invest in.

a. Consider the first scenario. The homeowner *already has* a 30-year fixed-rate mortgage, and is paying the interest rate on it in monthly installments that include principal and interest.
   - What would be the homeowner's primary concern in being locked into a fixed rate for 30 years?
   - Is the homeowner long or short in the spot bond mortgage market? Why?

Hint for part a. The homeowner has issued a mortgage bond requiring him to pay the 30-year fixed rate. The value of that bond represents the present value of what the homeowner owes on that loan. Now use your knowledge of bonds to analyze what happens to that bond value as mortgage rates increase or decrease.

b. Consider the second scenario discussed in the chapter, section 1.3. The homeowner is *considering issuing* a 30-year fixed-rate mortgage in 60 days.
   - What would be the homeowner's primary concern in this scenario?
   - Is the homeowner long or short in the spot mortgage market?
   - What position would the homeowner take in the forward mortgage-rate market? Why?

Hint for part b. The homeowner has not issued a fixed-rate mortgage yet but is planning on doing so in 60 days. Here we can take a hint from corporate behavior. In planning to issue securities (stocks or bonds), firms want to get the greatest proceeds from the issue which is equivalent to having to pay the lowest rates (costs of capital) on those securities once issued.

Now, analyze the effect of increasing and decreasing rates in 60 days on the homeowner *before* the mortgage bond is issued.

4. (*Global Derivatives Awareness*)

Answer the questions based on the most recent data on (Trading) Volume Statistics, which you can find at the FIA.org (Futures Industry Association) website. You are looking for the Annual Volume Survey under Volume Statistics.

SPOT, FORWARD, AND FUTURES CONTRACTING — 29

a. Identify the most actively traded derivative contracts. Consider each of the following sections separately:
  - Agricultural Futures and Options Contracts.
  - Energy Futures and Options Contracts.
  - Equity Index Futures and Options Contracts.
  - Foreign Exchange Futures and Options Contracts.
  - Metals Futures and Options Contracts.
  - Interest Rate Futures and Options Contracts.

b. What variable are the the rankings based upon?

c. Are there any other ways to rank 'actively traded' contracts?

■ SELECTED CONCEPT CHECK SOLUTIONS

Concept Check 1

a. On the quote date March 11, 2014 we found forward prices for the Australian dollar, the Japanese yen, the Swiss franc, and the UK pound (see Table 1.7 below).

b. One Euro was worth USD$1.3860.

c. There were 0.7215 Euros in one USD$. You can verify that 1/1.3860=0.7215.

Concept Check 3

a. When we did this exercise for March 7, 2014, we found a first entry of 4.54% which was an overnight average of the spot 30-year fixed-rate mortgage rate quoted by major financial institutions on the quote date. The second was the corresponding rate one week ago, 4.43 %. The third was the highest rate over the preceding 52 weeks, 4.80%, and the fourth was the 52-week low of 3.56%.

As you can see by looking at the high–low spread, there was considerable volatility in mortgage rates over the one-year period ending on March 7, 2014

Concept Check 5

a. Adams is *short* the futures contract. Therefore he has to deliver the spot commodity to the clearing house. The arrow indicates the direction of the underlying commodity flow.

TABLE 1.7 **Exchange Rates (March 11, 2014): New York Closing Snapshot**

IN US$	US$		VS. % CHG		PER US$	
Country/currency	Tues	Mon	1-Day	YTD	Tues	Mon
Americas						
Argentina peso	0.1272	0.1272	unch	20.6	7.8635	7.8599
Brazil real	0.4233	0.4256	0.55	unch	2.3627	2.3497
Canada dollar	0.9004	0.9005	unch	4.6	1.1106	1.1105
Chile peso	0.001738	0.001756	1.05	9.4	575.47	569.50
Colombia peso	0.0004890	0.0004898	0.16	5.9	2044.80	2041.60
Ecuador US dollar	1	1	unch	unch	1	1
Mexico peso	0.0753	0.0757	0.50	1.8	13.2827	13.2161
Peru new sol	0.3567	0.3566	unch	unch	2.8034	2.8045
Uruguay peso	0.04517	0.04512	−0.11	4.5	22.1405	22.1655
Venezuela b. fuerte	0.15748031	0.15748031	unch	unch	6.3500	6.3500
Asia-Pacific						
Australian dollar	0.8976	0.9021	0.50	−0.7	1.1140	1.1085
1-mos forward	0.8957	0.9001	0.49	−0.7	1.1164	1.1110
3-mos forward	0.8921	0.8965	0.49	−0.7	1.1209	1.1154
6-mos forward	0.8865	0.8911	0.51	−0.6	1.1280	1.1223
China yuan	0.1628	0.1629	unch	1.4	6.1411	6.1389
Hong Kong dollar	0.1288	0.1288	unch	0.1	7.7624	7.7613
India rupee	0.01638	0.01640	0.11	−1.3	61.04995	60.97995
Indonesia rupiah	0.0000870	0.0000874	0.48	−5.5	11494	11439
Japan yen	0.00971	0.00968	−0.25	−2.2	103.01	103.28
1-mos forward	0.00971	0.00968	−0.25	−2.2	103.00	103.26
3-mos forward	0.00971	0.00969	−0.25	−2.2	102.97	103.23
6-mos forward	0.00972	0.00969	−0.25	−2.2	102.91	103.17
Malaysia ringgit	0.3035	0.3045	0.32	0.4	3.2945	3.2839
New Zealand dollar	0.8470	0.8472	unch	−2.9	1.1807	1.1804
Pakistan rupee	0.00991	0.00991	unch	−4.2	100.945	100.895
Philippines peso	0.0224	0.0224	0.08	0.4	44.585	44.551
Singapore dollar	0.7889	0.7882	−0.08	0.4	1.2676	1.2687
South Korea won	0.0009387	0.0009374	−0.14	0.9	1065.32	1066.80
Taiwan dollar	0.03300	0.03298	−0.06	1.2	30.301	30.319

TABLE 1.7 *continued*

Country/currency	IN US$		US$ VS. % CHG		PER US$	
	Tues	Mon	1-Day	YTD	Tues	Mon
Thailand baht	0.03089	0.03088	unch	−1.1	32.368	32.380
Vietnam dong	0.00005	0.00005	unch	−0.2	21089	21090
Europe						
Czech Rep. koruna	0.05066	0.05072	0.12	−0.8	19.739	19.716
Denmark krone	0.1857	0.1859	0.12	−0.8	5.3845	5.3779
Euro area euro	1.3860	1.3877	0.13	−0.8	0.7215	0.7206
Hungary forint	0.00441714	0.00444008	0.52	4.7	226.39	225.22
Norway krone	0.1678	0.1679	0.07	−1.8	5.9594	5.9551
Poland zloty	0.3281	0.3294	0.37	0.8	3.0476	3.0363
Romania leu	0.3077	0.3086	0.30	−0.1	3.2500	3.2402
Russia ruble	0.02743	0.02751	0.30	10.7	36.459	36.351
Sweden krona	0.1569	0.1570	unch	−1.0	6.3743	6.3711
Switzerland franc	1.1387	1.1393	0.05	−1.7	0.8782	0.8777
1-mos forward	1.1389	1.1396	0.06	−1.7	0.8780	0.8775
3-mos forward	1.1395	1.1401	0.06	−1.7	0.8776	0.8771
6-mos forward	1.1405	1.1411	0.05	−1.7	0.8768	0.8764
Turkey lira	0.4452	0.4508	1.26	4.5	2.2464	2.2185
UK pound	1.6617	1.6645	0.17	−0.4	0.6018	0.6008
1-mos forward	1.6613	1.6641	0.17	−0.4	0.6020	0.6009
3-mos forward	1.6605	1.6633	0.17	−0.4	0.6022	0.6012
6-mos forward	1.6593	1.6621	0.17	−0.4	0.6027	0.6016
Middle East/Africa						
Bahrain dinar	2.6528	2.6525	unch	unch	0.3770	0.3770
Egypt pound	0.1437	0.1437	unch	0.1	6.9613	6.9609
Israel shekel	0.2883	0.2878	−0.17	unch	3.4688	3.4747
Jordan dinar	1.4143	1.4139	unch	−0.1	0.7071	0.7073
Kenya shilling	0.01159	0.01155	−0.29	−0.2	86.297	86.547
Kuwait dinar	3.5530	3.5532	unch	−0.4	0.2815	0.2814
Lebanon pound	0.0006642	0.0006643	unch	unch	1505.50	1505.45
Saudi Arabia riyal	0.2667	0.2666	unch	unch	3.7502	3.7504
South Africa rand	0.0921	0.0931	1.05	3.5	10.8587	10.7455
UAE dirham	0.2723	0.2723	unch	unch	3.6729	3.6731

Source: Tullett Prebon, historical data prior to 12/09/14:ICAP plc; historical data prior to 6/9/11: Thomson Reuters. Available online at: http://online.wsj.com/mdc/public/page/2_3021-forex-20140311.html?mod=mdc_pastcalendar (last accessed May 27, 2015). Reprinted with permission of online.wsj 2014.

Concept Check 7

a. 100*US$1366.00=US$136,000.

Concept Check 9

There is no one answer to this question.

a. You don't know that troughs have bottomed out without being able to foresee the future.
b. You don't know that peaks have peaked out without being able to foresee the future.
c. The general answer is that you will see upward and downward movements in gold prices. However, this does not mean that you can accurately predict the *next* move—either whether it will be up or down or the duration of the movement (when it will reverse itself).

Concept Check 11

a. 12,500,000*US$.009715=$121,437.50

CHAPTER 2

HEDGING WITH FORWARD CONTRACTS

2.1	Motivation for Hedging	33
2.2	Payoff to a Long Forward Position	37
2.3	Payoff to a Short Forward Position	39
2.4	Hedging with Forward Contracts	43
2.5	Profits to a Naked (Unhedged) Long Spot Position	45
2.6	Profits to a Fully Hedged Current Long Spot Position	47
2.7	Adding Profit Tables to Determine Profits from a Fully Hedged Position	50
2.8	Combining Charts to See Profits from the Hedged Position	54

Why are forward and futures contracts important for risk management? The fact that both forward and futures contracts *lock in* the future prices of volatile commodities for future delivery opens up risk management hedging possibilities.

2.1 MOTIVATION FOR HEDGING

Start with the simplest case. Say you are a wheat farmer, or grain merchant, and you plan to bring your crop to market in 4 months' time. In the meantime, you have to make many expenditures to actually produce a wheat crop. Your first objective is probably just to stay in business. The risk you face is that the future spot price of wheat in 4 months is not known. So the selling price of your wheat crop in 4 months' time is unknown.

Call that future, unknown wheat price $P_T(\omega)$. We are using the same notation as before: t is the current date, $T=t+4$ months is the future date, P_t is the current spot price of the grade of wheat you are growing, and $P_T(\omega)$ is the future unknown spot wheat price.

All the uncertainties associated with $P_T(\omega)$ are summarized in the state of nature, ω. Things that go into ω are: worldwide supplies of wheat from global wheat-producing economies, worldwide demand for wheat, the weather including possible droughts, wildfires, heatwaves, and other acts of nature.

The time line is, once again,

As a future *seller* of wheat, your first objective is just to protect yourself against falling wheat prices. How can you accomplish this using basic derivatives?

The simplest alternative is to sell some or all of your wheat forward at the current 4-month forward price for your grade of wheat. That is, take the *sell* side of a 4-month wheat forward contract. You arrange this in the (OTC) wheat forward market. This suits your needs since forward contracts are customizable.

The terms, which are between you and the buyer, include: delivery terms, delivery location, grade of wheat and quality specifications, deferred payment procedure, dispute resolution procedure, and cancellation provisions.

Note that, instead of the wheat farmer, you could think of a grain merchant who plans on obtaining wheat crops and marketing them in 4 months. They both have the same basic concern, which is *falling* prices over the 4-month time horizon.

Who would take the opposite (*buy*) side of this transaction? A firm in the business of processing your grade of wheat into other products. Examples include cereal producers (e.g. Kellogg's), bread producers (e.g. Pepperidge Farm), and other manufacturers who employ wheat as a raw material in their production processes.

Note that the producers worry about wheat prices *rising,* while farmers and grain merchants worry about wheat prices *falling.* So *their* risk management problem is to protect themselves against *rising* wheat prices. The same derivative works for them, except they need to take the *buy* side of the contract.

Let's put some real-world numbers on this. The first step is to get a number representing the spot price of wheat on the current date.

HEDGING WITH FORWARD CONTRACTS

Go to online.wsj.com, 'Market data', 'Commodities and futures', 'Cash commodity prices', and finally scroll to 'Grains and feeds'. You will see a variety of different grades of wheat all with different prices. These include: Wheat, Spring 14%-pro Mnpls; $/bu.-U; Wheat No. 2 soft red, St. Louis, bushel-BP,U; Wheat hard KC bu; Wheat, No. 1 soft white, del Portland, Ore-U.

You will notice bid and ask prices, but look for the prices on Thursday, March 13, 2014 which varied from a high of $9.7800 per bushel, to a low of $5.9875 per bushel. Thursday's price for Wheat hard KC/bu. was $ 5.9875/bu.

One of the important features of commodities like wheat is that they have to be delivered to alternative locations. This partially accounts for the differences in prices. Demand and supply for the different grades also determines the price differentials.

The standard for *futures* trading in hard, red winter wheat is now CME's Globex under the symbol KE, although some is traded by open outcry in the wheat futures trading pit (now on ClearPort) under the symbol KW. Kansas City (KC) wheat was formerly traded on the KCBT, but merged with the CME. The cash flow time line is,

$$\begin{array}{ccc} \$5.9875\text{ /bu} & & P_T(\omega) \\ \hline t & & T \end{array}$$

The next step is to get a price quote from the wheat forward market. This is not always easy to do, because of the lack of centralization of forward markets. So we use a trick. We go to the futures markets and look for wheat futures prices there.

For this example, the appropriate futures exchange is the cme.com which we just introduced. Looking up the July 2014 KC Wheat contract under settlements and choosing the date Thursday, March 13, 2014, we find a final (settlement) price of $7.31'4 per bushel. This means $7.31 and 4/8 of cent ($.005), or $7.315 per bushel.

The *settlement* price is a technical price used by futures exchanges to mark accounts to market. For our purposes, think of it as an indicator of futures price levels at the close of the market. Now our picture is fleshing out.

36 FORWARD CONTRACTS AND FUTURES CONTRACTS

$$Fut_{t,T}=F_{t,T}=\$7.315/bu$$
$$P_t=\$5.9875/bu \qquad\qquad P_T(\omega)$$

$t=$March 13, 2014 $\qquad\qquad$ $T=$July 14, 2014

Now, all our ingredients are in place to devise a hedging strategy. We'll assume that the wheat farmer could engage in a forward contract at the current forward price of $F_{t,T}=\$7.315/bu$, for delivery in Kansas City on July 14, 2014 for the number of bushels he wishes to sell. Assume that number is 500,000 bushels.

■ CONCEPT CHECK 1

a. What price would the wheat farmer receive for his 500,000 bushels if he sold his wheat in the July 14, 2014 forward market on March 13, 2014? When would he receive payment? Assume that the forward price is equal to the futures price.

b. Does the answer to a. depend on what happens in the world wheat market during the period March 13, 2014 to July 14, 2014?

Let's take a closer look at the wheat farmer's alternatives and decision-making process. The wheat farmer has the following information upon which to base a decision on how to protect his potential wheat crop.

1. The current spot wheat market is represented by the spot price of $P_t=\$5.9875/bu$. This may have some bearing on his decision but the crop is only potential. The farmer does not yet have wheat to sell. He is looking to protect the *potential* value of his crop.

2. He does have the ability to sell forward his entire crop by entering into the forward contract today. His entire wheat crop will then be delivered into the forward contract for $\$7.315/bu$. This will result in a cash flow of $\$3,657,500=500,000*\$7.315$.

    In this case, he will be *fully* hedged against any and all movements in the future spot price of wheat.

3. He could remain unhedged. In this case, he would have to sell his wheat crop for whatever the spot market wheat price turns out to be on

July 14, 2014. The cash flow from selling his crop is unknown today since wheat spot prices, when he sells his crop, are determined only on July 14, 2014. The spot price at that time, when the transaction occurs, will depend on conditions in the spot wheat market.

It is clear that alternative 3 is riskier than alternative 2. The question we ask in finance is whether the risk is worth it. The answer depends on a number of factors. First, the wheat farmer probably is risk-averse. He probably doesn't care to gamble with his wheat crop by 'playing the wheat market' (alternative 3).

Typically, people like wheat farmers (or grain merchants) are considered 'hedgers'. Hedgers are risk-averse individuals who are in business for the long run, and want to be in business next season. So, their economic survival is paramount. Having entered the wheat industry, they already take on numerous operational and competitive risks.

These include uncontrollable and unpredictable things, like worldwide weather during the crop season. These have already been mentioned at the beginning of this section, under ω.

Hedgers, like the wheat farmer or grain merchant, typically hedge at least some of their output to reduce the volatility in their cash flows, and thereby make it easier on themselves to effectively manage their businesses. In particular, one reason for managing the volatility of cash flows is the presence of debt and potential bankruptcy.

Lenders may *require* the borrower to at least partially hedge their output. This itself is a hedge strategy on the part of the lender. Hedging the *entire* output is what the *most* risk-averse hedger would do. Doing so reduces the risk of their cash flows to zero as we will now investigate. Later, we will consider partial hedges, hedging part but not all of their output.

So, how do we hedge with forward contracts? And, how do we map out the risk, expected return profiles of our hedges? The first step in addressing these questions is to understand the *payoff* from a (long, short) forward position.

2.2 PAYOFF TO A LONG FORWARD POSITION

We start by getting familiar with the terminology of long forward contract positions. The long in a forward contract is also called the buyer or in symbolic terms the +. 'Buyers' of forward contracts aren't really buying forward contracts.

They are just *obligating* themselves to buy the underlying commodity at the expiration date of the forward contract, at the forward price determined today, $F_{t,T}$. The terminology 'buyer of a forward contract' is unfortunate but persists as street lingo.

Example 1 (Individual Stock Forwards, Long Position)

Suppose that you are long a 3-month forward contract on IBM common stock. Such contracts on individual stocks are available as futures contracts at onechicago.com. The contract calls for delivery of 1000 shares of IBM stock. Assume that the forward price (=futures price) today is $190 per share and that IBM is currently trading at about $185 per share. What are the potential payoffs to the long forward position? Let's use our time line to map out the situation.

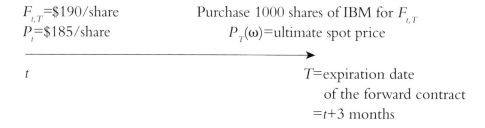

The payoff is unknown today because it depends on the ultimate IBM stock price $P_T(\omega)$, which will not be known until 3 months have passed. So we have to do 'scenario' (what-if) analysis.

Scenario 1 at *T*

Suppose that IBM's stock price in 3 months turns out to be $195/share. You take delivery of the 1,000 shares at the forward price of $190/share. Your expenditure is 1000*$190=$190,000.

What's your payoff? Well, you now own 1,000 shares of IBM stock, which the spot stock market values at $195/share. You could sell the 1,000 shares you own for 1000*$195=$195,000.

The payoff on this transaction is $195,000–$190,000=$5000. Here, we ignore any costs of trading shares and the like. These can be easily incorporated and add nothing at this point.

HEDGING WITH FORWARD CONTRACTS 39

Scenario 2 at *T*

As another possible scenario, suppose that IBM stock price in 3 months turns out to be $185/share. You would do well to buy the 1000 shares of IBM in the stock market at 1000*$185=$185,000.

But you cannot do so because, by taking the long forward position, you *obligated* yourself to buying the shares at the forward price of $190 per share. You now paid $190,000 for shares worth $185,000. This generates a *negative* payoff of $185,000–$190,000=–$5,000.

We learn from this that *the payoff to a long position in a forward contract can be positive or negative,* depending on whether the spot stock price at expiration of the forward contract is above or below the forward price at which you contracted at time *t*.

All other scenarios for $P_T(\omega)$ will show that the payoff to a long position in a forward contract on 1000 IBM shares will always be equal to $1,000*(+P_T(\omega)-F_{t,T})$. The minus sign because you buy at $F_{t,T}$ and the $+P_T(\omega)$ because you sell at $P_T(\omega)$.

■ CONCEPT CHECK 2

a. Fill in the third column of Table 2.1. Payoff means: payoff per share to a long forward position.

■ CONCEPT CHECK 3

a. Draw a Microsoft Excel chart of the payoff to the long forward position in Concept Check 2.

   The horizontal axis is the stock price at expiration, time *T*. The vertical axis is the payoff per share to the long forward position at time *T*.

2.3 PAYOFF TO A SHORT FORWARD POSITION

There are two ways to derive the payoff table and diagram for a short forward position. One is the 'cheat' method. Basically it says that for every long forward position, there is a corresponding short forward position. The payoff to the short forward position must be the negative (opposite) of the payoff to the long forward position, because every time the long makes money the short loses it and vice versa.

FORWARD CONTRACTS AND FUTURES CONTRACTS

TABLE 2.1 **Payoff to a Long Forward Position in IBM Contracted at $F_{t,T}$=\$190/share**

$F_{t,T}$	Stock Price @ Expiration	Payoff Per Share
190	145	
190	150	
190	155	
190	160	
190	165	
190	170	
190	175	
190	180	
190	185	
190	190	
190	195	
190	200	
190	205	
190	210	
190	215	
190	220	
190	225	
190	230	
190	235	
190	240	

Of course, this is all correct. But it is instructive to work out the payoff to a short forward position from scratch. When an individual 'sells a forward contract' he actually sells nothing. He merely *commits to sell* the underlying commodity in the future at the forward price agreed upon in the present. So selling a forward contract means *obligating oneself to a deferred sale commitment at the forward price*. Nothing more.

It doesn't mean 'selling the forward contract'. That's just imprecise street lingo which you should be familiar with. We will see later that, when initiated, a forward contract has zero value to all parties, so why would anyone want to sell something of zero value? The price would be zero.

HEDGING WITH FORWARD CONTRACTS 41

Key is that the forward price agreed upon today is a *commitment* price and it is fixed. Of course, the forward price for a given maturity contract does change over the life of the contract. But the changing forward price is for *new* commitments. That is, if you engage in a forward contract tomorrow with the same expiration date as mine today, you will almost certainly have a different forward price than mine.

However, both our forward prices are fixed as the commitment prices for our respective forward agreements. That is, upon delivery I will pay (receive) the forward price I contracted at as the buyer (seller). You, on the other hand will pay (receive) the forward price you contracted at as buyer (seller). Your forward price may be higher or lower than mine.

The point is that, at the specific time at which a forward contract is initiated, it *fixes* the transaction price at which the future transaction will take place, no matter what happens in the market in the period up to and including the expiration date.

To see what sellers face as shorts in forward contracts, note that the seller is *naked* the forward contract. This means that he does not have a position in the underlying spot market. In the example 1 we are discussing, the short currently owns no shares of IBM.

Nor did he own any underlying shares in the case of the long forward position. That was a naked long position also. Later, we will discuss what the payoffs look like for individuals who *combine* their spot positions with positions in forward contracts. Such individuals are typically hedgers.

Example 2 (Individual Stock Forwards, Short Position)

If I am *short* a forward contract on 1000 shares of IBM stock today for delivery in 3 months at the forward price today $F_{t,T}$=\$190/share, then I am obligated to deliver 1000 shares of IBM to the buyer on the delivery date agreed upon.

How do I do that given that I don't own any shares of IBM? I will have to go out and buy them in the spot market at the going price in 3 months of $P_T(\omega)$. Of course, that price is unknown today.

There will be an outflow of $1000*P_T(\omega)$ to pay for those shares at time T. Then, I will turn around and deliver those shares in fulfillment of my short forward position. On this leg of the transaction, I will receive $1,000*F_{t,T}$ =$1,000*\$190=\$190,000$ from the long counterparty in the forward contract.

What is my payoff? The answer is that we do not know until the expiration date of the contract arrives. Once again, we do scenario analysis across a range of ultimate (at expiration) stock prices $P_T(\omega)$.

42 FORWARD CONTRACTS AND FUTURES CONTRACTS

Scenario 1

Suppose that IBM's stock price in 3 months turns out to be $195/share. You purchase the 1000 shares at the spot market price of $195/share. Your expenditure is 1000*$195=$195,000.

Then, you turn around and deliver these shares to the long (as you obligated yourself to do at time t) for the forward price of $190/share resulting in an inflow of 1000*$190=+$190,000. The payoff on this transaction is+$190,000–$195,000=–$5000. Here, we ignore any costs of trading shares and the like.

Scenario 2

As another possible scenario, suppose that IBM stock price in 3 months turns out to be $185/share. You buy 1000 shares of IBM in the stock market at 1000*$185=$185,000. Then you deliver them into the forward contract to satisfy your short commitment. You get paid $190,000 for shares worth $185,000. That is a payoff of $190,000–$185,000=$5000.

We learn from this example that the *payoff to a short position in a forward contract can be positive or negative,* depending on whether the stock price at expiration of the forward contract is below or above the forward price. This is just the *opposite* of what we learned about the payoff to a long forward position.

We can now verify that the payoff to a short forward position in 1000 shares of IBM is always equal to $1,000*(+F_{t,T}-P_T(\omega))$. The minus $P_T(\omega)$ because you have to buy the spot commodity at $P_T(\omega)$ and the+$F_{t,T}$ because you sold it forward for $F_{t,T}$.

■ CONCEPT CHECK 4

a. Fill in the third column of Table 2.2. Payoff means: payoff per share to a short forward position.

■ CONCEPT CHECK 5

a. Draw a Microsoft Excel chart of the payoff to the short forward position in Concept Check 4. The horizontal axis is the stock price at expiration. The vertical axis is the payoff per share to the naked short forward position.

HEDGING WITH FORWARD CONTRACTS   43

TABLE 2.2 **Payoff to a Short Forward Position in IBM Contracted at $F_{t,T}=\$190$/share**

$F_{t,T}$	Stock Price @ Expiration	Payoff Per Share
190	145	
190	150	
190	155	
190	160	
190	165	
190	170	
190	175	
190	180	
190	185	
190	190	
190	195	
190	200	
190	205	
190	210	
190	215	
190	220	
190	225	
190	230	
190	235	
190	240	

Hint: one way that you can check your answers is to note that, in line with the 'cheat' method, the payoff to a short forward position is the mirror image in the horizontal axis of the payoff to a long forward position.

2.4 HEDGING WITH FORWARD CONTRACTS

We now go back to people like the wheat farmer (grain merchant) trying to protect his wheat crop (inventory) against essentially unforeseeable *declining* wheat spot prices. Simple as it sounds, we first have to determine what position the wheat farmer has in the spot market. Long or short?

44 FORWARD CONTRACTS AND FUTURES CONTRACTS

The wheat farmer (grain merchant) is *anticipating selling* his wheat crop (inventory) in 4 months' time, so he is currently long. His worry is that wheat spot prices will be lower than they are today. So the benchmark in his mind for wheat spot prices is the current wheat spot price. Most investors think that the 'best' indicator of the value of a commodity is the most recent price of that commodity.

Kansas City red, hard winter wheat was trading on the quote date at $5.9875/bu. Once again, we consider alternatives for the spot wheat price when the farmer delivers his 500,000 bushels to market.

Scenario 1

Suppose that the spot wheat price turns out to be $5.50/bushel in 4 months' time. The farmer, unhedged, could sell his wheat crop for $2,750,000. That sounds like a lot of money but compared to the benchmark of $2,993,750=500,000* $5.9875/bu., he lost $243,750. This loss is almost a quarter of a million dollars, and may be more than enough to put him out of business.

Alternatively, suppose that the farmer *sold* his wheat *forward* for $7.315/bu. This would result in a cash inflow of $3,657,500=500,000*$7.315. Compared to the benchmark represented by the current spot price of wheat, that is a profit of $663,750. This figure is just 500,000*($7.315–$5.9875).

Why? Because the farmer is selling his wheat forward for $7.315/bushel while people in the spot wheat market are currently selling spot wheat for $5.9875/bushel. The current spot wheat price is taken as the benchmark, just as before.

We can't line up time and take *future* wheat spot prices as the benchmark, because these are unknown today. Remember that the transaction in an ordinary forward contract means that delivery takes place later. The forward price, $F_{t,T}$, is determined today in the current forward market. Later we will consider how to calculate the *net profit* over the 4-month period, which must consider financing costs.

Scenario 2

Here is another scenario. Suppose that wheat appreciates to $7.605 per bushel by the end of 4 months. Then, unhedged, the wheat farmer would have made a gross profit of 500,000*($7.605–$5.9875)=$808,750. This is greater than he would have received by selling his crop forward which resulted in a gross profit, compared to the benchmark, of only $663,750. The difference is $808,750–$663,750=500,000*($7.605–$7.315), which represents the *extra* amount generated by selling the commodity in the spot market, rather than in the forward market.

Of course, there are many alternatives for the spot wheat price in 4 months. If the subsequent spot wheat price rises above the forward price, then the wheat farmer would have 'done better' in terms of gross profits by being unhedged. If the subsequent wheat price is lower than the forward price, he would have done worse.

How do we know which scenario will happen? We do not know. That is a matter of speculation. What we do know is that if the wheat farmer wants to stay in business for next season, he needs to manage the *risk* of his position. Not just the expected return. That's where derivatives, like forward contracts, enter the picture by providing risk-management tools.

2.5 PROFITS TO A NAKED (UNHEDGED) LONG SPOT POSITION

■ CONCEPT CHECK 6

a. Fill in the second column of Table 2.3. The position is fully unhedged and anticipates selling 500,000 bu. of wheat in 4 months in the spot market. The current spot price is $5.9875/bu.

■ CONCEPT CHECK 7

a. Draw a Microsoft Excel chart of the profit per bushel to the fully unhedged position in Concept Check 6. The horizontal axis is the spot wheat price at expiration. The vertical axis is the profit per bushel to the unhedged wheat position.

We see from this example that the unhedged position is fully exposed to uncertainty (volatility) in the subsequent spot price of wheat. If spot wheat prices *fall below* the current level of $5.9875 per bu., then the wheat farmer (grain merchant) will suffer a loss because the wheat farmer (grain merchant) will be forced to sell his wheat for a lower price than what sellers would transact at today.

FORWARD CONTRACTS AND FUTURES CONTRACTS

TABLE 2.3 **Profits to a Naked (Unhedged) Long Spot Position with the Current Spot Price=$5.9875/bu**

Wheat Spot Price @ Expiration	Profits from Wheat Position Unhedged
5.8	
5.85	
5.9	
5.95	
6	
6.05	
6.1	
6.15	
6.2	
6.25	
6.3	
6.35	
6.4	
6.45	
6.5	
6.55	
6.6	
6.65	
6.7	
6.75	

If wheat prices *rise above* the current level, the wheat farmer profits, because he can later sell his wheat for more than the going price today. We are ignoring carrying charges at the moment by considering gross profits. Later, we will consider *net* profits, which is defined as gross profits net (minus) carrying charges.

From this exercise, we also see that the profits for an unhedged position are just the profits from holding the commodity long. This amounts to (the number of units held long)*(the price *change* over the period). Or in our notation, $(500{,}000)*(+P_T(\omega)-P_t)$.

HEDGING WITH FORWARD CONTRACTS **47**

2.6 PROFITS TO A FULLY HEDGED CURRENT LONG SPOT POSITION

We want to recalculate the profits from ownership of the spot commodity *combined* with the forward sale of the farmer's (grain merchant's) wheat. Then, we will compare them to those from the unhedged position.

First, we need to discuss what goes into this profit calculation. As in the case of the unhedged position, the farmer calculates the profit from his forward sale relative to the current spot wheat price of $5.9875 per bu. This time he is *not* selling his wheat at the unknown going spot wheat price, $P_T(\omega)$. Instead, he is *selling it forward* for the fixed price $F_{t,T}$.

Per bushel profits on this strategy are $+F_{t,T}-P_t$ where P_t is the current (today) spot wheat price. Note the use of P_t because it represents the per unit price of the spot commodity today. For our case, $F_{t,T}=\$7.315/\text{bu}$. and $P_t=\$5.9875/\text{bu}$. The per bushel profit on the hedged position should be $\$7.315-\$5.9875=\$1.3275$. Multiplying by the scale factor (number of bushels) we obtain, $500{,}000*\$1.3275=\$663{,}750$, just as before.

In this case, the farmer (grain merchant) is *guaranteed* a gross profit of $663,750, *no matter what happens* in the spot market for wheat over the 4-month period. The forward sale is a far *safer* way of selling his wheat. In fact, it is riskless. That is its major benefit.

In order to obtain this benefit of risk reduction, the farmer has to give up some upside potential. That is, the forward sale gives him downside protection in return for giving up upside potential. Since the farmer probably doesn't want to gamble with his wheat crop, the forward sale is a useful alternative.

We have already seen the payoff graphs for a long and a short forward position, and for a naked (unhedged) long position. What does the picture look like if we *combine* a long spot position with a short forward position? This is a fairly easy exercise, but it is worth delving into it more thoroughly.

A fully hedged position will have a constant profit equal to (the number of units)$*(+F_{t,T}-P_t)$, which in our wheat example is $500{,}000*(\$7.315-\$5.9875)$ or $663,750. Let's take this apart a bit.

There are two components to a fully hedged position. First, there is the underlying commodity which we wish to hedge, the 1000 shares of IBM for the stock example or the 500,000 bushels of wheat.

Next comes the position one has in the underlying commodity. In both examples, the investor was *long* 1000 shares of IBM and the wheat farmer (grain merchant) was *long* 500,000 bushels of wheat. The profits to a naked

48 FORWARD CONTRACTS AND FUTURES CONTRACTS

long commodity position are equal to (the number of units)$*(+P_T(\omega)-P_t)$. The reason they are long is that both individuals anticipate *selling* their underlying commodity in the future. Even though the farmer may not have his crop available, he is still *implicitly long*.

The primary worry is that IBM's stock price will *fall* and the spot wheat price will *fall* by the time of the sale. To protect themselves, market participants take the opposite position in a derivative security; in this case, a short position in a forward contract. That is, they *sell forward at time t* their respective spot commodity, at the going forward price $F_{t,T}$.

This makes economic sense. If you are worried about price volatility of a commodity, sell it in a market for a price that has no volatility, a fixed price like the forward price, $F_{t,T}$.

The payoff to a short forward position depends on the spot price at expiration of the forward contract and is equal to (the number of units)$*$ $(+F_{t,T}-P_T(\omega))$. To get the *profit* from a short forward position, we would have to subtract the current cost of the forward contract. That cost is always zero, as we will shortly see, when the forward contract is initiated. So there is nothing to subtract.

Now we can combine both profit figures to get the profit figure for a fully hedged long spot position,

$$
\begin{aligned}
&\text{(the number of units)}*(+P_T(\omega)-P_t)+\text{(number of units)}*(+F_{t,T}-P_T(\omega))\\
&\quad=\text{(the number of units)}*(+P_T(\omega)-P_t+F_{t,T}-P_T(\omega))\\
&\quad=\text{(the number of units)}*(-P_t+F_{t,T})\\
&\quad=\text{(the number of units)}*(+F_{t,T}-P_t)
\end{aligned}
$$

Miraculously, the unknown spot price at expiration, $P_T(\omega)$, cancels out and we get what we derived before which is a *constant* profit that has nothing to do with what happens in the spot market between now and expiration of the forward contract. This means that we have successfully *hedged* our long spot position, if success means we have removed all of its risk.

■ CONCEPT CHECK 8

a. Fill in the third column of Table 2.4 below. Profit means: profit for the sale of all 500,000 bu. of wheat subsequent to a short forward position taken today.

HEDGING WITH FORWARD CONTRACTS — 49

TABLE 2.4 **Profits to a Long Spot Position Sold Forward at $F_{t,T}$**

$F_{t,T}$	Wheat Spot Price @ Expiration	Profit to a Spot Position in 500,000 bu. of Wheat Sold Forward by a Short Forward Contract
$7.315/bu	5.8	
	5.85	
	5.9	
	5.95	
	6	
	6.05	
	6.1	
	6.15	
	6.2	
	6.25	
	6.3	
	6.35	
	6.4	
	6.45	
	6.5	
	6.55	
	6.6	
	6.65	
	6.7	
	6.75	

■ CONCEPT CHECK 9

a. Draw a Microsoft Excel chart of the total profits to the fully hedged position in Concept Check 8.

The horizontal axis is the spot wheat price at expiration. The vertical axis is the profit for 5,000 bushels of the fully hedged wheat position.

50 FORWARD CONTRACTS AND FUTURES CONTRACTS

2.7 ADDING PROFIT TABLES TO DETERMINE PROFITS FROM A FULLY HEDGED POSITION

There is another very useful method for determining profits on relatively complex positions like hedged positions. The key is to recognize that such positions involve *combinations* of positions. For our wheat farmer (grain merchant) the components are,

1. A long position in 500,000 bu. of spot wheat. The current spot price is $P_t=\$5.9875$/bu.

2. A short forward position to sell 500,000 bushels of wheat in 4 months' time at the current forward price of $7.315/bu.

You have already derived the profit Table 2.3 for 1. in Concept Check 6, but we will reproduce it here in Table 2.5. The formula from which the numbers in Table 2.5 are derived is,

$$(\text{the number of units})*(+P_T(\omega)-P_t)=500,000*(+P_T(\omega)-P_t).$$

■ CONCEPT CHECK 10

a. Fill in the third column of Table 2.6. Profit means: profit to a naked short forward position in 500,000 bushels of wheat. Note that this is a *naked* short forward position.

Table 2.6 is derived from the formula,

$$(\text{the number of units})*(+F_{t,T}-P_T(\omega))$$
$$=500,000*(+F_{t,T}-P_T(\omega))$$
$$=500,000*(+\$7.315-P_T(\omega)),$$

since the forward price today for delivery of spot wheat 4 months from today is $F_{t,T}=\$7.315$/bu.

Now, we can combine the two tables, Table 2.5 and Table 2.6, and see what hedging does for us in this simple scenario. The combined Table 2.7 represents the profit from the fully hedged spot position. Table 2.7 is just the sum (combination of Table 2.5 and Table 2.6).

HEDGING WITH FORWARD CONTRACTS 51

TABLE 2.5 **Profits from a Fully Unhedged Spot Position in Wheat**

Wheat Spot Price @ Expiration	Profits from Wheat Position unhedged
5.8	−93750
5.85	−68750
5.9	−43750
5.95	−18750
6	6250
6.05	31250
6.1	56250
6.15	81250
6.2	106250
6.25	131250
6.3	156250
6.35	181250
6.4	206250
6.45	231250
6.5	256250
6.55	281250
6.6	306250
6.65	331250
6.7	356250
6.75	381250

Table 2.7 is exactly what we obtained before, but now we can get some further insight into what hedging does. Let's first summarize our price data in Table 2.8.

FORWARD CONTRACTS AND FUTURES CONTRACTS

TABLE 2.6 **Profits from a Short Forward Position in Wheat**

$F_{t,T}$	Wheat Spot Price @ Expiration	Profit to a Naked Short Forward Position in 500,000 bu. of wheat
$7.315/bu	5.8	
	5.85	
	5.9	
	5.95	
	6	
	6.05	
	6.1	
	6.15	
	6.2	
	6.25	
	6.3	
	6.35	
	6.4	
	6.45	
	6.5	
	6.55	
	6.6	
	6.65	
	6.7	
	6.75	

A little scenario analysis will serve to illustrate what is going on.

Scenario 1

First, suppose that the spot wheat price *drops* to $P_T(\omega)=\$5.85/bu$ at the end of 4 months. Compared to the current wheat spot price level, that is a loss of $500,000*(+P_T(\omega)-P_t)=500,000*(+\$5.85-\$5.9875)=-\$68,750$.

Fortunately, the farmer was hedged in the forward market where he made a profit of,

$$500,000*(+F_{t,T}-P_T(\omega))=500,000*(+\$7.315-\$5.85)$$
$$=+\$732,500.$$

Overall, his position *locked* in a profit of $732,500-$68,750=$663,750.

HEDGING WITH FORWARD CONTRACTS — 53

TABLE 2.7 **Profit from the Fully Hedged Spot Position**

Wheat Spot Price @ Expiration	Profits from a Naked (Unhedged) Long Spot Wheat Position	Profit To a Naked Short Forward Position in 500,000 bu. of wheat	Profits to the Combined (Fully Hedged) Position: Long Spot, Short Forward
5.8	−93750	757500	663750
5.85	−68750	732500	663750
5.9	−43750	707500	663750
5.95	−18750	682500	663750
6	6250	657500	663750
6.05	31250	632500	663750
6.1	56250	607500	663750
6.15	81250	582500	663750
6.2	106250	557500	663750
6.25	131250	532500	663750
6.3	156250	507500	663750
6.35	181250	482500	663750
6.4	206250	457500	663750
6.45	231250	432500	663750
6.5	256250	407500	663750
6.55	281250	382500	663750
6.6	306250	357500	663750
6.65	331250	332500	663750
6.7	356250	307500	663750
6.75	381250	282500	663750

TABLE 2.8 **Price Data Summary**

Current Spot Price	P_t	$5.9875 hu
Current Forward Price	$F_{t,T}$	$7.315 /bu
Ultimate Spot Price	$P_T(\omega)$	?

Scenario 2

Next, suppose that the spot price of wheat goes *up* in the next 4 months to $7.50/bu. Then the profit on the naked spot position would be,

$$500,000*(+\$7.50-\$5.9875)$$
$$=500,000*\$1.5125$$
$$=\$756,250.$$

However, we have to remember that we are hedged, so that we have to settle up on our obligatory short forward position on which there was a negative profit (loss) of $92,500=500,000*(+\$7.315-\$7.50)$.

The reason for the loss is that we pre-committed to sell the wheat forward at $7.315/bu and the spot market turned out to be higher by $7.50–$7.315 per bu. So we lost $.185 per bushel which is a grand total loss of $500,000*\$.185=\$92,500$.

Overall, our total profit is $756,250–$92,500=$663,750, which is the same as what it was under the first scenario.

Scenario 2 seems to imply that we could be 'worse off' by hedging. If we *knew in advance* that the spot price of wheat would be $7.50/bu with complete certainty, then clearly we *would* be better off in final wealth by *not* hedging.

However, we do not know. So, we have to be prudent and protect our spot wheat position against downside risk. In return for the protection afforded by forward contracting, we have to give up some upside profit potential in the event that the spot price of wheat goes up above the forward price.

These two scenarios for the ultimate spot price, indicate that the short hedge *locks in* the profit figure equal to (the number of units)$*(+F_{t,T}-P_t)$.

2.8 COMBINING CHARTS TO SEE PROFITS FROM THE HEDGED POSITION

Rather than just adding up the profits to the two components of the hedged position entry by entry, long spot wheat and short a forward contract, we can add up the *charts* for each of these components. This reduces the amount of work we have to do and will prove to be a useful technique when we get to options.

Figure 2.1 indicates the results of this process for our example.

HEDGING WITH FORWARD CONTRACTS

FIGURE 2.1 **Graphical Method to Get Hedged Position Profits**

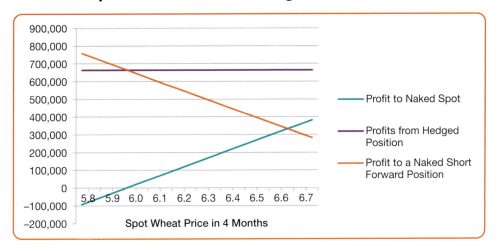

The orange line plus the blue line equals the purple line. In a sense, the orange line cancels out the blue line, the downward slope of the orange line (representing losses on the short forward position) are being exactly offset by the upward slope of the blue line representing profits on the long spot position.

That is, losses (gains) on the long spot position are being exactly offset by gains (losses) on the short forward position. The net effect is the *lock-in* of profits on the hedge at the fixed amount of $663,750. This amount is called the *time t basis* and will be discussed in detail in Chapter 6.

56   FORWARD CONTRACTS AND FUTURES CONTRACTS

■ KEY CONCEPTS

1. Motivation for Hedging.
2. Profits vs. Payoffs.
3. Payoff to a Long Forward Position.
4. Payoff to a Short Forward Position.
5. Hedging with Forward Contracts.
6. Profits to a Naked (Unhedged) Long Spot Position.
7. Profits to a Fully Hedged Current Long Spot Position.
8. Adding Tables to Determine Profits from a Fully Hedged Position.
9. Combining Charts to Determine Profits from the Hedged Position.

■ END OF CHAPTER EXERCISES FOR CHAPTER 2

1. You hold 1000 shares of IBM stock currently trading for P_t=\$185. You intend to hold the position for the next 3 months.

   a. Ignoring any dividends or payouts over the next 3 months, map out the profit per share diagram for your position.

   Note that $P_T(\omega)$ is on the horizontal axis and profits per share is on the vertical axis.

2. Referring back to Kansas City red winter wheat on the quote date, suppose that \$7.2650/bu. was the current spot wheat price.

   a. Fill in the second column of Table 2.9. The position is fully unhedged and anticipates selling 500,000 bu. of wheat in 4 months in the spot market.
   b. Draw a Microsoft excel chart of the profit per bushel to the fully unhedged position. The horizontal axis is the spot wheat price in 4 months. The vertical axis is the profit per bushel to the unhedged wheat position.

HEDGING WITH FORWARD CONTRACTS 57

TABLE 2.9 Data for End of Chapter 2, Exercise 2

Wheat Spot Price in 4 months	Profits from Wheat Position Unhedged
6.70	
6.75	
6.80	
6.85	
6.90	
6.95	
7.00	
7.05	
7.10	
7.15	
7.20	
7.265	
7.30	
7.35	
7.40	
7.45	
7.50	
7.55	
7.60	
7.65	

FORWARD CONTRACTS AND FUTURES CONTRACTS

3. a. Fill in the third column of Table 2.10. Profit means profit for the sale of all 500,000 bu. of wheat subsequent to a short forward position taken today. Assume the same current spot price as in exercise 2.

   b. Draw an Excel chart of the total profits for all 5,000 bushels to the fully hedged position. The horizontal axis is the spot wheat price at expiration. The vertical axis is the profit for 5,000 bushels of the fully hedged wheat position.

TABLE 2.10 **Data for End of Chapter 2, Exercise 3**

$F_{t,T}$	Wheat Spot Price @ Expiration	Profit to a Spot Position in 500,000 bu. of Wheat Sold Forward by a Short Forward Contract
$7.645/bu	6.70	
	6.75	
	6.80	
	6.85	
	6.90	
	6.95	
	7.00	
	7.05	
	7.10	
	7.15	
	7.20	
	7.265	
	7.30	
	7.35	
	7.40	
	7.45	
	7.50	
	7.55	
	7.60	
	7.65	

HEDGING WITH FORWARD CONTRACTS 59

4. a. Fill in Table 2.11 based on the information already given.
   b. Using the graphical method, draw an Excel chart of the unhedged spot position and the short forward position. Then combine the two to obtain the profits from the fully hedged position.

TABLE 2.11 **Data for End of Chapter 2, Exercise 4**

Wheat Spot Price @ Expiration	Profits from a Naked (Unhedged) Long Spot Wheat Position	Profits to a Naked Short Forward Position in 500,000 bu. of wheat	Profits to the Combined (Fully Hedged) Position: Long Spot, Short Forward
6.70			
6.75			
6.80			
6.85			
6.90			
6.95			
7.00			
7.05			
7.10			
7.15			
7.20			
7.265			
7.30			
7.35			
7.40			
7.45			
7.50			
7.55			
7.60			
7.65			

60 **FORWARD CONTRACTS AND FUTURES CONTRACTS**

5. Long positions in some underlier are not the only positions that require price protection. Think about firms like Kellogg's or Pillsbury which use wheat as a raw material in their production processes. Suppose that Pillsbury is planning, in mid-March of 2014, on buying KC hard, red winter wheat in mid-July of 2014.

   a. What is Pillsbury's primary worry? What position does Pillsbury have in the spot wheat market? Explain.
   b. How can Pillsbury risk manage its worry in a.?
   c. Fill in Table 2.12 for the payoffs to a naked long forward position. The 4-month wheat forward price is $F_{t,T}=\$7.645/bu$.

TABLE 2.12 **Data for End of Chapter 2, Exercise 5**

Wheat Spot Price @ Expiration	Profit to a Naked Long Forward Position in 500,000 bu. of Wheat
6.70	
6.75	
6.80	
6.85	
6.90	
6.95	
7.00	
7.05	
7.10	
7.15	
7.20	
7.265	
7.30	
7.35	
7.40	
7.45	
7.50	
7.55	
7.60	
7.65	

HEDGING WITH FORWARD CONTRACTS **61**

d. Draw a Microsoft Excel chart of the Payoff to a Long Forward Position in wheat forwards using the data. The horizontal axis is the wheat price at expiration. The vertical axis is the payoff per share to the naked long forward position.

e. Looking at the Excel chart in d. and explain exactly how the long forward position helps the producer manage the 4-month wheat price risk.

■ SELECTED CONCEPT CHECK SOLUTIONS

Concept Check 2

TABLE 2.1 ANSWER	**Payoff to a Long Forward Position in IBM contracted at $F_{t,T}=\$190$/share**	
$F_{t,T}$	**Stock Price @ Expiration**	**Payoff Per Share To a Long Forward Contract**
190	145	−45
190	150	−40
190	155	−35
190	160	−30
190	165	−25
190	170	−20
190	175	−15
190	180	−10
190	185	−5
190	190	0
190	195	5
190	200	10
190	205	15
190	210	20
190	215	25
190	220	30
190	225	35
190	230	40
190	235	45
190	240	50

Concept Check 3

FIGURE 2.2 **Payoff Per Share to a Long Forward Contract**

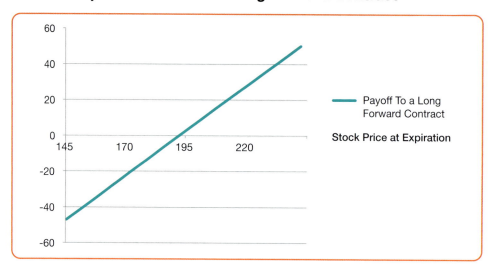

Concept Check 5

FIGURE 2.3 **Payoff Per Share to a Short Forward Contract**

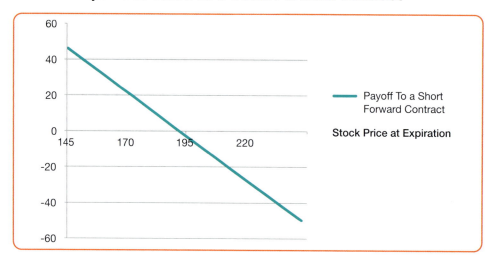

Concept Check 7

FIGURE 2.4 **Profits per bu. for the Unhedged Position**

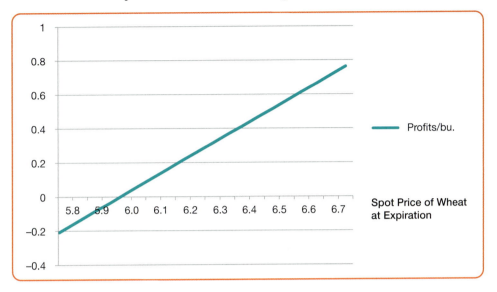

FORWARD CONTRACTS AND FUTURES CONTRACTS

Concept Check 10

TABLE 2.6 ANSWER	Profits from a Short Forward Position in Wheat	
$F_{t,T}$	Wheat Spot Price @ Expiration	Profit to a Naked Short Forward Position in 500,000 bu. of wheat
$7.315 /bu	5.8	757500
	5.85	732500
	5.9	707500
	5.95	682500
	6	657500
	6.05	632500
	6.1	607500
	6.15	582500
	6.2	557500
	6.25	532500
	6.3	507500
	6.35	482500
	6.4	457500
	6.45	432500
	6.5	407500
	6.55	382500
	6.6	357500
	6.65	332500
	6.7	307500
	6.75	282500

CHAPTER 3

VALUATION OF FORWARD CONTRACTS ON ASSETS WITHOUT A DIVIDEND YIELD

3.1	Comparing the Payoffs from a Naked Long Spot Position to the Payoffs from a Naked Long Forward Position	66
3.2	Pricing Zero-Coupon, Unit Discount Bonds in Continuous Time	66
	3.2.1 Continuous Compounding and Continuous Discounting	69
	3.2.2 Pricing Zero-Coupon Bonds	71
3.3	Price vs. Value for Forward Contracts	73
3.4	Valuing a Forward Contract at Expiration	74
3.5	Valuing a Forward Contract at Initiation	75
3.6	Interpreting Forward Contracts via Synthetic Forward Contracts	78

In this chapter, we start pricing derivative securities by pricing forward contracts, arguably the simplest derivatives form. You don't really understand financial securities until you can price them, and derivative financial securities are no exception. Pricing derivatives is a major industry both in academia and in industry, because to know how to trade one has to know the value of what one trades. Thinking for the moment of trading as finding undervalued and overvalued securities assumes that we must first have a reasonable idea of the *fair* value of securities. That is, trading opportunities based on mispriced securities are ultimately dependent on correct (neither over- nor under-valued) pricing.

One thing to note here is that when we talk about pricing, we mean *relative* pricing. That is, we aren't trying to find the absolute value of derivative securities, assuming that such a thing exists. Everything is priced relative to everything else. In the case of derivatives, which are based upon underlying securities, this is particularly relevant.

Derivative prices have to be strongly related to the prices of their underlying securities. The practical implication of this is that, the more you know about the securities underlying derivative securities, including how to price them, the better off you will be in attempting to understand the derivative securities based on these underlying instruments.

3.1 COMPARING THE PAYOFFS FROM A NAKED LONG SPOT POSITION TO THE PAYOFFS FROM A NAKED LONG FORWARD POSITION

To begin pricing forward contracts, we will compare two payoff charts that we already have. The first is the profits to a naked, long spot stock position. We will slightly modify this chart by showing just the *payoff* to a naked long spot stock position.

The difference between the payoff and the profit is that the profit subtracts the *current cost* of generating the payoff, which in this case is just the current stock price. Both the profit and the payoff diagram are given below. Here we are thinking of the stock price example given in Chapter 2. Here is a brief summary of that example.

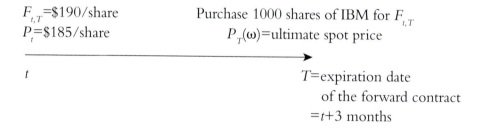

The *profit* (at time T) per share to a naked long position in IBM shares is $P_T(\omega) - P_t$, and is given in Figure 3.1. The *payoff* (at time T) per share to a naked long position in IBM shares is $P_T(\omega)$, and is given in Figure 3.2.

The third payoff chart that we have is the payoff per share to a naked long forward contract, which is $P_T(\omega) - F_{t,T}$. Why do we not also consider the profit chart for a long forward contract? To do so, we would have to subtract the current value of the forward contract to the long. There are several important things to note here. The first is that, unlike spot prices, the forward price is *not the value* of the forward contract!

FORWARD CONTRACTS WITHOUT A DIVIDEND YIELD

FIGURE 3.1 **Profits Per Share to a Naked Long Spot Position**

FIGURE 3.2 **Payoffs Per Share to a Naked Long Spot Position**

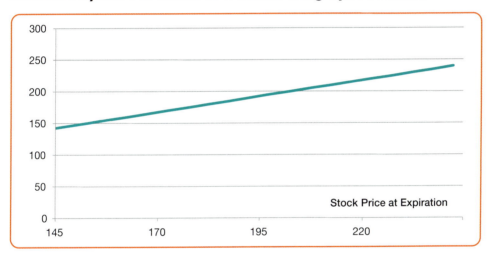

As discussed in Chapter 2, the forward price is not an asset price like a stock price. Remember, when you 'buy' a forward contract, you aren't really buying anything, despite the street lingo. You are simply taking on a *commitment* today to buy the underlying commodity at the forward price in the future. This is very different from a spot transaction like buying 1000 shares of IBM stock today.

Second, no payment is made today. Unless it is a prepaid forward contract, payment is usually deferred. What we need to determine is the current value of a forward contract. As we shall soon see, the current forward price is determined so that, at initiation of the forward contract, the current value of a forward contract is zero to all market participants, shorts and longs.

This implies that the payoff to a long forward contract is the same as the profit to a long forward contract, so there is no extra profits chart. Figure 3.3 illustrates the payoff profile to a long forward position.

FIGURE 3.3 **Payoffs (=Profits) Per Share to a Naked Long Forward Position**

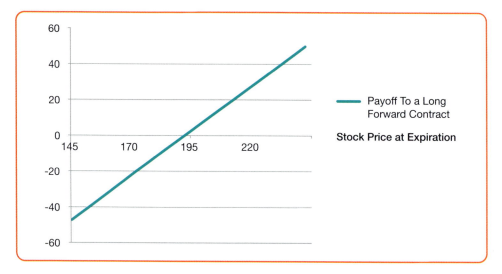

Comparing the payoff to a naked long spot position to the payoff to a long forward position on a single chart, we obtain the following combined chart in Figure 3.4.

FIGURE 3.4 **Payoffs Per Share to a Naked Long Spot Position and to a Naked Long Forward Position**

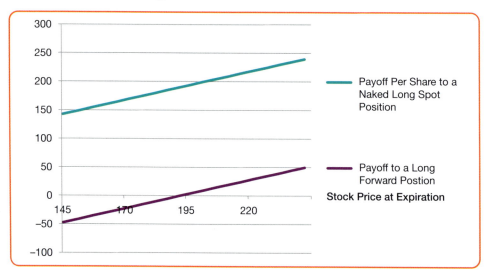

FORWARD CONTRACTS WITHOUT A DIVIDEND YIELD

Therefore, the payoff profiles for a naked long spot position and for a long forward position are essentially equivalent, except for the vertical distance between them. The vertical distance is just the current forward price, $F_{t,T}$, which in this case is $190 per share. This is going to prove very useful in pricing forward contracts. We have to take care of a few preliminaries first. For now, the brief summary of what we have just done is,

1. Payoff per unit to a naked long spot position = $+P_T(\omega)$,
2. Payoff per unit to a long forward position = $+P_T(\omega) - F_{t,T}$,
3. The difference between the payoff per unit to a naked long spot position and the payoff per unit to a naked long forward position,

$$= +P_T(\omega) - (+P_T(\omega) - F_{t,T})$$
$$= +F_{t,T}.$$

3.2 PRICING ZERO-COUPON, UNIT DISCOUNT BONDS IN CONTINUOUS TIME

3.2.1 Continuous Compounding and Continuous Discounting

In order to prepare the way for understanding derivatives including forward contracts, we have to deal with the idea and mechanics of compounding and discounting in continuous time. This is just the old familiar present value (PV) and future value (FV) found in all basic finance texts. Except that, in continuous time, we don't use $1/(1+r)^N$ nor $(1+r)^N$ or all the variations thereof for alternative cash flow streams.

What do we use? We will start with the simplest possible example. You put $100 into an account that pays interest continuously at an annualized rate equal to $r\%$ per year.

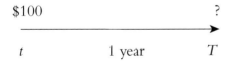

You leave the $100 in the account for 1 year. How much does it grow to by year end?

In order to answer this question, we can't use the FV function $(1+r)^N$, because that assumes discrete compounding. Our account, on the other hand, grows moment by moment.

We can divide the year interval into N little pieces. Then, associate to each time interval $(T-t)/N$ the appropriate interest rate which is r/N. The FV in the account will be equal to $\$100*(1+r/N)^N$.

But we have to go further. We have to let the chopping up of time become infinite, so that each sub-interval of time is just the moment. When we do that, mathematics tells us that $(1+r/N)^N$ becomes e^r where e is the exponential function, otherwise known as $\exp(.)$.

We can put our numbers into this: $r=5\%=.05$, and $T-t=1$ year$=1.0$. So $e^{r*1}=e^{.05}=1.051271$. Our $100 will compound at this rate and grow to $105.1271. This represents an equivalent annual rate (EAR) of 5.1271%, which is the *maximum rate* an account can grow by given the quote rate of 5% and the compounding method. That is, all other forms of compounding like semi-annually, quarterly, monthly, and even daily will result in a lower effective annual rate.

Continuous *discounting* is just the inverse of continuous compounding. The picture just looks a little different. Instead of putting $100 into an account today, we expect to receive $100 with certainty at the end of 1 year, where the continuously compounded annualized interest rate is equal to $r=5\%$ per year. What is this promise worth today?

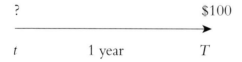

The answer is $\$100/e^{r*1}$ which is the same thing as $\$100*e^{-r}$. In our case, $e^{-.05}=1/1.051271$. So the $100 to be paid one year from now is worth $95.1229 in today's dollars.

What happens if $\tau=T-t$ is not equal to one year, as in our convenient example? The compounding growth factor becomes $e^{r\tau}$, where τ is measured in years or fractions thereof.

For example, suppose we are continuously compounding at an annualized rate of 10% per year but only for 3 months. Then $\tau=.25$, that is 1/4 of a year. Then $e^{r\tau}=e^{.10*.25}=e^{.025}=1.0253$. One hundred dollars placed into this account will grow to $102.53.

FORWARD CONTRACTS WITHOUT A DIVIDEND YIELD 71

■ CONCEPT CHECK 1

You expect to receive $100 at the end of 3 months where the annualized, continuously compounding rate is 10% per year.

a. What is that $100 promise worth in today's dollars?

■ CONCEPT CHECK 2

You put $1000 into an account today that pays interest at an annualized, continuously compounded rate of 6% per year. You leave it there for 1 year.

a. How much is in the account at the end of the year?
b. How much represents return of principal?
c. How much represents interest?

■ CONCEPT CHECK 3

The annualized, continuously compounded rate is 3% per year. You expect to receive $1000 at the end of 2 months.

a. What is that promise worth today?

3.2.2 Pricing Zero-Coupon Bonds

We are finally ready to do an important pricing exercise which is to price a unit discount bond in continuous time. The data for this is an annualized, continuously compounded rate of $r\%$ per year and a time to maturity of τ years. Note that in practice if τ is given in any other units than years (or fractions thereof), then it has to be converted into years. The conversion procedure was shown above.

Let's start with a simple unit discount bond in continuous time. Namely one that pays $1 at the end of a year.

? $1

t 1 year T

We want its price today (at time t). We will denote that price by $B(t,T)$; B for bond, t is the current time, and maturing at time T. The answer simply requires us to apply the discount factor which we know is $e^{-r\tau}$. The current price of the bond is therefore,

$$B(t,T)=e^{-r\tau}*\$1$$
$$=\$e^{-r\tau}.$$

We can use this result to price *any* zero-coupon bond. Suppose that its face value (value at maturity) is $\$F$, it has τ years to maturity and the annualized, continuously compounded rate is $r\%$ per year. Then the current price must be $e^{-r\tau}*F$.

■ CONCEPT CHECK 4

Given the information above, suppose that $F=\$1,000$, $\tau=2$ months, and $r=2\%$.

a. What is the current price of the corresponding zero-coupon bond?

Here is another interesting example. Suppose that the zero-coupon bond has face value equal to the current forward price of an underlying commodity, $F_{t,T}$. That is, this zero-coupon bond will have as its payoff the forward price $F_{t,T}$. An economic situation that corresponds to this payoff is that of the short in a forward contract. If you short a forward contract today (time t), then you are selling forward the underlying commodity for $F_{t,T}$. You will receive $+F_{t,T}$ when you deliver the commodity into the forward contract.

■ CONCEPT CHECK 5

Suppose you long a forward contract at time t at the forward price $F_{t,T}$.

a. What will be the cash flow due to settling the forward commitment at time T?

Note that we do not look at the cash flow from selling the asset we have acquired at time T for its going spot price $P_T(\omega)$. The question is about settling the forward commitment only.

CONCEPT CHECK 6

a. Price a zero-coupon bond with face value equal to $F_{t,T}$.

CONCEPT CHECK 7

a. Price a zero-coupon bond with face value equal to $F_{t,T}$=$190. The forward contract has 4 months to maturity (expiration) and the annualized, continuously compounded risk-free rate is 4%.

3.3 PRICE VS. VALUE FOR FORWARD CONTRACTS

We already discussed the difference between the forward *price* and the *value* of a forward contract. The forward price is simply a *commitment price* for a future transaction. The *value* of a forward contract is something *created* in the trading process as the spot price changes. This will become much clearer when we discuss futures contracts in Chapter 5, because their values are *realized* and *reconciled* daily.

This underscores the difference between derivatives and their underlying instruments. In the world of stock or bond prices, there is no difference between price and fundamental value. Bonds and stocks are primary financial securities that represent claims to the earnings' streams generated by specific real assets. Derivatives are not primary securities, they have no meaning when separated from the securities that underlie them.

Now, we need to investigate what is meant by *the value of a forward contract*. What creates this value and how is it related to the relationship between the spot price and the forward price? These are key questions that will give us a deeper understanding of how forwards work.

The first thing to note is that value is an ever-changing quantity that depends on time. So there are multiple valuation problems in valuing forward contracts. The easiest valuation problem is valuation at expiration, time T.

3.4 VALUING A FORWARD CONTRACT AT EXPIRATION

We already know the solution to this problem. But we will see that the value of a forward contract at expiration depends on whether you are the buyer or the seller.

In Chapter 2, we saw that the value of a forward contract at expiration depends on whether you took a long or a short position at time t (now). The payoff per unit to a long position in a forward contract will always be equal to $+P_T(\omega)-F_{t,T}$.

That's because the forward contract allows and obligates you to *purchase* a good for a per unit cost of $F_{t,T}$ which you can later sell in the spot market for its going price of $P_T(\omega)$ at time T. If the ultimate spot price, $P_T(\omega)$, is above the commitment forward price, $F_{t,T}$, then the payoff is positive. Otherwise, the payoff is negative. What does it cost today to engage in the long forward position? The answer is that it costs nothing today.

Next, consider the short forward position. A short position in a forward contract obligates you to *sell* the underlying commodity for the forward price $F_{t,T}$. Since we are considering a naked forward position, the assumption is that you have none of the underlying commodity.

At expiration of the forward contract, time T, you will need to go out and buy it in the spot market for $P_T(\omega)$, if only to be able to honor your commitment in the forward market. Then you will immediately sell the acquired commodity in the forward market for $+F_{t,T}$. Your payoff at time T is the forward price you receive minus the cost of the underlying commodity. The payoff to a short position in a forward contract will always be equal to $+F_{t,T}-P_T(\omega)$.

From this by now familiar material we can say that,

1. The per unit *Value of a Long Position* in a forward contract at expiration

    $=+P_T(\omega)-F_{t,T}$.

2. The per unit *Value of a Short Position* in a forward contract at expiration

    $=+F_{t,T}-P_T(\omega)$.

Note that this value can be positive or negative to either party. When it is positive (negative) to the long, it is negative (positive) to the short. This is what is usually meant when people say that (naked) forward positions are a

FORWARD CONTRACTS WITHOUT A DIVIDEND YIELD **75**

zero sum game. Your gains are my losses and vice versa. Of course, this assumes the long and short are holding *naked* forward positions.

If they were hedgers (holding explicit or implicit spot positions at time *t*) as well, then those positions need *not* constitute a zero sum game. That is, their overall positions in spot and forwards can be win-win for both the long and the short!

Unfortunately, a lot of the popular discussion simply drops the word 'naked' in its zero sum description and extrapolates to derivatives markets in general. The zero sum interpretation of derivatives markets applies, in general, to naked positions only.

3.5 VALUING A FORWARD CONTRACT AT INITIATION

We have succeeded in valuing forward positions, long and short, at expiration. Next, we turn to the much harder problem of valuing them today. In order to accomplish this, we need a pricing technique since it is not at all obvious how to price derivative securities.

We *could* use a very sophisticated version of the workhorse of basic finance, present value (PV). That procedure involves trying to find a risk-adjusted discount rate (RADR) to be used to discount the security's risky expected cash flows, and knowing the relevant probabilities. However, in practice, this could turn out to be very difficult because the data required to carry out this procedure is difficult to acquire. Fortunately, there is a much easier procedure.

Let's start with the observation that forward contracts involve no up-front payments. Usually, to acquire the expected cash flows from an asset, one has to pay its current value today. Since the usual forward contract's specifications involves zero cost today the forward market is telling us that, upon initiation, forward contracts are priced so as to force their current values to zero.

This is a very peculiar situation indeed. We can acquire the obligation today, at zero cost, to purchase an asset later. That obligation has potential positive value in the future. Isn't that an arbitrage opportunity? Not quite. Remember, as we have just seen: potential value can be negative as well as positive. So, this is puzzling, but it isn't an arbitrage.

Arbitrages will be discussed in detail in Chapter 4, section 4.6.1. But for now, an arbitrage opportunity (arb) is a strategy that costs nothing today and generates no negative cash flows (costs) in the future, and that generates at least one *positive* cash flow in the future under some scenario.

76 **FORWARD CONTRACTS AND FUTURES CONTRACTS**

Forward contracts don't accomplish this at all. In fact, at expiration you get the cards that nature deals to you in the form of a positive or a negative value based on your position today (short or long), and the outcome of the ultimate spot price relative to the forward price.

If you are a little confused at this point, don't worry. You are not alone. When people talk about swaps, which are simply chains of forward contracts as we will see in Chapter 8, they always seem to mention that the '*nominal*' value of such swaps is in the trillions of dollars. Despite the fact that the nominal value is not the correct value concept, the statement depends on when you are looking at them.

If you are looking at them at initiation, then their total value is actually zero. Just like forward contracts, from which they are constructed, their values at initiation are set to zero. Even at expiration, if we add up the value of all swaps (forwards) to all the shorts and longs, then that value is once again zero. This is because the gains (losses) to the longs are equal to the losses (gains) to the shorts, so that after the accounting is done, it's a grand wash in the end. That is just the definition of a zero sum game.

If one of the counterparties to a forward contract *defaulted,* then the other party would suffer the corresponding unpaid loss in value which is therefore destroyed. The same argument also holds for swaps. Also, at some intermediate time between now and expiration, there generally is some value created in forward contracts that is not yet transferred to the winning parties from the losing parties (see End of Chapter Exercise 2). The same holds for swaps discussed in Chapter 8. The existence of unpaid value creates incentives to default. Futures markets take care of this problem. A firm foundation in forwards is necessary for understanding swaps.

But how do we know that the current values of initiated forward contracts are actually zero? Maybe they are mispriced? What 'forces' their current values to be zero? Let's look into this. Well, spot prices are given (exogenously) today and we can't do much about current spot prices, other than simply taking them as given and not trying to mess with them too much. What else goes into forward prices?

Let's go back to our earlier discussion about the difference between the payoffs to long spot positions and long forward positions. We saw there that the only difference is the forward price, $F_{t,T}$. In symbols,

1. The payoff per unit to a naked long spot position

$$=+P_T(\omega)$$

FORWARD CONTRACTS WITHOUT A DIVIDEND YIELD

2. The payoff per unit to a naked long forward position

$$=+P_T(\omega)-F_{t,T}$$

3. The difference between the payoff per unit to a naked long spot position and the payoff per unit to a naked long forward position

$$=+P_T(\omega)-(+P_T(\omega)-F_{t,T})$$
$$=+F_{t,T}$$

At this point we can do a very useful exercise, the implications of which will be apparent momentarily. Suppose we want to engineer a financial security that has exactly the same payoff as the payoff to 3. That payoff is simply $+F_{t,T}$ at time T, and nothing before time T.

The time, cash flow line is,

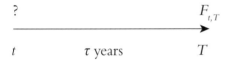

What would we have to do today in order to generate as payoff at time T the forward price at time t? We know the answer. This is just the payoff to a long position in a zero-coupon bond with face value equal to the forward price and maturing at the same time as the forward contract. We know exactly how to price this financial security from section 3.2. Its price today is $B(t,T)=e^{-r\tau}*F_{t,T}$.

To summarize, the payoff to the difference between a long spot position and a long forward position is exactly the same as the payoff to a long position in a zero-coupon bond with face value equal to the forward price, and maturing at the same time as the forward contract.

In the language of financial engineering, we have *replicated* the payoff to the original (natural) difference strategy by a synthetic strategy which is simply to buy the appropriate zero-coupon bond. Buy because we need to generate a positive cash flow equal to $+F_{t,T}$ at time T.

A basic principle of finance (the no-arbitrage principle, or the law of one price) is that if you can do what we just did, then the current costs of the two strategies must be the same. Otherwise, there *would be* a quick arbitrage opportunity. We will get into all this soon, but let's just follow through with what we have derived and see its pricing implications.

So, consider the *current cost(s)* of generating these alternative payoffs. To generate the payoff to a long spot position, we have to buy the spot commodity today for its current price $+P_t$.

In order to generate the payoff to a long forward position, we have to pay nothing today. Yet we get something that looks very much like the spot price. The only difference between the two strategies is the forward price $F_{t,T}$.

So, the combined payoff to the difference between long spot and long forward is just the forward price. The cost today of generating this combined payoff is just the current spot price P_t, because the forward position has no current cost.

The current cost of the replicating zero-coupon bond is $B(t,T)=e^{-r\tau}*F_{t,T}$. By the no–arbitrage principle, these two costs must be the same: $P_t=B(t,T)= e^{-r\tau}*F_{t,T}$. This simple relationship allows us to determine the forward price or, more precisely, the *equilibrium* forward price.

The *equilibrium forward price* is the forward price that makes the current value of the forward contract equal to zero. That is consistent with the absence of arbitrage opportunities.

All we have to do is multiply both sides of $P_t=e^{-r\tau}*F_{t,T}$ by $e^{r\tau}$ to obtain $F_{t,T}=e^{r\tau}*P_t$. Note that $1/e^{r\tau}=e^{-r\tau}$. Therefore, $F_{t,T}=e^{r\tau}*P_t$ is the equilibrium forward price.

■ CONCEPT CHECK 8

a. A forward contract has 3 months to maturity. It is written on an underlying commodity with a current price $P_t=\$151$. The annualized, continuously compounded risk-free rate is 3%. Calculate the equilibrium forward price.

3.6 INTERPRETING FORWARD CONTRACTS VIA SYNTHETIC FORWARD CONTRACTS

What accounts for this difference of $F_{t,T}$ between the long stock position and the long forward position?

The structure of a long position in a forward contract is to pay nothing today and then to pay the forward price at time T. The spot position is just the opposite. We have to pay the spot price P_t today, but then we don't have to pay out anything later.

That's the essential difference between a spot transaction and a forward transaction: a forward transaction is just a *deferred* spot transaction with a zero

FORWARD CONTRACTS WITHOUT A DIVIDEND YIELD   79

current cost. Pay nothing today but pay later. Vs. pay today for the spot commodity and pay nothing later.

But now we can pin down this difference to obtain a better understanding of what a forward contract is, and what it is not. When you take a long position in a forward contract, you get to buy the underlying commodity's payoff in the future at zero cost today.

When you buy the underlying commodity today, you obtain its payoffs in the future but you also pay the spot price today. In both cases, long forward and long spot, you obtain the same thing in the future: namely the underlying commodity and therefore its payoffs.

What is the missing ingredient in the long forward contract position that distinguishes it from the long spot commodity position? The answer is *embedded leverage*.

How can you purchase an asset without paying for it today? The answer is simple. Just borrow. In most cases, people do not typically borrow 100% of an asset's current cost, but they can come close. If you insist on literally paying nothing today, then you have no choice but to borrow the entire current cost of the asset.

Of course when the loan comes due, at expiration of the forward contract in our case, you will have to pay off the full amount of the loan which consists of the interest and the full amount of the principal. That's how loans work. All this suggests that *a long forward position is economically equivalent to a long spot position in the underlying commodity 100% financed by issuing a zero-coupon bond.*

We can follow this logic in detail for our case. Our strategy is to take a long spot position in the underlying commodity today and to *fully* finance it by issuing a zero-coupon bond. This is a (100% leveraged) strategy. Note that we are rewriting the equilibrium relationship between the forward price and the spot price in the form $P_t = e^{-r\tau} * F_{t,T}$.

1. Initiate a long spot position at time t for a current cost of P_t,
2. Borrow $P_t = e^{-r\tau} * F_{t,T}$ to fully finance 1.

The *payoffs* at time T to 1 and 2 are indicated in the cash flow time line below,

| 1. | $P_T(\omega)$ |
| 2. | $-F_{t,T}$ |

$t \qquad\qquad \tau \text{ years} \qquad\qquad T$

80 FORWARD CONTRACTS AND FUTURES CONTRACTS

Note that our bond, used to finance the spot position, is the zero-coupon bond with face value equal to the forward price $F_{t,T}$. Also note that the full payoff to this strategy is the payoff to a naked long forward position in the underlying commodity.

What have we accomplished? We have *replicated* the full payoff to a naked long forward position by a synthetic strategy using the underlying commodity and a position in a bond to finance it.

So now we have two ways to construct a long position in a forward contract. We can just initiate such a position naturally by entering into the forward market for the underlying commodity and taking the long position in the desired maturity contract.

Or, we can buy the underlying commodity today and pay nothing today, fully financing it by issuing a zero-coupon bond with face value equal to the forward price $F_{t,T}$ and maturity equal to the maturity of the natural forward contract. Either way, we get the *same* payoff at time T. The current costs are the same too. Zero in both cases.

So we have matched up the natural instrument (a long forward position) with the synthetic instrument (a 100% leveraged position in the underlying commodity) exactly. To all intents and purposes, the natural position and the synthetic position are economically equivalent (we ignore transactions costs).

What then is a long forward position? It is a 100% leveraged long position in the underlying commodity. That's the economics. The difference between a fully paid for long position in the underlying commodity and a fully financed long position in the underlying commodity is the zero-coupon bond issuance.

That's what accounts for the $-F_{t,T}$ component of the forward position, in the cash flow time line above. It corresponds to paying off the implicit loan embedded in the long forward position. Otherwise, a long position in the underlying commodity and a long forward position are identical.

We conclude that,

A. *A Long Forward Position=A Long Spot Position+Issuing a Zero-Coupon Bond with face value equal to the forward price.*

This is an important point to dwell on. What forward contracting adds to the mix is leverage—100% leverage. It's like buying a house. If it weren't for mortgages, you would have to pay the full price up front. Mortgage bonds allow you to cut your current cost at the future cost of having to pay off the mortgage's principal and interest.

FORWARD CONTRACTS WITHOUT A DIVIDEND YIELD · 81

Unlike a normal mortgage, with a forward contract full payment is expected when the contract matures. Also, unlike a normal mortgage, there is no (equity) down payment. Since leveraged securities are riskier than unleveraged securities, a naked long position in a forward contract is quite a risky position.

We will use the italicized relationship above in A. to derive the corresponding current costs for each component in A. That is, to translate each strategy into its corresponding cost,

a. Current Cost of a *Long Forward Position*=0,
b. Current Cost of a *Long Spot Position*=P_t,
c. Current Cost of *Issuing a Zero-Coupon Bond with face value equal to the forward price*$=-e^{-r\tau}*F_{t,T}$.

Putting the costs where they belong in the relationship we arrive at the equilibrium forward price relationship we already derived.

> A. *Cost of Long Forward Position=Cost of Long Spot Position*
> *+Cost of Issuing a Zero-Coupon Bond with face value equal*
> *to the forward price.*

$$0=P_t$$
$$+(-e^{-r\tau}*F_{t,T}) \qquad \textbf{(A.'s Costs)}$$

Note here that when we think of a *positive* cost like purchasing the underlying commodity, we list its price as$+P_t$. Borrowing is a negative cost, hence the minus sign in front of $e^{-r\tau}*F_{t,T}$ in the brackets.

We can also see this another way. When we considered the difference between a long spot position and a long forward position, we saw that the difference between the two was $+F_{t,T}$. This difference corresponds to *receiving* $F_{t,T}$ at time *T*.

This is what you would *receive* if you invested in a zero-coupon bond with face value $F_{t,T}$ payable at time *T*. So instead of borrowing the value of the underlying commodity, we invest (lend) in such a bond,

> B. *A Long Spot Position–A Long Forward Position=Investing in a Zero Coupon Bond with face value equal to the forward price.*

82   **FORWARD CONTRACTS AND FUTURES CONTRACTS**

Rearranging B., this says that,

> C. *A Long Spot Position=A Long Forward Position+Investing in a Zero Coupon Bond with face value equal to the forward price.*

Rearranging this, we get the same result as in A because—(investing in a zero-coupon bond with face value equal to the forward price) is the same as borrowing by issuing that zero-coupon bond.

That is,

> D. *A Long Forward Position=A Long Spot Position−Investing in a Zero-Coupon Bond with face value equal to the forward price, or*

> E. *A Long Forward Position=A Long Spot Position+Issuing a Zero-Coupon Bond with face value equal to the forward price.*

Note that E. is the same as our original A. All these modes of interpretation, A.–E., are economically equivalent.

■ ■ ■

FORWARD CONTRACTS WITHOUT A DIVIDEND YIELD **83**

■ KEY CONCEPTS

1. Payoff diagrams for: long spot, long forward position.
2. Pricing zero-coupon (discount) bonds in continuous time.
3. Price vs. Value for a forward contract.
4. Pricing a forward contract at initiation.
5. Pricing a forward contract at expiration.
6. Synthetic forwards.
7. Embedded leverage.

■ END OF CHAPTER EXERCISES FOR CHAPTER 3

1. *(Valuing a Forward Contract at t and at T)*

   a. We have valued a forward contract position at *initiation* of the position in the contract. What is that value to the long?
   b. What is the value to the long at *expiration* of the contract?
   c. What is the value to the short at initiation of the position in the contract?
   d. What is the value to the short at expiration of the contract?

2. *(Valuing a Forward Contract at t′ where t<t′<T)*

   a. Draw a time line and put t, t', and T on it. Also put the spot price at time t, P_t, on the time line at time t and the spot price at time t', $P_{t'}$.
   b. Next, suppose that the forward price at time t for expiration at time T is $F_{t,T}$. The proper notation for the forward price at time t' for expiration at time T would be $F_{t',T}$. Put both of these on the time line.
   c. What is the formula for $F_{t,T}$?
   d. What is the formula for $F_{t',T}$?
   e. Suppose you took a long position at time t in the forward contract maturing at time T. What would be the value of that position at time T?
   f. Subsequently, at time t', you took a short position in the same forward contract maturing at time T. What would be the value of that position at time T?
   g. Now think of the economics of e. and f. What would be the value of your combined position at time T (long the forward at time t and short the same forward at time t')?

FORWARD CONTRACTS AND FUTURES CONTRACTS

h. Ignoring discounting, what would be the value of your combined position at time t'?

i. Should we discount g. to get h.? That is, should we account for the time value of money to transform the value in g. to the value in h.?

Hint: What is your investment in the long position initiated at time t? What is your investment in the short position initiated at time t'? We discount in order to take into account the opportunity cost of an investment. What is the opportunity cost of your combined position?

3. *(Calculating Equilibrium Forward Prices)*

At 12:27 p.m. on March 26, 2014 Google stock was trading at $1,155.32. At that time, Google was not expected to pay any dividends to its shareholders for the next year. A roughly 3-month futures contract on Google stock was trading on the futures exchange onechicago.com on March 26, 2014 at $1154.5000 (bid) and $1159.400 (asked). You want to check whether this number is reasonable.

a. You decide to calculate the equilibrium 3-month forward price from the formula $F_{t,T} = e^{rT} * P_t$. Assuming an annualized, continuously compounded risk–free rate of .0004 calculate $F_{t,T}$.

b. If the answer to a. is within the bid–asked spread, it would be considered a reasonable number. Is it?

4. *(Short Positions in Forwards)*

A long position in a forward contract is just a long position in the underlier 100% leveraged by risk-free debt.

a. What is a short position in a forward contract?

5. *(Embedded Leverage)*

Embedded leverage is a characteristic of derivatives, but what does it really mean? We know that a long position in a forward contract is just a long position in the underlier 100% leveraged by risk-free debt.

a. Consider a long position initiated in a forward contract today, at time t, that matures at time T. The forward price is $F_{t,T}$. $F_{t,T}$ is also the face

FORWARD CONTRACTS WITHOUT A DIVIDEND YIELD — 85

value of the zero-coupon bond in the leveraged stock position that replicates the long forward position. What is the current value of the bond implicit in the long forward position? Assume an annualized, continuously compounded risk free rate of $r\%$.

b. Thinking of the long forward position as implicitly holding the underlying stock and fully borrowing to pay for it today, how are you going to pay the $F_{t,T}$ owed on the bond at time T?

c. Consider the two scenarios at time T. Fill in Table 3.1.

TABLE 3.1 **End of Chapter 3, Exercise 5c**

	Scenario 1: $S_T \geq F_{t,T}$	Scenario 2: $S_T < F_{t,T}$
Amount of Debt Repaid from Proceeds of the Stock Sale		
Value Remaining		

d. Looking at Table 3.1, what is the effect of the leverage embedded in the long forward position?

■ SELECTED CONCEPT CHECK SOLUTIONS

Concept Check 2

a. The compounding factor is $e^{.06}=1.061837$. One thousand dollars will grow to $1.061837*\$1,000=\$1061.837$.

b. Principal is $1000.

c. Interest is $61.837.

Concept Check 4

First, it is always a good idea to draw a time, cash flow line for the problem. Get into the habit of doing so, because time, cash flow lines reduce errors significantly.

a. For this problem, the time cash flow line is the following,

$$B(t,T) \qquad\qquad\qquad \$1000$$

$$t \qquad\qquad \tau \text{ years} \qquad\qquad T$$

Note that we have to first convert 2 months into years to get $\tau=2/12$ $=.1667$. The price

$$B(t,T)=e^{-r\tau}*F$$
$$=e^{-.1667*.02}*\$1000$$
$$=0.995011*\$1000$$
$$=\$995.011.$$

Concept Check 6

a. A zero-coupon bond with face value equal to $F_{t,T}$ is just like any other zero-coupon bond. Its price today is $e^{-r\tau}*F_{t,T}$.

Concept Check 8

a. After converting 3 months to years $\tau=0.25$, use the formula,

$$F_{t,T}=e^{r\tau}*P_t$$
$$=e^{.025*.03}*\$151$$
$$=1.007528*\$151$$
$$=\$152.1367.$$

CHAPTER 4

VALUATION OF FORWARD CONTRACTS ON ASSETS WITH A DIVIDEND YIELD

4.1	Stock Forwards when the Stock Pays Dividends	88
4.2	Modeling Continuous Yields: An Introduction to Non-Stochastic Differential Equations	90
	4.2.1 Modeling Zero-Coupon Bond Yields	90
	4.2.2 Modeling Continuous Dividend Yields for Stocks	93
4.3	How Dividend Payments Affect Stock Prices	94
4.4	How Capital Gains Affect Stock Prices	98
4.5	Pricing Forward Contracts on Stocks with a Dividend Yield Using the Net Interest Model	99
4.6	Pricing a Forward Contract on a Dividend-Paying Stock Using No-Arbitrage	100
	4.6.1 Arbitrage Definitions	100
	4.6.2 Forward Pricing Using No-Arbitrage	102
4.7	Currency Spot and Currency Forwards	103
	4.7.1 Price Quotes in the FX Market	103
	4.7.2 Pricing Currency Forwards	105
	4.7.3 Pricing FX Forward Contracts Using No-Arbitrage	106
	4.7.4 An Example of Pricing FX Forward Contracts	107
4.8	Appendix: Modeling Stock Returns with and without Dividends	109

88 FORWARD CONTRACTS AND FUTURES CONTRACTS

4.1 STOCK FORWARDS WHEN THE STOCK PAYS DIVIDENDS

In our discussion in Chapter 3 of pricing forward contracts on common stocks, we ignored the fact that many stocks pay dividends. That discussion works for stocks that do not pay dividends over the life of the forward contract. When dividends are paid, the critical question is whether they are paid or not paid *over the life* of the derivatives contract, not whether they are paid at all.

When they are paid, the dividend pricing model is essential for pricing stock index forwards (futures) and currency forwards (futures). Since stock index futures and currency futures are among the most popular derivative contracts, our time generalizing the no-payoff model will have its own payoffs.

As just noted, payouts on an instrument underlying a derivatives contract usually refer to payments made by that instrument *during the life* of the derivatives contract. Quarterly dividends on common stocks are the most familiar example. When we aggregate stocks into large portfolios, like the portfolio upon which the S&P 500 Index is based, the component stocks pay dividends at different times. So, we like to think of dividends as payable *continuously*.

Thinking in continuous time is useful and essential for understanding many of the more advanced applications. These applications include the Black–Scholes option pricing model. Also, continuous-time derivatives reasoning is so much neater than the discrete-time approach. The more technical aspects of this chapter are in the Appendix, section 4.8, and are well within your reach.

I suggest working through this material. It will help to open the door to the mystique of option pricing. All you might have to do is review a little standard calculus. In fact, modern option pricing theory is a major application and success story for non-standard (stochastic) calculus. We will give an introduction to stochastic calculus in Chapter 16 because the material in this chapter can be covered with ordinary calculus, but the material in Chapter 16 cannot.

For stock indices, we can think of dividend payments as being paid continuously at a certain, constant payout rate of ρ. For example, annualized dividend yields on large common stock portfolios in the USA are typically in the range of $\rho=3\%$ to 5%. This means 3% to 5% of the current value of the underlying stock index are paid out as dividends *on an annual basis*.

In symbols, over a small interval of time $[t,t+\Delta t]$, $\text{DIV}_{[t,t+\Delta t]}=\rho*\Delta t*I_t$ where $\text{DIV}_{[t,t+\Delta t]}$ are the dividends paid out over time $[t,t+\Delta t]$, ρ is the constant annualized dividend rate, I_t is the current value of the Index, and $\rho*\Delta t$ is the de-annualized dividend yield. One reason for this apparently low value is that a number of the S&P 500 stocks have zero-dividend yields.

FORWARD CONTRACTS WITH A DIVIDEND YIELD   89

The pricing concept we need in order to account for payouts on the underlier is called the *cost of carry*. There are benefits, as well as (borrowing) costs, to holding financial instruments. If you purchase individual stocks or a stock portfolio, you are entitled to receive the dividends those stocks pay over the holding period.

If you purchase bonds, you get the coupon (interest) payments those bonds pay over the holding period. When you purchase commodities like wheat or heating oil, you get the benefits resulting from the convenience of having them available in inventory. These benefits are usually summarized by what is called the *convenience yield* of the commodities held.

A simple example of convenience yield is the following. Suppose that you have an umbrella in your backpack as a hedge against the possibility of rain. There are costs to carrying the umbrella, such as the extra weight you have to lug around all day. But there are benefits as well. In case it does rain, you are covered and can save yourself the trouble of getting soaked or trying to find an umbrella for sale. Price gouging is possible in emergency situations, meaning that you are unlikely to get the best price for an umbrella in a rainstorm.

This kind of example is why many (but not all) firms keep excess (of what they can sell in the very short run) inventory in stock. Such *excess* inventory incurs costs of storage, but pays its way by earning a convenience yield. In the case of dividend-paying common stocks or stock portfolios, the dividend yield ρ is a *direct* benefit of holding stocks. In commodities, such as heating oil, the convenience yield is usually an *indirect* benefit. Whatever form it takes, there is value to it which must be taken into account in pricing derivatives.

■ CONCEPT CHECK 1

a. Discuss the *direct* and *indirect* costs of carrying (storing) inventories.
b. Is the *convenience yield* a direct or indirect cost or a benefit to the inventory holder? Why?
c. Can you tie convenience yield in with the concept of hedging?

Now suppose that you want to finance stock purchases today by borrowing the needed amount $\$S_t$ per share at the riskless rate r per annum. To do so, you issue enough zero-coupon bonds maturing at time T to currently generate $\$S_t$ per share. The holding period is $\tau=T-t$.

If you want to purchase 100 shares today you would borrow the amount $100*\$S_t$. If the stock pays zero dividends over the holding period you would owe $e^{r\tau}*S_t$ per share at the end of the borrowing period. However, if the stock pays a continuous dividend at the rate ρ, then you can use the dividends to pay off some of the interest on your loan. As an example, if r=5% and ρ=3% then your *net* cost of borrowing is $r-\rho$=2%, on an annual basis.

4.2 MODELING CONTINUOUS YIELDS: AN INTRODUCTION TO NON-STOCHASTIC DIFFERENTIAL EQUATIONS

4.2.1 Modeling Zero-Coupon Bond Yields

In order to properly incorporate a continuous dividend yield into the forward pricing mechanism, we have to first understand how to model continuous dividend yields. As already noted, this material will be very useful when we discuss continuous-time option pricing models in Chapter 16.

We have already done a bit of this when we priced zero-coupon bonds in continuous time in Chapter 3, section 3.2.2. Here, we focus on the idea of an *instantaneous* yield. As shown in Chapter 3, a zero-coupon bond paying $1 at maturity with time to maturity of $\tau=T-t$ is priced today at $B(t,T)=e^{-r\tau}$.

A little basic calculus, in the form of the 'chain rule', will provide us with some insight into where this formula comes from, and into modeling yields in continuous time, which is our objective.

Taking the derivative of $B(t,T)$ with respect to time,

$$\frac{dB(t,T)}{dt} = \frac{de^{-r\tau}}{dt}$$

$$= \frac{de^{-r\tau}}{d(-r\tau)}\frac{d(-r\tau)}{dt}$$

$$= e^{-r\tau}*\frac{d(-r(T-t))}{dt}$$

$$= e^{-r\tau}*(-r(-1))$$

$$= r*e^{-r\tau}$$

In the third equality, we used the fact that $de^x/dx=e^x$ where $x=-r\tau$. Taking a few mathematical liberties, by cross-multiplying, we can rewrite this as,

$$\frac{dB(t,T)}{B(t,T)} = r*dt \qquad \qquad \textbf{(Bond equation)}$$

FORWARD CONTRACTS WITH A DIVIDEND YIELD   91

which says that the *instantaneous* percentage rate of return on the bond–which is *defined* as the change in the bond price over a very small interval of time, $dB(t,T)$, divided by what you currently have to pay for the bond, $B(t,T)$— equals the instantaneous risk-free rate of $r*dt$. This shows that if the bond is priced at $B(t,T)=e^{-rT}$, then its instantaneous rate of return is $r*dt$.

We can also work backwards by solving (Bond equation) to get $B(t,T)=e^{-rT}$. This is rather important for understanding the current application as well as for later ones, so we will do it step by step. Working backwards means that we start from the assumption that $dB(t,T)/B(t,T)=r*dt$ expressed in (Bond equation).

We will work with the natural log function of the bond price: $\ln(\cdot)$ applied to $B(t,T)$ and use the 'chain rule' of calculus again,

$$\frac{d \ln\left(B(t,T)\right)}{dt} = \frac{d \ln\left(B(t,T)\right)}{dB(t,T)} * \frac{dB(t,T)}{dt}$$

$$= \frac{1}{B(t,T)} * \frac{dB(t,T)}{dt}$$

$$= \frac{\dfrac{dB(t,T)}{B(t,T)}}{dt}$$

$$= r \quad \text{from (Bond equation)}$$

From this last equation, after multiplying through by dt we obtain (Log Bond equation):

$$d \ln\left(B(t,T)\right) = r * dt \qquad \textbf{(Log Bond equation)}$$

This new (Log Bond equation) can be integrated using basic calculus. The definite integral of the left-hand side of (Log Bond equation) from t to T is,

$$\int_{t}^{T} \frac{d \ln\left(B(v,T)\right)}{dv} \, dv = \ln\left(B(T,T)\right) - \ln\left(B(t,T)\right) \qquad \textbf{(Integral of the}$$
$$\textbf{LHS of (Log}$$
$$= \ln\left(\frac{B(T,T)}{B(t,T)}\right) \qquad \textbf{Bond equation))}$$

By changing the dt to dv and integrating with respect to v, the definite integral of the right-hand side of (Log Bond equation) is,

FORWARD CONTRACTS AND FUTURES CONTRACTS

$$\int_t^T r * dv = r * T - r * t$$

$$= r * (T - t)$$

$$= r * \tau$$

(Integral of the RHS of (Log Bond equation))

Note that the price of the zero-coupon bond at maturity $B(T,T)=\$1.0$, by definition.

Equating the definite integral of the left-hand side of (Log Bond equation) to the definite integral of the right-hand side of (Log Bond equation) we find that,

$$\ln\left(\frac{1.0}{B(t,T)}\right) = r * \tau.$$

Applying the exponential function, $\exp(\cdot)$, to both sides of this equation we get

$$\exp\left[\ln\left(\frac{1.0}{B(t,T)}\right)\right] = \frac{1.0}{B(t,T)}$$

$$= e^{r\tau}$$

because the exp function and the ln function are inverse to each other. Therefore,

$$B(t,T) = \frac{1.0}{e^{r\tau}}$$

$$= e^{-r\tau},$$

based on a key property of the exp function.

This is what we wanted to prove. If the instantaneous rate of return is $r*dt$ then the bond is priced at $B(t,T)=e^{-r\tau}$. Combining the two results, we have proved what we set out to prove,

The instantaneous rate of return on a zero-coupon bond is $r*dt$ if and only if the bond price is given by $B(t,T)=e^{-r\tau}$ where τ is time to maturity $T-t$.

■ CONCEPT CHECK 2

Consider a 3-month zero-coupon bond with current price per dollar of face value of $B(t,T)=\$.0975$.

a. Use the relationship $\ln(1.0/B(t,T))=r*\tau$ to find r.

4.2.2 Modeling Continuous Dividend Yields for Stocks

Now that we have a good feel for what instantaneous returns mean, we will next consider an underlying stock with current price S_t that continuously pays dividends at a constant, annualized rate ρ. What this means is that the dividend payable at time t, $DIV_t = \rho * S_t * dt$ where dt is a very small interval of time called an *infinitesimal*.

We have to understand how to use this formula, because the idea of paying dividends at each instant of time is somewhat of an abstraction. A useful abstraction but nonetheless an abstraction since, in the real world, we usually deal with time discretely.

We will take a very short interval of time, from time t to time $t+\Delta t$. Keep in mind that this is a very small interval of time that happens almost instantaneously. By the time you have thought of it, it has already passed.

Here is a time, cash flow line of the stock and its dividend stream,

$$S_t \qquad\qquad\qquad\qquad S_{t+\Delta t}$$
$$DIV_t \qquad\qquad\qquad\qquad DIV_{t+\Delta t}$$

t	$t+\Delta t$

Our interval of time is Δt and total time intervals are usually measured in years in continuous-time finance. So, for example, 1 month would be recorded as 1/12 of a year or as .0833. The dividend yield is given *on an annual basis* as ρ. In order to apply the formula instantaneously to get the instantaneous dividend, we need the *instantaneous dividend yield*. We can approximate this as follows by de-annualizing the annualized dividend yield ρ.

Over an interval of length Δt as shown in the time, cash flow line, the appropriate de-annualized dividend yield is $\rho * \Delta t$. Now, if we make the time interval Δt small enough, then the stock price won't change much (unless it has jumps) over the interval $[t, t+\Delta t]$, and the dollar dividend payable over this interval will be roughly equal to $\rho * S_t * \Delta t$. As Δt gets smaller and smaller, it approaches what we call an *infinitesimal* amount of time, denoted as dt. The instantaneous dollar dividend is then equal to $\rho * S_t * dt$, or simply as $\rho S_t dt$, where we have dropped all the multiplication signs.

The bottom line on this discussion is that you can't simply multiply the annualized dividend rate ρ by the stock price at time t, S_t, to get the *instantaneous* dollar dividend. If dividends were always 3% of the stock price, then that would be a huge amount of dividends paid out over a year. In reality,

94 FORWARD CONTRACTS AND FUTURES CONTRACTS

the instantaneous dollar dividend is a very small amount. Nor can you multiply the annualized dividend rate ρ by the stock price at time t, S_t, to get the annualized dollar dividend. The procedure (formula) applies only to very small intervals.

■ CONCEPT CHECK 3

Suppose that $\rho=3\%$ and that the current stock price $S_t=\$100$.

a. What is the dollar amount of the dividend payable at time t, DIV_t, if $\Delta t=1$ day?

4.3 HOW DIVIDEND PAYMENTS AFFECT STOCK PRICES

Next, we want to more carefully consider the question of how dividend payments affect stock prices. You have undoubtedly learned that stock prices are the present values of the payouts generated by owning the stock, discounted at an appropriate risk-adjusted discount rate (RADR). The only *direct* cash payouts that common stocks pay are common dividends. Capital gains appear in the form of increased stock prices, and are not direct payouts like dividends. Stock dividends are payable in stock, not cash.

What happens to the stock price after the dividend is paid at time t? In a perfect capital market, the stock price should drop by the amount of the dividend because you just received it. The stock price represents the PV of all *subsequent* dividends–no dividends already paid in the past. Let's see if we can formalize this a bit using the analysis and notation we already have available.

We will again take a very short interval of time, from time t to time $t+\Delta t$. Keep in mind that this is a very small interval of time that happens almost instantaneously, as before.

S_t $\qquad\qquad\qquad\qquad\qquad\qquad\qquad\qquad$ $S_{t+\Delta t}$
DIV_t $\qquad\qquad\qquad\qquad\qquad\qquad\qquad$ $DIV_{t+\Delta t}$

t $\qquad\qquad\qquad\qquad\qquad\qquad\qquad\qquad\quad$ $t+\Delta t$

Our strategy is to buy the stock before time t to ensure that we have the right to receive all *subsequent* dividends. The ex-dividend date of the stock is time t. Let's say we pay roughly S_t for the stock with the dividend. When time t arrives, we receive the dividend DIV_t payable at time t, and owed to us. Assuming that nothing happens in the market to change the stock price other than the dividend payment, we look at what happened to our stock price.

It must have dropped by $DIV_t = \rho * S_t * \Delta t$. Looking at our current stock price *after* it has paid this dividend, but before the stock pays another dividend, we find that:

$$S_{t+\Delta t} = S_t - DIV_t$$
$$= S_t - \rho * S_t * \Delta t$$

In other words, $S_{t+\Delta t} - S_t = -DIV_t = -\rho * S_t * \Delta t$

Or we can say that the change in stock price, which we will write as ΔS_t:

$$\Delta S_t = S_{t+\Delta t} - S_t$$
$$= -DIV_t$$
$$= -\rho * S_t * \Delta t$$

We can get this into an integrable, calculus form by dividing both sides of this equation by S_t,

$$\frac{\Delta S_t}{S_t} = -\rho * \Delta t$$

This is a nice notation because then we can think of the *instantaneous* % change in the stock price dS_t due to the payment of the dividend (this is just $-DIV_t$) as,

$$\frac{dS_t}{S_t} = -\rho * dt \qquad\qquad\qquad (\mathbf{-DIV_t})$$

$(-DIV_t)$ is an equation we can easily solve using basic calculus.

We will solve the equation $(-DIV_t)$ using the same procedure we used to solve

$$\frac{dB(t,T)}{B(t,T)} = r * dt,$$

$$\frac{d \ln(S_t)}{dt} = \left(\frac{d \ln(S_t)}{dS_t}\right) * \left(\frac{dS_t}{dt}\right)$$

$$= \left(\frac{1}{S_t}\right) * \left(\frac{dS_t}{dt}\right)$$

$$= \frac{\frac{dS_t}{S_t}}{dt}$$

$$= -\rho \text{ from equation } (-\text{DIV}_t)$$

Or, taking a few mathematical liberties by cross-multiplying again,

$$d \ln(S_t) = -\rho * dt \qquad \qquad \textbf{(–Log DIV}_t\textbf{)}$$

This new equation (–Log DIV$_t$) can be integrated using basic calculus and a few little tricks. The definite integral of the left-hand side of equation (–Log DIV$_t$) is,

$$\int_t^{t+\Delta t} \frac{d \ln (S_v)}{dv} * dv = \ln (S_{t+\Delta t} - \ln (S_t) \qquad \textbf{(Integral of the}$$
$$\textbf{(–Log DIV}_t\textbf{))}$$

$$= \ln \left(\frac{S_{t+\Delta t}}{S_t}\right)$$

The last equality follows from the way the $\ln(\cdot)$ function works.

The definite integral of the right-hand side of (–Log DIV$_t$) is,

$$\int_t^{t+\Delta t} (-\rho) * dv = (-\rho) * (t + \Delta t) - (-\rho) * t \qquad \textbf{(Integral of the RHS}$$
$$\textbf{of (–Log DIV}_t\textbf{))}$$

$$= (-\rho) * (t + \Delta t - t)$$

$$= -\rho * \Delta t$$

Therefore, equating the left hand side to the right hand side, we obtain,

$$\ln \left(\frac{S_t + \Delta t}{S_\tau}\right) = -\rho * dt$$

FORWARD CONTRACTS WITH A DIVIDEND YIELD • 97

To get rid of the $\ln(\cdot)$ function standing in our way of $S_{t+\Delta t}/S_t$ (which is what we really want), we have to exponentiate both sides of this last equation and let the $\ln(\cdot)$ and $\exp(\cdot)$ functions cancel each other out. Since they are inverse to each other, we know this will happen. Taking the exponential of both sides we get the solution,

$$\frac{S_{t+\Delta T}}{S_t} = e^{-\rho*\Delta t} \quad \text{or}$$

$$S_{t+\Delta T} = S_t e^{-\rho*\Delta t}$$

(Dividend Payout Process)

The payment of dividends reduces the stock price process according to this last (dividend payout process) equation. Basically, the (dividend payout process) equation says that the continuously paid dividend results in a negative growth rate of $-\rho$. This makes sense, because as the stock pays dividends at the rate ρ, you receive those dividends and can do with them as you please.

For example, you could re invest them in the stock or you could strip them from the stock and place them in a risk-free account. Since they are no longer part of the stock (having been paid), the stock price has to decline by the amount of the dividend.

However, it is important to remember that the reason the stock can pay dividends at all is because it is earning an overall yield from which those dividends can be paid. We will call that overall yield μ. In general, μ represents the total reward for time preference (the risk-free rate) and for bearing risk (the capital gains yield).

This solves our problem of modeling the reduction in the stock price process due to it paying out its dividends, or what is the same thing, modeling the dividend payout process. The continuous dividend yield of ρ results in a negative growth rate in the stock of $-\rho$ which is what equation $(-DIV_t)$ says,

$$\frac{dS_t}{S_t} = -\rho * dt$$

■ CONCEPT CHECK 4

The current stock price $S_t=\$100$ and $\rho=2\%$.

a. How much would the stock price be reduced by the payment of dividends over a period of 3 months?

4.4 HOW CAPITAL GAINS AFFECT STOCK PRICES

We now model the *total return* process and the *capital gains* process associated with the original stock price process. Let's assume that every dollar invested in the stock, before it has paid its dividends, grows continuously at a risk adjusted rate of μ. We know from our basic finance, that μ is the *total yield* of the stock which consists of the dividend yield and the capital gains component.

In basic finance we learn that this expected return, μ, of a common stock comes from two sources. One is the dividend yield, the other is the capital gains (growth) component. This is usually written as $\mu=DIV_1/P_0+g$ in basic finance terms. Note that ρ corresponds to DIV_1/P_0 in our continuous–time model and g is the capital gains component, $(P_1-P_0)/P_0$. Together, they add up to the total return on the stock, $\mu=\rho+g$.

The stock price, *before* dividends are paid, grows at the continuously compounded rate μ and would look like,

$$\frac{dS_t}{S_t} = \mu \, dt \qquad \textbf{(Total Stock Return Process)}$$

Once the dividend rate of ρ is paid we are left with a stock process, S'_t, that earns its capital gains yield $g=\mu-\rho$, continuously compounded:

$$\frac{dS'_t}{S'_t} = (\mu - \rho) \, dt \qquad \textbf{(Capital Gains Process)}$$

The initial value of this capital gains process is $e^{-\rho*\tau}*S_t$, which will be demonstrated below. That is, $S_{t'}=e^{-\rho*\tau}*S_t$ is the capital gains component of the total stock price, which is $S_{t'}$. This capital gains component is the total stock price minus the present value of the dividends paid over the life of the derivative security.

For example, if the dividend yield $\rho=3\%$ and the total yield $\mu=10\%$ then the capital gains yield must be $\mu-\rho=10\%-3\%=7\%$. In terms of the ending stock price, since the original stock price is growing at a rate of μ, we would end up with a terminal stock price of $S_T=S_t e^{\mu*\tau}$ were it not for the payment of the dividends. This is the solution to (Total Stock Return Process).

To remove the dividends, we have to adjust the ending stock price using the factor $e^{-\rho*\tau}$. At time T, we look at our ending stock price and we find that $S_T'=S_t e^{\mu^* t^*}e^{-\rho^* \tau}=S_t e^{(\mu-\rho)^* \tau}$. This is the solution to (Capital Gains Process) which corresponds to the total return process minus the dividend yield.

For further details, see the Appendix, section 4.8, to this chapter which discusses how to model stock returns with and without dividends.

■ CONCEPT CHECK 5

For this example $S_t=\$150$, $\tau=6$ months, $\mu=10\%$, and $\rho=3\%$.

a. Calculate S_T' and interpret S_T'.

4.5 PRICING FORWARD CONTRACTS ON STOCKS WITH A DIVIDEND YIELD USING THE NET INTEREST MODEL

We are now in the fortunate position of being able to price forward contracts on stocks with a continuous dividend yield of ρ.

When you own the underlying stock you get the dividends. If you have a long position in a forward contract, you don't get the dividends paid on the underlying over the life of the forward contract. This is why we spent so much time looking at the stock price dynamics *after* the dividend had been paid. A forward contract is written on the stock *without* the dividends. This is the key issue in pricing forward contracts on dividend-paying stocks.

But now we fully understand that the stock price dynamics embeds the capital gains process, and that this capital gains process is the relevant stock process for pricing a forward contract.

Suppose that, once we receive the dividends from the stock, we use them to offset our borrowing cost represented by the riskless rate r. What this means is that as we receive the dividends on the underlying stock, we strip them (rather than re-invest them in the stock), and we place the stripped dividends in a continuously compounded riskless account.

At time T, when we owe the forward price (since we have a long forward position) we use the amount in the stripped dividends account to reduce our net borrowing cost to $r-\rho$. Recall what a synthetic long forward position is.

The fastest, intuitive way to price a forward contract in this scenario is to just substitute $r-\rho$ for r in our old forward pricing formula $F_{t,T}=e^{r\tau}*S_t$ to obtain,

$$F_{t,T}'=e^{(r-\rho)\tau}*S_t.$$

Here the $'$ indicates the forward price in the presence of dividends. That's the only difference between the forward pricing formula with and without dividends. Note that in both pricing formulas, S_t is just the normal stock price at time t.

All we have to remember is that our *net* borrowing cost is $r-\rho$ since we simply use the dividends paid by the stock to offset our borrowing cost of r. Stripping the stock of the dividends between times t and T and investing those dividends in a riskless savings account generates enough funds to reduce the continuously compounded borrowing rate to $r-\rho$.

4.6 PRICING A FORWARD CONTRACT ON A DIVIDEND-PAYING STOCK USING NO-ARBITRAGE

4.6.1 Arbitrage Definitions

We can also prove the forward pricing formula with a dividend yield using the usual arbitrage arguments. But first we must give the definitions for arbitrage. One of the most important definitions in derivatives is that of an *arbitrage opportunity*. We give three definitions. The first two are of a risk-free arbitrage opportunity and the third is of a risky arbitrage.

DEFINITION 1 (RISKLESS ARBITRAGE)

A *risk-free arbitrage opportunity* is one with the following properties:

1. It generates a *positive profit* (inflow) at time T, subsequent to today, represented by time t.
2. The *profit* generated at time T is *riskless*. That is, it is certain.
3. The *cost today* of generating that risk-free, positive profit at time T is *zero*.

DEFINITION 2 (RISKLESS ARBITRAGE)

A *risk-free arbitrage opportunity* is one with the following properties:

1. It generates a *positive profit* (inflow) today, time t.
2. The profit generated today is *riskless*.
3. There are *no subsequent outflows* (costs).

Under Definition 1, you get something later *for certain* for nothing today. Under Definition 2, you get something today *for certain* for nothing later. Sometimes, riskless arbitrage opportunities are called 'money machines'. If there were such machines, they wouldn't last long. Like the mythical perpetual motion machine which violates the principles of basic physics, arbitrage opportunities violate the principles of basic financial economics.

There is a third very important definition of arbitrage that does not require it to be risk-free.

DEFINITION 3 (RISKY ARBITRAGE)

A *risky arbitrage opportunity* is one with the following properties:

1. It does not cost anything today. This means that its cash flows today are all positive or zero (no negative cash flows).
2. In all states of the world after today, there are *no subsequent outflows* (costs).
3. In at *least one state* of the world subsequent to today, it generates a *strictly positive cash flow*.

Under Definition 3, as in Definition 1 and in Definition 2, there are no costs associated with a risky arbitrage at any time. However, there is only the *chance* of a positive cash flow, and you don't know under which scenario that will occur. So, you have nothing to lose in a risky arbitrage and the *potential* to gain. That potential is certain in the sense that it exists for sure, but the state of the world, ω, in which it does occur is uncertain. This is what makes it a risky arbitrage. An example of a risky arbitrage is an unexpired lottery ticket that someone lost and that you found at no cost to you.

■ CONCEPT CHECK 6

One good way to learn what an arbitrage opportunity is involves looking at some examples of opportunities that do not permit arbitrage.

a. Consider a long or a short position in an FX forward contract. It involves no up-front cost. Is it an arbitrage opportunity?
b. Explain why an unexpired lottery ticket that someone lost and that you found is a *risky* arbitrage. Check that an unexpired lottery ticket obtained at no cost, satisfies the three conditions for it to be a risky arbitrage.

102 FORWARD CONTRACTS AND FUTURES CONTRACTS

c. An option, call or put, does have non–negative payoffs in all states of the world. What must be true about options in order to prevent them from being arbitrage opportunities?

4.6.2 Forward Pricing Using No-Arbitrage

Using the methodology we used in this chapter, we showed in section 4.5 (using the net interest model) that the forward price on a dividend-paying stock must be $F'_{t,T}=e^{(r-\rho)\tau}*S_t$.

We want to now present the no-arbitrage opportunities argument for this result using exactly the same methodology we used in Chapter 3, section 3.5.

1. The payoff per unit to a long spot position in the stripped underlying stock is $S'_T=e^{(r-\rho)\tau}*S_t$. The stripped-of-dividends stock grows only at its capital gains rate $r-\rho$.

    Note that, since we are trying to replicate the forward contract, we buy the ordinary stock, receive its dividends (rather than re-invest them in the stock), re-invest them in a riskless savings account, and use the proceeds to reduce our borrowing rate from r to $r-\rho$.

2. The payoff per unit to a long forward position initiated at time t is equal to $S'_T-F'_{t,T}=e^{(r-\rho)\tau}*S_t-F'_{t,T}$ because the forward contract is written on the ex-dividend stock price (the capital gains component). When we take delivery of the stock underlying the forward contract, we get a stock at time T whose dividend yield has been stripped from it from time t to time T.

    That is, we get the capital gains component of the stock which is $e^{(r-\rho)\tau}*S_t$. Because it hasn't appreciated by the dividend yield, we can only expect to sell it for its fair market value which is $e^{(r-\rho)\tau}*S_t$ at time T. (We will address the issue of why we use the risk-free rate r, rather than the risk-adjusted expected return μ, when we discuss the risk-neutral valuation method for pricing derivatives in Chapter 13, Appendix, section 13.8, and in Chapter 15).

3. The difference between the payoff per unit to a naked long spot position, where we strip the subsequent dividends to defray borrowing costs, and the payoff per unit to a long forward position is therefore $S'_T-(S'_T-F'_{t,T})=F'_{t,T}$. The net *current cost* of 1.–2. is S_t, where S_t is the normal (unstripped) stock price. The forward contract involves no upfront current cost.

FORWARD CONTRACTS WITH A DIVIDEND YIELD — 103

4. We can replicate the payoffs to strategy 1.–2. by *buying* a zero-coupon bond with face value equal to $F'_{t,T}$. In this case, the current cost to us of doing so is $e^{-(r-\rho)\tau} * F'_{t,T}$ since we are lending, not borrowing. We are implicitly assuming that the borrowing rate is equal to the lending rate.

To avoid arbitrage these two strategies, strategy 1.–2., and lending the PV of $F'_{t,T}$ must have the same current cost, $S_t = e^{-(r-\rho)\tau} * F'_{t,T}$. To see this, you can construct the arbitrage opportunity directly, or use the law of one price (LOP), which follows from no-arbitrage. It follows that $F'_{t,T} = e^{(r-\rho)\tau} * S_t$. The ' indicates that we are solving for the forward price in the presence of dividends.

Note that this is the same pricing by replication argument that we gave in Chapter 3, section 3.5, for the no-dividend case. Also note that replication implies pricing because the replicating portfolio must have the same price as the strategy it replicates. Otherwise, there would be an arbitrage opportunity.

This methodology and result applies to other forward contracts including forward contracts where the underlying is a foreign currency. We just have to correctly identify the payout stream on the underlying asset.

But now it is time to delve more deeply into the FX market that we introduced in Chapter 1.

4.7 CURRENCY SPOT AND CURRENCY FORWARDS

One of the main forward markets is for FX (foreign exchange). This is a vast over-the-counter (OTC) market with trillions of dollars of FX trading on a daily basis. Forward contracts on FX give us a glimpse of the international flavor of derivatives. However, before we can discuss pricing of FX forward exchange contracts, we have to take a closer look at spot foreign exchange and the price quote mechanism than we did in Chapter 1.

4.7.1 Price Quotes in the FX Market

When looking at the FX market, we have to first decide what we choose to call the domestic economy (DE), and hence what we choose to call the foreign economy (FE). If we decide that the USA is the domestic economy and that, say Japan, is the foreign economy, then the exchange rate would be given as the number of US dollars per Japanese Yen, since we are thinking in terms of the US dollars of the domestic economy. We would be looking at Japanese

104 FORWARD CONTRACTS AND FUTURES CONTRACTS

Yen as a US investor would, and therefore at how many US dollars we would have to pay for each of them.

If Japan were the domestic economy and the USA the foreign economy, then the exchange rate would be in Japanese Yen per 1 US Dollar, since the Japanese are thinking in terms of their currency. A Japanese investor would want to know how much they would have to pay in Japanese Yen for each US dollar.

We can easily go back and forth once we have the exchange rate correctly interpreted, as will be seen below.

Go to wsjonline.com, '*Market data, FX*', scroll down to '*Complete Currencies*' data then to '*New York closing*'. Use the historical data for the quote date indicated. You will see a chart '*Exchange Rates: New York Closing Snapshot*' (Monday, April 7, 2014 U.S.-dollar foreign-exchange rates in late New York trading).

TABLE 4.1 **Exchange Rates (April 7, 2014): New York Closing Snapshot**

(U.S.-dollar foreign-exchange rates in late New York trading)

Country/currency	IN US$		US$ VS. % CHG		PER US$	
	Mon	Fri	1-Day	YTD	Mon	Fri
Argentina peso	0.1250	0.1250	unch	22.7	8.0003	8.0021
UK pound (spot)	1.6605	1.6577	−0.17	−0.3	0.6022	0.6033
1-mos forward	1.6602	1.6573	−0.17	−0.3	0.6024	0.6034
3-mos forward	1.6594	1.6565	−0.17	−0.3	0.6026	0.6037
6-mos forward	1.6582	1.6553	−0.17	−0.3	0.6031	0.6041

Source: online.wsj.com, reprinted with permission.

Table 4.1 gives the exchange rate in two equivalent forms. The first form tells you how many US dollars it costs to buy one 'foreign currency unit'. The second form tells you how many foreign currency units it costs to buy 1 US dollar.

For example, on the quote date April 7, 2014 the Argentinean peso had a cost of US$0.1250. If each Argentinean peso costs an eighth of a dollar, then there will be 8 Argentinean pesos to the dollar. That is, there will be 1.0/0.1250=8 Argentinean pesos in US$1. This is the second quote mechanism.

FORWARD CONTRACTS WITH A DIVIDEND YIELD 105

The first quote mechanism is the number of US dollars it takes to buy 1 Argentinean peso (the US investor's point of view). This is the first quote mechanism (IN US$). The second quote mechanism (PER US$) is how many Argentinean pesos it takes to buy 1 US dollar (the Argentinean investor's point of view). To go from one quote mechanism to the other, you just take the inverse of the given exchange rate.

4.7.2 Pricing Currency Forwards

It isn't hard to price currency forwards. The thing to remember is that there are two borrowing (lending) interest rates. One in the domestic economy (DE)–call it r_{DE}–applies to deposits made using the domestic currency. The other interest rate is the one in the foreign economy (FE). Call it r_{FE}. It applies to deposits made using the foreign currency.

We will take an example, and use it to familiarize ourselves with spot and forward price quotes. Using the same notation we have developed, let S_t represent the spot exchange rate between US dollars and British pounds today. Let's take this in US dollars per 1 foreign currency unit because we want to buy the foreign currency with our US dollars in order to price FX forward contracts.

From the point of view of a buyer of BP (seller of US$), the domestic economy is the US and the foreign economy is the UK. The foreign currency unit is 1 BP. Sellers of US dollars in the spot FX market for BP want to know how many US dollars there are in 1 BP (that is, the price of 1 BP in US$) on the quote date.

From the same quote we find that the spot exchange rate S_t=$1.6605 per 1 BP. The price of 1 BP in US dollars is $1.6605. From the point of view of a British investor who wants to buy US dollars, the BP price of 1 US dollar is the number of BP 'in' 1 US dollar. This is equal to USD$1/US Dollar Value of 1 BP=USD$1/USD$1.6605=0.6022BP. There are .6022 BP in 1 USD.

■ CONCEPT CHECK 7

You want to borrow US$100,000,000. Then convert (that is, sell US dollars for BP) them to BP at the going spot FX exchange rate S_t=$1.6605.

a. How many BP can you buy?

4.7.3 Pricing FX Forward Contracts Using No-Arbitrage

Now we can proceed with a no-arbitrage strategy needed to price an FX forward contract on BP. Let $F'_{t,T}$ be the current *forward exchange rate* for delivery of 1 BP at time T. The quote will be in the same units as the spot BP exchange rate, USD\$ per 1 BP. This allows us to compare spot and forward exchange rates. We do not know as yet what the equilibrium forward exchange rate should be, but we will now price it by no-arbitrage.

Based on what we previously did, we have to put the problem in context. Does the underlying spot exchange rate carry a 'dividend' or not? One way to think about this is as follows. When the underlying is something like shares of common stock that pay dividends and we hold the shares, we receive dividends and can use them to defray our cost of borrowing.

When we borrow US\$ and exchange them for BP, then we can place those BP in a bank in England and thereby earn the foreign interest rate, r_{FE}. The interest we earn on our foreign bank account is just like the dividends we receive on shares of stock. The foreign interest rate, r_{FE}, is just like a (continuous) dividend yield. We can use it to help defray our US borrowing cost of r_{DE}.

Our *net* borrowing cost is $r_{DE} - r_{FE}$. This is just like the framework of the dividend yield forward pricing model. In terms of our pricing model $r = r_{DE}$ and $\rho = r_{FE}$. Therefore, the dividend yield forward pricing model applied to FX says that the equilibrium forward price $F'_{t,T} = e^{(r_{DE} - r_{FE})\tau} * S_t$.

■ CONCEPT CHECK 8

Suppose you borrow the USD\$100,000,000 in the US at what is a US citizen's domestic interest rate, r_{DE}. Let's suppose that the 3-month (annualized) Treasury bill bond equivalent yield is 5%. This represents r_{DE}.

a. What will be the principal plus interest on this loan at the end of 3 months?

Note that, in order to implement the formula $F'_{t,T} = e^{(r-\rho)\tau} * S_t = e^{(r_{DE} - r_{FE})\tau} * S_t$, you have to know the appropriate interest rates. For example, on the quote date, annualized short-term rates in the UK were about $r_{FE} = .0003$ while they were about $r_{DE} = .0003$ in the USA. Therefore, the 3-month forward rate should be roughly equal to the spot rate.

FORWARD CONTRACTS WITH A DIVIDEND YIELD · **107**

For a 3-month forward contract $\tau=3/12=0.25$, and $e^{(.0003-.0003)*0.25}=1.00$. The equilibrium 3-month forward price should be about $1.0*\$1.6605$ $=\$1.6605$ which is the spot exchange rate. From Table 4.1, we find that the 3-month BP forward FX rate was $1.6594 per 1 BP or $.0011 below the spot rate. We don't know exactly what interest rates the market used for r_{FE} and for r_{DE}, but we aren't far off using the formula.

4.7.4 An Example of Pricing FX Forward Contracts

We will now derive the FX forward pricing formula in a slightly different manner than we did for stocks. We will change the respective interest rates in order to make the argument a little easier to follow, since interest rates in both the UK and the USA were at extraordinarily low levels on the quote date.

Suppose that the 3-month risk-free borrowing rate in the USA is $r_{DE}=5\%$ annualized and that the 3-month risk-free lending rate in the UK is $r_{FE}=4\%$ annually. We will reduce the amount of borrowings from US$100,000,000 to US$1,000,000 to get our answers in amounts per US$1,000,000.

Therefore, borrow US$1,000,000 for three months at the going de-annualized borrowing rate of $.05*.25=.0125$. At the end of 3 months you will have to pay back $e^{.0125}*\$1,000,000=\$1,012,578.45$ which is $1,000,000 in principal and $12,578.45 in interest.

Once the $1,000,000 is borrowed, immediately exchange it for BP at the going spot rate of $S_t=\$1.6605$ per 1BP (see Table 4.1). We will determine what the *equilibrium* (no-arbitrage) $F'_{t,T}$ should be. The number of BP one can buy with $1,000,000 is the number of BP 'in' USD$1,000,000. This is USD$1,000,000/USD$1.6605.=602,228.24 BP.

We are now in the fortunate position of being able to invest our 602,228.24 BP in a UK account and earn $r_{FE}=4\%$ annually or 1% for three months. That is, the BP constitute a dividend-paying asset which will have a payout of $e^{.01}*602,228.24$ BP=608,280.74 BP. This represents interest of 6,052.49 BP which will be in our British bank account at time T, when the forward contract expires.

Instead of pursuing the stripping strategy, as we did for stocks, we will indicate another method for obtaining the arbitrage-free forward price. We know that the accumulated amount of BP will be available at time T (3 months from today). That is, there will be 602,228.24 BP plus interest of 6,052.49 BP in the British bank account.

108   **FORWARD CONTRACTS AND FUTURES CONTRACTS**

The new strategy employed here is to sell *all* of the BP forward at time t for US dollar $F'_{t,T}$ per 1 BP. That is, we sell forward the full number of BP that are *expected* to be in our account at time T.

At the end of 3 months, we must unwind this entire strategy by delivering the full accumulated number of BP in our UK bank account into our short forward position. That is, we obligated ourselves to deliver the amount of BP at time T that we sold forward at time t at the agreed-upon forward price $F_{t,T}$. This generates a cash inflow of $e^{.01}*(\$1,000,000/S_t)*F'_{t,T}$, where $F'_{t,T}$ is quoted in US dollars per 1 BP as is the spot exchange rate S_t.

We have to also unwind the US borrowing side of our arb. This will generate a cash outflow of $e^{.0125}*\$US\,1,000,000$ because we borrowed US\$1,000,000 at time t at the de-annualized borrowing rate of .0125.

The current cost of this arb is zero since it costs nothing to engage in the forward contract and the borrowing is *currently* costless as well. In order to avoid arbitrage, the net cash flow from the arb must also be zero. You can't create something from nothing. Equating the arb's cash inflow to the arb's cash outflow we find that,

$$e^{.01}*\left(\frac{\$US1,000,000}{S_t}\right)*F'_{t,T}$$
$$= e^{.0125}*\$US1,000,000 \qquad \textbf{(equation Forward 0)}$$

All we have to do is solve (equation Forward 0) for the equilibrium (no-arbitrage) forward price $F'_{t,T}$,

First, divide both sides of (equation Forward 0) by \$1,000,000 to obtain,

$$e^{.01}*\left(\frac{1}{S_t}\right)*F'_{t,T} = e^{.0125} \qquad \textbf{(equation Forward 1)}$$

Then multiply both sides of (equation Forward 1) by S_t to obtain,

$$e^{.01}*F'_{t,T} = e^{.0125}*S_t \qquad \textbf{(equation Forward 2)}$$

We are almost done. Just divide both sides of (equation Forward 2) by $e^{.01}$ to obtain,

$$F'_{t,T} = \frac{e^{.0125}}{e^{.01}}*S_t \qquad \textbf{(equation Forward 3)}$$

FORWARD CONTRACTS WITH A DIVIDEND YIELD 109

A little simplifying of (equation Forward 3) by using the properties of the exponential function results in,

$$F'_{t,T} = e^{(.0125-.01)} * S_t \qquad \textbf{(equation Forward 4)}$$

Now we remember that the time horizon in this entire problem is $\tau = .25$, the domestic (US) borrowing rate $r_{DE} = .05$, and the foreign (UK) lending rate $r_{FE} = .04$. The effect of multiplying by τ is to de-annualize these interest rates. So (equation Forward 4) says that,

$$F'_{t,T} = e^{(r_{DE}*\tau - r_{FE}*\tau)} * S_t$$

There is no problem in factoring out the τ,

$$F'_{t,T} = e^{(r_{DE} - r_{FE})*\tau} * S_t$$

This is exactly what we know for stocks where $r = r_{DE}$ and $\rho = r_{FE}$. Our demonstration is a more appropriate way to do the arb for FX forward contracts because no stripping is necessary.

4.8 APPENDIX: MODELING STOCK RETURNS WITH AND WITHOUT DIVIDENDS

We want to model the different forms of stock returns, with and without dividends, and we now run into some thorny issues in the modeling of uncertainty. Unlike risk-free zero-coupon bonds, stocks are risky because their returns are not certain. That's why we generally use the term 'expected' in front of the term 'return' when discussing risky assets like real estate or common stocks.

We are going to ignore the uncertain component of a stock's return for the moment. This is *not* to say that it is unimportant. It is crucially important, and will be discussed when we get to options. We will just assume that the stock grows just like a bond (with no explicit uncertainty). Under this assumption of no uncertainty, the stock price dynamics look just like those of a bond except that we use the symbol μ instead of r.

110 **FORWARD CONTRACTS AND FUTURES CONTRACTS**

There are several questions here that focus on continuous time:

1. What does the underlying stock process look like when we think in continuous time?

2. What does the underlying stock process *without* dividends look like when we think in continuous time?

3. What does the underlying stock process *with* dividends look like when we think in continuous time?

The total stock process would look like this when we think in continuous time:

$$\frac{dS_t}{S_t} = \mu dt$$

(Total Stock Process with Dividends (before dividends are paid))

Here, μ is the stock's total expected rate of return on an annualized basis. It is the sum of the expected dividend yield (if the stock pays dividends) and the expected capital gains yield. In general, it incorporates a risk premium which we are initially going to ignore. In a competitive market, with no adjustment for risk, μ would be equal to the annualized risk-free rate r. Also, forward prices are determined under the risk-neutral measure, so any risk premium is irrelevant to pricing the forward contract (see Chapters 13 and 15).

EXERCISE A1

Look at the total stock process just given.

a. What would be the 'stock price' at time t, S_t, if it were a bond?
b. What would be the (expected) return, μ, if the stock were a bond?
c. Write down the solution to the Total Stock Process for the bond price $B(T,T)$.
d. Translate back to the stock price process to get the solution for the stock price at time T, S_T.

Solution

a. The stock price at time t would be the bond price $S_t = B(t,T)$.
b. The expected return would be $\mu = r$, the risk-free rate.
c. We did this earlier $B(T,T) = B(t,T) * e^{r\tau}$.
d. Translating back $S_T = S_t * e^{r\tau}$.

As we showed in this chapter in section 4.3, the dividend payout process is,

$$-\mathrm{DIV}_t = -\rho * S_t dt \qquad \textbf{(Dividend Payout Process)}$$

To get the stock price process *after* the dividend yield has been paid, just replace the original stock price process (with expected return=μ) by the stock price process with expected return=$\mu - \rho$. This produces the Capital Gains (CG) process which is defined as the stock process after the dividend yield is paid.

$$\frac{dS'_t}{S'_t} = (\mu - \rho)dt \qquad \textbf{(Capital Gains Process)}$$

Thus, there are three ways to look at a stock process, the effect of the dividend stream on the stock price process, and the stock process after the dividend stream is paid,

1. $\dfrac{dS_t}{S_t} = \mu dt$ $\qquad$ **(Total Stock Process** *before* **dividends are paid)**

2. $\mathrm{DIV}_t = \rho * S_t dt$ $\qquad$ **(Dividend Payout Process)**

3. $\dfrac{dS'_t}{S'_t} = (\mu - \rho)dt$ $\qquad$ **(Capital Gains Process)**

The Connection between 1. and 3.

Next, we want to explore the relationship between the Total Stock Process *before* dividends are paid and the Capital Gains Process. Specifically, we want to see how we can go from 1. to 3. Then, we want to see an easy way to go from the equilibrium forward price on 1. to the equilibrium forward price on 3. There is an extremely easy way to do so.

112   FORWARD CONTRACTS AND FUTURES CONTRACTS

Under risk-neutrality, the original process defined by 1. grows at the continuously compounded rate r. That is $\mu=r$. The terminal (time T) stock price is just $S_T=e^{r\tau}S_t$, as indicated in the time line below.

$$S_t \qquad\qquad\qquad\qquad\qquad S_T=e^{r\tau}S_t$$

$$t \qquad\qquad\qquad\qquad\qquad\qquad T$$

The terminal stock price under the Total Stock Return Process will grow based upon the Capital Gains (CG) component and the Dividend Yield component. The CG component of the terminal stock price is $e^{(r-\rho)\tau}*S_t$. This is just a definition which says that the Capital Gains component of the stock's return is just that component that grows the stock price at the Capital Gains rate of $r-\rho$.

To explore this further, suppose that we split up the current, time t stock price S_t into two parts. The first part is S_t minus the present value of the dividends paid out over the period $[t,T]$. We will denote this dividend amount by by $PV\{DIV_{[t,T]}\}$. The second part is just the dividend component, $PV\{DIV_{[t,T]}\}$. Then,

$$S_t = \left[S_t - PV\{DIV_{[t,T]}\}\right] + PV\{DIV_{[t,T]}\}$$

Every dollar invested in the stock grows at the same rate, r,

$$e^{r\tau}*S_t = e^{r\tau}*\left[S_t - PV\{DIV_{[t,T]}\}\right] + e^{r\tau}*PV\{DIV_{[t,T]}\}$$

The second term is the future value of the PV of the dividends paid out over $[0,T]$ re-invested at the continuously compounded rate r. It is the amount that would be in the 're-invested dividend account' at time T. We write it as $TV\{DIV_{[t,T]}\}$, the TV stands for terminal value.

Next, consider the first term. It represents the capital gains component of the stock's return. That is, if we remove $PV\{DIV_{[t,T]}\}$ from S_t, then the compounded difference represents the capital gains component of the terminal stock price. One way to think about this is to ask yourself how much you would be willing to pay for the capital gains component alone, without the dividends. The answer is $S_t-PV\{DIV_{[t,T]}\}$.

But this capital gains component can also be written as just $e^{(r-\rho)\tau}*S_t$. Therefore $e^{(r-\rho)\tau}*S_t=e^{r\tau}*[S_t-PV\{DIV_{[t,T]}\}]$. Multiplying both sides by $e^{-r\tau}$ the equation simplifies to, $e^{-\rho\tau}*S_t=[S_t-PV\{\mathrm{DIV}_{[t,T]}\}]$. This says that the stock price minus the PV of its dividend stream is equally well represented by $e^{-\rho\tau}*S_t$. This is a useful result as we now shall see.

We have just shown that the current stock price minus the PV of its dividends is just equal to the *normal* stock price S_t multiplied by the factor $e^{-\rho\tau}$. But this is the appropriate adjusted stock price for valuing the forward contract, because a forward contract is written only on the capital gains component of the stock price.

So we should be able to simply substitute $e^{-\rho\tau}*S_t$ into the zero dividend forward pricing model to obtain the dividend yield form of the forward price, $F'_{t,T}=e^{r\tau}(e^{-\rho\tau}S_t)=e^{(r-\rho)\tau}*S_t$. This is indeed the correct equilibrium forward price, also obtained by no-arbitrage arguments in section 4.6.2.

This argument shows that it makes sense to re-invest the dividends, when received, either into a continuously compounded risk-free account or into the risk-neutral stock.

We assumed in this chapter that we stripped dividends from the stock as we continuously received them, and re-invested them in a riskless account growing at the continuously compounded risk-free rate. Then, these cumulated dividends were used to reduce our borrowing cost from r to $r-\rho$. Re-investing the dividends into the stock produces the same net result. Therefore, both alternatives will result in the same terminal value in the dividend account.

There are equivalent standard arbitrage proofs of the result we obtained intuitively. In our currency forward hedging example, the problem that arises in the normal (zero dividend) arbitrage is that there are re-invested payouts or 'interest'. The problem, as we saw in the currency forward example, is that it won't do to just sell one forward contract for every unit of the spot commodity you hold. This is due to the fact that by the time the forward contract matures you have a position in the spot that is greater than 1 unit. This extra amount is called a *tail* and the procedure for hedging it is called 'tailing the hedge'. This problem arises in futures hedging as well. There are ways of dealing with this problem, as illustrated below.

Four Methods for Dealing with Dividends

There are four alternatives available when dividends on the stock are involved. We can either hold *fewer* than 1 unit of the stock, borrow the funds needed to finance it, and sell it forward using 1 forward contract. We just have to

114 FORWARD CONTRACTS AND FUTURES CONTRACTS

ensure that the future value of our stock position constitutes *one unit* of stock which can be delivered into the short forward position.

The other alternative is to hold *1 unit* of stock, borrow to finance it, and sell forward *more* than 1 forward contract in order to cover the future value of the stock with dividends re-invested in it.

Alternative 1

To pursue the first alternative, note that 1 unit of stock currently priced at S_t will appreciate to $e^{\rho\tau}S_t$ with dividends re-invested in the stock by maturity date T. Therefore, $e^{-\rho\tau}$ units of stock will appreciate to 1 unit of stock, with dividends re-invested, by time T.

The strategy is to borrow the current amount needed to finance $e^{-\rho\tau}$ units of stock, $e^{-\rho\tau}S_t$, and sell it forward with *one* forward contract at the forward price $F'_{t,T}$. This costs nothing today and produces a cash outflow consisting of the principal plus the interest on the loan equal to $e^{r\tau}(e^{-\rho\tau}S_t)$, and a cash inflow consisting of the proceeds from the short forward sale of $F'_{t,T}$. The net cash flow is equal to $F'_{t,T}-e^{r\tau}(e^{-\rho\tau}S_t)$. If this were different from zero, this would be an arbitrage strategy at time t.

Therefore, $F'_{t,T}=e^{r\tau}(e^{-\rho\tau}S_t)=e^{(r-\rho)\tau}*S_t$ which is our equilibrium forward price in the presence of dividends.

Alternative 2

Pursuing the second alternative method we will obtain exactly the same result. Under this alternative we simply purchase *one* unit of the spot commodity by borrowing its entire current value. We simultaneously sell forward the number of units of stock expected to be in the stock account at time T. The dividends continuously received on the stock over the period $[t,T]$ are re-invested in the stock. This re-investment strategy would result in a terminal stock account consisting of $e^{\rho\tau}$ units of stock. Just as in the forward currency example, we would have to sell forward this expected amount by selling $e^{\rho\tau}$ forward contracts.

The strategy costs nothing today and produces a cash outflow consisting of the principal plus the interest on the loan equal to $e^{r\tau}S_t$ and a cash inflow consisting of the proceeds from the short forward sale of $e^{\rho\tau}F'_{t,T}$. The net cash flow is equal to $e^{\rho\tau}F'_{t,T}-e^{r\tau}S_t$.

FORWARD CONTRACTS WITH A DIVIDEND YIELD · 115

If this were different from zero, there would be an arbitrage strategy at time t. Thus $F'_{t,T}=e^{-\rho\tau}e^{r\tau}S_t=e^{(r-\rho)\tau}*S_t$ which is again our equilibrium forward price in the presence of dividends.

Alternative 3

The third approach is to hold one unit of the spot commodity and fully finance it by riskless borrowing at the rate r, sell forward *one* forward contract, and strip the continuously received dividends as received, placing them into a riskless savings account. When the debt comes due, one uses the proceeds in this 'dividend re-invested account' to pay off some of the debt. The net effect is that the effective borrowing cost has been reduced to $r-\rho$. To obtain the equilibrium forward price, one then just substitutes $r-\rho$ for r in the no-dividend formula to obtain $F'_{t,T}=e^{(r-\rho)\tau}*S_t$.

Alternative 4

There is a fourth approach. That procedure is to note that the capital gains process is obtained from the total return process by the transformation $S'_t=e^{-\rho\tau}S_t$. This is how to transform the Total Stock Process *before* dividends are paid (the process in 1.) into the Capital Gains Process in 3. It is a nice little trick that will allow us to go freely back and forth between processes with dividends and processes without dividends. Note that this gets you the underlying process and not the forward price. That is more work.

But it is useful to know how to do this. Why? When we get to options, there are *transformation rules* that allow us to generate option pricing formulas from existing ones, by just knowing how to transform one underlying process into another. Knowing how to transform the original process 1. into the stripped–of–dividends (CG) process 3., combined with the transformation rules, essentially tells us how to go from the forward price for 1. (where we assume the process pays no dividends) to the forward price for 3. where the process does pay dividends. We illustrated this in this chapter.

116   **FORWARD CONTRACTS AND FUTURES CONTRACTS**

■ KEY CONCEPTS

1. Dividends (payouts) on the underlying.
2. Modeling Continuous Yields for zero-coupon bonds and for common stocks.
3. How Dividends Affect Stock Prices.
4. How Capital Gains Affect Stock Prices.
5. Pricing Forward Contracts on 'Stocks' paying a Continuous Dividend Yield using the Net Interest Model.
6. Pricing Forward Contracts on 'Stocks' paying a Continuous Dividend Yield using No-Arbitrage.
7. Three Definitions of an Arbitrage Opportunity.
8. Riskless Arbitrage.
9. Risky Arbitrage.
10. Forward Pricing using No-Arbitrage.
11. Currency Spot and Currency Forwards.
12. Price Quotes in the FX Market.
13. Pricing Currency Forwards.
14. Pricing FX Forward Contracts using No-Arbitrage.
15. An Example of Pricing FX Forward Contracts.

■ END OF CHAPTER EXERCISES FOR CHAPTER 4

1. Suppose that the underlying asset is the risk-free zero-coupon bond with price given by $B(t,T)=e^{-r\tau}$.

    a. Using the forward pricing formula at the end of Chapter 3, what would be the forward price today, $F_{t,T}$, for a forward contract on the zero-coupon bond?

    b. Does your answer to a. make economic sense? Why? or why not?

2. In the same scenario we just discussed in exercise 1, suppose that $F_{t,T}>P_T=B(T,T)=1.0$. Construct a risk-free arbitrage.

3. In the same scenario we just discussed in exercise 2, suppose that $F_{t,T}<P_T=B(T,T)$. Construct a risk-free arbitrage. Make sure that you check all three properties of a risk-free arbitrage opportunity.

FORWARD CONTRACTS WITH A DIVIDEND YIELD   117

4. Suppose that the stock price increases to $110 in the next instant $t+\Delta t$. That is $S_{t+\Delta t}=\$110$. The dividend yield ρ is equal to 3%. What is the dollar amount of the dividend payable at time $t+\Delta t$ if $\Delta t=1$ day?

5. Here is an example of the forward pricing formula for stocks paying dividends. Suppose that $r=5\%$ and that $\rho=3\%$. The current stock price S_t is $100. Time to expiration of the forward contract is 3 months.

   a. Calculate the forward price.
   b. Compare the forward price in a. to the forward price on the stock if it did not pay dividends.

6. Suppose that the 3-month risk-free borrowing rate in the US is $r_{DE}=3\%$ annualized and that the 3-month risk-free lending rate in the UK is $r_{FE}=5\%$ annually. The current spot rate is $S_t=\$1.6605/BP$.

   a. Calculate the 3-month forward rate.
   b. What do you conclude from this example about the relationship between the forward rate and the spot rate?

■ SELECTED CONCEPT CHECK SOLUTIONS

Concept Check 1

a. Direct costs of storing inventory are things like storage facilities (e.g. warehouses), and insurance. Direct costs appear in financial statements.

   Indirect costs are things like the *opportunity cost* of tying up one's money in commodities. This includes financing costs to purchase the inventory. The full opportunity cost does not typically appear in financial statements, although interest is usually reported.

b. The convenience yield is like a dividend yield in the sense that it is a benefit. It is unlike dividends in the sense that it is not *directly* paid. It is therefore an indirect benefit.

c. Convenience yield incorporates a risk-management component. The firm faces demand in two forms: the first is *expected* demand, and the second is *unexpected* demand. Expected demand can be planned for by holding enough inventory to cover it.

   Unexpected demand cannot be planned for in the same way because it is unexpected. But it can be hedged by holding excess inventory (above

118 FORWARD CONTRACTS AND FUTURES CONTRACTS

that needed to meet expected demand). The convenience yield of holding excess inventory is this *indirect* benefit it provides by allowing the firm to hedge the unexpected demand for its products.

Concept Check 3

First translate 1 day into its fraction of a year. A year consists of roughly 250 trading days due to holidays, weekends and other market closings. So a trading day is equal to 1/250 of a year, or about .004 of a year. This becomes our Δt. Then,

$$\mathrm{DIV}_t = \rho S_t \Delta t$$
$$= .03 * \$100 * .004$$
$$= \$0.012, \text{ or around a penny.}$$

Concept Check 5

$$S'_T = S_t e^{(\mu - \rho) * \tau}$$
$$= \$150 * e^{(10 - .03) * 0.5}$$
$$= \$155.343$$

Concept Check 6

a. A long or a short position in an FX forward contract meets only one condition of an arbitrage opportunity, namely zero cost today (see Definition 1, part 3., section 4.6.1). Unfortunately, we know that the payoff can be positive or negative at expiration so there is no guarantee of a positive profit in any state of the world. Therefore, such positions are clearly not riskless arbitrage opportunities (see parts 1. and 2. of Definition 1).

   Neither are they *risky* arbitrage opportunities even though they have a chance of a positive profit at expiration (see Definition 3, part 3., section 4.6.1). The reason is that part 2. of Definition 3 is violated, negative profits (costs) could arise at expiration.

b. An unexpired lottery ticket that someone lost and that you found is not a riskless arbitrage because winning is not a certainty. However, it is a *risky* arbitrage because there is a state of the world in which there is a (large) positive payoff, that in which you have the winning number. If you had to pay for it, it would involve a cost. Such investments are not arbitrages.

FORWARD CONTRACTS WITH A DIVIDEND YIELD **119**

c. It's nice that options, calls or puts, do have non-negative payoffs in all states of the world. This means that part 2. of definition 3 is satisfied. Part 2. is also satisfied because of the optional character of options.

   If you could get options for free (like the lottery ticket), then they would be risky arbitrage opportunities. This is why options cost money, the market acts to eliminate riskless and risky arbs. Therefore, options are related to forward contracts, but they are not forward contracts.

   What must be true about options in order to prevent them from being arbitrage opportunities is that they have to sell for positive prices.

Concept Check 7

The number of BP you can buy with $US100,000,000 is the number of BP 'in' $US 100,000,000. Since each BP costs $1.6605, this is,

$$\$100,000,000/\$1.6605=60,222,824.45BP.$$

The verification is easy,

$$60,222,824.45BP *\$1.6605=\$US100,000,000.$$

CHAPTER 5

FUTURES CONTRACTS: MARKET ORGANIZATION

5.1	Futures Market Participants	122
5.2	Three Phases of Futures Trading	125
5.3	'Buying' and 'Selling' Futures Contracts	126
5.4	Alternative Types of Orders: Market, Market with Protection, Limit	127
	5.4.1 Market Orders and Market Orders with Protection	127
	5.4.2 Limit Orders	129
	5.4.3 The Limit Order Book (LOB)	130
	5.4.4 Depth in the LOB	131
5.5	Globex and the Globex LOB	134
5.6	Pit Trading and the Order Flow Process	136
5.7	Operations and Functions of the Clearing House	139
	5.7.1 Matching Trades and Guaranteeing Futures Obligations	139
	5.7.2 The Clearing Process and Offsetting Futures Trades	141
	5.7.3 Marking to Market and the Daily Settlement Process	144
	5.7.4 Tracking the Equity in an Investor's Account	151
5.8	The Effective Price and the Invoice Price upon Delivery	153
	5.8.1 Offset vs. Delivery	155
5.9	Cash Settlement vs. Commodity Settlement	157

122 FORWARD CONTRACTS AND FUTURES CONTRACTS

We introduced futures trading in Chapter 1 as one of the three primary ways in which a commodity can be traded: in spot, forward, and futures markets. Despite its ups and downs which reflect the general economy, the markets for futures contracts, which are essentially *fancy* forward contracts, are expanding globally and will likely continue to do so into the indefinite future (see futuresindustry.org, Global Futures and Options Volume, annual volume survey. See also End of Chapter Exercise 4 in Chapter 1).

Our main purpose in this chapter is to take a closer look at the organization of modern futures markets and, in particular, at the structure of trading on futures markets. There is a fair amount of jargon in this chapter. That is because there is a lot of structure involved in creating and operating an organized futures exchange.

As a quick review the following Table 5.1 summarizes the major differences between forward contracts and futures contracts.

TABLE 5.1 **Forward Contracts vs. Futures Contracts**

Forward contract	Futures contract
Not standardized	Standardized
Not traded on an exchange	Exchange-traded
Between counterparties (OTC)	Between parties and the clearing house (not OTC)
Offsetting trade not usually possible	Offsetting trade usually possible
Delivery markets: underlying commodity must be delivered	Non-delivery markets: if contract is offset
Specific grade of the underlying commodity must be delivered	Seller's options: allowing a choice of grades to be delivered

5.1 FUTURES MARKET PARTICIPANTS

The first step in trading futures is to set up a futures trading account with a firm known as a *Futures Commission Merchant* (*FCM*). An FCM is just a firm that transacts futures positions on behalf of commercial users of futures contracts and the investment public. The FCM is going to accept your money in the form of initial margins and daily losses on futures positions held by you. On the other hand, it is going to pay you daily profits if you earn them.

Registered Commodity Representatives (*RCRs*) act like stock brokers, are individuals registered with the appropriate exchange(s), and solicit business for

FUTURES CONTRACTS: MARKET ORGANIZATION   123

a futures commission merchant. Or an *Introducing Broker (IB)* could solicit or accept your business to trade futures contracts. However, IBs do not accept money from customers. RCRs are employed by FCMs whereas IBs need not be.

While we are on the topic of participants at the order stage, here are a few more you should know. In addition to FCMs, RCRs, and IBs, there are *Commodity Pool Operators (CPOs)*. These are individuals or organizations who operate and solicit funds for commodity pools. A commodity pool does just that; it pools the funds of a number of persons for trading futures contracts, or possibly to invest in another commodity pool. A commodity pool is like a mutual fund in its pooling function. By pooling funds, a commodity pool or mutual fund provides access to investors that they would otherwise not have on their own.

For those who want advice, there are also *Commodity Trading Advisors (CTAs)* who are individuals or organizations which, for compensation or profit, advise others, directly or indirectly, as to the value of or the advisability of buying or selling futures contracts. Providing advice indirectly includes exercising trading authority over a customer's account as well as giving advice through written publications or other media. The analogy here is to a managed investment account. The unmanaged funds are less costly, but you do not receive investment advice and are therefore 'on your own'.

The National Futures Association (NFA), (www.nfa.futures.org/) provides a lot of interesting details on these matters under 'Compliance'.

When you open a futures trading account with an FCM you must deposit *initial* margins. As you trade, you make money and lose money. The net effect of all your transactions at a point in time is summarized in a number called the '*equity*' in your account. The FCM, with whom you have your trading account, must keep all these customer funds segregated and is not allowed to intermingle them with its other brokerage accounts. The reason for this is consumer protection. If the FCM goes bankrupt or experiences trading losses on its own accounts, you do not go bankrupt or lose any of your funds.

To get an idea of the scope of segregated customer funds held by FCMs, go to the CFTC report of February 28, 2014. (cftc.gov, Market Reports, Financial Data for FCMs). This contains data on 91 FCMs.

The total dollar value of segregated customer funds at that time was $165,839,817,851, which is not an insignificant amount to be protected. The full table is downloadable. We sorted the data and then excerpted the top 5 FCMs based on segregated customer funds in the following Table 5.2. From

FORWARD CONTRACTS AND FUTURES CONTRACTS

TABLE 5.2 — **Top 5 FCMs Ranked by Segregated Consumer Funds**

(February 28, 2014)

Ranking	Futures Commission Merchant/ Retail Foreign Exchange Dealer	Customers' Assets in Segregation*
Number 1	GOLDMAN SACHS & CO	21,582,534,364
Number 2	JP MORGAN SECURITIES LLC	19,103,116,743
Number 3	NEWEDGE USA LLC	15,881,233,323
Number 4	DEUTSCHE BANK SECURITIES INC	13,772,342,781
Number 5	MORGAN STANLEY & CO LLC	10,370,019,458

*This represents the total amount of money, securities, and property held in segregated accounts for futures and options customers in compliance with Section 4d of the Commodity Exchange Act.

Excerpted by the author from the source, cftc.gov, Market Reports, Financial Data for FCMs, February 28, 2014.

this, you can see that the major players include the top financial institutions in the USA and that the holdings are fairly vast: Goldman held over 21.5 billion US dollars!

Regulation of futures markets has always been a lively topic in the public eye. Every time there is a crisis in financial markets, it seems that derivatives are the first to be blamed. The most recent case is the financial debacle of 2007–2008. The federal agency governing futures trading in the USA is the *Commodity Futures Trading Commission (CFTC)*. There is a wealth of regulation of futures trading. One key law is the *Commodity Exchange Act*. *Dodd–Frank* also contains derivatives regulation. Regulation in general, and regulation of financial markets are interesting topics, as the following mini-case illustrates.

Mini-Case 1 (Segregation of Consumer Funds)

The theory of segregating consumer funds isn't just an academic exercise as the case of MF Global dramatically illustrates. To get started go to:

Website 1

http://www.bloomberg.com/news/articles/2011-11-02/corzine-s-lack-of-mf-global-controls-exposed-with-missing-customer-money (accessed May 27, 2015).

Website 2

http://www.cftc.gov/PressRoom/PressReleases/pr6776-13 (accessed May 27, 2015).

Then answer the following questions,

a. *What is the economic reasoning behind requiring FCMs to segregate consumer funds?*
b. The collapse of MF Global in 2011 was a major scandal. Estimates suggest that roughly 700 million dollars of segregated consumer funds (other estimates range as high as 1.7 billion) were 'lost' in the eighth largest bankruptcy in the USA.

   What effect would an event like this have on investor confidence in trading exchange traded futures? (See Website 1.)
c. In 2013, the CFTC ordered the return of 1.2 billion dollars to investors with funds at MF Global (see Website 2). Presumably investors were compensated 100% for their invested funds.

   Why is it critical for futures exchanges that the MF Global scandal be resolved?
d. *Do the MF Global and the Peregrine scandals imply that* all *FCMs are suspect? Or even that* most *of them are?*
e. Go to http://en.wikipedia.org/wiki/Fallacy_of_composition (accessed May 27, 2015) and absorb the information there. The *fallacy of composition* is a very common error in reasoning, occurring frequently in economic scenarios.

   Try to apply it to this mini-case.

5.2 THREE PHASES OF FUTURES TRADING

There are three phases to trading futures contracts and we will discuss each in turn. The first is *order submission*. Once all the paperwork associated with opening a futures trading account with an FCM is dealt with, you can *submit* futures trading orders. Once orders are submitted, buyers and sellers need to be *matched* up. This is the phase of *order execution*. In the old days, futures trading was done in pits. Pit trading still survives, mainly for S&P futures as well as futures options, but has been replaced by electronic trading such as the Globex system on the CME. Further, most European exchanges are fully automated.

Note that when we talk about electronic order execution, we aren't talking here about order *submission*, which usually is done electronically. Rather, pit trading vs. Globex trading refers to how buy and sell orders are *matched* (i.e. executed). It is during the execution of the trading process that futures (trade) prices are actually determined.

Since a futures contract is not an OTC instrument traded directly between counterparties, once trade orders are submitted and executed we are not done. The third phase is that the Clearing House associated to the futures exchange has to 'clear' all trades and thereby agree to be the counterparty to all parties. In summary, futures trading takes place in three stages:

1. Order *submission*;
2. Order *execution*; and
3. *Clearing* of trades (because the Clearing House is the counterparty to all trades).

5.3 'BUYING' AND 'SELLING' FUTURES CONTRACTS

The most basic types of futures orders are like those in any other market, buy or sell. In the world of futures 'buy' is a misnomer that means 'making a long commitment' and 'sell' means 'making a short commitment'. This is quite different than in the world of stocks and bonds, where you are buying or selling financial assets with value. Some derivatives like options, which confer rights, also have current value. However, when initiated, futures contracts do not involve the exchange of funds (except for initial margins), because their current values are set to zero to clear the market.

Keep in mind what we discussed when considering forward positions, because it is exactly the same here. You aren't buying or selling a futures contract, which is a piece of paper (or data entry) with no initial value. You are merely making a long or short commitment to take or make delivery of the underlying commodity in the future under the terms of the standardized contract. It is helpful here to recall the definition of a futures contract and its implications for order execution.

A Futures Contract is a standardized agreement between a buyer and the clearing house of an organized exchange to take delivery of a specified quantity and quality of a commodity, and between a seller and the clearing house of an organized exchange to *make* delivery of a specified quantity and quality of a commodity. Delivery is deferred and occurs during specified periods (delivery months) according to the rules of the futures exchange in which the specific futures contract is offered for trading.

(Reprinted with permission from CME Group Inc., 2014)

FUTURES CONTRACTS: MARKET ORGANIZATION   127

One thing to keep in mind here is that *futures contracts do not specify the futures price*. The futures price is determined through execution either on the floor of an exchange (in pit trading as for S&P500 futures), or through an electronic system that matches submitted buy orders with submitted sell orders to create a trade that is matched at the futures price mutually agreed to by both buyers and sellers.

5.4 ALTERNATIVE TYPES OF ORDERS: MARKET, MARKET WITH PROTECTION, LIMIT

The three basic types of trade orders are:

a. *Market orders* (pit trading);
b. *Market orders with protection* (Globex); and
c. *Limit orders.*

There are also combinations of the above types of orders, as well as other types such as stop and stop-limit orders. The types of orders available to a trader depend on the trading platform, the commodity traded, and the rules of the particular exchange. One example is stock trading on Nasdaq as an electronic trading platform.

When it comes to trading futures on the CME, the basic dichotomy is between open outcry (pit) trading and electronic matching systems such as Globex. One of the differences between pit trading and Globex is that you can enter market orders only in pit trading.

5.4.1 Market Orders and Market Orders with Protection

In a classical market order designed to trade common stock, or pit traded for futures (but not Globex futures), you do not specify the price. You let the market dictate the price and you accept the best price currently available. At any point in time in a real world dealer market there are usually at least two prices available, the bid and the asked. Actually, there are numerous prices available. We will get to this after discussing limit orders.

What traders mean by the *bid* and the *asked* is the *best (highest) bid* and the *best (lowest) asked*. The best bid is the highest bid currently available and the best asked is the lowest asking price currently available. Non-dealers buy at the asked price and sell at the bid price. Dealers buy at the bid and sell at the asked, thereby earning the bid–asked spread as a fee for providing liquidity.

Turning to market orders with protection, for a while Globex did not permit classical market orders, such as those we are all familiar with from stock trading. Now, classical market orders are still not permitted. They have been replaced by a type of order called *market order with protection*, which is a classical market order within price bands.

The precise CME specification is:

> Market with Protection Market orders at CME Group are implemented using a 'Market with Protection' approach. Unlike a conventional Market order, where customers are at risk of having their orders filled at extreme prices, Market with Protection orders are filled within a predefined range of prices (the protected range). The protected range is typically the current best bid or offer, plus or minus 50% of the product's Non-Reviewable Trading Range. If any part of the order cannot be filled within the protected range, the unfilled quantity remains on the book as a Limit order at the limit of the protected range.
>
> (Reprinted with permission from CME Group Inc., 2014)

This setup is designed to protect the investor against price spikes which, under a classical market order, could lead to a very unfavorable execution price. The general idea one gets from the CME literature is that it encourages investors to specify the price in their orders. That is, to submit limit orders. *Limit orders* are simply orders that must be fulfilled at a *given* limit price or better. That is, at the highest bid if a sale order or at the lowest offer if a buy order.

The nice thing about market orders is that they get immediately executed in a liquid stock or a liquid pit traded (e.g. S&P500) futures market. If you monitor the stock market (by observing the bids and asks) before you trade, you will probably get pretty close to what you think you are getting, unless there is a spike in stock prices. If you want some control over the price, then you will want to submit some kind of limit order.

■ CONCEPT CHECK 1

The following example is adapted from the CME literature (www.cmegroup.com/confluence/display/EPICSANDBOX/Order+Types+for+Futures+and+Options; accessed May 27, 2015) and it illustrates how the client interacts with CME Globex to process a market order with protection bid.

FUTURES CONTRACTS: MARKET ORGANIZATION · 129

The client sends a buy Market Order to CME Globex 'Bid 10 ESZ8'. Bid 10 means that the bid is for 10 contracts, ES is the symbol for the *E*-mini S&P 500 futures contract, Z represents December delivery, and the 8 refers to 2008.

At the time the bid was entered, the best offer was 90025 and the number of Protection Points was 600. This leads to a Protection Price Limit of 90025+600=90625.

a. *As a buyer, what do you think this should mean?*

The next step is that Globex attempts to fill the order with the following results:

1. CME Globex sends an Execution Report–Partial Fill 2-Lot @ 90025.
2. CME Globex sends an Execution Report–Partial Fill 3-Lot @ 90300.
3. CME Globex sends an Execution Report–Partial Fill 3-Lot @ 90550.

At this point, there are two remaining unexecuted buy orders. But the market has moved to the *next best offer of 90675.*

b. *What would happen if the order were an ordinary market order (without protection)?*

Unfortunately, the next best offer exceeds the protection price limit of 90625.

c. *What do you think happens to the remaining two unexecuted orders?*

5.4.2 Limit Orders

Limit orders are a lot more interesting when it comes to futures trading, particularly electronic trading. There are two types of Limit orders: Limit Bid (LBid) is a limit order *to buy*, and Limit Offer (LOff) is a limit order *to sell*. Unlike market orders or market orders 'with protection' on Globex, limit orders specify a price.

If you specify an LBid (to buy) at 100, you are requiring that the order be executed at a price *no higher* than 100. An LOff (to sell) order of 100 specifies that the order be executed at a price *no lower* than 100. Note here that 100 need not be in dollars, but is usually in units in which the contract is quoted. These could be in terms of an index such as the one used to quote the S&P 500.

The downside of limit orders is that they may not be executed immediately, if at all. If the market price represented by the best bid is *below* the sell price in the sell limit order, the sell limit order will not be executed. If the market price (lowest ask) is *above* the buy price in the buy limit order, the limit order will not be executed. Instead, the limit orders go into what is called the *Limit Order Book* (*LOB*). In order to understand electronic trading, an understanding of the Limit Order Book is essential.

■ CONCEPT CHECK 2

a. Suppose that the market price represented by the best bid is *below* the sell price in a sell market order *without* protection, what would happen?
b. Suppose that the market price represented by the best bid is *below* the sell price in a sell market order *with* protection, what would happen?

5.4.3 The Limit Order Book (LOB)

The limit order book comes into existence because traders submit limit orders, as opposed to market orders, with specified upper limits for buy orders and lower limits for sell orders. Unless these limits cross each other, a trade does not occur and the limit orders go into the limit order book as *unexecuted* trades. When new orders are submitted to the market they can 'pick off' existing buy or sell limit orders. These orders would then be executed, and therefore removed from the limit order book. In brief, the limit order book is the set of *unexecuted* limit buy and sell orders available in the market at a given point in time.

As a stock trading example, suppose that IBM shares are currently trading at a best bid of $200 per share and a best offer of $204 per share. We assume that the LOB for IBM is empty. This means that all of the market orders have already been fulfilled (why?), so that these bids and offers are irrelevant, except to get a barometer on the recent market price.

You own 100 shares of IBM and you want to sell them for *no less* than $205 per share. To do so, you submit a *limit sell order,* with the specified lowest limit price at which you are willing to sell. Your order goes into the limit order book as,

'100 IBM shares offered at $205/share'

FUTURES CONTRACTS: MARKET ORGANIZATION · 131

Note that identifiers such as your name would not go into the LOB, although you would have to provide identifiers and account information in order to submit the trade.

Another trader, on the other side of the market, wishes to *buy* IBM, but not at $204. Instead, he wants to pay at most $195/share. That trader submits a limit buy order which goes into the Limit Order Book as,

'100 IBM shares bid at $195/share'

We can now easily construct an elementary LOB by putting the limit buy order on one line and the limit offer directly above it (see Table 5.3). Sellers usually want to sell at prices higher than buyers are willing to pay, so this makes sense.

TABLE 5.3 **Simple Limit Order Book (Current Time)**

100 IBM shares offered at $205/share
100 IBM shares bid at $195/share

The best limit bid is $195/share and the best limit offer is $205/share so the limit bid–asked spread is $10 per share. In order for a trade to occur, new bids and offers have to be submitted.

Suppose that a *market order* to *sell* 100 shares enters the market. A market order says 'sell at the best available price', and that is what buyers are willing to pay, at a maximum. In this case, the *best* bid is $195/share so the market order would be immediately executed at $195/share.

If a *market order* to *buy* 100 shares is submitted to the market for execution, it would be executed at the best price at which people are willing to sell. In this case, at $205/share. The market order would be immediately executed at this price. If nothing else happened, the LOB would now be empty because the incoming market orders *picked off* the existing limit orders.

5.4.4 Depth in the LOB

A real-world LOB is more complex than in this simple example, so the next thing we want to see is how *depth* is added to the LOB. At any point in time, there are numerous individuals independently submitting buy and sell orders to the market for execution. Many of these orders may be market orders, or market orders with protection, which would 'pick off' the existing best bid or best offer as described above, depending on the quantities specified in the incoming orders.

Let's focus on incoming limit orders, still thinking in terms of our example. Suppose that some trader *really* wants to buy 100 shares of IBM and prefers not to wait for a better price. Assuming he has access to the standing limit orders, he sees that the current best offer price is $205 per share. There is no better offer. To get the 100 shares of IBM, the trader submits a limit order to buy at $205/per share,

'100 shares to buy at $205/share'

We know this is a limit order, because market orders do not specify a price. If the trader's order is appropriately situated in the queue, his limit buy order would 'pick off' the existing best offer of '100 shares to sell at $205/share'. A trade has just been executed, and therefore is dead to the trading world. Both limit orders to buy and sell at $205/share have been 'matched', creating a 'matched (executed) trade' and would be removed from the LOB because the LOB consists only of *unexecuted* limit orders.

■ CONCEPT CHECK 3

It is useful to pursue this example a bit more. Suppose someone submits a limit order to buy at $210 per share in the above example.

a. *At what price would the limit order be executed?*

Now we can turn to examine how depth is added to the LOB. As noted, there could be numerous buy and sell limit orders independently submitted all at different limit prices from which the *highest* limit bid and the *lowest* limit offer were extracted. This would add both height and depth to the LOB.

An example with the lowest five limit offers and the highest five limit bids illustrates this (see Table 5.4). Usually, the same number of shares are neither bid nor offered, and the numbers are not evenly spaced, so this example is simplified.

Also, once the current highest bid and offer are determined, new orders enter the market attempting to create an executed trade. What happens to these orders depends on whether they are market orders, market orders with

FUTURES CONTRACTS: MARKET ORGANIZATION — 133

TABLE 5.4 **Depth and Height of the LOB (Current Time)**

100 IBM shares offered at $209/share
100 IBM shares offered at $208/share
100 IBM shares offered at $207/share
100 IBM shares offered at $206/share
100 IBM shares offered at $205/share (Lowest Offer)
100 IBM shares bid at $195/share (Highest Bid)
100 IBM shares bid at $194/share
100 IBM shares bid at $193/share
100 IBM shares bid at $192/share
100 IBM shares bid at $191/share

protection, or limit orders. Market orders would be immediately executed at the best available prices.

Limit orders would go into the LOB. Limit orders within the current bid–asked spread would *change* the bid–asked spread.

Once again, at any point in time there are numerous traders submitting numerous limit orders to the market, and they are under no constraint to use the same limit prices as any other trader. So a trader could very well submit a limit to buy (sell) order above or below the current best bid (offer) of $195 ($205) per share. This would have the effect of changing the bid–asked spread

TABLE 5.5 **Trading within the Bid–Asked Spread (at a Later Time)**

100 IBM shares offered at $205/share (Old Lowest Offer)
100 IBM shares offered at $204/share
100 IBM shares offered at $203/share
100 IBM shares offered at $202/share
100 IBM shares offered at $201/share (New Lowest Offer)
100 IBM shares bid at $199/share (New Highest Bid)
100 IBM shares bid at $198/share
100 IBM shares bid at $197/share
100 IBM shares bid at $196/share
100 IBM shares bid at $195/share (Old Highest Bid)

FORWARD CONTRACTS AND FUTURES CONTRACTS

and potential market orders would be executed within the old bid–asked spread as in the example above (see Table 5.5).

In this example, limit orders get submitted within the bid–asked spread which is taken to be the prices between $195 and $205 per share as indicated. The new bid–asked spread becomes $199/$201 per share. New market orders would be executed at the new best prices available, market sell orders at the best bid of $199/share and market buy offers at the best offer of $201/share.

5.5 GLOBEX AND THE GLOBEX LOB

Up until now, our examples focused on stock trading. The next example, illustrated in Table 5.6, involves one of the most heavily traded financial futures contracts, the *E*-mini S&P 500. Here is a hypothetical example of the limit order book from Globex for the Sep 2014 E-mini S&P 500 futures contract at some time point on May 16, 2014.

TABLE 5.6 **Hypothetical Example 1 of a Globex LOB**

Bid Prices	Offer Prices
	1,868.50
	1,868.25
	1,868.00
	1,867.75
	1,867.50
	1,867.25
	1,867.00
	1,866.75
	1,866.50
Highest Bid	**1,866.25**
1,866.00	**Lowest Offer**
1,865.75	
1,865.50	
1,865.25	
1,865.00	
1,864.75	
1,864.50	

FUTURES CONTRACTS: MARKET ORGANIZATION **135**

In practice, as limit orders are submitted, that data is entered into the LOB. The bid (asked) size is the number of contracts in the bid (offer) (see Table 5.7). The price is always a limit price in the bids and offers.

Just as in our stock example, the asks and bids are 'stacked' from highest to lowest. The (highest) bid–(lowest) asked spread is clearly [1866.00,1866.25]. Note that these are not in dollar terms but are in S&P 500 Futures index points, which we will discuss in Chapter 7, section 7.4. One can translate these into dollar terms by multiplying by $50 (the current multiplier) for the E-mini S&P 500. This would give the value of the stock market underlying one E-mini Sep 2014 S&P 500 futures contract. Based on the best offer, this amounts to $50×1,866.25=$93,312.50.

The rule for recording of Globex trades is rule 536.B from www.cmegroup. com/rulebook/CBOT/I/5/5.pdf; accessed May 27, 2015), where we have excerpted the information:

'Each Globex terminal operator entering orders into Globex shall input for each order: a) the *user ID* assigned him by the Exchange, a clearing member or other authorized entity and b) the *price, quantity, product, expiration month, CTI (customer type indicator) code* and *account number* (except as provided in Section C.), and, for options, put or call and strike price. The Globex terminal operator's user ID must be present on each order entered. For a Globex terminal operator with access pursuant to Rule 574, clearing members authorizing such access will be responsible for the Globex terminal operator's compliance with this rule.'

(Reprinted by permission of the CME Inc., 2014)

■ CONCEPT CHECK 4

The Table 5.7 is built on data for contract ESZ8.cme (the December 2008 delivery E-mini S&P 500 futures contract traded on the CME).

a. Indicate the highest bid and the lowest offer.
b. The number of protection points is 200. What is the *highest* price at which a market buy order with protection would be executed?
c. What is the *lowest* price at which a market sell order with protection would be executed?
d. Suppose that a market order to buy with protection of 200 points for 200 contracts is submitted. Indicate at what prices it would be executed.

136 FORWARD CONTRACTS AND FUTURES CONTRACTS

e. Suppose that a market order to sell with protection of 200 points for 200 contracts is submitted. Indicate at what prices it would be executed.

TABLE 5.7 **Hypothetical Example 2 of a Globex LOB**

Bid Size	Bid Prices	Offer Prices	Ask Size
		832.50	
		833.25	
		832.00	
		831.75	
		831.50	468
		831.25	735
		831.00	317
		830.75	112
		830.50	44
108	830.25		
403	830.00		
218	829.75		
373	829.50		
415	829.25		
	829.00		

5.6 PIT TRADING AND THE ORDER FLOW PROCESS

In comparison to electronic trading, open outcry (pit) trading is easy to explain. Pit trading was effectively eliminated on July 6, 2015 for most, not all, commodities trading on the CME. It still exists for S&P Futures (and most futures options), among the most important commodities. Therefore, pit trading is still worth understanding. That understanding is an introduction to the type of information transfers needed in order to make electronic trading feasible.

The following schematic in Figure 5.1 describes the basic mechanism for pit trading, which is age-old. Academics describe it as a *double auction* open outcry system to be distinguished from electronic order matching systems like Globex which we have just described.

FUTURES CONTRACTS: MARKET ORGANIZATION

FIGURE 5.1 Order Flow Process (Pit Trading)

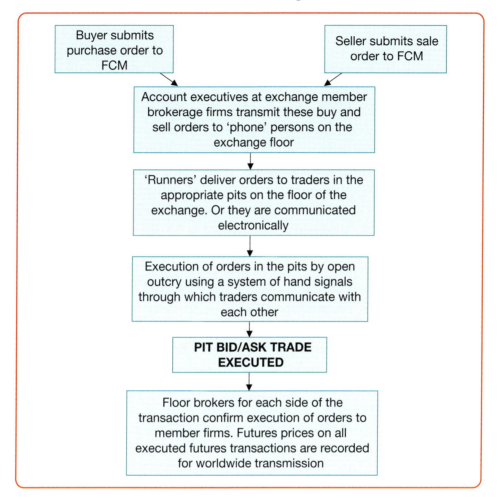

Note that we still do not have a valid open futures position because the clearing house has to intermediate it and assume the opposite side to the buyer and to the seller. The clearing process begins usually at the end of the day (now bi-daily) in part to facilitate this intermediation.

Here is the relevant quote from the CME Clearing House Rule Book, Rule 536.A (www.cmegroup.com/rulebook/CBOT/I/5/5.pdf; last accessed May 27, 2015):

General Requirements for Open Outcry Pit Trades

'At the time of execution, it shall be the duty of every member to record each trade on an approved electronic device or on pre-printed, sequentially pre-numbered trading cards in exact chronological order of execution. If recorded on trading cards, trades must be recorded on sequential lines of the card, and no lines may be skipped except that a member may use additional consecutive lines to record sufficient information concerning a particular trade type, including, but not limited to, spreads, exchange of futures or options for related positions and cabinet trades. Any lines that remain after the last execution recorded on the trading card must be marked through. No more than nine transactions may be recorded on each trading card. Every member must record *the date, price, quantity, product, expiration month, opposite trader, time of execution to the nearest minute* and, for options, put or call and strike price on the trading card or into the approved electronic device. Additionally, the trader must record a symbol which reflects whether the member was trading i) for his own account or an account controlled by such member, ii) for the proprietary account of his clearing member, iii) for another member present on the trading floor or for an account controlled by such other member, or iv) for any other account. Trades or order executions must either be recorded on an approved electronic device, or, if recorded on trading cards in non-erasable ink. Members using trading cards must use a new card at the start of each half-hour interval and at the start of the post settlement session.

Members must designate on the trading card whether such trade is a spread trade.

A member may correct any errors on written trading records by crossing out erroneous trade information without obliterating or otherwise making illegible any of the originally recorded information.

The seller or his designated representative ("the seller") must enter the trade into the clearing system within 30 minutes of execution. The seller must enter the material terms of the trade, including the information required in the first paragraph of this subsection, including the time of execution. Within 60 minutes of execution, the buyer or his designated representative ("the buyer") must review the seller's entry of the trade and affirmatively note any disagreement with any of the terms of the trade and enter a time of execution to the nearest minute except in a circumstance in which the buyer does not know the trade. The seller must allocate the trade to the correct clearing firm(s) within 30 minutes of the execution of the trade unless the trade will clear at the seller's qualifying clearing member firm. The buyer must allocate the trade to the correct clearing firm(s) within 60 minutes of the execution of the trade unless the

FUTURES CONTRACTS: MARKET ORGANIZATION **139**

trade will clear at the buyer's qualifying clearing member firm, however the buyer may not allocate a trade until the seller has entered the trade into the clearing system.

The original copy of trading cards must be submitted to the Exchange no later than 15 minutes after the end of each half-hour interval or the end of the closing range, whichever is earlier.

In addition, each member must maintain, and is accountable for, documents on which original trade information is recorded.

Trades that are not recorded contemporaneously due to an error or an out trade shall be recorded on the next available line of a member's pre-printed, sequentially numbered trading card or on a new trading card, and such trades must be denoted as being out of sequence.'

(Excerpted and reprinted by permission of the CME Inc., 2014)

I have reprinted most of the rule in order to indicate the level of detail under which a futures exchange, such as the CME, typically operates.

5.7 OPERATIONS AND FUNCTIONS OF THE CLEARING HOUSE

5.7.1 Matching Trades and Guaranteeing Futures Obligations

The basic role of the Clearing House is to *intermediate* trades as discussed in Chapter 1, section 1.5. By intermediating all executed futures transactions, whether pit or Globex, the clearing house is in a position to provide its guaranteeing function. In addition, this market organization provides liquidity in the form of an exit mechanism which may be executed through offsetting trades, as discussed.

In order to describe some of the other functions and operations of the clearing house, we need further definitions of the key market participants and some more futures trading terminology.

1. A *Member of an Exchange* is an individual or firm who qualifies for membership on the exchange and pays for one or more seats. Membership is important because only members are allowed to trade on the floor of the exchange. This may be important if you still want to trade pit-traded commodities through open outcry. Otherwise, futures trading involves fees and members get reduced fees.

Note that the terminology of membership has changed with the process of *demutualization*; changing futures exchanges from membership, non-profit

FORWARD CONTRACTS AND FUTURES CONTRACTS

member organizations into for-profit corporations. The CME did this in 2000–2001, eventually merging with its primary competitor, the CBOT, in 2007. In order to be allowed on the floor of such an exchange, the individual must own a specified number of class B shares.

Globex trading is significantly easier since Globex is based on *open access*. All you need is an account with an FCM or introducing broker. As long as they in turn have an account with a clearing member, you are good to trade on Globex.

However, pit trading is still available for the S&P 500 and futures options, so understanding its mechanics is worthwhile. Pit orders get routed to floor brokers who can trade for their own accounts or for the public. The first distinction in 2. and 3. is between a floor trader and a floor broker.

2. A *Floor-Trader (local)* is an exchange member who trades only for his account. Floor traders do not execute trades for the public.

3. A *Floor-Broker* is an exchange member who executes (public) customer orders. In order to execute public trades, a floor-broker must obtain the appropriate CFTC licensing.

4. A *Clearing House* is an adjunct to a futures exchange through which all futures transactions executed on the exchange are settled (or cleared), using a process of matching all long and short positions on all executed futures transactions.

5. *Clearing House members* are exchange members who also qualify for clearing house membership. In order to do so, you must meet certain stringent capital requirements and be a pillar of the community in terms of your business behavior.

Since all executed futures transactions have to be cleared through the clearing house in order to constitute valid futures transactions, every member of the exchange must be the customer of a clearing member simply in order to have their trades cleared. Once all trades are cleared, the clearing house becomes the *counterparty* to all futures transactions. The clearing house *guarantees* that the obligations created by all futures transactions will be met.

In addition to its role of controlling counterparty risk by guaranteeing all trades, the clearing house is also responsible for reconciling the financial implications of taking futures positions. Unlike forward contracts, this is done on a daily or semi-daily basis. Currently, the CME daily settles all futures positions twice a day.

FUTURES CONTRACTS: MARKET ORGANIZATION **141**

There are a number of important questions related to the organizational structure for trading futures contracts. We list them here.

a. What are the *financial implications* of trading futures contracts?
b. How does the clearing house monitor and reconcile these financial implications to the counterparties to all futures transactions?
c. How does the clearing house hold its counterparties accountable for the financial implications of their futures trades?
d. What value, if any, do future positions have to the respective short and long counterparties?
e. How and when are the values of futures positions realized?

We turn to a consideration of these questions next.

5.7.2 The Clearing Process and Offsetting Futures Trades

First, a couple of definitions are in order and we will continue from our previous list.

6. *The Clearing Process*

   a. Matching trades, interposition, and guaranteeing.
   b. Daily settlement: reconciliation on a daily basis, of the financial (cash flow) implications of all futures transactions.

7. *An Offsetting Trade* is an equal and opposite futures transaction prior to the last trading day ending up with a net zero position in futures. If originally long, you execute an offsetting trade by going short the same contract (delivery month) and the same number of contracts. The only other alternative is to take delivery or make delivery since, unless offset, you have one or more open long or short futures positions.

We return to the example of Smith and Adams from Chapter 1, section 1.5, in order to illustrate the offset process and its financial implications. We are going to add futures prices to that example. It is now September 1.

Suppose that a buyer named Smith submits a buy order for 10 Dec Wheat futures contracts. At the same time, a seller named Adams submits a sell order for 10 of the identical contract. These orders are executed through the trading

FIGURE 5.2 The Futures Clearing House

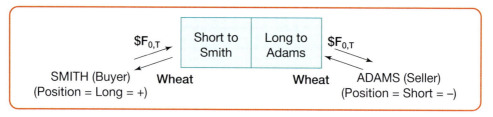

process on the floor of a futures exchange, or electronically. The futures price (think forward price) that emerges from this transaction is $F_{0,T}$. Figure 5.2 illustrates the situation.

Smith and Adams now have futures positions that obligate them to delivery commitments during the delivery month of the Dec wheat futures contract. The arrows above wheat indicate the direction of the commodity flows at delivery. Smith (long) will be receiving the commodity from the clearing house and Adams (short) will be delivering the underlying commodity to the clearing house.

Next, fast forward to the delivery date in December. Unless offsetting trades were made, each counterparty has a *fixed* obligation to take or make delivery of the underlying wheat. The dollar flows, per unit of wheat, are also indicated in Figure 5.2. If this was a forward contract, the contractual price $F_{0,T}$ would be exactly what would be exchanged at T, in exchange for a unit of wheat. This setup describes the cash flow implications of a standard forward contract held to expiration. We will discuss, in section 5.7.3, how the (daily) cash flow implications of a futures contract differ.

Now we are going to look at the *financial* implications of futures positions that are *offset* prior to delivery. Suppose that both Smith and Adams offset their futures positions at some intermediate time 1 at a futures price $F_{1,T}$. Most likely, $F_{1,T} \neq F_{0,T}$, if only due to the passage of time.

In this case, Smith makes an offsetting sell trade at $F_{1,T}$, and Adams makes an offsetting buy trade at $F_{1,T}$. Tracing through the implications of these new futures trades results in Figure 5.3.

The top portion of Figure 5.3 represents the implications of the *original* trade at time 0 at futures price $F_{0,T}$. The bottom portion represents the implications of the *subsequent* offsetting trades at time 1 at the futures price $F_{1,T}$. By implications, we mean the commodity flows and cash flows at delivery. We learn several important facts about futures trading from Figure 5.3.

FIGURE 5.3 **Offsetting Trades**

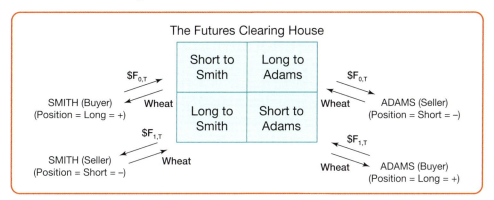

The first fact is that, once offsetting trades are executed, *physical* delivery of the underlying commodity is completely irrelevant! To see this, consider Smith. Originally Smith took a long position in 10 December wheat futures. This obligated Smith to *take* delivery of the contracted amount of wheat in December from the clearing house. Subsequently Smith took a short position in December wheat futures. This obligated Smith to *make* delivery of the contracted amount of wheat in December to the clearing house.

If the clearing house forced Smith to actually take delivery of the wheat, then Smith would simply redeliver it right back to the clearing house. The net result would be a wash. Delivery is irrelevant, given that Smith made an offsetting trade. Note that it is *not* that delivery is in general irrelevant. It would be highly relevant if Smith did not make an offsetting trade!

By making offsetting trades prior to the delivery month, both Smith and Adams have essentially exited the market. However, before they can fully do so, they have to meet the *financial* implications of all their futures positions.

Once again, consider Smith. Smith originally bought wheat for December delivery at a per unit price of $\$F_{0,T}$ per bushel. Smith subsequently sold the exact same amount of December wheat at a per unit price of $\$F_{1,T}$ per bushel. If $\$F_{1,T} > \$F_{0,T}$, then Smith made a profit of $\$F_{1,T} - \$F_{0,T}$ per bushel.

You can see this by looking at the cash flows to Smith in December on the left-hand side of Figure 5.3. It makes economic sense that the per unit profit to Smith (who is long) is just the futures price change. That is, the sell forward price $\$F_{1,T}$ minus the buy forward price $\$F_{0,T}$ per unit.

144 FORWARD CONTRACTS AND FUTURES CONTRACTS

The conclusions here are that:

a. The per unit overall profit to a *long* offset futures position is the change in the futures price in the *normal* direction, $\$F_{1,T}-\$F_{0,T}$.

b. The overall profit to a *short* offset futures position is the change in the futures price in the *opposite* direction, $\$F_{0,T}-\$F_{1,T}$. The short futures position is initially *selling* the commodity for deferred delivery at $\$F_{0,T}$. Subsequently, he offsets by *buying* the commodity back for deferred delivery at $\$F_{1,T}$. Hence the reversed profit figure.

We see from this discussion that the cash flow implications of trading futures are relevant. They are 'settled' on a bi-daily basis. The bi-daily settlement process formalizes and operationalizes the financial implications of trading futures contracts. The clearing house does not wish to wait for you to reverse your trades. The final settlement process marks all accounts to market (represented by the final settlement price) and essentially settles all open accounts on its books.

There are two perspectives on daily settlement. One is in the short run and the other is in the long run. In the long run, the clearing house has to design a settlement procedure that is consistent with the fact that a futures contract is just like a forward contract. Both lock in the futures price, or the forward price, as the effective price at which one is purchasing or selling the commodity in the future.

The difference between futures contracts and forward contracts, of course, is that futures contracts *also* reconcile the short–run financial implications of futures positions through the daily settlement process which we proceed to describe in detail.

5.7.3 Marking to Market and the Daily Settlement Process

As indicated at the beginning of this chapter, there is a lot of jargon that goes along with futures trading. This is also true for the bi-daily settlement process, so here is some of this essential jargon which continues our list. Continuing our list from section 5.7.2, we start with margins.

8. *Margins (Performance Bonds)*: in general, an amount deposited by *both* buyers and sellers to ensure performance of the terms of the contract. A margin in futures is not a down payment (as in equities) but rather is a performance

FUTURES CONTRACTS: MARKET ORGANIZATION · 145

bond. Customers of clearing member firms, and clearing member firms themselves, are required to keep margins on deposit. Margins come in two varieties.

a. *Initial Margins*: deposited by both sides of the contract. When you initiate a futures position (long or short) you are required to deposit, at a minimum, the appropriate initial margin.

Performance bond requirements are posted on the exchange's website. They depend on who you are, which is measured primarily by whether you are categorized as a speculator or as a hedger.

Initial margins are small compared to margins in equities (50% minimum). Roughly speaking, they constitute 5 to 10% of the current value of the underlying commodity at initiation of all positions. They do not change with every price movement in the underlying as this prescription suggests. However, when the price of the underlying dramatically increases (as in S&P 500 futures), one can expect initial margin requirements to also increase.

b. *Maintenance Margin* is a level. This level must be maintained at all times. Think of this as 75 to 80% of the initial margin level. The rule is that, if the equity in a customer's account falls below the maintenance margin level, then the customer gets a margin call requiring him to deposit funds into the account in order to bring the equity back to the *initial* margin level.

9. *The Equity* in a customer's account consists of initial margins plus unrealized gains on open futures positions minus any unrealized losses on open futures positions.

10. The *Close of the Market* is roughly the last 30–60 seconds of trading during the close. During the market's close, transactions take place frequently at a range of prices called the *Closing Range*.

11. An *Open Contract* is one that has not yet been offset by means of an offsetting trade.

12. The *Open Interest* is the number of open contracts at a point in time.

13. The *Settlement Price* is some kind of average of prices in the closing range. It is a measure of the condition of the market at the close and it is used

146 FORWARD CONTRACTS AND FUTURES CONTRACTS

by the clearing house to determine any final daily net gains and losses on all open futures positions.

14. *Marking to Market*: twice each trading day, the clearing house marks every account to 'market' (which for final settlement is represented by the settlement price). That is, all long and short futures positions are adjusted as to their *daily unrealized gains or losses*. These gains and losses are then realized. Each party either receives or pays off these amounts which are called Settlement Variation.

15. *Settlement Variation* are bi-daily profits and losses realized by the bi-daily settlement procedure.

16. The *Daily Value of a Futures Contract*: as the futures price fluctuates in the course of daily trading, a given futures position would sustain losses or gains. If the futures position was liquidated through offset, the daily value of this futures position would be equal to this unrealized profit or loss.

    The Daily Settlement process simply realizes the bi-daily value of all open futures positions to all counterparties, *whether they offset their open futures positions or not*. In sum, the daily value of a futures contract is nothing other than the daily price change measured relative to the initiation futures price if the position is initiated that day, or relative to yesterday's settlement price if the position was not initiated on that day.

One easy way to think about the daily value of a position in any financial instrument or portfolio is as follows. Suppose that at the beginning of the trading day, your investment portfolio is worth $1,000,000. By the end of the day (say at the close of the market) it is worth $1,100,000. Then you earned $100,000.

Marking your account to market there would be a $100,000 gain. In the case of an equity portfolio, you would also have the $1,000,000 principal value of the portfolio. In the case of futures or forward contracts, *the entire daily value of your investment is the daily profit or loss* because forward and futures contracts have zero value at initiation. They are priced that way to avoid arbitrage opportunities.

Investors typically mentally mark their accounts to market. Suppose you were actually paid the $100,000 gain *without* liquidating your portfolio. That is what the daily settlement process does. While this doesn't happen for most

FUTURES CONTRACTS: MARKET ORGANIZATION 147

financial instruments, it does happen on a bi-daily basis for all CME exchange traded futures contracts.

The clearing house acts not only as an intermediary but as a pay and collect agent to all counterparties. It's a quite interesting feature of futures trading! This is another way that the clearing house insures its positions against counterparty risk. You pay or get paid *as you go* in exchange-traded futures, unlike in forwards which are OTC instruments.

■ CONCEPT CHECK 5

Consider the CME crude oil futures. The symbol is CL. For this very popular contract, margins, initial and maintenance, vary by period. For example for the period July 2014–Aug 2014, the initial margin was $3190 while the maintenance margin was $2900.

Suppose that a crude oil futures trader initiates a long position in 100 August 2014 contracts at the futures price of $104.00 per unit.

a. What initial margin must be posted to his account?
b. The tick size in CL is $.01/bbl and the contract refers to 1000 bbl of underlying crude oil. Therefore a movement in the futures price of $.01/bbl corresponds to how many dollars?
c. How many ticks would the CL futures price have to move downward in order for the trader to receive a margin call?
d. How much must be deposited into the account once the margin call is received?

In order to understand the application of all of the definitions in this section, some examples will help.

Example 1

1. An individual sells (shorts) one Dec. Comex (part of the Cmegroup) gold futures contract at $F_{0,T}=\$1600/oz$. To get the specifications for this contract, one goes to cmegroup.com and looks under metals. The symbol for this contract is GC. The investor's short position represents a firm commitment to sell December gold at a fixed price of $100*\$1600= \$160,000$. (The contract size is 100 troy ounces, hence we multiply the futures price by 100.)

One can also find the performance bonds (margins). For what are called 'outrights' (naked, unhedged short or long futures positions) the current (2014) initial margin was set at \$7425 per contract. The maintenance margin level was set at \$6750 per contract. The investor is required by the exchange to deposit \$7425 into his account to cover the initial margin.

On the first day that the investor assumes the short position, the Dec. gold futures price settles at $\$F_{1,T}^{s}=\$1620$. The superscript 's' represents 'settlement', the subscript '1' represents Day 1, and T is the expiration date.

It is pretty clear that the investor lost money here due to the futures price rising against a short futures position. The amount of the loss is,

$$100*(F_{0,T}-F_{1,T}^{s})=100*(\$1600-\$1620)$$
$$=-\$2000.$$

The minus sign indicates a loss.

Would the investor receive a margin call? In order to answer this question, we have to calculate the 'equity' in the investor's account. The precise definition is given in definition 9 above.

Customer's Equity
=Initial Margin(s)+unrealized gains on open futures positions−
      unrealized losses on open futures positions
=\$7425−\$2000
=\$5425<\$6750=maintenance margin level.

Indeed, there would be a margin call. The investor would have to supply an additional amount into his account to bring the equity up to the *initial* margin (not just to the maintenance margin level). In this case, \$2000 would have to be put into the account. The *full* loss would have to be covered, because the equity fell below the maintenance margin level.

What would happen to the \$2000? It would go to pay the long on the other side of the short contract. That is, the account of the long would be credited the +\$2,000, which represents his profit on this trade. These funds would be channeled through the clearing house and would end up in the accounts of the respective clearing members representing the market participants.

Now repeat this procedure across all open positions in all contracts and you have the massive daily settlement process (we assume settlement is daily), which does two things:

FUTURES CONTRACTS: MARKET ORGANIZATION — 149

1. It *realizes* the daily value of all open futures positions through marking every contract to market based on the daily settlement price.

2. It *recontracts* all futures positions by setting their values to zero *after* all gains and losses have been paid out. We will discuss what daily recontracting means shortly.

Example 2

This example will be more dynamic in that it will involve multiple days and multiple trades. In this example, the investor originally goes long on Day 1. He maintains the long position by doing no trades on Day 2. On Day 3, he makes an offsetting trade by going short the original identical contract.

TABLE 5.8 **The Daily Settlement Process**

Day Transactions	Settlement Price	Daily Profit (Loss)
1. Buys 1 Dec. Gold at $F_{0,T}=\$1620$	$F^S_{1,T}=\$1616$	$F^S_{1,T}-F_{0,T}=-\$4*100$ $=-\$400$
2. Nothing	$F^S_{2,T}=\$1600$	$F^S_{2,T}-F^S_{1,T}=\$16*100$ $=-\$1600$
3. Short 1 June Gold at $F_{3,T}=\$1630$	$F^S_{3,T}=\$1640$	$F^S_{3,T}-F^S_{2,T}$ (long position) $=\$40*100$ $=+\$4000$
		$F_{3,T}-F^S_{3,T}$ (short position) $=-\$10*100$ $=-\$1000$

The transactions and daily settlements here should be transparent, and you should check them. However, we will go through them. In doing so, keep in mind that the clearing house settles positions *independently*. This is important to note on Day 3.

On Day 1, the investor simply longs 1 Dec. gold futures contract at the executed futures price $F_{0,T}=\$1620$. Unfortunately, by the end of the trading day, the futures price on the Dec. gold contract settles at the *lower* price represented by the settlement price, $F^S_{1,T}=\$1616$.

Here is the sum of all daily settlements, which represents the total profit/ounce on the futures trades.

Total profit per ounce

$$= \left(F_{1,T}^S - F_{0,T}\right) + \left(F_{2,T}^S - F_{1,T}^S\right) + \left(F_{3,T}^S - F_{1,T}^S\right) + \left(F_{3,T} - F_{3,T}^S\right)$$
$$= F_{3,T} - F_{0,T}$$
$$= \text{Selling futures price} - \text{Buying futures price}$$
$$= \$10$$

Adjusting for the contract size, we obtain the total profit per contract=($1,630–$1620)*100=+$1000.

This is what your *overall* profit should be because, if we fast forward to December, we see that the investor would be required to deliver gold to the clearing house in satisfaction of his short futures position struck at $1630, and buy gold from the clearing house for $1620 according to his long position. This is illustrated in Figure 5.4, and it yields an overall profit of $1000.

FIGURE 5.4 Overall Profits for Example 2

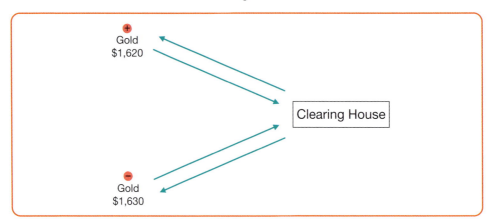

That the overall profit is consistent with the usual economics as sell price minus buy price is good to know. But, due to the daily settlement process, the overall profit is not paid out in this way. Rather, it is paid out as the *sum of the daily settlements*. That is, the overall profit is paid out in daily profits and losses.

Overall Profit=Sum of the daily settlements
=(–$400)–($1600)+($4000–$1000)
=+$1000

FUTURES CONTRACTS: MARKET ORGANIZATION 151

Summary

1. The *overall* profit or loss, per unit of the underlying, on a naked *long* futures position ultimately offset prior to the delivery month on day i, π^i_{Long}, equals the change in the futures price.

$$\pi^i_{\text{Long}} = \text{offset (sell price) on the } i\text{-th day} - \text{buy price at initiation}$$
$$= \Delta F$$
$$= F_{i,T} - F_{0,T}$$

2. The *overall* profit or loss, per unit of the underlying, on a naked *short* futures position ultimately offset prior to the delivery month on day i equals the change in the futures price in the opposite direction.

$$\pi^i_{\text{Short}} = \text{offset (buy price) on the } i\text{-th day} - \text{sell price at initiation}$$
$$= -\Delta F$$
$$= F_{0,T} - F_{i,T}$$

3. Settlement prices are completely irrelevant to the determination of the *final* (overall) profit or loss. They are relevant only to the determination of *daily* profits or losses.

4. The daily settlement process (marking to market and recontracting) is consistent with 1. and 2. That is, the daily settlement process is consistent with the economics of trading futures.

We can now add *recontracting* to our list of definitions.

17. *Recontracting* means that, once the daily values of all futures positions are realized by the daily settlement process and paid out or received by the respective counterparties, then there is no value left to all futures positions.

   The current value of all futures positions is then set to zero and the process restarts the next day, and so on until delivery. This contrasts with most non-derivative financial instruments like equities and bonds.

5.7.4 Tracking the Equity in an Investor's Account

Being able to track the investor's equity over the trading period is a useful skill, particularly in trading futures. We give an example of this process for Example 2.

152 **FORWARD CONTRACTS AND FUTURES CONTRACTS**

1. On Day 1, the investor must deposit the initial margin as required by his initiated long futures position. The investor's account is marked to market at the end of the trading day (we ignore the bi-daily feature) and reflects a loss of $400. This reduction in equity to $7025 does *not* violate the maintenance margin level. Day 1's ending equity carries forward to the beginning of trading Day 2, as indicated in Table 5.9.

2. The investor takes no trading action over Day 2, but his account is marked to market resulting in a loss of $1600. This reduces the equity to $5425 which *does* violate the maintenance margin level. Therefore, $2000 must be added to the account to get the equity up to the initial margin level which becomes the equity at the end of trading Day 2. As indicated, this equity carries over to the beginning of trading Day 3.

3. On Day 3, the investor makes $4000 on his long position, but his short offsetting trade position generates a loss of $1000. In sum, the equity increases to $10,425, which would be withdrawn from the account because the investor is now out of the market.

4. Let's see how much the investor deposits into his account and how much is withdrawn. On Day 1, he deposits $7425. On Day 2 he meets a margin call by depositing $2000. The total deposits were $9425. He withdraws $10,425 from his account at the end of Day 3 for a profit of $10,425–$9425=+$1000.

The following graphic Table 5.9 illustrates the equity account over the three trading days.

TABLE 5.9 **Tracking the Equity in an Investor's Account**

	Day 1	Day 2	Day 3
	+7425=IM on the initiated long position	7025	7425
Profit (Loss)	−400	−1600	+4000 (long position) −1000 (short position)
		5425<6750 therefore a *+2000*=MM call	10,425
EQUITY	7025	7425	10,425

FUTURES CONTRACTS: MARKET ORGANIZATION 153

Therefore, the overall profit

> =ending balance in customer's account–customer deposits
> =$10,425–($2000+$7425)
> =+$1000.

Deposits are indicated by italics in Table 5.9.

5.8 THE EFFECTIVE PRICE AND THE INVOICE PRICE UPON DELIVERY

What happens if a position in a futures contract is held to expiration and no other trading takes place over the life of the contract? The simple answer is that you would have to *make* delivery of the underlying commodity, if you went short at initiation. If you went long at initiation, you would have to *take* delivery of the underlying commodity during the delivery month. This is just the definition of a futures contract.

The trickier question is: what would be the *effective* price you would pay for the commodity? The answer is that if the contract was a forward contract, then you would simply pay the contracted forward price at delivery. Things are made slightly more complicated for a futures contract due to the daily settlement process. We look at this in general.

Suppose that you initiate a long position in a futures contract at the futures price $F_{0,T}$ and you hold it to expiration which is N days later. $t=0$ is the current time. The seller decides the exact date in the delivery month to deliver the underlying commodity. This is one of the seller's options.

The following graphic illustrates the sequence of daily settlements over the life of the contract where the superscript 's' indicates settlement price.

Daily Settlements

$$F_{0,T} \qquad \left(F^{S}_{1,T}-F_{0,T}\right) \quad \left(F^{S}_{2,T}-F^{S}_{1,T}\right) \quad \left(F^{S}_{3,T}-F^{S}_{2,T}\right) \qquad\qquad \left(F^{S}_{N,T}-F^{S}_{N-1,T}\right)$$

| 0 | 1 | 2 | 3 ... | N–1 | N DAY |

Note that when the long initiates the futures position, he is looking at it as a *fancy* forward contract. Therefore, he expects $F_{0,T}$ to be the *effective* price for the commodity, just as it would be if it were a forward contract. This makes economic sense.

However, let's see what the *invoice* price (actual price paid at delivery) is required to be in order for $F_{0,T}$ to be the buyer's *effective* price, after all the daily settlements are taken into account. When the underlying commodity is delivered by the clearing house to the long he will be *invoiced* for it. Call the price he *actually* pays for the commodity delivered, the *invoice price* at delivery, IP_N.

The total cash flows to the long is the sum of the daily settlements minus the invoice price (an outflow),

Total Undiscounted Cost

$$= \left(F_{1,T}^{S} - F_{0,T} \right) + \left(F_{2,T}^{S} - F_{1,T}^{S} \right) + \left(F_{3,T}^{S} - F_{2,T}^{S} \right) + \ldots + \left(F_{N,T}^{S} - F_{N-1,T}^{S} \right) - IP_N$$

$$= F_{0,T} + \left(F_{N,T}^{S} - IP_N \right)$$

Note that all the *intermediate* settlement prices wash out. The final settlement price on day N, $F_{N,T}^{S}$, cannot wash out of course. What must the invoice price be in order for longing futures at $F_{0,T}$ to lock in the *effective* price $F_{0,T}$?

In order for this to be the case, the second term above in total undiscounted cost must be zero. That is, the invoice price, IP_N, must be equal to the final settlement price, $F_{N,T}^{S}$.

Note that $F_{N,T}^{S}$ must also be equal to the ultimate spot price at delivery, because *the futures settlement price converges to the ultimate spot price*. That is, $F_{N,T}^{S}$ is the spot price at time N, P_N. Otherwise, there would be an arbitrage opportunity.

A futures contract with zero time to delivery represents a spot transaction. Therefore, you end up paying the ultimate spot price of the underlying commodity at delivery as the invoice price.

The conclusion we have reached is that:

1. *The invoice price paid for the commodity at delivery must be equal to the ultimate spot price, in order for the effective price paid for the commodity to be the contracted futures price.*

Because you end up paying the spot price at expiration for the commodity if delivered, new possibilities are created. One is that *any* futures contract could always be 'cash settled'. This means that, instead of taking delivery of the commodity (as the long) or making delivery of the commodity (as the short),

FUTURES CONTRACTS: MARKET ORGANIZATION **155**

one could simply purchase the commodity in the cash (spot) market (if long), or sell it in the spot market (if short).

As long as the ultimate settlement price $F_{N,T}^S$ is equal to the spot price at time N, P_N, the effective price paid (received) for the commodity is the contracted price, $F_{0,T}$, just as it would be for a forward contract.

5.8.1 Offset vs. Delivery

In this subsection we will examine when the total profit figures from offsetting a futures contract prior to delivery, or from delivering the underlying commodity, are equal. The notation is self-explanatory, but we will explain it anyway.

$F_{0,2}$ is the initial futures price at which the investor longs the futures contract for delivery at time 2. $F_{1,2}^S$ is the settlement price of that contract at the end of Day 1, $F_{2,2}^S$ is the settlement price of that contract at the end of Day 2, and P_2 is the ultimate spot price of the underlying commodity at the end of Day 2.

$$
\begin{array}{cccc}
 & & P_2 & \\
F_{0,T} & \left(F_{1,2}^S - F_{0,2}\right) & \left(F_{2,2}^S - F_{1,2}^S\right) & \\
\vdash\!\!\!-\!\!\!-\!\!\!-\!\!\!-\!\!\!-\!\!\!+\!\!\!-\!\!\!-\!\!\!-\!\!\!-\!\!\!-\!\!\!\dashv & & & \\
0 & 1 & 2 & \text{DAY}
\end{array}
$$

Next, we will contrast the two scenarios available to a trader at or close to expiration.

Case 1: The long trader takes delivery of the underlying commodity

In this case, there is no need to offset the long futures position. The long would receive (or pay) daily settlement variation in the amount $F_{1,2}^S - F_{0,2}$ at the end of Day 1, and in the amount $F_{2,2}^S - F_{1,2}^S$ at the end of Day 2. The sum of daily settlement variations over the two-day life of the contract is,

$$(F_{1,2}^S - F_{0,2}) + (F_{2,2}^S - F_{1,2}^S) = F_{2,2}^S - F_{0,2}.$$

Convergence, actual or forced, implies that $F_{2,2}^S = P_2$. Furthermore, we know by the result in section 5.8, that the invoice price paid for the underlying commodity by the long must be equal to the ultimate spot price P_2.

FORWARD CONTRACTS AND FUTURES CONTRACTS

Therefore the total cash flow to the long is,

$$(F_{1,2}^S - F_{0,2}) + (F_{2,2}^S - F_{1,2}^S) - P_2 = F_{2,2}^S - F_{0,2} - P_2$$
$$= P_2 - F_{0,2} - P_2$$
$$= -F_{0,2}$$

which is what it should be. Why?

Case 2: The long offsets his futures position just prior to expiration

In this case, the long offsets his futures position just prior to expiration, while the contract is still trading. He then purchases the commodity in the spot market. We could examine settlement variation each day on the long position initiated at time $t=0$ and the offsetting short position initiated at $N=2$.

But we can also use what we already know, which is that the overall profit (loss) on a long position offset by a short position is the *change* in the futures price, the futures sale price minus the futures buy price.

In this case, the short position was initiated at a price very close to $F_{2,2}^S = P_2$ near the end of Day 2 (this assumes convergence). The overall profit on the futures component of the strategy is $F_{2,2}^S - F_{0,2}$.

The remaining component is based on the purchase of the underlying commodity in the spot market at P_2.

$$\text{Total profits} = F_{2,2}^S - F_{0,2} - P_2$$
$$= -F_{0,2}$$

just as for case 1.

We conclude that, except for transactions costs:

1. The total profit figure to the long will be the same whether he takes delivery in the futures market, or offsets his position in the futures market by means of an offsetting trade, and takes delivery of the underlying commodity in the spot market.

2. *The necessary and sufficient condition in order for this to be true is convergence.*

The implication is that *any futures contract position could be cash settled.* In fact, very few of them are resolved by delivery in the futures market.

FUTURES CONTRACTS: MARKET ORGANIZATION — 157

5.9 CASH SETTLEMENT VS. COMMODITY SETTLEMENT

There are two ways that $F^S_{N,T}$ can be equated to the ultimate spot price. One way is through arbitrage. The other way is by *defining* $F^S_{N,T}=P_N$. That is, by *forcing convergence*. Therefore, contracts like the S&P 500 futures contract, where it would be very difficult or impossible to deliver the underlying commodity, can be cash settled. All the exchange has to do is to *force* convergence by equating the final settlement price to the ultimate spot price. Once this is done, a futures contract acts just like a fancy forward contract, which is the way we want it to act.

This paragraph describes what is meant by *cash settlement*. If you take a long position in a futures or a forward contract and the spot price at expiration is higher than the price at which you bought the commodity forward, $P_N>F_{0,N}$, then you made an overall profit equal to $P_N-F_{0,N}$. The corresponding short would have incurred an overall loss, because the profit (loss) to the short is $F_{0,N}-P_N$, which in this case would be negative. This *overall* profit or loss is paid out or received daily in the form of daily settlements, as described.

Cash settlement means that the longs and shorts would each have to pay up, or be paid, the respective daily values of their *last day's* futures positions based on the final settlement price being equated to the ultimate spot price in the cash market.

Hence the term *cash* settlement. In order to make the final profit figure work out, cash settlement requires that daily settlement on the last day, $F^S_{N,T}-F^S_{N-1,T}$, must be equal to $F^S_{N-1,T}$. It will be so equal if and only if $F^S_{N,T}=P_N$.

Further Implications

There are several important implications we can draw from this problem and our analysis of the the overall profits on a futures contract.

1. *The daily profits or losses to a futures position are unknown at time zero. However, with daily price limits they can be bounded.*

2. *If you persist until the end of the contract by steadfastly not offsetting your position when it appears to be generating losses, you will lock-in the futures price at which you originally contracted. Just as in a forward position. This is one reason that futures markets 'work'. They retain this feature of forward contracts but are just fancier instruments.*

158 FORWARD CONTRACTS AND FUTURES CONTRACTS

■ KEY CONCEPTS

1. Market Participants: FCMs, RCRs, IBs, CPOs, CTAs.
2. Three Phases Of Futures Trading: order submission, order execution, trade clearing.
3. Types of futures trade orders: Market with Protection, Limit, Stop orders.
4. Trading on Globex.
5. The Globex Limit Order Book (LOB).
6. Pit Trading and the Order Flow Process.
7. The Clearing House and its Functions: Interposing, Clearing, and Guaranteeing.
8. Margins in Futures as Performance Bonds.
9. Marking to Market and the Daily Settlement Process.
10. Daily Value of a Futures Contract.
11. Tracking the Equity in an Investor's Account.
12. The Effective Price and the Invoice Price.
13. Offset vs. Delivery.
14. Cash Settlement vs. Commodity Settlement.

■ END OF CHAPTER EXERCISES FOR CHAPTER 5

1. Define:

   (a) Member of an Exchange.
   (b) Clearing Member.
   (c) RCR.
   (*d*) FCM.
   (e) Floor Trader.
   (f) Floor Broker.

2. Review clearing.

   (a) What is meant by clearing trades?
   (b) Explain the relationship between the functions and operation of the Clearing House and the default risk on futures contracts.

3. Define the following terms:

   (a) Initial margin.
   (b) Maintenance margin.

FUTURES CONTRACTS: MARKET ORGANIZATION **159**

    (c) Variation margin call.

    (d) Settlement price.

    (e) Settlement variation.

    (f) Marking to market.

    (g) Open contract.

    (h) Open interest.

    (i) Equity.

    (j) Closing range.

    (k) Daily settlement.

4. Consider Adams in Figure 5.3.

    (a) Trace through the delivery obligations incurred by Adams as a result of his futures trades.

    (b) Is delivery relevant or irrelevant to the clearing house and to Adams?

    (c) What is the profit or loss to Adams in December as a result of his futures trades?

    (d) For what trade futures prices will Adams make a profit in December?

    (e) For what trade futures prices will Adams suffer a loss in December?

5. This problem refers to Example 1 in section 5.7.3. Suppose that the daily settlement price $F^S_{1,T}=\$1620$, but that the trader went long, instead of short, one Dec. Gold Comex contract at the futures price $\$F_{0,T}=\$1600/oz$.

    (a) Trace through the long investor's daily profit or loss by direct calculation.

    (b) Calculate the equity in the investor's account at the end of the trading day.

    (c) Would the investor receive a margin call?

6. Suppose there are $N=4$ days left until delivery on a futures contract.

    (a) Map out the daily cash flows to a long position in the futures contract.

    (b) Show what the invoice price must be, in order for the futures contract to lock in the contracted futures price $F_{0,4}$ as the effective purchase price of the commodity at $N=4$.

7. Is there any price volatility in a futures contract held to expiration? Explain.

160 FORWARD CONTRACTS AND FUTURES CONTRACTS

■ SELECTED CONCEPT CHECK SOLUTIONS

Concept Check 1

a. The answer follows from the definition of the protection price limit.
b. It would get executed at the *next best offer* of 90675.
c. 90675 exceeds the protection price limit of 90625, which represents the highest price that the investor is willing to pay. CME Globex places the remaining quantity (two contracts) on the limit order book at a protection price limit of 90625.

Concept Check 2

a. Market sell orders *without* protection are executed at the highest bid available in the market at the time. Therefore, it would be executed.
b. Market sell orders with protection are executed at the highest bid available in the market at the time, only if that highest bid is in the price band dictated by the market order with protection. Therefore, it would be executed if the price band was not violated.

   If the price band is violated, it would not be executed. Instead, it would go into the limit order book and await execution.

Concept Check 4

a. See Table 5.7 (Answer).
b. The best offer is 830.50 (which would be written as 83050) and the protection limit on the buy order is 83050+200=83250=832.50.
c. The best bid is 830.25 (83025) and the protection limit on the sell order is 83025−200=82825=828.25.
d. The order can only be executed for the available ask orders because the protection limit on a buy order is a 832.50 from part b. The first 44 would be executed 830.50, the next 112 would be executed at 830.75 and the remaining 44=200−112−44 would be executed at 831.00.
e. The best bid is 830.25 (83025) and the protection limit on the sell order is 83025−200=828.25. The order can be executed for the available bid orders because they lie above protection limit on the sell order. The first 108 would be executed 830.25, the remaining 92 would be executed at 830.00.

FUTURES CONTRACTS: MARKET ORGANIZATION **161**

TABLE 5.7 ANSWER	**Hypothetical Example 2 of a Globex LOB**		
Bid Size	**Bid Prices**	**Offer Prices**	**Ask Size**
		832.50	
		833.25	
		832.00	
		831.75	
		831.50	468
		831.25	735
		831.00	317
		830.75	112
	Lowest Offer	**830.50**	44
108	**830.25**	**Highest Bid**	
403	830.00		
218	829.75		
373	829.50		
415	829.25		
	829.00		

Concept Check 5

a. 100*$3190=$319,000.

b. 1,000*$.01=$10.

c. $3190–$2900=$290 which is 29 ticks, that is, if the futures price moves to $104–$0.29=$103.71.

d. $0.29*1,000*100=$29,000.

CHAPTER 6

HEDGING WITH FUTURES CONTRACTS, BASIS RISK, AND SPREADING

6.1	Hedging as Portfolio Theory	165
	6.1.1 Hedging as Synthesizing Negative Correlation	165
	6.1.2 Hedging's Objective	167
	6.1.3 Hedging Definitions	168
6.2	Traditional Theories of Hedging	168
	6.2.1 Traditional (One-for-One) Theory with No Basis Risk	168
	6.2.2 Profits in a Traditional Short Hedge and the Basis	171
	6.2.3 When is a Traditional (One-for-One) Hedge with No Basis Risk Consistent with No-Arbitrage?	172
	6.2.4 Traditional (One-for-One) Theory with Basis Risk	174
6.3	Basis Risk vs. Spot Price Risk	178
	6.3.1 When Does Traditional Hedging Reduce Risk?	179
6.4	Non-Traditional (λ-for-One) Hedging Theory	182
	6.4.1 When Does λ-for-One Hedging Reduce Risk?	183
	6.4.2 Minimum Variance Hedging	185
6.5	Carrying Charge Hedging	188
	6.5.1 Implications of Convergence	189
	6.5.2 Overall Profits in a Carrying Charge Hedge	189
	6.5.3 Equilibrium (No-Arbitrage) in a Full Carrying Charge Market	190
6.6	Comparing Equilibrium Forward Pricing and Equilibrium Futures Pricing	193
6.7	Storage and the Price (Cost) of Storage	195
6.8	Contango and Backwardation	198
6.9	Spreads as a Speculative Investment	199

In Chapter 2 we discussed hedging with forward contracts. When you hedge with a forward contract, you have to hold the hedge to maturity since a forward contract does not permit easy offset. This reduces the flexibility of the hedge. There is also default risk in a forward contract.

Using futures contracts as hedging vehicles opens up new possibilities: one could close the hedge by reversing out of the futures position and/or the spot position. The added cost of this flexibility is being subject to the daily cash flow implications based on daily settlement. As noted earlier, in order to engage in futures positions and meet one's objectives, one has to be able to 'weather the storm' of possible negative daily settlement cash flows.

In the case of hedging with forward contracts, one has to first decide what position one has in the underlying spot market. In the example given in Chapter 2, we considered a wheat farmer planning to sell his crop in the spot market in 4 months. The wheat farmer doesn't actually own any wheat today (at time t) because the crop has not yet come to fruition.

Therefore, the wheat farmer is not *explicitly* long. However, this does not mean that the wheat farmer has no position in the underlying wheat. The position the wheat farmer has depends on what he *plans* to do in the future. Since he anticipates *selling* wheat in the wheat market in four months, the farmer currently has a *long* position in spot wheat. Recall that an anticipated sell position means currently long and an anticipated buy position means currently short. This is summarized in Figure 6.1.

Now, looking forward to financial futures in Chapter 7, we will shift the focus away from agricultural commodities like wheat to financial 'commodities' like stock indexes and stock index futures contracts as their hedging vehicles.

FIGURE 6.1 Long vs. Short Positions

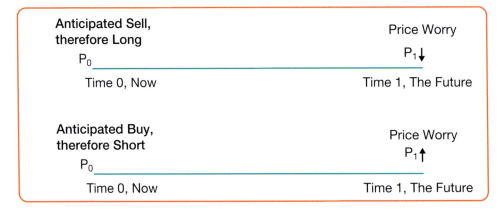

HEDGING, BASIS RISK, AND SPREADING

6.1 HEDGING AS PORTFOLIO THEORY

You are a mutual fund manager, which means that you manage a diversified portfolio. However, even after diversifying, market volatility remains. You don't want to jump around between asset classes attempting to execute a risky and questionably profitable market timing strategy. We will call this the Wall Street Journal strategy. Instead, you want to maintain your position in the portfolio, but you also want to protect it against adverse price movements.

The basic alternatives available to you are described in Figure 6.2.

FIGURE 6.2 **Synthetic Treasury Bill vs. Actual**

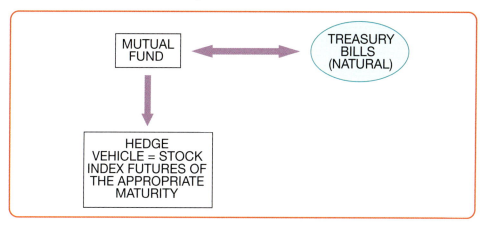

The difference between the left-hand side and the right-hand side of Figure 6.2 is that in order to get to the right-hand side you have to liquidate part or all of your mutual funds, and invest the proceeds in US Treasury bills. The left-hand side of the graphic involves *maintaining* your long position in the mutual fund, but hedging it in stock index futures contracts. In effect, you are synthesizing a natural US Treasury bill. The question, of course, is exactly how to accomplish this goal.

6.1.1 Hedging as Synthesizing Negative Correlation

The technique is hedging, which can be thought of as *synthesizing negative correlation*. The source of this idea is standard portfolio analysis. By combining assets into a portfolio, one obtains the '*correlation effect*'. This is illustrated in Figure 6.3. The returns to asset 1 are represented by the blue arrows and the returns to asset 2 are represented by the purple arrows.

FIGURE 6.3 Perfectly Negatively Correlated Asset Returns

These two assets exhibit counter-cyclical behavior as indicated by the direction of the arrows: when asset 1 is increasing, asset 2 is decreasing and when asset 1 is decreasing, asset 2 is increasing. If we form an equally weighted portfolio consisting of 50% of our wealth in asset 1 and 50% of our wealth in asset 2, then they will cancel each other out, resulting in a *synthetic* risk-free security!

FIGURE 6.4 Synthesizing a Treasury Bill

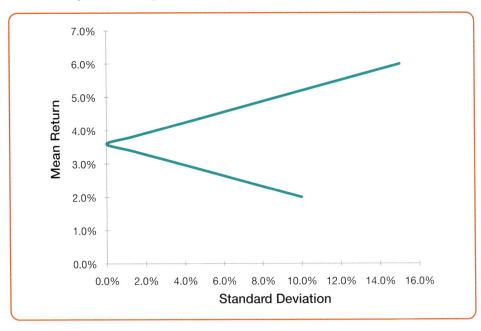

Figure 6.4 is another way to see the effect of combining two perfectly negatively correlated securities into a portfolio. If you can find a security that is perfectly negatively correlated with a given one (like the mutual fund of our example), then some combination of the portfolio weights will yield a portfolio with standard deviation equal to zero. Of course, it may be very hard to find such a security in the real world, because by diversifying the mutual fund you may have already exhausted your diversification possibilities.

This was the situation facing mutual fund managers prior to 1982. Then *stock index futures* contracts were introduced. This allowed investors to further 'diversify away' the *systematic* risk of their portfolios by hedging in stock index futures. In other words, hedging is just another kind of portfolio diversification–based on synthesizing the correlation that drives the diversification effect in the extreme case.

If the resulting zero risk portfolio does not have a return equal to the actual (non-synthetic) risk-free rate, then there is an arbitrage opportunity using the synthetic risk-free asset and the actual risk-free asset (US Treasury bill).

■ CONCEPT CHECK 1

We will put some numbers on this arbitrage. Suppose that the *bond equivalent yield (BEY)* of an actual one-year Treasury bill is 3%, and that there is a portfolio of spot and futures that is risk-free and carries a yield of 3.5% that is comparable to the BEY of the actual *T*-bill.

a. What exactly is meant by 'the synthetic *T*-bill'?
b. What is the synthetic *T*-bill in this example?
c. Construct an arbitrage strategy based on this scenario.
d. What is the implication of this exercise for the yield of the synthetic *T*-bill?

6.1.2 Hedging's Objective

The mutual fund manager's objective is to protect his position in the mutual fund over the next 3 months. The investor in the mutual fund benefits because, by diversifying his portfolio, he is already hedging. According to portfolio theory, individual stocks should *not* be held as isolated investments. Diversifying has the positive, risk-reducing effect of eliminating some of the avoidable risks of individual stocks.

168 **FORWARD CONTRACTS AND FUTURES CONTRACTS**

But the investor benefits further by having the mutual fund also protected against the *systematic, market* risk that remains after diversification. This is where stock index futures contracts enter the strategy, as we shall see in Chapter 7.

6.1.3 Hedging Definitions

1. *Hedging* is the simultaneous holding of a long or short position in an inventory (or commodity) and an opposite position in one or more futures contracts.

2. The nature of a hedge is determined with reference to the position in futures. A *short hedge* is a *selling hedge,* in which futures contracts are sold in conjunction with a long position in the underlying commodity. A *long hedge* is a *buying hedge,* in which futures contracts are bought in conjunction with a short position in the inventory.

6.2 TRADITIONAL THEORIES OF HEDGING

There are many theories of hedging, including one that says you should not hedge! We will cover the main theories, with applications. Always keep in mind the stated or assumed purpose of the hedge.

6.2.1 Traditional (One-for-One) Theory with No Basis Risk

The traditional theory maintains that hedging is used in order to *minimize* or indeed *eliminate* the risk of price fluctuations in some underlying inventory. That is, to protect the value of some existing inventory against price declines, assuming a long position in the underlying. We will start with the polar case, the traditional hedge eliminates all risk. This is illustrated by the following example 1.

Example 1 (Constant Basis)

Consider a precious metals merchant who buys 5000 ounces of silver on September 1 at $P_0=\$30.77/oz$. To protect the value of the inventory, which he now holds long, he simultaneously *sells* one December futures contract (in the deliverable grade) at, say $F_{0,1}=\$30.87/oz$. We will examine the realism of these numbers later and what determines $F_{0,1}$. We summarize his Sept. 1 position.

HEDGING, BASIS RISK, AND SPREADING · 169

Sept. 1 Position

Cash	Futures
Owns 5,000 oz. of silver at a cost of 30.77/oz.=P_0	Sells one December Silver futures contract at 30.87/oz.=$F_{0,1}$

Suppose that, by Nov. 15, both the cash and the futures price have fallen *by exactly the same dollar amount.* On Nov.15 the merchant's cash and futures positions appear as follows.

Nov. 15 Position

Cash	Futures
Owns 5,000 oz. of silver at a cost of 30.65/oz.=P_1	Short one December Silver futures contract at 30.75/oz.=$F_{1-,1}$

We aren't at expiration, time 1, so we denote the futures price on Nov. 15 by $F_{1-,1}$. 1− means a little before time $T=1$. The merchant decides to close out his position in the inventory by selling his silver in the spot silver market at a loss of $.12/oz. Simultaneously, he liquidates his futures position by making an offsetting purchase of one Dec. Silver futures contract at 30.75/oz.

The next step is to calculate the gain on the merchant's futures position. For the original seller of a futures contract, the net gain or loss through a subsequent purchase of a futures contract in the same grade and contract month will be $F_{0,1}-F_{1-,1}$. $F_{0,1}$ is the futures price at which he sold the futures contract at the beginning of the period, thus entitling him to receive $F_{0,1}$ at delivery. He is also obligated to pay $F_{1-,1}$ at maturity, due to his subsequent long position.

Another way to see this is to note that the buyer of a futures contract who offsets at $F_{1-,1}$ receives $F_{1-,1}-F_{0,1}$. Therefore, the opposite side of this position, the short, receives $-(F_{1-,1}-F_{0,1})=F_{0,1}-F_{1-,1}$.

In our example, the net gain to the merchant per ounce on the futures position is,

$$F_{0,1}-F_{1-,1}=\$30.87-\$30.75$$
$$=\$.12/oz.$$

Thus, on the merchant's *overall* position neither losses nor gains are sustained, because the loss on the spot position in silver was exactly offset by the gain on the short Dec. silver futures position. The loss per ounce on the spot silver position is just the spot price change $P_1-P_0=30.65-30.77=-\$.12$.

We can also calculate the total profits for the entire 5000 ounces of silver hedged in futures,

Total Profits,

$$\Pi=\Pi_S+\Pi_F=\text{Profits (Losses on the Spot Position)}+\text{Losses (Profits)}$$
$$\text{on the Futures Position}$$
$$=5000*(P_1-P_0)+5000*(F_{0,1}-F_{1-,1})$$
$$=5000*(30.65-30.77)+5000*(\$30.87-\$30.75)$$
$$=5000*(-\$.12)+5000*(+\$.12)$$
$$=-\$600+\$600$$
$$=\$0.0$$

The merchant 'broke even'. We conclude that, if the futures price was to fall by exactly the same amount as the price of the underlying commodity, then overall profits would be zero on the hedged position. This is to be compared to the potential loss such a merchant would sustain if he held the underlying commodity unhedged. In this case, that would be $-\$600$.

However, the hedge has an expected rate of return of zero which is only consistent with a risk-free rate of zero—a highly restrictive assumption. We will correct this soon by considering other more realistic hedging theories.

Profits on the hedge can be conveniently reformulated in terms of the important concept of the basis. The *basis* is the difference between the futures price and the spot price at a given point in time t, $B_t=F_{t,T}-P_t$. In our example, the September basis is given by

$$B_0=F_{0,1}-P_0$$
$$=\$.10 \text{ cents/oz.}$$

and the Nov. 15 basis is given by

$$B_1=F_{1-,1}-P_1$$
$$=-\$.10 \text{ cents/oz.}$$

Thus the *change* in the basis is $B_0-B_1=0$.

Note that the basis depends upon the contract month of the futures contract. If we take it to be the nearby futures contract, then we are considering the *nearby basis*.

The nearby futures contract is usually the most liquid contract and allows the merchant to easily close out his hedged position by making an offsetting trade, and selling the inventory in the cash market. Thereby, the merchant may take advantage of possibly favorable changes in the basis, if it does change.

Thus hedging does not preclude speculation but can incorporate speculation as '*speculating on the basis*'. We turn in section 6.2.2 to a general result on profits in a traditional short hedge which holds whether the basis changes (basis risk) or not (no basis risk).

6.2.2 Profits in a Traditional Short Hedge and the Basis

a. The net profit in a traditional (one-for-one) short hedge is the change in the basis measured as B_0-B_1.
b. Profits on a traditional short hedge will be zero if and only if the basis does not change.

To see a., we calculate the total profit in the hedging strategy defined by a short hedge. We did this above, but it is worth re-doing because now we will re-express it in terms of the basis. This total profit figure, Π, consists of two components:

1. Settlement variation from the futures positions$=F_{0,1}-F_{1-,1}=\Pi_F$,
2. Profit or loss from changes in the value of the underlying commodity$=P_1-P_0=\Pi_S$.

Thus total profits, Π, equals (1)+(2)=Settlement Variation+Profit (Loss) from value changes in the spot commodity,

$$
\begin{aligned}
\Pi &= \Pi_F + \Pi_S \\
&= (F_{0,1}-F_{1-,1}) + (P_1-P_0) \\
&= (F_{0,1}-P_0) - (F_{1-,1}-P_1) \\
&= B_0-B_1.
\end{aligned}
$$

172 FORWARD CONTRACTS AND FUTURES CONTRACTS

■ CONCEPT CHECK 2

a. Prove b. using a.
b. Can the hedger 'make money' on a traditional short hedge held to expiration?

6.2.3 When is a Traditional (One-for-One) Hedge with No Basis Risk Consistent with No-Arbitrage?

Is the traditional theory with no basis risk a reasonable (consistent with no-arbitrage) theory of how the basis does not change? Specifically, does the traditional theory of how the basis remains constant actually create a synthetic Treasury bill? In answering this question, we can bring to bear what we already know about futures (forward) pricing from Chapters 3 and 4 and learn something more about arbitrage opportunities and how to identify them in practice.

Case 1 (No Dividends and $r=0$)

Recall the forward pricing equation from Chapter 3, when there are no dividends on the underlier, $F_{t,T}=e^{rT}*P_t$. Suppose that time zero is the current date, $t=0$, and that time $T=1$ is the maturity date of the futures contract used to hedge the spot position.

If the hedger holds his hedged position until maturity then, as shown above, his total profit,

$$\Pi = B_0 - B_1$$
$$= \$0.$$

Another argument is that, at maturity, $B_1=\$0$ due to convergence (either natural or forced). If the basis at time 1 is zero and it didn't change from its value at time zero, then $B_0=\$0$ also. This means that $F_{0,1}=P_0$. The hedger's percentage rate of return on his investment of P_0 dollars is also 0% and the hedge is riskless.

In this no-dividend scenario, the only risk-free rate that is consistent with no-arbitrage is $r=0\%$ because $F_{0,1}=e^{r*1}P_0=P_0$ implies that r must be equal to zero. Note that this isn't so absurd. Short-term interest rates have been effectively equal to zero for at least the last 7 years in the USA, 2009–2015.

HEDGING, BASIS RISK, AND SPREADING 173

■ CONCEPT CHECK 3

a. In the scenario of Case 1 construct a risk-free arb if $r>0$. Assume, for example, that $r=3\%$.

Further, if $r=0\%$, then according to the forward pricing equation,

$$F_{t,T}=e^{r\tau}*P_t$$
$$=e^0*P_t$$
$$=P_t.$$

Since $t=0$, this says $F_0=P_0$ to use our previous notation. But then the time zero basis $B_0=0$. So not only does the basis not change, the basis is also a constant value of zero. Since r represents the cost of borrowing to finance the spot commodity, it represents financial 'carrying charges'.

We just proved that one scenario under which the basis can remain constant is that in which there are no carrying charges, financial, storage, or otherwise. In that case, the basis would equal the constant value of zero and the forward price equals the current spot price.

In general, the futures price can be equal, greater than, or less than the current spot price. This example illustrates one case when the two are equal. As noted, a risk-free rate of $r=0\%$ is not far-fetched. But, there is a second case in which $r>0$ but the basis does not change.

Case 2 (Dividends and $r>0$ and $r=\rho$)

This is the other case in which the basis does not change. In this case $r>0$. Suppose that the underlier carries a dividend yield of ρ where $\rho>0$ and that $r=\rho$. Using the dividend model of Chapter 4, we see that $F'_{t,T}=e^{(r-\rho)\tau}*P_t$. When $r=\rho$, the *net* cost of carry is zero and the forward price, $F'_{t,T}$, is once again equal to the spot price at time t, P_t. That is, the time t basis is equal to 0.

At any time subsequent to time t, say $t'>t$, the forward pricing relationship still holds. That is, $F'_{t',T}=e^{(r-\rho)\tau'}*P_{t'}$ where $\tau'=T-t'$ is the new time to maturity based on the new time t'. But $r=\rho$ is still true. Therefore, the time t' basis is also equal to zero. The basis has not changed.

174 **FORWARD CONTRACTS AND FUTURES CONTRACTS**

To summarize, the basis remaining constant is plausible under the two cases described above:

1. Either there are no dividends and $r=0$; or
2. there is a dividend yield and $r=\rho$.

These two cases correspond to the cost or the *net* cost of carry being zero. Equilibrium (no-arbitrage) considerations dictate that the basis must be equal to the (net) cost of carry in the (dividend) no-dividend model, as we shall see later in this chapter.

6.2.4 Traditional (One-for-One) Theory with Basis Risk

In the traditional theory there is no money to be made on a traditional short (or long) hedge if the basis does not change. In this case, which is only consistent with $r=0$ or with $r=\rho$, there is no basis risk in the hedge because the basis is riskless.

This is the extreme case of hedging in the sense that it doesn't just reduce risk. It eliminates it. There is no money to be made in a traditional hedge with zero (net) carrying charges, because there is no economic need to make money. The basis reflects (net) carrying charges (net storage costs), as we will see later in this chapter, in section 6.5.

When there are (net) carrying charges, these must be covered by the hedge. In order to generate the chance of *normal* profits, which are needed to cover (net) carrying charges, the basis *has* to change. Normal, not excess, profits means the profits needed to carry on an economic activity. Net carrying charges are part of the normal costs of doing commodity business. Speculative (excess) profits would be viewed as a reward for risk bearing. 'Making money' can mean making normal profits or making excess profits.

This allows us to address the question, 'Can you make money in a traditional short hedge?' Under conclusion b. of section 6.2.2, it is clear that the basis will generate no money whatsoever as long as the futures price moves by *exactly* the same dollar amount as the spot price, when it moves. The basis will remain constant, and profits (change in the basis by conclusion a.) will be zero. That will happen and be plausible as long as the cost of carry (net cost of carry) is zero.

The answer to our question is given in 3., which gives the technical condition for when you can make money and in 4., which gives the technical condition for when you lose money in a traditional short hedge.

HEDGING, BASIS RISK, AND SPREADING — 175

3. Overall profits, Π, in a traditional short hedge will be positive if and only if the basis narrows, $B_0 > B_1$.
4. Overall profits, Π, in a traditional short hedge will be negative if and only if the basis widens, $B_0 < B_1$.

If the hedge is held to maturity, $T=1$, and spot and futures prices converge, then the overall profits in a traditional short hedge are equal to the time 0 basis B_0 because $B_1 = 0$ if convergence occurs.

Both 3. and 4. are true because profits in a traditional (one-for-one) short hedge are equal to the change in the basis, $\Pi = B_0 - B_1$ by conclusion a. of section 6.2.2. The underlying reason for 3. and 4. is the cost-of-carry model described later in this chapter. If the net cost of carry is positive (negative), then the basis must narrow (widen) by it in order to maintain equilibrium.

To illustrate 3. and 4., we now consider an alternative example in which the basis does not remain constant, because in this example the futures price does not move by exactly the same amount as the price of the underlying commodity. The merchant's Sept. 1 position in cash and futures is as before.

Example 2 (Non-Constant Basis, Basis Widens)

Sept. 1 Position

Cash	Futures
Owns 5,000 oz. of silver at a cost of 30.77/oz.$=P_0$	Sells one December Silver futures contract at 30.87/oz.$=F_{0,1}$

Suppose that by Nov.15 both the cash and the futures price have *not fallen by exactly the same dollar amount*. On Nov.15 the merchant's cash and futures positions appear as follows.

Nov. 15 Position

Cash	Futures
Owns 5,000 oz. of silver at a cost of 30.65/oz.$=P_1$	Short one December Silver futures contract at 30.80/oz.$=F_{1-,1}$

176   **FORWARD CONTRACTS AND FUTURES CONTRACTS**

First note that we aren't quite at expiration on November 15. At expiration, the basis must be equal to zero. Total profits still equals the change in the basis $\Pi = B_0 - B_1$ but *the basis has widened*,

$$B_0 = F_0 - P_0$$
$$= \$30.87 - \$30.77$$
$$= \$.10/oz$$

and,

$$B_1 = F_{1-,1} - P_1$$
$$= \$30.80 - \$30.65$$
$$= .15/oz.$$

Thus total profits $= \$.10/oz - 15/oz.$
$$= -.05/oz \text{ which is negative (losses).}$$

Note that the cash price has fallen *more rapidly* than the futures price. This means that the basis has *widened*, or moved against the merchant. His losses, through relatively rapid spot price decline, have outweighed his gains on his short futures position. The result is a net loss on the hedged position.

■ CONCEPT CHECK 4

Here is a trick for understanding the economic effect of a *widening* basis in a traditional short hedge. Imagine that you are in an elevator. The floor represents the spot price and the ceiling represents the futures price. The elevator goes down.

a. What happens to the spot price?
b. What happens to the futures price?
c. Suppose that the floor falls faster than the ceiling. What happens to the basis?
d. The basis is the difference between the ceiling and the floor. If the floor falls faster than the ceiling, do you make money on the hedge?

Finally, we consider a third example in which the basis narrows.

HEDGING, BASIS RISK, AND SPREADING — 177

Example 3 (Non-Constant Basis, Basis Narrows)

Sept. 1 Position

Cash	Futures
Owns 5,000 oz. of silver at a cost of 30.77/oz.	Sells one December Silver futures contract at 30.87/oz.

Suppose that by Nov. 15 both the cash and the futures price have *not fallen by exactly the same dollar amount*. On Nov.15 the merchant's cash and futures positions appear as follows.

Nov. 15 Position

Cash	Futures
Owns 5,000 oz. of silver at a cost of 30.65/oz.	Short one December Silver futures contract at 30.70/oz.

The time 0 basis equals,

$$B_0 = F_0 - P_0$$
$$= \$30.87 - \$30.77$$
$$= \$.10/oz$$

and the time 1 basis equals,

$$B_1 = F_{1-,1} - P_1$$
$$= \$30.70 - \$30.65$$
$$= .05/oz.$$

Therefore, total profits,

$$\Pi = B_0 - B_1$$
$$= \$.10/oz - .05/oz.$$
$$= .05/oz.$$

Note that the basis has *narrowed* in this example. The futures price (above the cash price) has fallen more rapidly than the cash price. This means that the merchant's gains on his short position in futures has outweighed his losses on the underlying commodity.

178 FORWARD CONTRACTS AND FUTURES CONTRACTS

■ CONCEPT CHECK 5

Here is a trick for understanding the economic effect of a *narrowing* basis in a traditional short hedge. Imagine that you are in an elevator. The floor represents the spot price and the ceiling represents the futures price. The elevator goes down.

a. What happens to the spot price?
b. What happens to the futures price?
c. Suppose that the ceiling falls faster than the floor. What happens to the basis?
d. The basis is the difference between the ceiling and the floor. If the ceiling falls faster than the floor, do you make money on the hedge?

6.3 BASIS RISK VS. SPOT PRICE RISK

We see from these examples that merely holding a hedged position does not guarantee zero risk and zero return if the futures price does not change by exactly the same amount as the spot price. However, one can lock in a riskless positive profit, $B_0 = F_0 - P_0 > 0$, if the hedge is held to expiration and convergence occurs. This assume $r \neq 0$ or $r - \rho \neq 0$, (net) carrying charges are not zero.

One will not get rich doing so because the spread between the futures price and the spot price (the basis) just represents (net) carrying charges. To make speculative profits from a hedge, the hedger will have to lift the hedge prior to maturity and know when to do so. This involves *timing the basis*, which must narrow to profit (see 3. in section 6.2.4), and is quite a tall order.

The basis generally changes in unpredictable ways, except at expiration when it is expected to be zero, and so too will the hedger's profits, which are determined by the change in the basis. *When* the hedger offsets the hedge is also a factor. If the hedger holds the hedge to expiration then, due to convergence of the futures price to the ultimate spot price, the hedger will lock in the basis at the time the hedge was initiated. This is to be expected because the forward price and the futures price have this same 'lock-in' feature.

One can say though that, in a traditional short or long hedge, basis risk is being *substituted* for the risk of fluctuations in the spot price of the underlying commodity. Traditional hedging is based on the idea that the basis is generally less risky than the cash commodity, and therefore short and long hedgers are

HEDGING, BASIS RISK, AND SPREADING **179**

lowering their risk by traditionally hedging. This idea lies at the heart of some popular strategies such as spreading (see section 6.9). Note that risk here refers solely to total variability.

6.3.1 When Does Traditional Hedging Reduce Risk?

When does traditional hedging actually *reduce* risk relative to a fully unhedged spot position? Are there any conditions that must be satisfied? We can use some very basic portfolio theory to address this question.

We start with some time, t, between the current time which we will call time 0 and the expiration date which we will call time $1=T$. Let F_t denote the futures price at time t for delivery at time 1, and let P_t denote the cash price at time t (we drop the full notation $F_{t,1}$). Then $B_t(\omega)=F_t(\omega)-P_t(\omega)$. If we are standing at time 0, then the time t basis is unknown because $F_t(\omega)$ and $P_t(\omega)$ are random variables. The brief way to say this is that B_t is a random variable and to write B_t as $B_t(\omega)=F_t(\omega)-P_t(\omega)$.

We want to calculate the variance of $B_t(\omega)$, which we will abbreviate as $\mathrm{VAR}(B_t(\omega))$. To do this, we use the following result from statistics.

Portfolio Variance Calculation

If $X(\omega)$ and $Y(\omega))$ are two random variables and a and b are constants then we form the new random variable defined by $Z(\omega)=aX(\omega)+bY(\omega)$. It is straightforward to calculate the variance of $Z(\omega))$ as,

$$\mathrm{VAR}(aX(\omega))+bY(\omega))$$
$$=a^2\mathrm{VAR}(X(\omega))+b^2\mathrm{VAR}(Y(\omega))+2a*b*\mathrm{COV}(X(\omega)),Y(\omega)) \qquad \textbf{(VAR}_{\textbf{p}}\textbf{)}$$

where $\mathrm{COV}(X(\omega),Y(\omega))$ is the covariance between $X(\omega)$ and $Y(\omega)$.

Covariance is a measure of how two random variables *move together* and they can move in the same or in opposite directions, or not move together at all in the case of zero correlation.

We use this basic statistics result, (VAR_p), to calculate $\mathrm{VAR}(B_t(\omega)= \mathrm{VAR}(F_t(\omega)-P_t(\omega))$. Here $X(\omega)=F_t(\omega)$, $Y(\omega)=P_t(\omega)$, $a=+1.0$ and $b=-1.0$, so all we have to do is to apply the (VAR_p) formula,

$$\mathrm{VAR}(F_t(\omega)-P_t(\omega))$$
$$=a^2\mathrm{VAR}(F_t(\omega)+b^2\mathrm{VAR}(P_t(\omega)+2a*b*\mathrm{COV}(F_t(\omega),P_t(\omega))$$

180 FORWARD CONTRACTS AND FUTURES CONTRACTS

$$=(+1.0)^2 \text{VAR}(F_t(\omega)) + (-1.0)^2 \text{VAR}(P_t(\omega)) +$$
$$2*(+1.0)*(-1.0)*\text{COV}(F_t(\omega),P_t(\omega))$$
$$=\text{VAR}(F_t(\omega)) + \text{VAR}(P_t(\omega)) - 2*\text{COV}(F_t(\omega),P_t(\omega)).$$

The variance of a fully *unhedged* spot position is just the variance of the random spot price $\text{VAR}(P_t(\omega))$. So all we have to do is compare $\text{VAR}(B_t(\omega))$ to $\text{VAR}(P_t(\omega))$ and ask when is

$$\text{VAR}(B_t(\omega)) < \text{VAR}(P_t(\omega))?$$

That is, when is

$$\text{VAR}(B_t(\omega)) = \text{VAR}(F_t(\omega)) + \text{VAR}(P_t(\omega)) - 2*\text{COV}(F_t(\omega),P_t(\omega))$$
$$< \text{VAR}(P_t(\omega))?$$

Or the same question is, when is

$$\text{VAR}(F_t(\omega)) - 2*\text{COV}(F_t(\omega),P_t(\omega)) < 0?$$

We got this result by just canceling out $\text{VAR}(P_t(\omega))$ which appears on both sides of the second to last inequality. By bringing $-2*\text{COV}(F_t(\omega),P_t(\omega))$ over to the right-hand side of the last inequality we obtain the question:
When is

$$\text{VAR}(F_t(\omega)) < 2*\text{COV}(F_t(\omega)),P_t(\omega)))?$$

Since $\text{VAR}(F_t(\omega))$ is a positive number, we can divide both sides of the inequality by it to ask, when is

$$1.0 < 2\frac{\text{COV}(F_t(\omega),P_t(\omega))}{\text{VAR}(F_t(\omega))}?$$

Dividing this inequality through by 2 our question becomes, when is

$$\frac{1.0}{2} = 0.5 < \frac{\text{COV}(F_t(\omega),P_t(\omega))}{\text{VAR}(F_t(\omega))}?$$

HEDGING, BASIS RISK, AND SPREADING 181

Now all we have to do is to interpret the right-hand side of the last inequality. Another statistics result is called ordinary least squares regression (OLS).

OLS Regression

If we want to measure the correlation between $P_t(\omega)$, and $F_t(\omega)$, we run the regression,

$$P_t(\omega)=\alpha+\beta_{P_t(\omega),F_t(\omega)}*F_t(\omega)+\varepsilon_t$$

The coefficient $\beta_{P_t(\omega),F_t(\omega)}$ is called the *beta of the spot price on the futures price* and it is equal to,

$$\beta_{P_t(\omega),F_t(\omega)}=\frac{\mathrm{COV}(P_t(\omega),F_t(\omega))}{\mathrm{VAR}(F_t(\omega))}$$

Note that COV(,) isn't affected by the order, therefore

$$\mathrm{COV}(P_t(\omega),F_t(\omega))=\mathrm{COV}(F_t(\omega),P_t(\omega)).$$

Our result is that,

a. *Traditional hedging reduces risk if and only if the beta of the spot commodity price on the corresponding futures price is greater than 1/2.*

In other words, there has to be a sufficient degree of correlation between the spot price and the futures price in order for traditional hedging to 'work'. If there isn't enough correlation, traditional hedging would be counter-productive because it would *increase* risk, which is not what hedgers want to do.

Three questions with regard to the beta of the spot commodity price on the corresponding futures price naturally arise:

1. What is the beta of the price of the spot commodity on that of the futures price of the nearby contract?
2. Is it positive or negative?
3. If it is positive, how large is it?

Answers can be given in terms of *informational* effects. One would expect that those factors affecting the price of the spot commodity would also affect the nearby futures price. This common informational link would create a high degree of correlation between the two types of prices. The reason for considering the nearby futures price is that it would be more likely to be affected by the information set affecting the spot price than more distant futures.

A second factor creating a degree of correlation between spot and futures prices is that the price of the spot commodity is generally *determined* from the nearby futures price quote. Also, the forward pricing model says that the forward price depends *only* on the current spot price and the (net) cost of carry as expressed either by $F_{t,T}=e^{r\tau}*P_t$ or by $F'_{t,T}=e^{(r-\rho)\tau}*P_t$. According to this model, *nothing else* goes into the forward price.

The moral of the story is that one has to be careful in using traditional hedging. First, for the traditional theory with no basis risk, its basic assumption (equal dollar moves in futures and spot prices) holds in rather restrictive circumstances ($r=0$ or $r-\rho=0$).

The model cannot be used when neither of these conditions hold in the appropriate scenario (dividends or no dividends), because the model is then inconsistent with no–arbitrage. The correlation condition, however, is not a problem because in this case the (net) cost of carry is zero, futures prices and spot prices are identical. Then the beta of the spot price on the futures price is equal to 1.0 (why?) which is $>1/2$.

For the traditional theory with basis risk, one would have to check the condition $\beta_{P_t(\omega),F_t(\omega)}>0.5$. In a cross-hedging scenario, for example, this condition may fail. The point is that traditional hedging with basis risk only works under this condition and is not a universal risk reducer.

A similar issue occurs in portfolio theory. If you combine two stocks that are perfectly positively correlated into a portfolio, then there is no diversification effect.

The empirical issues associated with traditional hedging are discussed in the research literature. We turn next to other non-traditional forms of hedging.

6.4 NON-TRADITIONAL (λ-FOR-ONE) HEDGING THEORY

Rather than consider the one-for-one hedge we have been discussing, suppose that instead of selling one futures contract per unit of spot commodity we were to sell λ of them. We can conveniently call this λ-for-1 hedging.

The profits from a λ-for-1 hedge are very similar to the profits from a one-for-one hedge. In this case, profits are the change in the λ-basis where

HEDGING, BASIS RISK, AND SPREADING **183**

the definition of the λ-basis is, $B_{t,\lambda}=\lambda F_t-P_t$. This is demonstrated in the End of Chapter Exercise 3, which you should try now.

Note that when λ equals 1.0, we are right back to traditional hedging. When λ is different from 1.0, then we have a more general form of hedging. When λ is bigger than 1.0, we are *over hedging* the commodity. When λ is less than 1.0, we are *under hedging* the commodity.

6.4.1 When Does λ-for-One Hedging Reduce Risk?

Next, using the rule for calculating the variance of a portfolio, (VAR_p), with $a=\lambda$ and $b=-1.0$ we easily calculate $VAR(B_{t,\lambda})$ just as before for the case of $\lambda=1.0$.

$$
\begin{aligned}
VAR(B_{t,\lambda}) &= VAR(\lambda F_t(\omega)-P_t(\omega)) \\
&= \lambda^2 VAR(F_t(\omega))+(-1.0)^2 VAR(P_t(\omega))+ \\
&\quad 2*\lambda*(-1.0)*COV(F_t(\omega),P_t(\omega)) \\
&= \lambda^2 VAR(F_t(\omega))+VAR(P_t(\omega))-2*\lambda*COV(F_t(\omega),P_t(\omega)).
\end{aligned}
$$

Once again, we can ask when λ-for-one hedging reduces risk relative to a fully unhedged spot position. We simply compare the variance of the λ basis to the variance of the spot price.

When is

$$
\begin{aligned}
VAR(B_{t,\lambda}) &= \lambda^2 VAR(F_t(\omega))+VAR(P_t(\omega))-2*\lambda*COV(F_t(\omega),P_t(\omega)) \\
&< VAR(P_t(\omega))?
\end{aligned}
$$

Cancelling $VAR(P_t(\omega))$ from both sides we obtain the equivalent question, when is

$$
\lambda^2 VAR(F_t(\omega))-2*\lambda*COV(F_t(\omega),P_t(\omega))<0?
$$

Or, when is

$$
\lambda^2 VAR(F_t(\omega))<2*\lambda*COV(F_t(\omega)),P_t(\omega))?
$$

The answer is when

$$\frac{\lambda}{2} = \frac{\lambda^2}{2\lambda}$$

$$< \frac{\text{COV}(F_t(\omega), P_t(\omega))}{\text{VAR}(F_t(\omega))}$$

$$= \frac{\text{COV}(P_t(\omega), F_t(\omega))}{\text{VAR}(F_t(\omega))}$$

$$= \beta_{P_t(\omega), F_t(\omega)}$$

The right hand side of this inequality is once again the beta of the spot price on the futures price and the left-hand side is $\lambda/2$. So the inequality that must be satisfied is,

$$\frac{\lambda}{2} < \beta_{P_t(\omega), F_t(\omega)}$$

As long as $\beta_{P_t(\omega), F_t(\omega)}$ is positive we can always satisfy this inequality by making λ small enough.

■ CONCEPT CHECK 6

Suppose that $\beta_{P_t(\omega), F_t(\omega)} = 1/4$.

a. Does traditional hedging work?
b. Write out the condition on λ.

Traditional hedging fails to accomplish its goal in this case, which is to reduce risk relative to a naked spot position. In this case, all hope of reducing risk through traditional hedging is lost because there is simply not enough correlation between the spot price and the futures price to do so. Fortunately, this case is precisely one where we can use λ-for-one hedging to reduce risk relative to a fully unhedged spot position.

What happens when we are at the extreme value of $\lambda = 1/2$? We can't expect to reduce risk but we can hope to at least *match* spot price risk. We have to sell $1/2$ as many futures contracts as units of spot position held long.

This isn't hard to do because most traders do not hold a single unit of the spot commodity. For example, with 10 units of the spot commodity, one could sell 5 futures contracts as the hedge.

HEDGING, BASIS RISK, AND SPREADING **185**

We calculate the range of the λ hedge where $\lambda=1/2$ and the data is that $\beta_{P_t(\omega),F_t(\omega)}=1/4$ and,

$$
\begin{aligned}
F_0 &=6.00 \\
P_0 &=5.80 \\
P_1 &=5.55 \\
F_1 &=5.00.
\end{aligned}
$$

The time 0,1/2-basis is

$$
\begin{aligned}
B_{0,0.5} &=0.5F_0-P_0 \\
&=0.5\ (6.00)-5.80 \\
&=-2.80
\end{aligned}
$$

The time 1,1/2-basis is

$$
\begin{aligned}
B_{1,0.5} &=0.5F_1-P_1 \\
&=0.5\ (5.00)-5.55 \\
&=-3.05.
\end{aligned}
$$

Thus, the range in the $\lambda=1/2$ basis is equal to $-2.80-(-3.05)=0.25$. This is clearly equal to the range of the spot price $5.80-5.55=0.25$ so 1/2-for-one hedging has *equalized* risk relative to a naked spot position.

6.4.2 Minimum Variance Hedging

Minimum variance hedging is part of λ-for-one hedging and is therefore included in this section. The general principle is that, in order to minimize the variance of the λ-basis, one should choose $\lambda=$the beta of the spot price on the futures price$=\beta_{P_t(\omega),F_t(\omega)}$.

This result makes a lot of intuitive sense, because the beta of the spot price on the futures price tracks the co-movement between the futures price and the spot price. If the spot price moves roughly by $\beta_{P_t(\omega),F_t(\omega)}$ units every time the futures price moves by one unit then hedging will require that you adjust the hedge by selling $\beta_{P_t(\omega),F_t(\omega)}$ futures.

For example, if $\beta_{P_t(\omega),F_t(\omega)}=0.5$, then one must adjust for this risk-producing lack of dollar equivalence by selling fewer (half as many) futures per unit spot commodity you hold long. This is the art of λ-for-1 hedging.

A. Deriving the Risk-Minimizing Hedge Ratio

All this will come in handy when we talk about hedging using financial futures, such as stock index futures contracts. It also comes into play in the Black–Scholes formula and we will encounter it in the Binomial option pricing model (BOPM) as well. So it pays to understand it in this relatively simple context.

Our next task is to find the hedge ratio λ that will *minimize* the variance of dollar profits (the variance of the change in the λ-basis) over a given period. That minimum might not be zero, but it will be the *lowest* it can be. That is, the hedge will be risk minimizing, if not risk eliminating.

We have to set up the time dimension of the model. Suppose we are standing at time 0. The futures contract matures at time T and t is some intermediate time $0 < t < T$. The hedger has a fixed time horizon $[0,t]$, and wants to set up a *minimum variance hedge* over this time period.

Profits on the λ hedge are equal to,

$$\Pi_t(\omega) = \Delta B_{t,\lambda}$$
$$= B_{0,\lambda} - B_{t,\lambda}(\omega).$$

Of course, only the future (time t) λ basis is random at time 0, because $B_{0,\lambda} = \lambda F_0 - P_0$ is known once λ is determined.

Hence,

$$VAR(\Pi_t(\omega)) = VAR(\Delta B_{t,\lambda})$$
$$= VAR(B_{0,\lambda} - B_{t,\lambda}(\omega))$$
$$= VAR(B_{t,\lambda}(\omega))$$

So all we have to do is calculate $VAR(B_{t,\lambda}(\omega))$, which will be a function of λ. Then we take the first derivative of $VAR(B_{t,\lambda}(\omega))$ with respect to λ and set it equal to 0 to solve for the *optimal (risk-minimizing) hedge ratio* which we will call λ^*.

Finally, we check that the *second* derivative of $VAR(B_{t,\lambda}(\omega))$ with respect to λ is positive at λ^* to verify that λ^* is indeed the *minimum* variance hedge ratio.

We have already calculated the variance of the dollar profits of various hedges so this is an easy task.

$$VAR(B_{t,\lambda}(\omega))=VAR(\lambda F_t(\omega)-P_t(\omega))$$
$$=\lambda^2 VAR(F_t(\omega))-2\lambda COV(F_t(\omega),P_t(\omega))+VAR(P_t(\omega)).$$

Now, $VAR(F_t(\omega)),VAR(P_t(\omega))$, and $-2COV(F_t(\omega),P_t(\omega))$ are all considered to be constants when we look at how $VAR(B_{t,\lambda}(\omega))$ varies with λ. So the first derivative of $VAR(\lambda F_t(\omega)-P_t(\omega))$ with respect to λ is equal to,

$$2\lambda VAR(F_t(\omega))-2COV(F_t(\omega),P_t(\omega)).$$

Set this equal to zero and solve for λ^* to obtain,

$$\lambda^* = \frac{COV(P_t(\omega),F_t(\omega))}{VAR(F_t(\omega))}$$

$$= \beta_{P_t(\omega),F_t(\omega)}$$

λ^* is the beta of the spot price on the futures price. Note that you can always change the order in $COV(F_t(\omega),P_t(\omega))$ to $COV(P_t(\omega),F_t(\omega))$ without changing anything.

If we really want to know that we have obtained a minimum (rather than a *maximum*) value for the variance, we have to calculate the second derivative of $VAR(B_{t,\lambda}(\omega))$ (which is the first derivative of the first derivative). The first derivative of $2\lambda VAR(F_t(\omega))-2COV(F_t(\omega),P_t(\omega))$ with respect to λ is $2VAR(F_t(\omega))$ which is positive everywhere and specifically at λ^*. We have now completely shown that the risk-minimizing hedge ratio over the horizon $[0,t]$ is,

$$\lambda^* = \frac{COV(P_t(\omega),F_t(\omega))}{VAR(F_t(\omega))}$$

$$= \beta_{P_t(\omega),F_t(\omega)}$$

B. Estimating $\lambda^* = \beta_{P_t(\omega),F_t(\omega)}$

In order to implement this approach one has to estimate $\beta_{P_t(\omega),F_t(\omega)}$ based on running the ordinary least squares (OLS) regression,

$$P_t(\omega)=\alpha+\beta_{P_t(\omega),F_t(\omega)}F_t(\omega)+\varepsilon_t(\omega) \qquad \text{(OLS)}$$

188 FORWARD CONTRACTS AND FUTURES CONTRACTS

This is an estimation problem, and the results will be data-dependent and subject to error. Usually one uses past historical (in-sample) data on futures prices and spot prices to run the regression. Then one applies the estimated beta to the out-of-sample future period over which the hedger is hedging.

6.5 CARRYING CHARGE HEDGING

So far we have considered hedging under the assumption that, in holding a commodity, there are no 'carrying' charges or storage costs other than the normal (net) interest. In reality, a hedger who is long a commodity and hedges by shorting the appropriate number of the appropriate futures contracts will have to pay the costs associated with carrying the commodity over the hedging period.

Carrying charges include *direct* costs, such as warehousing and insurance, as well as *indirect* costs such as the *opportunity cost* of having funds tied up in inventory of the commodity. This opportunity cost is usually represented by the riskless rate of return on a riskless security. By having one's funds tied up in the inventory, one forgoes the interest one *could* have earned by putting those funds into a riskless 'bank account', instead of into the inventory.

To take a concrete example, consider an individual who buys the cash commodity at time zero at a per unit cash price of P_0. Simultaneously, he sells one futures contract at $t=0$ for delivery at $t=1$ at a per unit futures price of $F_{0,1}$. The individual is a traditional one-for-one short hedger. At time 1, he liquidates both his cash commodity position and satisfies his short futures commitment. This can be done simply by delivering the spot commodity into the short futures position.

Marginal carrying charges over the period [0,1], including storage, insurance, and excluding forgone interest, are expected to be CC[0,1] per unit of spot commodity carried. We calculate the dollar profits that the traditional short hedger expects to earn over the period [0,1].

We know that dollar profits, *ignoring* all carrying charges, are equal to the change in the traditional basis over the period, $\Pi[0,1]=B_0-B_1$ where $B_i=F_i-P_i$ for $i=0,1$ and we drop the full notation $B_{0,1}$ and $B_{1,1}$.

Let's take a closer look at the $t=1$ basis $B_1=F_1-P_1$. At $t=1$ the futures contract has matured. In the language of options, it has no time value. A futures contract on a cash commodity for immediate delivery must be priced at par with the cash market. That is, $F_1=P_1$. If this equality didn't hold, then there would be an arbitrage opportunity.

HEDGING, BASIS RISK, AND SPREADING 189

This phenomenon is called *convergence of futures to cash price at expiration*. We introduced this concept in Chapter 5, section 5.9, under the topic cash settlement vs. commodity settlement.

6.5.1 Implications of Convergence

a. For a traditional short hedge held to expiration, ignoring carrying costs, dollar profits equal the time zero basis $\Pi[0,1]=B_0$ where $B_0=F_0-P_0$.
b. Incorporating marginal carrying charges into traditional hedging is easy, just subtract $CC[0,1]$ from $\Pi[0,1]=B_0$ to obtain dollar profits adjusted for carrying charges of,

$$\Pi_{[0,1]}^{CC}=B_0-CC[0,1]$$
$$=F_0-P_0-CC[0,1].$$

6.5.2 Overall Profits in a Carrying Charge Hedge

This subsection mirrors section 6.2.2.

a. Overall profits in a traditional, carrying charge short hedge, $\Pi_{[0,1]}^{CC}$, are equal to the *change* in the traditional basis minus marginal carrying charges over the hedging period.
b. Overall profits, $\Pi_{[0,1]}^{CC}$, in a traditional, carrying charge short hedge will be *positive* if and only if the basis narrows by *more* than carrying charges, $B_0-B_1>CC[0,1]$.
c. Overall profits, $\Pi_{[0,1]}^{CC}$, in a traditional, carrying charge short hedge will be *negative* if and only if the basis narrows by *less* than carrying charges, $B_0-B_1<CC[0,1]$.
d. Overall profits, $\Pi_{[0,1]}^{CC}$, in a traditional, carrying charge short hedge if held to expiration equal the time zero basis minus carrying charges over the period ($CC[0,1]$), $\Pi_{[0,1]}^{CC}=B_0-CC[0,1]=F_0-P_0-CC[0,1]$.

This last result, *d.*, follows from convergence which implies that $B_1=F_1-P_1=0$. All of these implications should be clear, since they are generalizations of the results in section 6.2.2.

However, there is one very sticky point. All is well if $CC[0,1]>0$, but what happens when $CC[0,1]<0$, and how is that even possible? How can carrying charges be negative? We will consider this issue in the next subsection.

190 FORWARD CONTRACTS AND FUTURES CONTRACTS

6.5.3 Equilibrium (No-Arbitrage) in a Full Carrying Charge Market

We now want to look at what the futures price has to be if there are carrying charges and no-arbitrage. One way to do this is to try to set up a riskless arbitrage. Assuming that it's not possible to do so in equilibrium implies restriction(s) on the equilibrium (no-arbitrage) futures price.

We take the interval of time to be $[0,1]$ and the de-annualized risk-free rate appropriate to $[0,1]$ is denoted by $r[0,1]$. Also assume that compounding is simple so that \$1 borrowed at time $t=0$ grows to $\$1*(1+r[0,1])$ by time $t=1$.

Let's try to set up a (zero cost) arbitrage strategy using the spot commodity, the futures contract maturing at $t=1$, and riskless borrowing at $r[0,1]$.

A. Setting up the Arb

The two steps to the arbitrage are:

1. Take a long position in one unit of the spot commodity at a per unit price of P_0. We fully finance this position by borrowing the full amount P_0.

2. Simultaneously with the purchase of the spot commodity, we sell it forward in the futures market for the current futures price for delivery of the commodity at $t=1$ of $F_0=F_{0,1}$.

■ CONCEPT CHECK 7

a. Verify that the arb set up has no current cost.

B. Unwinding the Arb

We then hold all these positions until $t=1$ at which time we do three things:

a. We deliver the spot commodity to satisfy our short position in the futures contract. Then we *effectively* (after all the daily settlement) receive $+\$F_0$.
b. Pay off our loan at the payoff amount $\$P_0*(1+r[0,1])$.
c. Pay the carrying charges of $CC[0,1]$ that we incurred in carrying the spot commodity over the period $[0,1]$.

HEDGING, BASIS RISK, AND SPREADING 191

The overall (net) cash flow at time $t=1$ generated by this three-part strategy is equal to $+F_0-P_0*(1+r[0,1])-CC[0,1]$. In order to prevent arbitrage, we must have $F_0-P_0*(1+r[0,1])-CC[0,1]\leq0$ because if $F_0-P_0*(1+r[0,1])-CC[0,1]>0$ then we have constructed a riskless arbitrage opportunity.

■ CONCEPT CHECK 8

a. Verify that the arb is riskless.

We can actually show that $F_0-P_0*(1+r[0,1])-CC[0,1]$ must be equal to 0. That is, it cannot be strictly negative in equilibrium, $F_0-P_0*(1+r[0,1])-CC[0,1]<0$ is not possible (see C. below).

The resulting equation is,

$$F_0=P_0*(1+r[0,1])+CC[0,1] \qquad \textbf{(Cost-Of-Carry Model)}$$

In words, this says that the current no-arbitrage futures price must be equal to the current spot price plus interest over the holding period plus general (non-interest) marginal carrying costs, such as warehousing and insurance over the holding period.

The intuition is that the seller of a forward contract knows that he will have to deliver the spot commodity at expiration. Therefore, he purchases it today, carries it forward over the holding period, and pays carrying charges and the opportunity cost of the funds tied up in the spot inventory.

Knowing all the costs involved, he cannot sell forward the spot commodity for *less* than it will cost him to break even. He would like to sell the commodity forward for *more* than the break-even amount, but competitive forces in the market prevent him from doing so.

To show that $F_0-P_0*(1+r[0,1])-CC[0,1]<0$ leads to a formal arbitrage opportunity requires the assumption that the underlying commodity may be short sold. This holds for traded equity securities, but may be problematic for commodities. However, it is possible for some commodities such as stock indexes and bond indexes. Certain precious metals like gold and silver can be short sold.

It also depends who you are and what counterparties will agree to. J. P. Morgan can do a lot more than the private investor can on his own. Sometimes one can short an *Exchange Traded Fund (ETF)* related to the underlying commodity as a proxy for short selling the actual underlying commodity, because there are short ETFs available in the market.

Classical short selling a commodity, like an equity security, means borrowing it from a broker, selling it immediately, and placing the proceeds from that sale (in addition to required margins) in an account. The good news is that interest can be paid on that account, so in effect its opportunity cost is zero. The bad news is that eventually you have to 'cover' the short sale by replacing the borrowed stock. This means you have to buy it back at the going market price.

If the going market price P_1 is *lower* than the price at which you short sold, P_0, then you made money. But if the going market price P_1 is *greater* than P_0, you lost money. Anyway, that's the conventional story.

More accurately, if $P_1 < P_0*(1+r[0,1])$, you profit from the short sale and if $P_1 > P_0*(1+r[0,1])$ you lose. Adding interest earned on the short sale gives you a bit of a buffer zone. The stock price can rise by at most interest on the short sale before you start losing money.

C. $F_0-P_0*(1+r[0,1])-CC[0,1]<0$ Leads To a Formal Arbitrage Opportunity

C1. The Arb with no non-Interest Carrying Charges

In the arb we are going to do, we won't deal with P_1 at all, because P_1 is not known at time $t=1$. Instead, we will *buy* the commodity forward at F_0 in the futures market. This will cleverly allow us to accept delivery of the underlying commodity for F_0, no matter what it is selling for in the market. Then we turn right around and use the commodity to cover the short sale. The cash flow at $t=1$ from the commodity short sold at $t=0$ is $P_0*(1+r[0,1])$ because we placed the proceeds from the short sale into an account earning $r[0,1]$.

The long futures position created an effective cash outflow of F_0 at $t=1$. We would certainly have an arb if $F_0 < P_0*(1+r[0,1])$, that is if $F_0-P_0*(1+r[0,1]) < 0$, and there were no carrying charges.

The two steps in this arb are,

1. *Sell short* the commodity at time $t=0$ and place the proceeds from the short sale into an account earning $r[0,1]$.
2. *Buy* the commodity forward at $F_0=F_{0,1}$ in the futures market.

HEDGING, BASIS RISK, AND SPREADING 193

■ CONCEPT CHECK 9

1. Verify that the arb is an arb and it is riskless.

C2. The Arb with non-Interest Carrying Charges

If there are non-interest carrying charges CC[0,1] over the period, further analysis is needed. Carrying charges are usually incurred by individuals who are *long* the underlying commodity. But *not* paying carrying charges is a benefit (negative cost) to the short. We have already seen this, because the short earned interest on the proceeds of the short sale. Carrying charges include direct (accounting) charges as well as indirect (opportunity) costs.

Positive carrying charges (costs), direct and indirect, for the long become negative carrying charges (benefits) for the short. Negative carrying charges (benefits) for the long become positive carrying charges (costs) for the short.

So, in the presence of carrying charges, in the arb above (longing the futures and shorting the commodity) CC[0,1] will become an *addition* to the net cash flow of the arbitrageur at $t=1$. Recall that CC[0,1] are the *non-interest* carrying charges. Otherwise, we will be double counting. This doesn't imply CC[0,1] is positive. It could be negative, as we shall see below.

Thus the arb will be an arb if $F_0 < P_0*(1+r[0,1])+CC[0,1]$. The right-hand side is the cash flow to the short stock, and the left-hand side is the cost of the long futures position at $T=1$. Thus, to prevent arbitrage, the inequality cannot hold. We must have $F_0 \geq P_0*(1+r[0,1])+CC[0,1]$.

We showed that $F_0 \leq P_0*(1+r[0,1])+CC[0,1]$ in our first arb after Concept Check 7, so together these two inequalities imply that $F_0 = P_0*(1+r[0,1]) +CC[0,1]$ in order to avoid both arbitrages.

Thus our equilibrium futures price determination is the (*Cost-of-Carry Model*),

$$F_0 = P_0*(1+r[0,1])-CC[0,1] \qquad \text{(Cost-of-Carry Model)}$$

6.6 COMPARING EQUILIBRIUM FORWARD PRICING AND EQUILIBRIUM FUTURES PRICING

In our discussion of forward pricing *without* dividends in Chapter 3 we found that the no-arbitrage forward price is given by $F_0 = e^{r\tau}P_0$. In our model without

194 FORWARD CONTRACTS AND FUTURES CONTRACTS

carrying charges the equilibrium futures price is $F_0=P_0*(1+r[0,1])$. The only difference between these two results is the compounding method for interest and the time interval.

Suppose that $[0,1]$ corresponds to one year and therefore $\tau=1.0$. Then, under simple interest compounding, \$1 grows to $\$1*(1+r_A)$ where r_A is the *annual* interest rate under simple compounding. On the other hand, \$1 invested in an account that grows continuously at a *continuously* compounded rate of return r_c for one year is $\$1*e^{r_c}$.

If we equate these two terminal amounts, we get the continuously compounded rate r_c that is equivalent to the simple interest rate r_A. It is that rate that gives the same terminal amount as the simple rate, $\$1*e^{r_c}=\$1*(1+r_A)$.

We can carry out the exact same procedure when time to maturity is τ. We use the interval $[0,\tau]$ for simple compounding to obtain that \$1 grows to $\$1*(1+r[0,\tau])$ under simple compounding, and to $\$1*e^{r_c\tau}$. under continuous compounding. To get the equivalent continuously compounded rate r_c we equate the two accounts,

$$\$1*e^{r_c\tau}=\$1*(1+r[0,\tau]).$$

Applying this equivalence to F_0 we obtain,

$$F_0=e^{r_c\tau}*P_0$$
$$=(1+r[0,\tau])*P_0.$$

So there is no real difference between our old result for forward pricing and our new result for futures pricing, as long as we adjust for the time interval to be the same and for the compounding method.

None of this is surprising, of course, because the exact same no–arbitrage arguments, namely cash and carry arbitrage and reverse cash and carry arbitrage, were used to derive these relationships. Note here that we take interest rates to be non-stochastic so that there is no difference between futures prices and forward prices.

The other case for which we have to show equivalence is the dividend case. In the dividend case, the equilibrium forward price is $F'_{t,T}=e^{(r-\rho)\tau}*P_t$ where ρ is the dividend yield. The dividend yield is considered to be a benefit of holding the underlier, that is a *negative* carrying charge.

In our presentation, we used it to offset interest so it is part of interest-related carrying charges, or we could call $r-\rho$ the *net* interest cost of carry. The analogy of dividends to negative carrying charges indicates that there can be positive benefits, not just costs, associated with holding inventories.

HEDGING, BASIS RISK, AND SPREADING 195

The way a dividend yield would appear in the forward pricing formula is by setting $r'=r-\rho$ in the equation $F_0=P_0*(1+r[0,1])+CC[0,1]$ where $CC[0,1]$ is non-interest related carrying charges.

The equation analogous to $F'_0=e^{(r-\rho)\tau}*P_0$ is $F'_0=P_0*(1+(r-\rho)[0,1])$. It has the same equivalence as noted above for the zero-dividend case. Both models of forward prices, without dividends and with dividends, consider non-interest-related carrying charges, $CC[0,1]$, as well as interest-related carrying charges.

6.7 STORAGE AND THE PRICE (COST) OF STORAGE

The central point of the cost-of-carry model is that the *spread* between the nearby futures price and the spot price (the ordinary, traditional time $t=0$ basis) is simply the *price of storage*. Storage is the activity of having an inventory on hand and taking the trouble to carry it from one period, in which it is not consumed, forward in time to another period, in which it may be consumed. Storage can be thought of as *transportation across time*, only in the forward direction.

This activity goes back many, many years, at least to the time of the Egyptian empire as feast and famine taught people the importance of storage. One modern equivalent in financial terms is called 'saving', the transference of consumption today to increased consumption in the future. One can readily see the importance of saving (storage) for the benefit of numerous individuals. Further, one can view futures markets as providing an efficient (low transactions cost) mechanism for enabling storage.

An unhedged long position is going to incur storage charges, but there is no guarantee that such charges are recoverable through subsequent sale in the spot market. Here is where hedging shines. By selling that inventory forward today in the futures market *one locks in the subsequent sale price of the inventory,* thereby ensuring that the storer will be able to recover not only the current cost of the inventory, P_0, but also the cost of storage. It's a hedge against price uncertainty at time $t=1$.

Our cost-of-carry model tells us that storage cannot be an ex-ante unprofitable activity; otherwise people would not engage in it. Further, firms may have to do so in order to stay in business. The forward (futures) price has built-in compensation to the provider of storage services.

This is what $F_0=P_0*(1+r[0,1])+CC[0,1]$ says in economic terms. The seller of futures will understand that he cannot currently agree to sell forward the commodity below what it costs him, which, as noted earlier, is the spot price plus *interest-adjusted* marginal carrying charges. He cannot charge more on a forward sale because competition will not permit him to do so. Nor will the equilibrium imposed by the no-arbitrage condition.

If we roll interest costs, $r[0,1]*P_0$ into $CC[0,1]$ to obtain *interest-adjusted marginal carrying costs*, $CC'[0,1]=CC[0,1]+r[0,1]*P_0$, we find that $F_0=P_0+CC'[0,1]$, which more clearly shows that the spread between the nearby futures price and the spot price is simply the price of storage,

$$F_0-P_0=B_0$$
$$=CC'[0,1].$$

Providers of storage services (sellers of futures contracts) can then look at the simple time $t=0$ basis to get an estimate of how they can expect the futures market to pay them for supplying storage services.

Demanders of storage services (buyers of futures contracts) can also see what they will have to pay for storage services by looking at the time zero basis. Each value of the time zero basis implies a certain demand and supply of storage services. So, theoretically, the demand and supply curves can be estimated and, from these, the equilibrium amount stored.

This generalizes nicely to periods later than $[0,1]$. Suppose we have two periods $[0,1]$ and $[1,2]$.

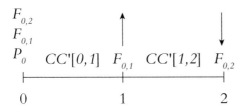

The notation should be fairly obvious. $F_{0,1}$ is the futures price at time $t=0$ for delivery of the underlying commodity at time $t=1$. $F_{0,2}$ is the futures price at time $t=0$ for delivery of the underlying commodity at time $t=2$. Both $F_{0,1}$ and $F_{0,2}$ are futures prices at time $t=0$, with the transactions consummated at $t=1$ and $t=2$ respectively.

Note that the storer who stores over *both* periods $[0,1]$ and $[1,2]$ incurs interest-adjusted storage costs of $CC'[0,2]=CC'[0,1]+CC'[1,2]$.

HEDGING, BASIS RISK, AND SPREADING   197

Now, the cost-of-carry model says that,

$$F_{0,2}=P_0+CC'[0,2]$$

and,

$$F_{0,1}=P_0+CC'[0,1].$$

By subtracting $F_{0,1}$ from $F_{0,2}$ we obtain,

$$F_{0,2}-F_{0,1}=CC'[0,2]-CC'[0,1]$$
$$=CC'[1,2],$$

which is the interesting result that the spread between subsequent futures price also represents the marginal cost of carry over the appropriate implied periods.

The suppliers and demanders of storage services can once again read off the prices of storage for subsequent *future* periods from the array of futures price spreads, $F_{0,2}-F_{0,1}$, $F_{0,3}-F_{0,2}$, $F_{0,4}-F_{0,3}$,... as long as and as far out as liquid contracts exist!

Current implementation of a storage service over a subsequent period, say [1,2], is easy. Just currently (at time $t=0$) go long at $F_{0,1}$ in the nearer contract and simultaneously go short the next out contract at $F_{0,2}$. This locks in the futures spread $F_{0,2}-F_{0,1}$ at time $t=0$.

What this amounts to is buying the commodity for delivery at $t=1$ for a price fixed at $t=0$, $F_{0,1}$. One also sells it at time $t=0$ for delivery at time $t=2$ for a price fixed today of $F_{0,2}$.

The whole transaction establishes a *short forward hedge* over [1,2] at currently fixed prices because one is buying the commodity at time $t=1$ for a fixed price determined at $t=0$ and also selling a futures contract (at time $t=0$) for delivery at time $t=2$.

That traditional, short forward hedge must be expected to earn the cost of storage over [1,2] which is determined at time $t=0$ as the futures price *spread*, $F_{0,2}-F_{0,1}$. In a similar manner, other futures spreads such as $F_{0,3}-F_{0,2}$ and $F_{0,4}-F_{0,3}$ establish the prices of storage over [2,3] and [3,4] respectively.

This construction is similar to implied forward rates in the current term structure of interest rates as predictive of expected spot interest rates under the expectations theory. Implied forward rates are discussed in Chapter 8, section 8.9.5. We mention them here in passing only.

6.8 CONTANGO AND BACKWARDATION

The cost-of-carry model seems to imply that futures prices will always be *above* the corresponding spot price $F_0>P_0$. However this situation, called *contango*, is only one of the possibilities in equilibrium. The other possibility is that $F_0<P_0$ which is called *backwardation*. In the event of backwardation, the cost of storage appears to be negative. Therefore we turn to examine *negative* storage charges.

Let's go back to our discussion of forward pricing with dividends. In that scenario, in addition to there being positive borrowing costs, there are benefits to holding securities. The benefits are in the form of some 'dividend' or payout stream. In the case of equities, the payouts would normally be in the form of dividends. Commodities can also provide 'dividends' (benefits) to the storer as well.

In Chapter 4, we saw that the equilibrium forward price in the presence of a dividend yield is $F'_{t,T}=e^{(r-\rho)\tau}*S_t$ where r represents the annualized, continuously compounded risk-free rate. r is the annualized cost of borrowing to finance the spot purchase at a per unit price of S_t, and ρ represents the annualized, continuously compounded dividend yield (payout rate) on the stock thereby financed. As argued in Chapter 4, $r-\rho$ is therefore the *effective,* annualized, continuously compounded borrowing rate.

Letting $t=0$ and writing P_t for the spot price at time $t=0$, then any futures price $F'_{0,T}=e^{(r-\rho)\tau}*P_0$ will be above (below) the corresponding spot price if and only if $r>\rho$ ($r<\rho$). This means that contango will prevail when the net borrowing rate $r-\rho$ is positive, and backwardation will prevail when the net borrowing rate $r-\rho$ is negative.

In the first case, interest-related carrying charges will be *positive* because the dividend yield *less than* offsets normal borrowing costs. In the second case, interest-related carrying charges will be *negative* because the dividend yield *more than* offsets normal borrowing costs. With minor modifications, the same applies to futures prices and commodities other than equities.

In general, one considers *all* carrying charges, not just the interest-related ones. Then we use the model $F_0-P_0=B_0=CC'[0,1]$ which says that $F_0>P_0$ (contango) prevails if and only if interest-adjusted carrying charges, $CC'[0,1]$, are positive. Backwardation, $F_0<P_0$, prevails if and only if interest-adjusted carrying charges, $CC'[0,1]$, are negative.

The paradox of backwardation is this. Why store a commodity when one appears to be negatively rewarded for doing so? That is, in a less than full carrying charge market. Note that the supply price of storage services is F_0-P_0. It is the buyer of the spot commodity, who simultaneously sells futures contracts (traditional one-for-one hedger), who *earns* the price of storage from the longs in futures, who *pay for* storage services.

One resolution of this paradox is that, just as in the case of equities, there are 'dividends' associated with storing a commodity. Therefore the direct, positive costs of storage can pay for themselves if the dividends (benefits) outweigh these direct costs which include interest charges, warehousing charges, and insurance.

Dividends for a general commodity come in the form of what is called a *convenience yield* that is generated by the commodity over its storage period. The convenience yield can be large enough to *offset* all the other positive costs, particularly when inventory levels of the commodity are low.

In this case, total storage costs *can* be negative, a net benefit rather than a net cost. Storers (short hedgers) will still supply storage services under these circumstances in order to earn the convenience yield.

We briefly discussed the convenience yield in Chapter 4, section 4.1. The idea behind what is called the convenience yield is that, while holding a commodity in inventory is costly, there are still reasons for holding inventory. One is the ability to meet unexpected demand at lower cost and without delay. This keeps customers happy. Firms do not sell all their stock before replenishing it. The reason is the convenience yield. In the event that a customer shows up, they will not be caught unprepared. To such firms, the inconvenience of stocking inventory is offset by the convenience of having it available 'just in case'.

By minimizing the carrying of inventory, the firm can certainly save itself some *direct* costs and *financing* costs as well. But there are also costs to *not* carrying inventory, and one of those costs is the loss of potential income associated with the inability to meet *unexpected* demand. This implies that firms should carry some inventory above and beyond what they need to hold in order to meet *expected* demand. And many firms do. Even firms that carry zero inventory can make sure that they can get inventories quickly.

6.9 SPREADS AS A SPECULATIVE INVESTMENT

So far, in section 6.7, we have talked about *calendar* spreads only. There are many types of spreads including *inter-commodity* spreads, *inter-market* spreads, and so on. Just as the ordinary basis can be viewed in a speculative way by not holding the hedge to maturity, one can also not lock in the spread between two futures. Rather, one obtains the change in the spread as the profit figure, where the change is calculated over the period that the spread is actually held.

Suppose that an investor initiates a spread by buying the nearby contract and selling the next-out contract. The usual picture applies,

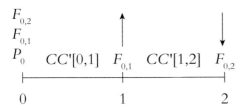

But this time, the spreader is considering *offsetting* the spread at some intermediate time, t', between $t=0$ and $t=1$, $0<t'<1$.

The mechanism for doing so is offsetting trades. Since the investor originally went long at $t=0$ at $F_{0,1}$ and short at $t=0$ at $F_{0,2}$ he can short the nearby contract at t' at $F_{t',1}$ and long the next-out contract at t' at $F_{t',2}$.

On the offset long position in the nearby contract the dollar profit figure per unit will be $\pi_{\text{Long Leg},t'} = F_{t',1} - F_{0,1}$.

The dollar profit figure per unit on the offset short position in the next-out contract will be $\pi_{\text{Short Leg},t'} = F_{0,2} - F_{t',2}$.

Combining these two profit figures we obtain the total dollar profits on the offset spread as,

$$\pi_{t'} = \pi_{\text{Long Leg},t'} + \pi_{\text{Short Leg},t'}$$
$$= (F_{t',1} - F_{0,1}) + (F_{0,2} - F_{t',2})$$
$$= (F_{0,2} - F_{0,1}) - (F_{t',2} - F_{t',1})$$
$$= \Delta \text{ spread basis}.$$

We define the *spread basis* at any point in time as $SB_t \equiv F_{t,2} - F_{t,1}$. This is by analogy with the ordinary basis defined as $B_{t,T} = F_{t,T} - P_t$. This makes sense because in a spread one longs the nearby contract, which takes the place of the spot commodity.

Our result then is completely analogous to the corresponding result that the net profit in a traditional short hedge is the change in the basis measured as $B_0 - B_1$. That is,

1. *The net profit in a traditional spread offset at time t' is the change in the spread basis measured as $SB_{0,t'} - SB_{1,t'}$.*

HEDGING, BASIS RISK, AND SPREADING 201

Now the beauty of spread trading, like that of basis trading, is that the spread basis is generally less volatile than the nearby futures price.

We will now find the condition under which this is true, just as we did for the ordinary basis. The derivation is basically a repeat of our proof that the traditional one-for-one basis is less volatile than the spot price when the beta of the spot price on the futures price is greater than $1/2$.

End of Chapter Exercise 7 shows that, in the spread, the long position in the nearby futures contract takes the place of the long spot position, and that the short position in the next-out futures takes the place of the short position in the nearby futures contract in the traditional basis. Then, everything goes through as before.

Assume that we are standing at time $t=0$ and looking ahead to some time $t<1$. We use the basic statistics result again to calculate,

$$\text{VAR}(\text{Spread } B_t(\omega))=\text{VAR}(F_{t,2}(\omega)-F_{t,1}(\omega))$$

where

$$X(\omega)=F_{t,2}(\omega),$$
$$Y(\omega)=F_{t,1}(\omega),$$
$$a=+1.0 \text{ and,}$$
$$b=-1.0.$$

So all we have to do is to apply the VAR formula,

$$\text{VAR}(F_{t,2}(\omega)-F_{t,1}(\omega))$$
$$=a^2\text{VAR}(F_{t,2}(\omega))+b^2\text{VAR}(F_{t,1}(\omega))+2a*b*\text{COV}(F_{t,2}(\omega),F_{t,1}(\omega))$$
$$=(+1.0)^2\text{VAR}(F_{t,2}(\omega))+(-1.0)^2\text{VAR}(F_{t,1}(\omega))$$
$$+2*(+1.0)*(-1.0)*\text{COV}(F_{t,2}(\omega),F_{t,1}(\omega))$$
$$=\text{VAR}(F_{t,2}(\omega))+\text{VAR}(F_{t,1}(\omega))-2*\text{COV}(F_{t,2}(\omega),F_{t,1}(\omega)).$$

Now, we compare this to the variance of a naked long position in the nearby futures contract, which is just the variance of the random futures price $\text{VAR}(F_{t,1}(\omega))$.

So all we have to do is compare $\text{VAR}(SB_t(\omega))$ to $\text{VAR}(F_{t,1}(\omega))$ and ask when is,

$$\text{VAR}(SB_t(\omega))<\text{VAR}(F_{t,1}(\omega))?$$

FORWARD CONTRACTS AND FUTURES CONTRACTS

This amounts to when is,

$$VAR(SB_t(\omega))=VAR(F_{t,2}(\omega))+VAR(F_{t,1}(\omega))-2*COV(F_{t,2}(\omega)),F_{t,1}(\omega))$$
$$<VAR(F_{t,1}(\omega))?$$

which in turn reduces to when is,

$$VAR(F_{t,2}(\omega))-2*COV(F_{t,2}(\omega),F_{t,1}(\omega))<0?$$

We got this result by just cancelling out $VAR(F_{t,1}(\omega))$ which appears on both sides of the inequality.

By bringing $-2*COV(F_{t,2}(\omega),F_{t,1}(\omega))$ over to the right-hand side of the inequality we obtain the inequality,

$$VAR(F_{t,2}(\omega))<2*COV(F_{t,2}(\omega),F_{t,1}(\omega))$$

Since $VAR(F_{t,2}(\omega))$ is a positive number, we can divide both sides of the inequality by it to get the condition,

$$1.0 < 2 * \frac{COV(F_{t,2}(\omega),F_{t,1}(\omega))}{VAR(F_{t,2}(\omega))}$$

Dividing through by 2.0 our condition becomes,

$$\frac{1}{2} < \frac{COV(F_{t,2}(\omega),F_{t,1}(\omega))}{VAR(F_{t,2}(\omega))}$$

Now we have to interpret the right-hand side of this last inequality. As earlier, if we want to measure the correlation between $F_{t,1}(\omega)$ and $F_{t,2}(\omega)$ we run the regression,

$$F_{t,1}(\omega)=\alpha+\beta F_{t,2}(\omega)+\varepsilon_t.$$

The coefficient $\beta_{F_{t,1}(\omega),F_{t,2}(\omega)}$ is equal to $\dfrac{COV(F_{t,1}(\omega),F_{t,2}(\omega))}{VAR(F_{t,2}(\omega))}$.

Since $COV(\ ,\ )$ isn't affected by the order, therefore $COV(F_{t,1}(\omega),F_{t,2}(\omega))$ $=COV(F_{t,2}(\omega),F_{t,1}(\omega))$.

Our result is that,

a. *Spreading reduces risk if the beta of the nearby futures price on the next-out futures price is greater than 1/2.*

In other words, there has to be a sufficient amount of correlation between the nearby futures price and the next-out futures price in order for spreading to 'work'.

If there isn't enough correlation, spreading would be counter-productive because it would *increase* risk, which is not what spreaders want to do.

Three questions with regard to the beta of the spot commodity price on the corresponding futures price naturally arise:

1. What is the beta of the nearby futures price on the next-out futures price?
2. Is it positive or negative?
3. If it is positive, how large is it?

Spreading in futures is one of the most popular strategies, so we suspect spreads work. In fact, some are pre-packaged by commodity futures exchanges as separate objects in which one can take positions without constructing each leg of the spread. We will see some examples in Chapter 7 on financial futures.

KEY CONCEPTS

1. Hedging as Portfolio Theory.
2. Hedging as Synthesizing Negative Correlation.
3. Hedging's Objective.
4. Hedging Definitions.
5. Traditional Theories of Hedging.
6. Traditional (One-for-One) Theory with no Basis Risk.
7. Profits in a Traditional Short Hedge and the Basis.
8. When is a Traditional (One-for-One) Hedge with no Basis Risk consistent with No-Arbitrage?
9. Traditional (One-for-One) Theory with Basis Risk.
10. Basis Risk vs. Spot Price Risk.
11. When Traditional Hedging Reduces Risk.
12. Non-Traditional (λ-for-One) Hedging Theory.
13. When λ-for-One Hedging Reduces Risk.
14. Minimum Variance Hedging.
15. Deriving the Risk-Minimizing Hedge Ratio.
16. Estimating $\lambda^* = \beta_{P_t(\omega), F_t(\omega)}$
17. Carrying Charge Hedging.
18. Implications of Convergence.
19. Overall Profits in a Carrying Charge Hedge.
20. Equilibrium (No-Arbitrage) in a Full Carrying Charge Market.
21. Setting up the Arb.
22. Unwinding the Arb.
23. $F_0 - P_0*(1+r[0,1]) - CC[0,1] < 0$ leads to a formal arbitrage opportunity.
24. The Arb with no non-Interest Carrying Charges.
25. The Arb with non-Interest Carrying Charges.
26. Comparing Equilibrium Forward Pricing and Equilibrium Futures Pricing.
27. Storage and the Price (Cost) of Storage.
28. Contango and Backwardation.
29. Spreads as a Speculative Investment.

HEDGING, BASIS RISK, AND SPREADING

■ END OF CHAPTER EXERCISES FOR CHAPTER 6

1. Given the data $\beta_{P_t(\omega),F_t(\omega)}=3/4$ and the vertical price chart

    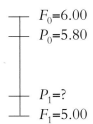

    $F_0=6.00$
    $P_0=5.80$

    $P_1=?$
    $F_1=5.00$

    a. Calculate the basis at time 0, B_0.
    b. Calculate the basis at time 0, B_1.
    c. Calculate the range of the basis.
    d. Calculate the range of the spot price.
    e. Did one-for-one hedging reduce risk relative to that of a naked spot position? Explain your answer in terms of the theory.

2. Given the data,

    $\beta_{P_t(\omega),F_t(\omega)}=1/4$ and,

    $F_0=6.00$
    $P_0=5.80$
    $P_1=?$

    $F_1=5.00$

    a. Calculate the basis at time 0, B_0.
    b. Calculate the basis at time 1, B_1.
    c. Calculate the range of the basis.
    d. Calculate the range of the spot price.
    e. Did one-for-one hedging reduce risk relative to that of a naked spot position? Explain in terms of the theory.

3. a. Show that overall profits in a λ-for-One (non-traditional) hedge is equal to the change in the 'λ-basis' where the definition of the λ-basis is $B_{t,\lambda}=\lambda F_t-P_t$.

206 **FORWARD CONTRACTS AND FUTURES CONTRACTS**

4. Using the data of exercise 2,

   a. Sell $\lambda=1/4$ futures contacts per unit of spot commodity and see what happens to the $\lambda=1/4$ basis.
   b. Does $1/4=\lambda$-for-One hedging reduce risk?

5. a. Verify all four implications of carrying charge hedging in section 6.5.2.

6. a. Show that the only difference between $F'_0=e^{(r-\rho)1}*P_0$ and $F_0=P_0*(1+(r-\rho)[0,1])$ is that the first is continuously compounded and the second is annually compounded. Assume that $[0,1]$ represents one year which is why we set $\tau=1$.

7. a. Look at the spread basis. Substitute the current spot price, P_0, for the nearby futures price and substitute the nearby futures price, $F_{0,1}$, for the next-out futures price in the spread basis. See if you can get the ordinary basis.

8. The following Table 6.1 is a set or price quotes on June 6, 2014 for the corn contract traded on the CME.

   a. Calculate the spread basis where time 1 is in July 2014 and time 2 is in September, 2014.
   b. What is the price of storage from July 2014–September 2014? Take the spot price to be 447. Using the settlement prices, is there contango or backwardation?
   c. Is the price of storage always positive?

HEDGING, BASIS RISK, AND SPREADING — 207

TABLE 6.1   CME Corn Contract Price Quotes

Month	Open	High	Low	Last	Change	Settle	Estimated Volume	Prior Day Open Interest
JLY 14	449'0	459'6	447'0	458'4	+10'0	459'0	163,794	459,758
SEP 14	444'2	457'2	442'6	455'4	+12'0	456'2	96,199	291,061
DEC 14	447'2	458'6	445'2	457'4	+10'4	457'6	81,047	441,580
MAR 15	457'0	468'0	455'0	—	+10'4	467'2	11,684	71,328
MAY 15	463'6	474'4	462'0	469'2	+10'0	473'6	2,596	16,284
JLY 15	469'6	480'2	468'0	—	+9'6	479'4	3,379	31,593
SEP 15	463'6	470'0	462'2A	—	+8'4	472'2	708	3,970
DEC 15	458'0	466'4	456'6	464'0	+8'0	465'6	2,506	48,666
MAR 16	470'0	470'0	469'0	—	+7'4	474'6	38	1,029

Reprinted by permission of the CME Inc., 2014.

■ SELECTED CONCEPT CHECK SOLUTIONS

Concept Check 1

a. The meaning of the words is: another portfolio of financial instruments that has the same risk, return characteristics as the actual T-bill. This means the same maturity, the same risk, and as we shall see in this example, the same yield.

Another way to think about the synthetic instrument is as a *replicating portfolio*. When we synthesized forward contracts, we saw that a *synthetic* forward contract is a portfolio consisting of the underlying spot instrument fully financed by a zero-coupon bond maturing at the expiration date of the forward contract.

b. The synthetic T-bill here is the portfolio of spot and futures, assumed to exist.

c. A simple comparison reveals the arb.

$$r_{actual}=3.00\%<r_{synthetic}=3.50\%.$$

The idea is to borrow at 3% and use the proceeds to buy the synthetic T-bill. Then we hold the synthetic portfolio until its maturity date, which is the same as the actual T-bill we effectively issued.

FORWARD CONTRACTS AND FUTURES CONTRACTS

We use the funds released from the synthetic T-bill to pay off our 3% loan. The profit generated is 3.50%–3.00%=0.50%, since the synthetic T-bill earns 3.50%.

We earned an arbitrage profit of 0.50% on this strategy at no current, nor subsequent cost.

The average investor may not be able to borrow at the actual T-bill rate but arbitrageurs can borrow at close to that using reverse repos. All that matters for the arbitrage is that, net of transactions costs, $r_{actual} < r_{synthetic}$.

d. Since the synthetic T-bill is a perfect substitute for the actual T-bill, it should sell for the same price (have the same BEY). Otherwise, there will be an arbitrage opportunity, and this means that the market will not be in equilibrium.

Concept Check 3

If $r=3\%$ on an annualized basis, for example, then you could borrow by selling the hedge (short the spot and long the futures) at time 0. This would release capital which could be invested in actual US Treasury bills. You would do so, and hold the Treasury bills to maturity earning the de-annualized rate of $3\%*\tau$ where τ is the length of the holding period.

Just before maturity, you would cover the short spot sale using the proceeds from the maturing T-bill, and you would offset your original long futures position by making an offsetting trade. This would fully unravel your selling the hedge position. The T-bill has also matured, so you are out of that as well.

The current net cost of executing this strategy would be $0 since you financed the purchase of the T-bill by shorting the spot commodity. You would earn the de-annualized T-bill rate of $3\%*\tau$ on this entire strategy because the percentage rate of return on selling the hedge would be 0% (just the negative of the percentage rate of return of longing the hedge.) This is clearly a riskless arbitrage opportunity!

Concept Check 5

a. The spot price declines.
b. The futures price declines with the spot price.
c. The basis narrows.

HEDGING, BASIS RISK, AND SPREADING

d. The basis is the difference between the ceiling and the floor. If the ceiling falls faster than the floor you make money on the hedge, because you recoup your losses through the decline of the futures price at a faster rate than you are accruing those losses through the decline of the spot price.

Concept Check 6

a. Note that traditional hedging without basis risk cannot apply because, when it does apply ($r=0$ or $r-\rho=0$), $\beta_{P_t(\omega),F_t(\omega)}=1.0$.

But our assumption is that $\beta_{P_t(\omega),F_t(\omega)}=1/4$ which rules it out. Traditional hedging with basis risk fails because $\beta_{P_t(\omega),F_t(\omega)}=1/4<1/2$.

b. The condition for λ-for-one hedging to work is that $\lambda/2<\beta_{P_t(\omega),F_t(\omega)}$ or that $\lambda<2*\beta_{P_t(\omega),F_t(\omega)}=2*1/4=1/2$.

Concept Check 9

There are no upfront costs to the set of transactions in 1. and 2. Shorting the commodity amounts to *borrowing it* and replacing it later at no cost today. Every term in $F_0-P_0*(1+r[0,1])$ is known at time $t=0$. If $F_0<P_0*(1+r[0,1])$ then the proceeds from the short sold commodity account, $P_0*(1+r[0,1])$, are greater than the cost of buying the commodity in the forward market based upon one's long forward position.

This results in an arbitrage profit of $P_0*(1+r[0,1])-F_0>0$. Since we have used the commodity delivered into the long forward position to cover the short sale, the arb has been properly unwound.

CHAPTER 7

INTRODUCTION TO FINANCIAL FUTURES CONTRACTS

7.1 Currency Futures 213

    7.1.1 Contract Specifications 213

    7.1.2 The Quote Mechanism: Futures Price Quotes ... 216

7.2 Risk Management Strategies Using Currency Futures ... 217

    7.2.1 Exchange Rate Risks and Currency Futures Positions 217

    7.2.2 The Rolling Hedge Strategy 220

    7.2.3 Interpretations of Profits from the Rolling Hedge ... 221

    7.2.4 Numerical Example of the Rolling Hedge Strategy 223

7.3 Hedging 224

    7.3.1 Issues in Hedging, Quantity Uncertainty 224

    7.3.2 Currency Futures Pricing vs. Currency Forward Pricing 225

7.4 Stock Index Futures 225

    7.4.1 The S&P 500 Spot Index 225

    7.4.2 S&P 500 Stock Index Futures Contract Specifications 227

    7.4.3 The Quote Mechanism for S&P 500 Futures Price Quotes 230

7.5 Risk Management Using Stock Index Futures 231

    7.5.1 Pricing and Hedging Preliminaries 231

    7.5.2 Monetizing the S&P 500 Spot Index 231

    7.5.3 Profits from the Traditional Hedge 235

212 FORWARD CONTRACTS AND FUTURES CONTRACTS

7.5.4	Risk, Return Analysis of the Traditional Hedge	236
7.5.5	Risk-Minimizing Hedging	238
7.5.6	Adjusting the Naive Hedge Ratio to Obtain the Risk-Minimizing Hedge Ratio	239
7.5.7	Risk-Minimizing the Hedge Using Forward vs. Futures Contracts	241
7.5.8	Cross-Hedging, Adjusting the Hedge for non S&P 500 Portfolios	243
7.6	The Spot Eurodollar Market	245
7.6.1	Spot 3-month Eurodollar Time Deposits	246
7.6.2	Spot Eurodollar Market Trading Terminology	248
7.6.3	$LIBOR_3$, $LIBID_3$, and Fed Funds	250
7.6.4	How Eurodollar Time Deposits are Created	252
7.7	Eurodollar Futures	254
7.7.1	Contract Specifications	254
7.7.2	The Quote Mechanism, Eurodollar Futures	256
7.7.3	Forced Convergence and Cash Settlement	258
7.7.4	How Profits and Losses are Calculated on Open ED Futures Positions	262

The crown jewels of futures contracts are the *financial* futures contracts which were introduced to the world in the late 1970s and early 1980s by the CME and the CBOT (since merged) in Chicago. These can be categorized by the underlying and the associated risk to be hedged in Table 7.1 below. We will be taking a look at *some* of the most important financial futures contracts, namely 1., 2., and 3., in this chapter.

FINANCIAL FUTURES CONTRACTS — 213

TABLE 7.1 **Selected Financial Futures Contracts**

Underlying Commodity	Associated Risk	Futures Contract= Hedging Vehicle	USA Trading Venue
1. Major Currencies	Foreign Exchange Rate Risk	Currency Futures	cmegroup.com
2. Stock Indices	Market Risk	Stock Index Futures	cmegroup.com
3. Three Month LIBOR (Eurodollar)	Short-Term International Borrowing/Lending Rate Risk	Eurodollar CD Futures	cmegroup.com
US Treasury Bond	Long-Term Borrowing/ Lending Rate Risk	US Treasury Bond Futures	cmegroup.com

7.1 CURRENCY FUTURES

We already discussed currency forwards and their pricing in Chapter 4. We also looked at some quoted FX spot and forward prices. As you know, when we move to FX futures we obtain standardization and all the features associated with futures trading, including margins and daily settlement. In other words, financial futures in general, and FX futures in particular, are just like any other futures contracts. They differ only in the details.

7.1.1 Contract Specifications

To get the details on any exchange–traded futures contract, the first place to look is at the contract specifications which are available for all futures contracts on the CME webpage for CME-traded contracts. For contracts traded on other exchanges, you should be able to find contract specifications, because futures are standardized instruments.

As an example of current interest, we will start with the Yen FX futures contracts. We first go to cmegroup.com and choose FX under 'Products and Trading'. Japanese Yen futures, denoted by JY for floor trading and 6J for Globex, will appear in the list. If we click 'Japanese Yen Futures', we will be taken to the contract specs which we reproduce in Table 7.2. Note that, as of July 06, 2015, Yen Futures no longer pit trade via open outcry.

FORWARD CONTRACTS AND FUTURES CONTRACTS

TABLE 7.2   JPY/USD Futures

Contract Size	12,500,000 Japanese yen
Contract Month Listings	Twenty months in the March quarterly cycle (Mar, Jun, Sep, Dec)
Settlement Procedure	Physical Delivery Daily FX Settlement Procedures (PDF) Final FX Settlement Procedures (PDF)
Position Accountability	10,000 contracts
Ticker Symbol	CME Globex Electronic Markets: 6J Open Outcry: JY AON Code: LJ View product and vendor codes
Minimum Price Increment	$.000001 per Japanese yen increments ($12.50/contract). $.0000005 per Japanese yen increments ($6.25/contract) for JPY/USD futures intra-currency spreads executed on the trading floor and electronically, and for AON transactions.
Trading Hours	GLOBEX (ETH)	Sundays: 5:00 p.m.–4:00 p.m. Central Time (CT) next day. Monday–Friday: 5:00 p.m.–4:00 p.m. CT the next day, except on Friday–closes at 4:00 p.m. and reopens Sunday at 5:00 p.m. CT.
	CME ClearPort	Sunday–Friday 6:00 p.m.–5:15 p.m. (5:00 p.m.–4:15 p.m. Chicago Time/CT) with a 45-minute break each day beginning at 5:15 p.m. (4:15 p.m. CT)
	OPEN OUTCRY (RTH)	7:20 a.m.–2:00 p.m.
Last Trade Date/ Time View Calendar	9:16 a.m. Central Time (CT) on the second business day immediately preceding the third Wednesday of the contract month (usually Monday).
Exchange Rule	These contracts are listed with, and subject to, the rules and regulations of CME.
Block Trade Eligibility	Yes. View more on Block Trade eligible contracts.
Block Trade Minimum	150 Contracts
EFP Eligibility	Yes. View more on EFPs.

Reprinted with permission from CME Group Inc., 2014.

FINANCIAL FUTURES CONTRACTS **215**

The main features of this contract are:

1. The *contract 'size'* refers to the number of units of the *underlying* commodity (JY) that must be delivered. In this case the number is 12,500,000 Japanese yen. With the spot yen price in US dollars about $.01, for example, the total spot value of the commodity underlying the JY contract (12,500,000 Japanese yen) is about $125,000=12,500,000 x $.01.

2. *Contracts are offered* according to delivery months in a way that is analogous to option 'cycles', which we will discuss in Part 3. The JY Futures contract follows the March cycle: 20 months in the March quarterly cycle (Mar, Jun, Sep, Dec). That covers 5 years forward, which you can confirm by looking at the quotes.

   For example, in June 2014 we found JY FX futures available from June 2014 to March 2019. Note that volume did taper off quickly to zero, after about a year.

   This is typical of futures contracts in that most of the trading interest is usually concentrated in the 'nearby' contract and the 'next-out' contract. As the nearby contract matures, trading transfers to the next available contract which then becomes the nearby contract.

3. *Delivery* is *physical* means that you have to deliver 12,500,000 Japanese yen into an account specified by the CME.

4. Once one accumulates a sufficient number of contract positions—10,000 in this case—they must be *reported* to the CFTC. This is what is meant under position accountability.

5. *Ticker* symbols have been explained. All-or-None (AON) orders are referred to by the AON code. All-or-None (AON) orders are orders executed in the open outcry venue that must be filled *in their entirety* at a single price.

6. The *tick size* is the *minimum* move in the futures price which in this case is $.000001 per Japanese yen increments ($12.50/contract). When one looks at a price quote below, multiply by $.000001 to get the dollar equivalent as a decimal. Note that the FX price quote in Futures is US dollars per 1JY. That is, as a direct price quote where the domestic currency is the US$.

The remaining entries are more or less self-explanatory. In cases of doubt, refer to the CME literature.

216   **FORWARD CONTRACTS AND FUTURES CONTRACTS**

7.1.2 The Quote Mechanism: Futures Price Quotes

The beauty of futures contracts is that futures price data is always readily available and easy to find, as long as there is (trading) volume in the futures contract under consideration. As the delivery month advances, trading volume tends to decline.

Futures market organization has been discussed in detail in Chapter 5. Here we will focus on the quote mechanism which is a product of futures trading as discussed in Chapter 5.

There are multiple sources for futures trade data. One source is the *Daily Settlements* which provide a summary of market activity and are used to settle all accounts as to daily profits and losses. Here is a price quote using the same access procedure as for contract specs (above). One of the tabs is called 'Quotes' then 'Settlements'.

TABLE 7.3   **Daily Settlements for Japanese Yen Future Futures (FINAL).**
Trade Date: 09/17/2013

Month	Open	High	Low	Last	Change	Settle	Estimated Volume	Prior Day Open Interest
DEC 13	10094	10105	10066	—	+4	10093	75,404	175,881

Reprinted with permission from CME Group Inc., 2014.

Commentary

1. The contract is the Dec. 2013 delivery month.
2. The quote is from the end of the trade date September 17, 2013.
3. The open (first) futures price on September 17, 2013 was 10094 which in US dollars means $.000001*10094=$.010094, a little over 1 cent.
4. The highest futures price for the day was $.010105.
5. The lowest futures price for the day was $.010066.
6. No 'last' futures price for the day was reported.
7. The change in the daily settlement futures price from the previous day was +4 which means up by $.000004. Therefore, yesterday's settlement price was $.000004 lower, 10089. You can confirm this by searching for the September 16, 2013 settlement price, which indeed is equal to this number.

FINANCIAL FUTURES CONTRACTS — 217

8. Today's settlement price was 10093 or $.010093.
9. Volume refers to the number of contracts traded (counting one side only). 75,404 JPY Dec. 2013 traded on September 17, 2013.
10. Prior Day Open Interest refers to the number of contracts (counting one side only) that were not offset by offsetting trades as of the end of the trade date September 16, 2013. That number was 175,881.

7.2 RISK MANAGEMENT STRATEGIES USING CURRENCY FUTURES

7.2.1 Exchange Rate Risks and Currency Futures Positions

Financial futures contracts are just like any other futures contracts, and futures contracts are just fancy forward contracts. Therefore, the hedging applications of currency futures are essentially the same as those of currency forwards. One has an explicit or an implicit long or short position in some underlying currency, and one wants to protect oneself or one's firm against adverse currency price movements. What is adverse depends on your position, long or short.

There are generally three or four different but related forms of exchange rate risk: transaction exposure, economic (operating) exposure, translation exposure, and contingent exposure. These distinctions are usually discussed in texts on international finance. Basically, exchange rate movements that affect the firm's domestic cash flows and/or the discount rate used to value these flows are causes of concern and would be subsumed under the exchange rate risk category.

If a firm has an explicit or implicit long position in some underlying currency, then it is planning on *selling* that currency in the future in exchange for some other currency. In order to hedge the anticipated sale, the firm could *sell forward* the underlying currency in the currency futures market.

There are other hedging alternatives as well, such as selling currency forwards depending on how they are quoted, or buying currency puts, or even setting up the short forward replicating strategy discussed in Chapter 4. In all cases, the idea is to *sell forward* the foreign currency in exchange for the domestic currency, thereby locking in the forward exchange rate.

Lufthansa Example

For example, the largest German airline, Lufthansa Airlines, faced this problem in January 1985. At that time, Lufthansa *pre-committed* to purchase

218   **FORWARD CONTRACTS AND FUTURES CONTRACTS**

US$500,000,000 worth of Boeing aircraft. Not an insignificant amount of money. Payment to Boeing (a US company) was due in January 1986 in US dollars, of course.

This would require Lufthansa to buy US$500,000,000 by *selling* an equivalent number of DM in return for those US dollars. The problem was that the spot exchange rate (US dollars per 1 DM) in January 1986 was currently (in January 1985) unknown. Lufthansa was exposed to a massive amount of exchange-rate risk.

To remove this uncertainty, Lufthansa could lock in the future sale price of DM in exchange for US dollars by selling DM forward at a fixed number of US dollars per 1 DM. That is, it could in January 1985 sell forward DM at a *fixed* rate of exchange for delivery in January 1986.

One thing to note here is that standardization prevails in currency futures. The underlying currency and the quote mechanism are also standardized. The Lufthansa problem could be rephrased in terms of *buying* US dollars forward.

Indeed, back in 1985 one could easily take a *long* position in a forward contract to buy US$500,000,000 for a *fixed* number of DM. The implied forward transaction is *selling DM and buying US dollars at the forward rate*.

When one compares this sequence to that in DM currency futures, one notes that the underlying currency in which one is taking a futures position is *not* US dollars. Note that, back then, the domestic currency of Germany was the Deutsche Mark. Since 2002, Germany, as part of the Eurozone, now uses the Euro. So you won't find any DM futures now. But you *will find* futures on the Euro. The Euro contract is very similar to the JY contract and has 125,000 Euros as its currency underlier.

The natural question arises,

What position in DM or Euro futures corresponds to buying US dollars?

■ CONCEPT CHECK 1

a. Convince yourself that the mechanism for Lufthansa to buy the US$500,000,000 is to sell the appropriate number of DM.

b. What are Lufthansa's two alternatives for selling the appropriate number of DM?

FINANCIAL FUTURES CONTRACTS 219

In order to answer the previous question, *always* go to the contract specifications and the basic definition of a futures contract. When one takes a long position in *any* futures contract, whether it be an ordinary commodity futures contract or a financial futures contract such as the DM or Euro futures contract, one is committing to *buying the underlying commodity* forward at a fixed price.

The commodity underlying the DM (Euro) futures contract is 125,000 DM (Euros). So a *long* position in the DM (Euro) currency futures contract corresponds to *buying* (receiving, taking delivery of) DM (Euros) in exchange for paying the requisite number of US dollars, based on the futures price when the position was initiated. You are in effect selling US dollars in exchange for receiving DMs (Euros). This is clearly *not* what Lufthansa wants to do.

However, by *shorting* DM (Euro) futures you commit to *selling* the underlying which is DMs (Euros) in exchange for US dollars. So a short position in this contract corresponds to selling (making delivery of) the underlying DMs (Euros), and receiving US dollars in exchange. You are in effect *buying* forward US dollars by *selling* forward DMs (Euros). This is exactly what Lufthansa wants to do because, by doing so, it locks in the number of US dollars it receives for its DMs.

This is a viable alternative to waiting until January 1986 and then doing a spot currency transaction at a spot exchange rate potentially unfavorable to the company. Of course, such a currency spot transaction *could* turn out favorable to the company. In fact, many companies do not hedge and the patterns of hedging also vary across different countries. Go back and look at the Southwestern Airlines example in Chapter 1.

■ CONCEPT CHECK 2

a. Is FX a raw material to a company like Lufthansa?
b. What is the main difference between Lufthansa's exposure in the jet fuel market and its exposure to FX risk?

The conclusion here is to be careful what position you take in a forward contract vis-à-vis a futures contract. If the currency underlying the forward is US dollars and the currency underlying the futures is the foreign currency (assuming domestic means the USA), then a long (short) position in US dollar forward contracts is equivalent (in terms of delivery) to a short (long) position in currency futures. If you think about this for a while, you will discover that it makes sense.

To nail the issue, we present Table 7.4 comparing US dollar forwards positions to Euro futures positions.

TABLE 7.4 **Currency Forward Positions vs. Currency Futures Positions**

Us Dollar-Euro Forwards	Euro Futures
Underlying: US Dollars	Underlying: Euros
LONG: receives (buys) US Dollars by selling Euros.	LONG: receives (buys) Euros by selling US Dollars.
SHORT: delivers (sells) US Dollars in exchange for Euros.	SHORT: delivers (sells) Euros in exchange for Euros.

Note how the positions line up. Of course, currency forward positions *could* match up perfectly if the forwards were quoted on the same terms as the futures. This may or may not happen, because forwards are not standardized like futures. Differing quote mechanisms are important in order to choose the appropriate hedge positions.

By selling DM (or Euro) currency futures, Lufthansa could lock in the DM (or Euro)–dollar exchange rate for delivery one year from today, thereby removing the risk of translating DM into US dollars in the spot market later. If Lufthansa does not wish to be a speculator in the FX market then this hedging strategy is worth considering. The problem is that there may not be liquidity in the distant (expiring in one year) futures contract. A *rolling hedge* could be implemented in this case.

7.2.2 The Rolling Hedge Strategy

When we discuss Eurodollar (ED) futures in the next chapter, we will refer to *strips* of Eurodollar futures. A *strip* involves currently taking positions in multiple futures contracts of different maturities. For ED futures, this can work because there is usually liquidity in multiple contracts at a given point in time. However, for contracts less liquid than ED futures there may be limited liquidity in the future, even up to a year.

Strips then become impractical or impossible. The nice thing about strips is that all the futures prices are currently known so there is complete lock-in. The *rolling hedge* strategy is a strip alternative because it concentrates on being in the most liquid (nearby) contract at each point in time over the duration of the hedge.

The rolling hedge short strategy is to currently sell forward the *nearby* futures contract, offset it just prior to maturity, then roll it over into a short position in the *next* futures contract. Prior to expiration of that contract, offset that position, and roll over into the next futures contract. Continue for three periods as indicated in Figure 7.1, where all the relevant prices and the relevant bases have been indicated. Note that, under the roll-over strategy, you will always have a short position in the nearby, most liquid contract.

FIGURE 7.1 **The Rolling Hedge Bases (4 Periods)**

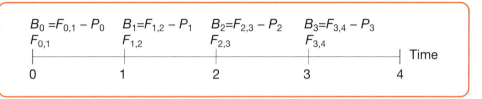

The first futures contract, held to maturity and offset prior to the last trading moment, locks in the time zero basis, $B_0 = F_{0,1} - P_0$. This is just the standard result that profits on a short hedge held to maturity are just equal to the basis at the time the hedge is initiated.

One then continues to carry the spot commodity and 'rolls' into a short position in the new nearby futures contract which matures at time $t=2$ and whose current (time $t=1$) futures price is $F_{1,2}$. Holding this contract to maturity and offsetting it prior to the last trading moment will lock in the time 1 basis, $B_1 = F_{1,2} - P_1$.

Proceeding in exactly the same manner, the roll-over hedger locks in $F_{2,3} - P_2$ over the third period. The last period, [3,4], produces the same form of basis profit figure, $F_{3,4} - P_3$, even though the spot currency position is liquidated by delivering it into the futures position. This is due to the result that profits from offsetting a contract at delivery and profits from delivering are equal, net of transactions costs, which was demonstrated in Chapter 5, section 5.8.1.

7.2.3 Interpretations of Profits from the Rolling Hedge

1. Adding up the profits on the rolling hedge we obtain that total profits,

$$\Pi = (F_{0,1} - P_0) + (F_{1,2} - P_1) + (F_{2,3} - P_2) + (F_{3,4} - P_3)$$
$$= B_0 + B_1 + B_2 + B_3$$
$$= 4 * \left(\frac{B_0 + B_1 + B_2 + B_3}{4} \right)$$

FORWARD CONTRACTS AND FUTURES CONTRACTS

This says that the roll-over strategy ends up with a total profit figure determined as the sum of the bases, or as the average of the time $t=i$ bases for $i=0,1,2,3$ times the number of periods.

2. Another way to look at total profits from the rolling hedge is as the *basis formed from the average of the prices*, as shown below, times the number of periods. Total Profits equals,

$$\Pi = (F_{0,1} - P_0) + (F_{1,2} - P_1) + (F_{2,3} - P_2) + (F_{3,4} - P_3)$$
$$= (F_{0,1} + F_{1,2} + F_{2,3} + F_{3,4}) - (P_0 + P_1 + P_2 + P_3)$$
$$= 4 * \left[\left(\frac{F_{0,1} + F_{1,2} + F_{2,3} + F_{3,4}}{4} \right) - \left(\frac{P_0 + P_1 + P_2 + P_3}{4} \right) \right]$$

Note that at time $t=0$, this is random because only the time $t=0$ basis is known (not random), while the subsequent bases $B_1(\omega)$, $B_2(\omega)$, $B_3(\omega)$ all depend on what happens at times $t=1,2$, and 3 represented by the state of nature ω.

The reason for this randomness is that all of the prices $F_{1,2}$, $F_{2,3}$, $F_{3,4}$, P_1, P_2, and P_3 are unknown at time $t=0$. However, we do know that, at expiration of each of the futures contracts, convergence implies that $F_{1,1}=P_1$, $F_{2,2}=P_2$, and $F_{3,3}=P_3$.

Thus, unlike in a normal one period short hedge or in a strip where all the futures prices are known in advance, you cannot *lock in* the bases. While this may appear to be a disadvantage of the roll-over strategy, it is better than not being able to hedge at all over the year with a single one-year futures contract that exists but is illiquid.

If one insists on a single hedging vehicle, then one is better off hedging with a one-year forward contract, which is likely to be available. Note however that it is going to be non-cancellable or it may be cancellable only under penalties. Liquidity is worth a lot, and futures strategies offer liquidity. They give the hedger better (lower transactions cost pricing) and the option of waiting to see what happens, and possibly to lift the hedge and to reinstate it as well.

In the roll-over strategy you aren't taking futures positions all at once but are taking positions sequentially. You are always in the most liquid contract, the nearby one. This gives you speculative options. You get the *average* futures price in a roll-over hedge, which is like *dollar-cost averaging* in the investment world. This smoothes out the volatility in futures prices.

Metallgesellschaft Example

A famous financial disaster occurred for a large company, Metallgesellschaft, using a roll-over hedge based on oil futures and other OTC derivatives. One of the issues in the case of Metallgesellschaft was the question of whether the company was hedging or speculating. This is part of a general debate, like that on the efficient market hypothesis (EMH), which will probably never be resolved.

The line between hedging and speculating is not written in stone. Not being able to lock in profits on a hedge doesn't mean that one is speculating. It does mean that you are taking some basis risk. One could say, very generically, that hedging is 'speculating on the basis'. But it depends; the basis is risky but less so than the underlying spot. In the extreme case one can remove all the risk, so there is no uncertainty whatsoever. No uncertainty means that there is nothing about which to speculate.

The idea behind hedging is to substitute 'basis risk' for 'spot price risk'. We gave the correlation condition under which this will occur in Chapter 6. The hedger removes some downside risk by giving up some upside profit potential. The hedger's goal is to *lower* the degree of risk by moving from an unhedged position to a hedged position. The extreme case of hedging is reduction of risk to zero, but this may not be possible.

The other extreme case is taking a naked position in a volatile commodity, such as oil. In between these two extremes are all the other cases of hedging, so that hedging is a matter of degree. Much of whether one is a hedger or a speculator depends on the motivation behind the trade.

7.2.4 Numerical Example of the Roll-Over Hedge Strategy

We will put numbers on the general scenario in Figure 7.2, but reduce the number of periods to three. Examples can be given where the basis goes from backwardation to contango to show what can happen.

FIGURE 7.2 The Rolling Hedge Bases (3 Periods)

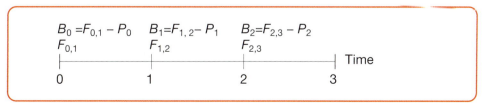

224 FORWARD CONTRACTS AND FUTURES CONTRACTS

Suppose that the current spot price is $P_0=\$17$ and that the subsequent spot prices turn out to be $P_1=\$18$, and $P_2=\$19$, while the current futures price is $F_{0,1}=\$17$, and that subsequent futures prices turn out to be $F_{1,2}=\$18.29$, and $F_{2,3}=\$19.44$. Note that at time $t=0$, only P_0 and $F_{0,1}$ are known with certainty.

The other prices would be revealed over time as indicated in Figure 7.2. With these numbers the bases would be determined as $B_0=F_{0,1}-P_0=\$0$, $B_1=F_{1,2}-P_1=\$0.29$, and $B_2=F_{2,3}-P_2=\$0.44$. Total profits on a traditional (one-for-one) rolling short hedge would then be the sum of the bases,

$$B_0+B_1+B_2=\$0+\$0.29+\$0.44$$
$$=\$0.73.$$

Thinking in terms of averages, the average spot price was $(P_0+P_1+P_2)/3=18$, and the average futures price was $(F_{0,1}+F_{1,2}+F_{2,3})/3=18.2433$ (the average futures price received was 18.2433). Therefore, total profits$=3*(18.2433-18)=.7299$ or .73.

■ CONCEPT CHECK 3

a. When was the market in contango?
b. When was the market in backwardation?
c. When was the market neither in contango nor in backwardation?

7.3 HEDGING

7.3.1 Issues in Hedging, Quantity Uncertainty

It should be noted that hedging using futures or forwards is not quite as simple as the above presentation would suggest. That's because, in addition to price (exchange rate) uncertainty, there may also be *quantity uncertainty*. This means that the number of units of the foreign currency one is trying to hedge may not be known when the hedge is placed.

In the case of a multinational corporation collecting revenues in foreign sales, the exchange rate risk is in translating the foreign currency units into the domestic currency. Even if one hedges the exchange rate risk perfectly, there may be quantity risk.

FINANCIAL FUTURES CONTRACTS · 225

Think of a multinational agricultural firm selling a crop in a foreign country in a foreign currency, and domesticating the foreign currency. The crop size is a random variable based on a number of risky sources such as the weather.

7.3.2 Currency Futures Pricing vs. Currency Forward Pricing

We have already priced forward contracts on underlyings without and with a dividend yield in Chapters 3 and 4 respectively. The pricing formula for the equilibrium *forward* price on underlyings with a dividend yield ρ, a risk-free rate r, and time to expiration τ is $F'_{t,T}=e^{(r-\rho)\tau}*S_t$.

It is a theoretical result, beyond the scope of this text, that if interest rates are non-stochastic, then equilibrium futures prices are equal to equilibrium forward prices. A constant risk-free rate is non-stochastic therefore the equilibrium *futures* price must also equal $F'_{t,T}=e^{(r-\rho)\tau}*S_t$ where S_t is the underlying stock price at time t.

7.4 STOCK INDEX FUTURES

7.4.1 The S&P 500 Spot Index

Stock index futures are financial derivative innovations that allow portfolio investors (for example, mutual fund managers and their customers) to hedge the *market risk* of their portfolios. According to portfolio analysis, common stocks and portfolios of common stock have at least two types of risk. Actually three.

First, there is the *total risk* of the risky asset or portfolio, by which is meant the variance of its percentage rates of return calculated over a specific holding period.

Second comes the *diversifiable risk*. Diversifiable means that we can eliminate the (diversifiable) risk just by diversifying, by forming portfolios. Diversifiable risks are also called *idiosyncratic risks* which means that they are specific to the company. An example would be the quality of the firm's management.

Finally, there is the *market risk* which is not diversifiable. Non-diversifiable risks are related to *economy-wide factors* such as inflation or GDP growth which affect all firms in varying degrees. No matter how many stocks you hold in your portfolio, the market risk remains. All of this is part and parcel of standard portfolio analysis which is usually covered in investments courses.

226 **FORWARD CONTRACTS AND FUTURES CONTRACTS**

The first step in understanding S&P 500 stock index futures is to examine the spot *S&P 500 stock index* which is a product of Standard & Poor's corporation. Full details on this index are available at standardandpoors.com. The reader is strongly encouraged to visit this site, where you will see the link to S&P 500 under S&P Dow Jones Indices.

A good starting point to understanding the S&P 500 spot index is the *S&P 500 fact sheet*, which reveals that the portfolio underlying the S&P 500 spot index includes most of the most heavily capitalized US companies such as Apple, Google, Microsoft, Exxon-Mobil, and others.

The ticker symbol for the S&P 500 spot index is SPX, although it is not traded directly, and 'price' quotes are available from the major financial reporting websites such as finance.yahoo.com, google.com/finance, marketwatch.com, and many others.

The alternative to trading S&P 500 spot index directly are exchange-traded funds (ETFs) that track the S&P 500 spot index.

The main thing to understand here is that the spot price quote mechanism is *not* in conventional dollars. Rather, it is in a scale-like temperature. The S&P 500 index is quoted in *index points*, determined relative to a *base value* which was set equal to 10.0 during the period 1941–1943, when the index was originated.

The early history of the S&P 500 is clouded in mystery, and the current version of it was introduced in 1957. For example, the early S&P 500 spot portfolio didn't even contain 500 stocks! It was expanded in 1957 to include 500 stocks. Of course, the company list has changed since many of the companies around today were not around in 1943 or in 1957. Remember, spot markets are not usually standardized. Standard & Poor's handles changes to the index by a divisor methodology.

What we observe today in the financial news is the *current* value of the index relative to its base value. At the close on Oct. 1, 2013 that value was 1695 index points. That seems like a huge value relative to what it was in 1941–1943. Indeed it is about 170 times larger if we round 1695 up to 1700.

The geometric average annual rate of return corresponding to this is the annualized percentage rate r_E that satisfies $10*(1+r_E)^{72}=1695$ because 10 S&P 500 index points in 1941 grew to 1695 S&P 500 index points in 2013, where we take 1941 to be the starting date.

Solving for r_E we obtain $r_E=(1695/10)^{1/72}=1.073892$. This says that the S&P 500 index grew on average only 7.3892% over the period 1941–2013, some 72 years. That seems like a rather paltry value, but one has to remember that the S&P 500 pays dividends and this calculation does not include the re-invested value of those dividends.

If we take that dividend yield to be approximately 3.5%–4.0%, we obtain a dividend-adjusted *geometric mean* for the S&P 500 of 10.8892%–11.3892%. This is in the ball park. One can check this against some online calculators and will get similar values. These calculations can be fine-tuned by getting the actual dividend yield.

7.4.2 S&P 500 Stock Index Futures Contract Specifications

We reproduce the contract specifications for the S&P 500 stock index futures contract from the CME Group Futures Exchange in Table 7.5.

The main features of this contract are:

1. The *contract 'size'* refers to a dollar value associated with the S&P 500 *futures price* which is quoted in index points, just like the spot S&P 500. The reason for this conversion to dollars is that people are not simply interested in calculating rates of return on the spot index. They are also interested in hedging portfolios worth billions of dollars.

This requires conversion of futures index points into dollar values. That way, they can figure out how many S&P 500 futures contracts to position in a hedge. The general principle is called *dollar equivalency*. We give an example right now.

Dollar Equivalents

To get the dollar equivalent, multiply the futures price by $250. When the S&P 500 spot index was a lot lower than it is now, the dollar multiplier was $500. Thus, one futures index point is worth $250.

On October 4, 2013 the December S&P 500 contract settled at 1684.80 futures index points. Thus the dollar equivalent of one December 2013 S&P 500 futures contract was $250*1684.80=$421,200.

2. *Contracts are offered* according to delivery months in a way that is analogous to option 'cycles'. The S&P 500 futures contract follows the March cycle: eight months in the March quarterly cycle (Mar, Jun, Sep, Dec) for outright positions.

That's 2 years forward. We found a few more quotes. For example, on the quote date that we looked at, we found S&P 500 futures available from

FORWARD CONTRACTS AND FUTURES CONTRACTS

TABLE 7.5 S&P 500 Futures

Contract Size	$250 × S&P 500 futures price	
Tick Size (minimum fluctuation)	OUTRIGHT	0.10 index points=$25
	CALENDAR SPREAD	0.05 index points=$12.50
Trading Hours All times listed are Central Time	Open Outcry	MON–FRI: 8:30 a.m.–3:15 p.m.
	CME Globex (Electronic Platform)	MON–FRI: 5:00 p.m. previous day–4:15 p.m. CT, trading halt from 8:15 a.m.–3:30 p.m.
Contract Months	Open Outcry	Eight months in the March Quarterly Cycle (Mar, Jun, Sep, Dec) plus three additional Dec contracts
	CME Globex	One month in the March Quarterly Cycle (Mar, Jun, Sep, Dec)
Last Trade Date/Time View Calendar	Open Outcry	3:15 p.m. on Thursday prior to 3rd Friday of the contract month
	CME Globex	On the rollingdate (typically eight days prior to last trade date for open outcry) when the lead month goes off the screen and the deferred month becomes the new lead month. View RollingDates
Settlement Procedure	Daily S&P Settlement Procedure (PDF) Final S&P Settlement Procedure (PDF)	
Daily Price Limits	View price limits details	
Position Limits	See: CME Rulebook Chapter 5 – POSITION LIMIT, POSITION ACCOUNTABILITY AND REPORTABLE LEVEL TABLE	
Block Trade Eligibility	No. View more on block-trade eligible contracts.	
Block Minimum	N/A	
Rulebook Chapter	351	
Exchange Rule	These contracts are listed with, and subject to, the rules and regulations of CME.	

Reprinted with permission from CME Group Inc., 2014.

December 2013 until December 2017. Volume was concentrated exclusively in the nearby contract.

3. *Delivery* is not physical. It would be quite difficult and costly to deliver units of a stock index. These are cash-settled contracts, as discussed in Chapter 5, section 5.9.

What this actually means is that absolutely nothing gets delivered at expiration, except for the settlement variation (cash value of open futures positions) from the 'losing' parties to the 'winning' parties. That is, only the cash flow implications of one's open futures positions have to be reconciled.

Here is the relevant quote from the CME Rule Book.

35103.B. Final Settlement

Clearing members holding open positions in a Standard & Poor's 500 Stock Price Index futures contract at the time of termination of trading in that contract shall make payment to or receive payment from the Clearing House in accordance with normal variation performance bond procedures based on a settlement price equal to the final settlement price.

> (Reprinted from the CME Rule Book with permission from CME Group Inc., 2014)

4. *Position limits* in the S&P 500 futures contracts equal 28,000 in all delivery months. Once one accumulates a sufficient number of contract positions, they must be *reported* to the CFTC which is the regulating body (cftc.gov).

5. *The Ticker* symbol for S&P 500 Futures is SP, which contrasts with the ticker symbol for the underlying S&P 500 index, .SPX.

6. The *tick size* is the minimum move in the futures price which in this case is .10 Index points. The dollar equivalent of a tick movement in the futures 'price' is therefore $250*.01=$25.

7. There are *Daily Price Limits* which are analogous to the circuit-breakers on US stock exchanges. These came about as a result of several stock market crashes.

8. The remaining entries are more or less self-explanatory. In cases of doubt, one refers to the CME literature.

7.4.3 The Quote Mechanism for S&P 500 Futures Price Quotes

Here is a price quote using the same access procedure as for contract specs (see above). One of the tabs is called 'Quotes' then 'Settlements'.

TABLE 7.6 **Daily Settlements for S&P 500 Futures, (FINAL). Trade Date: 10/04/2013**

Month	Open	High	Low	Last	Change	Settle	Estimated Volume	Prior Day Open Interest
DEC 13	1668.20	1685.50	1667.40	1684.80	+15.10	1684.80	4,193	151,223

Reprinted with permission from CME Group Inc., 2014.

Commentary

1. The contract is the Dec. 2013 delivery month.

2. The quote is from the end of the trade date 10/04/2013.

3. The open (first) futures price on 10/04/2013 was 1668.20 which, when translated into dollars, equals $250*1668.20=$417,050.

4. The highest futures price for the day was 1685.50 which, when translated into dollars, equals $250*1685.50=$421,375.

5. The lowest futures price for the day was 1667.40 which, when translated into dollars, equals $250*1667.40=$416, 850.

6. The 'last' futures price for the day was reported as 1684.80.

7. The change in the daily settlement futures price from the previous day was +15.10 which means up by 15.10 Index points. Therefore, yesterday's settlement price was 15.10 Index points lower, 1669.7. You can confirm this by searching for the 10/03/2013 settlement price which indeed is equal to this number.

8. Today's settlement price was 1684.80.

9. Volume refers to the number of contracts traded (counting one side only). 4,193 S&P 500 Dec. 2013 contracts traded on 10/04/2013.

10. Prior day open interest refers to the number of contracts (counting one side only) that were not offset by offsetting trades as of the end of the trade date 10/03/2013. That number was 151,223.

FINANCIAL FUTURES CONTRACTS   **231**

7.5 RISK MANAGEMENT USING STOCK INDEX FUTURES

7.5.1 Pricing and Hedging Preliminaries

The pricing methodology is to assume that index futures can be priced like forward contracts. Since stock market indexes are based on (large) portfolios of underlying stocks that typically pay dividends, we must use the forward pricing model from Chapter 4. We have already used this model for currency futures.

In our context, it says that the τ-period ahead futures price $F'_{t,T} = e^{(r-\rho)\tau} * I_t$ where r is the continuously compounded, annualized risk-free borrowing rate and ρ is the continuously compounded, annualized dividend yield on the spot index. I_t is the current value of the spot S&P 500 Index, $\text{S\&P500}_t$, $\tau = T-t$ is measured in years (or fractions thereof). In some of our applications we just take $t=0$ and T is the expiration date of the futures contract.

The theory of hedging with financial futures contracts basically follows from the theory of hedging in Chapter 6. There are a few tricks to learn when considering hedging with financial futures. One has to keep in mind that, like all futures contracts, a financial futures contract calls for delivery of an underlying commodity at expiration. In the case of financial futures, that underlying commodity is a particular financial instrument or some cash flow closely related to the price behavior of a particular financial instrument.

The mechanism of 'cash settlement' is a way around the problem of physical delivery. After all, shares of the S&P 500's underlying portfolio are a different 'commodity' than 100,000 bushels of corn. Something as abstract as an interest rate, like LIBOR_3, is hard to deliver.

However, as long as the cash flow implications of one's futures positions are taken care of, one can just offset the position(s) prior to maturity (see Chapter 5, section 5.8.1). If one really needs the actual commodity and is willing to forgo the liquidity provided by futures contracts, one can go to the forward market.

7.5.2 Monetizing the S&P 500 Spot Index

We will work through an example in detail. The numbers will be somewhat simplified in order to make the ideas as transparent as possible.

A portfolio manager has $20,000,000 in portfolio value to protect over a one-year period starting in December 2013. Shorting the 'appropriate' number of December 2014 S&P 500 futures contracts effectively *sells forward* the portfolio for a fixed price, as does any forward contract. The question is what is the appropriate number of December 2014 S&P 500 futures contracts to short?

We will start by setting up a traditional (one-for-one) short hedge. Suppose that the current S&P 500 spot index, I_0, is quoted at,

$$I_0 = \text{S\&P500}_0$$
$$= 1000 \text{ index points.}$$

We can easily determine the one-year forward price using the (net) cost-of-carry model from Chapter 4. That model says $F'_{0,1} = e^{(r-\rho)1} * \text{S\&P500}_0$ where r is the continuously compounded, annualized, risk-free borrowing rate and ρ is the continuously compounded, annualized, dividend yield on the S&P 500 spot index.

To keep life simple, assume that $r=5\%$ and $\rho=3\%$. These parameter values are consistent with historical experience. Transforming to decimals, the 'net' cost of carry is $r-\rho=.05-.03=.02$. Next, $e^{.02}=1.020201$ from which it follows that the current (December 2013) one-year ahead (delivery in December 2014) S&P 500 forward price,

$$F'_{0,1} = 1.020201 * \text{S\&P500}_0$$
$$= 1.020201 * 1000$$
$$= 1020.201 \text{ index points.}$$

We are going to have to select a way to *monetize* the S&P 500 Index in a way that makes it comparable to the way monetization is implicit in the specification of the S&P 500 futures price. Given that the current futures price of the December 2014 S&P 500 futures contract is 1020.201 *futures* index points, and that we understand the futures price quote mechanism, we see that $F_{0,1}=1020.201$ is associated with $\$250*1020.201=\$255,050.25$.

What exactly does this mean? It means that if you *shorted* one S&P 500 futures contract at time $t=0$ at $F'_{0,1}=1020.201$, you *effectively get to sell* the monetized (dollar) value of the S&P 500 Index at expiration, which is $\$250*\text{S\&P500}_1(\omega)$, for a *fixed* price of $\$250*1020.201=\$255,050.25$. When the contract specifies that the contract size is *$\$250 \times \text{S\&P500}$ futures price*, this is what those words actually mean.

Since a futures contract has the essential lock-in characteristic of a forward contract, this holds no matter what the actual spot Index price $250*S\&P500_1(\omega)$ turns out to be at expiration. If you were running a short hedge, you could deliver your spot commodity into the short futures position. The value of your spot commodity is the monetized value of the number of S&P 500 Index units it contains, $\$250*S\&P500_1(\omega)$ per each spot unit.

If $\$250*S\&P500_1(\omega)<\$250*1020.201$, you made money. If $\$250*S\&P500_1(\omega)>\$250*1020.201$, you lost money. You don't have to go through the trouble of making delivery of anything, because the cash settlement mechanism does all that for you.

After all daily settlements are taken care of, including that on the last day, your *effective* payoff will be $\$250*1020.201-\$250*S\&P500_1(\omega)$ because $F'_{0,1}=1020.201$.

This is the same payoff that you would receive if you had a *short* position in a forward contract otherwise identical to the S&P 500 futures contract. Only the pattern of the daily cash flows would be different, due to the daily settlement process, wherein the clearing house collects the daily settlement cash flows from the losers and delivers them to the winners.

Your effective payoff could be positive or negative, as indicated, depending on whether the ultimate spot price turns out to be below or above the initially contracted futures price. As noted earlier and in Chapter 3, this holds for any forward contract. We are just filling in the details for the financial futures contract under consideration.

While no underlying commodity actually gets delivered in a cash-settled futures contract, it is useful to know what actually *would* get delivered if physical delivery took place. In the case of any futures contract, the number of units of the underlying commodity specified in the contract would be the deliverable.

For the S&P 500 futures contract, this is in dollars and is the *monetized value* of the *spot* S&P 500 index. This monetized value is $\$250*S\&P500_1(\omega)$ per one futures contract, and it depends on what $S\&P500_1(\omega)$ turns out to be at expiration. That is, on a short futures position you deliver the spot commodity which is worth $250 times the spot S&P 500 index on the expiration date of the contract. This says that the commodity underlying the S&P 500 futures contract is the *spot commodity*.

The contract specs leave room for some confusion here. Don't confuse the *futures price* you effectively receive at time $t=1$, based on the short futures position you took at time $t=0$, for these spot S&P 500 index units themselves.

234 **FORWARD CONTRACTS AND FUTURES CONTRACTS**

You effectively receive $250 *F'_{0,1}$ per each spot S&P 500 index unit, as in any futures contract. At time $t=1$, each unit is worth its spot price in the spot market, $250*S\&P500_1(\omega)$.

For our portfolio manager, who wishes to hedge his $20,000,000 worth of portfolio value using S&P 500 futures contracts, we have to first determine how many monetized spot S&P 500 index units (the underlier) are 'in' the $20,000,000 portfolio value.

Call the $20,000,000 portfolio value VP_0. Note that we are maintaining *dollar equivalency* even though the hedge is one-for-one. This is easy to do. Just divide VP_0 by $250*I_0=\$250*1,000=\$250,000$ (we assumed earlier that $I_0=S\&P500_0=1000$ spot index points) to obtain what we will call the *Naive Hedge Ratio* (NHR),

$$\text{NHR} = \frac{\$20,000,000}{\$250 * S\&P500_0}$$

$$= \frac{\$20,000,000}{\$250 * 1,000}$$

$$= 80 \text{ monetized S\&P500 spot units.}$$

Therefore, in a one-for-one short hedge, the portfolio manager should short 80 December 2014 S&P 500 futures contracts simply because that is the number of units of spot commodity 'in' his $20,000,000 portfolio.

In brief, each futures contract has $250,000=\$250*1,000$ underlying value of stock index as its underlier. Therefore 80 contracts are needed to 'cover' the portfolio manager's $20,000,000.

■ CONCEPT CHECK 4

a. The S&P 500 is cash settled. However, as noted, it is useful to think about what would happen if you delivered the underlying commodity. Suppose that you delivered one S&P 500 spot index unit. How much would you receive for it?

b. What *effective* price would you receive for one S&P 500 spot index unit?

c. Explain when you would make money and when you would lose money on the futures transaction.

7.5.3 Profits from the Traditional Hedge

Without writing down a single number, we can say exactly what the overall profit figure is in a traditional short hedge held to expiration. It is the time zero basis, $B_0=F_{0,1}-P_0$, which must, in our case, be scaled by $N_{spot}=80*\$250$.

Let π_S be profits (or losses) from the long $\$20,000,000$ spot portfolio. Let π_F be losses (or profits) from the short S&P 500 December 2014 futures position in 80 contracts. Then $\pi=\pi_S+\pi_F$ equals total profits (or losses) on the overall hedge.

$$\pi_S=N_{spot}*(\text{S\&P500}_1-\text{S\&P500}_0)$$
$$=80*\$250*(I_1-I_0)$$
$$=(\text{the number of spot S\&P500 index units one is holding})*$$
$$(\text{the change in the spot index}),$$

since one is long the spot index $\text{S\&P500}_1$ is the spot index at expiration of the futures contract and $\text{S\&P500}_0$ is the current value of the spot S&P 500 index.

$$\pi_F=N_{futures}*(F'_{0,1}-F'_{1,1})$$
$$=80*\$250*(F'_{0,1}-F'_{1,1})$$

because you have a short position and in a one-for-one hedge $N_{futures}=-N_{spot}$. $F'_{1,1}$ is the S&P 500 Futures price at expiration, which by forced convergence, is equal to the ultimate spot index P_1.

Then total profits,

$$\pi=\pi_S+\pi_F$$
$$=80*\$250*(P_1-P_0)+80*\$250*(F'_{0,1}-F'_{1,1})$$
$$=80*\$250*[(P_1-P_0)+(F'_{0,1}-F'_{1,1})]$$
$$=80*\$250*(F'_{0,1}-P_0)$$
$$=80*\$250*B_0$$

because $F'_{1,1}=P_1$ by forced convergence.

Let's interpret this number for our case,

$$B_0=F'_{0,1}-P_0$$
$$=1020.201-1000$$
$$=20.201.$$

236   FORWARD CONTRACTS AND FUTURES CONTRACTS

Scaling by 80*$250 we obtain the monetized value of the basis (normally quoted in S&P 500 index points), $404,020. This amount is the *net* interest owed on a one-year loan (the net cost of carry) at a continuously compounded net borrowing rate of .02. Principal plus interest=$e^{.02}$*$20,000,000= $20,404,027. Subtracting the principal of $20,000,000, we obtain the net interest of $404,027 which, except for rounding error, is equal to $404,020.

This makes economic sense, of course. The basis is, in general, equal to the net cost of carry. Also, if we execute the arbitrage of Chapter 4, we would borrow $20,000,000 at a continuously compounded annual rate of $r=5\%$, and receive the continuously compounded, annual dividend yield $\rho=3\%$ on the index. Our *net* annualized borrowing cost would be 2%.

At the same time ($t=0$), we would sell forward 80 contracts on the spot S&P 500 index for one year at the futures price $F'_{0,1}=1020.201$ At the end of the year, we would owe $e^{.02}$*$20,000,000=$20,404,027 on the $20,000,000 loan.

We would pay off this amount from the proceeds of the forward sale which would also be equal to 80*$250*1020.201=$20,404,020. The difference is rounding error.

Our fully leveraged position in the $20,000,000 has no current cost, so it must generate a zero cash flow at expiration to avoid arbitrage.

$$\text{When } 80*\$250*F'_{0,1}=e^{.02} *\$20,000,000$$
$$=80*\$250*e^{.02}*S\&P500_0,$$

there is no-arbitrage.

This is just the equilibrium forward pricing relationship,

$$F'_{0,1}=e^{(r-\rho)1}*S\&P500_0.$$

7.5.4 Risk, Return Analysis of the Traditional Hedge

Is the one-to-one hedge the *best* hedging strategy available? Like most questions about investment strategies, we have to look at it from the point of view of *both* risk and expected return.

We first look at the expected return. We have $20,000,000 invested in the portfolio and the dollar return on the hedge is the scaled time $t=0$ basis $80*\$250*(F'_{0,1}-P_0)$.

FINANCIAL FUTURES CONTRACTS 237

The *Holding Period Rate* of return on the hedge is,

$$\begin{aligned}
\text{HPR} &= \frac{80 * \$250 * (F'_{0,1} - P_0)}{80 * \$250 * P_0} \\
&= \frac{F'_{0,1} - P_0}{P_0} \\
&= \frac{F'_{0,1}}{P_0} - 1.0 \\
&= e^{.02} - 1.0 \\
&= 0.0202013.
\end{aligned}$$

This rate is the simple interest rate (not compounded) equivalent to the continuously compounded 2% rate. The one-to-one hedge is just a synthetic Treasury bill, net of the dividend yield.

The risk analysis is based upon the timing of the hedge.

Case 1

If the hedge is held to expiration of the futures contract, then its basis risk is zero. Since this is the only kind of risk there is in a one-to-one hedge, its total risk is also zero. That's why its expected return is the *net* risk-free borrowing rate $r-\rho$. However, this is not the end of the story.

The main advantage of executing the hedge in futures markets, as opposed to in forward markets, is the liquidity provided. This gives the hedger the option to 'lift the hedge'. This could mean keeping the spot commodity, but in a partially or fully speculative (unhedged) position. For example, if underlying spot prices are moving in a favorable way, the hedger may want to (partially) lift the hedge in search of 'yield enhancement'. The hedger could subsequently put the hedge back on if he started to worry about unfavorable spot price movements. This kind of market timing strategy carries its own risks, *when to exit* and *when to re-enter* the hedge.

Case 2

The hedge is not held to maturity but rather to some intermediate time t where $0 < t < 1$. There are two scenarios here. One is that the intermediate time t is *fixed* in advance. The other scenario is that $t = t(\omega)$ is a *random* variable.

238 **FORWARD CONTRACTS AND FUTURES CONTRACTS**

We will only deal with scenario 1. Under scenario 1, the profits (ignoring the scale factor) on a traditional short hedge are still equal to the change in the basis, $\pi_t(\omega)=B_0-B_t(\omega)$ where $B_t(\omega)=F_t'(\omega)-P_t(\omega)$. However, unless $t=1$ which is expiration, we have no assurance that $F_t'(\omega)=P_t(\omega)$. This means that we have basis risk, $\mathrm{Var}(\pi_t(\omega))=\mathrm{Var}(B_t(\omega))$.

7.5.5 Risk-Minimizing Hedging

As discussed in Chapter 6, section 6.4.2, if we want to minimize this basis risk we have to match up dollar moves in the spot price with dollar moves in the futures price. The hedge ratio allows us to do this. Then the appropriate risk-minimizing hedge ratio is the beta of the spot price on the futures price,

$$\beta_{P_t(\omega),F_t'(\omega)} = \frac{\mathrm{COV}(P_t(\omega),F_t'(\omega))}{\mathrm{VAR}(F_t'(\omega))}$$

To estimate $\beta_{P_t(\omega),F_t'(\omega)}$, we start with the equilibrium forward pricing mechanism when the underlier pays a proportional dividend yield. It says that $F_{t,T}'=e^{(r-\rho)\tau}*P_t$ where P_t is the spot price and $F_{t,T}'$ is the forward price today (time=t) for a forward contract maturing at time T. We will assume that interest rates are non-stochastic and therefore that the corresponding futures price is equal to the forward price. We will also use the same notation for futures prices as for forward prices, $F_{t,T}'$.

From $F_{t,T}'=e^{(r-\rho)\tau}*P_t$,we can read off how a *fixed maturity* forward price varies with the spot price. It varies by $e^{(r-\rho)\tau}$ units every time the spot price changes by one unit. We can also read off how the spot price underlying a fixed maturity forward contract varies with the forward price associated to that contract from $P_t=e^{-(r-\rho)\tau}*F_{t,T}'$.

Suppose that the forward price $F_{t,T}'$ changes by one unit. Then the spot price P_t changes by the coefficient of $F_{t,T}'$ number of units. That is, it varies by $e^{-(r-\rho)\tau}$ units.

But this is pretty close to saying that $\beta_{P_t(\omega),F_t'(\omega)}=e^{-(r-\rho)\tau}$. It's not exactly the same, but if we restrict ourselves to fixed time-to-expiration forward contracts, τ is a constant, then $\beta_{P_t(\omega),F_t'(\omega)}=e^{-(r-\rho)\tau}$ is also a constant. This is the usual assumption about $\beta_{P_t(\omega),F_t'(\omega)}$.

Note that we are using the equilibrium forward pricing relation $P_t=e^{-(r-\rho)\tau}*F_{t,T}'$ to impute the beta, rather than a disequilibrium regression model such as the one in Chapter 5 which says that,

$$P_t(\omega) = \alpha + \beta_{P_t(\omega), F_t'(\omega)} * F_t'(\omega) + \varepsilon_t$$

Therefore, the risk-minimizing hedge ratio is $e^{-(r-\rho)\tau}$, based on our general result in Chapter 6. Note that $e^{-(r-\rho)\tau}$ is a number less than 1.0. For our example with $r=.05$, $\rho=.02$, and $\tau=1.0$, the optimal (risk-minimizing) hedge ratio is $e^{-(r-\rho)\tau}=0.980199$.

This makes economic sense because $P_t=e^{-(r-\rho)\tau}*F_{t,T}'$ says that the futures price is moving too fast relative to the spot price. We need to match up the relatively mismatched movements of spot and futures prices using a hedge ratio. The optimal (risk-minimizing) hedge ratio is $e^{-(r-\rho)\tau}$. We have to sell slightly less than one unit of futures per unit of spot.

7.5.6 Adjusting the Naive Hedge Ratio to Obtain the Risk-Minimizing Hedge Ratio

Now we can use this theory to answer an important question in stock index futures hedging. *Should we divide VP_0 by $\$250*I_0$ or by $\$250*F_0'$?* This is an issue that comes up when discussing hedging using stock index futures. Both answers appear in the literature. Fortunately, an answer can be given to this question. We start with what we already know about what it means to construct a dollar-equivalent one-for-one hedge.

There are two features of a dollar-equivalent one-for-one hedge. The first is *dollar equivalency* which is simply a question of matching spot units with futures underlying units. For example, if you were hedging 100,000 bushels of wheat in CME wheat futures you would need 100,000/5,000=20 CME wheat futures contracts to do so, since each CME wheat futures contract has only 5000 bushels of wheat as its underlier.

The hedge is still considered to be one-for-one because there are 20 underlying wheat spot units 'in' 100,000 bushels of wheat, 20*5,000=100,000. The term '*dollar equivalency*' to describe this straightforward adjustment is appropriate. This notion occurs in other applications, since investors rarely hold the exact number of units of the underlier specified in standardized futures contracts.

Similarly, for our portfolio manager's hedging problem $\$20,000,000/\$250*1,000=80$ futures contracts are needed to get dollar equivalency because, as discussed, there are 80 S&P 500 spot units 'in' the portfolio's current value of $\$20,000,000$. Note that we divide the spot commodity by the number of units of the *spot* index that underlie one S&P 500 futures contract. One such unit has a dollar value of $\$250*I_0$ where I_0 is the spot S&P 500 index.

240 **FORWARD CONTRACTS AND FUTURES CONTRACTS**

Dollar equivalency is a prerequisite for every hedge, *if* we decide that we want to hedge the *entire* amount of spot commodity in which we have a position. Otherwise one has a units mismatch. We don't have to hedge the entire amount, of course. What percentage of our spot commodity that we want to hedge, and what part we do not want to hedge, is part of the portfolio theory of hedging.

This one-to-one feature of the hedge comes into play explicitly once we have determined the 80 spot units and then we choose to *short 80* S&P *500 futures* contracts. But there are many alternatives to one-for-one hedging, as we know. Instead of setting up just a dollar-equivalent one-for-one hedge, we could set up a *risk-minimizing* hedge as in the next subsection.

The dollar equivalent one-for-one hedge matches up the number of units of the spot commodity with the correct number of futures contracts, but it does not generally match up the *risks* of the spot and futures prices movements because they don't generally move in the same way by the exact same dollar amount. To obtain the risk-minimizing hedge ratio, we have to apply the factor $e^{-(r-\rho)\tau}$.

Specifically, according to the equilibrium forward (futures) pricing relationship and for our example where $\tau=1.0$, for each dollar move in the futures price the spot price moves by $e^{-(r-\rho)*1}$ dollars. We should be selling *fewer* than 80 futures contracts, namely $e^{-(r-\rho)*1}*80=78.41589$ futures contracts. This assumes that $r>\rho$. In the alternative case of $r<\rho$ we would sell *more* than 80 futures contracts.

■ CONCEPT CHECK 5

Suppose that $r=.02$, $\rho=.05$, and $\tau=1.0$,

a. Calculate the optimal (risk-minimizing) hedge ratio.
b. How many futures contracts should one sell?

Ignoring the problem of fractional futures contracts, let's stay for a moment in the land of pure theory. In terms of our previous notation and generally for any $r>0$, $\rho>0$ and τ, the optimal hedge ratio is equal to,

$$e^{-(r-\rho)\tau} * \frac{VP_0}{\$250 * I_0} = e^{-(r-\rho)\tau} * \text{NHR}$$

where I_0 is the current index value of the spot S&P 500 index, τ is the hedging horizon, VP_0 is the current dollar value of the portfolio being hedged, and NHR is the naive hedge ratio.

Now, an interesting thing happens. Bring the optimal hedging factor $e^{-(r-\rho)\tau}$ to the denominator, changing the minus sign in the exponent to a plus sign, to obtain that the optimal hedge ratio is also equal to,

$$\frac{VP_0}{\$250 * e^{(r-\rho)\tau} * I_0}$$

Note that $\$250*e^{(r-\rho)\tau}*I_0$ is just the number of *futures* S&P 500 price units $\$250*F'_{0,T}$, where $F'_{0,T}=e^{(r-\rho)\tau}*I_0$ .This says that the optimal (risk-minimizing) hedge ratio is obtained by dividing VP_0 by $\$250*F'_{0,T}$, and not by dividing it by $\$250*I_0$ as does the naive hedge ratio. This answers our question: *should we divide VP_0 by $\$250*I_0$ or by $\$250*F'_0$?*

The answer is that in a straight, non–risk-minimizing hedge we should divide by the number of *spot* S&P 500 index units, $\$250*I_0$. If we want the *risk-minimizing* hedge, however, then we should divide by the number of *futures* S&P 500 index units, that is by $\$250*F'_0$. The optimal hedge ratio is $VP_0/\$250*F'_{0,T}$.

If you think about it for a moment, you will see that that number is the optimal hedge ratio. If we set the hedge ratio to equalize the number of futures units to the number of spot units being hedged, then we will have matched up respective dollar moves in the spot and in the futures. Thereby, risk has been minimized. This is the rationale for dividing by the number of futures units.

7.5.7 Risk Minimizing the Hedge Using Forward vs. Futures Contracts

In this subsection, we have to make a distinction between risk minimizing the hedge using forward contracts vs. risk minimizing the hedge using futures contracts because they mean different things. Sometimes, risk minimizing the hedge using futures contracts is called *tailing* the hedge using futures contracts.

Whatever the terminology, it is an interest-related adjustment process that attempts to adjust the hedge ratio for the financing costs or reinvestment returns due to the daily settlement variation feature of futures contracts.

There is no daily settlement variation for forward contracts, because the cash flows of a forward contract are exchanged only at expiration. But this only means that tailing the hedge in the futures contract sense is irrelevant for forward contracts. This logic does not dictate that there is no equally valid notion of tailing that applies to forward contracts.

The notion of tailing the hedge, appropriately defined, using forward contracts *could* still makes sense. For example, while there are no daily cash flows to incorporate when hedging with forward contracts, there is still the question of what the hedge ratio should be. Whether it is *necessary* to adjust the naive hedge ratio is another issue which we will now discuss as well.

The equilibrium pricing relationship $P_t = e^{-(r-\rho)\tau} * F'_{t,T}$ was derived for forward contracts in Chapter 4 and obviously holds for them. The same mismatch in futures vs. spot prices occurs, whether we are dealing with futures or forward contracts.

Consider a long forward position initiated on day zero at the forward price $F'_{0,T}$. Suppose that in the next instant, $0+\Delta t$, the forward price goes up to $F'_{\Delta t,T}$. A long forward position increased in value because you could now sell the commodity forward for the higher price of $F'_{\Delta t,T}$. Combined with your initial long forward position, you could buy the spot commodity at time T for $F'_{0,T}$.

The increased value embedded in the forward price movement is $F'_{\Delta t,T} - F'_{0,T}$, the change in the forward price. The only problem is that you have to wait until time T to *realize* this profit as a cash flow because there is no daily settlement procedure for forward contracts.

How should this profit on your long forward position be accounted for in your overall profit figure? The answer is that your current forward position has accrued a value increase equal to the *present value of the forward price change*. The appropriate discount rate to use in determining this present value is the net cost of borrowing $r-\rho$.

In current (time $t=\Delta t$) terms, the value of your forward position has increased by the present value of the forward price change, where the PV factor is $e^{-(r-\rho)\tau'}$ and τ' is the time to expiration from time $t=\Delta t$ to time T, $\tau' = T - \Delta t$ (i.e. after the price change). This says that the value of your current forward position has increased by $e^{-(r-\rho)\tau'} * (F'_{\Delta t,T} - F'_{0,T})$, and not by the undiscounted price change $F'_{\Delta t,T} - F'_{0,T}$.

If we think in terms of the profit figure on a risk-minimizing hedge for this scenario, the risk-minimizing hedge ratio is $e^{-(r-\rho)\tau'}$. This means that the profits on the forward position are $e^{-(r-\rho)\tau'} * (F'_{\Delta t,T} - F'_{0,T})$ over a short interval of time. This profit figure is simply the change in the forward price times a factor, $e^{-(r-\rho)\tau'}$, which is the risk-minimizing hedge ratio.

But this is how the profits on the forward position would *normally* be entered into the overall profit figure on the hedge simply because the raw price change, $(F'_{\Delta t,T} - F'_{0,T})$, is deferred until expiration. One can only put into the profit figure the *present value* of the raw price change on the forward position.

The conclusion is that the forward price hedge *automatically* adjusts for the risk-minimizing hedge ratio, so adding a separate hedge ratio would be double counting. The optimal hedge ratio for hedging with forward contracts is the naive, dollar equivalent, one-for-one hedge ratio (NHR).

Note that it isn't that forward prices do not require a matching of relative price moves. They do. However, the mechanism for creating this matching is *built into* forward price movements.

Futures contracts create *realized daily* cash flows in the form of daily settlement, so no waiting until realization of cash flows is required. Therefore, there is no discounting and daily settlement cash flows have to be hedged (discounted). The automatic adjustment that we just observed for forward hedging does not occur at the daily level for futures contracts.

So we can expect an adjustment to the NHR due to futures tailing. The adjustment is dynamic, and uses the changing discount factor $e^{-(r-\rho)\tau'}$. The technique behind tailing the hedge is to make the futures hedge replicate a forward hedge.

A more detailed discussion of tailing the hedge using futures contracts is beyond the scope of this text, and is discussed in the research literature.

7.5.8 Cross-Hedging, Adjusting the Hedge for non S&P 500 Portfolios

By now, you should appreciate the fact that hedging is both an art and a science. It can be a dynamic process that potentially involves numerous adjustments. We will see this later in our study of options hedging. Hedging applications also depend on the assumptions we make.

One of the assumptions made in our portfolio example is that the portfolio being hedged in S&P 500 futures *mirrors* the S&P 500 spot index. S&P 500 futures contracts are futures contracts designed to hedge movements in the underlying, which is the monetized spot index, $\$250*S\&P500_0$.

If a portfolio *does* mirror the underlying S&P 500 spot index, then we can assume that its *ordinary portfolio theory beta*, β_p, is equal to 1.0. Such a portfolio could be called an S&P *500 portfolio*. It isn't the portfolio underlying the S&P 500 index, but it mirrors it. The hedging impact of this assumption is that the instrument being hedged is, as far as its price behavior, identical to the instrument underlying the S&P 500 futures contract. We have a direct hedging vehicle capable of effectively hedging the instrument, and the portfolio manager's $20,000,000 can be naively hedged using S&P 500 futures contracts, with a possible adjustment for tailing.

However, a random portfolio may very well *not* be indexed to the S&P 500 spot index. We could call such a portfolio a *non-S&P 500 portfolio*. We can still use S&P 500 futures contracts to hedge our non-S&P 500 portfolio, but our hedge will be a *cross hedge*. That is, the hedge vehicle is written on an underlier *different* from the spot commodity we are trying to hedge.

The impact of *cross hedging* is basis risk. Cross hedging creates *extra* risks because the price behaviors of the spot instrument and the instrument underlying the futures contract would not be expected to mirror each other exactly. An example of a cross hedge is in attempting to hedge US hay, for which there are no futures contracts, using corn futures.

Figure 7.3 helps to explain how to adjust the hedge ratio for a cross hedge. The procedure is to adjust the hedge ratio for the portfolio's ordinary beta.

FIGURE 7.3 Hedging a Cross Hedge

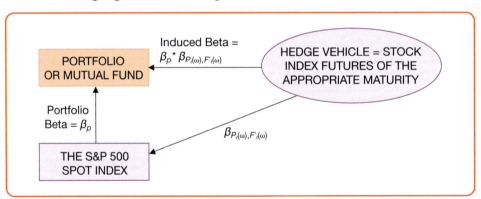

The ordinary portfolio beta, β_p, measures how the portfolio's value changes with changes in the S&P 500 spot index. That is our basic portfolio theory. Now we drill down to the next level. Changes in the S&P 500 stock index *futures* contract induce changes in the S&P 500 spot index based upon the beta of the spot on the futures, $\beta_{P_t(\omega),F'_t(\omega)}$, which measures that change.

Putting this information together, it follows that the beta of the portfolio on the S&P 500 stock index futures contract is $\beta_p * \beta_{P_t(\omega),F'_t(\omega)}$. This gives the co-movement in the portfolio being hedged with the S&P 500 stock index

FINANCIAL FUTURES CONTRACTS **245**

futures. Every time the futures price moves by one unit, the portfolio's price moves by $\beta_p * \beta_{P_t(\omega),F_t'(\omega)}$ units.

This means that we have to sell that many futures contracts to maintain dollar equivalency. For example, suppose that $\beta_{P_t(\omega),F_t'(\omega)}=0.8$ and that $\beta_p=3.0$. Then, the induced beta is 2.4 which means that, every time the futures price moves by one unit, the portfolio's price moves by 2.4 units.

The spot price moves much faster than the futures price. If, for each unit of spot portfolio we hold, we sell 2.4 futures contracts, then a one unit change in the futures price will correspond to a 2.4 unit change in the spot portfolio's price. This is equal to the change in the spot price, so we have matched price movements in the spot with price movements in the futures.

■ CONCEPT CHECK 6

Suppose that $\beta_p=0.90$ and that $\beta_{P_t(\omega),F_t'(\omega)}=0.75$.

a. Calculate the adjusted hedge ratio.

7.6 THE SPOT EURODOLLAR MARKET

The last financial futures contract that we want to discuss is also the world's most popular interest rate futures contract. It is also the most abstract.

Here are some numbers from futuresindustry.org showing that overall trading was up by 21.3% from the same period a year ago, with Eurodollar (ED) Futures ranked number 1 (by volume) of the world's 20 top interest rate futures and options contracts.

TABLE 7.7	Eurodollar Futures, CME (by Volume)				
Rank	Contract	Contract Size	Jan–Dec 2012	Jan–Dec 2013	% Change
1	Eurodollar Futures, CME	$1,000,000	426,438,437	517,250,183	21.3%

Source: FIA.org, Annual Volume Survey 2013, reprinted with permission.

FORWARD CONTRACTS AND FUTURES CONTRACTS

We started this chapter with currency futures, which are relatively straight-forward once FX risk is understood. Then we moved to stock index futures which are more abstract than currencies. Now we discuss LIBOR$_3$ futures which are quite abstract because the nominal underlier is a Eurodollar 3-month time deposit, but it is effectively the 3-month interest rate called LIBOR$_3$.

7.6.1 Spot 3-month Eurodollar Time Deposits

Our first objective is to get a rudimentary understanding of the spot Eurodollar (ED) time deposit market. That market is based upon ED time deposits with maturities ranging from 1 day to 5 years. The first problem is defining a spot Eurodollar (ED). Don't think of it as a US dollar 'sitting' in a non-US bank (e.g. in London). The international banking system is far too sophisticated for that interpretation to be correct.

Eurodollars are simply deposit *liabilities* of banks outside the USA that are denominated in US dollars.

The key to understanding Eurodollars is the word *liabilities*. The point being that foreign exchange transactions create assets and liabilities for the actors in those transactions, and US dollars to a non-US bank constitute a foreign currency.

The actual dollar size of the spot ED market is hard to determine because that market is unregulated and doesn't have to report to any government. However, the Bank for International Settlements (bis.org) collects data.

Also, the International Monetary Fund (imf.org) publishes some user-friendly numbers. Table 7.8 gives some useful information on the size of the market.

According to the IMF data, some $3,731,276,000,000 claims denominated in US$ were in the hands of foreign central banks outside the USA. That's almost $4 trillion dollars! Since banks and individuals can and do hold Eurodollars, the magnitude of all holdings could be much larger. Of course, there are foreign claims in other foreign currencies, most notably in Euros. US dollar claims accounted for 61.2% of the total allocated reserves, followed by Euro claims at 24.4%, as shown in Figure 7.4. Figure 7.5 is another representation of this data.

FINANCIAL FUTURES CONTRACTS

TABLE 7.8 Currency Composition of Foreign Exchange Reserves

(In millions of U.S. dollars)	2012-Q4	2013-Q1	2013-Q2	2013-Q3	2013-Q4
Total foreign exchange holidays	10,952,380	11,090,030	11,132,472	11,438,525	11,973,628
Allocated reserves	6,085,677	6,082,530	6,075,796	6,188,818	6,220,795
Claims in U.S. dollars	3,731,276	3,772,395	3,768,362	3,819,363	3,805,744
Claims in Pounds sterling	245,952	236,862	233,091	243,555	249,354
Claims in Japanese yen	248,780	239,914	237,098	239,933	244,804
Claims in Swiss francs	12,943	11,803	11,714	12,214	12,575
Claims in Canadian dollars	86,757	91,597	105,564	108,118	108,533
Claims in Australian dollars	88,511	97,955	100,499	101,123	100,141
Claims in Euros	1,474,397	1,435,117	1,450,987	1,491,583	1,520,969
Claims in other currencies	197,060	196,060	168,482	172,929	178,675
Unallocated reserves	4,866,703	5,007,500	5,056,677	5,249,707	5,452,832

Source: www.imf.org/external/np/sta/cofer/eng/index.htm (accessed May 27, 2015). Reprinted with permission of the International Monetary Fund (IMF), Data and Statistics, 'Currency Composition of Official Foreign Exchange Reserves (COFER)', March 31, 2014, Statistics Department of the IMF.

FIGURE 7.4 Currency Composition of Foreign Exchange Reserves (Pie Chart)

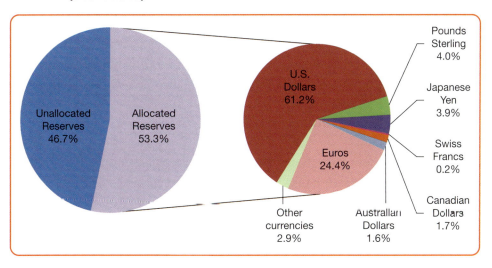

FIGURE 7.5 Currency Composition of Foreign Exchange Reserves (Graph)

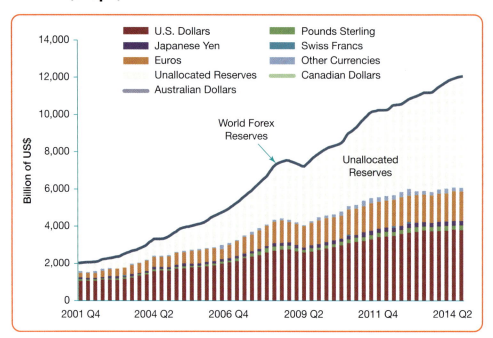

The definition of unallocated reserves is relevant here.

> Unallocated Reserves is the difference between the total foreign exchange reserves in the IFS (world table on Foreign Exchange) and the total allocated reserves in COFER. Thus Unallocated Reserves includes foreign exchange Reserves of those countries/territories that currently do not report to COFER but report the total foreign exchange reserves for publications in the IFS.
> (Source: email communication with StatisticsQuery@imf.org)

How do these claims come about? We will focus on one example of a *placement* of US dollars in a foreign bank. That is, of a *Eurodollar placement*.

7.6.2 Spot Eurodollar Market Trading Terminology

Placing Eurodollars means *selling* Eurodollars in return for Eurodollar time deposits. This is a lending scenario in which one bank *lends* another bank Eurodollars. One bank is exchanging one asset, say US$1,000,000, in return for another asset which in this case is a financial instrument, called a 3-month Eurodollar time deposit.

One easy way of rationalizing the terminology is to think in terms of (Euro) *dollars* vs. *securities* such as ED time deposits. When you *place* Eurodollars, you are giving them up (selling them), in return for something else. Now re-read the previous paragraph.

The investor (lender) pays US\$1,000,000 in return for a financial instrument that pays back the original principal plus interest at maturity in 3 months. The annualized (360 day) rate that the lender receives is called $LIBOR_3$.

$LIBOR_3$ is the rate at which prime London banks are willing to *lend* (make US dollar deposits) to other creditworthy banks in the interbank system. The 'OR' in $LIBOR_3$ indicates that it is an *offer* rate. Banks will *offer* 3-month US dollars in return for *receiving* $LIBOR_3/4$, where dividing by 4 represents the de-annualization appropriate for the 90-day holding period ($90/360=1/4$).

Taking Eurodollars means *buying* (receiving) Eurodollars in return for a Eurodollar time deposit *obligation*, which becomes the ED time deposit owner's liability to the lender who now owns the Eurodollar time deposit. This is a *borrowing* scenario. You are exchanging one asset, a financial asset in the form of a 3-month Eurodollar time deposit, in exchange for US\$1,000,000.

Again, one easy way of rationalizing the terminology is to think in terms of (Euro) *dollars* vs. *securities* such as ED time deposits. When you *take* Eurodollars, you are receiving them, in return for something else. Now re-read the previous paragraph.

The investor (lender) pays you US\$1,000,000 in return for a financial instrument that pays back the original principal plus interest at maturity in 3 months. The rate attached to this transaction is called $LIBID_3$.

$LIBID_3$ is the rate at which London banks are willing to *borrow* (receive US dollar deposits) from other credit worthy banks in the interbank system. The 'ID' in $LIBID_3$ indicates that it is a *bid* (buy=borrow) rate. Banks will accept 3-month US dollar deposits in return for *paying* $LIBID_3/4$. $LIBID_3$ is currently usually 0.125% lower than $LIBOR_3$.

So *selling Eurodollars* means *lending (offering) Eurodollars*. And *buying Eurodollars* means *borrowing (bidding for) them*. This is analogous to the situation in Federal Funds (FF) which are *excess reserves* traded, usually on an overnight basis, between Federal Reserve banks in the interbank FF market.

Selling FF means that one bank lends them to another bank effectively in return for receiving an FF time deposit (the promise of the return of the principal plus interest). Buying FF means that one bank borrows them from

250 FORWARD CONTRACTS AND FUTURES CONTRACTS

another bank, in return for paying principal plus interest to the lender at the end of the borrowing period. That is, in return for honoring the obligations incurred in the borrowing transaction.

An easy mnemonic is B in LIBID means buy or borrow Eurodollars. The O in LIBOR means offer or sell Eurodollars. It is also useful and important to think in terms of buying and selling *rates* such as the $LIBOR_3$, particularly when thinking about what position one has *in a rate* and therefore how to hedge that rate. We will discuss this important skill in Chapter 8 on swaps.

■ CONCEPT CHECK 7

1. Fill in Table 7.9.

TABLE 7.9 **Buying or Selling Spot Eurodollars**

	Placing (P) or Taking (T)	Position, Explicit Long (EL) or Explicit Short (ES)	Borrowing (B) or Lending (L)
Buy Eurodollars			
Sell Eurodollars			

■ CONCEPT CHECK 8

Consider a bank in the spot ED market that borrows $100,000,000.

a. At what annualized rate would the bank borrow?
b. Suppose the bank immediately lends out the $100,000,000. What annualized rate would the bank earn on its investment?
c. Is the above set of transactions an arbitrage opportunity?

7.6.3 $LIBOR_3$, $LIBID_3$, and Fed Funds

The annualized lending rate corresponding to a 3-month Eurodollar time deposit is called $LIBOR_3$ (London Interbank Offered Rate). Annual in the world of LIBOR means 360 days, by market convention. A 3-month (90 days) Eurodollar time deposit earns interest at the rate $LIBOR_3*(90/360)$ $=LIBOR_3/4$.

So, on $1,000,000 that amounts to $1,000,000*LIBOR$_3$/4. Say LIBOR$_3$= 3%. Interest would be,

$$1,000,000 * \frac{.03}{4} = \$1,000,000 * .0075$$
$$= \$7,500$$

On a Eurodollar placement of US$50,000,000 that amounts to 50*$7500= $375,000 which is not a bad 3 months work.

Fed Funds are quoted in exactly the same way, except that most FF transactions are on an overnight basis. They pay the de-annualized overnight Fed Funds rate (FFR) which would be FFR*(1/360)=FFR/360. It turns out that annualized LIBOR$_3$ and annualized FF are closely related. Why?

Figure 7.6, from the St. Louis Fed. indicates some fairly recent data. The blue graph represents LIBOR$_3$, based on the US dollar. The red graph represents the effective federal funds rate. The Federal reserve Bank of New York (newyorkfed.org) has all the definitions.

FIGURE 7.6 LIBOR$_3$ vs. Fed Funds

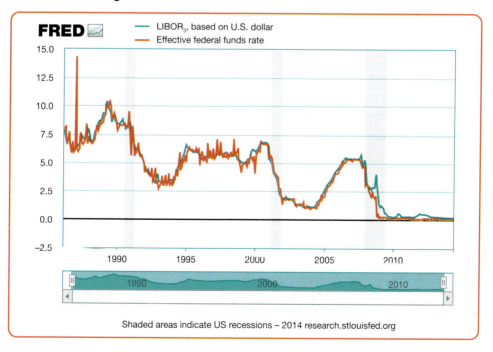

FORWARD CONTRACTS AND FUTURES CONTRACTS

There is no doubt that arbitrage drives the rates together. Of course, there is credit risk associated with Eurodollar time deposits with presumably little in the FF market. The *OIS* (average FF)–LIBOR *spread* is one of the spreads that market participants look at in order to monitor changes in credit and illiquidity risk which show up quickly in these active markets.

For example on the date June 23, 2014 $LIBOR_3$ was 0.23260%. $LIBID_3$ is typically about 1/8 % below $LIBOR_3$. These are virtually at 0.0.

7.6.4 How Eurodollar Time Deposits are Created

The next step in understanding the spot ED time deposit market is to run through an example showing how such deposits are created. This example owes a debt to *Stigum's Money Market* (McGraw-Hill, 2007), an excellent book written by Marcia Stigum.

Let's suppose that a wealthy US resident, say Warren Buffett (WB), decides to make a $100,000,000 Eurodollar placement in the London office of Bank of America (B of A).

Currently, WB has demand deposits in at least that amount of US dollars at Wells Fargo Bank (WF). He arranges a ED deposit by simply writing a cheque for $100,000,000 on his Wells Fargo account to B of A.

Wells Fargo does not cart over (or ship) the physical currency in the amount of $100,000,000 from WF and deposits it in the vaults of the London Branch of B of A. That's obviously absurd, and also not necessary. Both WF and the *New York branch* of B of A are *members* of the Federal Reserve system, and as such have accounts at the Fed.

This opens the door to the magic of accounting. The first effects of WB's drawing a cheque for $100MM are threefold. First, the effect on his balance sheet would be that his demand deposits at WF would *decrease* by $100MM. The second effect would be that reserves at WF would also *decline* by $100MM. Thirdly, the reserves at B of A (NY) would *increase* by $100MM, reflecting the transfer.

Let us illustrate these effects on the *T-accounts* (assets and liabilities) of these three economic units, WB, WF, and B of A (NY).

Please note several things here,

a. The exchange by WB through the ED placement shows up in his balance sheet as a *reduction in demand deposits* at WF of $100MM, but also as an *increase in financial assets* (ED time deposits) of $100MM.

FINANCIAL FUTURES CONTRACTS 253

FIGURE 7.7 Eurodollar Deposit Creation

WB's Balance Sheet

Assets	Liabilities
Demand Deposits @ WF −$100MM *ED Time Deposits* +100MM	

WF's Balance Sheet

Assets	Liabilities
Reserves −$100MM	*Demand Deposits* (*Liabilities to* WB) −$100MM

B of A's (NY) Balance Sheet

Assets	Liabilities
Reserves +$100MM	*Demand Deposits* (*Liability to* B of A (London)) +$100MM

B of A's (London) Balance Sheet

Assets	Liabilities
IOU from *B of A (NY)* +$100MM	*Time Deposit* (*Liability to* B of A (NY)) +$100MM

FED's Balance Sheet

Assets	Liabilities
	DD Liability to WF −100MM DD Liability to B of A (NY) +100MM

WB is exchanging one asset, US$100,000,000 for another financial asset (the ED time deposit).

b. WF's reserves declined by the withdrawal of $100MM. But now WF owes WB $100MM less. Therefore its liability to WB also declines by $100MM.

c. B of A's (NY) reserves went up by the amount of the deposit transferred from WF to B of A (NY), by $100MM.

So far it doesn't look like a Eurodollar account because the $100MM is in the NY branch of B of A. But it will remain there. There is no need to physically transfer anything.

Instead, B of A (NY) makes a *book entry* on its *liability* side that it *owes* B of A (London) $100MM.

d. The Fed is the (centralized) banker to its member banks, so to accomplish the transfer all it has to do are two book entries recording the transfer on its liabilities side.

The first decreases the liability it has to WF because the $100MM is no longer owed by the FED to WF. It is now owed to B of A (NY). That's what cheque writing does.

So the second book entry is the FED's increased liability to B of A (NY) which is recorded as +$100MM.

e. The only account missing here is that of B of A (London) which is a branch of the B of A entity. B of A London has an IOU from B of A (NY) in the amount of $100MM. It records it as an increase in its assets as such. But it also has a liability in the form of the $100 ED time deposit which Warren Buffett now owns. Someone has to pay WB. It records that as well. This closes the loop.

Note that book entry is the way to go. Eurodollars stay in the US. This should make it clear why it is not correct to think of Eurodollars as US dollars in non-US bank accounts. They are not. What is important to making the original transaction economically sound is simply that the asset and liabilities it creates are recorded.

7.7 EURODOLLAR FUTURES

Now that we have done all the necessary work to understand the spot ED market, ED futures are relatively straightforward. First, they constitute an *Interest Rate Derivative* (IRD).

Second, they are one of the slickest interest rate futures contract available today, and one of the most popular. Their connection to swaps is important as well, so this is part of the groundwork necessary for understanding Chapter 8.

One has to watch out for terminology shifts when thinking about ED futures vs. spot Eurodollars (see Table 7.9 and Table 7.11)

7.7.1 Contract Specifications

See Table 7.10.

FINANCIAL FUTURES CONTRACTS 255

TABLE 7.10 **Eurodollar Futures**

Underlying Instrument	Eurodollar time deposit having a principal value of USD $1,000,000 with a three-month maturity.
Price Quote	Quoted in IMM Three-Month LIBOR index points or 100 minus the rate on an annual basis over a 360 day year (e.g., a rate of 2.5% shall be quoted as 97.50). 1 basis point = .01 = $25.
Tick Size (minimum fluctuation)	One-quarter of one basis point (0.0025 = $6.25 per contract) in the nearest expiring contract month; One-half of one basis point (0.005 = $12.50 per contract) in all other contract months. The "new" front-month contract begins trading in 0.0025 increments on the same Trade Date as the Last Trading Day of the expiring "old" front-month contract.
Contract Months	Mar, Jun, Sep, Dec, extending out 10 years (total of 40 contracts) plus the four nearest serial expirations (months that are not in the March quarterly cycle). The new contract month terminating 10 years in the future is listed on the Tuesday following expiration of the front quarterly contract month.
Last Trading Day	The second London bank business day prior to the third Wednesday of the contract expiry month. Trading in the expiring contract closes at 11:00 a.m. London Time on the last trading day.
Settlement Procedure	Final Eurodollar Futures Settlement Procedure (PDF) Daily Eurodollar Futures Settlement Procedure (PDF)
Position Limits	None
Block Minimum	Block Trading Minimums
All or None Minimum	All or None Minimums
Rulebook Chapter	CME Chapter 452
Trading Hours (All times listed are Central Time)	OPEN OUTCRY MON–FRI: 7:20 a.m.–2:00 p.m. CME GLOBEX SUN–FRI: 5:00 p.m.–4:00 p.m. CT
Ticker Symbol	OPEN OUTCRY ED CME GLOBEX GE
Exchange Rule	These contracts are listed with, and subject to, the rules and regulations of CME.

Reprinted with permission from CME Group Inc., 2014.

7.7.2 The Quote Mechanism, Eurodollar Futures

The main features of this contract are:

1. The nominal underlier of the ED futures contract is a spot 3-month non-negotiable, Eurodollar time deposit with a face value of $1,000,000 (denominated in US dollars).

■ CONCEPT CHECK 9

TABLE 7.11 'Buying' and 'Selling' Eurodollar Futures

	Position in underlier	Future Borrowing (FB) or Future Lending (FL)
Buy ED Futures		
Sell ED Futures		

a.   Fill in Table 7.11.

Please note the difference between buy and sell positions in ED *spot* and 'buy' (long) and 'sell' (short) positions in ED *futures*.

2. The price quote is in terms of a *futures index* which is 100 minus the *Futures* LIBOR$_3$ (we will call this FLIBOR$_3$), not expressed as a decimalized percentage.

So a *Futures* LIBOR$_3$ of 2.5 would be quoted as a futures index value of 100–2.50=97.5. A *basis point* is .0001 (one hundredth of a percent written as a decimal) interest on $1,000,000 over 3 months which equals,

$$.0001 * \$1,000,000 * \left(\frac{90}{360}\right) = \frac{\$100}{4}$$

$$= \$25$$

Keep in mind what a forward (futures) contract is. It is an agreement to buy/sell an underlying commodity, in this case the 3-month Eurodollar time deposit (a financial instrument) *for future delivery* at a price agreed upon today. So the ED futures contract refers to something that doesn't even necessarily currently exist, an ED time deposit that, *on the expiration date*, has 3 months to maturity. That is, a *newly issued* 3-month ED time deposit that we have been discussing. (A longer maturity ED time deposit with 3 months left to maturity at expiration could also be delivered. For example, a spot 6-month ED time deposit with 3 months left.)

The *future* interest rate underlying a spot 3-month ED time deposit is the currently unknown $\text{LIBOR}_{3,T}(\omega)$ where T is the expiration date of the futures contract and $\text{LIBOR}_{3,T}$ means LIBOR_3 on that date.

If the expiration date of the futures contract is two months from today, then the futures contract refers to the 3-month LIBOR, $T=2$ months from today. Figure 7.8 is a schematic,

FIGURE 7.8 Timing in Eurodollar Futures

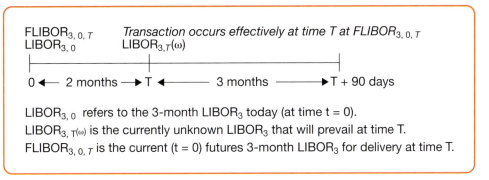

You can think of this as a pure bet (if you are a pure speculator) on the $\text{LIBOR}_{3,T}(\omega)$. If you are a hedger, you would think of it as the spot $\text{LIBOR}_{3,0}$ plus the cost of carry.

3. These contracts are so liquid that the *tick size,* the minimum move in the futures index, is one quarter of one basis point. Since one basis point has a dollar equivalent of $25 as we calculated, one quarter of one basis point has a dollar equivalent of $25/4=$6.25. Since the nearby contract is typically the most liquid, it price movement is fine-tuned the most. One half of a basis point is the tick size in all other contracts and has a dollar equivalent of $25/2= $12.50.

4. *Contracts offered* in the ED futures contract follow the March cycle (Mar, Jun, Sep, Dec.). Delivery months include 'the four nearest serial expirations (months that are not in the March quarterly cycle)' and they extend out for 10 years!

There is liquidity not only in the nearby contract. For example, Table 7.12 gives data from the trade date 10/25/2013. The four nearest serial month contracts are indicated.

The total *volume* across *all* contracts was 1,196,825 contracts for a nominal principal value of 1,196,825*$1,000,000=$1,196,825,000,000 or about 1.2 trillion US dollars.

Open interest was much larger (8 times) at 9,588,809 with a nominal principal value of 9,588,809*$1,000,000=$9,588,809,000,000, or about 9.6 trillion US dollars!

7.7.3 Forced Convergence and Cash Settlement

5. *Delivery* is not physical. These are *cash-settled* contracts just like the S&P 500 futures we studied. To reiterate, what this actually means is that absolutely nothing gets delivered at expiration, except for the daily cash value of the open futures position (for the last day) from the 'losing' party to the 'winning party'. Only the cash flow implications of one's open futures positions have to be reconciled. This was explained in Chapter 5.

The question is how to determine daily settlement variation on the last day, which is the same thing as determining the final settlement price. We know that futures trading only makes sense if there is convergence to the ultimate spot price. Here is the relevant quote from the CME Rule Book, Chapter 452.

45203.A. Final Settlement Price

The final settlement price of an expiring contract shall be 100 minus the *spot* [my emphasis] three-month Eurodollar interbank time deposit rate determined at the British Bankers' Association (BBA) LIBOR fixing on the second London bank Business Day immediately preceding the third Wednesday of the contract's named month of delivery. The value of such three-month Eurodollar interbank time deposit rate shall be rounded to the nearest 1/10,000th of a percentage point per annum. Tie values, *i.e.*, any such values ending in 0.00005 shall be rounded up. For example, a Three-Month BBA LIBOR fixing value of 8.65625% would be rounded up to 8.6563%, and then subtracted from 100 to determine a contract final settlement price of 91.3437.

(Reprinted with permission from CME Group Inc., 2014)

FINANCIAL FUTURES CONTRACTS · 259

TABLE 7.12 **Daily Settlements for Eurodollar Future Futures (Final)**

Trade Date: 10/25/2013
(Last Updated 10/25/2013 06:00 PM)

Month	Open	High	Low	Last	Change	Settle	Estimated Volume	Prior Day Open Interest
NOV 13	99.7600	99.7650	99.7600	–	+.0050	99.7625	8,486	42,591
DEC 13	99.7500	99.7550	99.7450	99.7500	UNCH	99.7500	72,761	879,949
JAN 14	99.7400	99.7450	99.7400	–	UNCH	99.7400	903	14,785
FEB 14	–	–	–	–	+.0050	99.7300	0	73
MAR 14	99.7100	99.7150	99.7050	99.7100	UNCH	99.7100	60,944	814,250
APR 14	–	–	–	–	+.0050	99.7000	0	0
JUN 14	99.6650	99.6750	99.6650	99.6700	UNCH	99.6700	58,982	776,182
SEP 14	99.6150	99.6250	99.6150	99.6200B	+.0050	99.6200	53,376	602,932
DEC 14	99.5350	99.5500	99.5350	99.5450A	+.0050	99.5450	86,744	899,264
MAR 15	99.4350	99.4550	99.4350	99.4450A	+.0050	99.4450	79,486	567,571
JUN 15	99.3050	99.3350	99.3050	99.3250A	+.0100	99.3200	106,087	784,846
SEP 15	99.1550	99.1850	99.1500	99.1750A	+.0200	99.1750	84,788	821,342
DEC 15	98.9600	98.9950	98.9550	98.9850A	+.0250	98.9850	145,342	814,890
MAR 16	98.7400	98.7750	98.7300	98.7700A	+.0300	98.7650	72,431	501,655
JUN 16	98.4900	98.5350	98.4850	98.5250A	+.0350	98.5250	78,308	334,029
SEP 16	98.2200	98.2750	98.2200	98.2650A	+.0400	98.2650	59,967	346,316
DEC 16	97.9600	98.0150	97.9550	98.0100B	+.0450	98.0100	65,427	364,916
MAR 17	97.7250	97.7900	97.7250	97.7800A	+.0500	97.7800	33,737	252,601
JUN 17	97.4850	97.5500	97.4850	97.5400A	+.0550	97.5450	26,874	177,433
SEP 17	97.2700	97.3300	97.2700	97.3200A	+.0550	97.3250	24,099	143,090
DEC 17	97.0450	97.1100	97.0450	97.1000A	+.0500	97.1000	35,238	159,853
MAR 18	96.8600	96.9150	96.8600	96.9100A	+.0500	96.9100	12,750	99,663
JUN 18	96.6950	96.7350	96.6900	96.7300A	+.0450	96.7250	11,382	72,745
SEP 18	96.5250	96.5700	96.5250	96.5650B	+.0400	96.5600	12,092	31,924
DEC 18	96.4000	96.4200	96.3750	–	+.0350	96.4050	2,451	25,734
MAR 19	96.2600	96.2850	96.2550	–	+.0300	96.2750	1,239	10,679
JUN 19	96.1450	96.1650	96.1300	–	+.0250	96.1550	804	9,561
SEP 19	96.0400	96.0550	96.0200	–	+.0200	96.0450	1,072	6,773
DEC 19	95.9350	95.9500	95.9150A	–	+.0150	95.9400	423	8,007
MAR 20	95.8550	95.8750	95.8350A	–	+.0100	95.8600	207	5,491
JUN 20	95.7750	95.7950B	95.7550A	–	+.0050	95.7800	207	4,542
SEP 20	95.7250	95.7300	95.6900A	–	UNCH	95.7100	218	1,801
DEC 20	–	–	–	–	UNCH	95.6450	0	1,157
MAR 21	–	–	–	–	+.0050	95.6050	0	2,287
JUN 21	–	–	–	–	+.0050	95.5450	0	4,106
SEP 21	–	–	–	–	+.0050	95.5000	0	724
DEC 21	–	–	–	–	+.0050	95.4500	0	510

TABLE 7.12 Daily Settlements for Eurodollar Future Futures (Final)—continued

MAR 22	–	–	–	–	+.0050	95.4250	0	506
JUN 22	–	–	–	–	+.0050	95.4000	0	999
SEP 22	–	–	–	–	+.0050	95.3650	0	1,384
DEC 22	–	–	–	–	+.0050	95.3300	0	499
MAR 23	–	–	–	–	+.0050	95.3050	0	628
JUN 23	–	–	–	–	+.0050	95.2700	0	519
SEP 23	–	–	–	–	+.0050	95.2450	0	2
Total							1,196,825	9,588,809

Reprinted with permission from CME Group Inc., 2014.

Rule 45203.A is describing *'forced convergence'*. Normally, the pressures of arbitrage will make the futures price on an expiring futures contract converge to the spot price in the market. Otherwise, net of transactions costs, there would be an arbitrage opportunity. Forced convergence makes this happen, regardless of natural arbitrage. Going back to the usual schematic in Figure 7.9, remember that all futures contracts are subject to daily settlement.

FIGURE 7.9 Forced Convergence of ED Futures

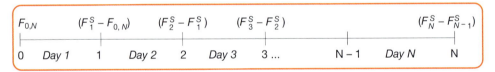

Forced convergence sets the final settlement price on day N (expiration date of the contract) $F_N^S = P_N$, the spot price on day N.

Here is the settlement procedure for the last day.

45203.B. Final Settlement

Clearing members holding open positions in a contract at the time of termination of trading in that contract shall make payment to or receive payment from the Clearing House in accordance with normal variation performance bond procedures based on a settlement price equal to the final settlement price.

Reprinted with permission from CME Group Inc., 2014)

FINANCIAL FUTURES CONTRACTS 261

Rule 45203.B describes what is meant by *cash* settlement. If you take a long position in a futures or a forward contract and the spot price at expiration is higher than the price at which you bought the commodity forward, $P_N > F_{0,N}$, then you made an overall profit equal to $P_N - F_{0,N}$.

The corresponding short would have incurred an overall loss because the profit (loss) to the short is $F_{0,N} - P_N$ which in this case would be negative. This overall profit or loss on a futures contract, as opposed to a forward contract, is not paid out as a lump sum in this manner. Rather, the same effective profit (loss) comes, and is received daily, in the form of daily settlements as described in Chapter 5.

Final cash settlement means that the longs and shorts would each have to pay up or be paid the respective daily values of their *last* day's futures positions based on the final settlement price being equated to the ultimate spot price in the cash market. Hence the term *cash* settlement.

In order to make the final profit figure work out to what it should be, cash settlement requires that daily settlement on the last day, $F_N^S - F_{N-1}^S$, must be equal to $P_N - F_{N-1}^S$. It will be so equal if and only if $F_N^S = P_N$.

6. There are no position limits in the ED futures, so you can load up on as many short or long positions as you want.

7. *The Ticker* symbol for ED Futures depends on the trading venue because it is dual traded using open outcry and on Globex. The symbol on open outcry is ED and the symbol is GE on Globex. Please note that this applies before July 6, 2015. After that date, open outcry (pit) trading was ended for most futures contracts on the CME.

8. There are no daily price limits on ED futures.

9. The remaining entries are more or less self-explanatory. In cases of doubt, one refers to the CME literature.

■ CONCEPT CHECK 10

Suppose that the long in an ED futures contract wants to obtain the underlying spot 3-month Eurodollar time deposit as an investment vehicle.

a. *Since the contract is cash settled, what would he have to do?*

7.7.4 How Profits and Losses are Calculated on Open ED Futures Positions

In this section we will take a look at how traders would calculate profits (losses) on open ED futures positions. We will take some numbers away from zero in order to make the presentation clearer. An important clarification is needed before we do the profit (loss) calculations.

Think in terms of buying or selling the *forward* $LIBOR_3$ *rate*, $FLIBOR_{3,0,T}$, at time $t=0$. *Buying the* $LIBOR_3$ today for *forward* delivery at the fixed rate $FLIBOR_{3,0,T}$ means that you are buying a fixed rate for investment (lending) at time T.

Selling the $LIBOR_3$ today for *forward* delivery at the fixed rate $FLIBOR_{3,0,T}$ means that you are selling a fixed rate for borrowing at time T.

Cash settlement means that when time T arrives, you make the lending or borrowing transaction in the spot 3-month ED time deposit market. You will have settlement variation in hand at that time which will determine the effective lending or borrowing rate you locked in at time $t=0$.

Example

Suppose that it is October 17, 2013 (time $t=0$) and that the current, nearby (December 2013) ED futures price (quoted as an Index) is 96.00.

A trader takes a *long* position in 10 December 2013 ED futures contracts. Since the trader went long the ED futures contracts, that trader is buying an investment rate,

$$\frac{FLIBOR_{3,0,T}}{4} = \frac{100 - 96.00}{4}$$
$$= 1.0\%$$

for the subsequent 3-month period, starting on the delivery date in December 2013. This is the effective forward rate that the trader is locking in today.

What subsequently happens depends on what $LIBOR_{3,T}(\omega)$ turns out to be at time T.

FINANCIAL FUTURES CONTRACTS   263

Case 1 (LIBOR$_3$ goes down)

Suppose that LIBOR$_{3,T}(\omega_{\text{Down}})$=2.00 % on an annualized basis. Note that by forced convergence F_T^S=100–P_T=98.00. The investor would lend \$10,000,000 in the spot market for 3 months at (100–98.00)/4=2.00%/4.

\$10,000,000 invested at 0.5% for 3 months generates interest of \$10,000,000 *(.005)=\$50,000 which appears as quite a disappointing investment result.

However, there is settlement variation gained on the 10 long ED futures position. Let's calculate that the way a trader would. The futures price went from $F_{0,T}$=96.00 to F_T^S=100–P_T=98.00. What does this mean to the trader?

It means that the trader bought the 3-month lending rate of 4%/4=1% at time T and he also effectively sold (borrowed at) the 3-month borrowing rate of 2%/4=.50% at time T.

The dollar profits on this transaction at time T+3 months would be equal to \$10,000,000*(.005)=\$50,000. Therefore, the trader has actually earned \$100,000 on his investment at time T: the \$50,000 from the spot ED time deposit investment plus the \$50,000 in profits on his long ED Futures position.

This corresponds to a 3-month HPR rate of return of (\$10,100,000–\$10,000,000)/\$10,000,000=.01 over the period $[T,T+3]$. On an annual basis, this is 4*.01=4%, which is precisely what the trader contracted at at time 0 because FLIBOR$_{3,0,T}$=100–96.00=4.00%.

In order to calculate the profits on his long ED futures position, the trader would take a short cut and calculate his profit or loss in basis points. First, the futures (index) price went up from 96.00 to 98.00. A movement of the futures index up constitutes a profit on a long position. That's why the futures price is quoted this way: futures index up (down) means profit (loss) on long futures positions. The rationale, of course, is that the prices of the underlying financial securities are inversely related to interest rates.

One basis point on a single ED futures contract has a dollar equivalent value of \$25. The trader is long 10 contracts and the basis point move in the index was up by 2.00%=200 basis points. This generates a gain of 10*200*\$25=\$50,000 as calculated in the long manner.

Case 2 (LIBOR$_3$ goes up)

Suppose that LIBOR$_{3,T}(\omega_{\text{Up}})$=6.00 % on an annualized basis. Note that, by forced convergence, F_T^S=100–P_T=94.00. The investor would lend \$10,000,000 in the spot market for 3 months at,

$$\frac{100 - 94.00}{4} = \frac{6.00\%}{4}$$
$$= 1.5\%$$

$10,000,000 invested at .015 for 3 months generates interest of $10,000,000 $*(.015)=\$150,000$ which appears as quite a fantastic investment result. It looks like the trader made a killing in the lending market.

However, there is settlement variation lost on the 10 long ED futures position. Let's calculate that the way a trader would. The futures price went from $100\text{–FLIBOR}_{3,0,T}=96.00(\text{FLIBOR}_{3,0,T}=4.00\%)$ to $F_T^S=100-P_T=94.00$ $(P_T=\text{LIBOR}_{3,T}\omega_{Up})=6.00\%)$.

What does this mean to the trader? It means that the trader gets to buy the 3-month lending rate of 4%/4=1% at time T, and he also sold (gets to borrow) the 3-month borrowing rate of 6%/4=1.50% at time T.

The dollar profits (loss) on this transaction at time $T+3$ months would be equal to $10,000,000*(.01-.015)=-\$50,000$. Therefore, the trader has actually earned $100,000=\$150,000-\$50,000$ on his investment at time T: the $150,000 from the spot ED time deposit investment minus the $50,000 in losses on his long ED futures position.

This corresponds to a 3-month HPR rate of return of ($10,100,000–$10,000,000)/$10,000,000=.01. On an annual basis this is 4*.01=4%, which is again precisely what the trader contracted at at time 0 because $\text{FLIBOR}_{3,0,T}=100-96.00=4.00\%$.

In order to calculate the profits on his long ED futures position the trader could take a short cut, and calculate his profit or loss in basis points. First, the futures (index) price went *down* from 96.00 to 94.00. A movement of the futures index down constitutes a loss on a *long* position.

One basis point on a single ED futures contract has a dollar equivalent value of $25. The trader is long 10 contracts and the basis point move in the index was down by 2.00%=200 basis points. This generates a loss of 10*200*$25=$50,000 as calculated in the long manner.

We will end this chapter here, because we have set the stage for the next chapter where we will continue the discussion of hedging using ED futures, and we will introduce swaps. Swaps are very closely related to strips of ED futures and such strips are actually used to hedge positions in swaps. That will be our main example of hedging using ED futures.

FINANCIAL FUTURES CONTRACTS   265

■ KEY CONCEPTS

1. A Financial Futures Contract is like any other Futures Contract, only the Underlier is different.
2. Currency Futures as a way to Manage Exchange Rate Risk.
3. Contract Specifications.
4. Reading Futures Price Quotes.
5. Daily Settlements.
6. Types of Exchange Rate Risk.
7. Position Types, Long vs. Short.
8. Classifying Positions in Currency Futures vs. Currency Forwards.
9. Lufthansa example, DMs vs. Euros.
10. Risk Management using Currency Futures: the Rolling Hedge.
11. Profits from the Rolling Hedge.
12. Interpreting Rolling Hedge Profits.
13. Metallgesellschaft Disaster.
14. Hedging as Speculating on the Basis.
15. Was Metallgesellschaft a Hedger or a Speculator?
16. Currency Futures vs. Currency Forward Pricing.
17. Quantity Uncertainty vs. Price Uncertainty in Hedging.
18. Stock Index Futures.
19. S&P 500 Stock Index Futures Contract Specifications.
20. The Quote Mechanism, S&P 500 Futures Price Quotes.
21. Risk Management Using Stock Index Futures.
22. Pricing and Hedging Preliminaries.
23. Monetizing the S&P 500 Spot Index.
24. Profits from the Traditional Hedge.
25. Risk, Return Analysis of the Traditional Hedge.
26. Risk-Minimizing Hedging.
27. Adjusting the Naive Hedge Ratio to obtain the Risk-Minimizing Hedge Ratio.
28. Risk Minimizing the Hedge using Forward Contracts.
29. Adjusting the Hedge for non S&P 500 Portfolios.
30. The Spot Eurodollar Market.
31. Spot Eurodollar 3-month Time Deposits.
32. Spot Eurodollar Market Trading Terminology.
33. $LIBOR_3$, $LIBID_3$, and Fed Funds.
34. How Eurodollar Time Deposits are Created.

266 FORWARD CONTRACTS AND FUTURES CONTRACTS

35. Eurodollar Futures.
36. Contract Specifications.
37. The Quote Mechanism: Eurodollar Futures.
38. Forced Convergence and Cash Settlement.
39. How Profits and Losses are Calculated on Open ED Futures Positions.

■ END OF CHAPTER EXERCISES FOR CHAPTER 7

1. a. Rewrite the equilibrium forward pricing relationship by solving it for the spot price.
    b. Interpret the spot price in a.

2. Given the data r=5.5%, ρ=3.2% and τ=6 months, a portfolio manager has $100,000,000 invested in a portfolio which he wishes to protect by hedging in S&P 500 stock index futures. Assume that the current value of the spot S&P 500 index is 2,000.

    a. Calculate the naive hedge ratio (NHR).
    b. Calculate the optimal hedge ratio.

3. This exercise shows what happens when $r<\rho$. Given the data r=3.2%, ρ=5.5% and τ=6 months, a portfolio manager has $100,000,000 invested in a portfolio which he wishes to protect by hedging in S&P 500 stock index futures. Assume that the current value of the spot S&P 500 index is 2,000.

    a. Calculate the naive hedge ratio.
    b. Calculate the optimal hedge ratio.

4. This exercise is about interpreting $\dfrac{VP_0}{\$250 * e^{(r-\rho)\tau} * I_0} = \dfrac{VP_0}{\$250 * F'_{0,T}}$

    Think of VP_0 as the spot price of the portfolio being hedged. $\$250*F'_{0,T}$ is a futures S&P 500 unit in dollars.

    a. Interpret $VP_0/(\$250*F'_{0,T})$.

FINANCIAL FUTURES CONTRACTS

5. Consider a US importer who imports goods from the UK. Let's say that in one month's time, the importer will have to pay for the goods. The UK exporter expects to receive BP for the goods and hence the US importer is subject to FX risk.

   a. What position does the US importer currently have in the FX market?
   b. What risk is the US importer subject to due to his position in a.?
   c. In order to hedge using forward contracts, what position in forward FX would the US importer have to take?
   d. In order to hedge using FX futures contracts, what position in futures FX would the US importer have to take?

6. This exercise is for our portfolio manager's $20,000,000 portfolio.
   Suppose that $\beta_{P_t(\omega),F'_t(\omega)}=0.9$. The one extra piece of information that we need is the (ordinary) portfolio beta which we estimate to be $\beta_p=2.0$.

   a. What is the adjusted hedge ratio?

7. a. Calculate $LIBID_3$, assuming that $LIBOR_3=0.23260\%$.

8. Given the data above in exercise 7, suppose that a bank borrows US$100,000,000 for three months (90 days) and lends it out for three months.

   a. What is the 90 day de-annualized borrowing rate?
   b. What is the 90 day de-annualized lending rate?
   c. How much (in US dollars) does the bank earn?

9. This exercise is for the case wherein $LIBOR_3$ goes down. Start with Figure 7.8 reproduced below.

   a. What is time 0?
   b. What is time T?
   c. What would the investor do at time T?

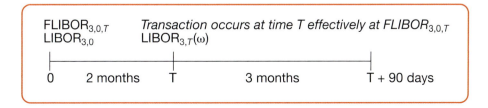

10. This exercise is for the case wherein $LIBOR_3$ goes up. Start with Figure 7.8,

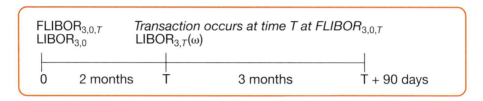

a. What is time 0?
b. What is time T?
c. What would the investor do at time T?

■ SELECTED CONCEPT CHECK SOLUTIONS

Concept Check 1

a. Since Lufthansa is a German firm, it will most likely use its own DM currency to buy the US$500,000,000. It could have reserves of other currencies. However, these would have to be exchanged for US dollars at some point. The exchange would be subject to exchange rate risk. Even if it had US dollar reserves, there would still be an opportunity cost associated to the exchange rate between the US dollar and the DM one year from today.
b. Lufthansa could wait a year and then buy the $500 million with DM at the going exchange rate in the spot FX market. This would expose it to exchange rate risk.

   Alternatively Lufthansa could currently buy forward the $500 million (sell forward the appropriate number of DM) at the current going forward rate for delivery of deutsche mark in one year. This would eliminate the exchange rate risk.

Concept Check 2

a. FX is not a raw material to Lufthansa unless FX is used as part of its regular operations.
b. Lufthansa's exposure in the jet fuel market is periodic and occurs on a regular basis. Lufthansa only occasionally buys jet planes. However, the

FINANCIAL FUTURES CONTRACTS 269

magnitude of the transaction is so large that it is worth considering and hedging.

Concept Check 4

a. You would receive the *invoice price*, as for any futures contract. The invoice price is the spot price at expiration, $\$250*S\&P500_1(\omega)$.
b. The *effective price* you would receive for one S&P 500 spot index unit is the forward price you contracted at, $\$250*1020.201$.
c. Thinking of a futures contract as a 'fancy' forward contract, the profit on a short forward position is the forward price minus the ultimate spot price (see Chapter 3, section 3.4).

   That is, $250*1020.201-\$250*S\&P500_1(\omega)$. Therefore, you made money if $\$250*1020.201>\$250*S\&P500_1(\omega)$ and you lost money if $\$250*1020.201<\$250*S\&P500_1(\omega)$.

Concept Check 6

Suppose that $\beta_p=0.90$ and that $\beta_{P_t(\omega),F_t'(\omega)}=0.75$.

a. The adjusted hedge ratio$=\beta_p*\beta_{P_t(\omega),F_t'(\omega)}=0.90* 0.75=0.675$.

Concept Check 8

Consider a bank in the ED market that borrows ED$100,000,000 for 3 months.

a. The annualized rate is $LIBID_3$. Banks in the ED market buy (borrow) spot Eurodollars at $LIBID_3$.
b. The annualized rate is $LIBOR_3$. Banks in the ED market sell (offer, lend) spot Eurodollars at $LIBOR_3$.
c. The $LIBOR_3$, $LIBID_3$ spread is typically 0.125%. If a bank borrows at one rate, $LIBID_3$, in this case and lends at a higher rate, $LIBOR_3$, then that has the appearance of an arbitrage strategy.

However, there are transactions costs to the bank of arranging these transactions, and these costs can eat up the apparent arbitrage profits. What looks like arbitrage profits are just compensation for the services provided.

270 FORWARD CONTRACTS AND FUTURES CONTRACTS

The same thing happens in many markets in which there is a bid–asked spread, and that includes most markets. The spread represents transactions costs and the dealer offering the ability to transact is just earning those transactions costs.

Concept Check 10

The dealer would have to go out, at time T, into the spot market for 3-month Eurodollar time deposits and purchase it for the going spot price As shown in Chapter 5, section 5.8.1, he would still effectively pay the futures price he contracted at for the investment vehicle, due to his long ED futures position.

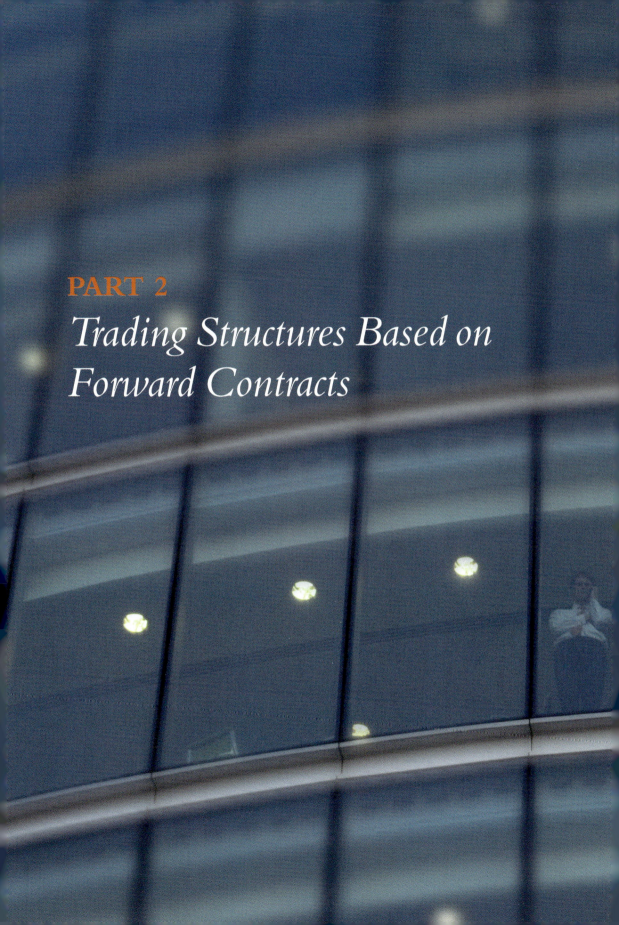

PART 2
Trading Structures Based on Forward Contracts

CHAPTER 8

STRUCTURED PRODUCTS, INTEREST-RATE SWAPS

8.1	Swaps as Strips of Forward Contracts	274
	8.1.1 Commodity Forward Contracts as Single Period Swaps	275
	8.1.2 Strips of Forward Contracts	277
8.2	Basic Terminology for Interest-Rate Swaps: Paying Fixed and Receiving Floating	278
	8.2.1 Paying Fixed in an IRD (Making Fixed Payments)	278
	8.2.2 Receiving Variable in an IRD (Receiving Floating Payments)	279
	8.2.3 Eurodollar Futures Strips	280
8.3	Non-Dealer Intermediated Plain Vanilla Interest-Rate Swaps	281
8.4	Dealer Intermediated Plain Vanilla Interest-Rate Swaps	284
	8.4.1 An Example	284
	8.4.2 Plain Vanilla Interest-Rate Swaps as Hedge Vehicles	286
	8.4.3 Arbitraging the Swaps Market	292
8.5	Swaps: More Terminology and Examples	293
8.6	The Dealer's Problem: Finding the Other Side to the Swap	294
8.7	Are Swaps a Zero Sum Game?	298
8.8	Why Financial Institutions Use Swaps	299
8.9	Swaps Pricing	301

TRADING STRUCTURES BASED ON FORWARD CONTRACTS

8.9.1	An Example	301
8.9.2	Valuation of the Fixed-Rate Bond	303
8.9.3	Valuation of the Floating-Rate Bond	305
8.9.4	Valuation of the Swap at Initiation	308
8.9.5	Implied Forward Rates (IFRs)	309
8.9.6	Three Interpretations of the Par Swap Rate	311

8.1 SWAPS AS STRIPS OF FORWARD CONTRACTS

In this chapter, we give an introduction to structured products in the form of plain vanilla interest-rate swaps. Swaps are very widely traded and measuring their value in terms of notional principal produces some outrageous numbers. For example, at the end of June 2013 the *notional value* of interest-rate swaps as reported by bis.org (Statistical release, OTC Derivatives Statistics at end-June 2013, Monetary and Economic Department, November 2013) stood at US\$437,066,000,000,000 which is more than \$437 trillion dollars!

The *notional* value of *currency* swaps was US\$26,318,000,000,000 which is a mere 26.318 trillion US dollars. Gold commodity contracts, which we will be using for illustration, amounted to US\$1,051,000,000,000 (about a trillion US\$). For comparison, US GDP at the end of 2012 was, according to the World Bank (data.worldbank.org/indicator; last accessed May 27, 2015), US\$15,684,800,000,000, or about 16 trillion US dollars.

It is hard to believe that so much wealth was invested in swaps. And in fact, it was not. As we shall see, this is not a correct way to measure the *value* of swaps outstanding.

A swap is a financial instrument based on the idea behind forward contracts of *paying* (receiving) *fixed* and *receiving* (paying) *floating*. Swaps therefore reflect the properties of forward contracts which we have discussed in detail throughout this text. A plain vanilla interest-rate swap is very closely related to a *financial* forward contract.

In the case of plain vanilla interest-rate swaps the financial forward contract that delivers the $LIBOR_3$ is the closely related instrument. The liquid version of this interest-rate forward contract is the corresponding Eurodollar futures contract, which is subject to all the rules for exchange-traded futures contracts including daily settlement.

OTC MARKETS AND SWAPS — 275

Interest rates come in different maturities. There is 3-month LIBOR, denoted by $LIBOR_3$; 6-month LIBOR, denoted by $LIBOR_6$; and 12-month LIBOR, denoted by $LIBOR_{12}$, to keep things under a year. We have discussed the 3-month Eurodollar time deposit futures contract in Chapter 7, section 7.6.1, which can also be viewed as a futures contract on the future 3-month LIBOR at expiration of the futures contract, time T, $LIBOR_{3,T}(\omega)$. We will have to be flexible in thinking about the deliverable which can also be thought of as a 3-month spot ED time deposit as of the maturity date of the ED Futures contract, time T.

8.1.1 Commodity Forward Contracts as Single Period Swaps

Once the idea behind forward contracts is grasped, it is a short step to understanding how and why swaps work.

Let's take yet another look at how forward contracts work. We will start with a 3-month gold forward contract. An investor goes long today (time t) 1 gold forward contract for delivery of 100 troy ounces of gold in 3 months, at time $T=t+3$. He contracts today at the current forward price $F_{t,T}$ for delivery of the commodity at time T.

$$\text{Long } @F_{t,T}(\omega) \qquad \text{Purchase gold for } F_{t,T}(\omega)$$

$$\xrightarrow{\hspace{6cm}}$$

$$t \qquad\qquad\qquad\qquad T=t+3 \text{ months}$$

The implication of his time t position is that the investor will have to buy 100 troy ounces of gold for the fixed per troy ounce price $F_{t,T}$, *no matter what happens* to spot gold prices in the interim $[t,T]$. That's the whole idea of a forward contract. At time T, the investor could then sell the gold at the per unit going spot price $P_T(\omega)$, which is currently (time t) unknown.

The market value of his position at time T would thus be $100*(P_T(\omega)-F_{t,T})$, as we discussed in Chapter 3, section 3.4. Since $P_T(\omega)$ is not a currently fixed cash amount, it makes sense to think of it as generating a variable (*floating*) cash flow.

The commodity flows and the cash flows that would occur at time T as a result of these transactions are shown in Figure 8.1.

Note that the time T market value of the gold delivered by the seller to the buyer is $100*P_T(\omega)$ where $P_T(\omega)$ is the gold spot price per ounce at expiration. The profit (loss) on the forward transaction is $100*(P_T(\omega)-F_{t,T})$, in accord with our results from Chapter 3.

FIGURE 8.1 Paying Fixed, Receiving Floating in a Commodity Forward Contract

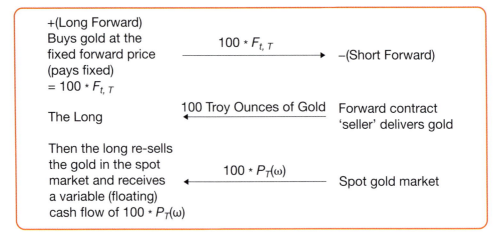

We conclude that:

1. The *long side* of an ordinary commodity forward contract is an individual who today contracts to *pay fixed,* and *receive floating* for an underlying commodity.

2. The *short side* of an ordinary commodity forward contract is an individual who today contracts to *receive fixed,* and *pay floating* for an underlying commodity.

There is another way to express these results that shows the strong connection between forward contracts and swaps terminologies.

1'. The *buy* side in an ordinary forward contract is 'Swapping' *Fixed for Floating* payments (i.e. paying fixed, receiving floating).

2'. The *sell* side in an ordinary forward contract is 'Swapping' *Floating for Fixed* payments (i.e. paying floating, receiving fixed).

The implication is that a standard forward contract is a kind of swap with a single set of cash flows at expiration. It turns out that a swap is also a product structured from forward contracts, in this case a *strip* of forward contracts.

■ CONCEPT CHECK 1

a. Convince yourself of the truth of 1 and 2.

8.1.2 Strips of Forward Contracts

You can see this strip feature in Figure 8.2. On the horizontal axis is time, measured in 6-month intervals (0.5=6 months, 1.0=1 year, etc.). FIX denotes a *fixed* payment (based on the appropriate forward price) and FLO denotes a *floating* receipt. At time $t=0$, the trader takes a long position in 6 forward contracts for delivery of gold at times $t'=0.5, 1.0, 1.5, 2.0, 2.5,$ and 3.0.

The current forward prices are $F_{0,0.5}, F_{0,1.0}, F_{0,1.5}, F_{0,2.0}, F_{0,2.5},$ and $F_{0,3.0}$ using our previous notation $F_{t,T}$ for forward prices. This is known as a *strip* of gold forward contracts and it would have the cash flow implications indicated in Figure 8.2.

FIGURE 8.2 Long's Position in a Strip of Forward Contracts

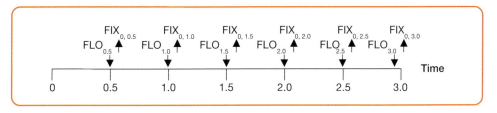

Note that a downward arrow is an inflow (receipt) and an upward arrow is an outflow (payment).

Time t=0 Transactions Generating the Strip Cash Flows in Figure 8.2 (Long)

1. Long gold for delivery at time $t'=0.5$ at $F_{0,0.5}$
2. Long gold for delivery at time $t'=1.0$ at $F_{0,1.0}$
3. Long gold for delivery at time $t'=1.5$ at $F_{0,1.5}$
4. Long gold for delivery at time $t'=2.0$ at $F_{0,2.0}$
5. Long gold for delivery at time $t'=2.5$ at $F_{0,2.5}$
6. Long gold for delivery at time $t'=3.0$ at $F_{0,3.0}$

The investor would effectively pay the contracted forward price, $F_{0,t'}$, at each of the times $t'=0.5, 1.0, 1.5, 2.0, 2.5,$ and 3.0. Note that $FLO_{t'}$ represents the variable (floating) spot price of gold at time t', which is what the long would receive after re-selling the gold in the spot market.

■ CONCEPT CHECK 2

a. Replicate Figure 8.2 (Long) for the *short's* position in a strip of forward contracts.

8.2 BASIC TERMINOLOGY FOR INTEREST-RATE SWAPS: PAYING FIXED AND RECEIVING FLOATING

Our gold forward example is an example of a *commodity* swap. Paying fixed and receiving floating is clear in the case of commodities, because fixed and floating refer to the *price* of the underlying commodity which is the commodity—gold in this case.

Interest rate derivatives (IRDs) are a little more complex, particularly if one thinks in terms of rates. As discussed in Chapter 7, section 7.7, the *nominal* underlier for the Eurodollar (ED) futures contract is a spot 3-month ED time deposit that pays interest at $\text{LIBOR}_{3,t'}$ where $t'=T$ is the maturity date of the futures contract.

However, the ED futures contract is usually thought of in terms of *Futures LIBOR$_3$* which we denote by $\text{FLIBOR}_{3,t,T}$. Indeed the futures 'price' is quoted in rate terms as $100-\text{FLIBOR}_{3,t,T}$. So it is clear that traders, at least, are thinking in terms of rates and not directly in terms of the underlying financial instrument which is a type of short-term money market instrument. Being able to think in both ways is a very useful skill.

8.2.1 Paying Fixed in an IRD (Making Fixed Payments)

Swaps are over-the-counter (OTC) bilateral agreements between one party who pays a fixed *rate* at regular intervals and receives a variable rate, and a counterparty who pays a variable rate and receives the fixed rate. Think of the variable rate as (spot) $\text{LIBOR}_{3,t'}(\omega)$ where t' could be 0.5, 1.0, 1.5, 2.0, 2.5, and 3.0, as in our gold forward strip example illustrated in Figure 8.2.

If someone wants to arrange to *pay* a fixed interest rate at specified time intervals over some specified period, then that person would be in a *borrowing* scenario. Good examples are mortgage loans, car loans, or student loans. The mortgage loan, car loan, or student loan enables people to receive monies today in return for their promise to pay it back plus interest.

OTC MARKETS AND SWAPS   **279**

Each loan creates a financial instrument called a mortgage bond, a student loan (repayment) bond, or a car loan (repayment) bond. The forward (futures) markets permit *future* borrowing and lending at *fixed* rates determined today.

What position in the bond is taken by the individual who takes out a loan either currently or in the future? The person would be *issuing (shorting, selling)* the financial instrument created as a result of the loan agreement. Then the individual would typically pay a fixed rate—unless the loan was a variable-rate bond like a variable-rate mortgage.

The same reasoning applies to forward loans. Note that 'selling' here doesn't mean selling something you already own. It refers to what a hedger in an *implicit* long position would want to do in order to protect the anticipated sale of something they do not currently own. To be short, such a forward loan means to arrange today to borrow in the future at a *fixed rate* for a specified period, no matter what happens to rates in the spot market at the time the loan is actually originated. Once again, that's the nature of any forward contract.

What this means is that in the world of ED futures contracts, *paying a fixed rate* means that you must *short* ED futures, because the nominal underlying is the 3-month security. This differs from the interpretation of paying a fixed *price* in a commodity futures or forward contract, which involves taking a long position as discussed.

■ CONCEPT CHECK 3

a. Discuss the ED futures contract with emphasis on the underlier.
b. Convince yourself that if you take a *short* position in a single ED futures contract, you will end up *borrowing* (paying a fixed rate) in the spot market at its expiration date, time T.

8.2.2 Receiving Variable in an IRD (Receiving Floating Payments)

Where does the 'receiving variable' component enter the picture? As previously discussed in Chapter 5, section 5.9 under 'cash settlement of futures contracts', the short would actually borrow in the spot market at maturity of the ED futures contract. Due to the daily and cash settlement procedures on ED futures positions, the short's *effective* borrowing rate would be the rate he originally contracted at in the short futures position.

280 TRADING STRUCTURES BASED ON FORWARD CONTRACTS

When I borrow in the spot 3-month ED time deposit market, let's say I borrow US$1,000,000. That $1,000,000 could be immediately lent out at the going 3-month rate $LIBOR_{3,T}(\omega)$, and I would receive the appropriately de-annualized $LIBOR_{3,T}$ for the subsequent 3-month period commencing at time T.

Of course, at time t when the short ED futures position was initiated that rate, $LIBOR_{3,T}(\omega)$ was unknown which is why it is said to be variable. We conclude that *paying a future fixed rate and receiving a future variable rate* is equivalent to *shorting* an ED futures contract.

■ CONCEPT CHECK 4

a. Convince yourself that if you take a *long* position at time t in a single ED futures contract, you will end up lending (receiving a fixed rate) in the spot market at its expiration date, time T.
b. Also, that you will be paying a floating rate.

8.2.3 Eurodollar Futures Strips

It is a small step to looking at a strip of ED futures contracts and re-interpreting in terms of rates. $L_{3,0.5}$ will be our short form for *spot* $LIBOR_{3,0.5}$ and $FL_{0,0.5}$ will be short form for *futures* $LIBOR_{3,0,0.5}$. $L_{3,0.5}$ denotes *spot* $LIBOR_{3,0.5}(\omega)$, and it means the currently (time $t=0$) unknown $LIBOR_3$ at the future time $t=0.5$.

The notation for *futures* $LIBOR_{3,0,0.5}$ means 3 for 3 months, 0 for today's time ($t=0$), and the 0.5 for delivery at time $t'=0.5$. The short form is $FL_{0,0.5}$. We can drop the 3 in futures $LIBOR_3$ because of the ED futures contract specifications that specify the deliverable, which is the 3-month ED time deposit based on $LIBOR_3$.

Note in Figure 8.3 that the short the ED futures strip always pays the fixed rates (which are fixed in advance, but usually differ from 3-month period to subsequent 3-month period based on the ED futures rates) $FIX_{0,t'}=FL_{0,0.5}$, $FL_{0,1.0}$, $FL_{0,1.5}$, $FL_{0,2.0}$, $FL_{0,2.5}$, $FL_{0,3.0}$ and receives the floating rates (which again change from 3-month period to subsequent 3-month period) $FLO=L_{3,0.5}$, $L_{3,1.0}$, $L_{3,1.5}$, $L_{3,2.0}$, $L_{3,2.5}$, $L_{3,3.0}$.

FIGURE 8.3 Cash Flows to the Short in an ED Futures Strip

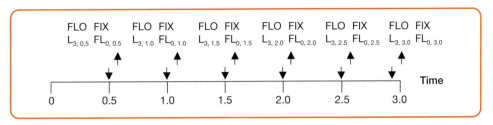

Time t=0 Transactions Required to Generate the Cash Flows for the Short Futures Strip in Figure 8.3

1. Short 1 ED futures at time $t=0$ for delivery at 0.5 at $FL_{0,0.5}$
2. Short 1 ED futures at time $t=0$ for delivery at 1.0 at $FL_{0,1.0}$
3. Short 1 ED futures at time $t=0$ for delivery at 1.5 at $FL_{0,1.5}$
4. Short 1 ED futures at time $t=0$ for delivery at 2.0 at $FL_{0,2.0}$
5. Short 1 ED futures at time $t=0$ for delivery at 2.5 at $FL_{0,2.5}$
6. Short 1 ED futures at time $t=0$ for delivery at 3.0 at $FL_{0,3.0}$

A swap accomplishes all this in a *single* contract and we will see how this is done with a *single* fixed rate over the life of the swap (not multiple fixed rates), when we discuss the par swap rate below.

The CME introduced *packs* and *bundles* of ED futures contracts in 1994. These allow investors to simultaneously take positions in multiple ED futures contracts, thereby capturing this aspect of the swap transaction. There are other significant differences between ED futures strips (packs and bundles) and plain vanilla interest-rate swaps.

But it is time to give some swap examples in order to have a baseline for the instrument. Remember, swaps are OTC instruments. That means non-standardization. ED futures, on the other hand, are fully standardized, as are all exchange-traded futures contracts.

8.3 NON-DEALER INTERMEDIATED PLAIN VANILLA INTEREST-RATE SWAPS

We start with an example from the ISDA (International Association of Swaps Dealers, source: www.isda.org/educat/pdf/irs-diagram1.pdf; accessed May 27, 2015).

In this example, the two counterparties enter into a direct (unintermediated) bilateral swap agreement with the following terms:

- Fixed rate payer: Alfa Corp.
- Fixed rate: 5%, semiannual (s.a.).
- Floating rate payer: Strong Financial Corp.
- Floating rate: 3-month USD LIBOR quarterly.
- Notional amount: US$ 100 million.
- Maturity: 5 years.

FIGURE 8.4 Cash Flows in a Non-Intermediated Swap

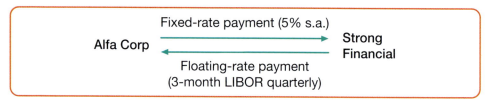

Copyright 2004 International Swaps and Derivatives Association, Inc. Reproduced with the permission of the International Swaps and Derivatives Association, Inc.

More specifically, here are the precise terms of the non-dealer intermediated swap agreement.

a. Alfa Corp agrees to pay 5.0% of $100 million on a *semiannual* (s.a.) basis to Strong Financial for the next five years. That is, Alfa will pay 2.5% of $100 million, or $2.5 million, twice a year to Strong Financial Corp.

b. Strong Financial agrees to pay 3-month LIBOR (as a percent of the notional amount) on a *quarterly* basis to Alfa Corp. for the next five years. This floating rate $LIBOR_{3,t'}(\omega)$ gets reset to the spot $LIBOR_{3,t'}$ prevailing at time t' at the beginning of every 3-month period, starting three months from today.

For example, if 3-month LIBOR is 2.4% on the first reset date ($t'=0.25$), then Strong will be obligated to pay Alfa an amount equal to .024/4* $100,000,000=$600,000 at time t'. Note that Alfa's first payment occurs at time 0.50 so there is no payment at time 0.25.

Looking at the financial obligations of each party, one sees that on the second reset date ($t'=0.50$) Alfa owes Strong $2,500,000 at t' and that Strong owes Alfa $600,000 on that date. The *net amount* Alfa owes Strong is therefore

OTC MARKETS AND SWAPS 283

$2,500,000–$600,000=$1,900,000 and this is the amount that Alfa would *actually* be obligated to pay Strong.

This illustrates the magic of *'netting'*. Only *net* obligations are transferred from the winner to the loser on reset dates at which payments are due from both parties. Note that a winner can become a loser and vice versa depending on where spot $LIBOR_{3,t'}$ ends up. For example, spot $LIBOR_{3,t'}$ would have to be less than 10% for Strong to be the winner at t'.

Also note that the notional principal, $100,000,000 in this case *never gets transferred*. Therefore, it is absurd to measure the value of outstanding swaps in terms of the notional principal underlying swaps contracts. So numbers like US$437,066,000,000,000 are fun to look at but represent an absurd measure of the amount at risk represented by swaps. The amount at risk is much, much smaller (see bis.org for other measures).

c. In practice, the (de-annualization) fractions used to determine payment obligations could differ according to the *actual* number of days in a period. If there are 91 days in the relevant quarter then, using the market convention for quoting $LIBOR_3$ which is to use a 360-day year (actual/360), the floating rate payment obligation incurred by Strong and owed to Alfa in the above example will be $91/360 \times .024*$100,000,000=$606,666.67$.

■ CONCEPT CHECK 5

(Graphical Representation of Swap's Cash Flows)

a. Construct a graphic illustrating the swap's cash flows from Alfa's point of view. The vertical arrows pointing upwards represent fixed cash outflows owed by Alfa. The arrows pointing downwards represent floating cash inflows received by Alfa.
b. Draw the appropriate arrows in Figure 8.5.
c. How much and how often does the swap obligate Alfa to pay?
d. How much and how often will Alfa will receive as a floating payment?

In practice, swaps dealers take the role of counterparties in swaps transactions. That is, the swaps market is a dealer-brokered market.

This is the process we will look at in section 8.4.

FIGURE 8.5 Cash Flows to Alfa in the Non-Intermediated Swap

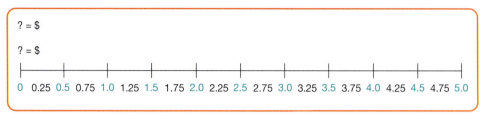

8.4 DEALER INTERMEDIATED PLAIN VANILLA INTEREST-RATE SWAPS

8.4.1 An Example

A firm, BBB (BBB refers to its credit rating) wants fixed-rate financing for 5 years (quarterly). Of course, BBB could just go out into the fixed-rate bond market and issue a 5-year bond with quarterly coupon payments. The fixed rate at which BBB can borrow directly in the 5-year fixed-rate market is 6.20%.

But BBB thinks that it may be able to do better via a swaps strategy. In return for such fixed-rate payments arranged in the swaps market, BBB is willing to pay a variable rate based on $LIBOR_{3,t'}(\omega)$. Instead of searching for a counterparty as in our previous example, BBB finds a swaps dealer who is willing to be BBB's counterparty to the swap agreement.

If a swaps dealer enters into a swaps agreement with a single counterparty, then it faces some credit risk. The dealer may want to hedge its position, using an appropriate position in an appropriate ED futures strip going out 5 years. In this situation the swaps dealer is said to be *warehousing* the swap.

This is a temporary situation and will be resolved once the swaps dealer finds a true counterparty to the swap. Swaps dealers aren't interested in being more than temporary counterparties. Their role is as *intermediaries* between the buy side and the sell side of swaps which is why they are called dealers.

There is another way in which a swaps dealer can partially control the credit risk associated with a fixed payer defaulting on his payments, and that is in the schedule of terms it offers to the fixed-rate payer, based on his credit rating. Here is an example of a swaps dealer's schedule for firms with BBB's credit ratings.

OTC MARKETS AND SWAPS **285**

TABLE 8.1 **Swaps Dealer's Schedule for BBB-Type Firms for 5-year Swaps**

Dealer Pays (BID) the	Dealer Receives (ASK) the
5-year T-note Rate+48bps (quarterly) in exchange for $\text{LIBOR}_{3,t'}(\omega)$.	5-year T-note rate+54 bps (quarterly) in exchange for $\text{LIBOR}_{3,t'}(\omega)$.
That is, paying a fixed rate and receiving a floating rate (a *short* forward position).	That is, paying a floating rate and receiving a fixed rate (a *long* forward position) .

Note that such a schedule has two sides depending on whether the swaps dealer is receiving fixed payments and paying floating–rate payments (the ASK side), or the swaps dealer is paying fixed payments and receiving floating payments (the BID side).

Note from the schedule that when the dealer pays the fixed rate then the dealer is short an equivalent ED futures strip. When the dealer pays the floating rate, $\text{LIBOR}_{3,t'}(\omega)$ in this case, the dealer is *long* an equivalent ED futures strip.

Suppose that, at the time the swap agreement was made, the 5-year Treasury-Note rate was 5.00%. A basis point is 1/100 of one percent. Then the dealer agrees to pay 5.48%/4 (quarterly) on a notional principal. In return for doing so, the swaps dealer would receive (quarterly) from BBB a variable amount equal to $\text{LIBOR}_{3,t'}(\omega)/4$ on the same notional principal.

The cash flow picture is as follows in Figure 8.6, where NP means notional principal (e.g. NP=US$100,000,000).

FIGURE 8.6 The Bid Side in a Dealer-Intermediated Swap with BBB

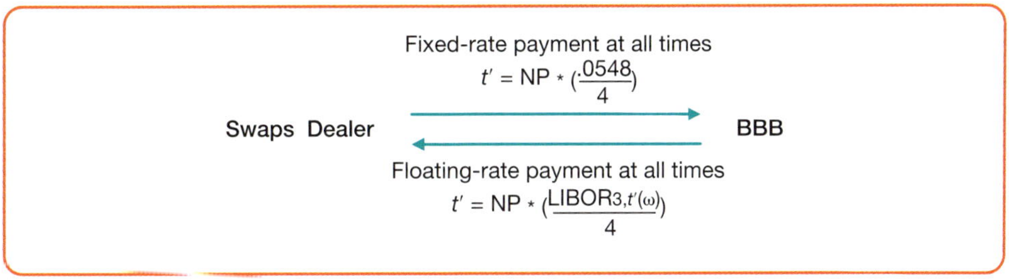

A similar picture, Figure 8.7, shows the asking side of the swap from the dealer's point of view. In this case, BBB pays the swaps dealer a fixed–rate payment every three months equal to Notional Principal*(.0554/4) and BBB receives a floating-rate payment at time $t'=\text{NP}*(\text{LIBOR}_{3,t'}(\omega)/4)$. This is the relevant scenario for BBB because BBB wants to make fixed–rate payments.

FIGURE 8.7 The Asked Side in a Dealer-Intermediated Swap with BBB

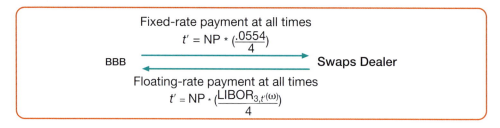

Before we continue, note that the *dealer's spread* on transactions with BBB-type firms is 54 bps−48bps=6bps because if it took the role of counterparty to 2 firms with credit ratings of BBB, it would make NP*(.006/4) on the round-trip transaction.

For the dealer could buy the swap (pay annualized fixed of .0548), and then sell the swap (receive annualized fixed of .0554). On an annualized basis, the swaps dealer makes a percentage rate of return of (.0554−.0548). Trading multiple lots of swaps creates a living for a swaps dealer. And don't forget that there is the potential other side of the swap.

In this example, BBB takes a buy position in the swap. It is called a buy position by convention which is defined as the *payer of the fixed rate (receiver of floating)* who is said to be *buying the swap*. Analogously, *the payer of the floating rate (receiver of fixed)* is said to be *selling the swap,* the dealer in this case.

We know from our previous discussion that *buying* the swap is economically equivalent to *shorting* a strip of ED futures contracts. Shorting because the participant who issues the underlying 3-month ED time deposit ends up *paying the fixed rate* on those ED time deposits, assuming they sold them forward at the futures prices. Since the swap reset dates are quarterly in our example, the short strip would have to have maturity dates that coincide with the swaps reset dates.

8.4.2 Plain Vanilla Interest-Rate Swaps as Hedge Vehicles

Why would anyone take a position like the one BBB takes in the swap? Here we can simply turn hedging on its head, as it were, to back out BBB's likely position in the spot market. BBB is effectively short an ED futures (forward) strip. If BBB is a hedger, BBB must therefore be long something else that is correlated with future spot $LIBOR_{3,t'}(\omega)$ rates.

Recall that a long position in a spot commodity is one that, either explicitly or implicitly, plans to *sell* that commodity in the future and therefore worries about price declines in the underlying commodity. That is the motive for hedging. If the underlying commodity declines in price, then the corresponding hedging vehicle's (futures) price will also decline and a short futures position will recoup some of the losses incurred in the spot market, subject to basis risk.

Note that a price decline in the 3-month Eurodollar time deposit's value corresponds to an increase in the spot $LIBOR_{3,t'}(\omega)$ rate used to price the underlying financial instrument. This is just a statement of the fact that bond prices move inversely with the discount rates used to price them.

Suppose that BBB has currently (at time $t=0$) issued short-term financing financed at $LIBOR_{3,0}+50bp$ (its natural rate in the floating market, given its credit risk) which will be *rolled over* every 3 months for 5 years. BBB requires quarterly financing for 5 years (20 periods).

The *first* 3-month borrowing period is covered by the current $LIBOR_{3,0}$ +50bp financing and requires no hedging. BBB's worry is in selling (issuing) *future* 3-month financial securities to re-finance its short-term debt. The worry is that short-term rates will *increase* in the future, when the periodic 3-month re-financing dates arrive.

BBB would have to issue new spot securities every three months and those securities have currently unknown rates which will be determined by $LIBOR_{3,t'}(\omega)+50bp$ prevailing at $t'=0.25$, 0 .50, 0.75, 1.00, 1.25, 1.50, 1.75, 2.00, 2.25, 2.50, 2.75, 3.0, 3.25, 3.50, 3.75, 4.00, 4.25, 4.50, and 4.75 (every 3 months). The current quarterly rate is $LIBOR_{3,0}$ which is known, so we don't include it in the future unknown quarterly $LIBOR_{3,t'}$ rates.

The risks to BBB, if it remains unhedged, are that any of the above spot $LIBOR_{3,t'}$ rates could rise by the time the re-financing dates t' arrive. Suppose that you never heard of swaps. They are a relatively recent innovation and hedging was accomplished before swaps.

But, you have read Chapter 7 and are familiar with ED futures. Further, you have fully absorbed and integrated the idea of the lock–in feature of a forward contract into your financial thinking. You also know that futures contracts are just 'fancy' forward contracts, and therefore they incorporate the same lock-in feature.

How could BBB hedge itself against potentially higher re-financing rates?

To hedge itself, it locks in these future rates by *selling* $FLIBOR_{3,0,t'}$ forward now (at time $t=0$) for $t'=0.25$, 0.50, 0.75, 1.0, 1.25, 1.50, 1.75, 2.00, 2.25, 2.50, 2.75, 3.00, 3.50, 3.75, 4.00, 4.25, 4.50, and 4.75 (every 3 months). That is, BBB *sells* a ED futures strip today.

To incorporate the swaps concept, we simply recognize that a buy (long) position (pay fixed, receive floating) in a swap is equivalent to a *short* ED futures strip. Note the *terminology shift*–paying fixed, receiving floating is called 'buy' in the swaps world, and is called 'short' in the ED futures world. Thus BBB could buy the appropriate swap thereby taking a pay fixed, receive floating position in the swap.

The swaps market allows BBB to come up with a customized (vs. non-standardized) solution to its hedging problem. One advantage of the swap solution is that things happen at the reset dates, but not daily as for exchange-traded futures contracts.

BBB's Complete Hedging Strategy

Let's review BBB's situation:

1. BBB needs to arrange financing for five years. BBB prefers fixed-rate financing as opposed to rolling over variable-rate financing.

2. Whatever the form of financing, BBB wants to hedge it.

3. At the end of the 5-year period, BBB will have to pay back the principal which we will assume is $100,000,000.

We will discuss 1., 2., and 3. in turn.

1. The initial step is that BBB will raise $100,000,000 at time $t=0$. The choice is whether to issue 5-year bonds with a fixed rate over the life of the bond, or to issue 3-month securities and to roll them over every three months over the five-year period.

Rolling over the 3-month (variable) rate debt coming due means to pay off the principal by issuing new 3-month debt every 3 months. This rolls over the interest payments on that variable-rate debt to the next 3-month period. Note that the issuance of debt, whether fixed rate or variable rate, is a purely spot market transaction.

One of the factors that the firm considers when it makes a choice between fixed-rate and variable-rate financing is the structure of its real assets. We will discuss this shortly under *gap management*. Another factor is the rate that the firm faces in variable-rate debt vs. the rate that the firm must pay to arrange for fixed-rate financing. This depends on the term structure of rates in the financial markets, as well as upon the firm's credit rating.

A firm, like an individual, has a credit score that reflects the risk to the lender that the firm might default. This credit score is instrumental in determining the rates that the individual or firm is able to borrow at in the fixed and floating interest rate markets. In practice, these are usually quoted as a *spread* to certain benchmark rates such as the 5-year T–Bond (for fixed) and $LIBOR_3$ for floating.

For example, firms with a BBB credit rating might face the following spreads. The rate schedule would be much more detailed than this, but this suffices to get the idea.

TABLE 8.2 Credit Spreads in the Spot Market for BBB-Type Firms

Credit-Rated Firms	Fixed rate	Floating rate
BBB	5 year T-Note rate+120 bp	$LIBOR_3$+50bp

If the 5–year T–Note rate were 5.00% at time t=0, as in our example, then BBB would face 5-year fixed-rate borrowing of 6.20%. In the short term variable-rate market, then whatever $LIBOR_{3,t'}(\omega)$ turned out to be at time t', BBB would face a borrowing rate 0.5% higher.

2. Issuing variable-rate debt creates a hedging problem for BBB. As discussed, the problem is potentially *rising short-term rates* at refinancing dates. We have seen how to hedge this rate uncertainty by taking a short position in an ED futures strip.

Then, if variable rates do increase, the firm pays these higher rates in the spot market (remember that ED futures are cash settled). To offset these increased rates are the profits on the *short* ED futures strip. Equivalently, BBB takes a *buy* position in a fixed for floating rate swap.

One way to avoid the uncertainty associated with variable-rate financing is not to issue it. Rather, BBB could issue fixed–rate financing. This hedges against the risk of rising variable rates, but it creates another hedging problem which we will discuss under the section that describes how the swaps dealer finds a counterparty firm AAA.

We confine our attention to BBB issuing variable-rate financing. Of course, this won't make BBB happy, because BBB wants fixed-rate financing. As financial engineers, we are going to give BBB fixed-rate financing. The only thing is that it will be *synthetic* fixed-rate financing, as opposed to the *natural* fixed-rate financing available to it in the fixed–rate bond market.

290 TRADING STRUCTURES BASED ON FORWARD CONTRACTS

Synthetic fixed-rate financing is a product structured from variable-rate financing *in combination* with a swap.

It is not hard to see this by considering Figure 8.8. The synthetic fixed rate strategy, made available by the swaps market, is for BBB to issue variable-rate financing. Then BBB gets the swaps dealer to pay off all or most of this variable-rate financing, in exchange for quarterly fixed payments. The swap component is evident. BBB is swapping fixed payments for floating payments with the swaps dealer. That is, it is taking a pay fixed, receive floating (buy) position in the swap.

FIGURE 8.8 Synthetic Fixed-Rate Strategy for BBB

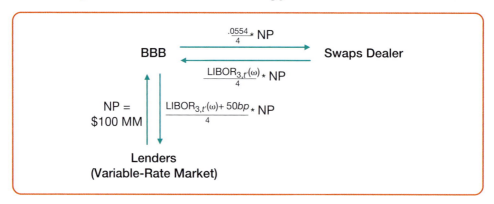

BBB's Strategy

The strategy, which we will call *synthetic fixed-rate financing*, that generates this set of cash flows and rates is,

1. At each time t' including $t=0$, BBB simply issues 3-month securities in the principal amount of NP=\$100,000,000 paying $[(LIBOR_{3,t'}(\omega)+50bp)/4]$ *NP quarterly. The first short-term rate is not random at time $t=0$ and is $(LIBOR_{3,0}+50bp)/4$ on NP.

2. At time $t=0$, BBB enters into the 5-year swap described paying a fixed rate of .0554/4 quarterly, based on the swap dealer's schedule for BBB-type firms. In return, BBB is to receive the floating rate $LIBOR_{3,t'}(\omega)/4$ quarterly. This rate would be adjusted at the beginning of every subsequent quarter based upon the then current $LIBOR_{3,t'}(\omega)/4$.

Implications of BBB's Swaps Hedging Strategy

Now look at what has happened as a result of this hedge strategy. First, note that the swap is an imperfect (but good enough, and in some ways better) substitute for a short ED futures strip, which is a clear hedge vehicle against short-term interest rates rising.

The swaps hedge *synthesizes* fixed-rate financing where the rate one is trying to beat is the natural fixed-rate financing rate of 6.20%. The synthetic fixed-rate bond is an alternative to direct borrowing in the fixed-rate market at an annualized rate of 6.20%.

First, even though BBB has issued floating-rate debt, BBB is fortuitously *not* exposed to the risks of a rising $LIBOR_{3,t'}(\omega)$. Why is that? Thanks to the swap, BBB has essentially *passed on* the variable part of its variable-rate debt obligation (everything but the 50 bp penalty) and the consequent risks to the swaps dealer!

BBB did not have to hold a gun to the head of the swaps dealer to do so, because it was a voluntary transaction and the swaps dealer, by agreeing to do the swap, is saying that he is willing to take on the variable-rate risk.

In effect, BBB pays off the interest on the bulk (except for 50bp) of its floating rate debt by *passing through* the swaps dealer's floating rate payment to its lenders (see Figure 8.8).

In turn, BBB's obligation is the fixed-rate payment of (.0554/4)* $100,000,000=$1,385,000 quarterly. Thus, BBB *transforms* its variable-rate debt into fixed-rate debt, thereby removing the variable-rate risk from its balance sheet. It does so by '*doing the opposite*' of what it really wants to do, which is to issue fixed-rate debt directly, and BBB simultaneously enters into the swap.

If the fixed rate it ultimately achieves by virtue of this strategy is lower than its 'natural rate' in the fixed-rate debt market (6.20%) , then BBB has made itself better off.

BBB's natural fixed rate is 6.20% annualized and the fixed rate it achieved via the swap strategy is equal to the sum of the fixed rate it pays plus the 50 bp part of the floating rate not covered by the swaps dealer's payment,

$$5.54\%+50bp=5.54\%+.50\%$$
$$=6.04\%.$$

So the savings to BBB is,

$$6.20\%-6.04\%=.16\%$$
$$=16bp.$$

292 TRADING STRUCTURES BASED ON FORWARD CONTRACTS

Note that BBB's natural variable rate is 50bp above $\text{LIBOR}_{3,t'}(\omega)$ because flat (no add-on) $\text{LIBOR}_{3,t'}(\omega)$ is defined as the rate for *prime* credit risks, and BBB is not a prime credit risk.

3. Of course, BBB is liable for paying back the principal of $100,000,000 at the end of five years. Neither the swap transaction, that involves no exchange of notional principal, nor the variable-rate rollovers, which presumably end at the last rollover at $t'=4.75$ address this issue.

Note the net effect of the hedging strategy. BBB makes quarterly payments for 5 years at a rate of 6.04% annualized. Interest is computed on the amount borrowed, which is the notional principal. Plus, BBB makes a full payment of the notional principal $100,000,000. The variable-rate payments have washed out. The overall effect is that the resulting strategy represents a *synthetic fixed-rate* bond.

8.4.3 Arbitraging the Swaps Market

There appears to be an arbitrage opportunity in BBB's use of the swap hedge because synthetic fixed-rate debt should carry the same rate as natural fixed-rate debt in a competitive debt market, provided that it exactly replicates it.

However, there has been a lot of research trying to show that what appears to be an arbitrage opportunity is in fact not. Here, we will give one of the many available arguments.

As noted, in an interest-rate swap, the notional principal is never exchanged. One sometimes sees the argument that therefore, the fixed rate implied by the swap is lower than the fixed-rate BBB can obtain in the normal 5-year fixed-rate debt market. This is because the credit risk and the interest-rate risk of the fixed payments in the swap, which does not include the principal repayment, are lower than the corresponding risks for normal fixed-rate debt, that *does* include the principal repayment.

The problem here is that this argument only considers the swap component of the synthetic fixed-rate debt. As noted in 3., BBB has also issued debt in the variable-rate debt market and that debt has principal which must ultimately be repaid.

Another more plausible argument is that only the *net* interest payments get transferred in the swap. In fixed-rate debt, the *full* amount of the coupons must be paid. This means that, all else equal, the credit risk of the natural fixed-rate debt issuer must be higher than that of the synthetic fixed-rate swaps strategy (borrow floating then swap fixed for floating). Therefore, there should be a rate advantage to the synthetic fixed-rate strategy.

There are many other arguments attempting to debunk the arbitrage rationale for swaps and we will revisit this issue when we discuss complete markets in Part 3 of this text.

Our next task, however, is to see how the dealer would go about finding the other side of the swap. Before proceeding, we will first introduce some more useful swaps terminology.

8.5 SWAPS: MORE TERMINOLOGY AND EXAMPLES

1. The party to the swap *paying fixed and receiving floating* is said to have *bought (long)* the swap.

2. The party to the swap *receiving fixed and paying floating* is said to have *sold (short)* the swap. In our example, BBB has bought the swap for 5.54%, and the dealer has sold the swap for 5.54%.

3. *Trade Date*: the date at which the parties agree to the swap and lock in the fixed rate and the initial floating rate.

4. *Effective Date*: the date at which the initial fixed and floating payments begin to accrue. For Eurodollar interest rate swaps this is two London business days subsequent to the trade date.

    Example: In a generic swap with a trade date of 02/15/2014 the effective date would 02/17/2014 (2 days after the trade date) and the first payment date would be 8/17/2014 (6 months from the effective date).

5. *Reset Date*: the date at which the floating rate is set for the next period.

6. *Swap's Tenor*: the life of the swap, starting from the effective date (not the trade date) to the maturity date of the swap.

7. *Resetting The Floating Rate*: the initial floating rate is first set on the trade date and then reset at specified intervals specified in the swap. The reset date is usually two London business days before the next payment date.

    Example: On the reset date for the next set of payments, the LIBOR appropriate to the swap is observed and becomes applicable to the next period.

8. *The Floating Leg* is the sequence of floating-rate payments.

9. *The Fixed Leg* is the sequence of fixed-rate payments.

10. *The Front Stub Period* is the effective date to the first payment date. In the example in 4. above, the front stub period is from 2/17/2014 to 8/17/2014.

11. *The Back Stub Period* is the last period covered by the swap.
    Note: the length of the back stub period could be shorter than the preceding payment periods.

12. *The Swap Spread*: The spread over the T-Note rate corresponding to the swap's maturity (similar to the bid–ask spread but tailored to credit ratings). *Exampl*e: see Table 8.3.

TABLE 8.3 **Generic Example: a 5-Year Swap**

	Dealer Pays	Dealer Receives
AA	50 bps+5 yr T-Note	52 bps+5 yr T-note
	The swap spread for AA is 50 to 52 bps.	
	Dealer Pays	**Dealer Receives**
BBB	48 bps+5 yr T-Note	54 bps+5 yr T-note
	The swap spread for BBB is 48 to 54 bps.	

13. *Par Swap Rate*: the fixed rate at which the swap has a current zero present value. Otherwise, there would be an arbitrage opportunity.

14. *Pricing a Swap*: determination of the fixed rate (par swap rate) in a generic fixed for floating-rate swap. This is what is meant by *pricing* the swap. There are two swap pricing problems. The first is pricing the swap at initiation. The second is pricing after initiation.

8.6 THE DEALER'S PROBLEM: FINDING THE OTHER SIDE TO THE SWAP

As discussed, the dealer may wish to act only as an intermediary and not warehouse swaps. If it does warehouse swaps, then it usually wants to hedge them. The best solution for the dealer is to find a *natural* hedge, which is to fill the other side of the swap with some other counterparty.

Suppose that the swaps dealer does find another firm, AA, now with an AA credit rating. It has a different swap schedule for AA-type firms. Note that the swaps dealer is willing to pay a higher rate (a spread of 50 bps) to the

OTC MARKETS AND SWAPS — 295

better rated firm AA, and is willing to take a lower fixed rate from AA (a spread of 52 bps).

The corresponding spreads for BBB-type firms were 48 bps and 54 bps. This is one way that the swaps dealer adjusts for the alternative credit risks associated with AA and BBB.

TABLE 8.4 Dealer Swap Schedule for AA-Type Firms

Dealer Pays (BID) the	Dealer Receives (ASK) the
5-year T-note Rate+50bps (quarterly) in exchange for $LIBOR_{3,t'}(\omega)$.	5-year T-note rate+52 bps (quarterly) in exchange for $LIBOR_{3,t'}(\omega)$.
That is, paying fixed and receiving floating (a short forward position).	That is, paying floating and receiving fixed (a long forward position).

What we did for BBB applies here and there is nothing really new. The cash flow diagrams just have different numbers attached to them. We once again assume that the 5-year *T*-Note rate is 5.00% and that NP stands for notional principal.

FIGURE 8.9 Bid Side in a Dealer-Intermediated Swap with AA

Fixed-rate payment at all times
$$t' = NP * \left(\frac{.0550}{4}\right)$$
Swaps Dealer → AA
Floating-rate payment at all times
$$t' = NP * \left(\frac{LIBOR_{3,t'}(\omega)}{4}\right)$$

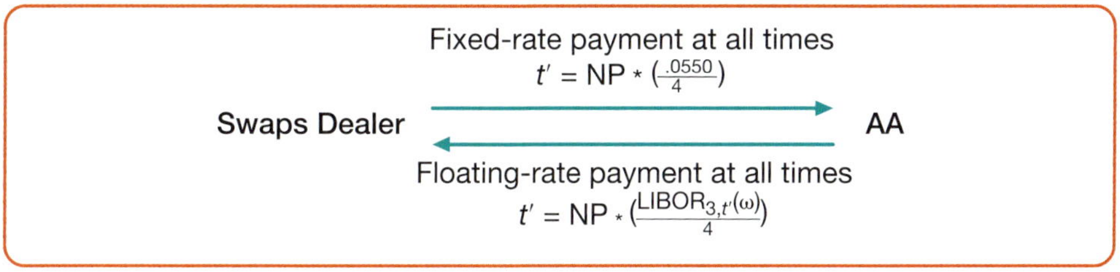

A similar picture shows the asking side of the swap from the dealer's point of view. In this case, AA pays the swaps dealer a fixed-rate payment every 3 months equal to Notional Principal*(.0552/4) and receives a floating rate payment at time t'=NP*(LIBOR$_{3,t'}(\omega)$/4).

FIGURE 8.10 Asked Side in a Dealer-Intermediated Swap with AA

Fixed-rate payment at all times
$$t' = NP * \left(\frac{.0552}{4}\right)$$
AA → Swaps Dealer
Floating-rate payment at all times
$$t' = NP * \left(\frac{LIBOR_{3,t'}(\omega)}{4}\right)$$

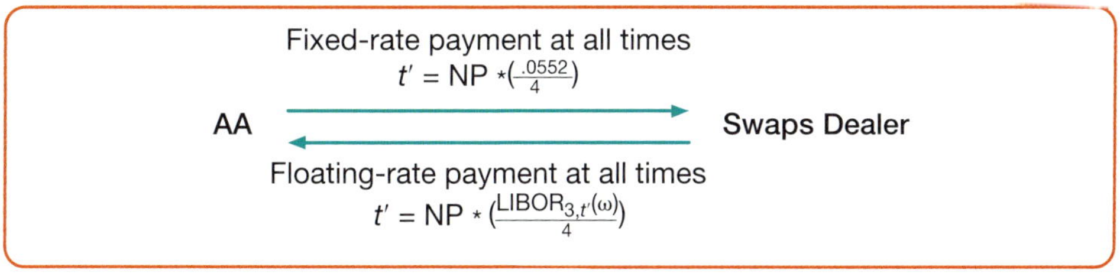

TRADING STRUCTURES BASED ON FORWARD CONTRACTS

Now, for whatever reason as we shall soon see, AA wishes to take a *sell* position in the swap (pay floating and receive fixed). Remember that *the receiver of fixed (payer of the floating rate)* is said to be *selling the swap.*

We know from the previous discussion that selling the swap is economically equivalent to *longing* a strip of ED futures contracts. Longing because the participant who buys the underlying 3-month ED time deposit ends up receiving the fixed rate on those ED time deposits, assuming they bought them forward at the futures prices. Once again, since the swap reset dates are quarterly in our example, the long strip would have to have maturity dates that coincide with the swap's reset dates.

Why would anyone take a position such as AA in the swap? Just as we did for BBB, we turn hedging on its head to back out AA's likely position in the spot market. Since AA is long an ED futures (forward) strip AA must, if AA is a hedger, be short something else that is correlated with future $LIBOR_{3,t'}(\omega)$ rates.

Recall that a short position in a spot commodity is one that either explicitly or implicitly plans to *buy* that commodity in the future and therefore worries about price increases in the underlying commodity. That is the motive for hedging. If the underlying commodity increases in price (rates decline), then the corresponding hedging vehicle's (futures) price will also increase and a long futures position will recoup some of the losses incurred in the spot market, subject to basis risk of course.

So we know that AA is short something. Suppose that AA has currently (at time $t=0$) issued long–term (5–year) financing at its natural rate in the fixed-rate market which is 5.30%. See the chart below, Table 8.5, for AA's respective borrowing rates in fixed and floating markets, given its credit risk.

TABLE 8.5 Credit Spreads in the Spot Market for AA-Type Firms

Credit Rating	Fixed rate	Floating rate
AA	5-year T-Note rate+30bp	$LIBOR_3$ flat

Note that AA is a borrower in the spot fixed-rate bond market who has *locked into* paying the fixed rate of 5.30% for five years. This puts AA at a potential disadvantage if rates *decrease* across the board.

If that happens, then AA is locked into too high a rate for the remaining life of the loan. An analogous situation is the homeowner with a fixed–rate mortgage who sees the fixed rate decline, and therefore wishes to refinance.

OTC MARKETS AND SWAPS

If rates do decline, then AA could repurchase the bonds previously issued, but they would be selling at a higher price than originally issued, creating a loss for AA. After repurchasing the existing bonds, AA could refinance by issuing new bonds at lower rates. However, it would be easier for AA to hedge itself using swaps.

What AA really wants is floating rate financing rather than fixed-rate financing, because floating-rate financing adjusts to interest rate changes. The question is how to most cost effectively achieve it. Of course, AA can go out into the floating-rate market and get quarterly financing at flat $\text{LIBOR}_{3,t'}(\omega)/4$.

AA notices, though, that it could issue fixed-rate debt at annualized 5.30% and simultaneously enter into a swap with the dealer in which AA pays to the dealer annualized $\text{LIBOR}_{3,t'}(\omega)$ flat and receives from the dealer the fixed rate of 5.50%.

When the coupons become due every quarter, AA uses the dealer's fixed payment to pay off the annualized 5.30% and keeps the extra .20% to offset its flat $\text{LIBOR}_{3,t'}$ borrowing rate thereby *reducing* it to $\text{LIBOR}_{3,t'}(\omega)-.20\%$.

This *transforms* AA's fixed-rate borrowing into floating rate borrowing at an annualized savings of 20bp relative to direct floating rate financing. Figure 8.11 illustrates the situation.

FIGURE 8.11 Synthetic Floating-Rate Financing for AA

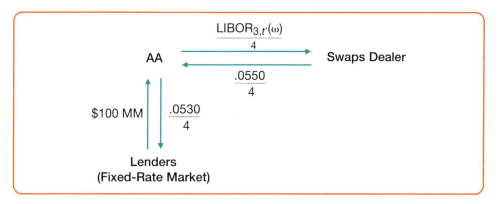

Note that the net overall quarterly cost to AA due to this strategy is,

$$\frac{\text{LIBOR}_{3,t'}(\omega)}{4} + \left(\frac{.0530}{4} - \frac{.0550}{4}\right) = \frac{\text{LIBOR}_{3,t'}(\omega)}{4} - \frac{.002}{4}$$

which is $\text{LIBOR}_{3,t'}(\omega)-.002$ annualized.

Therefore, AA has saved 20 basis points (.002=.2 of a percent) by issuing floating-rate debt and swapping fixed for floating with the swaps dealer. It has *effectively* achieved fixed-rate financing as well.

Figure 8.12 shows the complete set of cash flows generated by the swap with both counterparties AA and BBB.

FIGURE 8.12 **Full Set of Swap Cash Flows for BBB, AA, and the Dealer**

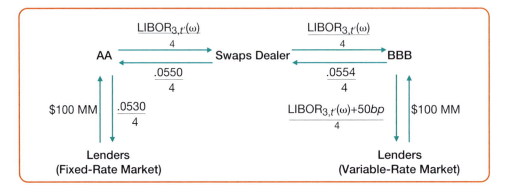

8.7 ARE SWAPS A ZERO SUM GAME?

We see from Figure 8.12 the net gains to AA, BBB, and to the swaps dealer. The dealer makes 4 bp on NP annualized because it receives 5.54% annualized from BBB and pays out 5.50% annualized to AA.

BBB effectively arranges fixed-rate financing and pays out 5.54% (annualized) plus .50%=6.04% which represents a savings of 16 bp over its natural fixed-rate borrowing rate of 6.20%(annualized).

Finally, AA has arranged floating-rate financing at a cost of $LIBOR_{3,t'}(\omega)$–20bp which is 20 bp below what it would naturally pay in the floating-rate market. The sum of cost savings to all parties is therefore 4bp+16bp+20bp=40bp.

There is a nice way of seeing where these 40bps come from. To explain this will require a few definitions. Recall the natural rates available to AA and BBB summarized in Table 8.6.

TABLE 8.6 **Credit Spreads for AA and BBB**

Credit-Rated Firms	Fixed rate	Floating rate
AA	5.30% (530bps)	$LIBOR_3$
BBB	6.20% (620bps)	$LIBOR_3$+0.5%

Definitions

1. *The Quality Spread in Fixed is*

   (QSFIX)=Fixed-rate differential between AA and BBB
   =620bps–530bps
   =90bps.

2. *The Quality Spread in Floating is*

   (QSFLO)=Floating rate differential between AA and BBB
   =(LIBOR$_3$+0.5%)–LIBOR$_3$
   =50bps.

Then the sum of all gains to all parties is the difference between QSFIX and QSFLO. In our example, that difference is 90bps–50bps=40bps.

The economic argument behind this result is called *comparative advantage* and the process described in our extensive example was known as '*Arbitraging the Swaps Market*'. As noted, many researchers and practitioners question whether there is a real arbitrage opportunity here.

8.8 WHY FINANCIAL INSTITUTIONS USE SWAPS

We have skirted by the issue of why parties such as AA and BBB would want to transform fixed to floating-rate liabilities, or floating to fixed-rate liabilities. That is, why would AA and BBB want to restructure their balance sheets in the first place?

As an example, let's look at a financial intermediary (FI) such as Bank of America (B of A). Below is a look at what B of A's partial balance sheet might look like.

TABLE 8.7 **Bank Of America's Simplified Balance Sheet**

Assets	Liabilities
Fixed-rate 30-year mortgages earning ROA=r_A	6-month CDs with cost of capital=r_D

An immediate problem is apparent here and it goes under the title '*Gap Management*'.

Asset Portfolio	GAP	Liability Portfolio

300 **TRADING STRUCTURES BASED ON FORWARD CONTRACTS**

Bank of America is in a risky position, because it has funded long-term assets such as 30-year fixed-rate mortgages with short-term liabilities such as 6-month certificates of deposit (CD). The latter are floating-rate securities because B of A will have to roll them over, reborrowing the principal every 6 months, most likely on a rate based on $LIBOR_6$. B of A is thus exposed to potentially *increasing* financing costs.

The principle that attempts to avoid this issue is called the '*Matching Principle*' which is to match the duration of your assets with the duration of your liabilities.

Duration has a technical meaning in that it measures the interest rate sensitivity of a firm's asset and liability portfolio. If one could apply the matching principle perfectly, then the duration of the firm's balance sheet would be zero and the pure interest-rate risk of the portfolio would be neutralized.

Interest-rate swaps provide a low-cost method for a firm to accomplish this goal. Note that the relevant measure of the life of an investment is not generally its stated maturity. Rather, duration is the correct concept which captures the risk of an interest-rate sensitive investment. Thirty-year fixed-rate mortgages appear to be very long-term assets but their duration is in the 7–8 year range. This means that a 7–8 year interest rate swap would be an appropriate hedging vehicle.

To pursue this example a little more, we first focus on the market participants. The *issuer* of a mortgage is the homeowner, who is a borrower in this case. The investor in the mortgage is Bank of America, who is the lender in the mortgage transaction. B of A expects to earn the spread between the rate of return on its fixed-rate mortgages and its cost of funds. This can be written as $r_A - E(r_D(\omega))$.

What is the primary risk to B of A in this scenario? The risk is that $r_D(\omega)$ increases and B of A's spread narrows. Potential solutions to this gap management problem include:

a. Sell the fixed-rate mortgages in the secondary mortgage market. To reduce the risk of these 30-year mortgages, sell them to Freddie Mac or Fannie Mae. Then buy them back as mortgage-backed securities.
b. Don't issue fixed-rate mortgages. Use variable-rate mortgages instead.
c. Hedge with strips of Eurodollar futures (ED futures).
d. Lock in the future costs of funding by forward rate agreements (FRAs).
e. Use swaps (Fixed-for-Floating Plain Vanilla Swaps) to transform floating-rate costs of funds into fixed-rate costs of funds.

OTC MARKETS AND SWAPS **301**

Each of the above solutions has costs and benefits. Instead of describing those costs and benefits, it is time to turn to the pricing swaps.

8.9 SWAPS PRICING

What does it mean to price a generic swap? The answer is that it means the same thing as to price a forward contract, which is to determine the equilibrium forward price. Swaps are forward strips, so pricing generic swaps is more complicated than pricing an individual forward contract.

Pricing a generic swap means that the swaps market, and therefore the swaps dealer, has determined the fixed rate that the fixed-rate payer pays in a generic fixed for floating-rate swap. This amounts to 'pricing the swap currently'.

Note that swap pricing includes pricing *at origination* which we will focus on. It also includes pricing *after origination*. Just as a forward contract has zero value at origination, but assumes positive and negative values to market participants, so for swaps the swap can assume a positive or negative value as the underlying spot price changes.

How does the swaps market come up with the base fixed rates to charge alternative credit risks such as AA and BBB? Recall definition 13 which is repeated here.

> The *Par Swap Rate* is the fixed rate at which the swap has a zero present value at initiation.

Otherwise, there would be an arbitrage opportunity.

We know from our study of forward contracts that the value of a forward contract is zero at initiation. We also looked at the arbitrage opportunity available if this were not true. Since a swap is just a strip of forward contracts, the same valuation must apply to swaps. The details follow.

When a swaps dealer takes the opposite side of a swaps transaction with a firm such as BBB who has bought the swap, it ends up *receiving fixed* and *paying floating* periodically. To get a handle on the pricing problem, we can interpret the swaps dealer's positions in terms of bonds.

8.9.1 An Example

Consider a 3-year swap. Suppose that $LIBOR_{12,0}$ is the spot 1-year $LIBOR_{12}$ at the beginning of year 1. It applies to determine cash flows to be received at the end of year 1 and is known at $t=0$.

Also, $LIBOR_{12,1}(\omega)$ is 1-year spot $LIBOR_{12}$ at the beginning of year 2. Finally, $LIBOR_{12,2}(\omega)$ is 1-year spot $LIBOR_{12}$ at the beginning of year 3. We will assume that notional principal (NP) is $100,000,000.

The swap's floating payments are,

$FLO_1 = NP*LIBOR_{12,0}$,
$FLO_2 = NP*LIBOR_{12,1}(\omega)$,
$FLO_3 = NP*LIBOR_{12,2}(\omega)$.

The swap's fixed payments are,

$FIX_1 = NP*R$,
$FIX_2 = NP*R$,
$FIX_3 = NP*R$,

where R is the par swap rate.

Note that all the fixed payments are the same: $FIX_1 = FIX_2 = FIX_3 = FIX$, as is characteristic of a fixed-for-floating swap. The swap's cash flows are illustrated in Figure 8.13:

FIGURE 8.13 Cash Flows for an Annual Rate Swap from the Dealer's Point of View

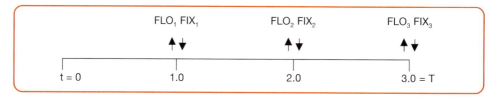

But we can write the cash flows of the swap in terms of two bonds, a floating-rate bond and a fixed-rate bond. Bonds differ from swaps in that, for bonds, NP must be repaid at maturity $T=3$.

Note that NP is a wash in the swap because it gets paid out via the floating-rate bond and it is received from the fixed-rate bond. Also note that the swap's cash flows are equal to the *vertical sum* of the two bonds' cash flows, as illustrated in Figure 8.14.

The swaps dealer has *effectively* issued (shorted) a floating-rate bond and invested in (longed) a fixed-rate bond. Long the fixed-rate bond because he is *receiving* the fixed rate from the counterparty, and short the floating-rate bond because he is *paying* $LIBOR_{12,t'}$ to the counterparty at each time t'.

FIGURE 8.14 Decomposing the Swap's Cash Flows into its Implicit Bonds

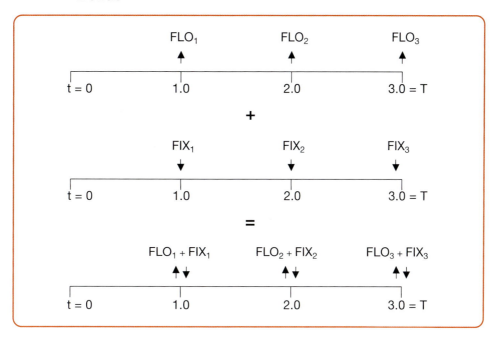

The conclusion here is that the swap, from the dealer's point of view, is economically equivalent to *short the floating-rate bond* and *long the fixed-rate bond*.

The next step is to value each of these bonds and thereby to value the swap. To do so, we need the appropriate discount rates.

8.9.2 Valuation of the Fixed-Rate Bond

In order to value the fixed-rate bond in which the dealer is long, we need the appropriate discount rates to apply to the bond's cash flows. We are in the world of interest-rate swaps which is a LIBOR world.

So we need the current ($t=0$) spot LIBOR yield curve. It gives the rates to be applied to zero-coupon Eurobonds for alternative maturities. Assume that it is as in Table 8.8.

Our long position in the fixed-rate bond can be decomposed as the sum of three *zero-coupon* bonds, and one NP repayment bond as indicated in the multi-level cash flow diagram, Figure 8.15.

TABLE 8.8	LIBOR Yield Curve (Spot Rates)
Maturity	Zero-Coupon Bond Yields
1 year	6.0%
2 years	6.5%
3 years	7.0%

FIGURE 8.15 **The Implicit Fixed-Rate Bond in a Swap, Written in Terms of Zero-Coupon Bonds**

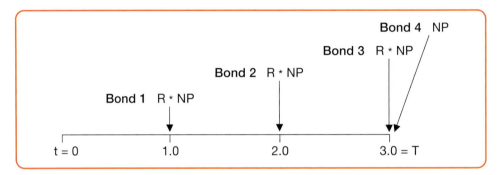

The LIBOR zero-yield curve says that the appropriate discount rate to apply to the cash flow from Bond 1 is 6.00%, the appropriate discount rate to apply to the cash flow from Bond 2 is 6.5%, and the appropriate discount rate to apply to the cash flows from Bond 3 and from Bond 4 is 7.0%.

This leads to the pricing formulas for the three zero-coupon bonds indicated: $B_{0,1}$, $B_{0,2}$, $B_{0,3}$, and the notional principal bond $NPB_{0,3}$. The first three bonds pay exactly the same coupon, $R*NP$ where R is the par swap rate. The fourth bond represents the return of the principal NP and is therefore denoted as $NPB_{0,3}$.

The time at which we have to value these bonds is $t=0$, as indicated by the notation. Given this preliminary setup work, it is now easy to value each bond.

$$B_{0,1} = \frac{R * NP}{1.0600}$$
$$= R * NP * \frac{1.0}{1.0600}$$
$$= R * NP * B'_{0,1}$$

$$B_{0,2} = \frac{R * NP}{(1.065)^2}$$

$$= R * NP * \frac{1.0}{(1.065)^2}$$

$$= R * NP * B'_{0,2}$$

$$B_{0,3} = \frac{R * NP}{(1.070)^3}$$

$$= R * NP * \frac{1.0}{(1.070)^3}$$

$$= R * NP * B'_{0,3}$$

$$NPB_{0,3} = \frac{NP}{(1.070)^3}$$

$$= NP * B'_{0,3}$$

where we have written these bond values in terms of $B'_{0,1}$, $B'_{0,2}$, and $B'_{0,3}$ which are the *unit* ($1 payoff) discount bonds maturing at times $t'=1$, 2, and 3.

Therefore, the current value of the fixed-rate bond is,

$$B_{0,\text{Fixed Rate}} = \frac{R * NP}{1.0600} + \frac{R * NP}{(1.065)^2} + \frac{R * NP}{(1.070)^3} + \frac{NP}{(1.070)^3}$$

$$= B_{0,1} + B_{0,2} + B_{0,3} + NPB_{0,3}$$

$$= R * NP * B'_{0,1} + R * NP * B'_{0,2} + R * NP * B'_{0,3} + NP * B'_{0,3}$$

8.9.3 Valuation of the Floating-Rate Bond

The floating-rate bond is described by its cash flow diagram in Figure 8.16.

In order to price such a set of cash flows with *random* variable payoffs, we have to take expected values and then discount them appropriately. This means that, in order to come up with a price for the variable-rate bond, we have to replace its cash flows by its *expected* cash flows, where the expectation is with respect to information currently available.

FIGURE 8.16 The Floating-Rate Bond Implicit in the Swap

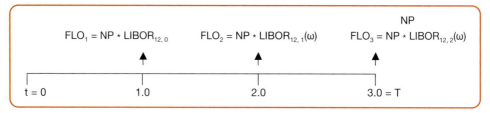

FIGURE 8.17 Floating-Rate Payments as Expected Cash Flows

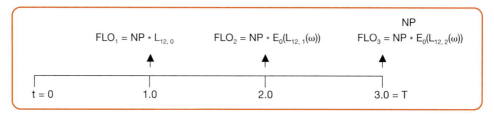

Note that the first cash flow is equal to its expected value because it is based on current $LIBOR_{12,0}$. Also, we have abbreviated $LIBOR_{12,1}(\omega)$ by $L_{12,1}(\omega)$ to save space in Figure 8.17.

There is a fairly easy way of seeing that the variable-rate bond must sell at par, at initiation of the swap. That is, $B_{0,\text{Floating Rate}} = NP$. Start at one time period before maturity of the swap, time $t=2.0$, in the above cash-flow diagram.

At time $t=2.0$, $LIBOR_{12,2}$ is known and is used to determine the next coupon payment which is,

$$FLO_3 = NP * E_0(L_{12,2}(\omega))$$
$$= NP * LIBOR_{12,2}.$$

Note that we can drop both the expectation, E_0, and the randomness ω because $LIBOR_{12,2}$ is known at time 2.0. The cash flow picture follows in Figure 8.18.

FIGURE 8.18 Valuing the Floating-Rate Bond One Period Prior to Maturity

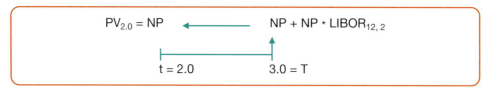

The appropriate discount rate for this cash flow stream is $\text{LIBOR}_{12,2}$ because the cash flow is based upon $\text{LIBOR}_{12,2}$,

$$PV(NP * \text{LIBOR}_{12,2} + NP) = PV(NP * (1 + \text{LIBOR}_{12,2}))$$

$$= \frac{NP * (1 + \text{LIBOR}_{12,2})}{1 + \text{LIBOR}_{12,2}}$$

$$= NP$$

This says that, at the second reset date $t=2$, the value of the remaining one period bond maturing at time $T=3$ is par, which in this case is NP. We replace this last period bond by its PV at time $t=2$, as indicated in the cash flow diagram, Figure 8.18. We can do this because replacing a cash flow by its economic present value is economically neutral.

Now we move back in time to the first reset date $t=1.0$. The cash flow receivable at time $t=2.0$ from this one-period bond is NP times the time $t=1.0$ $\text{LIBOR}_{12,1}$ reset at $t=1.0$. Once again, the appropriate discount rate for this cash flow stream is $\text{LIBOR}_{12,1}$ because the cash flow is based on $\text{LIBOR}_{12,1}$. Figure 8.19 illustrates the discounting procedure.

FIGURE 8.19 Valuing the Floating-Rate Bond Two Periods Prior to Maturity

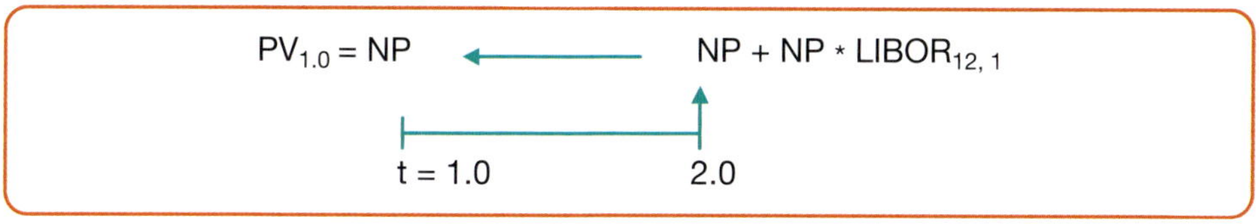

We repeat the calculation to find that the PV of this bond at time $t=1$ is once again equal to NP,

$$PV(NP * \text{LIBOR}_{12,1} + NP) = PV(NP * (1 + \text{LIBOR}_{12,1}))$$

$$= \frac{NP * (1 + \text{LIBOR}_{12,1})}{1 + \text{LIBOR}_{12,1}}$$

$$= NP$$

By repeating this line of reasoning, we find that the PV at time $t=0$ of the corresponding one-period bond is NP. But this contains the collapsed value of *all* the cash flows generated by the multi-period bond.

FIGURE 8.20 Complete Valuation of the Implicit Floating-Rate Bond in an Interest-Rate Swap

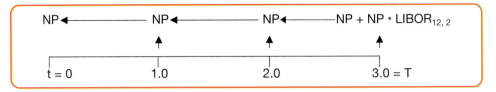

We just successively discount the cash flows starting at $T=3$ and move backwards. So the value of the floating rate bond at initiation of the swap, and at all the reset dates is par=NP, as indicated in Figure 8.20.

8.9.4 Valuation of the Swap at Initiation

Since the swap, from the dealer's point of view, is economically equivalent to short the floating and long the implicit fixed-rate bonds, its current value must be equal to,

$$PV(\text{Fixed-Rate Bond}) - PV(\text{Variable-Rate Bond})$$

and this quantity, just as for a forward contract, must be zero at initiation to avoid arbitrage. That is,

$$B_{0,\text{Fixed Rate}} - B_{0,\text{Floating Rate}} = \frac{R*NP}{1.0600} + \frac{R*NP}{(1.065)^2} + \frac{R*NP}{(1.070)^3} + \frac{NP}{(1.070)^3} - NP$$
$$= 0$$

Divide this equation through by NP to obtain,

$$\frac{R}{1.0600} + \frac{R}{(1.065)^2} + \frac{R}{(1.070)^3} + \frac{1.0}{(1.070)^3} - 1.0 = 0$$

Solving this equation for the par swap rate R yields,

$$R = \frac{1.0 - \dfrac{1.0}{(1.070)^3}}{\dfrac{1.0}{1.0600} + \dfrac{1.0}{(1.065)^2} + \dfrac{1.0}{(1.070)^3}}$$
$$= \frac{1.0 - B'_{0,3}}{B'_{0,1} + B'_{0,2} + B'_{0,3}}$$

where we have expressed the par swap rate in terms of the unit discount bonds, $B'_{0,1}, B'_{0,2}$, and $B'_{0,3}$ introduced above.

8.9.5 Implied Forward Rates (IFRs)

We give one economic interpretation of the par swap rate in this sub-section. We first need the useful notion of *Implied Forward Rate* (IFR). Take the first two periods of our example. An investor with a 2-year horizon has two alternatives,

1. He can invest in a two-year bond for two years.

2. He can invest in a 1-year bond, hold it until maturity for one year, and then roll it over into a 1-year bond for the second year.

The difference between these two investment strategies is that in 1. the rate is known, while in 2. the second year rate becomes known one year later, just as in the floating leg of an interest-rate swap. Now, we examine the payoffs to these strategies.

The payoff at time $t=2$ from an investment of $1 in 1. made at time 0 is $1*(1+\text{LIBOR}_{2,0})^2$ where $\text{LIBOR}_{2,0}$ is the 2-year LIBOR at time 0.

The payoff at time $t=2$ from an investment of $1 in 2. made at time 0 is $1*(1+\text{LIBOR}_{1,0})*(1+\text{LIBOR}_{1,1}(\omega))$ where $\text{LIBOR}_{1,0}$ is the 1-year LIBOR at time 0 and $\text{LIBOR}_{1,1}(\omega)$ is the one-year LIBOR at time 1 as indicated in Figure 8.21.

FIGURE 8.21 The Two Strategies that Generate Implied Forward Rates

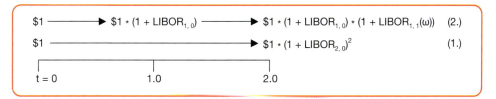

The payoff to 2. is clearly random as of time $t=0$, and it depends on what occurs for $\text{LIBOR}_{1,1}(\omega)$ one year from time 0. However, we can also think in terms of *expected* payoffs. The expected payoff to 2. is $(1+\text{LIBOR}_{1,0})*(1+E_0(\text{LIBOR}_{1,1}(\omega)))$.

310 TRADING STRUCTURES BASED ON FORWARD CONTRACTS

Then we can define the important notion of the *Implied Forward Rate* (*IFR*) on one-year loans one year from today as the *artificial, non-random* rate that equates the expected payoffs of strategies 1. and 2.

That is, it is the rate, denoted by $IFR_{1,1}$, such that $(1+LIBOR_{2,0})^2=(1+LIBOR_{1,0})*(1+IFR_{1,1})$. The $IFR_{1,1}$ is given by,

$$IFR_{1,1} = \frac{(1+LIBOR_{2,0})^2}{(1+LIBOR_{1,0})} - 1.0$$

Similarly, the Implied Forward Rate on one-year loans *two* years from today, denoted by $IFR_{1,2}$, is defined as the artificial rate such that,

$$(1+LIBOR_{3,0})^3 = (1+LIBOR_{2,0})^2(1+IFR_{1,2}) \text{ or}$$

$$IFR_{1,2} = \frac{(1+LIBOR_{3,0})^3}{(1+LIBOR_{2,0})^2} - 1.0$$

Implied Forward Rates are obtained from the LIBOR yield curve, or from the prices of Eurodollar futures contracts. For example, based on the LIBOR yield curve given in Table 8.8, we can imply 1-year forward rates one year from today and two years from today.

■ CONCEPT CHECK 6

a. Calculate, based upon Table 8.8, the IFR for 1-year loans one year from today, $IFR_{1,1}$.
b. Also, calculate the IFR for 1-year loans two years from today, $IFR_{1,2}$.

Implied Forward Rates are useful because, under certain assumptions, they are *unbiased* estimates of future 1-year LIBOR. That is,

$$IFR_{1,1}=E_0(LIBOR_{1,1}(\omega)) \text{ and } IFR_{1,2}=E_0(LIBOR_{1,2}(\omega)).$$

This follows from the no-arbitrage assumption and the expectations theory of the term structure of interest rates.

The expectations theory says that long-term rates are determined by the current short-term rate and expected future short-term rates. For example, the current 2-year LIBOR rate, $LIBOR_{2,0}$, is determined by the current 1-year $LIBOR_{1,0}$ and the *expected* one-year $E_0(LIBOR_{1,1}(\omega))$ one year from today,

$$(1+LIBOR_{2,0})^2=(1+LIBOR_{1,0})(1+E_0(LIBOR_{1,1}(\omega))).$$

If this holds, then it immediately follows directly from the definition of IFR that $IFR_{1,1}=E_0(LIBOR_{1,1}(\omega))$.

8.9.6 Three Interpretations of the Par Swap Rate

With this brief introduction to IFRs we can now properly interpret the par swap rate in three different ways.

Interpretation 1

We will take the 3-year example. Obtain the IFRs from the LIBOR yield curve. The LIBOR appropriate to the first year of the swap is already known and is $LIBOR_{1,0}$. For the second period we want $E_0(LIBOR_{1,1}(\omega))$ and for the third period $E_0(LIBOR_{1,2}(\omega))$. These last two are each equal to the appropriate IFR, $IFR_{1,1}=E_0(LIBOR_{1,1}(\omega))$ and $IFR_{1,2}=E_0(LIBOR_{1,2}(\omega))$.

The floating leg of the swap is not a bond in the normal sense of having fixed coupons and has the following *expected* cash flows indicated in Figure 8.22.

FIGURE 8.22 The First Interpretation of the Par Swap Rate in Terms of Implied Forward Rates

The PV of this cash-flow stream is PV (expected cash flows from the floating leg)

$$= \frac{NP*LIBOR_{1,0}}{(1+r_1)} + \frac{NP*IFR_{1,1}}{(1+r_2)^2} + \frac{NP*IFR_{1,2}}{(1+r_3)^3}$$

where r_1, r_2, and r_3 are the one-year discount rates from the spot LIBOR yield curve.

The *PV* of the fixed leg (there is no *NP*) has already been calculated as

$$PV(\text{Fixed Leg}) = \frac{R*NP}{(1+r_1)} + \frac{R*NP}{(1+r_2)^2} + \frac{R*NP}{(1+r_3)^3}$$

where R is the Par Swap Rate.

312 **TRADING STRUCTURES BASED ON FORWARD CONTRACTS**

No-arbitrage requires that these two present values must be equal. That is, at initiation, the value of the swap must be zero,

$$\frac{R*NP}{(1+r_1)} + \frac{R*NP}{(1+r_2)^2} + \frac{R*NP}{(1+r_3)^3}$$

$$= \frac{NP*LIBOR_{1,0}}{(1+r_1)} + \frac{NP*IFR_{1,1}}{(1+r_2)^2} + \frac{NP*IFR_{1,2}}{(1+r_3)^3}$$

Dividing through by NP yields,

$$\frac{R}{(1+r_1)} + \frac{R}{(1+r_2)^2} + \frac{R}{(1+r_3)^3} = \frac{LIBOR_{1,0}}{(1+r_1)} + \frac{IFR_{1,1}}{(1+r_2)^2} + \frac{IFR_{1,2}}{(1+r_3)^3}$$

Factoring out the par swap rate R yields,

$$R*\left[\frac{1.0}{(1+r_1)} + \frac{1.0}{(1+r_2)^2} + \frac{1.0}{(1+r_3)^3}\right]$$

$$= \frac{LIBOR_{1,0}}{(1+r_1)} + \frac{IFR_{1,1}}{(1+r_2)^2} + \frac{IFR_{1,2}}{(1+r_3)^3}$$

$$R*\left[B'_{0,1} + B'_{0,2} + B'_{0,3}\right]$$

$$= LIBOR_{1,0}*B'_{0,1} + IFR_{1,1}*B'_{0,2} + IFR_{1,2}*B'_{0,3}$$

where we have used the notation $B'_{0,1}$ for the unit discount bonds indicated with payoff \$1.0 at their respective maturity dates.

This yields the solution for R as,

$$R = \frac{LIBOR_{1,0}*B'_{0,1} + IFR_{1,1}*B'_{0,2} + IFR_{1,2}*B'_{0,3}}{B'_{0,1} + B'_{0,2} + B'_{0,3}}$$

$$= \frac{LIBOR_{1,0}*B'_{0,1}}{B'_{0,1} + B'_{0,2} + B'_{0,3}} + \frac{IFR_{1,1}*B'_{0,2}}{B'_{0,1} + B'_{0,2} + B'_{0,3}} + \frac{IFR_{1,2}*B'_{0,3}}{B'_{0,1} + B'_{0,2} + B'_{0,3}}$$

$$= \frac{B'_{0,1}}{B'_{0,1} + B'_{0,2} + B'_{0,3}}*LIBOR_{1,0} + \frac{B'_{0,2}}{B'_{0,1} + B'_{0,2} + B'_{0,3}}*IFR_{1,1}$$

$$+ \frac{B'_{0,3}}{B'_{0,1} + B'_{0,2} + B'_{0,3}}*IFR_{1,2}$$

This provides our *first* interpretation of the par swap rate as a weighted average of current LIBOR and the IFRs. For the first period, the current 1-year $LIBOR_{1,0}$ can be thought of as the IFR for period one, denoted by $IFR_{1,0}$. Thus the *par swap rate is a weighted average of all the IFRs.*

The weights add up to 1.0 and are the current prices of 1, 2, and 3-year unit discount LIBOR bonds each expressed as a percentage of the sum of the values of those bonds,

$$R = \frac{B'_{0,1}}{B'_{0,1} + B'_{0,2} + B'_{0,3}} * LIBOR_{1,0} + \frac{B'_{0,2}}{B'_{0,1} + B'_{0,2} + B'_{0,3}} * IFR_{1,1}$$

$$+ \frac{B'_{0,3}}{B'_{0,1} + B'_{0,2} + B'_{0,3}} * IFR_{1,2}$$

Interpretation 2

This representation is equivalent to that given in section 8.9.4 of the par swap rate as

$$\frac{1.0 - B'_{0,3}}{B'_{0,1} + B'_{0,2} + B'_{0,3}}$$

To establish this equivalence, all we have to do is to show that,

$$1.0 - B'_{0,3} = LIBOR_{1,0} * B'_{0,1} + IFR_{1,1} * B'_{0,2} + IFR_{1,2} * B'_{0,3}$$

Re-write $LIBOR_{1,0}$ as r_1, where r_1 is the LIBOR zero yield curve rate used to price $B'_{0,1}$, r_2 is the LIBOR zero yield curve rate used to price $B'_{0,2}$, and r_3 is the LIBOR zero yield curve rate used to price $B'_{0,3}$.

Using the definitions of the IFRs we obtain that the right hand side of the required equality, $LIBOR_{1,0}*(B'_{0,1})+[IFR_{1,1}]*(B'_{0,2})+[IFR_{1,2}]*(B'_{0,3})$, is equal to,

$$\frac{r_1}{(1+r_1)} + \left[\frac{(1+r_2)^2}{(1+r_1)} - 1.0\right] * \left(\frac{1}{(1+r_2)^2}\right) + \left[\frac{(1+r_3)^3}{(1+r_2)^2} - 1.0\right] * \left(\frac{1}{(1+r_3)^3}\right)$$

$$= \frac{r_1}{(1+r_1)} + \left[\frac{1}{(1+r_1)} - \frac{1}{(1+r_2)^2}\right] + \left[\frac{1}{(1+r_2)^2} - \frac{1}{(1+r_3)^3}\right]$$

$$= \frac{r_1}{(1+r_1)} + \frac{1}{(1+r_1)} - \frac{1}{(1+r_3)^3}$$

$$= \frac{r_1+1}{(1+r_1)} - \frac{1}{(1+r_3)^3}$$

$$= 1 - B'_{0,3}$$

314 **TRADING STRUCTURES BASED ON FORWARD CONTRACTS**

This is what we wanted to demonstrate because it is the left side of

$$1.0 - B'_{0,3} = LIBOR_{1,0} * B'_{0,1} + IFR_{1,1} * B'_{0,2} + IFR_{1,2} * B'_{0,3}$$

Interpretation 3

There is a third useful interpretation of the par swap rate that follows from basic bond finance. The short (seller) in a swap (the dealer counterparty in the BBB example) has issued (shorted) a floating-rate bond and invested in (longed) a fixed-rate bond. Verify that the swaps dealer would be *receiving fixed* and *paying floating*.

Therefore, the value of the swap to the *short* the swap is the difference between the value of the variable-rate bond he issued and the fixed-rate bond he has invested in. This value must be zero at initiation of the swap, just as for a single forward contract.

The variable-rate bond is priced at par, as we have seen, while the fixed-rate bond is priced in the usual manner. Equating the values of the two bonds, we see that the fixed-rate bond must have a coupon rate (the par swap rate) that equates the value of the fixed-rate bond to par.

This is where our basic bond finance enters. A fixed-rate bond will sell at par if and only if its coupon rate is equal to its yield to maturity (YTM). Therefore, the *par swap rate is the YTM on the fixed-rate bond implicit in the swap.* This is our third interpretation of the par swap rate.

Summary

Thus, you can think of the par swap rate in three ways:

1. As a *weighted average* of the implied forward rates where the current spot rate is taken as the first implied forward rate.

2. As *interest*, $1 - B'_{0,3}$, on the zero-coupon bond maturing at time $t=3$ (see Figure 8.15) as a percentage of the sum of the bond prices.

3. As the *YTM* of the fixed-rate bond implicit in the swap.

Using these interpretations, we will explore valuation of the swap *after* initiation in the End of Chapter Exercise 4. Just as for a single forward contract, the value of a swap after initiation depends on who you are (the long or the short), and upon what happens in the spot market.

OTC MARKETS AND SWAPS — 315

■ KEY CONCEPTS

1. Commodity Forward Contracts as Single Period Swaps.
2. Strips of Forward Contracts.
3. Swaps as Strips of Forward Contracts.
4. Interest-Rate Swaps Basic Terminology, Paying Fixed and Receiving Floating.
5. Paying Fixed in an IRD (Making Fixed Payments).
6. Receiving Floating in an IRD (Receiving Variable Payments).
7. Eurodollar Futures Strips.
8. Non-Dealer Intermediated Plain Vanilla Interest-Rate Swaps.
9. Dealer Intermediated Plain Vanilla Interest-Rate Swaps.
10. Plain Vanilla Interest-Rate Swaps as Hedge Vehicles.
11. Arbitraging the Swaps Market.
12. Swaps Terminology.
13. The Dealer's Problem, Finding the Other Side to the Swap
14. Are Swaps a Zero Sum Game?
15. Why Financial Institutions Use Swaps.
16. Swaps Pricing.
17. Valuation of the Fixed-Rate Bond.
18. Valuation of the Floating-Rate Bond.
19. Valuation of the Swap at Initiation.
20. Implied Forward Rates (IFRs).
21. Three Interpretations of the Par Swap Rate.

■ END OF CHAPTER EXERCISES FOR CHAPTER 8

1. *(This problem generalizes concept check 4.)*

   a. Convince yourself that if you take a long position at time t in a strip of ED futures contracts, you will end up lending (receiving a fixed rate) in the spot market at the expiration dates of each contract in the strip.
   b. Also, you will be paying a floating rate.

2. *(This problem looks at the swaps-as-a-hedge strategy from section 8.4.2.)*

   a. Draw the cash flow diagram for the swaps hedge strategy.
   b. Convince yourself that this is none other than issuing a fixed-rate bond priced at par where the coupon rate is 6.04%.

316 TRADING STRUCTURES BASED ON FORWARD CONTRACTS

3. *(This exercise is on the groundwork needed to understand swap value.)*

   a. Does the value of a swap depend on who you are, long or short? Explain.
   b. Is there any value to either longs or shorts in a swap at initiation?
   c. Consider the swaps dealer of section 8.9.1. What position does he have in the swap? Why?
   d. What types of bonds are implicit in the swaps dealer's position?
   e. What does the par swap rate do to the value of the bonds implicit in the swaps dealer's position?
   f. Explain the YTM interpretation of the par swap rate.

4. *(This exercise indicates one quick way to see where the value of a swap at an intermediate time, restricted to rate reset dates after initiation, comes from.)*

   a. The swaps dealer is _____ the fixed-rate bond and _____ the floating rate bond.
   b. Does the variable-rate bond change in value as the short–term rate, in terms of which it is defined, changes?
   c. From where and only from where can any value changes to the swaps dealer's position come from?
   d. Suppose that the YTM on the fixed-rate bond that the dealer is _____ goes up. What happens to the value of the swaps dealer's position in the fixed-rate bond?

(*Hint*: the coupon rate on the fixed-rate bond, the par swap rate, doesn't change because it is fixed at initiation of the swap.)

   e. Based on d. what happens to the value of the swaps dealer's position in the swap as interest rates increase across the board?
   f. Repeat d. and e. for a decline in interest rates.
   g. Summarize your conclusions on the intermediate value of a swap to the swaps dealer.

5. Repeat exercise 4 for the counterparty on the opposite side of the swap, like BBB in our discussion.

OTC MARKETS AND SWAPS 317

■ SELECTED CONCEPT CHECK SOLUTIONS

Concept Check 1

The truth of 1. is the argument in the text. The long gets to *buy* the underlying commodity at time T at the fixed forward price contracted at time t, $F_{t,T}$. This means that he pays fixed. But then he owns a commodity that is worth its spot price, $P_T(\omega)$. So he could either sell that commodity at time T in the spot market for its spot price, which is variable (floating) as of time t, or he could *mark to market* his commodity position. Either way, he is effectively receiving the floating value of his spot commodity.

The only question is the meaning of 'swaps'. It means he *pays* fixed in return for *receiving* floating. He is swapping (exchanging) his fixed payment for a floating receipt.

Concept Check 2

The truth of 2. is just the opposite side of the argument for 1. The short gets to *sell* the underlying commodity at time T at the fixed forward price contracted at time t, $F_{t,T}$. This means that he receives fixed. But, in order to sell the underlying commodity at time T, he has to first somehow acquire it. That is, he has to acquire an asset that is worth $P_T(\omega)$ at time T. That acquisition corresponds to a floating outflow.

The meaning of 'swaps' for the short is that he *receives* fixed in return for *paying* floating. He is swapping (exchanging) his floating payment for a fixed receipt.

Concept Check 3

a. First, we always have to keep in mind the underlier in a futures contract and not speculate as to what it is. The potential confusion is between the *quote mechanism*, which is in terms of rates, and the *contract specifications* which are in terms of the underlying money market instrument.

According to the contract specifications, the underlier for the ED futures contract traded on the CME is a 3-month Eurodollar time deposit that has 3 months to expiration on the delivery date, time T.

b. What this means is that if you take a short position in the contract, you are selling forward (issuing) the underlying 3-month ED time deposit. As such, you are making a forward borrowing commitment.

318 TRADING STRUCTURES BASED ON FORWARD CONTRACTS

In the world of forward (futures) contracts this means that you are committing to *pay* a fixed rate over the life of the forward loan. You could always borrow in the spot loan market at the future times. What the forward concept buys you is the ability to do so at *fixed rates in the future*.

The mechanics of ED futures are a little tricky because they are cash-settled contracts. This means that, to do the actual borrowing, you have to go into the spot market at time T and arrange the loan.

It would therefore appear that you are getting a variable loan rate, because the spot rate on 3-month loans at time T is not known at time t.

However, as discussed in Chapter 7, combined with daily settlement cash flows, the *effective* borrowing rate is the rate you contracted at when you took the short position in the ED futures contract, that is, $FLIBOR_{3,t,T}$.

Concept Check 5 (Graphical Representation of Swap Cash Flows)

a. The swap obligates Alfa to pay a fixed amount equal to $(.05/2)*$100,000,000=$2,500,000$ every six months for the next 5 years (10 semi-annual periods).

b. In return for this $2,500,000, Alfa will receive a floating payment equal to $LIBOR_{3,t'}(\omega)/4*$100,000,000$ where t' is alternatively time 0.25, 0.5, 0.75, 1.0, 1.25, 1.5, 1.75, 2.0, 2.25, 2.5, 2.75, 3.0, 3.25, 3.5, 3.75, 4.0, 4.25, 4.5, 4.75, and 5.0 (every 3 months), and $LIBOR_{3,t'}$ is the spot 3-month LIBOR rate prevailing in the market at time t'.

The vertical arrows pointing upwards represent the fixed cash outflows owed by Alfa. The arrows pointing downwards represent floating cash flows received by Alfa.

FIGURE 8.5 (Solution) Cash Flows to Alfa in the Non-Intermediated Swap

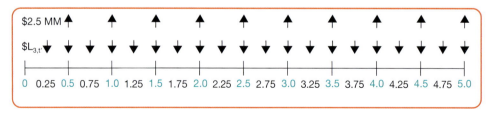

Concept Check 6

a. The implied forward rate on 1-year loans one year from today,

$$IFR_{1,1} = \frac{1.065^2}{1.06} - 1.0 = 7.002\%$$

b. The implied forward rate on 1-year loans two years from today,

$$IFR_{1,2} = \frac{1.07^3}{1.065^2} - 1.0 = 8.0071\%$$

PART 3
Options

CHAPTER 9

INTRODUCTION TO OPTIONS MARKETS

9.1	Options and Option Scenarios	323
9.2	A Framework for Learning Options	326
9.3	Definitions and Terminology for Plain Vanilla Put and Call Options	327
9.4	A Basic American Call (Put) Option Pricing Model	332
9.5.	Reading Option Price Quotes	334
9.6	Going Beyond the Basic Definitions: Infrastructure to Understand Puts and Calls	337
9.7	Identifying Long and Short Positions in an Underlying	339

9.1 OPTIONS AND OPTION SCENARIOS

We have discussed forward contracts in detail. These are fundamental derivative securities. For example, both futures contracts and swaps are based on the forward contract concept, and we have emphasized this connection. This chapter introduces another category of basic derivative securities—put and call options.

These options can be viewed as the most fundamental derivative securities because they serve as the building blocks for constructing other derivative securities, including forward contracts and swaps. Synthesizing and pricing complex derivative securities from simpler, relatively well-known financial instruments such as stocks, bonds, and plain vanilla options is the subject of financial engineering.

Options are important to both professionals and the average investor because they appear in many different financial scenarios that investors will routinely encounter. Most investors are familiar with ordinary securities like stocks and bonds. The stock market is constantly in the limelight. Due to the financial crisis of 2007–2008, credit (bond) markets are also being increasingly publicized.

Far less familiar and less understood are the options embedded in ordinary securities. Many examples abound: the conversion feature in a convertible bond, the callability provision in callable bonds, the pre-payment option in fixed-rate mortgages, the variable-rate feature in variable-rate mortgages, lease arrangements wherein the lease holder has the option to buy, and many, many more.

Options occur not only in the field of investments, but also in corporate finance. For example, understanding something as basic as the common stock of a corporation is a conceptual hurdle, if you think about it. If you go back to your basic corporate finance course, you probably learned that the common stock of a corporation is a claim on the *residual* cash flows of the firm. While this is true, by definition as an accounting definition, it does not fully explain the equity of a firm. Using options analysis, researchers have found that the equity of a firm can be better explained as an option on total firm value with exercise price equal to the face value of the debt of the firm.

Options also frequently arise in strategic, option-like scenarios. For example, many options are neither traded as financial instruments (like ordinary stock options), nor embedded in financial instruments (like pre-payment features). Options of this type are called *real asset options* because they are built upon real assets rather than upon financial assets as the underlying security.

Key examples are the growth opportunities of a firm, the research and development efforts of a firm, or the option of a corporation to abandon a project, or wait to invest in one.

Many examples of corporate and other real-world decision making are not fully understandable without appealing to the option concept. As just one important example, starting up a firm could be a losing proposition when viewed in isolation of the expansion opportunities it creates. But investing in the start-up creates the option to invest in the growth opportunities it may create.

When a Hollywood studio introduces a film to the public, it also obtains the valuable option to introduce sequels. These options may or may not be exercised, depending on the success or failure of the first films. But the point is that sequels aren't even feasible without the initial film.

Table 9.1 indicates the variety of options currently traded on the *Chicago Board of Options Exchange* (www.cboe.com). In general, exchange-traded options are subject to the rules of the specific exchanges, like futures contracts.

Further, a large part of option trading occurs in the OTC (over-the-counter market) and are tailor-made to the needs of the counterparties without intermediation by an options exchange.

TABLE 9.1 Exchange-Traded (CBOE) Option Contracts

Individual Equity Options
Equity Options (100 shares)
Mini Options (10 shares)
Equity Leaps
Equity Flex
Index Options
Volatility Indexes
Broad Based Indexes
Standard & Poor's Indexes
Dow Jones Indexes
Nasdaq Indexes
Russell Indexes
CBOE Sector Indexes
Morgan Stanley Indexes
International Indexes
Options on Exchange-Traded Products (ETPs)
Commodity-based
Currency-related
Global-related ETP
Interest-rate-related (bond funds)
Alternative Expiration Options
Weeklys
Quarterlys
Binary Options
S&P 500 Index (SPX)
Volatility Index (VIX)
Credit Events (CEBOs)

Reprinted with permission from CBOE.com

326 OPTIONS

■ CONCEPT CHECK 1

a. Go to www.cboe.com and check out the product specifications for individual equity options.
b. Do CBOE individual equity options specify cash or physical delivery?
c. Who would be doing the delivering?

■ CONCEPT CHECK 2

a. Go to www.cboe.com and check out the product specifications for *mini* equity options.
b. Do CBOE mini options specify cash or physical delivery?
c. Who would be doing the delivering?

9.2 A FRAMEWORK FOR LEARNING OPTIONS

With some web research, you can gain a basic appreciation for the vast array of options' applications in finance. Options are complex instruments with significant subtleties and nuances. They are best understood through mastering basic concepts, with numerical and strategic examples.

Moving forward in section 9.3, we will explore the basic definitions and terminology for call and put options, and present a basic American option pricing model that decomposes option prices into *Intrinsic Value* and *Time Premium* in section 9.4. We will learn how to read actual price quotes in section 9.5, and then immediately apply this pricing model to actual option price quotes.

In order to obtain a deeper understanding of puts and calls, we introduce the definitions of payoff and profit diagrams in section 9.6. This is an important first step in learning how to identify and analyze the economic characteristics of put and call options, and how to use them strategically.

We defer the application of the profit, payoff diagram methodology to the six different naked positions that can be held in an underlying and in puts and calls until Chapter 10. Finally, we revisit how to identify long and short positions in section 9.7 and give some new examples thereof.

While studying the following material, keep in mind the context in which we are studying options as described by the following three points:

INTRODUCTION TO OPTIONS MARKETS 327

1. Naked (unhedged) long (short) positions abound in practice, and are subject to price volatility. Profitability comes only from an increase (decrease) in the price of the underlying. Therefore, holding such positions unhedged is a speculative strategy.

2. A call (put) option is different from a naked underlying position, and therefore is not a substitute for it. Like a forward contract, it is the leveraged *right* (but not the obligation) to take a long (short) position in some underlying financial asset, or scenario, at a fixed cost at any time prior to and including a fixed date in the future.

   Options incorporate both leverage and insurance features. *You cannot directly compare two financial instruments with differing degrees of leverage.*

3. While one can also *speculate* on option prices, options can be used in *hedging* strategies to limit the volatility of naked long (short) positions. They fulfill a hedging function just as forwards, futures, and swaps do. However, not in the exact same way, because their payoff profiles differ.

9.3 DEFINITIONS AND TERMINOLOGY FOR PLAIN VANILLA PUT AND CALL OPTIONS

Since there is such a wide array of options and options scenarios, the following definitions will be rather general. Put options seem more intuitive than call options because they embody the idea of insurance for long positions.

However, we will see later that call options provide the appropriate insurance for *short* positions. So we treat puts and calls symmetrically. European puts and calls are very closely connected through Put-Call Parity, which will be discussed in Chapter 11.

At this general level, it is not possible to fully understand put options without understanding call options (and vice versa). Later, when we introduce the Binomial option pricing model and the Black–Scholes model, this circularity problem will be resolved because these models give actual pricing formulas for European puts and calls under specific assumptions.

1. The *underlying* is the financial asset or the scenario upon which the option is based. In a naked *long* position in an underlying, an increase (decrease) in the price of the underlying will be profitable (unprofitable).

   In a naked *short* position in an underlying, an increase (decrease) in the price of the underlying will be unprofitable (profitable).

328 **OPTIONS**

2. A *call (put) option* is the right, but not the obligation, to take a *long (short)* position in some underlying financial asset or scenario at a fixed cost at any time prior to and including a fixed date in the future.

There are at least two kinds of options. An *American* option has nothing to do with America, and is an option that can be exercised at any time point prior to and including the expiration date.

A *European* option (nothing to do with Europe) is an option that can be exercised only at the expiration date.

3. The *exercise price* (also called the *strike price*) of an option is the *fixed* price specified in the option contract.

4. *Exercising the option* is making the transaction specified in the option contract.

One exercises a standard stock *call* option by *buying* 100 shares of the specific underlying stock at the exercise price per share.

One exercises a standard stock *put* option by *selling* 100 shares of stock at the exercise price per share.

Exercising the option is never mandatory.

The alternatives to exercising an option are to sell it (trade it out) or to continue to hold it unexercised.

5. The *maturity date* (also called the *expiration date*) is the fixed final date specified in the contract.

6. The *call (put) premium* (also called the *option market premium*) is the price at which the option contract trades in the options market.

7. The *option buyer* (also called the *long, denoted* **+**) is the individual who has the right(s) specified in the option contract.

8. The *option seller* (also called the *short, denoted* –) is the individual with respect to whom the option buyer can exercise the right(s) specified in the option contract.

In return for giving away this right, the option seller receives the option's market premium.

The *Options Clearing Corporation* (OCC) acts as an intermediary between buyers and sellers of options.

9. The next concept is *moneyness* of calls and puts.

Let t be the current time, T the expiration date of the call option, S_t the current price of the underlying financial asset or scenario, and E the exercise price of the option.

A *call* option is said to be,

   a. in-the-money [ITM] at time t if $S_t > E$.
   b. at-the-money [ATM] at time t if $S_t = E$.
   c. out of-the-money [OTM] at time t if $S_t < E$.

Note that this is a dynamic concept. An option can change its moneyness status at any point in time. In fact this dynamic quality (volatility) is what makes options useful and interesting.

Turning to put options, a *put* option is said to be,

   a. in-the-money [ITM] at time t if $S_t < E$.
   b. at-the-money [ATM] at time t if $S_t = E$.
   c. out of-the-money [OTM] at time t if $S_t > E$.

That is, the moneyness of a put option is just the opposite of a call. Figure 9.1 illustrates the moneyness concept and its dynamic character for a call (put) option. Note that both puts and calls are at-the-money at the stock prices which cross the E line.

FIGURE 9.1 Moneyness of a Call (Put) Option

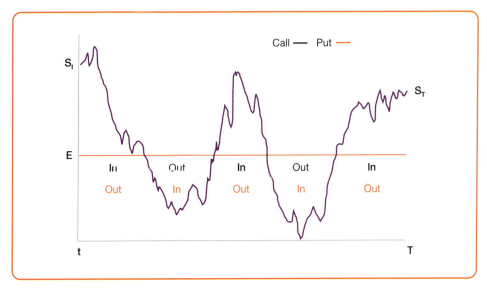

OPTIONS

10. A *call option's Intrinsic Value (Immediate Exercise Value)* at a specific time t is,

$$\text{MAX}[S_t-E, 0]=S_t-E \text{ if } S_t \geq E$$
$$=0 \text{ if } S_t < E$$

One can think of the Intrinsic Value of a call option as its immediate value *if* one could exercise it immediately. That is, if the option is an American option. The reason is that if one could exercise the call option at time t, then one buys the underlying for \$$E$ per unit by exercising the option. This is the definition of a call option.

One could then sell the underlying asset at its market price, S_t. These actions would *realize* the American option's intrinsic value.

The only time it *might* make economic sense to exercise the call option is when the exercise price is less than, or possibly equal to, the underlying's market price. Otherwise, one does not exercise the call and its payoff is zero as indicated.

11. A *put option's Intrinsic Value (Immediate Exercise Value)* at a specific time t is,

$$\text{MAX}[E-S_t, 0]=E-S_t \text{ if } S_t \leq E$$
$$=0 \text{ if } S_t > E$$

One can think of the Intrinsic Value of a put option as its value *if* one could exercise it immediately. Once again, this is only possible for American puts. The reason is that if one exercises the put option at time t, one *sells* the underlying for \$$E$ per unit (by definition of the put option). Of course, to sell it, one has to first acquire the underlying asset in the market at its market price S_t.

The only time it *might* make economic sense to exercise the put option is when the exercise price is greater than the market price. Otherwise, one does not exercise the put and its payoff is zero as indicated.

12. A *call (put) option's Time Premium* is the value associated with the ability to exercise the call (put) option at *any time in the future* (not immediately) prior to and including the expiration date.

INTRODUCTION TO OPTIONS MARKETS

Another term for an option's time premium is the *Delayed Exercise Premium*, because one is looking at that part of the option's value that corresponds to delayed exercise.

■ CONCEPT CHECK 3

a. Who gets the option's rights?
b. Who gets the option's market premium?
c. What are the right(s) associated to a European call option?
d. What are the right(s) associated to a European put option?
e. What are the right(s) associated to a American call option?
f. What are the right(s) associated to a American put option?

■ CONCEPT CHECK 4

Here is Figure 5.2 from Chapter 5. In this concept check, we will modify it for option positions.

FIGURE 5.2 The Futures Clearing House

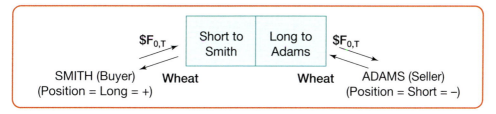

Smith takes a *long* position in a single IBM equity *call* option. Adams is on the other side of this trade. Fill in the commodity flows, cash flows, and positions as indicated by question marks in Figure 9.2.

FIGURE 9.2 The Options Clearing House (Calls)

OPTIONS

■ CONCEPT CHECK 5

Here is Figure 5.2 from Chapter 5. In this concept check, we will modify it for put option positions.

FIGURE 5.2 **The Futures Clearing House**

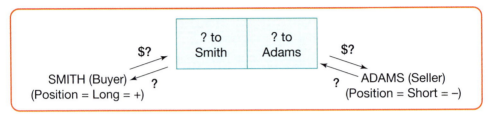

a. Smith takes a *long* position in a single IBM equity *put* option. Adams is on the other side of this trade. Fill in the commodity flows, cash flows, and positions as indicated by question marks in Figure 9.3.

FIGURE 9.3 **The Options Clearing House (Puts)**

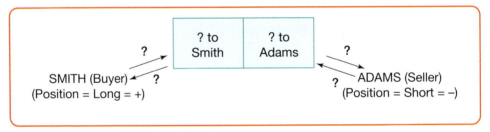

9.4 A BASIC AMERICAN CALL (PUT) OPTION PRICING MODEL

With this minimal set of definitions one can construct an American call (put) option pricing model! An American call (put) option confers on its owner only two rights:

1. The right to exercise the option *immediately*.
2. The right to exercise the option in the *future*.

■ CONCEPT CHECK 6

a. When you sell an option, what does the prospective buyer buy?
b. When you sell an option, what does the option seller sell?

Some might think that there is another right which is to sell the option to someone else. This could be called the *liquidity* option. From a valuation perspective, liquidity is not a separate right distinct from 1. and 2.

On the other hand, liquid options could command a liquidity premium and the bid–asked spread could be lower for liquid vs. illiquid options. This is more of a transactions costs phenomenon, as opposed to an embedded rights feature.

The first right is worth the option's intrinsic value, and the second right is currently worth the option's time premium.

Denote the current (time t) value of the American call option by C_t^A and let P_t^A denote the American put option price at time t. The basic American option pricing model says:

$$C_t^A = (\text{Call Intrinsic Value})_t + (\text{Call Time Premium at time})_t$$
$$= IV(C_t^A) + TP(C_t^A)$$

$$P_t^A = (\text{Put Intrinsic Value})_t + (\text{Put Time Premium at time})_t$$
$$= IV(P_t^A) + TP(P_t^A).$$

The idea behind this American option pricing model is simply that, if the financial instrument we are attempting to value—an American call (put) option in this case—has an implicit or explicit payoff associated to it, then its price must incorporate the PV of those payoffs. Otherwise, there would be mispricing and an arbitrage opportunity.

That's the idea, but how do you *prove* our American option pricing model? The proof is 'by definition'. One simply *defines* the time premium, $TP(C_t^A)$ in the case of calls or, $TP(P_t^A)$ in the case of puts, as the difference between the option's premium and intrinsic value. That is, *define* the time premia by,

$$TP(C_t^A) \equiv C_t^A - IV(C_t^A),$$

$$TP(P_t^A) \equiv P_t^A - IV(P_t^A).$$

This is a neat trick, but only a trick. This American option pricing model is interesting because it uses only the basic definitions. However, it is not well-suited to European options because, for a European option, ordinary intrinsic value is not immediately *realizable*, since you can't early exercise a European option.

We will discuss an analogous model for European put and call options in Chapter 11, in the context of rational option pricing.

334 **OPTIONS**

At this point, we can immediately apply this American option pricing model to examine market option prices. Note that CBOE individual equity options *are* all American (see concept check 1). Therefore, it is legitimate to apply our American option pricing model.

9.5 READING OPTION PRICE QUOTES

The most important stock option exchange in the USA is the Chicago Board Options Exchange (www.cboe.com). One can obtain the full specifications of equity call options traded on the CBOE by going to the site and hitting 'products', then 'equity options' (see concept check 1).

A standard stock option is the right, but not the obligation, to purchase 100 shares of a publicly traded common stock at a fixed price, the strike price, at or before a fixed date, the expiration date.

Let's consider the nearby call options for Merck Inc. To obtain the following list of price quotes go to www.cboe.com, select '*products*', then '*options on single stocks and Exchange Traded Products*', hit '*quotes and data*', then hit '*delayed quotes classic*' and insert the symbol *Mrk*. Then choose '*list near term at-the-money options & Weeklys if avail*'.

The quote date and time for this particular quote was Feb 22, 2008 @ 15:54 ET as indicated. Just around financial crisis time. You are asked to do an update in End of Chapter Exercise 1.

One sees, in Table 9.2, that numerous Merck options were traded. Here we have taken the *nearby* options only. These are the options that mature in the closest several months to the observation date. In this case, these are the call and put options on Merck maturing in March and April of 2008.

Note that Merck has an option series based upon exercise prices changing in $2.50 intervals around $45. This procedure captures options that are in-the-money and out-of-the-money. As the stock price changes, new options will be issued with new exercise prices reflecting the current stock price level.

Note that the *underlying* (Merck stock) is traded on the NYSE, not on the CBOE. So, we have no guarantee that the stock price observation was made at the same time as the observation for Merck options. This leads to the *non-simultaneous price quote* problem.

Prices in alternative markets need to be compared at the same time. If you think you have discovered an arbitrage opportunity by reading the *Wall Street Journal*, or other summary data, the opportunity probably is not real. However,

TABLE 9.2   **Merck Options Price Quotes**

MRK (MERCK & CO INC)   **45.63** −0.50

Feb 22, 2008 @ 15:54 ET   Bid **N/E** Ask **N/E** Size **N/ExN/E** Vol **9241648**

Calls	Last Sale	Net	Bid	Ask	Vol	Open Int	Puts	Last Sale	Net	Bid	Ask	Vol	Open Int
08 Mar 42.50 (MRK CV-E)	4.10	0.0	3.40	3.60	0	786	08 Mar 42.50 (MRK OV-E)	0.42	+0.12	0.35	0.45	260	2804
08 Mar 45.00 (MRK CI-E)	1.65	−0.40	1.60	1.70	267	2355	08 Mar 45.00 (MRK OI-E)	1.25	+0.25	1.05	1.15	604	14110
08 Mar 47.50 (MRK CW-E)	0.60	−0.20	0.55	0.60	26	7651	08 Mar 47.50 (MRK OW-E)	2.70	+0.50	2.55	2.65	45	17273
08 Mar 50.00 (MRK CJ-E)	0.20	−0.10	0.15	0.20	702	15476	08 Mar 50.00 (MRK OJ-E)	4.20	0.0	4.60	4.80	0	19148
08 Apr 42.50 (MRK DV-E)	5.60	0.0	4.10	4.30	0	646	08 Apr 42.50 MRK PV-E)	0.90	0.0	1.00	1.10	0	3182
08 Apr 45.00 (MRK DI-E)	2.95	0.0	2.55	2.65	0	2595	08 Apr 45.00 (MRK PI-E)	2.15	+0.45	1.95	2.05	52	8611
08 Apr 47.50 (MRK DW-E)	1.35	−0.30	1.40	1.50	24	5905	08 Apr 47.50 (MRK PW-E)	2.85	0.0	3.30	3.40	0	6755
08 Apr 50.00 (MRK DJ-E)	0.70	−0.20	0.70	0.80	30	15176	08 Apr 50.00 (MRK PJ-E)	5.40	+1.19	5.10	5.20	3	6078

Reprinted with permission from CBOE.com.

336 OPTIONS

TABLE 9.3 **A Particular Merck Option Price Quote**

Calls	Last Sale	Net	Bid	Ask	Vol	Open Int
08 Mar 45.00 (MRK CI-E)	1.65	−0.40	1.60	1.70	267	2355

Reprinted with permission from CBOE.com.

the stock price of $45.63 on the observation date gives us a rough, but not exact, idea of the stock price at the quote time.

Consider the price quote for the second call option in Table 9.3 which was excerpted from Table 9.2. We will discuss each component of the basic call option price quote in Table 9.3.

a. 08 Mar refers to the *expiration date* in March 2008.
b. The *exercise price* of the call is $45.00.
c. C is the CBOE's *expiration month code* for March calls (O is the code for puts).
d. I is the *strike price code* for 45.00 (http://en.wikipedia.org/wiki/Option_naming_conventionStrike_Price_Codes; accessed May 27, 2015).
e. E indicates that the option was traded on the CBOE Chicago Board Options Exchange (www.cboe.com/delayedquote/quotehelp.aspx; accessed May 27, 2015).
f. The *Last Sale* gives the asked price at which this option was last traded prior to the observation time.
g. *Net* represents the change in the asked option price relative to the previous trade. Investors (not dealers), who buy options, buy at the ask (offered) price and sell options at the bid price.
h. The *Bid* and *Asked prices* were $1.60 and $1.70 for the call.
i. A *standard* equity option always refers to *100* shares of underlying Merck stock, unless it is a mini–option (see concept check 2). In that case, it refers to *10* shares of the underlying stock,
j. *Volume* represents the number of such options traded at the observation date which is 267 (each based on 100 shares of Merck stock).
k. The *Open Interest*, 2355, represents the number of outstanding options (counting one side only) in which investors have taken a buy position as observed on the observation date and time.

This particular call option matures on the Saturday immediately following the third Friday of the expiration month, March 22, 2008. This was the CBOE rule until February 15, 2015. After that date, the expiration date became the third such Friday.

INTRODUCTION TO OPTIONS MARKETS **337**

This option entitles the option buyer (the long) to purchase 100 shares of Merck common stock at $45 per share (100*$45=$4500), on any business day before the expiration date.

This call was *in-the-money* because the stock price was $45.63 which is above the exercise price by $45.63–$45.00=$0.63. So, based on the asked option price of $1.70, the *option's market premium* per share is $1.70.

Since *intrinsic value* is $0.63 per share, using our basic American option pricing model, the rest of the option premium $1.70–$0.63=$1.07 must be *time premium*.

That is, options investors are paying $1.07 per share for the right to exercise this option on any business day prior to the expiration date, except the current date. That is, $1.07 is the *delayed exercise premium* per share. The price they are paying for the ability to exercise this option immediately is $0.63 per share,

$$\$1.70=(\text{Intrinsic Value})_t+(\text{Time Premium at time})_t$$
$$=\$0.63+\$1.07.$$

To get these corresponding values for the entire option, multiply the per share amounts by 100 (for 100 shares).

The basic American option pricing model also explains why out-of-the-money options command a positive price prior to expiration. While out-of-the-money options have zero intrinsic value, they will have time premia at all times except at expiration. From this we see that the value of a call option must equal its intrinsic value when it matures.

■ CONCEPT CHECK 7

a. Explain in detail the 08 Mar 42.50 (MRK OV-*E*) price quote in Table 9.2.

9.6 GOING BEYOND THE BASIC DEFINITIONS: INFRASTRUCTURE TO UNDERSTAND PUTS AND CALLS

In the field of options and derivatives in general, the definitions are more or less straightforward. Learning why these objects are important, recognizing options in far-flung scenarios, and knowing how to use derivative securities, all require a knowledge deeper than the mere definitions.

Our goal will be to provide some techniques of financial engineering (synthesizing complex derivatives) for obtaining this deeper knowledge.

OPTIONS

In the next chapters, we will give many applications of these techniques. For example, we can *break down* European call and put options into their fundamental economic components. This goes a long way towards answering the following basic question,

> *Question*: What do put and call options provide to investors, in terms of profit (net of investment cost) or payoff profiles, that are not immediately or easily available to investors otherwise?

The technology we will develop is simple, yet powerful when pushed to its logical conclusion. It is the systematic use of payoff diagrams and profit diagrams to analyze option strategies.

1. *Payoff diagrams* describe the dollar cash flow (ignoring the investment cost) at the option's expiration date as a function of the underlying stock price at expiration.

2. *Profit diagrams* describe the dollar profits (net of the investment's cost) at the option's expiration as a function of the underlying stock price at expiration. We will pursue this and give many examples in Chapter 10.

■ CONCEPT CHECK 8

a. Draw the payoff diagram for a call's Intrinsic Value function in definition 10 in section 9.3.
b. Draw the payoff diagram for a put's Intrinsic Value function in definition 11 in section 9.3.

Note that the *stock's price at expiration* of the option, S_T, is on the horizontal axis and the *payoff* is on the vertical axis. Thus the payoff diagram gives the payoff to the intrinsic value function, in this case, as a function of the terminal stock price.

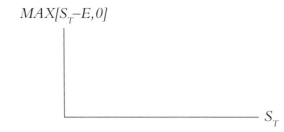

9.7 IDENTIFYING LONG AND SHORT POSITIONS IN AN UNDERLYING

We briefly discussed identifying long and short positions in Chapter 6, Figure 6.1.

Here we will extend the discussion. Derivative securities are all based upon some underlying asset or scenario. The underlying is the financial asset or the scenario upon which the option is based. There are two kinds of positions one can take in an underlying, long or short.

To be long something means that we worry about *selling* it at some point in the future and therefore the worry is that the price declines. For example, we could be long 100 shares of IBM Corp. common stock.

Don't think of long as being equivalent to outright ownership, because long positions can be more sophisticated. A long position could just involve the *anticipation* of selling something in the future. One need not own it today.

For example, suppose that a privately held firm is planning an IPO, and therefore it has an anticipation of selling stock at some future date. Therefore, it is long the IPO and it worries about a price decline, just like an investor who holds publicly traded common stock.

Investigating the subtleties of this kind of distinction is important for applications. Developing an extended notion of long (and short) will reveal that there are many more long (and short) positions lurking out there. Further, they may very well require the hedge protection that derivatives, financial and real-asset based, can provide.

We have defined a current long position in some underlying as any position that *anticipates selling* the underlying at some future point in time, and therefore is concerned about potential price declines. That is, we work backwards from the future to discover the current position. If the future anticipated transaction is to *sell*, then one is long today (see Figure 9.4).

Short positions are harder to understand, and to identify, but no less important than long positions. In a classical short sale of common stock, one borrows the stock from a broker, sells it immediately and then incurs the future obligation to *cover the short sale*.

That is, one must *buy back* the stock at some later time and then return it to the broker. Here the anticipated future transaction is *buying*. As an *anticipatory buyer*, one worries about price increases. So much is clear.

One could define a *short* position in an underlying as any position that anticipates a *buy* transaction in the future. Thus, short doesn't mean selling

340 OPTIONS

something one owns today. Rather, one can sell something one doesn't own! Then one incurs the obligation to buy back the underlying.

An instructive example is the individual who is *naked short a call option*. The individual never owned the option, but they got payment from the option buyer for the option. In return, they are potentially liable for buying the underlying stock and delivering it to the buyer in exchange for the exercise price.

Does this example illustrate our definition of short? First, the option short is naked short, he owns no underlying stock. Second, the option short worries about price *increases*, because the option buyer *could* exercise the option thereby forcing the short to go into the market and buy the stock. Yes, it fits.

Next, consider a short real asset example. It is well known that current energy sources are going to be unable to meet world energy demand 50 years from today. At that time, we will have to *buy* energy at possibly prohibitive prices. That is, we are now in an anticipated buy position, which is the hallmark of a current short energy position.

Understanding this is the key to hedging the short position. One hedge vehicle is energy R&D, a real–asset call option. This shows that a government agency responsible for energy policy must understand the notion of a short option position.

The point is that it is important to recognize the many *implicit short positions* out there and the need to hedge the risk of prices *rising*. Figure 9.4 illustrates how to determine whether one is long or short the underlying.

FIGURE 9.4 Long vs. Short Positions

Anticipated Sell, therefore Long	**Price Worry**
P_0	$P_1\downarrow$
Time 0, Now	Time 1, The Future
Anticipated Buy, therefore Short	**Price Worry**
P_0	$P_1\uparrow$
Time 0, Now	Time 1, The Future

INTRODUCTION TO OPTIONS MARKETS 341

■ KEY CONCEPTS

1. Options and Option Scenarios.
2. Framework For Learning Options.
3. Option Definitions For Plain Vanilla Calls and Puts.
4. A Basic American Call (Put) Option Pricing Model.
5. Reading Option Price Quotes.
6. Going Beyond the Basic Definitions, Infrastructure to Understand Puts and Calls.
7. Identifying Long and Short Positions in an Underlying with Examples.

■ END OF CHAPTER EXERCISES FOR CHAPTER 9

1. (*Price quotes*)

    Go to CBOE.com and update the Merck example in Table 9.2 by answering the following questions:

    a. What has happened to the underlier (Merck stock) since 2008?
    b. What are the exercise prices for some of Merck's liquid options?
    c. Are the increments in Merck's option prices still $2.50?
    d. What option cycle does Merck belong to?

2. (*Embedded options*)

    a. List some embedded options that investors are likely to encounter.
    b. List some real asset options that financial managers are likely to encounter.
    c. Name an option that incorporates futures contracts. Where are these typically traded?

3. (*American option pricing model*)

    a. State the American option pricing model of section 9.4.
    b. What is the methodology used to prove the result of a.?
    c. Why doesn't the methodology in b. immediately apply to European options?
    d. 'An in-the-money American option is a combination of IV and TP'. Explain.
    e. 'An out-of-the-money American option is pure TP'. Explain.
    f. What happens to TP as time to maturity, τ, approaches zero?

342 OPTIONS

g. What happens to an American option's market premium as τ approaches zero?

h. What happens to IV_t as τ approaches zero?

4. (*Long and short positions in real asset options*)

Consider the timely topics, health care and health insurance. Most people consider the status of their own health and its health care.

a. What position do most people have in their own health, long or short?

b. What are some natural hedges for the concern in a.?

c. What is a financial hedge for the concern in a.?

d. What position would you take in c. in executing the hedge?

e. How does the issue of rapidly rising health care costs fit into this discussion?

f. How does the issue of rising health care insurance premiums fit into this discussion?

◼ SELECTED CONCEPT CHECK SOLUTIONS

Concept Check 1

a. According to Figure 9.5, under 'Settlement of Option Exercise', the actual shares of the underlying stock would have to be delivered.

b. The option seller always does the delivery.

Concept Check 2

b. See Figure 9.6, under 'physical settlement'.

c. The option seller always does the delivery.

Concept Check 6

a. The option buyer buys the rights, and only the rights, that the option confers on the option's owner.

b. The seller sells those rights, and only those rights, in return for the premium.

INTRODUCTION TO OPTIONS MARKETS · 343

FIGURE 9.5 CBOE Equity Option Specifications

Equity Options

Exchange traded equity options are "physical delivery" options. This means that there is a physical delivery of the underlying stock to or from your brokerage account if the option is exercised. The owner of an equity option can exercise the contract at any time prior to the exercise deadline set by the investor's brokerage firm. Generally this deadline occurs on the option's last day of trading. The expiration date for equity options is the Saturday immediately following the third Friday of the expiration month until February 15, 2015. On and after February 15, 2015, the expiration date will be the third Friday of the expiration month. If this third Friday happens to be an exchange holiday, then the last day is the third Thursday of the month. Check with your brokerage firm about its procedures and deadlines for instruction to exercise any equity options. After the option's expiration date, the equity option will cease to exist.

For additional information on equity options, visit the Equity Option Strategies section of the web site.

Equity Options Product Specifications

Symbol:
The option symbols are the same as for the underlying equity security. Visit the CBOE Symbol Directory for specific symbols.

Underlying:
Generally, 100 shares of the underlying equity security.

Strike Price Intervals:
Generally, 2 1/2 points when the strike price is between $5 and $25, 5 points when the strike price is between $25 and $200, and 10 points when the strike price is over $200. Strikes are adjusted for splits, re-capitalizations, etc.

Strike (Exercise) Prices:
In-, at- and out-of-the-money strike prices are initially listed. New series are generally added when the underlying trades through the highest or lowest strike price available.

Premium Quotation:
Stated in decimals. One point equals $100. Minimum tick for options trading below 3 is .05 and for all other series, .10.

Expiration Date:
Saturday immediately following the third Friday of the expiration month until February 15, 2015. On and after February 15, 2015, the expiration date will be the third Friday of the expiration month.

Expiration Months:
Two near-term months plus two additional months from the January, February or March quarterly cycles.

Exercise Style:
American-Equity options generally may be exercised on any business day before the expiration date.

Settlement of Option Exercise:
Exercise notices properly tendered on any business day will result in delivery of the underlying stock on the third business day following exercise.

Position and Exercise Limits:
Limits vary according to the number of outstanding shares and past six-month trading volume of the underlying stock. The largest in capitalization and most frequently traded stocks have an option position limit of 250,000 contracts (with adjustments for splits, re-capitalizations, etc.) on the same side of the market; smaller capitalization stocks have position limits of 200,000, 75,000, 50,000 or 25,000 contracts (with adjustments for splits, re-capitalizations, etc.) on the same side of the market. The number of contracts on the same side of the market that may be exercised within any five consecutive business days is equal to the position limit. Equity option positions must be aggregated with equity LEAPS positions on the same underlying for position and exercise limit purposes. Exemptions may be available for certain qualified hedging strategies.

Reporting Requirements:
Please refer to Exchange Rule 4.13 for information pertaining to reporting requirements for positions in excess of 200 contracts.

Margin:
Purchases of puts or calls with 9 months or less until expiration must be paid for in full. Writers of uncovered puts or calls must deposit/maintain 100% of the option proceeds* plus 20% of the aggregate contract value (current equity price x $100) minus the amount by which the option is out-of-the-money, if any, subject to a minimum for calls of option proceeds* plus 10% of the aggregate contract value and a minimum for puts of option proceeds* plus 10% of the aggregate exercise price amount. (*For calculating maintenance margin, use option current market value instead of option proceeds.) Additional margin may be required pursuant to Exchange Rule 12.10.

Last Trading Day:
Trading in equity options will ordinarily cease on the business day (usually a Friday) preceding the expiration date.

Trading Hours:
8:30 a.m. – 3:00 p.m. Central Time (Chicago time).

Reprinted with permission from CBOE.com, 2014.

FIGURE 9.6 CBOE Mini Equity Option Specifications

CBOE Mini Options

New CBOE Mini options with physical settlement began trading on March 18, 2013. The new Mini options represent a deliverable of 10 shares of an underlying security, whereas standard equity options represent a deliverable of 100 shares. The options symbol for the new Mini options will be the underlying security symbol followed by the number 7 (see examples in the table below).

In addition, please note that the cash-settled Mini-SPX options (ticker XSP (1/10th the size of SPX, with a multiplier of 100)) have been listed since 2006 www.cboe.com/XSP.

The Mini options are designed to provide added investment flexibility. For example, for an investor who holds 10 to 90 shares of AAPL or GOOG stock, the new mini options could provide that investor with tools that have the potential to be more efficient and tailored for strategies such as covered call writing or hedging.

SECURITY	MINI OPTIONS SYMBOL*	UNDERLYING SECURITY SYMBOL	MINI OPTIONS MULTIPLIER	NOTIONAL VALUE COVERED BY MINI OPTION (IF OPTION WERE OFFERED ON FEBRUARY 8, 2013, APPROXIMATE)
Mini options with physical settlement; launched in March 2013–				
Amazon.com Inc.	AMZN7	AMZN	10	$2,620 (10 × $262)
Google Inc.	GOGL7	GOOG	10	$7,850 (10 × $785)
SPDR Gold Trust	GLD7	GLD	10	$1,620 (10 × $162)
SPDR S&P 500	SPY7	SPY	10	$1,520 (10 × $152)
Mini options with cash settlement; launched in 2005–				
Mini-SPX Index (1/10 the size of SPX)	XSP	XSP	100	$15,200 (100 × $152)

* The options symbol for the new Mini options usually is the underlying security symbol followed by the number 7 (see examples in the table above). However, if there is a corporate action, the symbol could be further modified and appended with an 8 such as "XYZ8." Investors can access the options chain for standard and Mini-sized options at the CBOE Delayed Quotes web page. (Reprinted with permission from the CBOE.com, 2014)

Reprinted with permission from CBOE.com, 2014.

CHAPTER 10

OPTION TRADING STRATEGIES, PART 1

10.1	Profit Diagrams	346
10.2	Eight Basic (Naked) Strategies Using the Underlying, European Puts and Calls, and Riskless, Zero-Coupon Bonds	347
	10.2.1 Strategy 1. Long the Underlying	347
	10.2.2 Strategy 2. Short the Underlying	349
	10.2.3 Strategy 3. Long a European Call Option on the Underlying	351
	10.2.4 Strategy 4. Short a European Call Option on the Underlying	355
	10.2.5 Strategy 5. Long a European Put Option on the Underlying	357
	10.2.6 Strategy 6. Short a European Put Option on the Underlying	359
	10.2.7 Strategy 7. Long a Zero-Coupon Riskless Bond and Hold it to Maturity	360
	10.2.8 Strategy 8. Short a Zero-Coupon Riskless Bond and Hold it to Maturity	362

In this chapter, we will first define and then map out the profit diagrams for the eight basic strategies one can employ using long and short positions in an underlying, in calls and puts, and in riskless zero-coupon bonds. These are naked strategies which means that they are fully unhedged and subject to price volatility.

When considering long and short positions in the underlying, obviously they need not have expiration dates. However, we are correlating option payoffs with underlying payoffs, and so we use a finite time horizon and the option's expiration date to make the connection.

This chapter is preparation for Chapter 11, which is much more abstract. It takes us beyond the first level of understanding options which was discussed in Chapter 9.

10.1 PROFIT DIAGRAMS

Before we get into mapping these strategies by profit diagrams, we want to show where profit diagrams come from. Consider the following historical price chart of Merck stock over a few months of a historically turbulent period (source: www.nasdaq.com).

FIGURE 10.1 **Merck Stock Price (11/30/2007 through 2/29/2008). (Actual path in blue, simulated paths in red and black)**

Note that the Merck stock price was $59.36 on 11/30/2007 and it was $44.30 on 2/29/2008. Figure 10.1 gives the *actual* price path from December 2007 through February 2008. The blue path is the actual data. If we were standing at the end of November 2007, Merck was trading at $59.36, and a

3-month in-the-money Feb. 2008 call option on Merck, Inc. with exercise price $50 could be purchased. The horizontal black line indicates the exercise price of $50, which is *roughly* situated at $50.

Of course, at that date we would not know whether this 50 Feb. call would end in the money or not. If we could roll forward time, as in the chart, we would see that the 50 Feb. call remained in-the-money for a significant amount of time (through the 3rd week in January 2008), but then the tide turned. There was a precipitous drop in the stock price through the entire month of February 2008. The option ended up out of the money on the expiration date on February 16, 2008.

Now we move back to November 30, 2007, and we run the ticker tape forward, imagining other price paths for Merck. There are an *infinite* number of potential price paths. Two such paths, one in black and the other in red, indicate two other possibilities. If Merck followed the red path, the option would have ended up roughly at the money and if Merck had followed the black path it would have ended in the money also.

Profit (subtracts current cost) and payoff (does not subtract current cost) diagrams indicate the profits and payoffs that *would* have resulted from a given strategy based on all the possibilities for the stock price at expiration.

10.2 EIGHT BASIC (NAKED) STRATEGIES USING THE UNDERLYING, EUROPEAN PUTS AND CALLS, AND RISKLESS, ZERO-COUPON BONDS

Table 10.1 lists the eight basic strategies which we will analyze in sections 10.2.1–10.2.8. All options are European.

10.2.1 Strategy 1. Long the Underlying

Let the current time be t, and let T be the expiration date of the call option. Only the current stock price, S_t, is known today. The stock price at expiration, S_T, is unknown and depends on what happens between today and the option's expiration date. That is, S_T is a random variable, which could be written as $S_T = S_T(\omega)$.

The profit figure, π_T, from long an underlying stock today is also a random variable equal to the price difference. If the price goes up, you make money and if the price goes down, you lose money,

$$\pi_T(\omega) = S_T(\omega) - S_t$$

TABLE 10.1 The Eight Basic Naked Strategies

STRATEGY 1	Go long the underlying
STRATEGY 2	Go short the underlying
STRATEGY 3	Go long a call option on the underlying
STRATEGY 4	Go short a call on the underlying
STRATEGY 5	Go long a put option on the underlying
STRATEGY 6	Go short a put option on the underlying
STRATEGY 7	Go long a riskless bond with face value equal to the option's exercise price
STRATEGY 8	Go short a riskless bond with face value equal to the option's exercise price

For example, if one buys a stock today for $S_t=\$50$ and it ends up at time T (say 3 months' later) at $S_T=\$60$, then one's profit is $\$10=\$60-\$50$. If the stock price ends up at time T at $S_T=\$40$, then one's profit is $-\$10=\$40-\$50$.

The following graphic, Figure 10.2, displays the profits from a long position in an underlying as a function of the underlying price at expiration, $S_T(\omega)$. The underlying price starts at time t at its current value S_t.

FIGURE 10.2 Strategy 1: Profits from a Long Position in an Underlying

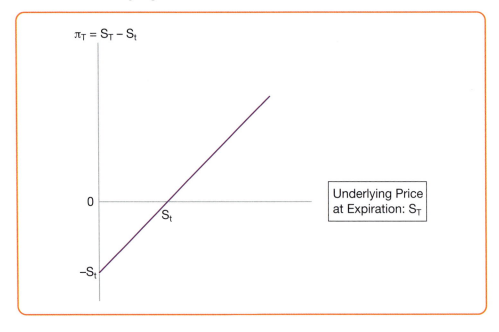

Time passes and we reach expiration, time T. If the stock price has not changed, profits are zero as depicted. If the stock price completely collapses to zero, we lose our entire investment. If the stock price takes off, we make potentially unlimited profits equal to $S_T - S_t$.

Strategy 1, long the stock today, has two economic characteristics:

1. *Limited Liability on the Downside*: You can lose at a maximum your investment S_t.
2. *Unlimited Upside Potential*: Because stock prices are potentially unlimited.

One should understand the risk in any long, unprotected position in any underlying, like the common stock of a company. Since the price can drop to zero, losing one's entire investment is a significant economic event.

A naked long position in any underlying is always subject to the maximum impact of severe downside volatility. Such positions require protection and derivatives can offer downside protection, as we shall see.

10.2.2 Strategy 2. Short the Underlying

We use the same notation as for strategy 1. The current time is t, and T is the expiration date of the call option. Only the current stock price, S_t, is known today. The stock price at expiration, S_T, is unknown and depends on what happens between today and the option's expiration date. That is, $S_T(\omega)$ is a random variable.

A short position in an asset, like the common stock of a company, is a rather complex transaction involving borrowing the stock from a broker, selling it immediately in the market, fulfilling the margin requirements, and then incurring the obligation to cover the short sale later by buying back the asset.

In derivatives markets, it is considerably easier to take short positions. Short positions have the characteristic of having a positive cash flow equal to the current value of the underlying, $+S_t$, and a negative cash flow by buying back the underlying at time T for S_T.

The profit figure, π_T, from shorting an underlying today is simply the price difference between the current price and the future spot price. If the price goes *down* you make money, because you buy it back for a lower price than what it generated for you at time t. If the price goes up, you lose money because you have to buy back the underlying at time T at a higher price than it was at time t,

$$\pi_T(\omega) = S_t - S_T(\omega).$$

For example, if you short a stock today for $S_t=\$50$ and it ends up at time T (say 3 months' later) at $S_T=\$60$, then one's profit is $-\$10=\$50-\$60$, because you have to buy it back for $S_T=\$60$.

If the stock price ends up at time T at $S_T=\$40$, then one's profit is $+\$10=\$50-\$40$ because you have to buy it back for $\$40$ and, when you sold it immediately upon the short sale, it generated $S_t=\$50$.

The following graphic, Figure 10.3, displays the profits from a short position in an underlier as a function of the underlying price at expiration, $S_T(\omega)$. The underlying price starts at time t at its current value S_t.

Time passes and we reach expiration, time T. If the stock price has not changed, profits are zero as depicted. If the stock price completely collapses to 0, we make the full profits from the short sale at time t, which is S_t, with zero buy-back cost at time T.

If the stock price takes off above S_t we incur potentially unlimited losses equal to $S_t - S_T(\omega)$, because we have to buy back the underlying at potentially unlimited prices.

Note that the profit profile for a short position is just the negative of the profit profile for a long position.

FIGURE 10.3 Strategy 2: Profits from a Short Position in an Underlying

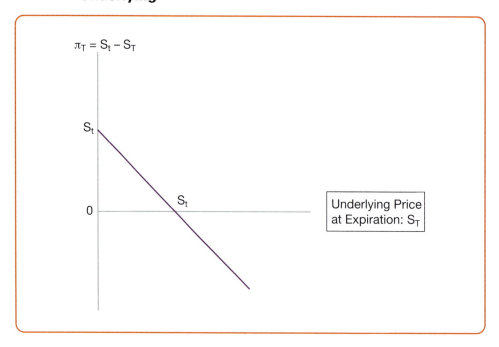

OPTION TRADING STRATEGIES, PART 1   **351**

Strategy 2, short the stock today, has two economic characteristics:

1. *Limited Upside Potential on the Downside*: You can gain at most S_t if the stock price collapses to zero.
2. *Unlimited Downside Potential*: Because stock prices are potentially unlimited.

One should understand the risks in any short unprotected position in any underlying, like the common stock of a company. Since the price can precipitously *rise*, potentially unlimited losses could be incurred due to the obligation to *buy back* the asset at such prices. Thus, a naked short position in any underlying is a risky position.

Some stock exchanges prohibit short positions in certain highly volatile stocks under volatile market conditions because of this fact. Such positions require protection and derivatives can offer the protection needed.

This is an interesting case, because the risk is driven by *upside* volatility. There are many scenarios in which this is the case, including real asset options, and derivatives can protect against upside volatility in real asset prices. A prime example of a real asset underlier with significant upside volatility is energy, as discussed. You could also add health care and education costs to this list.

10.2.3 Strategy 3. Long a European Call Option on the Underlying

We denote the European call premium by C_t. In order to derive the profit profile for a European call option, we have to know the optimal exercise policy at expiration. This is easy.

A *European* option's market premium consists of *adjusted* intrinsic value, which we will discuss in Chapter 11, and time premium. At time T (expiration) there is no time premium left, therefore the option's market premium consists entirely of (adjusted=unadjusted) intrinsic value,

$$C_T = \text{MAX}[S_T - E, 0]$$
$$= S_T - E \quad \text{if } S_T \geqslant E$$
$$= 0 \qquad \text{if } S_T < E.$$

It is very easy to value options at expiration, when there is no further time value. For example, if the exercise price is \$50 and the stock price ends up at \$60 then intrinsic value is $S_T - E = \$60 - \$50 = +\$10$.

If the stock price is $40 at expiration, the option is worth zero and not −$10 because you don't have to exercise the option.

In fact, no matter how far the stock price falls below the exercise price, the option is always worthless. This is one of the fundamental differences between holding the stock and holding a long position in a call option on the stock.

The optimal exercise policy is to exercise if $S_T \geq E$ and not to exercise if $S_T < E$.

The option costs C_t today, so profits are as follows,

$$\pi_T = (S_T - E) - C_t \quad \text{if } S_T \geq E$$
$$= -C_t \quad \text{if } S_T < E.$$

For example, if the cost of the option today is $5 and the stock price ends up at $60 then the profits to the long call position equals $60−$50−$5=$5. Note that, for every single stock price below $50, the profits to the long call position are a constant

−$5=−$C_t$ (that is, the cost of the option).

FIGURE 10.4 Strategy 3: Profits from a Long Position in a European Call Option on an Underlying

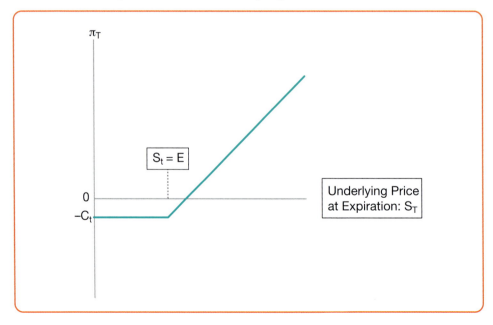

Figure 10.4, depicts the profit profile from a long position in a European call option. In the graph, we have indicated an *at-the-money* European call, $S_t=E$.

Here we start to notice some *new* economic characteristics, which are not obtainable simply by taking long (or short) positions in some underlying.

Strategy 3, long the call option today, has two economic characteristics:

1. *Unlimited Upside Potential On The Upside*: You participate fully in upward underlying price movements.
2. *Limited Downside Potential:* Limited to the loss of the option premium. If the stock price ends out-of-the-money at expiration you don't exercise the option, and you lose the call option premium paid at time t.

Note that call options share feature 1 of naked spot positions in the underlying, but differ from them because call options appear to *insure* against downward price movements. The potential downside loss is truncated and limited to the option premium, which is typically a fraction of the underlying's price.

Hence the horizontal section of the graph in Figure 10.4. We will see exactly why this is so in Chapter 11.

If one holds a long position in an underlying, then one is *fully* exposed to its price volatility. If one holds a long position in a call option, one is still exposed to the underlying's volatility. However, one consequence of that volatility is on the downside, and can be defined in terms of the probability that the underlying asset price ends up below the exercise price at expiration.

For all values of S_T below E, one sustains the *same* loss of the entire option's original market premium, C_t, because one simply does not exercise the option for all such values $S_T<E$.

Contrast this with the effect of downside price volatility on a naked long underlying position. Every dollar decline fully impacts the price change.

■ CONCEPT CHECK 1

Take a standing position. Hold your left hand out horizontally at a level which will represent the exercise price. The floor represents a stock price level equal to $0. Your other hand represents the stock price and it is fluctuating above the exercise price. Time is passing.

a. Which has a *greater* probability, the stock price falling to the floor or to below the exercise price?

b. What would you conclude about the relative (bankruptcy) risk of the underlying stock vs. the European call option?

Caution

A superficial understanding of the difference between a long call position and a long underlying position, by focusing on economic characteristic 1., might tempt one to think that it is always better to hold the option position. That is, the option always *dominates* the stock as an investment. The opposite is in fact true, the stock dominates the option as will be seen in Chapter 11, where we will define what it means to dominate.

A more careful analysis indicates that there are key differences between the two positions. The first is that options are *finite-maturity* financial instruments with a finite expiration date. Underlyings, like common stock, tend to be long-lived securities (perpetuities). Hence one can 'ride one's losses' in the underlying market whereas, in the option's market, everything is over at expiration. This creates a risk factor in options that is not shared by the underlying stock.

Next, while options are cheaper than stocks, this does not make them a less risky and hence a better choice. The financial way to measure risk is in *relative*, not absolute, terms. That is, as the risk *per dollar* invested in the financial instrument.

Options are riskier in relative terms because they are leveraged instruments and leverage increases the risk per dollar invested. They *seem* 'cheaper' only because they implicitly are financed by debt, just like forward contracts. Unlike for forward contracts however, the percentage debt does not have to be 100% (see Chapter 11, section 11.8.1).

The marketing of call options is mainly based on their upside profit potential, *'for a fraction of the price of the underlying stock price, one can fully participate in upward stock price movements'*.

■ CONCEPT CHECK 2

a. Evaluate the above statement.
b. How can one get the same feature of the stock at no cost?

OPTION TRADING STRATEGIES, PART 1   355

Imagine a scenario in which an investor in \$100,000,000 worth of a stock portfolio liquidated his portfolio and placed the funds in an equivalent dollar amount of Index call options. Then it would *not* be cheaper to make this investment, and the risk of one's position against complete downward loss would be significantly magnified.

The moral of the story is that options are not *perfect substitutes* for underlying positions. Rather, they are vehicles that can effectively be used to manage the risk of price volatility in the underlying. We will take up this important topic in the advanced strategies discussed in Chapter 12, which include hedging using options.

10.2.4 Strategy 4. Short a European Call Option on the Underlying

This is an instructive strategy to examine because it illustrates what it means to take a short position in an option. To take a short position ('sell' an option) means to sell the rights contained in the option to the option buyer.

In return for this two things happen. First, one always obtains the option premium. Second, one could find oneself *exercised against*.

That is, the option buyer could choose to exercise the option according to the optimal exercise decision in strategy 3. So one's fate as an option seller depends upon what the buyer does. The call buyer's profit function is,

$$\pi_{T,\text{Long}} = (S_T - E) - C_t \quad \text{if } S_T \geq E$$
$$= -C_t \quad \text{if } S_T < E.$$

Now we consider the short call.

Case 1

If $S_T \leq E$, then the call option buyer will not exercise. The short's profit is then equal to the current call option premium generated by shorting the option, $+C_t$.

Case 2

If $S_T > E$, then the call option buyer will exercise the option. Buyers notify the OCC (Options Clearing Corporation) of their intent to exercise the call.

The option short must deliver stock to the OCC in return for E per share. This means that the short must first obtain the underlying for its going market price, S_T, and then deliver it (sell it) to the OCC for E per share. The profits to the short generated by these actions are,

$$\pi_{T,Short} = (E-S_T)+C_t \quad \text{if } S_T \geq E$$
$$= +C_t \quad \text{if } S_T < E.$$

For example, if the exercise price is $50 and the stock price ends up at $60, the long the call option (buyer) will exercise. This will force an option short, assigned to the long's exercise notice, to sell his stock for $50 to the option buyer when the stock is worth $60.

After all, that is precisely the position one is putting oneself into as an option short. In return, shorts get the premium, say $C_t=\$5$. Overall profits equal $50-$60+$5=-$5. If the stock price ends up at any value below $50, the short can rest assured that the long will not exercise and he keeps the $5 call option premium.

Figure 10.5 exhibits the profit diagram for a short European call position.

FIGURE 10.5 Strategy 4: Profits from a Short Position in a European Call Option on an Underlying

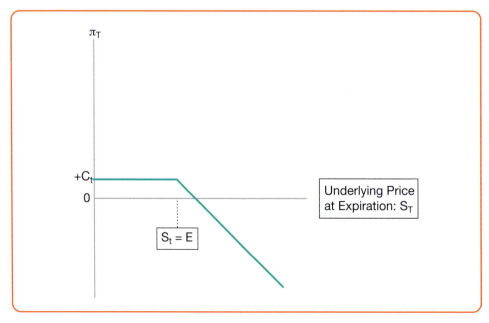

OPTION TRADING STRATEGIES, PART 1   357

■ CONCEPT CHECK 3

a. Rationalize every component of the short's profit figure in the equations above.

Note that this profit profile is just the *opposite* of that to the long call strategy. This makes economic sense but it was important not to 'cheat' and to derive it from first principles. This way, we learn exactly what is involved when one shorts an option. The 'cheat' method is to take the mirror image in the horizontal axis of the profits of the long the call.

The economic characteristics of a short call option position are:

1. *Limited Upside Profit Potential*: Limited to the current option premium C_t.
2. *Unlimited Potential Downside Losses*: In parallel to the unlimited upside gains of the call option exerciser.

10.2.5 Strategy 5. Long a European Put Option on the Underlying

Whenever one takes a long position in an option, the buyer obtains the rights, but not the obligation, to do what the option allows one to do. In this case, a put option gives the put buyer the right to *sell* the underlying at expiration for $\$E$ per share. The notation for the European put premium at the current time t is P_t.

In order to derive the profit profile for a European put option, we have to again know the optimal exercise policy at expiration. Given our basic option pricing model, modified for European options, this is easy. At time T, there is no time premium left, the option premium consists entirely of intrinsic value,

$$
\begin{aligned}
P_T &= \text{MAX}[E-S_T,0] \\
&= E-S_T \quad \text{if } S_T < E \\
&= 0 \qquad\ \text{if } S_T \geq E.
\end{aligned}
$$

The optimal exercise policy is to exercise if $S_T < E$ and not to exercise if $S_T \geq E$. The put option costs P_t today so profits are as follows,

$$
\begin{aligned}
\pi_T &= (E-S_T)-P_t \quad \text{if } S_T < E \\
&= -P_t \qquad\qquad \text{if } S_T \geq E.
\end{aligned}
$$

The following graph, Figure 10.6, depicts the profit profile from a long position in a European put option. In the graph we have indicated a currently at-the-money European put $S_t=E$.

FIGURE 10.6 Strategy 5: Profits from a Long Position in a European Put Option on an Underlying

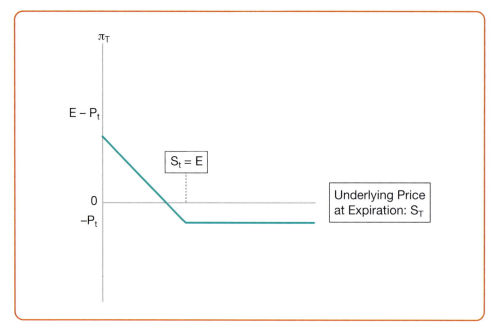

Here we start to notice some new economic characteristics which are not obtainable simply by taking long (or short) positions in some underlying. Strategy 5, long the European put option today, has two economic characteristics:

1. *Limited Upside Potential on the downside*: If the market moves down you sell at the exercise price something that is worth less than the exercise price. Your maximum potential profit occurs if the stock price completely tanks.
2. *Limited Downside Potential*: Limited to the loss of the put option premium on the upside. If the stock price rises above the exercise price at expiration, you simply don't exercise the put option, and you lose the put option premium paid at time t, P_t.

OPTION TRADING STRATEGIES, PART 1 · 359

Put options share features of naked short positions in the underlying but they also appear to have an insurance component, that insures against movements of the market above the exercise price E. Put options are not like naked short positions in the underlying, because they appear to insure against *upward* price movements by truncating the potential upside loss to the put option premium, which is typically a fraction of the underlying's price. Hence the horizontal section of the graph above E.

If one holds a short position in an underlying, one is fully exposed to its price volatility because one is obligated to *buy back* the underlying. If one holds a long position in a put option, one is still exposed to the underlying's volatility. However, for all values of S_T above E, one sustains the *same* loss because, for all such values, one simply does not exercise the put option.

Contrast this with the effect of price volatility on a naked short underlying position. Every dollar increase fully impacts the profit position because one's profit equals the reversed normal (long) price change. In the case of short positions, it is *upside* volatility that becomes the risk factor.

■ CONCEPT CHECK 4

a. In the case of short positions, it is *upside* volatility that becomes the risk factor. Why?

The conclusion is that a rising price is not always a good thing.

10.2.6 Strategy 6. Short a European Put Option on the Underlying

Again, the short in an option trade sells the rights embodied in the option contract to the buyer (typically the OCC for CBOE equity options). This is in return for the current put option premium, P_t. Thus the fate of the short is in the hands of the long.

Case 1

If $S_T < E$, then the put option buyer exercises the put.

Then, the short's profit$=(E-S_T)+P_t$.

Case 2

If $S_T \geq E$, then the put option buyer does not exercise.
Then, the short's profit=P_t.
Figure 10.7 exhibits the profit diagram for a short European put position.

FIGURE 10.7 Strategy 6: Profits from a Short Position in a European Put Option on an Underlying

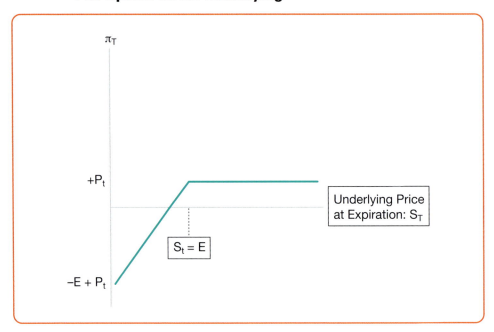

Strategy 6, short the European put option today, has two economic characteristics:

1. *Limited Upside Potential on the upside*: If the market moves up, the put buyer does not exercise and you (the short) earn the put premium.
2. *Downside Potential*: This is based on the put buyer exercising, but it is offset partially by the put premium.

10.2.7 Strategy 7. Long a Zero-Coupon Riskless Bond and Hold it to Maturity

This means *investing* in the bond, which is the same thing as *lending* the money required to purchase it.

OPTION TRADING STRATEGIES, PART 1

The cash outflow at time t will be $B(t,T) = -e^{-r\tau}*E$ and the payoff at time T will be $+E$.

In this case, the profit is very simple and is independent of the underlying stock price,

$\pi_T = E - e^{-r\tau}*E$ for all S_t.

The cash flow time line is given below.

```
-e^{-rτ} *E                +E
────────────────────────────▶
    t                       T
```

The economic characteristic of this strategy (see Figure 10.8) is that the profit is a constant which is equal to the interest earned on the initial investment.

FIGURE 10.8 Strategy 7: Profits from Longing the Risk-Free Bond

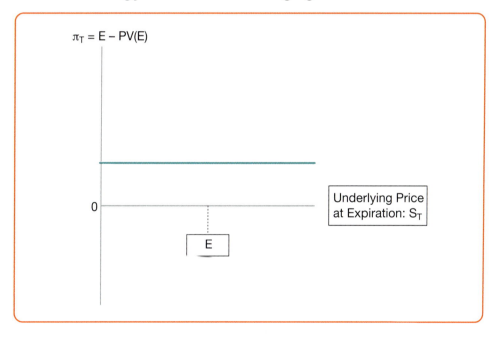

■ CONCEPT CHECK 5

a. Convince yourself that $e^{-r\tau}*E$ is the present value of the payoff, E, under continuous discounting.
b. Show that the profit figure is just the interest earned over the period, $[t, T]$, on the initial investment and paid out at time T.

10.2.8 Strategy 8. Short a Zero-Coupon Riskless Bond and Hold it to Maturity

This means *issuing* the bond which is the same thing as *borrowing* its current value in the bond market.

The cash flow at time t will be $+e^{-r\tau}*E$ and the payoff at time T will be $-E$.

```
+e^{-rτ} *E                           -E
──────────────────────────────▶
    t                                  T
```

FIGURE 10.9 **Strategy 8: Profits from Shorting the Risk-Free Bond**

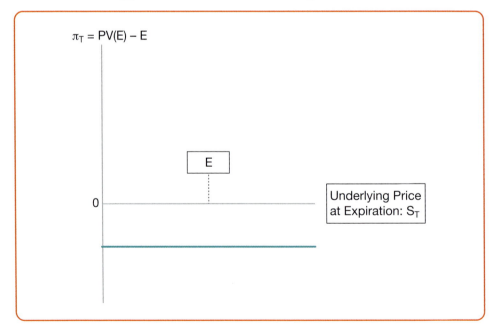

In this case, you receive $e^{-r\tau}*E$ as an inflow at time T and you pay it (plus interest) back at time T.

This results in a profit figure of,

$$\pi_1 = +e^{-r\tau}*E - E$$
$$= PV(E) - E \text{ for all } S_t.$$

The economic characteristic of this strategy (see Figure 10.9) is that the profit is a constant, which is equal to a negative value consisting of the interest paid on the initial borrowing strategy, $-(E-PV(E))$. It is just the negative of the profits from strategy 7.

■ ■ ■

364 **OPTIONS**

■ KEY CONCEPTS

1. Profit Diagrams.
2. Eight Basic (Naked) Strategies Using the Underlying, European Puts and Calls, and Riskless, Zero-Coupon Bonds.
3. Strategy 1. Go Long the Underlying.
4. Strategy 2. Go Short the Underlying.
5. Strategy 3. Go Long a European Call Option on the Underlying.
6. Strategy 4. Short a European Call Option on the Underlying.
7. Strategy 5. Long a European Put Option on the Underlying.
8. Strategy 6. Short a European Put Option on the Underlying.
9. Strategy 7. Long a Zero-Coupon Riskless Bond and Hold it to Maturity.
10. Strategy 8. Short a Zero-Coupon Riskless Bond and Hold it to Maturity.

■ END OF CHAPTER EXERCISES FOR CHAPTER 10

1. The chapter has discussed the profit diagrams for the eight basic strategies. It is also important to develop facility using the payoff diagrams. This exercise is to draw the *payoff* diagrams for the eight basic strategies.

   Recall that the payoff represents the outcomes, in the relevant states of the world, *without* adjusting for the cost of the strategies.

2. *(This question does some basic numerical calculations for some of the basic strategies.)*

   We will re-consider the Merck data in Figure 10.1 where Merck stock price was \$59.36 on 11/30/2007 and it was \$44.30 on 2/29/2008. The date range 11/30/2007–2/29/2008 is roughly a 3-month period.

   Assume that 3-month European calls and puts were available with an exercise price of $E=\$50$ on this stock. We will assume that a 3-month European call is trading at $C_t^E=\$10$ (per share).

   The pricing bounds in Chapter 11 are consistent with this for $\tau=0.25$ and $r=3.00\%$, continuously compounded. Then European Put-Call Parity generates the value of the corresponding European put option as $P_t^E=\$0.266$ (per share).

   Fill in Table 10.2 which gives profit (loss) figures for alternative terminal stock prices, S_T, where T is 2/29/2008.

OPTION TRADING STRATEGIES, PART 1 — 365

TABLE 10.2 **Profits for Alternative Terminal Stock Prices, S_T**

Merck Stock on 2/29/2008	Long Stock	Short Stock	Long Call	Short Call	Long Put	Short Put	Long Bond	Short Bond
60								
55								
50								
45								
40								
35								

3. Consider the long call option strategy (see Figure 10.4). Answer the following questions.

   a. Where does the profit diagram cross the S_T axis? This is called the *break-even stock price*.
   b. Suppose that $E < S_T <$ break-even stock price. Should you exercise the call option? Why or why not?
   c. When is the exercise of a European call option profitable?

4. You think that Exxon Mobil stock is going to appreciate substantially in the next 6 months. Exxon Mobil stock is currently trading at $100 per share, while an at-the-money 6-month call option on Exxon Mobil is currently trading at $10 per share.

   As usual, one contract involves 100 shares of Exxon Mobil stock. You have a total of $10,000 to invest and you are considering the following two investment alternatives.

Investment Strategy 1

Invest all $10,000 in Exxon Mobil stock, buying 100 shares.

Investment Strategy 2

Invest all $10,000 in Exxon Mobil call options, purchasing 10 contracts. That is, you are taking the *entire* money you would have invested in Investment Strategy 1 and, instead, you are investing it in options.

   a. Calculate the *dollar returns* for each investment strategy in Table 10.3 for the alternative end-of-period stock prices given. Show your calculations in the spaces provided.

366 OPTIONS

TABLE 10.3	**Total Dollar Returns ($10,000 Initial Investment)**		
S_T	$80	$100	$120
Investment Strategy 1			
Investment Strategy 2			

b.   Calculate the *percentage rates of return* for each investment strategy in Table 10.4 for the alternative end–of period stock prices given. Show your calculations in the spaces provided.

TABLE 10.4	**Percentage Rates of Return ($10,000 Initial Investment)**		
S_T	$80	$100	$120
Investment Strategy 1			
Investment Strategy 2			

c.   Discuss the relative riskiness of the two investment strategies using your table calculations.

6.   (*This question develops facility in adding up payoff diagrams.*)

a.   Consider a European call option with exercise price E. Draw its payoff diagram on the usual graph.

b.   Consider a European put option also with exercise price E and identical in all terms to the European call option in a. Draw its payoff diagram on the same usual graph in a.

c.   Now add up the two payoff profiles on the same graph.

d.   What financial instrument does the resulting payoff profile look like?

■ SELECTED CONCEPT CHECK SOLUTIONS

Concept Check 1

a.   To see this, consider the probability of losing one's *entire* investment in the underlying. That probability is the probability that the stock price falls to zero.

OPTION TRADING STRATEGIES, PART 1 367

b. Alternatively, the probability of losing one's entire investment in the long option position is the probability that the stock price falls below the exercise price E.

Since $E>0$, this is a greater probability. It is more likely that the stock price will fall below any given positive price level, for example the exercise price, than that it will completely collapse. Hence, on the downside per dollar invested, call options are riskier than naked long position.

Concept Check 2

a. Only if the stock price goes up above E at expiration. Otherwise one loses the *entire* investment.

b. Finance students are familiar with the concept of leverage and can recognize it in the quote. They are also aware that leverage is a two-sided sword that needs to be carefully risk-managed.

You aren't getting the stock's upside potential at no cost, as the quote seems to imply. There is a *hidden* cost in the form of taking on the risks associated with the option's embedded leverage.

Concept Check 5

b. Principal plus interest at time T is equal to $e^{r\tau}e^{-r\tau}*E=E$. Subtracting the initial investment of $e^{-r\tau}*E$ yields the interest earned over $[t,T]$, which is $E-e^{-r\tau}*E$. That interest, as is customary, is paid out after it is earned at time T.

CHAPTER 11

RATIONAL OPTION PRICING

11.1 Model-Independent vs. Model-Based Option Pricing   370

11.2 Relative Pricing Trades vs. Directional Trades   371

11.3 The Dominance Principle   373

11.4 Implications of the Dominance Principle, ROP for Puts and Calls   374

    11.4.1 Lower Bound for an American Call Option on an Underlying with no Dividends (LBAC)   374

    11.4.2 Lower Bound for a European Call Option on an Underlying with no Dividends (LBEC)   375

    11.4.3 Lower Bound for an American Put Option on an Underlying with no Dividends (LBAP)   378

    11.4.4 Lower Bound for a European Put Option on an Underlying with no Dividends (LBEP)   380

    11.4.5 Lower Bound for a European Call Option on an Underlying with Continuous Dividends (LBECD)   382

    11.4.6 Lower Bound for an American Call Option on an Underlying with Continuous Dividends (LBACD)   383

    11.4.7 Lower Bound for a European Put Option on an Underlying with Continuous Dividends (LBEPD)   386

    11.4.8 Lower Bound for an American Put Option on an Underlying with Continuous Dividends (LBAPD)   387

370 OPTIONS

11.5 Static Replication and European Put-Call Parity
(No Dividends)   388

   11.5.1 Partially Replicating a European Call Option
   (the Embedded Forward Contract)   388

   11.5.2 Fully Replicating a European Call Option
   (the Embedded Insurance Contract)   391

   11.5.3 From Strategies to Current Costs and Back   393

   11.5.4 Working Backwards from Payoffs to Costs
   to Derive European Put-Call Parity   393

11.6 Basic Implications of European Put-Call Parity   394

   11.6.1 What is a European Call Option?   394

   11.6.2 The Analogue of the Basic American Option
   Pricing Model for European Options   396

   11.6.3 What is a European Put Option?   398

11.7 Further Implications of European Put-Call Parity   399

   11.7.1 Synthesizing Forward Contract from
   Puts and Calls   399

11.8 Financial Innovation using European Put-Call Parity   401

   11.8.1 Generalized Forward Contracts   401

   11.8.2 American Put-Call Parity (No Dividends)   403

11.9 Postscript on ROP   405

11.1 MODEL-INDEPENDENT VS. MODEL-BASED OPTION PRICING

In Chapter 9, section 9.4, we introduced a basic American option pricing model which says that the value of an American call or put option is the sum of intrinsic value and time premium, also known as the delayed exercise premium. In this chapter, we start pricing options in more detail. Before doing so, it's useful to define and think about the different types of option pricing models and their objectives.

RATIONAL OPTION PRICING — 371

There are two kinds of option pricing models. The first type is called *'rational'* *option pricing* (ROP) and it starts by not making any assumptions about the process generating the underlying's prices. For any underlying asset price process that itself does not admit arbitrage opportunities, it asserts that there must be some intuitive, obvious relationships between options and their underlying instruments. Or between plain vanilla European puts and calls.

Basically, rational option pricing tries to put *bounds* on option prices without attaching actual, unique numbers or formulas to them, because this is all ROP can do. Doing the latter is a much harder task, requires additional assumptions, and is the object of *model-based option pricing* (MBOP). We will discuss such models, which include the Binomial and the Black–Scholes models, in the next chapters.

A result is a ROP result if and only if it holds for *all* arbitrage-free processes underlying the derivative security. A single counter-example is enough to disqualify a result as a ROP result. An example of ROP is the result that an option's price can never be greater that the price of the underlying (assumed to be a limited liability asset). This result seems obvious, but ROP tries to proves results such as these. Intuitive or obvious in this context means that, if these relationships did not hold, then market forces in the form of trading activity would spontaneously arise, pushing relative prices back to where these relationships do hold.

You are already familiar with the notion here. If something is known to be under-priced relative to something else many people will want to buy it, and they will do so. But the under-pricing cannot persist forever, because the buying pressure of many buyers will 'bid' the price up. The same idea applies to the over-priced something else. Many people will want to sell it, thereby driving its price down. These market forces will restore both the over-priced and the under-priced to an equilibrium where neither is over-priced nor under-priced relative to the other.

11.2 RELATIVE PRICING TRADES VS. DIRECTIONAL TRADES

Relative price trading is a very special type of trading based on exploiting known relationships between the relative prices of various commodities. It differs from the type of trading described as *'directional'*. Directional trading tends to be based on divergent opinions as to where the market price will go in the future.

372 OPTIONS

For example, you might think that gold prices will go up in the next 3 months and so you go long gold. You might be wrong though, and see gold prices decline over your horizon. This is called *model risk* and it is the job of the financial engineer both to recognize model risk and to manage it.

Alternatively, you might not care to hazard a guess, nor base a trading strategy on, the absolute level of gold prices. You might think that gold is over-priced *relative* to silver. In this case, you would *sell* gold and *buy* silver. If many people shared your model, they would do the same, thereby driving up the price of silver and driving down the price of gold.

As the equilibrium relationship between gold and silver prices is restored you would make money on both legs of the trade, short gold with gold prices declining and long silver with silver prices increasing. There might still be some risk to this strategy but it would probably be less than that of a naked bet on either the absolute level of gold prices or on the absolute level of silver prices. In other words, you are a 'spread' trader. Since spreads are less volatile than their underlyings under mild conditions, trading them is less risky (see Chapter 6, section 6.9).

Rational option pricing is based only on the principle of *No-Arbitrage in Equilibrium* (NAIE). Theoretically, every result of ROP could be derived by showing that an arbitrage strategy could be constructed, if the result did not hold. In practice, it is more streamlined to use a principle derived from NAIE called the *'Dominance' Principle*.

■ CONCEPT CHECK 1

It is important to understand the difference between directional trades and relative trades because the possibility of financial disaster is, in part, based on this distinction.

a. Think of an example of a *directional* trade, keeping in mind that such a trade is a pure bet on the direction that some underlying variable moves. Feel free to review the relevant portions of Part 1 of the text.
b. Think of an example of a *relative* trade, which depends on the relative price movement of several variables.
c. Where does arbitrage more naturally fit? Into directional or relative trades?
d. What does our basic economics say about pricing? Is it relative or absolute?
e. Which type of trade would be riskier and why?

11.3 THE DOMINANCE PRINCIPLE

The dominance principle compares financial packages (strategies) to each other. It uses the idea of relevant '*states of the world*' for pricing. The concept is easy: an example of relevant states of the world for travel tomorrow might be whether it is going to rain or shine tomorrow. We know these states but we can't say with absolute certainty which one will occur. We might attach subjective probabilities to them, as in 'rain (60% probability)' and 'shine (40% probability)'. Of course, we could add more states or refine the given ones.

The *Dominance Principle* says that if we have two financial packages, call them A and B, and that A has payoffs in all relevant states of the world that are *at least as great* as the corresponding payoffs of financial package B, then the price today of A, $P_{A,t}$, must be at least as great as the price today of B, $P_{B,t}$. That is $P_{A,t} \geq P_{B,t}$. Otherwise, there would be an arbitrage opportunity.

If $P_{A,t} < P_{B,t}$ then A would be underpriced relative to B. We could short sell B, earning $P_{B,t}$, and use the proceeds to buy A for $P_{A,t}$. This would earn us an immediate, positive cash flow of $P_{B,t} - P_{A,t}$. Now that we own A, we would cover the short sale by replacing B with A. No one would complain because the payoffs of A are at least as great as the payoffs of B in all states of the world. So people would be as happy owning A as they were by owning B. We would be happy too, because we got it cheap relative to B.

Our strategy would yield an immediate riskless arbitrage profit of $P_{B,t} - P_{A,t} > 0$, and no subsequent cash flow implications because we have unwound all positions. The short sale of B has been closed out by covering the short sale. The long position we acquired in A has been liquidated by using A to cover the short sale, after which we own no position in A nor in B. Further, if we short sell B and purchase A fast enough, the immediate cash flow will be almost riskless. Now, recall definition 2 of (riskless) arbitrage given in Chapter 4, section 4.6.1.

Risk-Free Arbitrage Definition 2

A *risk-free arbitrage opportunity* is one with the following properties:

1. It generates a *positive profit* (inflow) today, time *t*.
2. There are *no subsequent outflows* (costs).
3. The profit generated today is *riskless*.

374 OPTIONS

11.4 IMPLICATIONS OF THE DOMINANCE PRINCIPLE, ROP FOR PUTS AND CALLS

There are at least three dichotomies in classifying options: European vs. American, call vs. put, and dividends vs. no dividends. Dividends can also be discrete vs. continuous but we will restrict the discussion to continuous dividends. This leads to the eight possible combinations as listed in Table 11.1.

TABLE 11.1 **Classification of Options**

American (11.4.1)	Call	No Dividends
European (11.4.2)	Call	No Dividends
American (11.4.3)	Put	No Dividends
European (11.4.4)	Put	No Dividends
European (11.4.5)	Call	Continuous Dividends
American (11.4.6)	Call	Continuous Dividends
European (11.4.7)	Put	Continuous Dividends
American (11.4.8)	Put	Continuous Dividends

11.4.1 Lower Bound for an American Call Option on an Underlying with no Dividends (LBAC)

Let $C^A(S_{T,\tau}, E)$ denote the current value of an American call option with current stock price $S_{T,\tau}$ to maturity, and exercise price E. The *nominal* lower bound is intrinsic value $IV_t = \text{MAX}[S_t - E, 0]$. A lower bound ROP result for American calls on underlyings that pay no dividends over the life of the option is,

$$C^A(S_t,\tau,E) \geqslant \text{MAX}[S_t - E,\ 0] \qquad \textbf{(Lower Bound American Calls (LBAC))}$$

for all underlying stock prices S_t and all times t prior to the maturity date.

First, at maturity it is clear that $C^A(S_T, 0, E) = \text{MAX}[S_T - E, 0]$ because, by our basic American option pricing model, there is no time premium. In the End of Chapter Exercise 1, you work through an exercise that shows that if LBAC does *not* hold, there would be an arbitrage opportunity. This exercise uses the proof by contradiction technique.

Example of the Intrinsic Value Lower Bound for an American Call

Here we will take an American option's price quote and examine whether it satisfies $C^A(S_t,\tau,E){\geq}MAX[S_t{-}E,0]$. Google's official closing stock price on Nasdaq was approximately \$575.62 on September 12, 2014. The GOOG\14J18\500.0 (2014 Oct 500.00 Call) was trading at that time for an offer price of \$78.80.

Intrinsic value was therefore \$575.62–\$ 500.00=\$75.62, which is below the option price of \$78.80. The difference of \$78.80–\$75.62=\$3.18 consisted of time premium per share.

The story does not end here, however, because the American feature, which seems to enhance the value of an American call option relative to an otherwise identical European call option, is illusory if there are no payouts to the underlying over the life of the option. We will discuss this in section 11.4.6.

11.4.2 Lower Bound for a European Call Option on an Underlying with no Dividends (LBEC)

In the case of European call options with no dividends, we can get a *higher* lower bound than the intrinsic value bound. (This bound also holds for American call options where there are no dividends (see section 11.4.6)). In the case of European options, early exercise is not possible so the arbitrage opportunity we constructed in terms of intrinsic value does not work.

Ordinary intrinsic value is not an appropriate immediate value concept for European options because, to wring the value out of a European option, you have to wait until expiration. However, instead of using E in the definition of intrinsic value, we can simply use the present value of E, $PV(E)=e^{-r\tau}E$. This leads to a useful way to adjust intrinsic value for European call options.

Definition of Adjusted Intrinsic Value (AIV) for a European Call

Adjusted intrinsic value is intrinsic value with E replaced by $e^{-r\tau}E$,

$$AIV_t=MAX[S_t-e^{-r\tau}E, 0]$$

A proven lower bound for a *European* (note the E in C^E below) call option on an underlying asset that has no payouts over the life of the option is adjusted intrinsic value.

$$C^E(S_t,\tau,E){\geq}MAX[S_t-e^{-r\tau}E, 0] \qquad \textbf{(Lower Bound European Calls (LBEC))}$$

376 OPTIONS

We will prove this using the dominance principle, not by constructing an arbitrage strategy explicitly. To do so, we look at the right-hand side of (LBEC) and work back from current costs to strategies. This technique is discussed in section 11.5.4, but simply involves taking costs (and benefits) and working backwards to uncover the strategies that generate them.

The strategy represented by the current cost of $S_t - e^{-r\tau}E$ is simply to borrow $\$e^{-r\tau}E$ and purchase the stock for $\$S_t$. This will be called *Strategy B*.

Strategy A will be purchasing a European call option. Table 11.2 describes the payoffs to each strategy in each relevant state of the world at expiration.

TABLE 11.2 Proving LBEC

State of the World at Expiration	$S_T \geqslant E$	$S_T < E$
Strategy A		
Payoff to Long European Call Option	$S_T - E$	0
Strategy B		
i. Long the stock	S_T	S_T
ii. Borrow PV(E)	$-E$	$-E$
Total Payoff to Strategy B	$S_T - E$	$S_T - E$

Note that Strategy A has payoffs at least as great as the payoffs to Strategy B in all states of the world. Note that the payoff to Strategy B is $S_T - E$ which is negative if $S_T < E$ while the payoff to Strategy A is 0. The current value of Strategy B is $S_t - e^{-r\tau}E$.

■ CONCEPT CHECK 2

Show, by using the dominance principle, that the value of a European call option also cannot be negative.

By the dominance principle, the current value of Strategy A must be greater than or equal to the current value of Strategy B. Therefore, adjusted intrinsic value is a lower bound for the value of a European call option with no payouts over the life of the option, $C^E(S_t, \tau, E) \geqslant \text{MAX}[S_t - e^{-r\tau}E, 0]$.

There are several important things to note about (LBEC). First, note that this lower bound is higher than intrinsic value.

RATIONAL OPTION PRICING   377

■ CONCEPT CHECK 3

a. Show that adjusted intrinsic value for calls is greater than (unadjusted) intrinsic value, except at maturity.
b. Show that adjusted intrinsic value for calls is equal to (unadjusted) intrinsic value, at maturity.

Implications of the Lower Bound for European Calls

One of the implications is that the underlying asset itself can be interpreted as a European call option. There are two interpretations:

Interpretation 1

The exercise price $E=0$. In this case, the underlying asset is economically equivalent to a European call option with exercise price equal to zero and with any maturity.

Interpretation 2

The exercise price $E>0$. In this case, the underlying asset is economically equivalent to a European call option with any exercise price greater than zero and infinite maturity.

To prove interpretation 1, we compare the payoffs to holding any European call option with $E=0$ and any maturity to that of holding the stock. There is only one relevant state of the world since $S_T<0=E$ cannot occur for a limited liability asset. This is described in Table 11.3.

TABLE 11.3   **Interpretation 1 of the Underlying Asset as a European Call Option**

State of the World at Expiration	$S_T \geqslant 0$
Strategy A Long European Call Option with $E=0$	$S_I - E - S_T$
Strategy B Long the Stock	S_T

It's clear that the two strategies have exactly the same payoffs when $E=0$, so they are economically equivalent and therefore have the same current costs,

$S_t = C^E(S_t, \tau, 0)$. The value of any European call option with $E=0$ is equal to the current underlying asset price S_t.

To prove interpretation 2, all we need to do is note that as the time to maturity τ increases the $PV(E) = e^{-r\tau}E$ approaches zero. Furthermore,

$$MAX[S_t - e^{-r\tau}E, 0] \leqslant C^E(S_t, \tau, E) \leqslant S_t.$$

The first inequality is (LBEC), and the second inequality follows because the call option price cannot be greater than the underlying asset price. But as τ increases without bound, $MAX[S_t - e^{-r\tau}E, 0]$ approaches $MAX[S_t, 0] = S_t$, since a limited liability asset always sells for at least a zero price.

Thus $S_t \leqslant C^E(S_t, \tau, E) \leqslant S_t$. This says $C^E(S_t, \tau, E) = S_t$, as long as τ becomes infinitely large, *no matter what the exercise price is.* This is interpretation 2.

We next turn to the ROP bounds for American and European puts, once again for assets with no payouts over the life of the option.

11.4.3 Lower Bound for an American Put Option on an Underlying with no Dividends (LBAP)

The *nominal* lower bound for an American put option is intrinsic value for a put $IV_t = MAX[E-S_t, 0]$. We say nominal because there is a very real possibility that the American put will be exercised prior to maturity. Once an option is exercised it is dead and gone and no bounds can hold for its price.

$$P^A(S_t, \tau, E) \geqslant MAX[E-S_t, 0] \qquad \textbf{(Lower Bound American Puts (LBAP))}$$

We can prove this by contradiction. If (LBAP) were not true, then $P^A(S_t, \tau, E) < MAX[E-S_t, 0]$ and an immediate arbitrage opportunity would arise. Note that $E > S_t$ and $MAX[E-S_t, 0] = E-S_t$, otherwise the assumption implies that $P^A(S_t, \tau, E) < 0$ which is not possible (the put premium cannot be negative).

The arbitrage strategy would be to buy the put for $P^A(S_t, \tau, E)$, then acquire the stock underlying the put by purchasing it. Then you would exercise the put by delivering the stock in return for $\$E$. This would leave you with the positive amount $E-S_t$ since $E > S_t$.

RATIONAL OPTION PRICING

The *net* cash flow from this set of transactions is $E - S_t - P^A(S_t, \tau, E)$, which is positive by the assumption that $P^A(S_t, \tau, E) < \text{MAX}[E - S_t, 0] = E - S_t$. There are no further implications to your trades—the put has been exercised, and you disposed of the stock. Nothing is left to do except to walk away with your arbitrage profits.

Example of the Intrinsic Value Lower Bound for an American Put

Here we will take an American put option's price quote and examine whether it satisfies $P^A(S_t, \tau, E) \geq \text{MAX}[E - S_t, 0]$. Google's official closing stock price on Nasdaq was approximately \$575.62 on September 12, 2014. The GOOG\14V18\500.0 (2014 Oct 500.00 Put) was trading at that time for an offer price of \$1.30.

Intrinsic value was $\text{MAX}[E - S_t, 0] = 0$ since the stock price was *above* the put's exercise price. Therefore, the entire value of the option, \$1.30 per share, consisted of time premium.

FIGURE 11.1 Optimal Early Exercise for an American Put Option (No Underlying Dividends) Along the Early Exercise Boundary

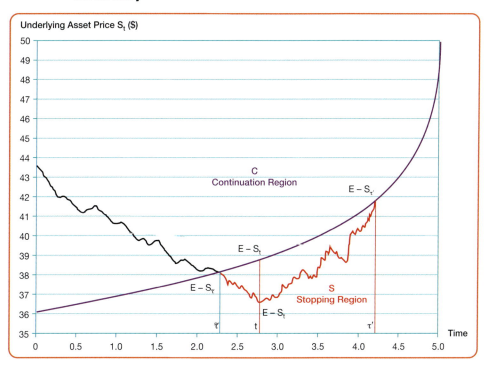

The story of American puts doesn't end here. Early exercise of American put options is an advanced topic. However, we can give some idea of the flavor of this important topic. First, once you have read section 11.4.6 below, compare it to this section.

Early exercise of American put options is not driven by dividends. For each time t prior to maturity, there is a certain level called the *early exercise boundary*. When the underlying asset price declines to and hits the early exercise boundary *for the first time*, it is optimal to exercise the American put option. Figure 11.1 illustrates. Note that τ' is the *second* time the early exercise boundary is hit. Too late.

The optimal time to exercise the American put option is the random time $\tilde{\tau}$ (not normal time to expiration τ, but the *effective random* time to early exercise) and the optimal early exercise price is $S_{\tilde{\tau}}$. At this critical stock price the value of the American put comes into equality with intrinsic value, $P^A(S_{\tilde{\tau}},\tilde{\tau},E)=$ MAX$[E-S_{\tilde{\tau}}, 0]=E-S_{\tilde{\tau}}$, since the American put option has to be in-the-money in order to justify exercising it.

11.4.4 Lower Bound for a European Put Option on an Underlying with no Dividends (LBEP)

In the case of European put options, we can get a lower bound that is lower than unadjusted intrinsic value for an American put. In this case, early exercise is not possible, so the arbitrage opportunity we just constructed in terms of intrinsic value again does not work.

However, instead of using E in the definition of intrinsic value we can use the present value of E, $PV(E)=e^{-r\tau}E$. This is the corresponding way to adjust intrinsic value for European puts.

Definition (Adjusted Intrinsic Value for a European Put Option)

Adjusted intrinsic value is ordinary intrinsic value with E replaced by $e^{-r\tau}E$, $AIV_t=$MAX$[e^{-r\tau}E-S_t, 0]$. We use the same notation as for calls. The context dictates which form to use.

The lower bound for a European put option is then adjusted intrinsic value.

$$P^E(S_t,\tau,E)\geqslant\text{MAX}[e^{-r\tau}E-S_t, 0] \qquad \textbf{(Lower Bound European Puts (LBEP))}$$

We will prove this using the dominance principle, not by constructing an arbitrage strategy explicitly. To do so, we look at the right-hand side of (LBEP)

RATIONAL OPTION PRICING **381**

TABLE 11.4 **Lower Bound for a European Put Option**

State of the World at Expiration	$S_T \geq E$	$S_T < E$
Strategy A		
Payoff to Long European Put Option	0	$E-S_T$
Strategy B		
i. Short the Stock	$-S_T$	$-S_T$
ii. Lend PV(E)	E	E
Total Payoff to Strategy B	$E-S_T$	$E-S_T$

and work back from current costs to strategies. The strategy represented by the current cost of $e^{-r\tau}E-S_t$ is simply to lend \$$e^{-r\tau}E$ and short sell the stock, thereby cutting current costs by S_t. This will be Strategy B. Strategy A will be purchasing a European put option.

Table 11.4 describes the payoffs to each strategy in each relevant state of the world at expiration.

Note that Strategy A has payoffs at least as great as the payoffs to Strategy B in all states of the world. The payoff to Strategy B is $E-S_T < 0$ if $S_T \geq E$, while the payoff to Strategy A is 0. The current value of Strategy B is $e^{-r\tau}E-S_t$. The value of a European put option also cannot be negative because its payoffs dominate the zero–payoff strategy.

By the dominance principle the current value of Strategy A must be greater than or equal to the current value of Strategy B. The maximum of adjusted intrinsic value and zero is a lower bound for the value of the European put option,

$$P^E(S_t,\tau,E) \geq \text{MAX}[e^{-r\tau}E-S_t, 0] \qquad \textbf{(Lower Bound European Puts}$$
$$\textbf{(LBEP))}$$

Note that adjusted intrinsic value for a European put option this time is *lower* than unadjusted intrinsic value.

■ CONCEPT CHECK 4

a. Show that adjusted intrinsic value (AIV) for puts is lower than (unadjusted) intrinsic value, except at maturity.
b. Show that adjusted intrinsic value for puts is equal to (unadjusted) intrinsic value, at maturity.

11.4.5 Lower Bound for a European Call Option on an Underlying with Continuous Dividends (LBECD)

This material is similar to Chapter 4, sections 4.5 and 4.6, on the valuation of forward contracts when the underlying carries a continuous dividend yield. As we shall see after discussing put–call parity, European call and put options are closely related to their corresponding forward contracts.

There are a number of ways of generating a lower bound in this scenario, just as there were for forward contracts. The objective is to replicate Table 11.2 by adjusting for dividends. This is done in Table 11.5.

Let the stock price at time T, with dividends paid over $[t, T]$ and re-invested in the stock, be denoted by S_T. Let S_T' be the terminal (time T) stock price *without* the re-invested dividends. This is the terminal value of the capital gains process, to use the terminology of Chapter 4, section 4.4. It is also the future value of the current stock price S_t minus the PV(dividends paid out over $[t, T]$).

Denote the current stock price, S_t, minus the PV(dividends paid out over $[t, T]$) by S_t'. We showed, in Chapter 4, Appendix 4.8, that the quick way to calculate S_t' is $S_t' = e^{-\rho\tau} S_t$. That is, multiply the current stock price S_t by the discount factor $e^{-\rho\tau}$.

The key thing to remember in this case is that the European call entitles the exerciser to the terminal stock price at expiration, S_T, minus the re-invested dividends paid out over the life of the option $[t, T]$. That is, only to the adjusted terminal stock price S_T'.

We start with a long position in a single European call option as our strategy A. The payoff is in terms of the dividend-adjusted stock price so it doesn't pay to exercise unless $S_T' > E$. (In terms of the normal stock price, it has to be larger than the exercise price, E, plus the FV of the re-invested dividends for this to occur.)

We now have to figure out how to partially replicate the call option's payoffs. Provided that we accomplish this with payoffs that are no larger than the payoffs to the call option, the dominance principle will provide a lower bound to the option's current price.

Under strategy B, we purchase the current stock price, S_t, minus the PV (dividends paid out over $[t, T]$) for the price $S_t' = e^{-\rho\tau} S_t$. That is, we purchase fewer than one unit of underlying stock since $e^{-\rho\tau} < 1.0$. This is a form of tailing the hedge, because we now can match up that part of the option's payoff corresponding to S_T'. Note that S_t' grows to S_T' by definition. The other part

RATIONAL OPTION PRICING **383**

TABLE 11.5 **Lower Bound for a European Call Option with Dividends**

State of the World at Expiration	$S_T' \geqslant E$	$S_T' < E$
Strategy A		
Payoff to a Long European Call Option	$S_T' - E$	0
Strategy B		
i. Long $e^{-\rho\tau}$ units of the underlying stock	S_T'	S_T'
ii. Borrow PV(E)=$e^{-r\tau}*E$	$-E$	$-E$
Total Payoff to Strategy B	$S_T'-E$	$S_T'-E$

of strategy B is the usual borrowing of $PV(E)=e^{-r\tau}*E$, which will result in an outflow of $-E$ at time T.

We have matched up the option's payoff in state of the world $S_T' \geqslant E$. In state $S_T' < E$, we underperformed the option because our payoff $S_T' - E < 0$, whereas the payoff to the option is 0.0. This is perfectly fine. The dominance principle tells us that the current price of strategy A, $C^E(S_t, \tau, E)$, must be greater than or equal to the current price of strategy B, $e^{-\rho\tau}S_t - e^{-r\tau}E$. It is also greater than 0. Therefore, our lower bound in this case is,

$$C^E(S_t, \tau, E) \geqslant \text{MAX}[S_t' - e^{-r\tau}E, \, 0] = \text{MAX}[e^{-\rho\tau}S_t - e^{-r\tau}E, \, 0] \qquad \textbf{(LBECD)}$$

Note that $e^{-\rho\tau}S_t - e^{-r\tau}E = S_t - PV(\text{dividends payable over } [t, T]) - e^{-r\tau}E$.

11.4.6 Lower Bound for an American Call Option on an Underlying with Continuous Dividends (LBACD)

Once we enter the world of American options, the waters of ROP are muddied because early exercise complicates the ROP discussion considerably. One has to carefully distinguish between ROP results, which hold for all models, and model-based results which hold only for the assumed processes, unless proven otherwise.

However, the first thing to note is that, even when early exercise is possible, it is not always *optimal* to early exercise an American call option just because it happens to be in-the-money. This is true whether or not the underlying pays dividends. In the case of no dividends on the underlier, an unambiguous exercise policy can be given, which is *never* to early exercise.

Case 1: An American call on an underlier with no dividends over the life of the option

In this case, it is *never* optimal to *early* exercise an American call option. Therefore, while one *can* early exercise it due to the American feature, the value of being able to do so is zero. It will consequently sell for the same current market premium as an otherwise identical European option, $C^A(S_t,\tau,E)=C^E(S_t,\tau,E)$.

This result is not hard to prove using the tools we already have. But we will defer its proof to End of Chapter Exercise 2. This result is a famous result due to Robert Merton in 1973, and we will take the reader systematically through all the steps.

Case 2: An American call on an underlier with continuous, proportional dividends over the life of the option

In this case, it *may* be optimal to early exercise an American call. That depends on the relative magnitude of the dividend to the loss of interest on the exercise price, which will be incurred by exercising. Using the proportional dividend model, the instantaneous dividend is $\rho S_t \Delta t$ over a small interval of time Δt. Instantaneous interest, if the option were not exercised and the strike price E were not lost, would be equal to $e^{r\Delta t}E$ over the same small interval of time Δt.

Thus, a necessary condition for early exercise at time t is that $\rho S_t \Delta t > e^{r\Delta t}E$, which says that the instantaneous dividend is greater than the loss of instantaneous interest. The condition is roughly equivalent to $\rho S_t > rE$, which will hold at each time t prior to maturity if the stock price S_t is sufficiently large.

Thus, early exercise of American call options is a *dividend capture play,* since the option is written on the ex-dividend underlying asset price. Just as it is for forward contracts. If the dividend one can capture by exercising the option is relatively large enough, it can be optimal to early exercise. Otherwise, not.

Any ROP result that we obtain for American calls on dividend-paying underlying assets carries the qualifier '*only when the option is unexercised*'. After the option is exercised, it is extinguished, and no results can apply to an option that has ceased to exist. Option pricing bounds only apply to alive options.

More precisely, option pricing bounds apply where the underlying asset price is in the *continuation region* (see Figure 11.1). When the underlying asset price hits the early exercise boundary, its value is exactly equal to intrinsic value. Beyond the early exercise boundary, in the *stopping region* exclusive of the early exercise boundary, the option is no longer alive, if one has rationally exercised it.

We now turn to show that the no-arbitrage lower bound in this American scenario, for an American call on an underlier with proportional, continuous dividends over the life of the option is the same as that for an American call option on an underlying with no dividends given in section 11.4.1.

$$C^A(S_t, \tau, E) \geqslant \text{MAX}[S_t - E, 0]$$ **(Lower Bound American Calls (LBACD)=(LBAC))**

The implication of the dividend-adjusted lower bound, both for European calls and European puts, discussed in sections 11.4.6 and 11.4.7 is that, if you initiate a long position in a European call option at time t, then at expiration, time T, you will receive only the adjusted terminal stock price S_T'. As discussed, this is the stock price with dividends re-invested, S_T, minus the future value of the re-invested dividends paid out over the life of the option $[t, T]$.

In the case of a European put, you only have to deliver S_T' and make no adjustment for the dividends paid over the period $[t, T]$. It is important to note that it is the time difference $T-t$ that creates the dividend adjustment issue. And it is the European feature that precludes early exercise. These problems go away when we turn to American options.

In the case of American options, early exercise is instantaneous so there is no lag between the initiation date, t, of the long call or put position and the potential exercise date T. That is, we can assume $T=t$ if we want to do so. When we do the arb discussed in End of Chapter Exercise 1, dividends will not impact the value proposition, because we can buy the call option at time t and then instantaneously exercise it, without losing any past dividends. Since we can do this at any time t in a continuous-time, continuous-trading model, the value of the American call must be no smaller than ordinary intrinsic value, without any adjustment for dividends. That is, LBAC must prevail at all times t' in the maturity range of the option $[t, T]$.

To connect up this lower bound with early exercise, it is the possibility of *attaining* the lower bound in a world of dividends that drives early exercise.

386 OPTIONS

11.4.7 Lower Bound for a European Put Option on an Underlying with Continuous Dividends (LBEPD)

In order to understand this section, one has to know several facts about the institutional structure of the spot and put options markets. The institutional fact is that:

> A short seller of underlying shares must pay any dividends distributed to shareholders while the short position is held; a put holder does not.
>
> (Source: www.cboe.com/learncenter/concepts/ beyond/general.aspx; accessed May 27, 2015)

Basically, we have to replicate Table 11.4 for this scenario. We start with a long position in a single European put option as our strategy A. The payoff is in terms of the dividend–adjusted stock price (see the above quote) so it doesn't pay to exercise unless $S'_T < E$. When you exercise the European put at time T, you deliver the stock *without* its dividends over $[t, T]$ re-invested and you receive \$$E$ for it. The value of that stock at time T is S'_T because it is the dividend–adjusted stock. (Note that the normal stock price with dividends re-invested has to be less than the exercise price, E, plus the FV of the re-invested dividends for this to occur).

We now have to figure out how to *partially* replicate the put option's payoffs. Provided that we accomplish this with payoffs that are no larger than the payoffs to the put option, the dominance principle then will provide a lower bound to the put option's current price.

In order to partially replicate the long European put option position, we have to short sell *less* than one unit of underlying stock, because the short position in the spot market has to restitute the option seller for the dividends paid out over $[t, T]$. If we short sell $e^{-\rho\tau}$ units of underlying stock at time t, everything works out fine because, once again, $e^{-\rho\tau}S_t$ grows to S'_T, by definition. Table 11.6 indicates the partial replication strategy.

Note that Strategy A has payoffs at least as great as the payoffs to Strategy B in all states of the world. The payoff to Strategy B is $E - S'_T \leq 0$ if $S'_T \geq E$ while the payoff to Strategy A is 0.

The current value of Strategy B is $e^{-r\tau}E - e^{-\rho\tau}S_t = e^{-r\tau}E - (S_t - PV(\text{DIVs})) = e^{-r\tau}E + PV(\text{DIVs}) - S_t$. The value of a European put option also cannot be negative because its payoffs dominate the zero-payoff strategy. By the dominance principle, the current value of Strategy A must be greater than or

RATIONAL OPTION PRICING 387

TABLE 11.6 **Lower Bound for a European Put Option with Dividends on the Underlier**

State of the World at Expiration	$S_T' \geq E$	$S_T' < E$
Strategy A		
Payoff to Long European Put Option	0	$E-S_T'$
Strategy B		
i. Short $e^{-\rho\tau}$ units of the underlying stock	$-S_T'$	$-S_T'$
ii. Lend PV(E)	E	E
Total Payoff to Strategy B	$E-S_T'$	$E-S_T'$

equal to the current value of Strategy B. The lower bound for the value of the European put option is dividend-adjusted intrinsic value,

$$P^E(S_t,\tau,E) \geq MAX[e^{-r\tau}E+PV(DIVs)-S_t, 0] \quad \textbf{(Lower Bound European}$$
$$=MAX[e^{-r\tau}E-e^{-\rho\tau}S_t, 0] \quad \textbf{Puts (LBEPD))}$$

The equality follows because $S_t-PV(DIVs)=e^{-\rho\tau}S_t$.

11.4.8 Lower Bound for an American Put Option on an Underlying with Continuous Dividends (LBAPD)

The same argument given in section 11.4.6 for the no-arbitrage lower bound, but not the rationale for early exercise, applies in this scenario. The lower bound is exactly the same as if there were no dividends,

$$P^A(S_t,\tau,E) \geq MAX[E-S_t, 0] \quad \textbf{(Lower Bound American Puts}$$
$$\textbf{(LBAPD)=(LBAP))}$$

We can prove this by contradiction. If (LBAPD) were not true, then $P^A(S_t,\tau,E)<MAX[E\ S_t, 0]$, and an immediate arbitrage opportunity would arise. Note that $E>S_t$ and $MAX[E-S_t, 0]=E-S_t$ otherwise the assumption implies that $P^A(S_t,\tau,E)<0$, which is not possible (the put premium cannot be negative). So, the assumption to be disproven is that $P^A(S_t,\tau,E)<E-S_t$.

The arbitrage strategy would be to acquire the stock underlying the put by buying it for its current market value S_t, buy the put for $P^A(S_t,\tau,E)$, and immediately exercise it by delivering the stock (without any dividend

388 OPTIONS

adjustment) in return for E. The stock and exercise part of the transaction would leave you with the positive amount $E-S_t$ since $E>S_t$.

The *net* cash flow from this set of transactions is $E-S_t-P^A(S_t,\tau,E)$, which is positive by the assumption that $P^A(S_t,\tau,E)<\text{MAX}[E-S_t,0]=E-S_t$. There are no further implications to your trades, the put has been exercised and the stock delivered into the put. You walk away with your arbitrage profits.

11.5 STATIC REPLICATION AND EUROPEAN PUT-CALL PARITY (NO DIVIDENDS)

The principle of *Static Replication* follows directly from the dominance principle and forms the basis of much of financial engineering. It is very simple. It compares financial packages A and B, once again, and concludes that if A has payoffs in all relevant states of the world that are *exactly equal* to the corresponding payoffs of financial package B, then the price today of A must be *equal* to the price of B, $P_{A,t}=P_{B,t}$. Otherwise, there would be an arbitrage opportunity.

One easy way to demonstrate this is to note that in the case of replication, financial package A dominates financial package B, so $P_{A,t}\geqslant P_{B,t}$. But B also dominates financial package A, so $P_{B,t}\geqslant P_{A,t}$. Since $P_{A,t}\geqslant P_{B,t}$ and $P_{B,t}\geqslant P_{A,t}$, together these imply that $P_{A,t}=P_{B,t}$.

11.5.1 Partially Replicating a European Call Option (the Embedded Forward Contract)

Using the principle of *Static Replication,* we are going to prove one of the most important results in Rational Option Pricing. This is called *Put-Call Parity for European puts and calls* on stocks paying no dividends over the life of the option. This result has many applications and implications, including an explanation of what a European call option is in economic terms.

The payoff table for a European call option on an underlying stock paying no dividends over the life of the option contract is Table 11.7.

According to the principle of static replication, we attempt to *break down* the long call position into 'simpler' financial instruments and positions. That is, we attempt to replicate the payoffs from the long call position in all relevant states of the world at expiration (there are only two). When we replicate, we do so through a synthetic portfolio of financial instruments, our replicating portfolio (RP) of simpler financial instruments.

RATIONAL OPTION PRICING

TABLE 11.7 **States of the World for a European Call Option (No Dividends)**

State of the World at Expiration, time T	$S_T \geq E$	$S_T < E$
European Call Option Payoff	$S_T - E$	0

If we can manage to accomplish this replication, then the current price of our replicating portfolio must be equal to the current price of the 'natural' call position (the call premium). That's what the *Static Replication Principle* says, otherwise there would be an immediate arbitrage opportunity.

Further, the long call position is economically equivalent to the replicating portfolio's components. In effect, we will have succeeded in breaking down the long call position into its fundamental components; positions in the simpler financial instruments in the replicating portfolio.

So, let's try it! To get started, what should go into our synthetic call option?

Since the actual call option is a derivative security, the simplest financial instrument to put into the replicating portfolio is the underlying 'stock'.

Clearly, the most fundamental financial instrument in determining the behavior of the call option and its price is the instrument underlying it.

What next? Look at the payoff diagram for a long call position given in Figure 11.2.

FIGURE 11.2 Payoff to a Long Position in a European Call Option on an Underlying Stock

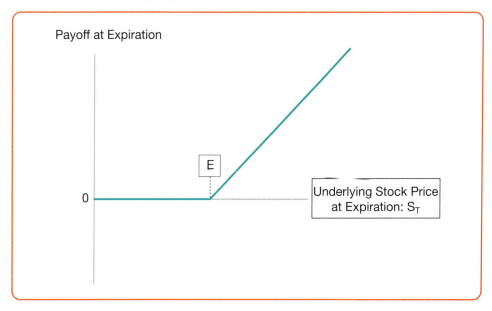

390 OPTIONS

We see two characteristics of a European call option from this payoff diagram:

1. It looks like the underlying stock for upward stock price movements.
2. It has a floor on the downside.

It is important to understand what we *don't* see from the picture, which is the leverage embedded in the option. This embedded leverage is the same as that for forward contracts, except that it need *not* be 100%, as it is for a forward contract. This strongly suggests including bonds (a borrowing position) in our replicating portfolio.

TABLE 11.8 **Partially Replicating the Payoffs to a European Call Option (No Dividends)**

State of the World at Expiration	$S_T \geq E$	$S_T < E$
Partial Replicating Portfolio		
1. Long Stock at time t for S_t	S_T	S_T
2. Borrow PV(E)=$e^{-r\tau} * E$	$-E$	$-E$
Payoffs to the Partially Replicating Portfolio	$S_T - E$	$S_T - E$

The payoffs to the long stock position are clear. No matter what the state of the world turns out to be, the payoff is just the terminal stock price S_T. (Remember that for payoff diagrams and payoff tables, we never subtract the initial cost of the investment.)

The payoff at time T to the short bond position (borrowing PV(E) today) is principal plus interest, which is an *outflow* of the FV of PV(E))=$-E$. This is just as we did for forward contracts.

Note that the payoffs to the partially replicating portfolio are less than or equal to the payoffs to the European call option in both states of the world. It follows from the dominance principle that the current cost of the partially replicating portfolio must be no larger that than current cost of the European call option,

$$C^E(S_t, \tau, E) \geq \text{MAX}[S_t - e^{-r\tau}E, \ 0].$$

But this is just our old friend, the adjusted intrinsic value lower bound for European calls (LBEC) of section 11.4.2, this time wearing a different hat.

RATIONAL OPTION PRICING **391**

■ CONCEPT CHECK 5

a. In forwards, the fixed price is the forward price. When we talk about options, instead of the *forward* price, the fixed price is the *exercise* price of the option, E. Write $E = F_{t,T}$. Now consider $S_t - e^{-r\tau}E = S_t - e^{-r\tau}F_{t,T}$. Interpret this quantity in terms of forward contract value.

b. What must the option's exercise price E be, if $F_{t,T}$ is the *actual* forward price?

c. Does the option exercise concept restrict E, as in b.?

d. What are the other possibilities for the sign of $S_t - e^{-r\tau}E$, and therefore for where E lies?

11.5.2 Fully Replicating a European Call Option (the Embedded Insurance Contract)

Note that Table 11.8 illustrates *partial* replication only. Namely, it replicates a type of forward contract embedded in a European call option. Concept Check 5 was an introduction to this forward contract concept, which we will fully flesh out in section 11.8.1 of this chapter.

As can be seen from the third column in Table 11.8, there must be one more ingredient needed to fully replicate a European call option, because a leveraged stock is never going to look like the payoff to a European call option in Figure 11.2.

We know that a *fully* leveraged stock position is just a forward contract, and a forward contract is a linear (not piece-wise linear) instrument that has no floor. We will find out exactly what the mystery ingredient is by using a mechanical approach to replicating the European call option.

See Table 11.9 below, where we have indicated the target of our replicating portfolio as the payoffs to the European call option.

Let's summarize what we have accomplished in Table 11.9. In one state of the world, $S_T \geqslant E$, our replicating portfolio adds up correctly to $S_T - E$. Unfortunately, it doesn't add up to zero in the other state of the world, $S_T < E$. In that out-of-the-money state it is supposed to add up to 0, the payoff for an out-of-the-money European call option.

How can we fix this? By visual inspection alone, the mystery ingredient in our replicating portfolio has to have a payoff of 0 if $S_T \geqslant E$, and it has to have a payoff of $E - S_T$ if $S_T < E$. The payoff diagram that describes this instrument is clearly that for a long put position, given in Figure 11.3.

OPTIONS

TABLE 11.9 Fully Replicating the Payoffs to a European Call Option

State of the World at Expiration	$S_T \geq E$	$S_T < E$
Fully Replicating Portfolio Constructed today at time t.		
1. Long Stock	S_T	S_T
2. Borrow $PV(E) = e^{-r\tau}E$	$-E$	$-E$
3. ?	?	?
The Target is the Payoff to a Long European Call Option	$S_T - E$	0

FIGURE 11.3 Payoff to a Long Position in a European Put Option on an Underlying Stock

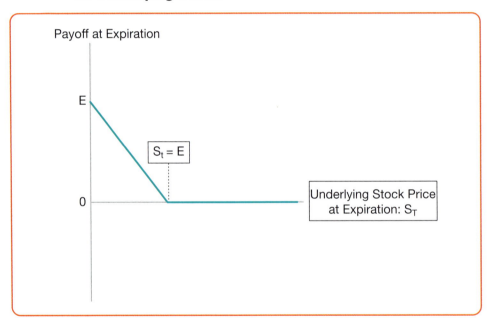

Before completing the full replication of a European call option, we want to first discuss an important technique used in the derivation. Further, it has numerous applications.

11.5.3 From Strategies to Current Costs and Back

This is a very useful technique, rarely discussed, in the study of derivatives securities. It is the method of going back and forth between current costs and the strategies that correspond to them. It isn't rocket science.

Rather, it is a purely mechanical technique that is foolproof if applied methodically. The first thing to note is the convention regarding current costs that we make. A *positive* current cost (an outflow) is recorded as a positive number. A *negative* current cost (an inflow) is a benefit, or a reduction, in positive current costs, and is recorded as a negative number.

■ CONCEPT CHECK 6

a. Suppose that we see a current cost recorded as S_t=\$725.06. The technique is just to ask, what strategy generated this current cost?
b. Suppose we see that the current cost is recorded as $-PV(E)=-e^{-r\tau}E$. What strategy generated this current cost?
c. Suppose we see that the current cost is recorded as $P^E(S_t,\tau,E)$. What strategy generated this current cost?

11.5.4 Working Backwards from Payoffs to Costs to Derive European Put-Call Parity

We now use the *static replication principle* to work back to the initial costs of all the strategies involved in replicating the long European call option position. Table 11.10 summarizes the initial costs. Note that a positive cost will be indicated as a positive number. A positive cost creates an outflow. A negative

TABLE 11.10 **Current Costs of the Synthetic Call Option and of the Natural Call Option**

Synthetic Call	Current Costs
Long Stock	S_t
Borrow *PV(E)*	$-PV(E)$
Long Put	$P^E(S_t, \tau, E)$
Total Cost of the Synthetic Call	$S_t - PV(E) + P^E(S_t, \tau, E)$
Cost of the Natural Call	$C^E(S_t, \tau, E)$

394 **OPTIONS**

cost is a benefit and it creates an inflow, such as when we borrow. The final replicating portfolio is indicated in Table 11.10.

The static replication principle says that the price of the synthetic European call option must be equal to the price of the *actual* European call option, $C^E(S_t, \tau, E)$. Otherwise, there would be an immediate arbitrage opportunity. Recognizing that $PV(E) = e^{-r\tau}E$, we obtain put-call parity for European call and put options with no dividends on the underlying over the life of the option.

$$C^E(S_t, \tau, E) = S_t - e^{-r\tau}E + P^E(S_t, \tau, E) \qquad \textbf{(European Put–Call Parity,}$$
$$\textbf{no Dividends)}$$

11.6 BASIC IMPLICATIONS OF EUROPEAN PUT-CALL PARITY

11.6.1 What is a European Call Option?

The European Put-Call Parity equation is a very important result for several reasons. First, it explains the economic effects of a European call option. A European call option is the combination of the underlying stock, leverage as a means of *partially* financing it, and an insurance policy in the form of a European put option.

The first two effects are fairly clear. The call option allows the investor to invest in the stock at a fraction of the price of the underlying stock. But this cannot be the case in an arbitrage-free market. How could you get the underlying stock without paying for it?

The answer is that you cannot. Borrowing to finance the stock gives one the *illusion* of getting something for nothing. In reality, borrowing simply *defers* the otherwise up-front payment until later. And its cost is that you may not be able to pay back the amount borrowed (plus interest) later. Thus, leverage exposes the leveraged investor to their own default risk and to potential bankruptcy. So one is hardly getting something for nothing.

Note also that leverage increases the *risks to equity holders*, which is a basic finance result. Therefore, one cannot compare an unleveraged stock to a leveraged one. That's like comparing apples to oranges.

The third component of a European call option is its embedded European put option. The put option's role is to provide insurance for our leveraged stock position. We have to carefully consider the European put option embedded in the European call option. Exactly what does it insure and how does it work? Suppose that one does borrow $PV(E) = e^{-r\tau}E$ right now, at time t. Note that this may be less than, equal to, or greater than the current cost of the stock S_t. The three cases are,

Case 1: $S_t > e^{-r\tau}E$

Note that in this case $E < e^{r\tau}S_t = F_{t,T}$, which is the forward price from Chapter 3. The option's exercise price is *below* the corresponding forward price.

Case 2: $S_t = e^{-r\tau}E$

Note that in this case $E = e^{r\tau}S_t = F_{t,T}$, the option's exercise price is *equal* to the corresponding forward price.

Case 3: $S_t < e^{-r\tau}E$

Note that in this case $E > e^{r\tau}S_t = F_{t,T}$, the option's exercise price is *above* the corresponding forward price.

So it appears that European call options are closely related to, and embed, generalized forward contracts on the underlying. We will discuss this important connection in section 11.8.1.

We use the borrowed amount to finance the stock purchase at time T. In Case 1, the borrowing *under*-finances the stock purchase, in Case 2 it *exactly* finances it, and in Case 3 it *over*-finances it. In all three cases, the amount borrowed needs to be repaid in the amount $FV(PV(E)) = E$. That is, principal plus interest amounts to $\$E$. This is where the leverage risk enters the picture.

What assets do we have that will allow us to pay off the debt? The stock is the most natural asset, since we own it. Its value at time T is S_T. If $S_T > E$ or if $S_T = E$ at time T, we remain solvent since we can sell the stock for S_T and use the proceeds to pay off the debt of $\$E$.

However, if $S_T < E$, then owning the stock will not fully cover the debt owed. If we *just* held the stock, then we would technically be bankrupt. An insurance policy is what is needed in order to insure that you are able to pay off the *full* amount of the debt at time T, by allowing you to sell your stock for $\$E$ in the event that $S_T < E$. (In the event that $S_T \geq E$ you wouldn't exercise your insurance policy.)

This is exactly what a long put allows you to do. When $S_T < E$, the payoff to the long stock position embedded in the European call option is S_T. The payoff to the leverage is $-E$. The net payoff to the leveraged stock is $S_T - E$, which is a negative amount interpreted as the shortfall in the stock as repayment of the debt. The European put option has a (positive) payoff precisely equal to this amount $E-S_T$ (see Figure 11.3).

Paying off the debt by exercising the European put option results in the ability to *fully* cover the debt when the stock itself cannot do so. A zero cash flow results.

This is why the European call option has a floor for stock prices $S_T<E$. The reason for the floor on a European call option is exercise of the implicit European put option embedded in it.

11.6.2 The Analogue of the Basic American Option Pricing Model for European Options

The American option pricing model introduced in Chapter 9, section 9.4, certainly does apply, in one sense, to European call options. Consider the no-dividend case. Then $C_t^E=C_t^A$ (see End of Chapter Exercise 2). Therefore,

$$C_t^E=C_t^A$$
$$=\text{(Intrinsic Value)}_t + \text{(Call Time Premium at time)}_t$$
$$=IV(C_t^A) + TP(C_t^A).$$

In the case of dividends, $C_t^E \leq C_t^A$ with the difference $C_t^A-C_t^E=EEP_t$ which is called the *early exercise premium* (see End of Chapter Exercise 4). Typically, for the dividend case, $C_t^E \lesseqgtr C_t^A=IV(C_t^A)+TP(C_t^A)$, so we obtain an inequality.

Going back to the no-dividend case, we encounter a problem in *interpreting* $C_t^E=IV(C_t^E)+TP(C_t^A)$ in terms of *early* exercise rights. Since a European option does not permit early exercise, $IV(C_t^E)$ is not something to which we have rights. Therefore, we cannot realize $IV(C_t^E)$.

However, there is a value quantity that we do have access to, in the sense that it is embedded in the option price. That quantity is adjusted intrinsic value (AIV) and the AIV bound, $C^E(S_t,\tau,E) \geq MAX[S_t-e^{-r\tau}E,0]$ (LBEC), tells us that it is embedded in the call option price. But what exactly is it in terms of rights? We shall see momentarily.

But first, our adjusted European option pricing model should say that, $C_t^E=\text{(Adjusted Intrinsic Value)}_t+(\textit{Adjusted}\text{ Call Time Premium at time})_t$, which in notation is,

$$C_t^E=\text{AIV}(C_t^E)+\text{ATP}(C_t^E) \quad \textbf{(Basic European Option Pricing Model)}$$

RATIONAL OPTION PRICING   397

Note that, the *adjusted time premium*, $ATP(C_t^E)$, is defined in terms of $AIV(C_t^E)$ (not in terms of unadjusted $IV(C_t^E)$). That is, the proof of the analogous European option pricing model is just by *defining* $ATP(C_t^E) \equiv C_t^E - AIV(C_t^E)$.

Interpretation of (Basic European Option Pricing Model)

This European option pricing model can be also be interpreted in terms of the rights associated with *relative risks*, in perfect analogy with the *rights* interpretation option for the American case.

To understand the relative risk rights, ask yourself the question: to what does a European call option entitle the option holder? The answer is clearly only the right to exercise the option at expiration, time T. There are no further rights associated with a European call option. So its time t value should be the risk-neutral current value of this right.

Interestingly, we can break down this single right into two sub rights, based on relative risk considerations. Imagine a scenario in which you knew for sure at time t, that you would exercise the option at time T. That is, it is assumed for certain that $S_T > E$, and consequently an expenditure of $\$E$ would be made for certain at time T, in exchange for each unit of the stock. Note that the assumption is that the event $\{S_T > E\}$ would occur with probability 1.0.

Since this entire scenario is riskless, the present value of the certain cash flow associated with this scenario is equal to the present value of the ultimate stock price minus the present value of the exercise price. That is, discounting would occur at the risk-free rate. This results in a present value of $S_t - e^{-r\tau}E$. You could call this the *certainty equivalent* (*CE*) of the ultimate cash flow associated with the option's exercise.

If indeed $S_t - e^{-r\tau}E > 0$, this represents the minimum amount that you would accept for the option. If $S_t - e^{-r\tau}E < 0$, then the certainty equivalent present value is zero. That is, adjusted intrinsic value, $MAX[S_t - e^{-r\tau}E, 0]$, represents the present value of the *certainty equivalent* cash flow associated with the precommitment to exercise the option at time T.

Now, ask yourself the question: would you accept $\$0$ in return for the option in the case in which adjusted intrinsic value is equal to zero? Most investors would answer no because, even though the option is currently *out-of-the-money* in the adjusted sense, there is a *chance* that it *could* be *in-the-money* at expiration. As you can see, this introduces risk into the previously riskless scenario.

The option's market premium at time t should include a dollar risk premium payable to the investor, in return for taking the risk associated with the option. That risk premium is precisely the time premium associated with the option, where in this case it incorporates the volatility of the ultimate stock price in the random event $\{S_T(\omega)>E\}$.

Thus, the current call option premium is the sum of adjusted intrinsic value plus this risk-adjusted dollar time premium. The two rights incorporated into the option value are the rights to the certainty equivalent cash flow of the event $\{S_T>E\}$, and to the dollar risk premium of the event $\{S_T(\omega)>E\}$, which would be calculated as a risk-neutral discounted expected value. We will see how this is done for the MBOP models in Chapters 13, 14, and 16.

This is about as far as we can get in a ROP sense. MBOP models such as Black–Scholes effectively pin down the European call option's current time premium. There is nothing to compute in adjusted intrinsic value, because it is perfectly known at time t.

11.6.3 What is a European Put Option?

Now that we have interpreted a European call option as a leveraged stock insured by a European put, we can give a similar interpretation to a European put option.

If we simply re-arrange Put-Call Parity for European options to have the put premium on the left-hand side and the other three positions on the right-hand side, then we just apply our technique of working backwards from current costs to strategies.

$$P^E(S_t,\tau,E)=-S_t+e^{-r\tau}E+C^E(S_t,\tau,E) \qquad \textbf{(European Put–Call Parity re-arranged)}$$

Table 11.11 indicates the strategies that correspond to each term on the right-hand side of the re-arranged European Put-Call Parity equation.

Since the sign of S_t is negative, the position in the underlying stock must be a short sale, borrowing by selling stock you don't own. The position in $PV(E)$ has a positive cost, so it must be lending, investing in the stock. The sign of $C^E(S_t,\tau,E)$ is positive, so we must be investing in the call (purchasing it).

All this tells us that a long European put option is economically equivalent to a short stock position, a lending position in $PV(E)$, and a long European call option.

RATIONAL OPTION PRICING 399

TABLE 11.11 **Current Costs of the Synthetic Put Option and of the Natural Put Option**

Underlying Strategy	Current Costs
Short Stock	$-S_t$
Lend PV(E)	$+PV(E)$
Long Call	$C^E(S_t,\tau,E)$
Total Cost of the Synthetic Put	$-S_t+PV(E)+C^E(S_t,\tau,E)$
Cost of the Natural Put	$P^E(S_t,\tau,E)$

■ CONCEPT CHECK 7

a. What is the risk in the short stock position?
b. How does the lending position in $PV(E)$ help to control the risk in a.?
c. What residual risk is not managed by the lending position in $PV(E)$?
d. How does longing the European call option control the residual risk in c.?

11.7 FURTHER IMPLICATIONS OF EUROPEAN PUT-CALL PARITY

11.7.1 Synthesizing Forward Contract from Puts and Calls

We start again from the European Put-Call Parity relationship,

$$C^E(S_t,\tau,E)=S_t-e^{-r\tau}E+P^E(S_t,\tau,E) \qquad \textbf{(European PC-Parity, no Dividends)}$$

We are familiar with another financial instrument with a fixed price built into it, a forward contract with forward price $F_{t,T}$.

Let $t=0$ and write F_0 for $F_{t,T}$. Suppose $E=F_0$. Substitute this into the PC-Parity relationship and let's see what happens,

$$C^E(S_t,\tau,E)=(S_t-e^{-r\tau}F_0)+P^E(S_t,\tau,E).$$

So far nothing too exciting, until we remember that the equilibrium forward price $F_0=e^{r\tau}S_t$ which means that $S_t-e^{-r\tau}F_0=0$. Let's think in terms of replication for a moment. Look at the quantity $S_t-e^{-r\tau}F_0$. It represents the current cost of a certain strategy. We can easily determine the strategy using our technique of going from current costs to underlying strategies. This is accomplished in Table 11.12.

400 OPTIONS

TABLE 11.12 **Current Costs of a Natural Forward Contract**

Long Forward Contract	Current Costs
Long stock	S_t
Borrow $PV(F_0)$	$-e^{-r\tau}F_0$
Total Cost of the Natural Long Forward Contract	$S_t - e^{-r\tau}F_0 = 0$

The total cost of replicating the long forward contract position is its current value which, due to the principle of no arbitrage in equilibrium, equals 0. Now we will construct a synthetic long forward contract position.

According to European Put-Call Parity,

$$C^E(S_t, \tau, E) - P^E(S_t, \tau, E) = S_t - e^{-r\tau}F_{t,T}$$

The right-hand side is the current value of a long forward contract. The left-hand side is the cost of the synthetic long forward contract. See Table 11.13.

TABLE 11.13 **Current Costs of a Synthetic Forward Contract**

Synthetic Long Forward Contract	Current Costs
Long European Call Option	$C^E(S_t, \tau, E)$
Short European Put Option	$-P^E(S_t, \tau, E)$
Total Cost of the Synthetic Long Forward Contract	$C^E(S_t, \tau, E) - P^E(S_t, \tau, E)$

This says that a synthetic long forward contract is a long European call and a short European put, both with exercise price equal to the equilibrium forward price $E = F_{t,T} = e^{r\tau}S_t$. The intuition behind this is that if $S_T \geq E$, then you will exercise the long call, buying the underlying commodity for $\$E$, but the buyer of the put will not exercise the put because it is not in-the-money.

On the other hand, if $S_T < E$, the buyer of the put will exercise the put forcing you to buy the underlying commodity for $\$E$. You won't exercise the call because it is out-of-the-money in this case.

So no matter what state of the world prevails, you will end up having to buy the underlying commodity for $\$E$. But that is exactly what a long forward contract is; the obligation to buy the underlying commodity for $\$E$, no matter what happens at time T.

RATIONAL OPTION PRICING **401**

11.8 FINANCIAL INNOVATION USING EUROPEAN PUT-CALL PARITY

11.8.1 Generalized Forward Contracts

Using these ideas linking forward contracts to European puts and calls, we can do a little financial innovation. When you take a long position in a 'normal' forward contract, the forward price must equal $F_{t,T}=e^{r\tau}S_t$ in order to avoid arbitrage. There is no up-front payment required because, at this forward price, the current value of the forward contract to all longs and shorts is zero.

This creates a limitation on the types of forward contracts that can be written. Given zero up-front costs, the number of 'exercise prices' for forward contracts is precisely one. Also, what happens when a forward contract begins to assume value as time progresses?

Surely it is possible to write forward contracts with $F_{t,T}\neq e^{r\tau}S_t$. There would be no problem in doing so. But if the current value of such contracts were set to be equal to zero, then there would be arbitrage opportunities and some participants would be 'winners', while others would be 'losers' from the get go.

We know that a forward contract can have positive or negative value to the long at expiration, depending on whether $S_T>F_{t,T}$ or $S_T<F_{t,T}$. This value creation can, and usually does, occur prior to expiration as $S_{t'}$ moves away from $F_{t,T}$ with time $t'>t$.

An important point to remember is that the current value of forward contracts is set to 0 *at initiation*, time t. *After* initiation the value of forward contracts is free to go where it wants to go based on the movement of the underlying commodity prices.

There is no reason that forward contracts cannot be written at all forward prices, just as options are written at different exercise prices and could, in theory, be written at all exercise prices. So long as we eliminate the arbitrage opportunities. To do so, we have to drop the constraint of zero initiation value for generalized forward contracts. That's because they no longer have zero value at initiation when $F_{t,T}\neq e^{r\tau}S_t$.

To see this, look back at European Put-Call Parity. Re-arranging it slightly, it then says $C^E(S_t,\tau,E)-P^E(S_t,\tau,E)=S_t-e^{-r\tau}F_{t,T}$. You will immediately see that the current (time=t) value of the synthetic long forward contract position is the difference between a European call and a European put option written at the exercise price $E=F_{t,T}$. And this difference is $S_t-e^{-r\tau}F_{t,T}$ (see Chapter 3 and concept check 5 in that chapter).

402 **OPTIONS**

Since the synthetic long forward contract is, to all intents and purposes, economically equivalent to the long forward position, and options have current value, the right-hand side is the current value of the long forward position. Note that this current value can be positive, zero, or negative depending on the three possible cases; $S_t > e^{-r\tau}F_{t,T}$, $S_t = e^{-r\tau}F_{t,T}$, or $S_t < e^{-r\tau}F_{t,T}$.

If we think about this for a moment, we will see exactly what is going on here. We need a notation for the *equilibrium* forward price at time t, so we will call it $F_{t,T}^* = e^{r\tau}S_t$. Think of $F_{t,T}$ as a *generalized* forward price, or as the exercise price of the put and call options that generate the forward contract by European Put-Call Parity.

If $S_t > e^{-r\tau}F_{t,T}$ then $F_{t,T}$ is below the equilibrium forward price, $F_{t,T}^* = e^{r\tau}S_t$. A long would then be contracting to pay for the commodity at a lower price than the market specifies to prevent arbitrage. There would indeed be an arbitrage opportunity here, yielding an arbitrage profit equal to $S_t - e^{-r\tau}F_{t,T}$, assuming that there were no up-front (or time T compensating) payment from the long to the short on the forward contract.

So to eliminate this arb, we just charge the long for what he is receiving, either currently or at time T. Currently, the long would pay to the short the amount $S_t - e^{-r\tau}F_{t,T}$.

This leads to a categorization of three different types of forward contracts, analogous to the categorization for options, as indicated in Table 11.14. However, for forward contracts the correct comparison of the underlying 'stock' price is to the discounted forward price. Note that $E = F_{t,T}$ is the forward price at which you want to write the forward contract, analogous to the exercise price of the options generating the forward contract.

TABLE 11.14 **Generalized Forward Contracts**

Type of Forward Contract		Premium (Discount)
$E^* = e^{r\tau}S_t > E = F_{t,T}$	(in-the-money forward)	$S_t - e^{-r\tau}F_{t,T} > 0$ (premium)
$E^* = e^{r\tau}S_t = F_{t,T}^*$	(at-the-money forward)	None, an ordinary forward contract
$E^* = e^{r\tau}S_t < E = F_{t,T}$	(out-of-the-money forward)	$S_t - e^{-r\tau}F_{t,T} < 0$ (discount)

RATIONAL OPTION PRICING 403

■ CONCEPT CHECK 8

a. Show that if $e^{r\tau}S_t = E^* < E = F_{t,T}$, then the long is *overpaying* for the long position (acquiring a position that has negative current value).
b. How much would he have to be compensated by the short in order to be coaxed to take this currently negative-value long forward position?

Under these arrangements, there are no arbs and everyone (longs and shorts) is currently happy. Remember, the ultimate payoff comes at time T and, from a speculative point of view, can still be expected to be positive.

11.8.2 American Put-Call Parity (No Dividends)

American Put-Call Parity, even in the absence of dividends on the underlier, comes in the form of *inequalities*. That is, it bounds the prices of American call options in terms of well-known bounds and the prices of corresponding American puts. It says,

$$(S_t - E) + P^A(S_t, \tau, E) \leq C^A(S_t, \tau, E) \leq (S_t - e^{-r\tau}E) + P^A(S_t, \tau, E)$$

(American Put–Call Parity, no Dividends)

Another commonly used equivalent format, which bounds the American call and American put option price differential, is

$$(S_t - E) \leq C^A(S_t, \tau, E) - P^A(S_t, \tau, E) \leq (S_t - e^{-r\tau}E)$$

(American Put–Call Parity, no Dividends)

That is, the difference between an American call and an otherwise American put option on an asset that carries no dividends over the life of the option is bounded by something that looks like the usual American intrinsic value bound, and by something that looks like the corresponding adjusted intrinsic value bound.

Note that ordinary intrinsic value is $\text{MAX}[S_t - E, 0]$, which is bounded below by zero. The lower bound in the above inequalities is $S_t - E$ which is negative when $S_t < E$.

Similarly, the upper bound is *not* adjusted intrinsic value which is $AIV_t = \text{MAX}[S_t - e^{-r\tau}E, 0] > 0$. Our bound, $S_t - e^{-r\tau}E$, can and will be negative when $S_t < e^{-r\tau}E$.

404 OPTIONS

This subtle difference suggests that we are dealing with three different forward contracts in (American Put-Call Parity, no Dividends), $(S_t-E) \leqslant C^A(S_t,\tau,E) - P^A(S_t,\tau,E) \leqslant (S_t-e^{-r\tau}E)$.

The interpretation of these inequalities is probably more interesting than the proofs, which will be deferred to End of Chapter Exercise 10, because interpreting them affords us an opportunity to learn something more about forward contracts, as suggested above.

Instead of giving the mechanical proofs of *sub-replication* for the first inequality and *super-replication* for the second inequality, we will discuss the intuition behind this pair of inequalities.

The first preliminary result we need is that a generalized forward contract is increasing in current value as its time to expiration, τ, increases.

■ CONCEPT CHECK 9

a. What is the current value of a generalized forward contract with forward price E?

b. What happens to the current price of a zero-coupon bond $B(t,T)=e^{-r\tau}$ as τ increases?

c. What happens to $PV(E)=e^{-r\tau}E$ as τ increases, for a given E?

d. What happens to the the current value of a generalized forward contract with forward price E as τ increases?

The result d. of this concept check is important for interpreting American Put-Call Parity, no Dividends. Consider $S_t-e^{-r\tau}E$ on the right-hand side of the inequality. It is just the current value of an ordinary, generalized forward contract which can only be 'exercised' (the long takes delivery of the underlying commodity) at its maturity date, time T. Not before. You can also write it, by European Put-Call Parity as $C^A(S_t,\tau,E)-P^E(S_t,\tau,E)=S_t-e^{-r\tau}E$.

Next, consider the left-hand side quantity, S_t-E. We can interpret it as the value of a specific forward contract! The *shortest* maturity forward contract is the one that calls for *immediate* delivery. That is, a spot transaction. Recall our discussion in Chapter 1 of the three ways one can transact in an underlying commodity. A forward contract is a *deferred* spot transaction. Alternatively, a spot transaction is an *immediate* forward transaction.

Of course, if you could contract to pay for a commodity an amount $\$E$ when it was selling for $S_t>E$, that would be an immediate arbitrage opportunity. To remove it, you would have to compensate the short in the immediate forward

RATIONAL OPTION PRICING 405

contract by the amount S_t-E. Overall, you would end up paying the short $\$E+\$(S_t-E)=\$S_t$ which is what the commodity is worth at time t.

Now for the punch line. The value of an *immediate* forward contract must be less than that of an otherwise identical, deferred forward contract, $S_t-E<S_t-e^{-r\tau}E$ as long as the interest rate $r>0$. Of course, we already know this. But there is a higher payoff to the forward contract interpretation.

Let's look at the middle quantity, $C^A(S_t,\tau,E)-P^A(S_t,\tau,E)$ and interpret it as the value of a specific, albeit somewhat weird, forward contract. In the world of no dividends on the underlier over the life of an American call option, we know that it would never be exercised early and therefore commands the same current market value as an otherwise identical European call option, $C^A(S_t,\tau,E)=C^E(S_t,\tau,E)$ (see section 11.4.6, Case 1, and End of Chapter Exercise 2). Therefore, $C^A(S_t,\tau,E)-P^A(S_t,\tau,E)=C^E(S_t,\tau,E)-P^A(S_t,\tau,E)$.

This implies that you, the long in some kind of forward contract whose current value is represented by $C^E(S_t,\tau,E)-P^A(S_t,\tau, E)$, would never willingly take delivery early if that choice was based on the call option you implicitly hold. However, the short American put position that you implicitly hold might be exercised by the put's long.

Therefore, $C^E(S_t,\tau,E)-P^A(S_t,\tau,E)$ represents the value of a forward contract with a *random* maturity date, based on the exercise of the American put by the long. Since $P^E(S_t,\tau,E)\leq P^A(S_t,\tau,E)$, therefore,

$$C^E(S_t,\tau,E)-P^A(S_t,\tau,E)\leq C^E(S_t,\tau,E)-P^E(S_t,\tau,E)=S_t-e^{-r\tau}E,$$

which is the right-hand side of the inequality defining American put-call parity with no dividends, $C^A(S_t,\tau,E)-P^A(S_t,\tau,E)\leq(S_t-e^{-r\tau}E)$.

The left side of the inequality, $(S_t-E)\leq C^A(S_t,\tau,E)-P^A(S_t,\tau,E)$, follows because the generalized forward contract represented by $C^A(S_t,\tau,E)-P^A(S_t,\tau,E)$ has a random maturity date which is greater than or equal to the current time t. Therefore, it has a greater current value than an immediately exercisable forward contact, S_t-E.

11.9 POSTSCRIPT ON ROP

ROP is a very powerful technique but it can't do everything. For example, it cannot generate *unique* option prices, unless other conditions such as replicability or market completeness hold (see Chapter 13, section 13.5). ROP is based upon *No-Arbitrage In Equilibrium* (NAIE), which is a minimal necessary condition for being able to price financial instruments, including derivatives.

ROP typically leads to a *range* of option prices or relative pricing relationships such as European Put-Call Parity, which has a circularity in it. We can't dispense with NAIE, because then we would have no hope of generating any reasonable pricing mechanism, albeit non-unique.

As an example of something that is *not* an ROP result, consider the proposition that call options always increase as the underlying stock price increases. This seems obvious but there are some processes for which it is not true. Therefore, obvious and being a ROP result are not the same thing.

Another proposition that cannot be proven without further conditions is *convexity* of the option price in the underlying stock price. There are examples in which the option price can have concavities.

One of the challenges in option pricing is justifying the following Figure 11.4, which graphs the current (time t) European call option price, $C^E(S_t,\tau,E)$, for a given time to maturity, $\tau=T-t$, as a function of the current stock price S_t. It illustrates the AIV bound, $C^E(S_t,\tau,E) \geq \text{MAX}[S_t - e^{-r\tau}E, 0]$ (LBEC) which consists of the two red lines indicated.

We *hope* that European call option prices look like the graph in Figure 11.4, and for many underlying processes they do. But not for all. Therefore, one cannot prove the content of Figure 11.4 as a ROP result. So Figure 11.4 expresses a MBOP result. (However, one can make some assumptions about the underlying process and derive Figure 11.4.)

FIGURE 11.4 **European Call Option Price, $C^E(S_t,\tau,E)$, for a Given Maturity $\tau=T-t$**

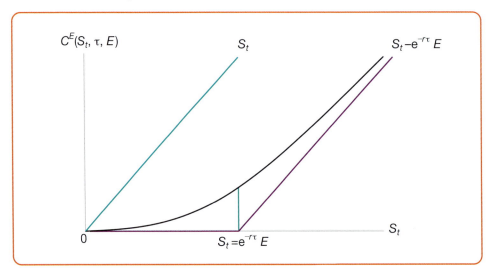

The conclusions usually drawn from Figure 11.4 are,

1. $C^E(S_t,\tau,E)$ is an *increasing* function of the underlying stock price S_t (the *monotonicity* property).

2. $C^E(S_t,\tau,E)$ is a *convex* function of the underlying stock price S_t (the *convexity* property).

3. $C^E(0,\tau,E)=0$.

4. The time premium (defined in terms of AIV) starts at zero, reaches a maximum at $e^{-r\tau}E$, then declines (see the blue vertical line in Figure 11.4).

■ CONCEPT CHECK 10

a. Which of the above conclusions are ROP?
b. Which of the above conclusions are MBOP?

408 OPTIONS

■ KEY CONCEPTS

1. Rational (Model-Independent) Option Pricing (ROP) vs. Model-Based Option (MBOP) Pricing.
2. Relative Pricing Trades vs. Directional Trades.
3. The Dominance Principle.
4. Classification of Options.
5. Implications of the Dominance Principle, ROP for Puts and Calls.

   a. Lower Bound for an American Call Option on an Underlying with no Dividends (LBAC).
   b. Lower Bound for a European Call Option on an Underlying with no Dividends (LBEC).
   c. Lower Bound for an American Put Option on an Underlying with no Dividends (LBAP).
   d. Lower Bound for a European Put Option on an Underlying with no Dividends (LBEP).
   e. Lower Bound for a European Call Option on an Underlying with Continuous Dividends (LBECD).
   f. Lower Bound for an American Call Option on an Underlying with Continuous Dividends (LBACD)=(LBAC).
   g. Lower Bound for a European Put Option on an Underlying with Continuous Dividends (LBEPD).
   h. Lower Bound for an American Put Option on an Underlying with Continuous Dividends (LBAPD)=(LBAP).

6. Static Replication and European Put-Call Parity (No Dividends).
7. Partially Replicating a European Call Option by Replicating its Embedded Forward Contract.
8. Fully Replicating a European Call Option by Replicating its Embedded Insurance Contract.
9. The Technique of Working from Strategies' Payoffs to Current Costs and Back.
10. Applying the Technique to Derive European Put-Call Parity.
11. Basic Implications of European Put-Call Parity.

    a. What is a European Call Option?
    b. The analogue of our Basic American Option Pricing Model for European Call Options.
    c. What is a European Put Option?

RATIONAL OPTION PRICING 409

12. Further Implications of European Put-Call Parity.
13. Synthesizing Ordinary Forward Contract from Puts and Calls.
14. Generalizing Forward Contracts.

    a. Construction.
    b. American Put-Call Parity (No Dividends).

15. Postscript on ROP.

■ END OF CHAPTER EXERCISES FOR CHAPTER 11

1. *(Arbitrage Opportunities)*

   In this exercise, you will construct an arbitrage strategy using an American call option. Let $C^A(S_t,\tau,E)$ be the current value of an American call option on an underlying stock with current price S_t, time to expiration τ, and exercise price E.

       a. What is the Intrinsic Value of the American call option?
       b. Construct an arbitrage strategy if $C^A(S_t,\tau,E)<$Intrinsic Value in a.

2. Assume that the underlier, a stock for example, has no payouts over its life $[t,T]$. The underlier could also be a real asset with no cash flows paid out over the option's life.

   Also, consider an American call option written on the underlier over the period $[t,T]$ with current value $C^A(S_t,\tau,E)$. An otherwise identical European call option has current value $C^E(S_t,\tau,E)$.

       a. What must the relationship, as an inequality, be between $C^A(S_t,\tau,E)$ and $C^E(S_t,\tau,E)$?
       b. Write out the (LBEC).
       c. Refer to Concept Check 3. Assuming that both $\mathrm{MAX}[S_t-e^{-r\tau}E,\,0]$ and $\mathrm{MAX}[S_t-E,\,0]$ are positive and that $\tau>0$, which is larger?
       d. Assume that the un–adjusted intrinsic value $\mathrm{MAX}[S_t-E,\,0]$ is positive. Is adjusted intrinsic value also positive in this case?
       e. What does (LBEC) say under the assumption that $\mathrm{MAX}[S_t-e^{-r\tau}E,\,0]$ >0?
       f. Now combine $S_t-e^{-r\tau}E \gtreqless S_t-E$ at any time prior to maturity, given the assumption that the American call option is in-the-money ($S_t-E>0$), with the result of a. What do you get?

410 **OPTIONS**

g. We now have to interpret the result of f. which asserts that, with no dividends on the underlier over $[t,T]$, and that we are prior to maturity $(t>0)$, the value of an American call option will always be *strictly greater* than its immediate exercise value.

Recall the three alternatives available to the long an American call option point in time in $[t,T]$. List them in the spaces below.

He can _____ , _____ , or _____ the option. The payoffs to these three alternatives are _____ , _____ , or _____ .

h. On a pure cost-benefit basis, which alternative should you *always* choose for an American option prior to maturity? What does it mean to kill an option? What does it mean to keep an option alive?

3. The basic American option pricing model presented in Chapter 9, section 9.4, could be called the intrinsic value (lower) bound model or it could be called the delayed exercise premium (DEP) model. The DEP could be written as DEP_t or as $DEP_{[t,T]}$, to indicate that it changes over time and represents the present value, at each time t, of being able to delay exercise until sometime after t, including at time T.

a. Does the DEP model apply to American puts and American calls?
b. Does the DEP model apply to European options?
c. When $DEP_t>0$, what does the DEP model say that you should do?
d. When $DEP_t=0$, what does the DEP model say that you should do?

4. Here is another model that decomposes American option prices. It says that an American option's premium is the sum of its corresponding European option value plus a premium.

a. Using the exercise premium terminology, what would you call the value of a European call option?
b. We need some terminology for that *extra* part of an American option's premium that does not correspond to the European feature. What should it be called, using the exercise premium terminology once again?

5. a. Show, using the model in exercise 4. that any lower bound for the value of a European option is also a lower bound for the value of an American option.

b. Does it follow that a lower bound for the value of a European option is always a *better* bound than the intrinsic value bound? Assume no dividends on the underlier.
c. Give an example of b. illustrating a better lower bound. Assume no dividends on the underlier.

6. First review Tables 11.5 and 11.6.

   a. What do these two tables do in terms of replication?
   b. Now refer to Table 11.9 for the no-dividend case. Fill in 3. under fully replicating portfolio.
   c. Now, generalize Table 11.9 to the proportional dividend case. Start by getting the two correct states of the world in this scenario. Then make the necessary changes to the target payoff of the European call option. Finally, make the necessary changes to the replicating portfolio.

7. *'One of the nice things about generalized forward contracts is that they allow you to control the leverage in your position.'* Explain the statement.

   a. Start by examining the leverage in an ordinary forward contract. Refer to Chapter 3 as needed.
   b. Next, consider the case $S_t - e^{-r\tau}F_{t,T} > 0$ and examine its degree of leverage relative to an ordinary forward contract in a.
   c. Finally, consider the case $S_t - e^{-r\tau}F_{t,T} < 0$ and examine its leverage relative to an ordinary forward contract in a.

8. *'Which comes first, the chicken or the egg?'*

   a. What does European Put-Call Parity say about the relationship between European options and (ordinary) forward contracts?
   b. When is the European call option premium equal to that of an otherwise identical European put option?
   c. When is the European call option premium greater than that of an otherwise identical European put option?
   d. When is the European call option premium less than that of an otherwise identical European put option?

412 OPTIONS

9. Explain what a European call option is in terms of forward contracts and European puts.

    a. Use European Put–Call Parity in order to make the connection.
    b. Is this essentially the same relationship we discussed in section 11.6.1? Why or why not?
    c. Explain what a European put option is in terms of forward contracts and European calls.
    d. Is this essentially the same relationship we discussed in section 11.6.2? Why or why not?

10. This problem addresses the first (easier) part of American put-call parity, no dividends, $C^A(S_t,\tau,E)-P^A(S_t,\tau,E)\leq S_t-e^{-r\tau}E$.

    a. In order for any inequality to make sense, the things in it have to exist. Refer to Figure 11.1. In what region do all of the quantities in the above inequality exist?
    b. Therefore the correct statement of the inequality is $C^A(S_t,\tau,E)-P^A(S_t,\tau,E)\leq S_t-e^{-r\tau}E$ for all S_t in the _____ _____ . Is this the same statement as $C^A(S_t,\tau,E)-P^A(S_t,\tau,E)\leq S_t-e^{-r\tau}E$ for all S_t?
    c. If the underlier pays no dividends over the life of the option, what can we say about $C^A(S_t,\tau,E)$? How does the inequality simplify?
    d. Write $P^A(S_t,\tau,E)$ in terms of the corresponding European put option and the early exercise premium, and substitute into the inequality. Also substitute the correct option representation for $S_t-e^{-r\tau}E$.
    e. What remains to be proven? Is it true?
    f. How does the value of the generalized, early exercisable, forward contract whose current cost is represented by $C^A(S_t,\tau,E)-P^A(S_t,\tau,E)$ differ from that of an ordinary deferred generalized forward contract, whose current cost is represented by $S_t-e^{-r\tau}E$?
    g. What does the quantity in f. represent in terms of the value of rights?

RATIONAL OPTION PRICING **413**

■ SELECTED CONCEPT CHECK SOLUTIONS

Concept Check 2

Because its payoffs dominate the zero–payoff strategy.

Concept Check 3

a. Since with a positive interest rate and a positive time to expiration $PV(E)<E$, it follows that $-PV(E)>-E$. Therefore $S_t-PV(E)>S_t-E$. It also follows that $MAX[0, S_t-PV(E)]>MAX[0, S_t-E]$.

b. At maturity $\tau=0$, $PV(E)=E$, so the two bounds are equal.

Concept Check 4

a. This is because $PV(E)<E$ so we are subtracting S_t from a smaller number, which will produce a higher number.

b. At maturity $\tau=0$, $PV(E)=E$, so the two bounds are equal.

Concept Check 6

a. The answer is to go long the stock. Simply purchase it.

b. Since $-PV(E)$ is a negative number (if $E>0$), we must have done something to cut our current costs. That is, to generate an inflow. Borrowing does this. So the strategy is to borrow the $PV(E)$.

c. Since $P^E(S_t,\tau,E)\geq0$ we must have done something to create an outflow. Buying a put for its market premium will do just that. So the underlying strategy is to buy an American put option.

Concept Check 7

a. The risk of the short stock position is that the stock may rise in price and you will have to cover the short sale at a much higher price than the price at which you short sold the stock.

b. Since we lend $PV(E)$ at time T, we will have $\$E$ in a savings account. If the stock price rises to no more than $\$E$, we can use these funds to repurchase the stock and cover the short sale. Therefore, the lending position in $PV(E)$ *partially* covers the risk of the stock rising, up to $\$E$ per share.

c. That part of the rise in the stock price, if it indeed rises above E, is not covered by the lending position in $PV(E)$.

d. The long European call option is an insurance policy for the short stock position. If the stock price rises above E to $S_T > E$, all you have to do is exercise the call and purchase the stock for $\$E$ per share. Then you would use these stocks to cover the short sale.

The floor on the long European put position in Figure 11.3 comes about because of this exercise strategy. You use the positive cash flow of $S_T - E$ to cover your loss of $E - S_T$ on the short sale.

CHAPTER 12

OPTION TRADING STRATEGIES, PART 2

12.1	Generating Synthetic Option Strategies from European Put-Call Parity	416
12.2	The Covered Call Hedging Strategy	419
	12.2.1 Three Types Of Covered Call Writes	420
	12.2.2 Economic Interpretation of the Covered Call Strategy	426
12.3	The Protective Put Hedging Strategy	427
	12.3.1 Puts as Insurance	427
	12.3.2 Economic Interpretation of the Protective Put Strategy	429

There are at least two ways to think about option trading strategies more advanced than the eight basic ones presented in Chapter 10. One way requires mathematical genius in order to figure out, both as to where they come from and how they operate in practice. The other way is to *systematically* generate them, for example, from rational option pricing restrictions of the type discussed in Chapter 11. Since I believe that much of derivatives analysis is *not* rocket science and partial differential equations, we will take the latter approach.

Which strategies will be appropriate for specific investors depends on their risk, expected-return preferences and price expectations.

We discussed the eight basic naked strategies in Chapter 10 and European Put-Call Parity in Chapter 11. In this chapter, we put these components together and interpret the eight basic strategies in terms of their *synthetic* equivalents. Then we generate and interpret the classical hedging strategies—covered call writes and protective puts.

416 **OPTIONS**

12.1 GENERATING SYNTHETIC OPTION STRATEGIES FROM EUROPEAN PUT-CALL PARITY

We will start with ROP as a method for generating new option strategies. Specifically, remember that European Put-Call Parity says that,

$$C^E(S_t,\tau,E)=(S_t-e^{-r\tau}E)+P^E(S_t,\tau,E) \qquad \textbf{(European Put-Call Parity)}$$

By re-arranging (European Put-Call Parity, No Divs) we generate eight different *synthetic* strategies, each of which is equivalent to its respective natural strategy.

The *natural strategy* is to take an outright position, such as long a traded call option.

The corresponding *synthetic strategy* is the replicating portfolio that replicates the natural position.

European Put-Call Parity says that the replicating portfolio for the natural long call position is long the stock, borrow $PV(E)$, and long an otherwise identical European put option. One reads this off from $C^E(S_t,\tau,E)=(S_t-e^{-r\tau}E)+P^E(S_t,\tau,E)$, by backing out the strategies that give rise to each of the costs on the right-hand side of this equation, as discussed in Chapter 11, section 11.5.3.

We will abbreviate $C^E(S_t,\tau,E)$ to C^E and $P^E(S_t,\tau,E)$ to P^E. Also, we will write $PV(E)$ for $e^{-r\tau}E$. There are two easy steps followed to generate Table 12.1.

Step 1

Re-arrange European Put-Call Parity to get the cost of the *natural* strategy (also called the natural, actual, or non-synthetic) in the first column and the costs of the synthetic strategy in the second column.

Step 2

Work backwards from the costs of the synthetic strategy in the second column to the strategies required to generate those costs as discussed in Chapter 11, section 11.5.3. Note that this is a very mechanical but useful technique.

To illustrate these two steps, we will go through Step 1 and Step 2 for actual strategy 5, which is long the stock. It is interesting that the underlying itself, which is not a derivative security, can be synthesized from derivative securities and lending. (Actually the synthesis is from a generalized forward contract, with its leverage neutralized.)

OPTION TRADING STRATEGIES, PART 2 · 417

TABLE 12.1 The Eight Synthetic Equivalents to the Eight Basic Strategies

Natural (Actual) Strategy Cost	Synthetic Strategy and its Cost
1. LONG CALL C^E	Long Stock, Borrow $PV(E)$, Long Put $S_t - PV(E) + P^E$
2. SHORT CALL $-C^E$	Short Stock, Lend $PV(E)$, Short Put $-S_t + PV(E) - P^E$
3. LONG PUT P^E	Long Call, Short Stock, Lend $PV(E)$ $C^E - S_t + PV(E)$
4. SHORT PUT $-P^E$	Short Call, Long Stock, Borrow $PV(E)$ $-C^E + S_t - PV(E)$
5. LONG STOCK S_t	Long Call, Lend $PV(E)$, Short Put $C^E + PV(E) - P^E$
6. SHORT STOCK $-S_t$	Short Call, Borrow $PV(E)$, Long Put $-C^E - PV(E) + P^E$
7. BORROWING $-PV(E)$	Long Call, Short Stock, Short Put $C^E - S_t - P^E$
8. LENDING $+PV(E)$	Short Call, Long Stock, Long Put $-C^E + S_t + P^E$

Recall that a positive cost is an outflow, while a negative cost is a benefit (inflow); for example, shorting a financial instrument to generate benefits or borrowing. That is the convention we are making here.

Step 1

Re-arrange European P-C Parity to obtain the stock price S_t on the left-hand side of the equation. Then $C^E + PV(E) - P^E$ will be on the right-hand side.

Step 2

Note that $+S_t$ represents the cost of purchasing one unit of the stock. Hence the strategy that corresponds to $+S_t$ is just going long the stock. Now look at each term in $C^E + PV(E) - P^E$ and interpret each by backing out the strategies that generated them as respective costs.

a. C^E is the cost of purchasing the call option. Therefore, the strategy that generates C^E is just longing the call.
b. $+PV(E)$ is the cost of lending (that is, investing) $PV(E)$. Hence the strategy is just lending (investing) $PV(E)$.

418 OPTIONS

c. $-P^E$ is the cost of shorting the put option. Shorting because it is a negative cost.

The conclusion is that the natural strategy of going long the stock is *economically equivalent* to its synthetic equivalent, which is to long a call with exercise price E, lend the PV of the option's exercise price, and short an otherwise identical put option. Note that the stock price doesn't depend on E. So neither does the synthetic strategy; any E will do.

■ CONCEPT CHECK 1

a. Draw the profit diagram for the long call position. Where does it intersect the $S_T=0$ axis?
b. On the same graph, draw the profit diagram for lending $PV(E)$.
c. On the same graph, draw the profit diagram for shorting the put option. Where does it intersect the $S_T=0$ axis?
d. Add up the $S_T=0$ intercepts from a., b., and c. Use European P-C Parity to verify that it adds up to the correct quantity.
e. Add up the profit diagrams from a., b., and c. Convince yourself that it looks like the profit diagram from a long stock position.

From Table 12.1, we see our eight basic natural strategies in the first column. In the second column, we see the *synthetic equivalent* of each of the eight basic strategies. So, in addition to the eight basic natural strategies, we now have eight equivalent synthetic strategies.

Further, the synthetic strategies are (economically) equivalent to their corresponding natural strategies. Therefore, except for transactions costs, they should have the same prices. Otherwise, there would be arbitrage opportunities.

If there are transactions costs, then there *could* be infinitely more synthetic strategies that would not be arbitrage strategies *if* their execution prices differ by *more* than the transactions costs of executing the arbs, depending on by how much they differ. If the difference between the cost of executing the synthetic strategies and the cost of executing the natural strategies is *less* than the transaction costs involved, then these could be arbitrage strategies.

In total, there are 16 no-arbitrage strategies described in Table 12.1, and a host of other potential arbitrage strategies.

12.2 THE COVERED CALL HEDGING STRATEGY

We can also use European P-C Parity to generate some not-so-basic hedging strategies as indicated in Table 12.2. These are classic basic hedging strategies using plain vanilla European puts and calls. Two new strategies are introduced in this chapter. Strategy 9 is called the *covered call* strategy and strategy 10 is called the *protective put* strategy. Both are option hedging strategies, allowing an investor with a spot position in some underlying to protect that position against adverse price movements.

Note that, as usual, whether a price movement is adverse depends on whether you are short or long. Long positions are the ones most often discussed, but short positions are equally important. We will discuss the covered call strategy in this section, 12.2, and the protective put strategy in section 12.3.

TABLE 12.2 Covered Calls and Protective Put Strategies

Natural (Actual) Strategy Cost	Synthetic Strategy Cost
9. LONG STOCK, SHORT CALL $S_t - C^E$	Short Put, Lend $PV(E)$ $-P^E + PV(E)$
10. LONG STOCK, LONG PUT $S_t + P^E$	Long Call, Lend $PV(E)$ $C^E + PV(E)$

Here is a common financial scenario. You own 1000 shares of Bank of America (BAC) stock. You are worried about downward movements over the next 3 months in BAC as a result of regulation, competition, or general market movements. Your horizon of worry is the holding period of 3 months.

Your objective is to protect your position over the next 3 months. There are alternative ways to hedge your position. One is to note that you shouldn't be holding any stock as an isolated investment. Rather, individual stocks should be held in portfolios. This has the positive effect of diversifying away some of the avoidable risk of individual stocks.

However, we also know from portfolio analysis that there are limits to diversification. You can't diversify away the *non-diversifiable (market)* risks of your portfolio.

We also know that the *maximum* effect of diversification occurs when we add perfectly *negatively* correlated assets to our portfolio. So, the alternative ways to hedge your position are:

420 **OPTIONS**

1. *(Naive) Diversification*: add securities to form a portfolio with BAC. This gets you the diversification effect.
2. *Synthetically create negative correlation*: find another type of security that is highly positively correlated with BAC stock and short it!

Under 2., candidate hedging vehicles include standard plain vanilla call options on BAC. There are many choices, varying by maturity and exercise price. One could also use forward contracts, or liquid futures contracts on BAC to hedge. Futures contracts on individual stocks are now traded on onechicago. com, as noted earlier in Chapter 2. Here we will focus on highly liquid call options as hedging vehicles.

Since call options are typically highly correlated with their underlying stock, a viable hedging strategy to protect 1000 long shares of BAC would be to short (sell) 10 call options on BAC. The resulting strategy is called the *covered call* strategy.

It consists of multiple positions; long the underlying shares, and short an equivalent number of call options. Several questions have to be addressed in executing covered call strategies and these include:

1. Option *Expiration* dates. Which call option series? This choice is related to your time horizon for the hedge.
2. Which particular call option, by *exercise price*? This addresses the moneyness factor through the choice of exercise price.

12.2.1 Three Types of Covered Call Writes

There are three types of covered call writes based upon the moneyness of the options employed.

a. *In-the-Money* covered call. These are defined by the requirement that the call option being used as the hedging vehicle is currently in-the-money. That is, $S_t > E$ where S_t is the current stock price and E is the exercise price.
b. *At-the-Money* covered call. In this case, $S_t = E$ currently (at time t).
c. *Out-of-the Money* covered call. In this case, $S_t < E$ currently (at time t).

OPTION TRADING STRATEGIES, PART 2 421

Examples of Covered Call Writes

We will now give an example that illustrates how the moneyness of a covered call strategy affects its payoffs. XYZ stock has a current price per share of $45. Two 3-month ($\tau=.25$) covered call writes are being considered:

1. An In-the-Money covered-call write, $E_1=\$40<\$45=S_t$ and $\tau=.25$,
2. An Out-of-the-Money covered-call write, $E_2=\$50>\$45=S_t$ and $\tau=.25$.

The corresponding call prices are $C_{t,1}=\$8$ and $C_{t,2}=\$1$, where we have just taken more or less arbitrary values for $C_{t,1}$ and $C_{t,2}$, based upon the normal ROP result that the In-the-Money call with the same maturity will be worth more than the Out-of-the-Money call (call prices decrease with the exercise price).

Our first objective is to map out the profits of these two covered call writes as a function of the ultimate stock price at expiration, S_T.

1. *The In-the-Money Covered Call Write*

TABLE 12.3 **Profits for the In-the-Money Covered Call Write, $E_1=\$40$, $S_t=\$45$ and $C_{t,1}=\$8$**

S_T	Profits for the In-the-Money Covered Call Write ($E_1=\$40$, $C_{t,1}=\$8$)
35	100*(35–45)+100*8=–200
37	100*(37–45)+100*8=0
$E_1=40$	100*(40–45)+100*8=300
$S_T=45$	100*(40–45)+100*8=300
50	100*(40–45)+100*8=300
60	100*(40–45)+100*8=300

■ CONCEPT CHECK 2

a. With reference to Table 12.3, explain what happens once the underlying stock price, S_T, reaches $E_1=40$ and above.

422 **OPTIONS**

Figure 12.1 illustrates the profit diagram for this In-the-Money covered call strategy. It has two characteristics. First, it provides $800 worth of *downside protection* on the long stock position, because a call option with market premium has been sold for $8 per share. For a standard call option with 100 underlying shares, that sale generates $8*100=$800 dollars.

In practice this means that the stock price could drop by $8 and the investor in the covered call would still break even. Such is the price protection offered by selling calls. The sale of the call option releases funds that act as a cushion against potential price declines.

■ CONCEPT CHECK 3

You are jumping out of an airplane with a parachute. The parachute may or may not work. However, you sold call options, to act as a cushion on the ground to hedge against parachute failure.

a.   *Which calls, In-the-Money or Out-of-the-Money provide more cushioning?*

The price protection obtained by selling call options comes at a cost. The investor has to give up the unlimited upside that he would have had on a naked long stock position. The reason for this is that, as long as $S_T>E_1$, the underlying stock would be '*called away*' by the buyer of the call.

By selling the call, the investor in the covered call write has given away the right to the call buyer to buy the stock for E_1 in the event that $S_T>E_1$. But this is precisely what the long the call would do when $S_T>E_1$.

In our Table 12.3 we see this, because when $S_T>E_1$ the covered call writer can no longer obtain the normal profit figure that he would have obtained from a naked stock position, which is $100*(S_T-S_t)$. Rather, he obtains only $100*(E_1-S_t)$ as indicated in Table 12.3, and in Figure 12.1.

Thus the covered call write has a limited upside equal to $100*(E_1-S_t)+100*C_{t,1}$ in general.

This is equal to $100*(\$40-\$45)+100*\$8=\$300$ in our case.

■ CONCEPT CHECK 4

a.   Show that the maximum upside potential per share on a covered call write is equal to $100*(E-S_t)+100*C_t$ where C_t is the market premium of the written call and the other notation is self-explanatory.

FIGURE 12.1 An In-the-Money Covered Call Write

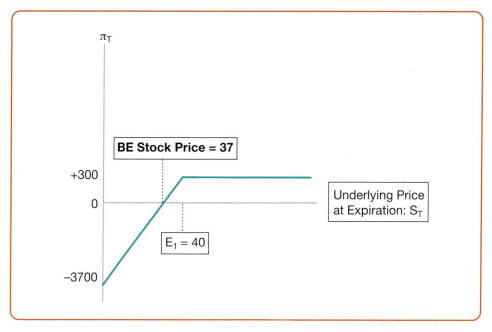

Figure 12.1 illustrates the maximum potential *loss* outcome of the covered call write. If the stock completely tanks one would *normally* lose,

$$100*S_t = 100*\$45$$
$$= \$4500.$$

However, in the case of the covered call write, one has,

$$100*C_{t,1} = 100*\$8$$
$$= \$800$$

in sold call option premium to partially offset the complete loss on the long stock position.

Therefore, the net, or overall loss on the hedge is only $\$4500-\$800=\$3700$. The *maximum upside potential* of $100*(E_1-S_t)+100*C_{t,1}=\$300$ for our case is also illustrated.

424 **OPTIONS**

The *break-even* (BE) stock price is also apparent, $S_T=\$37$. At this stock price, one loses,

$$100*(\$45-\$37)=100*\$8$$
$$=\$800$$

on the declined stock price, but one gains $800 in sold call option premium. The two offset each other resulting in the break-even scenario.

2. The Out-of-the-Money Covered Call Write

We now illustrate the Out-of-the-Money covered write. Here, the writer generates only $100*C_{t,2}=100*\$1$ in call premium income, which is a lot less than from the sale of an In-the-Money call. But the upside is also much higher,

$$100*(E_2-S_t)+100*C_{t,2}=100*(50-45)+100*\$1$$
$$=\$600.$$

In this case, the call option will not be exercised by the long call holder until $S_T>E_2=\$50$.

TABLE 12.4 **Profits for the Out-of-the-Money Covered Call Write ($E_2=\$50$, $S_t=\$45$, and $C_{t,2}=\$1$)**

S_T	Profits for the Covered Call Write ($E_2=\$50$, $C_{t,2}=\$1$)
35	100*(35–45)+100*$1=–$900
37	100*(37–45)+100*$1=–$700
40	100*(40–45)+100*$1=–$400
$S_t=45$	100*(45–45)+100*$1=$100
$E_2=50$	100*(50–45)+100*$1=$600
60	100*(50–45)+100*$1=$600
65	100*(50–45)+100*$1=$600

Figure 12.2 (not to scale) illustrates the maximum potential loss outcome of the covered call write. If the stock completely tanks, the strategist who is simply naked long the stock, would normally lose,

$$100*S_t=100*\$45$$
$$=\$4500.$$

OPTION TRADING STRATEGIES, PART 2

FIGURE 12.2 An Out-of-the-Money Covered Call Write

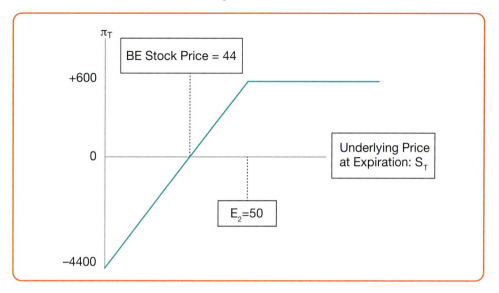

However, the covered call strategist has,

$$100*C_{t,2} = 100*\$1$$
$$= \$100$$

in sold call option premium to partially offset the complete loss on the long stock position. Therefore the net, or overall loss on the hedge is only $4500-$100=$4400.

The maximum upside potential of $100*(E_2-S_t)+100*C_{t,2}=\$600$ for our case is also illustrated. The break-even stock price is also apparent, $S_T=\$44$. At this stock price, one loses,

$$100*(\$45-\$44) = 100*\$1$$
$$= \$100.$$

on the declined stock price, but one gains $100 in sold call option premium. The two offset each other resulting in the break-even scenario.

Therefore, the difference between an In-the-Money covered write and an Out-of-the-Money covered write is that the In-the-Money covered write affords more downside protection in return for giving up a greater amount of upside potential than an Out-of-the-Money covered write.

■ CONCEPT CHECK 5

a. Is there a speculative component to the choice of which type of covered call strategy to employ?

b. If yes to a., then one learns that hedging can have a speculative component. Explain.

12.2.2 Economic Interpretation of the Covered Call Strategy

Looking at the profit diagrams for the covered call writes, we see that they look remarkably like the profit diagram for a short put illustrated in Figure 10.7 in Chapter 10, section 10.2.6.

Are they in fact economically equivalent? Namely, is the synthetic equivalent of the covered call strategy simply a short put?

In order to answer this question, note that this is precisely where having an analytic result, like (European Put-Call Parity, No Divs), comes in very handy. By re-arranging it to get the costs of the covered call write on the left-hand side, we can read off the equivalent synthetic strategy, the costs of which will be on the right-hand side.

We want to re-arrange European Put-Call Parity so that $S_t - C^E(S_t, \tau, E)$, the total cost of the covered-call write, is on the left-hand side. This produces the re-arranged Put-Call Parity equation, $S_t - C^E(S_t, \tau, E) = e^{-r\tau}E - P^E(S_t, \tau, E)$.

From this, we conclude that the actual covered write is economically equivalent to a short put *and* a long (lending) position in a zero coupon bond, with face value equal to the exercise price of the call option written in the covered-call strategy.

TABLE 12.5 Current Costs of the Natural Covered Call Write and of the Synthetic Covered Call Write

Current Costs	Underlying Strategy
S_t	Long Stock
$-C^E(S_t, \tau, E)$	Short Call
$S_t - C^E(S_t, \tau, E)$	*Natural Covered Call Write*
$PV(E)$	Lend $PV(E)$
$-P^E(S_t, \tau, E)$	Short Put
$PV(E) - P^E(S_t, \tau, E)$	*Synthetic Covered Call Write*

Note that the synthetic covered-write has no position in the underlying stock! Yet it is economically equivalent to one that *does* have a stock position.

A covered-write is like being short a put, but not naked short. The long put position holder has the right to sell the underlying stock to the short put position in exchange for E. If one were naked short, then one might find oneself in the scenario of having to come up with E per share to pay for the stock underlying the put being exercised against you.

To hedge against this potential possibility, the short put position puts $PV(E)$ in the bank today. At time T, this will grow to E and the short put has the funds necessary to deal with the exercised put. Note that, not only can we correctly interpret the covered-call strategy, but we can also look at its relative risk characteristics.

■ CONCEPT CHECK 6

a. Define the type of risk described in the paragraph immediately above.
b. Which is riskier? A naked short put position or a short put position combined with lending $PV(E)$?
c. Using synthetic equivalence, which is riskier? The covered call position or a naked short put position? Explain your reasoning.

12.3 THE PROTECTIVE PUT HEDGING STRATEGY

Once again, the scenario is that one has a long position in some underlying inventory to protect against declining prices. For example, a mutual fund manager constantly worries about the impact of *market (non-diversifiable)* risk on his position. Being full diversified only protects one from *diversifiable* risk.

12.3.1 Puts as Insurance

Instead of *selling* call options, an alternative is to *buy* insurance in the form of put options. If the underlying stock price or index price falls below the exercise price of the put option, one could sell the stock or the index for the exercise price.

A classic example is purchasing insurance in the form of index puts to protect stock portfolios against potential market declines. Index puts can prove to be very valuable when stock markets decline. Of course, one has to pay for the puts, just as one pays insurance premiums, in order to obtain insurance.

OPTIONS

Here is an example, which has the same exercise price as the first covered call write we considered. $S_t=\$45$ and $E_1=\$40$, so a put with exercise price E_1 would currently be *out-of-the-money*. Suppose that the put sells for $P_{t,1}=\$1$.

TABLE 12.6 Profits for the Out-of-the-Money Protective Put with $E_1=\$40$, $S_t=\$45$, and $P_{t,1}=\$1$

S_T	Profits for the Protective Put
35	100*(40–45)–100*$1=–$600
37	100*(40–45)–100*$1=–$600
$E_1=40$	100*(40–45)–100*$1=–$600
$S_t=45$	100*(45–45)–100*$1=–$100
50	100*(50–45)–100*$1=$400
55	100*(55–45)–100*$1=$900
60	100*(60–45)–100*$1=$1400

FIGURE 12.3 Out-of-the-Money Protective Put Profits ($E_1=\$40$, $P_{t,1}=\$1$, $S_t=\$45$)

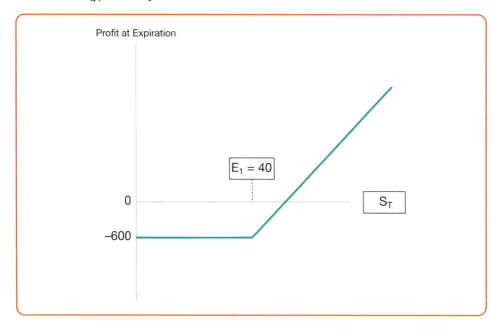

Profits (at time T) for the protective put strategy are,

$$\Pi_T = 100*(E_1-S_t)-100*P_{t,1} \quad \text{if } S_T < E_1$$
$$ = 100*(S_T-S_t)-100*P_{t,1} \quad \text{if } S_T \geq E_1$$

because when the put is in-the-money at time T, it will be exercised and the underlying stock will be sold for E_1. This will always happen when $S_T < E_1$ because, in this case, it is more advantageous to sell the stock for E_1 than for S_T.

When the put is out-of-the-money it would be more advantageous to sell it for S_T than for E_1 because $S_T \geq E_1$. Of course, one has to always pay for the put at time t, hence the subtraction of $100*P_{t,1}$.

The two characteristics of the protective put strategy are downside protection and unlimited upside potential. Thus the protective put does not sacrifice upside potential like the covered-call write. The sacrifice here for downside protection is that you have to pay the put premium, just as in any insurance policy.

12.3.2 Economic Interpretation of the Protective Put Strategy

Figure 12.3 looks very much like a naked long call option profit diagram with $E_1 = 40$. It is not quite that.

Again, (European Put-Call Parity, No Divs) will clarify the situation. We want the current costs associated with the protective put strategy on one side of the re-arranged P-C parity equation and whatever remains on the other side. This is no problem,

$$S_t + P^E(S_t, \tau, E) = C^E(S_t, \tau, E) + e^{-r\tau}E.$$

Now we can back out the synthetic equivalent of the protective put in Table 12.7, just as we did for the covered-call write.

From Table 12.7, we learn that the synthetic equivalent of the natural protective put is a long call position combined with a *lending* position in the amount $PV(E)$.

The economic rationale for the lending position in the synthetic position is to allow the long call position to cover the cash flow required to exercise the call option. In the event of exercise, the long call holder will need $\$E$ per share to purchase the underlying stock. Investing in $PV(E)$ at the current time t will pay off with the *exact* correct amount needed to cover the call exercise.

430 OPTIONS

TABLE 12.7 **Current Costs of the Natural Protective Put and of the Synthetic Protective Put**

Current Costs	Underlying Strategy
S_t	Long Stock
$P^E(S_t, \tau, E)$	Long Put
$S_t + P^E(S_t, \tau, E)$	*Natural Protective Put*
$PV(E)$	Lend $PV(E)$
$C^E(S_t, \tau, E)$	Long CALL
$PV(E) + C^E(S_t, \tau, E)$	*Synthetic Protective Put*

One concludes that, in this sense, the protective put strategy is similar to a long call position, but also has coverage in the form of the lending position.

The moneyness of the put determines the degree of downside protection with an in-the-money put offering more protection, and costing more than an out of-the-money put. An in-the-money protective put is discussed in the End of Chapter Exercise 4.

OPTION TRADING STRATEGIES, PART 2 — 431

■ KEY CONCEPTS

1. Generating Synthetic Option Strategies from European Put–Call Parity.
2. The Covered Call Hedging Strategy.
3. Three Types Of Covered Call Writes.
4. Economic Interpretation of the Covered Call Strategy.
5. The Protective Put Hedging Strategy.
6. Puts as Insurance.
7. Economic Interpretation of the Protective Put Strategy.

■ END OF CHAPTER EXERCISES FOR CHAPTER 12

1. XYZ stock is currently trading at $48 per share. The XYZ 3-month European call, with exercise price of $45, is selling at $4.

   a. Compute the *maximum profit* potential on a covered call write using the stock and the option.
   b. Compute the *break-even* stock price level for the covered call write.
   c. Compute the *maximum loss* potential on the covered call write.
   d. Draw a labeled graph illustrating your answers above.

2. You have just purchased 100 shares of an indexed stock fund, currently selling at $400 per share. To protect yourself against potential losses, you have also purchased an at-the-money European index put option for $20 per share (100 shares) with three months to expiration.

   a. What is the name of this strategy? _____
   b. What are the two relevant 'states of the world' at expiration?

      State of the World 1 at expiration _____
      State of the World 2 at expiration _____

      Why are these the only relevant 'states of the world' at expiration?

   c. Present the *profit table* for this investment strategy that describes the profits at expiration for each relevant state of the world. Clearly indicate what all the numbers and/or symbols represent.
   d. Present the profit diagram (*i.e.* graph) that describes this investment strategy. Label the axes.

432 OPTIONS

3. *(Replicating a long put position)*
   a. Draw the profit diagram for the long call position. Where does it intersect the $S_T=0$ axis?
   b. On the same graph, draw the profit diagram for lending $PV(E)$. Where does it intersect the $S_T=0$ axis?
   c. On the same graph, draw the profit diagram for shorting the stock. Where does it intersect the $S_T=0$ axis?
   d. Add up the $S_T=0$ intercepts from a., b., and c. Use European Put-Call Parity to verify that it adds up to the correct quantity.
   e. Add up the profit diagrams from a., b., and c. Convince yourself that it looks like the profit diagram from a long put position.

4. The following chart is an Microsoft Excel version of Figure 12.3 in the text, produced from the data in Table 12.6.

FIGURE 12.3 (PP-Out) Excel Chart for the Out-of-the-Money Protective Put Profits (E_1=\$40, $P_{t,1}$=\$1, S_t=\$45)

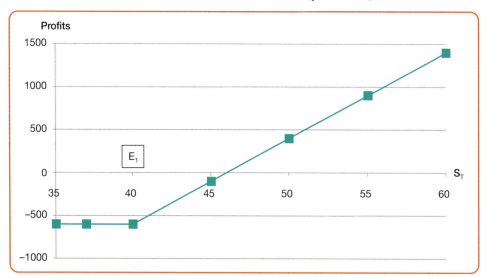

   a. See if you can reproduce it.
   b. We didn't do an example of an In-the-Money protective put in the chapter. We will do it here. Take E_2=\$50, S_t=\$45, and $P_{t,2}$=\$6. These parameters are analogous to the parameters for the covered call write in Table 12.4.

Now, take Table 12.8 and fill it in for this In-the-Money protective put. To get you started the empty table is appended.

OPTION TRADING STRATEGIES, PART 2   433

TABLE 12.8 **Profits for the In-the-Money Protective Put with E_2=\$50, S_t=45 and $P_{t,2}$=\$6**

S_T	Profits for the Protective Put
35	100*(?)–100*\$?=\$?
37	100*(?)–100*\$?=\$?
40	100*(?)–100*\$?=\$?
S_t=45	100*(?)–100*\$?=\$?
E_2=50	100*(?)–100*\$?=\$?
55	100*(?)–100*\$?=\$?
60	100*(?)–100*\$?=\$?

c. Draw an Excel chart for the data in b. Table 12.8. Call the resulting Excel chart Figure 12.3 (PP-in).

d. Now put both Excel charts on the same chart, and compare the profit profile for the In-the-Money protective put, Figure 12.3 (PP-in), to the profit profile for the Out-of-the-Money protective put in Figure 12.3 (PP-out).

What do you conclude about the differences between an Out-of-the-Money protective put and an In-the-Money protective put, based on this example?

■ SELECTED CONCEPT CHECK SOLUTIONS

Concept Check 2

a. Referring to Table 12.3, when the stock price reaches \$40, the long the call will exercise it. This means that he will buy it for the exercise price E_1=\$40.

Concept Check 4

a. The maximum profit potential on a covered call write occurs at the exercise price and remains there (see Figure 12.1). The profit consists of profits from the exercise call, $100*(E_1-S_t)$, plus premium income from the sale of the calls, $+100*C_{t,1}$.

434 OPTIONS

Concept Check 5

a. The speculative element in covered call writing is reflected in the choice of the moneyness of the option. It is a trade-off between protection on the downside and profits on the upside. This is speculative because of the uncertainty as to which way the stock price will actually go.

b. Covered call writing shows that hedging can have a speculative component. That is, the covered call writer is neither a 100% hedger nor a 100% speculator. He has combined position that represents *both* hedging and speculating.

CHAPTER 13

MODEL-BASED OPTION PRICING IN DISCRETE TIME, PART 1: THE BINOMIAL OPTION PRICING MODEL (BOPM, $N=1$)

13.1	The Objective of Model-Based Option Pricing (MBOP)	437
13.2	The Binomial Option Pricing Model, Basics	437
	13.2.1 Modeling Time in a Discrete Time Framework	437
	13.2.2 Modeling the Underlying Stock Price Uncertainty	438
13.3	The Binomial Option Pricing Model, Advanced	440
	13.3.1 Path Structure of the Binomial Process, Total Number of Price Paths	440
	13.3.2 Path Structure of the Binomial Process, Total Number of Price Paths Ending at a Specific Terminal Price	442
	13.3.3 Summary of Stock Price Evolution for the N-Period Binomial Process	444
13.4	Option Valuation for the BOPM ($N=1$)	445
	13.4.1 Step 1, Pricing the Option at Expiration	445
	13.4.2 Step 2, Pricing the Option Currently (time $t=0$)	446
13.5	Modern Tools for Pricing Options	448
	13.5.1 Tool 1, The Principle of No-Arbitrage	448
	13.5.2 Tool 2, Complete Markets or Replicability and a Rule of Thumb	449
	13.5.3 Tool 3, Dynamic and Static Replication	450
	13.5.4 Relationships between the Three Tools	450
13.6	Synthesizing a European Call Option	453

13.6.1	Step 1, Parameterization	454
13.6.2	Step 2, Defining the Hedge Ratio and the Dollar Bond Position	455
13.6.3	Step 3, Constructing the Replicating Portfolio	456
13.6.4	Step 4, Implications of Replication	462
13.7	Alternative Option Pricing Techniques	464
13.8	Appendix: Derivation of the BOPM ($N=1$) as a Risk-Neutral Valuation Relationship	467

In this chapter we study the simplest model-based, yet still rational (arbitrage-free) option pricing model. This model is called the *Binomial Option Pricing Model* (BOPM) and it is a discrete time model. The Binomial option pricing model uses a decision tree framework but goes beyond it. In fact, the Binomial option pricing model shows how to correctly discount option payoffs in a discrete, decision tree context.

Most of the central option valuation concepts, including discounting option payoffs, can be understood in the context of the Binomial option pricing model. One of the main ideas that comes out of this model is the notion of static vs. dynamic hedging. This is a rarely stressed feature of the BOPM but if one wants, as we do, to understand continuous-time option pricing models like Black–Scholes, then it is crucial that we appreciate the importance of dynamic hedging.

The lesson we learned from Chapter 11 on Rational Option Pricing is that, in order for any option pricing model to make economic sense, it should be arbitrage-free. That is the equilibrium concept. It provides a basis upon which to price, trade, and to use options.

Pricing options in a market that admits arbitrage opportunities is like standing on quicksand. Arbitrageurs will usually try to take advantage of arbitrage opportunities. As they do so, there will be buying and/or selling pressure that will change prices as they attempt to reach an equilibrium. In brief, there does not exist a consistent, linear, positive pricing mechanism in the presence of arbitrage opportunities.

To put the Binomial option pricing model in context, we recall the distinction between two kinds of models, ROP and MBOP.

1. *Rational option pricing* models make no restrictions on the process generating underlying spot prices, other than that they are arbitrage-free.

2. *Model-based option pricing* models place restrictions on the process generating underlying spot prices.

The thing to note here is that model-based option pricing models must also be arbitrage-free. Otherwise they make little economic sense. That was the challenge for 73 years from 1900–1973. It's relatively easy to come up with an option pricing model, by perhaps adding an additional parameter or two. It's much harder to come up with an arbitrage-free option pricing model. Apparently, the Black–Scholes option pricing model, to be discussed in Chapter 16, was the first such model.

In its wake, derivatives trading displayed explosive growth and has by now become a global phenomenon.

13.1 THE OBJECTIVE OF MODEL-BASED OPTION PRICING (MBOP)

The objective is to develop a 'rational' (arbitrage-free) valuation formula for a European call option on an underlying asset whose price follows a Binomial process with no dividends. We will discuss the Binomial process shortly.

Before proceeding, recall from Chapter 11 that rational option pricing (ROP) does not accomplish this objective. As discussed in Chapter 11, ROP usually looks for *relationships* between puts and calls, or for *bounds* on option prices. The net result of ROP is usually a *range* of option prices rather than specific option prices.

In model-based option pricing, we try to find actual values (specific and unique numbers) for option prices, not just bounds.

13.2 THE BINOMIAL OPTION PRICING MODEL, BASICS

13.2.1 Modeling Time in a Discrete Time Framework

The current date is time t and the option's expiration date is T, which is now called N because the BOPM is a discrete time model. For example, N could be the number of days to expiration. Time to expiration is $\tau = N - t$. We divide τ into N sub-intervals of length $\Delta t = \tau / N$, a day in our example.

FIGURE 13.1 Modeling Time in the Binomial Model

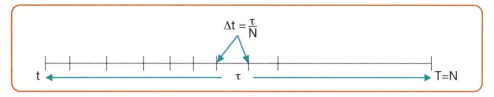

13.2.2 Modeling the Underlying Stock Price Uncertainty

Only the current stock price, S_0, is known today, which we will take to be $t=0$. Future stock prices $S_1, S_2, \ldots, S_N$ are *random* variables and are therefore unknown today. However, the possible values of the future stock prices are *not* completely unknown. Their randomness is generated by a Binomial process, which we will now describe for $N=1$, and for general $N>1$.

Given the current stock price, S_0, the stock price can *only* do one of two things over the next day. It can go up to $uS_0=(1+u')S_0$ with probability p, or it can go down to $dS_0=(1+d')S_0$ with probability $1-p$. Here, u' is the *percentage* return *if* the stock price goes *up* over the first period, and d' is the percentage return *if* the stock price goes *down* over the first period.

■ CONCEPT CHECK 1

An example illustrates the Binomial process. Suppose that the current stock price S_0 is $100, and the stock price can go up by 10% or it can go down by 5%. The probability of an up move is 0.75 and therefore the probability of a down move is 0.25.

a. What is u'?
b. What is d'?
c. What is u?
d. What is d?

Figure 13.2 illustrates modeling stock price uncertainty for any N, and Figure 13.3 illustrates the Binomial approach to modeling that uncertainty over one period, $N=1$. Note that in Figure 13.2 that it is the *percentage* (not the absolute) up and down moves that remain constant.

FIGURE 13.2 **Stock Price Uncertainty in the BOPM, any N**

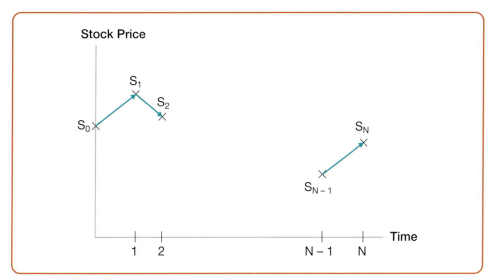

FIGURE 13.3 **The Binomial Process (N=1), Example (S_0=100, u'=.10, d'=–05, u=1.1, d=.95)**

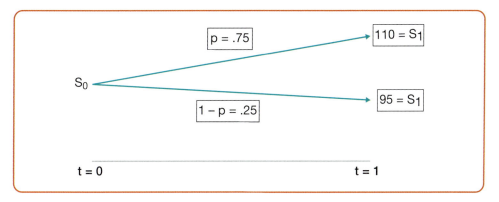

This is all there is to the one-period Binomial process. To extrapolate the process to more than one period, the Binomial process simply assumes that the future evolution of the (random) stock price follows the exact same process in terms of the parameters (u,d,p) as over the first period. That is, everything stays the same.

Figure 13.4 illustrates this for a Binomial process for N=2, for the same parameters that we have been using. In parentheses, we have indicated the appropriate up or down move with the associated probability, either p for an up move or $1-p$ for a down move.

FIGURE 13.4 Stock Price Evolution for the Binomial Process (N=2)

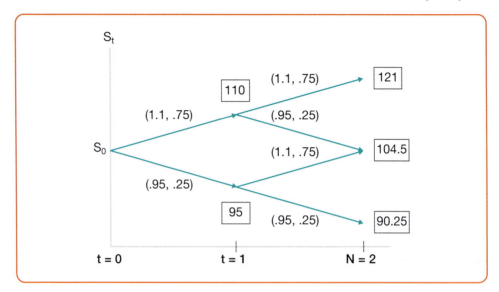

13.3 THE BINOMIAL OPTION PRICING MODEL, ADVANCED

13.3.1 Path Structure of the Binomial Process, Total Number of Price Paths

In order to understand how the Binomial option pricing model works, it is essential to study the path structure of the Binomial process. This is essentially a counting exercise. We want to count the number of paths (this section 13.3.1), and the number of paths ending at given possible terminal stock prices (section 13.3.2). For the example just given, we can make a table of all the paths generated by the Binomial process for $N=2$.

We can see in the above example that there is one stock price path ending at 121, there is one stock price path ending at 90.25, and there are two stock price paths ending at 104.5.

For the Binomial process for $N=2$, note that there are in total four paths but only three terminal stock prices at expiration. (This is because $udS_0=duS_0$, and therefore the two inner stock price paths terminate in the same terminal stock price.) Each path is described by whether the stock experiences an up move or down move that day. See Table 13.1.

Let's go one step further and look at the *total* number of stock price paths for $N=3$. For each day the stock price can either go up or down. This

OPTION PRICING IN DISCRETE TIME, PART 1   441

TABLE 13.1 Binomial Process (N=2), Price Paths Structure

Path Structure	Terminal Stock Price
a. uu (up, up)	$u^2 S_0$
b. ud (up, down)	$du S_0$
c. du (down, up)	$ud S_0$
d. dd (down, down)	$d^2 S_0$

corresponds to either a d or a u. There are therefore two ways to fill the box labeled Day 1 in Figure 13.5. Subsequently, there are two ways to fill the box labeled Day 2. On the third day there are, once again, two ways to fill the box labeled Day 3.

Therefore, the total number of ways of filling the three days with either u or d is $2*2*2=8$. Thus there are in total eight paths for the Binomial process for $N=3$. Figure 13.5 illustrates the process of creating paths by assigning either d or u to each day for $N=3$.

■ CONCEPT CHECK 2

a. Construct a table similar to Table 13.1 for a Binomial process for $N=3$, listing all the price paths. I suggest doing it systematically. Start with all the possible paths starting on day one with an up move. Then move on

FIGURE 13.5 Stock Price Evolution, Total Number of Price Paths, BOPM, $N=3$

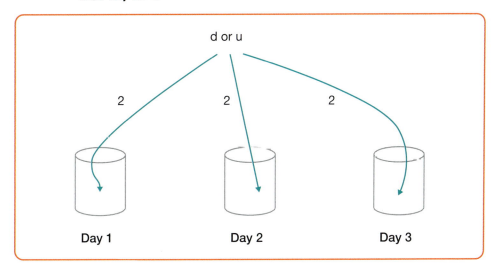

to all the possible paths starting on Day 2 with a down move. Make sure you get all the possible paths.

■ CONCEPT CHECK 3

a. For reference later, for an N-period Binomial model, what is the total number of price paths?
b. Explain your answer to a. in terms of the counting argument presented.
c. How many different terminal (at time N) stock prices are there?

13.3.2 Path Structure of the Binomial Process, Total Number of Price Paths Ending at a Specific Terminal Price

Each terminal stock price is determined by the number of ups and downs over the life of the option. Let us suppose that, over the life of the option, the stock price experiences j up moves and therefore $N-j$ down moves. Then the terminal stock price corresponding to j up moves and $N-j$ down moves is $S_N = u^j d^{N-j} S_0$.

For example, for $N=3$ assume that there are $j=2$ up moves over the 3-day life of the option. Then there can only be one down move. The situation is illustrated in Figure 13.6. *Any* two up days will lead to the *same* terminal stock price $S_3 = u^2 d^1 S_0$. Since there are $N=3$ days, two up moves can occur on any two of those three days: Day 1 and Day 2; Day 1 and Day 3; or Day 2 and Day 3.

This is illustrated by the colored lines in Figure 13.6. The figure also shows that the number of paths corresponding to two up moves and one down move is just the number of ways of putting two up symbols, u, into three boxes.

■ CONCEPT CHECK 4

a. Verify that there are three ways to put two d's into three boxes (days).
b. List the ways in a.

OPTION PRICING IN DISCRETE TIME, PART 1   443

FIGURE 13.6 Stock Price Evolution, Total Number of Price Paths Ending at a Specific Price, BOPM, N=3

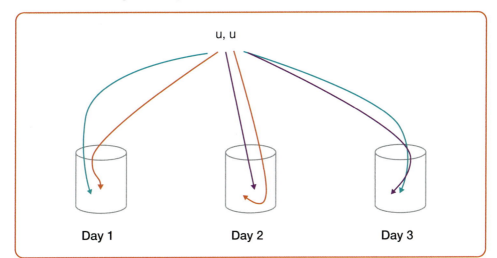

The Combination Function C(N,j)

There is a very useful mathematical formula which answers our question in the title of section 13.3.2. The question is, how many ways are there of putting two identical things into three boxes? The order is unimportant.

The terminology for this quantity is the *number of combinations* of three boxes two at a time. For $N=3$ and $j=2$, the formula is,

$$C(3,2) = \frac{3!}{1! 2!}$$
$$= \frac{3*2*1}{(1)*(2*1)}$$
$$= 3$$

since the definition of 3! (called 3 factorial) is that $3!=3*2*1$, $1!=1$, and similarly $2!=2*1$.

In general, the number of combinations of N things j at a time is the number of ways you can put the j up moves, u, into N boxes, given that the order is not important. The formula for the number of combinations of N things j at a time is,

$$C(N,j) = \frac{N!}{(N-j)! * j!}$$

444 OPTIONS

where $N!=N*(N-1)*(N-2)*\ldots*2*1$ is the factorial function. The factorial function just multiplies all the numbers equal to and below a given number.

■ CONCEPT CHECK 5

a. Calculate $C(3,0)$, $C(3,1)$, and $C(3,3)$.
b. What do the symbols in a. correspond to in our terms of up and downs and days?

The Joint Probability of a Given Path

What is the probability that the stock price will follow a given path consisting of j up moves and $N-j$ down moves over its life of N days? Remembering that the probability of an up move over an individual day is p, and therefore the probability of a down move over an individual day is $1-p$, it follows that the *joint* probability of j up moves in N days is obtained by multiplying p, j times, $p*p*p*\ldots*p=p^j$.

The joint probability of down moves over each of the remaining $N-j$ days is $(1-p)^{N-j}$. Putting these two joint probabilities together, we obtain that the probability of a path consisting of j up moves and $N-j$ down moves is simply $p^j*(1-p)^{N-j}$.

From what we just learned, this is *also* the probability that a given path ends at the terminal stock price $S_N=u^jd^{N-j}S_0$. Remember also that there are $C(N,j)$ paths terminating at $S_N=u^jd^{N-j}S_0$, because the order of the up moves is unimportant.

Figure 13.7 summarizes the information we have derived. This information fully describes the general $N=$period Binomial process, which is the underlier for the BOPM, $N>1$.

13.3.3 Summary of Stock Price Evolution for the *N*-Period Binomial Process

See Figure 13.7.

FIGURE 13.7 **Summary of Stock Price Evolution (*N*-Period BOPM)**

Terminal Stock Price	Number of Price Paths Terminating in Terminal Stock Price	Joint Probability
$S_N = u^j d^{N-j} S_0$	$C(N, j)$	$p^j (1 - p)^{N-j}$

13.4 OPTION VALUATION FOR THE BOPM (*N*=1)

Now that we have a detailed understanding of the underlying Binomial process and how the paths of the Binomial process work, we can turn to the main objective which is to price plain vanilla European put and call options on underlying processes following the Binomial process for $N=1$ and, in the next chapter, for $N>1$.

We will start by trying to price a European call option with one period to expiration. There are two steps to doing so. The first step is to price the option at expiration. This is easy. The second step is much harder. It is to price the option at the current time.

13.4.1 Step 1, Pricing the Option at Expiration

The reason that this is easy to do is that at the expiration date of an option, there is no time premium. This is a fairly obvious statement, because at expiration the option has no further time over which it could have a time premium.

From the model we previously developed for European options in Chapter 11, section 11.6.2, modified by using adjusted intrinsic value instead of unadjusted intrinsic value, the entire value of a European option at any point time is adjusted intrinsic value plus adjusted time premium.

Its *entire* value is intrinsic value at the expiration date of the option, recalling that adjusted intrinsic value equals unadjusted intrinsic value at expiration.

So, all we have to do is write down an expression for the intrinsic value of a European call option at expiration, which we will call time N. Again, this is very easy to do. We can even do this for $N>1$. Let E be the exercise price, S_0 the current stock price, and S_N the stock price at expiration. Then,

$$C_N = MAX[0, S_N - E]$$
$$= MAX[0, u^j d^{N-j} S_0 - E]$$
$$= IV_N$$

where j is the number of up moves experienced by the underlying Binomial stock price process. Note that j can run from 0 to N, because there can be between 0 and N up moves over the entire life of the option.

To summarize the result, option valuation at expiration is easy. The value of the option is just intrinsic value.

■ CONCEPT CHECK 6

a. Apply this result to our $N=2$ period model obtain the terminal option prices in Figure 13.8.

FIGURE 13.8 **European Call Option Valuation at Expiration ($E=100$)**

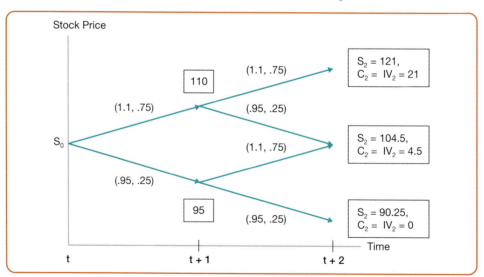

13.4.2 Step 2, Pricing the Option Currently (time $t=0$)

This is the hard part. We will take the $N=1$ case of the BOPM using the example provided below. The question is, how do we determine the option value C_0 at time 0? A little option pricing history is useful here. Much of what we know as finance would respond that the solution is obtained by using standard discounting techniques. Let's explore this potential avenue to pricing options.

The standard discounted cash flow (DCF) approach has two steps,

Step 1
Calculate the expected value of the option's payoffs using the *actual* probabilities p and $1-p$ of up and down moves respectively in the Binomial process.

Step 2
Discount the result of Step 1 by an appropriate risk-adjusted discount rate (RADR). Note that, in order to accomplish this, one needs the option's risk premium, since an option is a risky asset.

Note that, even if we could do Steps 1 and 2, we would still have to show that the resulting option price is arbitrage-free. We are looking for the arbitrage-free option price, not simply a number which is the result of a financial discounting technique.

Let's try to carry out a DCF valuation of European call option using Steps 1 and 2.

Step 1
We would need to estimate the (physical=actual) probability p of an up move in the accompanying diagram, Figure 13.9. This is by no means an easy estimate to obtain. It is based on the *actual* probability distribution of the stock price.

Assuming that we did obtain such an estimate p, the expected value of the option's payoff is then simply $p\mathrm{MAX}[uS_0{-}E, 0]+(1{-}p)\mathrm{MAX}[dS_0{-}E, 0]$, since $N=1$ and the option's payoffs at expiration are just the intrinsic values corresponding to an up or down move.

Step 2
How do we *discount* the option's expected payoffs? As noted, we need to calculate an aggregate (market) risk premium appropriate to the risk of the option in order to do this. Standard models like the CAPM apply with difficulty to financial securities with payoffs like options. It would appear that we have reached a dead-end.

FIGURE 13.9 **The Binomial Process, *N*=1 (*E*=100)**

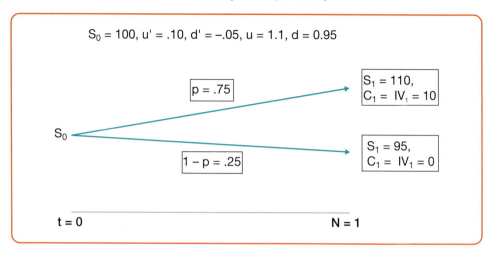

However, under some assumptions, Step 2 can actually be done but the assumptions that are needed make it needlessly difficult.

In fact, we have reached a dead-end using the standard DCF approach because, while generally non-uniquely possible under no-arbitrage, it isn't at all obvious how to apply that approach to option valuation. Therefore, we need to search for more robust and easier-to-apply pricing techniques than standard discounting techniques.

Instead of standard discounting techniques, we're going to use three modern tools that belong in the toolbox of every financial engineer. These are presented in section 13.5.

13.5 MODERN TOOLS FOR PRICING OPTIONS

13.5.1 Tool 1, The Principle of No-Arbitrage

Basically, *the market does not admit any (riskless or risky) arbitrage opportunities* in the three senses we discussed in Chapter 4, section 4.6.1. This is a critical assumption, and it is needed to generate at least one positive, linear pricing mechanism. In other words, one cannot reasonably price financial instruments in a market that admits arbitrage.

13.5.2 Tool 2, Complete Markets or Replicability and a Rule of Thumb

We start with a weaker version of completeness. A financial instrument is said to be *replicable* if it can be *spanned* by a set of 'primitive' securities. Primitive securities could be Arrow–Debreu (AD) securities which we will discuss in Chapter 15, section 15.1. Or they could be a stock and a riskless bond. The key point is that all arbitrage-free pricing mechanisms yield the same, therefore unique, price on *replicable claims.*

A market is *complete* if *all* reasonable contingent claims are replicable. That is, they can be *spanned* by a set of primitive securities. Only in the case that a market is complete will there then be a *unique* pricing mechanism. This result, uniqueness, is usually called the '*Second Fundamental Theorem of Asset Pricing*' (FTAP$_2$).

Tool 2 is the theoretical foundation for Tool 3, replication, because it means that any reasonable contingent claim, not just European puts and calls, can be replicated. In order to be replicable, it has to be spanned by other traded (marketed) financial instruments that can be uniquely priced. The idea of *hedging* is also based on the complete market concept.

Note that the simplest, traditional securities are the underlying security and a default-free zero-coupon bond maturing at the expiration date of the option. We will show in Chapter 15, section 15.1, that the AD securities can be priced in terms of them.

A Rule of Thumb

A very useful rule of thumb is that *if there are as many independent primitive securities as there are states of the world,* then the market is complete. This is a sufficient, but not a necessary condition, for market completeness.

■ CONCEPT CHECK 7

a. What are the independent 'states of the world' in the Binomial model?
b. Do you think the Binomial model is complete? Use the rule of thumb in the above paragraph.

13.5.3 Tool 3, Dynamic and Static Replication

This means that *the payoffs to a contingent claim can be replicated in all relevant states of the world by a static or dynamic (replicating) portfolio consisting of the minimal number of simpler securities.*

For example, for the case of European call options, dynamic (static) replication means that there is a portfolio (with constant portfolio weights in the case of static replication) of primitive securities that replicates the payoffs of a European call option in all relevant states of the world (see Chapter 15, section 15.2.1).

We will see that *static* replication only works in the BOPM for $N=1$. Therefore, for $N>1$, we are going to need to use *dynamic* replication. This will be discussed in detail in Chapter 14.

13.5.4 Relationships between the Three Tools

No-arbitrage, replicability and market completeness, and dynamic and static replication are perhaps the most important tools of the financial engineer. So we are going to explain them and their relationships in detail.

We have already given several definitions of an arbitrage opportunity, both risky and riskless, in Chapter 4, section 4.6.1. The principle of no-arbitrage is one of the most minimal equilibrium conditions that can be imposed on a market of financial securities. All that is required for it to hold as an equilibrium notion is that one or more investors prefers more to less. And that they are rational enough that they will attempt to exploit opportunities for obtaining more than less, if they can do so at no current or future cost, resulting in an optimal demand.

From a pricing point of view, no-arbitrage is an *essential* tool. Without it, pricing financial securities is in general impossible, a hopeless endeavor. The reason for this is that the *existence* of at least one (and generally many) linear, positive pricing mechanisms is equivalent to the absence of arbitrage in one sense or another.

This result is called the *First Fundamental Theorem of Asset Pricing* ($FTAP_1$). Thus, no-arbitrage is a *necessary* condition for pricing derivative securities.

Unfortunately, contrary to intuition, the no-arbitrage condition is not enough machinery to *uniquely* price derivative securities. That is, no-arbitrage is *not a sufficient* condition for *uniquely* pricing derivative securities. There are generally many linear, positive pricing mechanisms, all consistent with no-arbitrage, for non-replicable financial claims!

Another way to say this is that in an *incomplete* market, there can be many equally valid (no-arbitrage) pricing mechanisms.

We already have an inkling of this through our study of ROP. Rational option pricing, which is exclusively based on the foundation of the no-arbitrage principle, produces pricing relationships (such as European Put-Call Parity) and pricing *bounds* or *ranges* into which rational option prices must fall.

ROP does not produce specific, *unique* prices. But this is precisely what we want, and (complete market) model-based derivatives pricing is designed to accomplish this. The idea is to *pin down* the price of a European call option, for example, to a unique price.

In order to accomplish this goal, which is to uniquely price derivative securities, we need another result stronger than simple no-arbitrage. The key to being able to do this is *replication*, not simply no-arbitrage. We can't, of course, do without no-arbitrage because sensible pricing requires it as a necessary existence condition. Tools 2 and 3 are the appropriate tools, in conjunction with Tool 1.

Replicability (complete markets) is the foundation for the ability to statically or dynamically replicate some (all) reasonable derivative securities.

Market completeness means that *any* reasonably behaved contingent claim, such as a plain vanilla European put or call option, can be statically or dynamically replicated. This also forms a foundation for hedging.

If a contingent claim can be *replicated*, then the implication is that it can be *hedged,* because its synthetic, equivalent replicating portfolio can serve as the hedge vehicle. This is very good to know from a practical perspective.

Market completeness guarantees that, when we start on our journey to replicate (hedge) derivative securities, we are confident that we can, in principle, be successful. Without this guarantee, our efforts to find a unique replicating portfolio may indeed fail because we will not be able to distinguish between the multiple, no-arbitrage pricing mechanisms available in a simply no-arbitrage market.

Note that once we have a unique pricing mechanism, which is guaranteed by market completeness, then we get no-arbitrage by the *First Fundamental Theorem of Asset Pricing*. The only case in which this is not true is when there *does not exist* a linear, positive pricing mechanism. In that case, there would also be arbitrage opportunities, in which case linear, positive pricing wouldn't even make sense.

Furthermore, why would anyone want to replicate derivative securities if not for the fact that the pricing mechanism emerges from that exercise, as we

452 **OPTIONS**

will shortly see in the single period BOPM? Replication is an academic exercise in a world with arbitrage opportunities because no linear, positive pricing mechanism exists in that world. In that case, hedging also hardly makes sense.

Once we have a replicating portfolio, then market completeness implies that its price must be equal to the price of the derivative being replicated, because market completeness implies no-arbitrage (according to our interpretation). So, we do not need an independent application of the principle of no-arbitrage to show that the current cost of the replicating portfolio must be equal to the price of the derivative security. Market completeness guarantees that, because it implies no-arbitrage, in our interpretation.

The usual argument given for equality between the cost of the replicating portfolio and the derivative it is replicating is that no-arbitrage implies the *Law of One Price* (LOP), which says that the two economically equivalent financial instruments cannot trade for different prices. This is pretty clear.

If LOP did not hold, then there would be an arbitrage opportunity. The LOP construct is cute, and weaker than no-arbitrage, but not needed. Furthermore, there is no particular benefit to considering a market in which just the weaker LOP holds.

The relevant market is one in which there are linear, positive pricing mechanisms, that is, markets in which there are no arbitrage opportunities. No-arbitrage is a stronger condition than LOP. Under LOP you wouldn't be able to derive option prices. You wouldn't be able to uniquely derive them simply under no-arbitrage either, but you would be closer to doing so.

What breaks the loop of not being able to solve the option pricing problem (remember that this took 73 years) is replicability, which when applied to all reasonable assets is market completeness.

All we really need is market completeness, where the definition does not preclude the existence of one linear, positive pricing mechanism. This is an absurd case. It doesn't make a lot of economic sense to say that market completeness means that the pricing mechanism is unique *if* it exists. That constitutes an artificial separation of no-arbitrage from market completeness. Market completeness includes no-arbitrage when it is simply described as '*a linear, positive pricing mechanism exists (no-arbitrage) and is unique (market completeness)*'.

Once we have a linear, positive pricing mechanism, then no-arbitrage follows from the *First Fundamental Theorem of Asset Pricing* ($FTAP_1$). Market completeness (replication through spanning), ($FTAP_2$), then gives us uniqueness of the pricing mechanism.

As noted, *replication* is just another word for *hedging*. Replication gives us the ability to actually determine the unique price of the derivative security. Why? Because replication synthesizes the derivative in terms of simpler securities, such as the stock and a bond in the Binomial model.

The prices of these simpler (spanning) securities are usually taken as given. In *partial equilibrium* (PE) models, a given set of marketed (traded) underliers is usually given exogenously (without explanation as to how they arise). *General equilibrium* (GE) models would also consider the pricing of such underliers.

We haven't mentioned *risk-neutral valuation* in the above. That's because we are deferring that confusing notion to our concluding Chapter 17, where we will discuss it in detail. It will also be important to understand Chapter 15, before grappling with the notion of 'risk-neutral' valuation. However, a first attack on the issue of risk-neutral valuation is given in the Appendix to this chapter, section 13.8.

13.6 SYNTHESIZING A EUROPEAN CALL OPTION

In this section, we are going to replicate the payoffs to a relatively complex financial instrument, a European call option, with the combined payoffs of two relatively simpler financial instruments. These two relatively simpler financial instruments will form what is called the *replicating portfolio* (*RP*).

Our first question is what goes into the replicating portfolio? We already know the answer, but it is worth thinking about this a little more. A natural choice is the underlying stock, since the European call option is a derivative security, based primarily on the underlying stock. We also know from European Put-Call Parity that options embody leverage, so unit discount bonds are also a good candidate.

One would also think, based on European Put-Call Parity, that a European put option is required. However, we aren't going to use a European put option because doing so would just lead to a ROP result. Furthermore, we only need *two* financial securities, not three, to hedge out *all* of the risk associated with movements in the underlying stock. From our discussion of complete markets embodied in the rule of thumb in section 13.5.2, we only need two independent financial instruments (see Concept Check 7).

We already know quite a bit about bond pricing in continuous time. The BOPM is a purely discrete-time model, so we should be using discretely compounded interest rates. Let r' be the one-period percentage interest rate appropriate to the discrete time interval defining the single-period BOPM. r' represents the de-annualized risk-free rate. In the following, we will also need to define $r=1+r'$ which represents the future value of \$1 placed into an account paying r' over the time interval.

If the unit discount bond matures at its face value of \$1 at time 1, then the current price of the unit discount is $B(t, T)=B(0,1)=1/(1+r')$. We know this from our basic present value. We can now divide the work of pricing a European call option into several steps.

13.6.1 Step 1, Parameterization

Parameter 1

$u=1+u'$ which represents 1 plus the percentage up move in the stock *if* it goes up over the period.

Parameter 2

$d=1+d'$ which represents 1 plus the percentage down move in the stock *if* it goes down over the period.

Parameter 3

$r=1+r'$ which represents 1 plus the riskless rate over the period.

An example we have been considering is $u'=.10$, $d'=-.05$. Then $u=1+u'=1.10$ and $d=1+d'=0.95$.

The first question is, what can we say about the relative magnitude of $r=1+r'$? In order to say anything, we have to use one or more of our basic tools. Tool 1 is sufficient. If there is no arbitrage then we must have $d<r<u$. This implies that $r'<.10$, r' can be no larger than 10%. Otherwise there would be an arbitrage opportunity.

The basic idea is that the bond market (riskless rate) cannot be expected to grow faster than the underlying stock. If it did, there would be an arbitrage opportunity.

The other half is easier, if $r<d$ then $r'<d'<0$ which means that interest rates are negative. This is a rather unlikely possibility in the USA, although it has occurred in Japan. Our conclusion from no-arbitrage is that, $d<r<u$.

13.6.2 Step 2, Defining the Hedge Ratio and the Dollar Bond Position

First, we need a definition of '*hedge ratio*'. In this context the hedge ratio is the number of underlying stocks to hold in the replicating portfolio. At first thought, one would think that this should *always* be 1.0. After all, when we replicated a European call option in deriving European Put-Call Parity we did use 1.0 and that construction was a one-for-one hedge.

Depending on the position, the hedge ratio *could* be 1.0, as we shall see under Case 1 in section 13.6.3. For many models (not all), except for certain perverse cases, option prices are convex in the underlying stock price. This means that the change in the option price as a result of a stock price change is *less* than the given change in the stock price. However, these changes would have to be equal in order for a one-for-one hedge to be able to replicate the option, no matter what the bond position.

In order to hedge the option in the Binomial model, we have to have a hedge ratio different from 1, except for Case 1. Further, it generally has to be less than 1.0 in order to hedge the option.

When we replicated the option for European Put-Call Parity, we also had a European put option that we used as the 'fudge' factor. Here, we only have the stock and the bond. So we have to do better than we did in proving European Put-Call Parity. How can we do better, given that we lost the put option? The answer is that we have been given something we didn't have for proving European Put-Call Parity.

We now get to choose the hedge ratio and make it different from 1.0. (We also get to *change* the hedge ratio in the Binomial model for $N>1$ as the underlying stock price changes, and thereby dynamically hedge the option.) Neither of these two possibilities were available to us in proving European Put-Call Parity. We do not have access to the European put, but we do have access to new trading opportunities.

So this highlights one of the essential differences between ROP and MBOP, model-based option pricing. The difference is that hedging in the case of $N=1$ will not necessarily be one-for-one, and that dynamic hedging will be necessary in the case of $N>1$.

We can't expect to always be able to hedge the option's payoffs with a simple *static* portfolio consisting of one unit of stock (and bonds) to each share defining the option.

456 OPTIONS

13.6.3 Step 3, Constructing the Replicating Portfolio

1. Let Δ be the number of shares to hold in the replicating portfolio per share of stock underlying the option.

2. Let B be the dollar position in riskless bonds. Note that $B<0$ means we *borrow* at the riskless rate.

3. Let C_0 be the current value of the European call option per share. C_0 depends on the current value of the underlying stock, S_0, the number of periods to expiration, $N=1$, and the exercise price E. So we can write $C_0=C(S_0,1;E)$.

Our goal is to determine the current, unique, no-arbitrage value of C_0.

Starting at time zero, we now let time pass and see what happens to the option's value as the stock price either goes up or goes down. If the stock price goes up, the option price will also go up. If the stock price goes down, then the option price will also go down. (This assumes the monotonicity property of European call options, which holds in the BOPM case.)

4. Let C_u be the value of the option at time $N=1$ *if* the stock price goes up. Using our notation $C_u=C_u(uS_0,0;E)$, which represents the value of the option based on the new stock price uS_0, no time to expiration since $N-1=0$, and exercise price E.

5. Let C_d be the value of the option at time $N=1$ *if* the stock price goes down. Using our notation again $C_d=C_d(dS_0,0;E)$, which represents the value of the option based on the new stock price dS_0, no time to expiration since $N-1=0$, and exercise price E.

We know that $C_u=IV_u=\text{MAX}[0,uS_0-E]$ and that $C_d=IV_d=\text{MAX}[0,dS_0-E]$ where IV_u means intrinsic value if the stock price goes up, and IV_d means intrinsic value if the stock price goes down over the only period.

The schematic is given in Figure 13.10, which we will call the 'natural' or actual call option's price dynamics. This is the object to be synthesized by the replicating portfolio.

Next, we represent the replicating portfolio in Figure 13.11.

Note that replication must be done for both the up-state and the down-state. *Up-state* means that the stock price goes up over the single period. *Down-state* means that the stock price goes down over the single period.

FIGURE 13.10 **Option Price Dynamics (BOPM, N=1)**

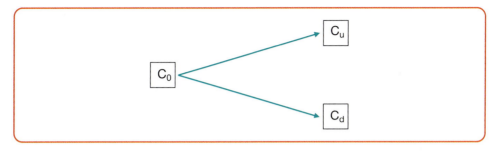

FIGURE 13.11 **Replicating Portfolio Price Dynamics (BOPM, N=1)**

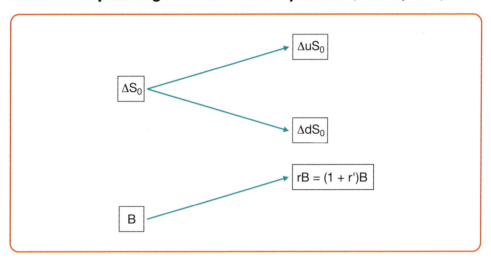

A. Replication in the Up-State

The call option's payoff=C_u, and the replicating portfolio's payoff=payoff to Δ shares of stock and $B in bonds=$\Delta u S_0 + rB$. Therefore, replication means that,

$$\Delta u S_0 + rB = C_u \qquad \text{(up)}$$

B. Replication in the Down-State

The call option's payoff=C_d, and the replicating portfolio's payoff=payoff to Δ shares of stock and $B in bonds=$\Delta d S_0 + rB$. Therefore, replication means that,

$$\Delta d S_0 + rB = C_d \qquad \text{(down)}$$

C. Solving the Two Equations for Δ and B

We now have two equations in two unknowns which must hold simultaneously, and it is a simple mathematical exercise in equation-solving to solve them simultaneously. In other words, there is no economics here. The economics will come into play when we try to *interpret* the solutions to these two equations,

$$\Delta u S_0 + rB = C_u \qquad \text{(up)}$$
$$\Delta d S_0 + rB = C_d \qquad \text{(down)}$$

To solve for Δ, just subtract (down) from (up) to obtain, $\Delta u S_0 - \Delta d S_0 = C_u - C_d$ which when solved gives the hedge ratio Δ,

$$\Delta = \frac{(C_u - C_d)}{(u S_0 - d S_0)} \qquad \textbf{(Δ equation)}$$
$$= \frac{(C_u - C_d)}{((u - d) S_0)}$$

In order to interpret this hedge ratio, note that the numerator $C_u - C_d$ is just the *spread* in the option price. The denominator, $u S_0 - d S_0$, is the *spread* in the stock price. So the hedge ratio, Δ, is the change in the option price relative to the change in the stock price, which is how the option price changes when the stock price changes.

It is the *beta* of the option price with respect to the stock price and we know from Chapter 6, section 6.4, that this is the optimal (risk-minimizing) hedge ratio.

Write the hedge ratio as,

$$\Delta = \frac{\text{Change in the option price}}{\text{Change in the stock price}} \qquad \textbf{(Hedge Ratio equation)}$$

$$= \text{the 'Delta' of the option price with respect to the stock price}$$

$$= \frac{dC}{dS}$$

This should remind you of the derivative of the option price with respect to the stock price because this is essentially what it is in discrete time.

OPTION PRICING IN DISCRETE TIME, PART 1   459

Next, we solve for the dollar position in bonds. Substitute (Δ) into (up):

$$\Delta uS + rB = \left[\frac{(C_u - C_d)}{((u-d)S_0)}\right] * (uS_0) + rB$$

$$= C_u$$

But,

$$\left[\frac{(C_u - C_d)}{((u-d)S_0)}\right] * (uS_0) = \left[\frac{(C_u - C_d)}{(u-d)}\right] * u$$

Therefore,

$$\left[\frac{(C_u - C_d)}{(u-d)}\right] * (u) + rB = C_u$$

and,

$$rB = C_u - u * \left[\frac{(C_u - C_d)}{(u-d)}\right]$$

$$= \frac{(u-d) * C_u - u * (C_u - C_d)}{(u-d)}$$

$$= \frac{(uC_d - dC_u)}{(u-d)}$$

Therefore, dividing by r, we find that the bond position is,

$$B = \frac{(uC_d - dC_u)}{r(u-d)} \qquad \textbf{(Bond Position equation)}$$

There is no immediate interpretation to B, except to note that it is the *required* dollar bond position to make replication possible.

The Sign of B

Let's consider the sign of B, where it is understood that $B<0$ means that we take a *borrowing* position, and $B>0$ means that we take a *lending* position. To determine the sign of B note that $B<0$ if and only if $uC_d - dC_u < 0$.

Remember that $C_u = IV_u = MAX[0, uS_0 - E]$ and that $C_d = IV_d = MAX[0, dS_0 - E]$. Thus, there are four separate cases to consider.

Case 1: $C_u = uS_0 - E > 0$ and $C_d = dS_0 - E > 0$

Then

$$
\begin{aligned}
uC_d - dC_u &= u*(dS_0 - E) - d*(uS_0 - E) \\
&= -u*E + d*E \\
&= -(u-d)*E \\
&< 0
\end{aligned}
$$

because $u-d > 0$.

Therefore $uC_d - dC_u < 0$ which implies that $B < 0$.

Case 2: $C_u = uS_0 - E > 0$ and $C_d = 0$

Then

$$
\begin{aligned}
uC_d - dC_u &= u*0 - d*(uS_0 - E) \\
&= -d*(uS_0 - E) \\
&< 0
\end{aligned}
$$

because $uS_0 - E > 0$. This implies that $B < 0$.

Case 3: $C_u = 0$ and $C_d = 0$

In this case, $uC_d - dC_u = 0$. So $B = 0$ in this case.

Case 4: $C_u = 0$ and $C_d > 0$

If $C_u = 0$ then $uS_0 - E < 0$.

But $d < u$ so $dS_0 < uS_0$

Next, $dS_0 - E < uS_0 - E < 0$

This implies $C_d = 0$, so this case is not possible.

Magnitude of the Hedge Ratio

We can also determine the relative magnitude of the hedge ratio, Δ, in all four cases. For example, can Δ be equal to 1.0? The answer is yes, as in Case 1.

Case 1: $C_u=uS_0-E>0$ and that $C_d=dS_0-E>0$

Then,

$$C_u-C_d=(uS_0-E)-(dS_0-E)$$
$$=(u-d)S_0$$

Therefore,

$$\Delta = \frac{(C_u-C_d)}{(u-d)S_0}$$
$$= \frac{(u-d)S_0}{(u-d)S_0}$$
$$= 1.0$$

It is *possible* that the hedge ratio can be 1.0, if both outcomes for the option are in-the-money at expiration. This can happen if the exercise price, E, is low enough.

Case 2: $C_u=uS_0-E>0$ and that $C_d=0$

Then,

$$\Delta = \frac{(C_u-C_d)}{(u-d)S_0}$$
$$= \frac{C_u}{(u-d)S_0}$$
$$= \frac{(uS_0-E)}{(u-d)S_0}$$

But since $dS_0<E$ it follows that $-dS_0>-E$ and that

$$uS_0-dS_0>uS_0-E.$$

462 **OPTIONS**

Therefore, the denominator of Δ is greater than the numerator. This means that $\Delta<1.0$.

Case 3: $C_u=0$ and that $C_d=0$

So

$$\Delta = \frac{(C_u - C_d)}{(u - d)S_0}$$

$$= 0$$

There is nothing to hedge.

Case 4: $C_u=0$ and that $C_d>0$

This case is not possible, as shown above.

13.6.4 Step 4, Implications of Replication

Once we have the hedge ratio, Δ, and the dollar bond position B, then we can calculate the current cost of the replicating portfolio. It is just the current cost of buying Δ shares of underlying stock per share referred to by the option and borrowing $\$B$ per share referred to by the option. This means that you would borrow $100*\$B$ to replicate the entire option, in addition to buying $100*\Delta$ shares of underlying stock.

Since option prices are usually quoted on a per share basis, we will stick to that convention. The current cost of the replicating portfolio per share, RP_0, is just,

$$\Delta * S_0 + B$$

where,

$$\Delta = \frac{(C_u - C_d)}{(u - d)S_0}$$

and,

$$B = \frac{(uC_d - dC_u)}{r(u - d)}$$

OPTION PRICING IN DISCRETE TIME, PART 1 463

The usual argument for this equality is an application of LOP which (as a consequence of no–arbitrage) implies that this must also be the current cost of the option. That is,

$$C_0 = RP_0$$
$$= \Delta * S_0 + B$$

where,

$$\Delta = \frac{(C_u - C_d)}{(u - d)S_0}$$

and,

$$B = \frac{(uC_d - dC_u)}{r(u - d)}$$

Otherwise, you could arbitrage between the natural option and the replicating portfolio. Replicability also implies (includes) no-arbitrage, so it too implies equality of the price of the replicating portfolio and the European call option.

This completes the complete markets replication approach to pricing a European call option, which is succinctly summarized in the statement that *'the unique, arbitrage-free price of the option is the price of its replicating portfolio'*.

Before we leave this proof of the BOPM($N=1$) we give Table 13.2, indicating what techniques are used and when. That way, the logic of the BOPM model for $N=1$ will become apparent.

We see from Table 13.2 that it isn't simply no-arbitrage that drives the BOPM, $N=1$. Most of the pricing technique is based on replicability (in general, complete markets).

The pricing technique that follows from complete markets is *pricing by replication*. In order to replicate the option's payoffs in all states of the world, we have to first know that this is possible.

TABLE 13.2 **Logic of the BOPM ($N=1$) and its Drivers**

Step Number	Technique
1. Preliminaries : $d<u<r$	No-Arbitrage
2. Defining the Hedge Ratio, Δ, and the Dollar Bond Position B ($N=1$)	Replicability Static Replication ($N=1$)
3. Constructing the Replicating Portfolio	Replicability and Equation Solving
4. Implications of Replication	Replicability or No-Arbitrage

464 **OPTIONS**

No-arbitrage does not guarantee the ability to replicate. However, no-arbitrage is important to assume because, without it, there aren't any equilibrium prices at all.

With no-arbitrage *alone,* there are multiple prices in general (FTAP$_1$). The assumption that a given financial claim is replicable, or that each reasonable ones are (complete markets), gets you a single price for each reasonable contingent claims. We use the word 'reasonable' because technical, mathematical conditions have to be satisfied. These need not concern us here.

In the very early days of option pricing theory, researchers spoke of '*pricing by arbitrage*', apparently suggesting that no-arbitrage alone would always generate unique prices. It was later discovered that no-arbitrage alone *does not* get you unique prices, unless the contingent claim in question is attainable (replicable). This is precisely the issue addressed by completeness.

The reason that the BOPM (*N*=1) *appears* to be priced by no-arbitrage alone, an *illusion*, is that it is a complete model. Thus, it merely *appears* that all one needs is no-arbitrage. *Given* completeness, this is true.

If the model was incomplete, no-arbitrage wouldn't get you very far because there would be multiple pricing mechanisms. An example of an incomplete model is a *Trinomial* model (three stock outcomes) with just the stock and bond in the replicating portfolio.

13.7 ALTERNATIVE OPTION PRICING TECHNIQUES

There are other, *equivalent* pricing methods and interpretations of the option price in the BOPM (*N*=1). But it is important to recognize that, in complete markets, there can only be *one* arbitrage-free price for each contingent claim. All pricing mechanisms, while they might look different, will produce *exactly the same price* on *replicable* claims.

We know that there is a no-arbitrage price, because we just calculated one. Its existence is predicated on no-arbitrage. Therefore all pricing methods, when the underlying model is complete, must lead to the same result given by replication. Without no-arbitrage, either built into the definition of complete markets or assumed, there is no viable pricing mechanism at all. Even with no-arbitrage, there are *multiple* viable pricing mechanisms. Complete markets *filter* them down to one by implying a unique pricing mechanism, the one generated by the replicating portfolio.

OPTION PRICING IN DISCRETE TIME, PART 1 — 465

The BOPM is known to be a complete model, so once we get a linear, positive pricing mechanism we know that it is the correct and only one. The quick way to see completeness of the BOPM ($N=1$) is to use our rule of thumb.

All of the uncertainty in the model is embodied in the stock price movement up or down. There are no other sources of uncertainty. The two risks, up or down, can be '*spanned*' by two independent securities in the model. With two states of the world and two independent securities, the underlying stock and bond, the BOPM is complete.

A detailed numerical example of pricing using the BOPM, $N=1$ is given in the End of Chapter Exercise 4. The solution to that question is also given at its end, so you can test your understanding.

In Chapter 14 we will look at alternative interpretations of the price produced by replication in the BOPM ($N=1$) and generalize the BOPM to $N>1$. One such interpretation is discussed in the Appendix, section 13.8, to this chapter. We will now see what is new for the case $N>1$.

■ KEY CONCEPTS

1. The Objective of Model-Based Option Pricing (MBOP).
2. Modeling Time in a Discrete Time Framework.
3. Modeling the Underlying Stock Price Uncertainty.
4. Path Structure of the Binomial Process, Total Number of Price Paths.
5. Path Structure of the Binomial Process, Total Number of Price Paths ending at a Specific Terminal Price.
6. The Combination Function $C(N,j)$.
7. The Joint Probability of a Given Path.
8. Summary of Stock Price Evolution for the N-Period Binomial Process.
9. Option Valuation for the BOPM (N=1).
10. Step 1, Pricing the Option at Expiration.
11. Step 2, Pricing the Option Currently (time t=0).
12. Modern Tools for Pricing Options.
13. Tool 1, The Principle of No-Arbitrage.
14. Tool 2, Complete Markets.
15. Tool 3, Dynamic and Static Replication.
16. Relationships between the Three Tools.
17. Synthesizing a European Call Option.
18. Step 1, Parameterization.
19. Step 2, Defining the Hedge Ratio and the Dollar Bond Position.
20. Step 3, Constructing the Replicating Portfolio.
21. Replication in the Up-State.
22. Replication in the Down-State.
23. Solving the Two Equations for Δ and B.
24. Case 1: $C_u=uS_0-E>0$ and that $C_d=dS_0-E>0$.
25. Case 2: $C_u=uS_0-E>0$ and that $C_d=0$.
26. Case 3: $C_u=0$ and that $C_d=0$.
27. Case 4: $C_u=0$ and that $C_d>0$.
28. Implications of Replication.
29. Logic of the BOPM (N=1) and its Drivers.
30. Alternative Option Pricing Techniques.
31. The BOPM (N=1) as a Risk-Neutral Valuation Relationship.

OPTION PRICING IN DISCRETE TIME, PART 1   467

13.8 APPENDIX: DERIVATION OF THE BOPM (*N*=1) AS A RISK-NEUTRAL VALUATION RELATIONSHIP (RNVR)

To interpret the BOPM replicating formula as a RNVR, substitute into it the hedge ratio, Δ, and the dollar bond position, B.

$$C_0 = RP_0$$
$$= \Delta * S_0 + B \qquad\qquad (C_0)$$

where,

$$\Delta = \frac{(C_u - C_d)}{(u-d)S_0} \qquad\qquad (\Delta)$$

$$B = \frac{(uC_d - dC_u)}{r(u-d)} \qquad\qquad (B)$$

Substitute (Δ) and (B) into (C_0), and perform some algebraic manipulations, the reasons for which will become apparent as we go along,

$$C_0 = \Delta * S_0 + B$$
$$= \frac{(C_u - C_d)}{(u-d)S_0} * S_0 + \frac{uC_d - dC_u}{r(u-d)}$$

Cancel S_0 in the first term above to obtain,

$$\frac{(C_u - C_d)}{(u-d)S_0} * S_0 + \frac{uC_d - dC_u}{r(u-d)} = \frac{(C_u - C_d)}{(u-d)} + \frac{uC_d - dC_u}{r(u-d)}$$

Then, take a common *denominator* to obtain,

$$\frac{(C_u - C_d)}{(u-d)} + \frac{uC_d - dC_u}{r(u-d)} = \frac{r*(C_u - C_d) + (uC_d - dC_u)}{r(u-d)}$$

Now, collect terms in the numerator involving C_u and C_d,

$$\frac{r*(C_u - C_d) + (uC_d - dC_u)}{r(u-d)} = \frac{(r-d)*C_u + (u-r)*C_d}{r(u-d)}$$

Next, for an important little trick, bring the $(u{-}d)$ in the denominator *upstairs* to the numerator to obtain,

$$\frac{(r-d)*C_u+(u-r)*C_d)}{r(u-d)} = \frac{\left\{\dfrac{r-d}{u-d}*C_u+\dfrac{u-r}{u-d}*C_d\right\}}{r}$$

Now *define* $p'\equiv(r{-}d)/(u{-}d)$. Then a little algebra will show that $1{-}p'{=}(u{-}r)/(u{-}d)$, the conclusion of which is that p' and $1{-}p'$ act just like probabilities, because they add up to 1.0

They aren't, except under one scenario, equal to the true probabilities p and $1{-}p$.

Our final presentation of the current BOPM, $N{=}1$ option price C_0 is,

$$C_0 = \frac{\left[p'*C_u+(1-p')*C_d\right]}{r} \qquad \textbf{(BOPM, N=1)}$$

$$\text{where } p' = \frac{r-d}{u-d}$$

Interpretation of the (BOPM, *N*=1) as a Risk-Neutral Valuation Relationship

The risk-neutral value interpretation of (BOPM, $N{=}1$) is clear. Since p' and $1{-}p'$ act as probabilities, the numerator is the expected value (the probability-weighted average) of the option's payoffs in the up state and in the down state, using the risk-neutral probabilities p' and $1{-}p'$ to weight the payoffs. The denominator is one plus the risk-free rate $r{=}1{+}r'$.

The intuitive rationale for the term 'risk-neutral' is that p' and $1{-}p'$ are the probabilities that a risk-neutral investor would use in pricing the option. They must be, because the expected value in the numerator of (BOPM, $N{=}1$) is being discounted by the risk-free rate.

Therefore, (BOPM, $N{=}1$) is the discounted expected value of the option, where the expectation is based on the risk-neutral probabilities p' and $1{-}p'$, *not* on the real-world ones p and $1{-}p$, and discounting is at the risk-free rate, *not* at a risk-adjusted discount rate, as would be customary for risky assets like stocks.

The only remaining issue is exactly why and in what sense our formula, (BOPM, $N{=}1$), is risk-neutral. In the modern approach to derivatives valuation, Chapter 15 is a prerequisite for understanding what risk-neutral valuation is supposed to mean. It will be also be further discussed in detail in our concluding Chapter 17.

OPTION PRICING IN DISCRETE TIME, PART 1   469

■ END OF CHAPTER EXERCISES FOR CHAPTER 13

1. The following data is to be used in this question,

$$S_0=\$129, \; E=\$80, \; u=1.5, \; d=0.5, \; r=1.1, \; \tau=1 \text{ year.}$$

  a. Draw the *one period* Binomial tree showing the potential stock prices. Label everything.

  b. Price a European call option *at expiration*, maturing in 1 year for each of the potential stock prices in a.

  c. Calculate the appropriate probability, p', needed to price the option today. $p'=$_____ .

  d. Calculate the current value of the European call option, C_0.

  e. What does the replicating portfolio consist of?

    Define Δ _____

    Calculate $\Delta=$_____

    Define B _____

    Calculate $B=$_____

2. The current price of a share of RJR Nabisco Co. common stock is $100. The stock price can only go up by 10% with probability 0.5 or it can go down by 5% with probability 0.5 in each period.

    Consider a *two-period* European call option written on RJR Nabisco Co. stock with current value C_0. The call option is written so that it is currently at the money and the riskless rate per period is 7%.

  a. Draw the Binomial tree for the underlying asset price.

  b. Calculate the expiration prices of the European call option according to the two-period Binomial option pricing model.

3. Suppose that $u'=10\%$, $d'=-5\%$, $S_0=\$50$, $p=0.4$, and $N=3$.

  a. Derive the Binomial tree for a stock price evolving according to the above parameters in this three-period Binomial model.

  b. Calculate the option prices at expiration for the terminal stock prices indicated in a.

4. Here, we will take an at-the-money European call option. The current stock price is $S_0=\$40$. The stock price can go up by 50% or it can go down by 50% over the year, which is the single period. The annual interest rate is $r'=.10$.

470 OPTIONS

a. What is the value of E?

b. What are the values of u', d', u, and of d?

c. What is the value of r?

d. In order to replicate the option, all we have to do is to calculate Δ and B. To calculate Δ, we need C_u and C_d which are just intrinsic values if the stock price goes up or down respectively. Calculate C_u and C_d.

e. Calculate the hedge ratio Δ.

f. All that is left is the bond position. Calculate B. Interpret B.

g. How much should we borrow per share?

h. What is the current cost per share of the replicating portfolio?

i. What is the current price of the European call option? Why?

j. Fill in Table 13.3, which is a schematic by level of complexity. We use the relatively simpler _____ to price the relatively complex financial derivative, _____ .

TABLE 13.3 **Schematic by Level of Complexity**

	Relatively Complex	Relatively Simple
	_____	_____
	_____	_____
Current Costs	$C_0=\$\_\_\_\_\_$	$RP_0=\$\_\_\_\_\_$

Solution to Exercise 4

a. $E=\$40$ since the option is at-the-money.

b. $u=1+u'=1.5$ and $d=1+d'=0.50$.

c. $r=1+r'=1.10$

d. $C_u=IV_u=\text{MAX}[0,uS_0-E]=\text{MAX}[0,60-40]=\text{MAX}[0,20]=20$

   $C_d=IV_d=\text{MAX}[0,dS_0-E]=\text{MAX}[0,20-40]=\text{MAX}[0,-20]=0$

e. The Hedge Ratio $\Delta=(20-0)/(60-20)=1/2$
   which means that for 1 option (100 shares) you would hold 50 shares in your replicating portfolio.

OPTION PRICING IN DISCRETE TIME, PART 1 **471**

f.   All that is left is the bond position

$$B = \frac{uC_d - dC_u}{r(u-d)}$$
$$= \frac{u*0 - .50*20}{1.1*1}$$
$$= \frac{-10}{1.1}$$
$$= -9.09.$$

g.   Therefore we need to borrow $9.09 per share.

h.   Combined with the stock position of 0.50 shares of underlying stock, the current cost of the Replicating Portfolio=ΔS_0+B=0.50($40)–$9.09 =$10.91 per share of stock referred to by the option. (The replicating portfolio for the entire option—for 100 shares—would cost 100* $10.91=$1091.00.)

i.   We have succeeded in pricing the option. Its price is the current cost of its Replicating Portfolio: C_0=RP_0=$10.91.

j.   The schematic for this is shown below by level of complexity. We use the relatively simpler replicating portfolio to price the relatively complex financial derivative.

TABLE 13.3   **Schematic by Level of Complexity**

	Relatively Complex Actual (Natural) Option	Relatively Simple Synthetic Option (Replicating Portfolio)
Current Costs	C_0=$10.91	RP_0=$10.91

■ SELECTED CONCEPT CHECK SOLUTIONS

Concept Check 3

a.   The answer is 2^N.
b.   There are two possibilities for each day (u or d) and there are N boxes to put these two possibilities into, for a total of 2^N paths. This can be a very, very large number. Calculate it for N=91 days (a 3-month option).

Concept Check 4

In this example, Intrinsic Value at time 2 equals,

$$IV_2=C_2$$
$$=MAX[0,S_2-100]$$

which is 21, 4.5, or zero depending on whether the stock price ends up at 121, 104.5, or 90.25.

Concept Check 7

a. There are only two *independent* states in the Binomial model, the up state and the down state.
b. Yes, two independent securities will do. The underlying stock and a risk-free bond work just fine. In the Binomial model, these are enough to span any reasonable contingent claims, including the European puts and calls that we have effectively demonstrated. The Binomial model is intuitively complete, by our rule of thumb.

CHAPTER 14

OPTION PRICING IN DISCRETE TIME, PART 2: DYNAMIC HEDGING AND THE MULTI-PERIOD BINOMIAL OPTION PRICING MODEL, *N*>1

14.1	Modeling Time and Uncertainty in the BOPM, *N*>1	475
	14.1.1 Stock Price Behavior, *N*=2	475
	14.1.2 Option Price Behavior, *N*=2	476
14.2	Hedging a European Call Option, *N*=2	477
	14.2.1 Step 1, Parameterization	477
	14.2.2 Step 2, Defining the Hedge Ratio and the Dollar Bond Position	478
	14.2.3 Step 3, Constructing the Replicating Portfolio	478
	14.2.4 The Complete Hedging Program for the BOPM, *N*=2	484
14.3	Implementation of the BOPM for *N*=2	485
14.4	The BOPM, *N*>1 as a RNVR Formula	490
14.5	Multi-period BOPM, *N*>1: A Path Integral Approach	493
	14.5.1 Thinking of the BOPM in Terms of Paths	493
	14.5.2 Proof of the BOPM Model for general *N*	499

We have studied the BOPM, *N*=1 in detail. Most of the basic ideas of option pricing are included in that model. There is one very important idea that is *not* included in the BOPM, *N*=1, and that is called *dynamic hedging*. When we consider multi-period models, we can no longer replicate the option *statically*.

That is, we have to change the hedge ratio and the bond position as we move from period to period. However, the good news is that both the hedge ratio and the bond position will have exactly the same *form* in the BOPM, *N*>2 as in the BOPM, *N*=1.

474 **OPTIONS**

In terms of 'states of the world', there appear to be many more possible states, even in a two-period Binomial model. If we were limited to static hedges, the BOPM, $N=2$ model would not be complete, and therefore it would not be possible to replicate all contingent claims statically. It would not be possible to statically replicate even a standard European call option.

However, note that in the BOPM, $N=2$, while there are three terminal states for the stock price (three distinct states at expiration), there are still only the same *two sources of uncertainty;* whether the stock price will go up or down over each period. Just as in the BOPM, $N=1$. Not only that. The percentage upward and downward moves, u and d, are the same over all periods as well as the risk-free rate. The process is self-replicating.

Thus two independent securities, the stock and the bond, are enough to replicate contingent claims, provided that we allow *more trading opportunities.* This is what dynamic hedging enables. We *can* replicate contingent claims in the multi-period Binomial model by *changing* our trading strategy as we move backwards from period to period. In fact, we generally *have to* change the hedge ratio as we move from period to period. That is the other half of the BOPM, $N>1$, which is the purely mathematical technique of backward dynamic programming.

Remember that it is easy to value a European call option at the end of its life, at time N. Then, using the single-period BOPM, we can move back one step to time $N–1$. Having done so for each node in the tree at time $N–1$, we reapply the single period BOPM to get option prices at time $N–2$. Repeating this procedure, we eventually get the option price at time 0, C_0.

The economic content of this procedure is the unique, arbitrage-free, risk-neutral valuation relationship implied by the single-period BOPM. Arbitrage opportunities exist in the multi-period model only if they exist at some point in the Binomial tree. Thus, this procedure is guaranteed to produce an arbitrage-free option price. This model is also complete, due to the two hedge-able sources of uncertainty and the dynamic trading opportunities required to hedge them. Therefore the option price generated is unique.

There is nothing really new in the BOPM, $N>1$ from a valuation perspective. It is just the repeated application of the single-period BOPM. The new component is dynamic hedging. In the single-period BOPM, we use the *static* hedge ratio and bond position. In the multi-period BOPM this will not work. The hedge ratio and bond position required to replicate the option is now dependent upon the period. We gave a numerical example of the (BOPM, $N=1$) in Chapter 13.

OPTION PRICING IN DISCRETE TIME, PART 2

Here we will do the *general* case for N=2. Once again, a good notation will help to properly understand this material.

14.1 MODELING TIME AND UNCERTAINTY IN THE BOPM, $N>1$

14.1.1 Stock Price Behavior, $N=2$

We first indicate the evolution of the stock price over the $N=2$ periods in Figure 14.1. The intermediate outcomes at the end of the first period, $N=1$, are also indicated.

FIGURE 14.1 Stock Price Behavior (BOPM, $N=2$)

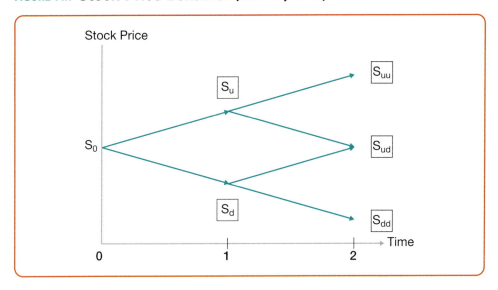

The setup here is the same as in Chapter 13. Four things can happen to the stock price over the $N=2$ periods. The outcomes at $N=2$ are described in Table 14.1. Note that there are only $N+1=3$ different outcomes at time $N=2$, because $S_{ud}=duS_0=udS_0=S_{du}$. Note the order in S_{ud}. The u corresponds to the first move (over the first period) and the d corresponds to the price move over the second period. Thus $S_{ud}=duS_0$. The order turns out not to matter, but it is better to have a consistent, defined notation.

TABLE 14.1 Stock Price Behavior (BOPM, N=2)

1. *uu* (up, up) — $S_{uu} = u^2 S_0$
2. *ud* (up, down) — $S_{ud} = du S_0$
3. *du* (down, up) — $S_{du} = ud S_0 = du S_0 = S_{ud}$
4. *dd* (down, down) — $S_{dd} = d^2 S_0$

14.1.2 Option Price Behavior, N=2

The European call option price can also do four things over the $N=2$ periods. The three distinct outcomes at $N=2$ are described in the Table 14.2. Note that there are only $N+1=3$ different outcomes at time $N=2$, because $C_{ud} = C_{du}$. Keep in mind that the change in the option price is generally, but not always, less than the change in the stock price as indicated in Figure 14.2.

TABLE 14.2 Option Price Behavior (BOPM, N=2)

1. *uu* (up, up) — $C_{uu} = C(S_{uu})$
2. *ud* (up, down) — $C_{ud} = C(S_{ud})$
3. *du* (down, up) — $C_{du} = C(S_{du}) = C(S_{ud}) = C_{ud}$
4. *dd* (down, down) — $C_{dd} = C(S_{dd})$

FIGURE 14.2 Option Price Behavior (BOPM, N=2)

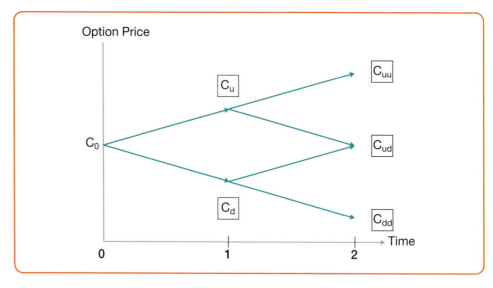

OPTION PRICING IN DISCRETE TIME, PART 2 **477**

■ CONCEPT CHECK 1

a. Explain why $C_{ud} = C_{du}$.

14.2 HEDGING A EUROPEAN CALL OPTION, *N*=2

We'll work our way through the general case of the BOPM, N=2 to show how to hedge the option at each step and to derive the option price at time 0, C_0, just as we did for the BOPM, N=1. We take the BOPM, N=1 as our starting point.

■ CONCEPT CHECK 2

a. How many ultimate 'states of nature' are there in the BOPM for N=2?
b. How many *distinct* ultimate option prices are there in the BOPM for N=2? List them.
c. Recall the useful *rule of thumb* from Chapter 13, section 13.5.2.
d. If we only have the underlying stock and a risk-free bond and a static hedge ratio at our disposal, what does c. suggest about our ability to replicate a European call option?
e. Recall also that the rule of thumb is a sufficient, but not a necessary condition, for market completeness. What does that mean?
f. How do you expect that more trading opportunities will help us to replicate a European call option with only our two independent securities?

We will follow the procedure we developed for the BOPM, N=1 step by step. The difference in the BOPM, N=2, is that we have to replicate the option's payoffs over three different scenarios. As discussed, we start at the last period and move backwards, in accord with the method of dynamic, backward programming.

14.2.1 Step 1, Parameterization

The assumption of the multi-period BOPM is that the future evolution of the stock price beyond period 1 is determined by exactly the same parameters as over the first period. This is a *stationarity* assumption which says that u, d, and r stay the same over subsequent periods.

Parameter 1

$u=1+u'$ represents 1 plus the percentage up move in the stock, *if* it goes up over the second period.

Parameter 2

$d=1+d'$ represents 1 plus the percentage down move in the stock, *if* it goes down over the second period.

Parameter 3

$r=1+r'$ represents 1 plus the riskless rate over the first and second period.

Further, under the standing assumption of no arbitrage, we must have $d<r<u$, as shown in Chapter 13, section 13.6.1.

14.2.2 Step 2, Defining the Hedge Ratio and the Dollar Bond Position

Just as for the BOPM, $(N=1)$, the hedge ratio is the number of underlying stocks to hold in the replicating portfolio over the second period. However, it doesn't have to be, nor could it in general be, equal to the hedge ratio over the first period. The dollar bond position is also potentially different over each period and each different scenario.

14.2.3 Step 3, Constructing the Replicating Portfolio

Before doing the replication, we should describe the *three* scenarios involved in the BOPM for $N=2$. There are two scenarios for period 2, and one scenario for period 1.

Replication over period 2 involves,

Scenario 1:
At the end of the first period, the stock price has increased to S_u and the option price to C_u, or

Scenario 2:
At the end of the first period, the stock price has decreased to S_d and the option price to C_d. This is apparent from Figure 14.1 and Figure 14.2.

OPTION PRICING IN DISCRETE TIME, PART 2 **479**

Replication over period 1 involves,

Scenario 3:
Is the usual BOPM, $N=1$ case. The stock price starts at S_0 and the corresponding option price is the current option price, C_0. At the end of the first period, the stock price either goes up to S_u or it goes down to S_d.

Replication over Period 2, under Scenario 1

1. Let Δ_u be the number of shares to hold in the replicating portfolio per share of stock underlying the option, assuming that the stock price has gone up to S_u over the first period. The subscript u helps us remember that we are constructing the hedge over the second period, based on S_u.

2. Let B_u be the dollar position in riskless bonds at time 1. Note that $B_u<0$ means that we borrow at the riskless rate.

3. Let C_u be the current (time 1) value of the European call option when the stock price is S_u. C_u depends on the current (time 1) value of the underlying stock, S_u, on the number of periods to expiration, $N-1=1$, and on the exercise price E. So we can write $C_u=C(S_u,1;E)$. This is what we are trying to replicate at this first stage.

We are at time $t=1$, and we now let time pass and see what happens to the option's value as the stock price either goes up or goes down over the *second* period. If the stock price goes up over the second period, the option price will also go up. If the stock price goes down, then the option price will also go down.

4. Let C_{uu} be the value of the option at time $N=2$ *if* the stock price goes up over the second period. Using our notation $C_{uu}=C_{uu}(u^2S_0,0;E)$, which represents the value of the option based on the new stock price u^2S_0, no time to expiration since we are then at expiration $N=2$, and exercise price E.

5. Let C_{ud} be the value of the option at time $N=2$ *if* the stock price goes down over the second period. Using our notation again, $C_{ud}=C_{ud}(duS_0,0;E)$, which represents the value of the option based on the new stock price duS_0, no time to expiration since $N=2$, and exercise price E.

Option valuation is easy *at expiration* since the option's value must be intrinsic value, because there is no time value left. Therefore, we know that,

$$C_{uu} = IV_{uu}$$
$$= \text{MAX}[0, u^2 S_0 - E]$$

and that,

$$C_{ud} = IV_{ud}$$
$$= \text{MAX}[0, du S_0 - E],$$

where IV_{uu} means intrinsic value, if the stock price goes up over the second period, and IV_{ud} means intrinsic value if the stock price goes down over the second period.

The schematic, given in Figure 14.3, describes what we have called the *natural* or *actual* call option. This is the object to be synthesized by the replicating portfolio, at this first stage.

FIGURE 14.3 The Natural Call Option under Scenario 1

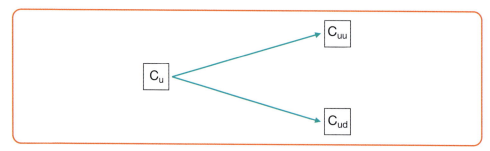

Next, we represent the replicating portfolio in Figure 14.4.

As always, replication must be done *simultaneously* for both the up state and the down state. Up state means that the stock price goes up over the second period. Down state means that the stock price goes down over the second period. Now we proceed to replicate in each state.

A. Replication in the Up State

The call option's payoff, if the stock price goes up over the second period, is equal to C_{uu}. The replicating portfolio's payoff is the sum of the payoff to Δ_u stocks and $\$B_u$ in bonds which is $\Delta_u S_{uu} + rB_u$.

Replication means that $\Delta_u S_{uu} + rB_u = C_{uu}$ (up state)

FIGURE 14.4 The Replicating Portfolio under Scenario 1

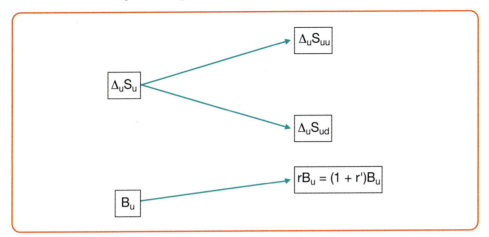

B. Replication in the Down State

The call option's payoff, if the stock price goes down over the second period, is equal to C_{ud}. The replicating portfolio's payoff is the sum of the payoff to Δ_u stocks plus \$$B_u$ in bonds. This combined payoff is, $\Delta_u S_{ud} + rB_u$.

Replication means that $\Delta_u S_{ud} + rB_u = C_{ud}$ (down state)

C. Solving the Two Equations for Δ_u and B_u

We now have two equations, (up state) and (down state) in two unknowns, Δ_u and B_u, which must hold simultaneously, and it is a simple mathematical exercise in equation solving to solve them simultaneously. This is just as for the BOPM, $N=1$.

$\Delta_u S_{uu} + rB_u = C_{uu}$ (up state)
$\Delta_u S_{ud} + rB_u = C_{ud}$ (down state)

To solve for Δ_u, just subtract (down state) from (up state) to obtain $\Delta_u S_{uu} - \Delta_u S_{ud} = C_{uu} - C_{ud}$ which when solved gives the hedge ratio Δ_u,

$$\Delta_u = \frac{C_{uu} - C_{ud}}{S_{uu} - S_{ud}} \quad\quad\quad (\Delta_u)$$
$$= \frac{C_{uu} - C_{ud}}{(u^2 - du)S_0}$$

482 OPTIONS

Interpretation of the Hedge Ratio, Δ_u

In order to interpret this hedge ratio, note that the numerator $C_{uu}-C_{ud}$ is just the *spread* in the option price, but now over the second period, *if* the stock price went up over the first period. The denominator $(u^2-du)S_0$ is the corresponding *spread* in the stock price.

So, the hedge ratio, Δ_u, is the change in the option price relative to the change in the stock price, which is how the option price changes when the stock price changes.

Note here that the *form* of the hedge ratio is exactly the same as it was in our analysis of the BOPM ($N=1$). Of course, the numbers will change because the *curvature* of the option price is changing (see Figure 11.4 in End of Chapter Exercise 2).

In order to perform its main function of hedging, the hedge ratio (HR) is always,

$$
\begin{aligned}
\text{HR} &= \frac{\text{change in the option price}}{\text{change in the stock price}} \\
&= \text{Beta} \\
&= \frac{dC}{dS} \\
&= \beta_{?,?}
\end{aligned}
$$

(Hedge Ratio)

■ CONCEPT CHECK 3

a. We derived the optimal (risk-minimizing) hedge ratio for hedging a spot position in λ futures in Chapter 6, section 6.4.2.

It was $\lambda^*=\beta_{P_t(\omega),F_t(\omega)}$, the beta of the spot on the futures. Intuitively, why does this minimize risk? Take an example, say $\beta_{P_t(\omega),F_t(\omega)}=0.50$.

b. We could turn a. on its head and hedge the futures using $\lambda^{*\prime}=(1/\lambda^*)=\beta_{F_t(\omega),P_t(\omega)}$ units of the spot commodity.

What is the numerical value of $\beta_{F_t(\omega),P_t(\omega)}$ if $\beta_{P_t(\omega),F_t(\omega)}=0.50$?

Does this make sense?

c. In the replication problem for options, what exactly is being hedged—the stock or the option?

d. What is the risk-minimizing hedge ratio, $\beta_{?,?}$, in the context of c.?

OPTION PRICING IN DISCRETE TIME, PART 2 — 483

D. Solving for the Dollar Position in Bonds over Period 2, under Scenario 1

Next, we solve for the dollar position in bonds, B_u. Substitute the result of equation (Δ_u) into (up),

$$\Delta_u S_{uu} + rB_u = \left[\frac{(C_{uu} - C_{ud})}{(u^2 - du)S_0} \right] * (u^2 S_0) + rB_u$$

$$= C_{uu}$$

But,

$$\left[\frac{(C_{uu} - C_{ud})}{(u^2 - du)S_0} \right] * (u^2 S_0) = \left[\frac{(C_{uu} - C_{ud})}{(u - d)} \right] * u$$

So,

$$\left[\frac{(C_{uu} - C_{ud})}{(u - d)} \right] * u + rB_u = C_{uu}$$

Therefore,

$$rB_u = C_{uu} - u * \left[\frac{(C_{uu} - C_{ud})}{(u - d)} \right]$$

$$= \frac{\left[(u - d)C_{uu} - u * (C_{uu} - C_{ud}) \right]}{(u - d)}$$

$$= \frac{\left[uC_{ud} - dC_{uu} \right]}{(u - d)}$$

Therefore, dividing by r, we find that the dollar bond position is,

$$B_u = \frac{\left[uC_{ud} - dC_{uu} \right]}{r(u - d)} \qquad \textbf{(Dollar Position in Bonds)}$$

The interpretation of B_u is as the *required* dollar bond position to make replication possible over the second period, *if* the stock price went up over the first period.

484 OPTIONS

Replication under Scenario 2, over Period 2

The next step is to construct the hedging strategy for scenario 2 over period 2. It follows exactly the same procedure as for scenario 1, so you should do it in End of Chapter Exercises 3 and 4. We include these exercises for completeness, since we already know the form of the hedge ratio and the dollar bond position.

14.2.4 The Complete Hedging Program for the BOPM, *N*=2

We now have a complete hedging program for replicating the option which we will now summarize. Table 14.3 makes apparent the common form of the hedge ratio and the dollar bond position across and within periods.

TABLE 14.3 **The Complete Hedging Program for the BOPM, *N*=2**

Period	Δ, the Hedge Ratio	*B*, the Dollar Bond Position
1 (Scenario 3)	$\Delta = \dfrac{C_u - C_d}{(u-d)S_0}$	$B = \dfrac{uC_d - dC_u}{r(u-d)}$
2 (up) (Scenario 1)	$\Delta_u = \dfrac{C_{uu} - C_{ud}}{(u^2 - du)S_0}$	$B_u = \dfrac{uC_{ud} - dC_{uu}}{r(u-d)}$
2 (down) (Scenario 2)	$\Delta_d = \dfrac{C_{du} - C_{dd}}{(du - d^2)S_0}$	$B_d = \dfrac{uC_{dd} - dC_{du}}{r(u-d)}$

Note that 2(up) refers to the appropriate hedging strategy over period 2 if the stock price goes up over period 1 (scenario 1), while 2(down) refers to the appropriate hedging strategy over period 2 if the stock price goes down over period 1 (scenario 2). This is the nature of dynamic hedging, it adjusts to the particular scenario.

To see the commonality in all the Δs and the Bs, first start with the Bs. Examining *B* for period 1, the algorithm it expresses is,

1. Take the down value of the option, C_d, and multiply it by the up parameter.

2. Take the up value of the option, C_u, and multiply it by the down parameter.

3. Subtract 2. from 1.

4. Divide 3. by $r(u-d)$.

OPTION PRICING IN DISCRETE TIME, PART 2 **485**

Now, examine B_u. Since the stock price has gone up over the first period, the current corresponding option price is C_u.

Let's apply the algorithm and see if it gives the correct result for this case,

1. Take the down value of the option, $(C_u)_d$, and multiply it by the up parameter u. This gives $u(C_u)_d$.

2. Take the up value of the option, $(C_u)_u$, and multiply it by the down parameter d. This gives $d(C_u)_u$.

3. Subtract 2. from 1. This gives $u(C_u)_d - d(C_u)_u$.

4. Divide 3. by $r(u-d)$ which gives $[(uC_{ud} - dC_{uu})/r(u-d)] = B_u$.

■ CONCEPT CHECK 4

a. Confirm that B_d conforms to the algorithm for determining B by verifying that steps 1.–4. directly above result in the correct value B_d.

14.3 IMPLEMENTATION OF THE BOPM FOR *N*=2

This section discusses the actual implementation of the BOPM for $N=2$, whereas section 14.2 has discussed the full, dynamic replicating (hedging) strategy.

If you look at the hedge ratios and bond positions in Table 14.3, you will see that one must know the values of C_u, C_d, C_{ud}, C_{uu}, and C_{dd} in order to implement them!

Therefore, we have to solve the pricing problem at least for C_u and C_d. Note that C_{ud}, C_{uu}, and C_{dd} are determined at expiration as the appropriate intrinsic values. That is,

$$C_{ud} = IV_{ud}$$
$$= \text{MAX}\left[0, duS_0 - E\right]$$
$$C_{uu} = IV_{uu}$$
$$= \text{MAX}\left[0, u^2 S_0 - E\right]$$

and

$$C_{dd} = IV_{dd}$$
$$= \text{MAX}\left[0, d^2 S_0 - E\right]$$

These intrinsic values can be read off the stock price evolution chart (Figure 14.1).

In order to determine C_u and C_d, we have to understand how the BOPM, $N>1$ works. It is simply a collection of single period BOPM ($N=1$) models which we already know exactly how to solve.

The algorithm here is,

1. Given the option parameters d, r, and u calculate the 'risk-neutral' (certainty-equivalent) probabilities $p'=(r-d)/(u-d)$ and $1-p'=(u-r)/(u-d)$ (see the Appendix, section 13.8, to Chapter 13).

2. Then, no matter what node one is at in the tree, the option value at that node is simply the risk-neutral quantity.

$$C_{\text{current node}} = \frac{p' * C_{\text{current node,up}} + (1-p') * C_{\text{current node,down}}}{r} \quad \text{(BOPM for } N=1\text{)}$$

This formula is simply the BOPM for $N=1$. It is usually called a *risk-neutral valuation relation* (RNVR) and it emerges directly from the replication strategy, as we have seen in Chapter 13.

Note that $C_{\text{current node,up}}$ refers to the value of the option if the stock price goes up over the immediately following period, and $C_{\text{current node, down}}$ refers to the value of the option if the stock price goes down over the immediately following period.

As an example, suppose that we are in the BOPM, $N=2$ situation, and the stock has gone up over the first period. Therefore, we want to value C_u. This scenario is illustrated in Figure 14.5.

FIGURE 14.5 Valuing C_u

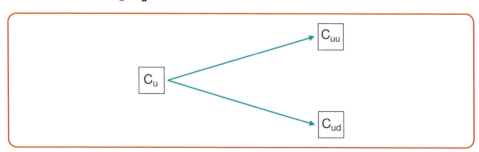

Applying the algorithm yields,

$$C_u = \frac{p' * C_{uu} + (1-p') * C_{ud}}{r}$$

The values of C_{uu} and C_{ud} are determined by the intrinsic values at the corresponding terminal stock prices u^2S_0 and duS_0.

Next, we can determine C_d in an identical manner using the relevant part of the Binomial tree reproduced below in Figure 14.6. The algorithm yields,

$$C_d = \frac{p' * C_{du} + (1-p') * C_{dd}}{r}$$

FIGURE 14.6 Valuing C_d

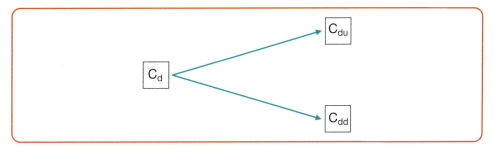

Now, we have all the information needed to determine the complete hedging program in Table 14.3, because that entire program is based on C_u, C_d, $C_{ud} = C_{du}$, C_{uu}, C_{dd}, the parameters d, u, r, and the current stock price S_0.

A Numerical Example of the BOPM, N=2

An example illustrating the calculation of the hedge program follows. The basic parameters in this model are, $u'=.10$, $d'=-.05$, $r'=.06$, $S_0=E=100$.

Then $u=1+u'=1.10$, $d=1+d'=0.95$, $r=1+r'=1.06$.

Figure 14.7 illustrates the stock price Binomial tree from which it is easy to read off the relevant intrinsic values, C_{uu}, C_{ud}, and C_{dd}.

Based on these ultimate stock price values, we obtain,

$C_{uu} = IV_{uu}$
   $= MAX[u^2S_0 - E, 0]$
   $= MAX[121-100, 0]$
   $= 21$,

FIGURE 14.7 Stock Price Tree for the BOPM, N=2

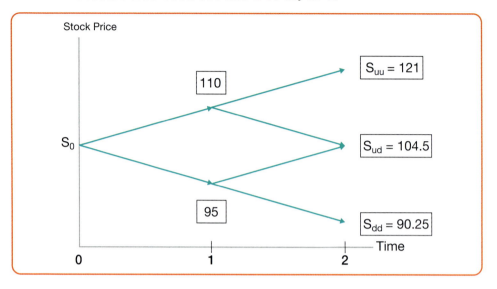

$$C_{ud} = IV_{ud}$$
$$= MAX[duS_0 - E, 0]$$
$$= MAX[104.5 - 100, 0]$$
$$= 4.5,$$

and

$$C_{dd} = IV_{dd}$$
$$= MAX[d^2 S_0 - E, 0]$$
$$= MAX[90.25 - 100, 0]$$
$$= 0.$$

To determine C_u and C_d we apply the algorithm,

a. Given the option parameters d, r, and u, calculate the 'risk-neutral' (certainty-equivalent) probabilities $p' = (r-d)/(u-d)$ and $1-p' = (u-r)/(u-d)$.
   This produces $p' = (1.06 - 0.95)/(1.10 - 0.95) = .11/.15 = .7333$, and therefore $1-p' = .2667$.
b. Then, no matter what node one is at in the tree, the option value at that point is simply the RNVR,

OPTION PRICING IN DISCRETE TIME, PART 2 — 489

$$C_u = \frac{p' * C_{uu} + (1 - p') * C_{ud}}{r}$$

$$= \frac{[.7333 * 21 + .2667 * 4.5]}{1.06}$$

$$= 15.66038$$

and,

$$C_d = \frac{p' * C_{du} + (1 - p') * C_{dd}}{r}$$

$$= \frac{[+.7333 * 4.5 + .2667 * 0.0]}{1.06}$$

$$= \frac{3.3}{1.06}$$

$$= 3.113$$

Now we can fill in the entire hedging strategy in Table14.4.

TABLE 14.4 **Complete Hedging Strategy for the BOPM ($N=2$) Example**

Period	Hedge Ratio	Bond Position
1	$\Delta = 0.836492$	$B = -72.031830$
2 (up)	$\Delta_u = 1.0$	$B_u = -94.3396$
2 (down)	$\Delta_d = 0.3158$	$B_d = -26.8868$

Using the period 1 hedge ratio, Δ, and the dollar bond position B, we can easily price the option at time $t=0$ as the price of its replicating portfolio,

$$C_0 = \Delta S_0 + B$$

$$= 0.836492 * 100 - 72.0318$$

$$= 11.61737$$

■ CONCEPT CHECK 5

a. Verify the numbers in Table 14.4.

490 **OPTIONS**

■ CONCEPT CHECK 6

The other way to directly value this option at time $t=0$ is using the RNVR,

$$C_{\text{current node}} = \frac{p' * C_{\text{current node,up}} + (1-p') * C_{\text{current node,down}}}{r} \qquad \textbf{(RNVR)}$$

a. What is the current node in this case?
b. What is $C_{\text{current node,up}}$ in this case?
c. What is $C_{\text{current node,down}}$ in this case?
d. Use (RNVR) in conjunction with p' and $1-p'$ to calculate C_0.
e. Do you get the same answer as the replicating portfolio method generates?

We can also look at the BOPM, $N>1$ as a pure formula, that essentially gives European option prices in closed form. We will do this in section 14.4. Then, we want to understand the BOPM, $N>1$ formula as the result of a more general option pricing technique in section 14.5.

That approach weaves together the individual BOPMs in the model and takes a bigger, more macro, path approach to option pricing. It forms part of the foundation for Chapter 16, where we price options in continuous time.

14.4 THE BOPM, *N*>1 AS A RNVR FORMULA

First note that replicating (hedging) implies no–arbitrage, unique pricing, as we have discussed and just seen. The price of any reasonable contingent claim in complete markets is just the price of its replicating portfolio.

We can sometimes write down a closed–form equation formula for the current option price without going through all the individual hedges. However, ultimately such formulas are the results of this process. The hedging process is just hidden away.

Remember that the ability to *uniquely* price a contingent claim rests on the ability to replicate (hedge) it. This is the key lesson of the *Second Fundamental Theorem of Asset Pricing* (FTAP$_2$), that hedging is intimately tied in with unique pricing. The two cannot be separated. At least, this is what FTAP$_2$ says. In brief, it says that *'unique, arbitrage-free pricing is equivalent to replicability'*.

It is easier to at first focus on the case $N=2$. So we will do so. The concept in (pure) pricing is to recognize that the BOPM, $N=2$ is simply a set of BOPMs,

OPTION PRICING IN DISCRETE TIME, PART 2

FIGURE 14.8 The BOPM, $N=2$, as a Set of BOPMs, $N=1$

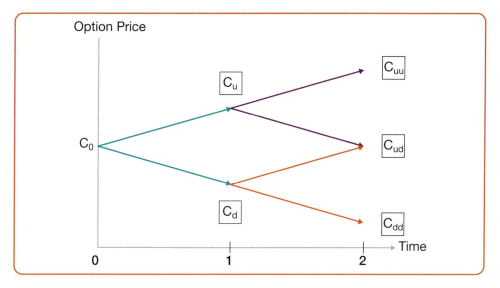

$N=1$. This is also true for $N>2$. By examining the option tree in Figure 14.8, this becomes apparent.

There are three distinct single-period BOPMs embedded in Figure 14.8 and they are indicated by the three colors. Option pricing for each of these three imbedded single-period BOPMs is easily given by the RNVR algorithm,

$$C_{\text{current node}} = \frac{p' * C_{\text{current node,up}} + (1-p') * C_{\text{current node,down}}}{r} \quad \text{(RNVR)}$$

1. One BOPM emanating from C_0 (blue) giving,

$$C_0 = \frac{p' * C_u + (1-p') * C_d}{r}$$

2. One BOPM emanating from C_u (purple) giving,

$$C_u = \frac{p' * C_{uu} + (1-p') * C_{ud}}{r}$$

3. One BOPM emanating from C_d (orange) giving,

$$C_d = \frac{p' * C_{ud} + (1-p') * C_{dd}}{r}$$

The quickest and slickest proof of the BOPM, $N=2$ is to substitute both the option pricing formula in 2. for C_u and the option pricing formula in 3. for C_d into C_u and C_d as they appear in 1. It's slick but not particularly enlightening, and it's hard to apply for $N>2$, so we will pursue other pricing methods below.

Carrying out the substitution procedure described above,

$$C_0 = \frac{p' * C_u + (1-p') * C_d}{r}$$

$$= \frac{p' * \left[\dfrac{p' * C_{uu} + (1-p') * C_{ud}}{r}\right] + (1-p') * \left[\dfrac{p' * C_{ud} + (1-p') * C_{dd}}{r}\right]}{r}$$

$$= \left[\frac{p'^2 * C_{uu} + p'(1-p') * C_{ud}}{r^2}\right] + \left[\frac{(1-p') * p' * C_{ud} + (1-p')^2 * C_{dd}}{r^2}\right]$$

$$= \frac{p'^2 * C_{uu} + 2p'(1-p') * C_{ud} + (1-p')^2 * C_{dd}}{r^2}$$

$$= \frac{\sum_{j=0,1,2} C(2,j)\,(p')^j (1-p')^{2-j} C_{u^j d^{2-j}}}{r^2}$$

we can guess that the general Binomial option pricing formula for all N is,

$$\frac{\sum_{j=0,1,\dots N} C(N,j)\,(p')^j (1-p')^{N-j} C_{u^j d^{N-j}}}{r^N} \qquad \textbf{(BOPM, all } N\textbf{)}$$

where we use the notation we developed in Chapter 13. In our case of $N=2$, our result is the same as the general formula for $N=2$.

Recall that $C(N,j)$ is the number of ways of choosing j up moves from among N periods. $C_{u^j d^{N-j}}$ is the option's intrinsic value at time N, based upon j up moves and $N-j$ down moves in the stock over the N periods.

This is the usual formula for BOPM, $N=2$, and we can verify that it gives the same option value C_0 as the replicating portfolio method, where $p'=.7333$, $C_{uu}=21$, $C_{ud}=4.5$, $C_{dd}=0$ and $r=1.06$.

Using Microsoft Excel, we obtain $C_0=11.6174$, which is the same answer we obtained earlier using replicating portfolio method.

OPTION PRICING IN DISCRETE TIME, PART 2 **493**

■ CONCEPT CHECK 7

a. Verify that (BOPM, N=2) gives the same option value C_0 as the replicating portfolio method, where p'=.7333, C_{uu}=21, C_{ud}=4.5, C_{dd}=0 and r=1.06.

We now want to present a different, but equivalent method, of pricing in the BOPM for general N. Hopefully, it helps to explain the rather cumbersome formula,

$$\frac{\sum_{j=0,1,\dots N} C(N,j)\,(p')^j(1-p')^{N-j}C_{u^j d^{N-j}}}{r^N} \qquad \textbf{(BOPM, all } N\textbf{)}$$

However it cannot, of course, give a *different price* than either the replicating portfolio method or the RNVR method; or, for that matter, different from the price generated by *any* other arbitrage-free procedure applied to the BOPM. You should think about why this is true.

14.5 MULTI-PERIOD BOPM, N>1: A PATH INTEGRAL APPROACH

14.5.1 Thinking of the BOPM in Terms of Paths

The idea behind the derivation of the BOPM for N=2 is to start from what is currently known, which consists of the option values at expiration. Then, one moves backwards one period to time N=1 and reaches the nodes C_u and C_d, the values of which are unknown.

In order to determine their values, one simply applies the single-period BOPM, (N=1) at each node C_u and C_d. Having done so, one moves back to time N=0. One again applies the single-period BOPM, (N=1) in order to determine C_0, which is possible because both C_u and C_d are known.

The exact same procedure works for N>2. Look at Figure 14.9 describing the evolution of the option price for N=3.

We start at the *highest* node in the tree, namely C_{uuu} at expiration. Now we move back in the tree to the highest node at N–1=2, which is C_{uu}. To determine C_{uu}, we apply the single-period BOPM using the known values of C_{uuu} and C_{uud}.

Similarly, we determine *all the other* nodal values at N–1 by repeatedly applying the single-period BOPM at each node. C_{ud}, for example, is determined from C_{uud} and C_{udd}. C_{dd} is determined from C_{udd} and C_{ddd}.

FIGURE 14.9 The BOPM for N=3

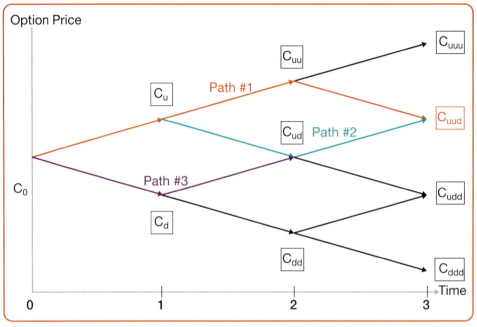

Then, we move back another step to N=1 and determine C_u and C_d by reapplying the single-period BOPM. Finally, we determine C_0 from a single application of the single-period BOPM, applied to the now known values of C_u and C_d.

There is another approach which is based on the *paths* of the process and does not calculate the *full* option value at each node. Rather, it looks at the tree in terms of individual paths and just values the *contribution* of cash flows at the end of path segments to the full nodal value, which is at the beginning of the given path.

This approach is consistent with the way the formula is usually written,

$$\frac{\sum_{j=0,1,\ldots N} C(N,j)\,(p')^j (1-p')^{N-j} C_{u^j d^{N-j}}}{r^N} \quad \text{(BOPM, all } N\text{)}$$

and helps to elucidate it. We want to be able to fully explain each term in this formula.

In order to tackle the general case, we will start with the BOPM for N=3 to get the basic idea of valuation in terms of individual paths. So, re-consider Figure 14.9.

OPTION PRICING IN DISCRETE TIME, PART 2 · 495

As an example, we focus on a terminal option value at $N=3$, say C_{uud} indicated by the color orange. We first ask how many paths terminate at C_{uud}. The answer is clearly the three paths indicated or $C(3, 2)$ paths where $N=3$ and the number of up moves over the life of the option is $j=2$. We list all the paths terminating at C_{uud}.

1. *Path 1 (all orange)* is $C_0 C_u C_{uu} C_{uud}$.
2. *Path 2 (orange, blue, blue)* is $C_0 C_u C_{ud} C_{uud}$.
3. *Path 3 (purple, purple, blue)* is $C_0 C_d C_{ud} C_{uud}$.

We want to move *backwards* along each path to the previous node on each path. This time, instead of calculating the *full* option value at each previous node using the single-period BOPM, we will calculate the *contribution* to the full nodal value made by the the value at the end of each path segment. This is easier to show than to explain in words, but it will become clear as we work through our example.

Using our example again, re-consider Path 1 and start at C_{uud}. Moving backward to the previous node on that path along the path segment $C_{uu} C_{uud}$, we easily arrive at C_{uu}. Then, we *partially* apply the single-period BOPM to calculate the *contribution* to the full option value of C_{uu} made by what is at the end of the path segment, C_{uud}.

This means that we are at C_{uu} and that we apply the appropriate risk-neutral probability to C_{uud} and discount by the risk-free rater (as opposed to including C_{uuu} as well and calculating the full option value C_{uu}). That is, we are simply calculating *that part* of the full option value C_{uu} contributed by the end point of Path 1, namely by C_{uud}.

The first step is, of course, to determine the correct risk-neutral probability. Since the path segment $C_{uu} C_{uud}$ corresponds to a *down* move from C_{uu}, the risk-neutral probability is $(1-p')$ where p' is defined as before.

Then the value of the contribution of C_{uud} to C_{uu} is its correctly discounted present value. This is clearly $(1-p')*C_{uud}/r$ where p' is the risk-neutral probability. Keep in mind that this path contribution is *part*, but *not all*, of the full value of C_{uu}.

Next, we examine the *previous* path segment of Path 1, $C_u C_{uu}$, imagining that we are now standing at C_u. Here, we want to calculate the *contribution* to the full option value C_u made by the path segment $C_u C_{uu}$. The answer is $p'*C_{uu}/r$ since $C_u C_{uu}$ constitutes an *up* move from C_u.

496 OPTIONS

Note that this is how one would value the *entire* value of C_{uu}. But we only want the value *contributed* to C_{uu} by the path segment $C_{uu}C_{uud}$. So, we need to link up the path segment $C_{uu}C_{uud}$ to the path segment $C_{u}C_{uu}$ in terms of the risk-neutral probabilities.

The subsequent path segment $C_{uu}C_{uud}$ only contributes $(1-p')*C_{uud}/r$ to C_{uu}, as demonstrated in the second previous paragraph, and it is *this* value that we are interested in.

Remember that the *full* value of C_{uu} does not matter, only the *contribution* to its value made by the path segment $C_{uu}C_{uud}$ is relevant. We computed this contribution as $(1-p')*C_{uud}/r$. Applying p' to this *contributed* quantity, rather than to the full C_{uu}, and discounting by r, we obtain $[p'*[((1-p')*C_{uud})/r]]/r$ or $[p'*(1-p')*C_{uud}]/r^2$. This represents the *contribution* to C_u made by the ultimate endpoint of the path, C_{uud}.

Finally, we look at the *contribution* to the time 0 option value made by the last path segment of Path 1, C_0C_u, and that is $p'C_u/r$. Of course, the *whole* of C_u is not relevant for our purposes. Only $[p'*(1-p')*C_{uud}]/r^2$ is relevant, as just demonstrated. This corresponds to the time 0 value of $[(p'*[p'*(1-p')* C_{uud}])/r^2]/r$ or $[p'*p'*(1-p')*C_{uud}]/r^3$.

Thus, we have calculated that part of the value of C_{uud} which is contributed to the time-zero option value C_0 by Path 1 as $[p'*p'*(1-p')*C_{uud}]/r^3$. Another equivalent way to write this quantity is as $[(p')^2*(1-p')*C_{uud}]/r^3$.

This is useful, as we will see. Notice that it is the discounted, risk-neutral, present value of the product of C_{uud} times the joint probability of its occurring at the end of Path 1.

■ CONCEPT CHECK 8

a. Run through the path *contribution analysis* for Path 2 to obtain the contribution made by C_{uud} to C_0 along Path 2.

■ CONCEPT CHECK 9

a. Run through the *path contribution analysis* for Path 3 to obtain the contribution made by C_{uud} to C_0 along Path 3.

OPTION PRICING IN DISCRETE TIME, PART 2 **497**

To summarize, each path segment of each of the three paths terminating at C_{uud} makes a *contribution* to the option price at time 0 in accordance with the risk-neutral path probability assigned to it.

If we look at the path segments of path 2, for example, $C_0 C_u$ has risk-neutral probability p', because it corresponds to an up move in the underlying stock from C_0. $C_u C_{ud}$ has risk-neutral probability $(1-p')$, because it corresponds to a down move in the underlying stock from C_u. Finally, $C_{ud} C_{uud}$ also has risk-neutral probability p', because it corresponds to an up move in the underlying stock from C_{ud}. Thus the (joint) path probability for path 2 is $p'*(1-p')*p'$.

Similarly, Path 1 has risk-neutral path probability $p'*p'*(1-p')$ and Path 3 has risk-neutral path probability $(1-p')*p'*p'$. Note that all these three paths have the *same* joint risk-neutral probability $(p'^2)*(1-p')$. So, the *sum* of their path probabilities is just $3*(p'^2)*(1-p')$.

The contribution to C_0 of the terminal option price C_{uud}, made through all the paths terminating at C_{uud}, is its risk-neutral discounted value which is simply equal to $[3*(p'^2)*(1-p')C_{uud}]/r^3$.

If we perform this counting exercise for the remaining three outcomes of the option price process, C_{uuu}, C_{udd} and C_{ddd}, discount by r^3, and add them up, we will end up with the BOPM, $N=3$ value of C_0. To accomplish this, we reproduce the relevant information from Chapter 13 in Table 14.5.

TABLE 14.5 **Path Structure of the BOPM, $N=3$**

Terminal Stock Price	Terminal Option Price	Number of Option Price Paths Terminating in Terminal Option Price	Risk-Neutral Path Probability
S_{uuu}	C_{uuu}	$C(3, 3)=1$	p'^3
S_{uud}	C_{uud}	$C(3, 2)=3$	$p'^2*(1-p')$
S_{udd}	C_{udd}	$C(3, 1)=3$	$p'*(1-p')^2$
S_{ddd}	C_{ddd}	$C(3, 0)=1$	$(1-p')^3$

Then, Table 14.6 gives the contribution to C_0 made by all the paths. Outside the brackets on the left are the number of paths terminating in the given terminal option value. Inside the bracket is the joint risk-neutral probability of arriving at the given terminal option value times that terminal option value. Outside the brackets on the right, is the compounded risk-free rate.

498 OPTIONS

TABLE 14.6 **Value Contributions to C_0 made by the Paths of the BOPM, $N=3$**

Terminal Option Price	Contribution to C_0
C_{uuu}	$1 * \dfrac{p'^3 * C_{uuu}}{r^3}$
C_{uud}	$3 * \dfrac{p'^2 * (1-p') C_{uud}}{r^3}$
C_{udd}	$3 * \dfrac{p' * (1-p')^2 C_{udd}}{r^3}$
C_{ddd}	$3 * \dfrac{(1-p')^3 C_{ddd}}{r^3}$

When we add all these contributions up we obtain the European option price at time 0,

$$C_0 = 1 * \frac{p'^3 * C_{uuu}}{r^3} + 3 * \frac{p'^2 * (1-p') * C_{uud}}{r^3} + 3 * \frac{p' * (1-p')^2 * C_{udd}}{r^3}$$

$$+ 1 * \frac{(1-p')^3 * C_{ddd}}{r^3}$$

$$= \frac{p'^3 * C_{uuu} + 3 * p'^2 * (1-p') * C_{uud} + 3 * p' * (1-p')^2 * C_{udd} + (1-p')^3 * C_{ddd}}{r^3}$$

But, this is exactly the same as the (BOPM, $N=3$) pricing formula, as it must be,

$$C_0 = \frac{\sum_{j=0,1,2,3} C(3,j) \, (p')^j (1-p')^{3-j} C_{u^j d^{3-j}}}{r^3}$$

■ CONCEPT CHECK 10

a. Verify the last statement that,

$$\frac{p'^3 * C_{uuu} + 3 * p'^2 * (1-p') * C_{uud} + 3 * p' * (1-p')^2 * C_{udd} + (1-p')^3 * C_{ddd}}{r^3}$$

$$= \frac{\sum_{j=0,1,2,3} C(3,j) \, (p')^j (1-p')^{3-j} C_{u^j d^{3-j}}}{r^3}$$

OPTION PRICING IN DISCRETE TIME, PART 2 — 499

14.5.2 Proof of the BOPM Model for general *N*

Now we can give an easy proof of the BOPM for *any* N based on the summary Figure 14.10. It's a simple counting exercise based on the path analysis we accomplished.

FIGURE 14.10 **Summary of Stock Price Evolution (*N*-Period Binomial Process)**

Terminal Stock Price	Number of Price Paths Terminating in Terminal Stock Price	Risk-Neutral Path Probability
$S_N = u^j d^{N-j} S_0$	$C(N, j)$	$(p')^j (1 - p')^{N-j}$

1. For each terminal option price $C_{u^j d^{N-j}}$ corresponding to j up moves and $N-j$ down moves in the underlying stock price, there are $C(N,j)$ paths terminating at $C_{u^j d^{N-j}}$.

2. The risk-neutral path joint probability of each one of these paths is $(p')^j (1-p')^{N-j}$.

3. The *contribution* of $C_{u^j d^{N-j}}$ to C_0 is the number of paths times the risk-neutral path probability times the terminal value $C_{u^j d^{N-j}}$ discounted by r^N. That is,

$$\frac{C(N,j) * (p')^j (1 - p')^{N-j} * C_{u^j d^{N-j}}}{r^N}$$

4. Now, add up all these contributions across all the paths corresponding to $j=0, 1,\ldots,N$ to obtain the multi-period BOPM for any N where we factored out r^N because it is common to all terms in the sum,

$$C_0 = \frac{\sum_{j=0,1,\ldots N} C(N,j) * (p')^j * (1 - p')^{N-j} * C_{u^j d^{N-j}}}{r^N} \qquad \textbf{(BOPM, all } N\textbf{)}$$

500   **OPTIONS**

We know that this is the correct option price, because *it is exactly the same one that would be generated by dynamic replication*. There can't be anything too new in a complete model. However, there are some new ideas in the proof. It's part of the martingale approach to pricing derivatives which we turn to in Chapter 15.

OPTION PRICING IN DISCRETE TIME, PART 2 **501**

■ KEY CONCEPTS

1. Modeling Time and Uncertainty in the BOPM, $N>1$.
2. Stock Price Behavior, $N=2$.
3. Option Price Behavior, $N=2$.
4. Hedging a European Call Option, $N=2$.
5. Step 1, Parameterization.
6. Step 2, Defining the Hedge Ratio and the Dollar Bond Position.
7. Step 3, Constructing the Replicating Portfolio.
8. Replication under Scenario 1, over Period 2.
9. Replication in the Up State.
10. Replication in the Down State.
11. Solving the Two Equations for Δ_u and B_u.
12. The Complete Hedging Program for the BOPM, $N=2$.
13. Implementation of the BOPM for $N=2$.
14. The BOPM, $N>1$ as a RNVR Formula.
15. Multi-period BOPM, $N>1$: A Path Integral Approach.
16. Thinking of the BOPM in Terms of Paths.
17. Proof of the BOPM Model for general N.

■ END OF CHAPTER EXERCISES FOR CHAPTER 14

1. The current price of a share of RJR Nabisco Co. common stock is $100. The stock price can only go up by 10% with probability 0.5, or it can go down by 5% with probability 0.5 in each period.

   Consider a *two-period* European call option written on RJR Nabisco Co. stock with current value C_0. The call option is written so that it is currently *At-the-Money* and the riskless rate per period is 7%.

   a. Refer to the Binomial tree for the underlying asset price in Chapter 13, End of Chapter Exercise 2, part a.
   b. Calculate the current price of the European call option according to the two-period binomial option pricing model.

2. Consider Figure 11.4 from Chapter 11, reproduced below. Answer the following questions:

   a. What is the monotonicity property?
   b. What is the convexity property?

c. Are a. and b. *rational* option properties?
d. Pick a stock price, on the horizontal axis around E. Go directly up to the European option price and draw a tangent to the option price graph. What does the slope of that tangent line represent?
e. What happens to the slope of the tangent line in d. as the stock price changes from $S_t=0$ to above E?
f. Interpret the result of e. in terms of the replicating portfolio.

FIGURE 11.4 A European Call Option Price, $C^E(S_t,\tau,E)$, for a Given Maturity $\tau=T-t$

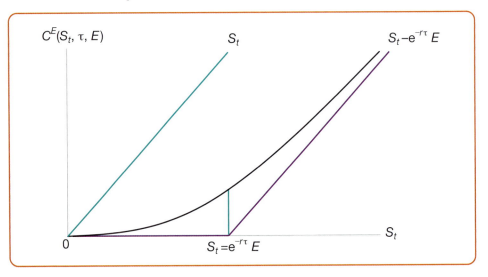

3. *(Constructing the Replicating Portfolio under Scenario 2)*

First, recall *Scenario 2*, which is that at the end of the first period the stock price has decreased to S_d and the option price to C_d.

Step 1, Parameterization, is the same in that u, d, and r are the same constants and $d<r<u$ to avoid arbitrage.

For Step 2, defining the hedge ratio and the dollar bond position, let Δ_d be the number of shares to hold in the replicating portfolio per share of stock underlying the option. The subscript d helps us remember that we are constructing the hedge based on a starting stock price equal to S_d.

Let B_d be the dollar position in riskless bonds needed to replicate the option over period 2. Note that $B_d<0$ means we borrow at the riskless rate.

Let C_d be the current value of the European call option when the stock price is S_d. C_d depends on the current value of the underlying stock, S_d, the number of periods to expiration, $N-1=1$, and the exercise price E. So we can write $C_d = C(S_d, 1; E)$. This is what we are trying to determine.

Now we let time pass, and see what happens to the option's value as the stock price either goes up or goes down over the second period. If the stock price goes up, the option price will also go up. If the stock price goes down, then the option price will also go down.

Let C_{du} be the value of the option at time $N=2$ *if* the stock price goes up over the second period. Using our notation $C_{du} = C_{du}(udS_0, 0; E)$, which represents the value of the option based on the new stock price udS_0, no time to expiration since $N-2=0$, and exercise price E.

Let C_{dd} be the value of the option at time $N=2$ *if* the stock price goes down over the second period. Using our notation again, $C_{dd} = C_{dd}(d^2 S_0, 0; E)$, which represents the value of the option based on the new stock price $d^2 S_0$, no time to expiration since $N-2=0$, and exercise price E.

We know that $C_{du} = IV_{du} = \text{MAX}[0, udS_0 - E]$ and that $C_{dd} = IV_{dd} = \text{MAX}[0, d^2 S_0 - E]$, where IV_{du} means intrinsic value if the stock price goes up, and IV_{ud} means intrinsic value if the stock price goes down over the second period.

The schematic is given in a. and is what we call the 'natural' or actual call option under Scenario 2. This is the object to be synthesized by the replicating portfolio.

a. Fill in the question marks in all of the figures below.

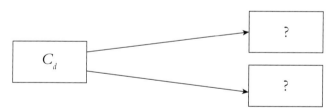

Next, we represent the replicating portfolio,

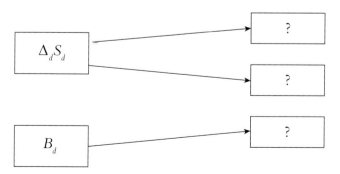

504 OPTIONS

Replication must be done for both the up state and the down state. Up state means that the stock price goes up over the second period. Down state means that the stock price goes down over the second period.

A. Replication in the Up State

b. The call option's payoff if the stock price goes *up* over the second period= _____ .

c. The replicating portfolio's payoff=payoff to _____ stocks and $_____ in bonds= _____+_____.

d. Replication in the up state over the second period means that

$$_____ + _____ = _____. \qquad \textbf{(up)}$$

B. Replication in the Down State

e. The call option's payoff if the stock price goes *down* over the second period=_____ .

f. The replicating portfolio's payoff=payoff to _____ stocks and $_____ in bonds=_____ _____ .

g. Replication in the down state means that

$$_____ + _____ = _____. \qquad \textbf{(down)}$$

We now have two equations in two unknowns which must hold simultaneously in exercise 4.

4. *(This exercise is a continuation of exercise 3.)*

C. Solving the Two Equations for Δ_d and B_d

h. The two equations are,

$$_____ = _____ \qquad \textbf{(up)}$$
$$_____ = _____ \qquad \textbf{(down)}$$

i. To solve for Δ_d, just subtract (down) from (up) to obtain,

$$_____ = _____$$

which when solved gives the hedge ratio Δ_d,

$$\Delta_d = _____ \qquad \textbf{(Δ_d)}$$

j. Interpret the hedge ratio Δ_d

OPTION PRICING IN DISCRETE TIME, PART 2 — 505

k. Next, solve for the dollar position in bonds, B_d. Substitute (Δ_d) into (down) to obtain,

$$\underline{\hspace{2cm}} + \underline{\hspace{2cm}} = \underline{\hspace{2cm}} \ .$$

Therefore,

$$B_d = \underline{\hspace{2cm}} \ .$$

l. Interpret B_d.

■ SELECTED CONCEPT CHECK SOLUTIONS

Concept Check 2

a. There are $N+1=2+1=3$ ultimate 'states of nature' in the BOPM for $N=2$.

b. There are three distinct ultimate option prices in the BOPM for $N=2$. These are the three distinct option prices C_{uu}, C_{ud}, and C_{dd} corresponding to the driving ultimate stock prices, S_{uu}, S_{ud}, and S_{dd}.

c. Recall the useful rule of thumb from Chapter 13: *if there are as many independent primitive securities as there are states of the world, then the market is complete.*

d. It suggests that it might be impossible if we take that rule literally. From our rule of thumb presented in Chapter 13, it would appear that two securities are insufficient to span these outcomes and thereby hedge the option.

e. It means that the rule describes a condition under which the market is complete. That is what '*sufficient*' means. However, the market can be complete without the condition in the rule of thumb holding. This is what '*not necessary*' means. There could be other sufficient conditions for the market to be complete *even if* there are more states of nature than independent hedging securities.

f. More trading opportunities, specifically dynamic hedging, will help us replicate a European call option with only our two independent securities. The proliferation of dynamic trading strategies makes up for this gap.

 We still only need the stock and a riskless bond to dynamically hedge the option, because there are only two sources of uncertainty in the dynamic BOPM model. In effect, the model is reduced to a sequence of single-period BOPMs, with *different* hedge ratios Δs and dollar bond positions Bs for each period.

OPTIONS

A more refined version of the rule of thumb from Chapter 13, section 13.5.2, would say that: *if there are as many independent securities as there are sources of risk in the model, then the model is* dynamically *complete.* Under this interpretation, the $N=2$, BOPM is *dynamically* complete. However, you still need dynamic hedging in order to be *dynamically complete.*

Concept Check 8

The answer is the risk-neutral path probability $p'*(1-p')*p'$ times C_{uud}, discounted by r over three periods. That is, $[p'*(1-p')*p'*C_{uud}]/r^3$.

Concept Check 9

The answer is the risk-neutral path probability $(1-p')*p'*p'$ times C_{uud}, discounted by r over three periods. That is, $[(1-p')*p'*p'*C_{uud}]/r^3$.

CHAPTER 15

EQUIVALENT MARTINGALE MEASURES: A MODERN APPROACH TO OPTION PRICING

15.1 Primitive Arrow–Debreu Securities and Option Pricing ... 508

    15.1.1 Exercise 1, Pricing $B(0,1)$ ... 510

    15.1.2 Exercise 2, Pricing $AD_u(\omega)$ and $AD_d(\omega)$ ... 511

15.2 Contingent Claim Pricing ... 514

    15.2.1 Pricing a European Call Option ... 514

    15.2.2 Pricing any Contingent Claim ... 515

15.3 Equivalent Martingale Measures (EMMs) ... 517

    15.3.1 Introduction and Examples ... 517

    15.3.2 Definition of a Discrete-Time Martingale ... 521

15.4 Martingales and Stock Prices ... 521

    15.4.1 The Equivalent Martingale Representation of Stock Prices ... 524

15.5 The Equivalent Martingale Representation of Option Prices ... 526

    15.5.1 Discounted Option Prices ... 527

    15.5.2 Summary of the EMM Approach ... 528

15.6 The Efficient Market Hypothesis (EMH), A Guide To Modeling Prices ... 529

15.7 Appendix: Essential Martingale Properties ... 533

508 OPTIONS

We will start by revisiting risk-neutral valuation in the context of the BOPM, $N=1$, and looking at it from the perspective of modern (post late 1970s) developments in asset pricing. The central notion here is that of an *equivalent martingale measure* (EMM). The name sounds intimidating but the underlying concept is quite simple.

The BOPM, $N=1$ is a two-state model, as discussed in Chapter 13, section 13.2.2. Let $\omega_1=\omega_u$ denote the state of the world, corresponding to the underlying stock going up to uS_0 at the end of the first and only period. Let $\omega_2=\omega_d$ denote the state of the world, corresponding to the underlying stock going down to dS_0 at the end of the first and only period. We collect these two possible states of the world to be revealed at the end of period one into one 'big' collection $\Omega=\{\omega_u,\omega_d\}$ which we will call the *'state space'*.

This is a finite, hence discrete state space, as opposed to the continuous state spaces corresponding to the continuity of the time and state (stock price) variables that we will discuss in continuous time in Chapter 16. Getting used to this jargon and notation helps orient one to the world of modern asset pricing.

15.1 PRIMITIVE ARROW–DEBREU SECURITIES AND OPTION PRICING

Now we introduce the key idea of (primitive) *Arrow–Debreu* (AD) securities. A (primitive) AD security is a *state-contingent* financial security that pays \$1 if a pre-specified state of the world occurs, and nothing if that state does not occur. In our simple BOPM, $N=1$ there are two primitive AD securities corresponding to the two states in $\Omega=\{\omega_u,\omega_d\}$,

$$AD_1(\omega)=AD_u(\omega)=1 \quad \text{if and only if } \omega=\omega_u$$
$$=0 \quad \text{if and only if } \omega=\omega_d$$

$$AD_2(\omega)=AD_d(\omega)=1 \quad \text{if and only if } \omega=\omega_d$$
$$=0 \quad \text{if and only if } \omega=\omega_u$$

Note here that we can form a new security $AD_{sum}(\omega)=AD_u(\omega)+AD_d(\omega)$, the sum of the two AD securities. However, $AD_{sum}(\omega)$ isn't a primitive AD security because it pays off \$1 in *both* states of the world ω_u and ω_d,

$$AD_{sum}(\omega_u)=AD_u(\omega_u)+AD_d(\omega_u)$$
$$=\$1+\$0$$
$$=\$1$$

EQUIVALENT MARTINGALE MEASURES **509**

and,

$$AD_{sum}(\omega_d)=AD_u(\omega_d)+AD_d(\omega_d)$$
$$=\$0+\$1$$
$$=\$1.$$

A financial security that pays a *certain* amount \$1, no matter what the state of the world turns out to be, is called a riskless bond. It is the easiest financial security to price, and we already did so both in discrete and in continuous time. Here, we price it in discrete time using the AD approach, since the BOPM is a discrete-time, discrete-state space model.

We assume that the market permits no-arbitrage. Then, by the first fundamental theorem of asset pricing (FTAP$_1$), there is a positive, linear pricing functional, $P_0(\cdot)$, that prices all reasonable contingent claims, which justifies the first equality below. The second equality is linearity. The third equality follows by replicating the riskless bond using the stock and the riskless bond. This is illustrated in the exercise 1 immediately following. We also assume that there is a riskless percentage rate of interest, r', and define $r=1+r'$ as one plus the riskless rate.

$$P_0\left(AD_{sum}(\omega)\right) = P_0\left(AD_u(\omega)+ AD_d(\omega)\right)$$
$$= P_0\left(AD_u(\omega)\right)+ P_0\left(AD_d(\omega)\right)$$
$$= \frac{1}{r}$$
$$= \frac{1}{1+r'}$$

The following set of exercises first shows, in exercise 1, how to use replication to price a unit discount bond in discrete time. Then, the primitive AD securities in the BOPM, $N=1$ model, $AD_u(\omega)$ and $AD_d(\omega)$ will be priced in exercise 2.

This is called *pricing the states*, u and d. Using these '*state prices*', in section 15.2.1 we price a European call option, for example. We can also price *any* contingent claim using the state prices.

510 **OPTIONS**

15.1.1 Exercise 1, Pricing $B(0,1)$

This exercise shows where the usual present value (PV) operator and pricing method comes from, at least when applied to riskless bonds. The PV method of pricing a riskless bond with a payoff of $1 at maturity (no matter what the state of the world) says that its price, $B(0,1)=PV(\$1$ to be received with certainty at the end of the period)$=1/r$, where r is the appropriately de-annualized risk-free rate. The exercise is to prove this result by replication.

Solution to Exercise 1

Form a replicating portfolio consisting of Δ units of the stock and a dollar position of $\$B$ in the riskless bond. For replication to occur, the following two equations must hold, because the riskless bond pays $1 in each state,

$$\Delta(uS_0)+rB=1.0 \qquad \textbf{(up)}$$

$$\Delta(dS_0)+rB=1.0 \qquad \textbf{(down)}$$

Solving, by subtracting (down) from (up) we obtain $\Delta=0$ (why?) and therefore $rB=1.0$ from which $B=1/r$. Note that B is the same as $B(0,1)$, because B is the dollar amount of bonds to hold, which is just the price of the bonds being held.

We realize that this replication is 'trivial', because to replicate the bond with the stock and the bond all we have to do is zero out the stock price and hold a dollar bond position equal to $\$1/r$. This demonstration shows that you can do it mechanically.

By no-arbitrage, the usual PV formula results,

$$
\begin{aligned}
B(0,1) &= \Delta S_0 + B \\
&= 0 * S_0 + B \\
&= B \\
&= \frac{1}{r} \\
&= PV \ (\$1 \text{ to be received with certainty at the end of the period})
\end{aligned}
$$

15.1.2 Exercise 2, Pricing $AD_u(\omega)$ and $AD_d(\omega)$

First, note that because $P_0(AD_u(\omega))+P_0(AD_d(\omega))=B(0,1)=1/r$, our workload in pricing $AD_u(\omega)$ and $AD_d(\omega)$ is cut in half. If we can price either $AD_u(\omega)$ or $AD_d(\omega)$ then the price of the other follows from $P_0(AD_u(\omega))+P_0(AD_d(\omega))=1/r$. Say we have priced $AD_u(\omega)$. Then $P_0(AD_d(\omega))=1/r-P_0(AD_u(\omega))$.

So how do we price $AD_u(\omega)$? Static replication using the underlying stock and the riskless bond is the pricing tool of choice because, if it is replicable, then it is therefore *uniquely* priced by replication (FTAP$_2$).

Just as in the BOPM, (N=1), we have at our disposal the underlying stock and the riskless bond with which to replicate the first AD primitive security $AD_u(\omega)$. Replication has the usual meaning of finding the hedge ratio, Δ, and the dollar position, B, in the riskless bond so that the resulting replicating portfolio (RP) has exactly the same payoffs as $AD_u(\omega)$ in all states of the world in $\Omega=\{\omega_u,\omega_d\}$.

This means that the following two equations hold,

$$\Delta u S_0+rB=AD_u(\omega_u)$$
$$=1.0 \qquad\qquad\qquad \textbf{(up)}$$

$$\Delta d S_0+rB=AD_u(\omega_d)$$
$$=0.0 \qquad\qquad\qquad \textbf{(down)}$$

To solve for Δ, just subtract (down) from (up) to obtain,

$$\Delta u S_0-\Delta d S_0=1.0-0.0$$
$$=1.0,$$

which when solved gives the hedge ratio Δ,

$$\Delta = \frac{1.0}{(uS_0 - dS_0)}$$
$$= \frac{1.0}{(u - d)S_0}$$

512 OPTIONS

To solve for B just solve (down),

$$rB = -\Delta dS_0$$

$$= \left[\frac{-1.0}{(u-d)S_0}\right]dS_0$$

$$= \left[\frac{-dS_0}{(u-d)S_0}\right]$$

$$= \frac{-d}{u-d}$$

Dividing by r we obtain the required dollar bond position,

$$B = \frac{-d}{r(u-d)}$$

We've just demonstrated that $AD_u(\omega)$ is replicable. Therefore, by FTAP$_2$, its no-arbitrage price must be equal to the price of its replicating portfolio. (This is what FTAP$_2$ says: replication identifies the unique, no-arbitrage price associated with the replicated asset).

$$P_0\left(AD_{sum}(\omega)\right) = \Delta * S_0 + B$$

$$= \left[\frac{1.0}{(u-d)S_0}\right]S_0 + \left[\frac{-d}{r(u-d)}\right]$$

$$= \left[\frac{S_0}{(u-d)S_0}\right] - \left[\frac{d}{r(u-d)}\right]$$

$$= \left[\frac{1}{(u-d)}\right] - \left[\frac{d}{r(u-d)}\right]$$

$$= \left[\frac{r}{r(u-d)}\right] - \left[\frac{d}{r(u-d)}\right]$$

$$= \frac{r-d}{r(u-d)}$$

If we go back to the BOPM, ($N=1$), we find that the risk–neutral probability in that model is p' where,

$$p' = \frac{r-d}{u-d}$$

From this, it follows that the price of the first primitive AD security is the risk neutral probability corresponding to the up state, p', divided by one plus the risk-free rate r.

$$P_0\left(AD_u(\omega)\right) = \frac{p'}{r}$$

The argument for why this makes economic sense is that the risk-averse option valuation exercise performed by any risk-averse investor generates exactly the same option valuation that would be produced by a risk neutral investor (see Chapter 17). This is because replication (hedging) implies that the resulting option valuation doesn't depend on investors' risk preferences. Thus, the risk-neutral investor's valuation would be universally accepted by all investors, provided they accept replication. This is called *consensus*.

We don't have to ban risk preferences in valuing options. Far from it. They wash out on their own in the riskless hedge, as can be precisely demonstrated. What we can do for simplicity is just start with a risk-neutral investor and let him generate the option valuation. Why? It's just simpler that way. This is called *convenience*.

Now $AD_u(\omega)$ is a security paying \$1 if state ω_u occurs and \$0 if state ω_d occurs. The risk-neutralized probability of ω_u occurring is p' and therefore the risk-neutralized probability of ω_d occurring is $1-p'$.

The expected value of $AD_u(\omega)$'s payoffs at time $t=1$ is $p'(\$1)+(1-p')(\$0)=p'$. Of course, we have to discount this back to time $t=0$ to get its current price, $P_0(AD_u(\omega))$. Since the expected value is risk neutralized, meaning that it is calculated with respect to the risk neutral measure $(p', 1-p')$, the appropriate discount rate is therefore the risk-free rate $r=1+r'$.

Now, we can also price the second primitive AD security as discussed earlier as,

$$P_0\left(AD_d(\omega)\right) = \frac{1}{r} - P_0\left(AD_u(\omega)\right)$$

$$= \frac{1}{r} - \frac{p'}{r}$$

$$= \frac{1-p'}{r}$$

514 OPTIONS

Therefore, the second primitive AD security is also the risk-neutral probability corresponding to the down state, $1-p'$, divided by one plus the risk-free rate r. By exactly the same reasoning above as for $AD_u(\omega)$, this is exactly what it should be.

■ CONCEPT CHECK 1

a. Convince yourself why.

15.2 CONTINGENT CLAIM PRICING

We can actually use these primitive AD security prices as a *basis*, in the sense of linear algebra, for pricing *any* contingent claim in terms of the 'state prices'.

15.2.1 Pricing a European Call Option

For example, the price of a European call option, with payoff C_u in the up state and payoff C_d in the down state, is just,

$$
\begin{aligned}
C_0 &= P_0\big(AD_u(\omega)\big) * C_u + P_0\big(AD_d(\omega)\big) * C_d \\
&= \frac{p'}{r} * C_u + \frac{1-p'}{r} * C_d \\
&= \frac{p'C_u + (1-p')C_d}{r}
\end{aligned}
$$

■ CONCEPT CHECK 2

a. Interpret the quantity

$$
\frac{p'C_u + (1-p')C_d}{r}
$$

Comparing this to the BOPM, ($N=1$) formula, you will see that it is *exactly the same*. We know this *has to* happen. Why?

EQUIVALENT MARTINGALE MEASURES   515

We next turn to the question of why we can price any contingent claim if we can price the primitive AD securities.

15.2.2 Pricing any Contingent Claim

Consider a general contingent claim G that pays off $\$G_u$ if and only if the up state occurs, and it pays off $\$G_d$ if and only if the down state occurs. G_u doesn't have to be intrinsic value, because it is a general claim, which is not necessarily a European call option. Nor does G_d have to be intrinsic value.

Now, define a new state claim, G_u, that also pays off $\$G_u$ if and only if the up state occurs,

$$G_u(\omega)=\$G_u \quad \text{if and only if } \omega=\omega_u$$
$$=0 \quad \text{if } \omega=\omega_d$$

Also, define a new state claim that pays off $\$G_d$ if and only if the down state occurs. Again, G_d doesn't have to be intrinsic value, because it is a *general* claim which is not necessarily a European call option,

$$G_d(\omega)=\$G_d \quad \text{if } \omega=\omega_d$$
$$=0 \quad \text{if } \omega=\omega_u$$

Now consider the sum claim defined by,

$$G_{sum}(\omega)=G_u(\omega)+G_d(\omega).$$

Then,

$$G_{sum}(\omega_u)=G_u(\omega_u)+G_d(\omega_u)$$
$$=\$G_u+\$0$$
$$=\$G_u$$

and,

$$G_{sum}(\omega_d)=G_u(\omega_d)+G_d(\omega_d)$$
$$=\$0+\$G_d$$
$$=\$G_d$$

516 OPTIONS

Therefore, $G_{sum}(\omega)$ is a claim that pays off $\$G_u$ if and only if the up state occurs, and it pays off $\$G_d$ if and only if the down state occurs.

This security has exactly the same payoffs at time $t=1$ as our general contingent claim, $G(\omega)$. That is, $G(\omega)=G_u(\omega)+G_d(\omega)$ at time $t=1$, no matter what state occurs. To prevent arbitrage, the *current price* of G must be equal to the sum of the current prices of G_u and G_d.

Next, we can interpret $G_u(\omega)$ and $G_d(\omega)$ in terms of the primitive AD security state prices, $AD_u(\omega)$ and $AD_d(\omega)$, because there is very little difference between a security that pays \$1 if and only if state ω_u or state ω_d occurs and one that pays a constant dollar amount, $\$G_u$ or $\$G_d$ in these cases if and only if state ω_u or state ω_d occurs respectively.

Consider the new security defined by $\$G_u*AD_u(\omega)$. Its payoff is clearly $\$G_u$ if and only if $\omega=\omega_u$, and zero otherwise. But this is exactly the same payoff structure as $G_u(\omega)$. Therefore $G_u(\omega)=\$G_u*AD_u(\omega)$ and similarly $G_d(\omega)=\$G_d*AD_d(\omega)$. Why?

The only difference between $G_u(\omega)$ and $AD_u(\omega)$ is that $G_u(\omega)$ pays off $\$G_u$ while $AD_u(\omega)$ pays off \$1 if and only if state ω_u occurs. This is called *scaling*.

We have written the non-primitive AD securities, $G_u(\omega)$ and $G_d(\omega)$, in terms of the primitive AD securities. It follows that,

$$
\begin{aligned}
G(\omega)&=G_u(\omega)+G_d(\omega)\\
&=G_u*AD_u(\omega)+G_d*AD_d(\omega)
\end{aligned}
$$

Note that this shows that if we can price the primitive AD securities $AD_u(\omega)$ and $AD_d(\omega)$, then we can price *any* contingent claim.

By linearity of the pricing functional P_0 we obtain,

$$
\begin{aligned}
P_0(G(\omega))&=P_0(G_u*AD_u(\omega)+G_d*AD_d(\omega))\\
&=P_0(G_u*AD_u(\omega))+P_0(G_d*AD_d(\omega))\\
&=G_u*P_0(AD_u(\omega))+G_d*P_0(AD_d(\omega))
\end{aligned}
$$

The fact that any contingent claim can be written as a linear combination of the primitive AD securities shows that it can be priced, if the AD securities can be priced (if there is no-arbitrage). But all contingent claims can be so written. It follows that if we can obtain some set of 'state prices'—by which is meant prices for the (primitive) AD securities—then we can price all contingent claims.

Note that you don't get uniqueness at this stage because the above arguments only depend on no-arbitrage which, by $FTAP_1$, implies the existence of at least one positive, linear pricing functional $P_0(\cdot)$.

However, if we can *replicate* the primitive AD securities in terms of some other marketed securities, then their prices will be unique, by $FTAP_2$. It then follows that the prices of all contingent claims will also be unique. (We just showed that they are replicable.) This is what we showed for the Binomial, (N=1) model. Therefore we actually proved that the BOPM, (N=1) is complete.

The proof has three parts,

1. Every contingent claim is a unique linear combination of primitive AD securities.

2. Every primitive AD security can be replicated by a replicating portfolio consisting of a position in the underlying security and a position in the riskless bond. We demonstrated this in section 15.1.2. Therefore, every AD security can be uniquely priced as the unique price of its replicating portfolio.

3. 1. and 2. imply that every contingent claim can be *uniquely* priced. That is, the market is complete.

The same procedure shows that the BOPM, N>1 is also complete. The key step is to price the N+1 primitive AD securities. There are N+1 primitive AD securities in the BOPM, (N>1), because there are N+1 distinct states at time N.

15.3 EQUIVALENT MARTINGALE MEASURES (EMMS)

15.3.1 Introduction and Examples

The modern way of thinking about 'risk neutral' valuation is in terms of martingales, more precisely *equivalent martingale measures* (EMMs). Part of this approach is just a change of terminology; the other part is in order to use the heavy machinery of martingale theory in mathematical finance.

Knowing where this concept comes from is important. It's just *formal* 'risk-neutral' valuation in disguise. It also connects up to the *efficient market hypothesis* (EMH) as a basis for modeling underlying asset prices. This connection will be discussed in section 15.6.

518 OPTIONS

The easiest way to think about martingales is in terms of the notion of a *'fair game'*. This is an idea that comes from utility theory, and is applied to investment decision-making in portfolio analysis. A fair game is also a concept that appears in the gambling literature. It is a risky gamble in which you can expect to break even. Here is an example.

Example 1 A Fair Game

Toss a 'fair' coin. If it lands on heads (*H*), you win $1. If it lands on tails (*T*), you lose $1.

TABLE 15.1 **A Fair Game with Equal Probabilities**

Outcome	Winnings/Losses	Probability
H	$X_1=\$1$	$p_H=0.5$
T	$X_2=-\$1$	$p_T=0.5$

This is clearly a *risky* gamble, unlike a riskless bond, because we could either win or lose and we do not know in advance which will happen. Nature or chance, that is ω, will determine whether a *H* or a *T* occurs on any trial of the game.

Calculate the *expected value* of the fair coin toss. Before doing so, a little notation. This is a *two-state* model again with the 'state-space' $\omega=\{\omega_H,\omega_T\}$, where ω_H corresponds to heads occurring and ω_T corresponds to tails occurring. Fairness is implied by the equal probabilities p_H and p_T (but there are other fair games in which the probabilities are not equal).

The random variable $X(\omega)$ is given by,

$X(\omega_H)=\$1$ and
$X(\omega_T)=-\$1$.

The expected value of $X(\omega)$ is then the probability-weighted average of the coin tosses outcomes,

$$E(X(\omega))=p_H*X(\omega_H)+p_T*X(\omega_T)$$
$$=(0.5)*(\$1)+(0.5)*(-\$1)$$
$$=\$0.$$

EQUIVALENT MARTINGALE MEASURES

You *break even*, which is the hallmark of a fair bet. You take the risk, but you get nothing for your risk taking. Here is another example that incorporates and extends the concept of a fair game.

Example 2 A Two-Period Example

In this example, an investor starts out life, at time $t=0$, with an endowment of wealth equal to W_0. W_0 is clearly *certain* today, although it could have been generated by risky processes in the past.

The investor is a bit of a gambler and knows that the maximum *certain* yield obtainable on W_0 at the end of period 1 is rW_0, by investing in the risk-free rate. $r=1+r'$ is, as always, appropriately de-annualized to reflect the length of the period. You can think of it as a year for now.

In an attempt to augment his potential future expected income, the investor takes on a risky gamble X_1 at time $t=0$. The payoff to X_1 at the end of the period, time $t=1$, is the random variable $X_1(\omega)$.

All that we want to assume about $X_1(\omega)$ is that it is a fair game, meaning that $E(X_1(\omega))=0$. You can think of it as a fair coin toss for now, though equal and opposite outcomes with equal probabilities are sufficient, but not necessary to define a fair game.

Using this information, we can define *random*, end-of-the-period wealth as $W_1(\omega)$ where $W_1(\omega)=W_0+X_1(\omega)$ is the sum of certain current wealth and end-of-the-period random wealth, $X_1(\omega)$. We ignore interest on W_0 which would make W_0 grow to rW_0, provided that none of W_0 was spent on acquiring $X_1(\omega)$.

The reason for this assumption is that the martingale hypothesis, which we are going to introduce, is only consistent with zero interest rates, $r'=0$. Also, a risk-averse investor would spend no money on a fair bet because of its unattractive risk, expected return profile.

Figure 15.1 summarizes the investment strategy over the two periods.

FIGURE 15.1 Strategy for Example 2

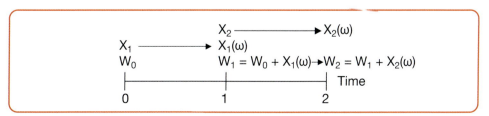

520 **OPTIONS**

The investor starts at time $t=0$ with current wealth of W_0 and acquires a fair game bet, X_1, that pays off $X_1(\omega)$ at time $t=1$.

The investor's new wealth at time $t=1$ is now $W_1=W_0+X_1(\omega)$. At time $t=1$, the investor acquires another independent fair game bet, X_2, that pays off $X_2(\omega)$ at time $t=2$. The investor's new wealth at time $t=2$ is now $W_2=W_1+X_2(\omega)$. At this point, the investor can liquidate his position.

Note that the *change in wealth* is given by the fair games $X_i(\omega)$, $i=1,2$,

$$W_1-W_0=X_1(\omega),$$
$$W_2-W_1=X_2(\omega).$$

Now we calculate the *conditional* expectation of W_2, given W_1 at time $t=1$. This is like an ordinary expectation except that it assumes that the conditioning variable is known and non-stochastic at time 1.

Keep in mind that you are standing at time $t=1$ when calculating $E(W_2(\omega)\,|\,W_1)$. At time $t=1$, $X_1(\omega)$ is known so we write it as X_1, which is not random,

$$
\begin{aligned}
E(W_2(\omega)\,|\,W_1) &= E(W_1+X_2(\omega)\,|\,W_1)\\
&= E(W_1\,|\,W_1)+E(X_2(\omega)\,|\,W_1)\\
&= E(W_1)+E(X_2(\omega)\,|\,W_0+X_1(\omega))\\
&= W_1+E(X_2(\omega)\,|\,W_0+X_1)\\
&= W_1+E(X_2(\omega))\\
&= W_1+0\\
&= W_1.
\end{aligned}
$$

Therefore,

$$E(W_2(\omega)\,|\,W_1)=W_1.$$

The first equality above follows by substituting the definition of $W_2(\omega)$, and the second by linearity of conditional expectations. The third equality follows because $E(W_1\,|\,W_1)$ means the expectation of W_1, assuming W_1 is known. In this case, it is actually known at $t=1$. The second part of the third equality follows by substitution of the definition of W_1 as the conditioning variable.

The fourth equality reflects the fact that at time $t=1$, both W_0 and the outcome of $X_1(\omega)$ are known. The fifth equality follows because $X_2(\omega)$ is assumed to be independent of both W_0 and the outcome of $X_1(\omega)$. The final

EQUIVALENT MARTINGALE MEASURES   **521**

equality is due to the fact that $E(X_2(\omega))=0$, because it is a fair game by assumption. We can also prove that $E(W_1(\omega)\,|\,W_0)=W_0$.

■ CONCEPT CHECK 3

a. Prove that $E(W_1(\omega)\,|\,W_0)=W_0$, where we are standing at time $t=0$.

We now have two results,

$E(W_1(\omega)\,|\,W_0)=W_0$ and,
$E(W_2(\omega)\,|\,W_1)=W_1$.

15.3.2 Definition of a Discrete-Time Martingale

A discrete-time stochastic process $(X_n(\omega))_{n=0,1,2,3,...}$ is called a *martingale* if,

1. $E(X_n)<\infty$ and $E(X_n^2)<\infty$ for all n and,
2. $E(X_{n+1}(\omega)\,|\,X_n)=X_n$ for all $n=0,1,2,3,...$

Note that our martingales have finite first and second moments. As we have seen in example 2, martingales are constructed from independent fair games. If we add independent fair games to a given starting wealth process, we will end up with a wealth process that is a martingale.

Conversely, if the wealth process is a martingale with finite means and variances, then it must have been generated in this way, by adding uncorrelated fair games to an initial wealth process and proceeding in this way. This shows where martingales come from.

15.4 MARTINGALES AND STOCK PRICES

At this point, the reader might be wondering what martingales have to do with pricing derivatives. The brief answer, which we will expand upon, is that the risk-neutral valuation procedure is equivalent to a martingale measure representation; more precisely, to an equivalent martingale measure (EMM) representation for the 'discounted' price process.

Consider the risk-neutral investor. A risk-neutral investor would not require a *risk premium* on any risky security, such as the underlying stock or the option. That is, he would value *both* the stock and the option as risk-neutral

522 OPTIONS

investments, therefore expected to earn only the *risk-free* rate $r=1+r'$ over the term to expiration of the option. That is, risk-neutral investors still require compensation for waiting (time preference).

The risk-neutral investor uses risk-neutralized probabilities p^r and $(1-p^r)$ to value all investments. The expected value used by the risk-neutral investor is notated by $E^r(\cdot)$.

The actual (physical), risk-adjusted probabilities and expectation used by real *risk-averse* investors in the real world are p and $1-p$, and $E(\cdot)$. No one claims that $p=p^r$ or therefore that $E(\cdot)=E^r(\cdot)$.

The risk-neutral investor looks at the stock and says that his required rate of return on the stock investment over the period must be $r=1+r'$, no more, no less,

$$\frac{E^r(S_1(\omega)\,|\,S_0)}{S_0} = 1 + r'$$

Evaluating $E^r(S_1(\omega)\,|\,S_0)$ we obtain,

$$E^r(S_1(\omega)\,|\,S_0) = p^r S_u + (1-p^r) S_d$$
$$= p^r(uS_0) + (1-p^r)(dS_0)$$

Therefore,

$$\frac{E^r(S_1(\omega)\,|\,S_0)}{S_0} = \frac{p^r(uS_0) + (1-p^r)(dS_0)}{S_0}$$
$$= p^r u + (1-p^r)d$$

since S_0 cancels out.

Equating this to r, and solving for p^r we obtain,

$$p^r u + (1-p^r)d = r \text{ or,}$$
$$p^r(u-d) = r-d$$

Therefore $p^r = \dfrac{r-d}{u-d}$ and $1-p^r = \dfrac{u-r}{u-d}$

These are our familiar 'risk neutralized' probabilities, p' and $1-p'$, that we discussed in the Appendix to Chapter 13. This shows that they indeed are

EQUIVALENT MARTINGALE MEASURES 523

the risk-neutral probabilities that would actually be used by a risk-neutral investor. We henceforth do not distinguish between p' and p'. They are just two different notations for the same thing.

And they reflect the risk neutral investor's private, risk-neutral valuation of the underlying stock. To summarize, here are the steps leading to the risk-neutralized S_0 which would more appropriately be called S_0^r.

$$\frac{E'(S_1(\omega)\,|\,S_0)}{S_0} = 1 + r'$$

Therefore,

$$E'(S_1(\omega)\,|\,S_0) = (1+r')S_0$$

$$S_0 = \frac{E'(S_1(\omega)\,|\,S_0)}{(1+r')}$$

$$= \frac{p'uS_0 + (1-p')dS_0}{(1+r')}$$

with $p' = \dfrac{r-d}{u-d}$

Let's examine the connection between this clearly risk-neutral valuation and martingales. First, note that under the risk-neutral probability measure E^r, the risk-neutralized stock price (which we will continue to call S_0) is clearly *not* a martingale, unless riskless interest rates actually are equal to zero. The second equation above says that,

$$E^r(S_1(\omega)\,|\,S_0) = (1+r')S_0 > S_0 \text{ unless } r'=0.$$

Even under risk neutrality (which doesn't mean zero interest rates), the martingale requirement that $E^r(S_1(\omega)\,|\,S_0) = S_0$ is clearly violated. *Stock prices under risk neutrality are not martingales.* However they aren't very far from martingales.

Definition of a Sub (Super) Martingale

1. A discrete-time stochastic process $(X_n(\omega))_{n=0,1,2,3,\ldots}$ is called a *sub-martingale* if $E(X_n)<\infty$, $E(X_n^2)<\infty$ and $E(X_{n+1}(\omega)\,|\,X_n)>X_n$ for all $n=0,1,2,3,\ldots$

2. A discrete-time stochastic process $(X_n(\omega))_{n=0,1,2,3,\ldots}$ is called a *super-martingale* if $E(X_n)<\infty$, $E(X_n^2)<\infty$, and $E(X_{n+1}(\omega)\,|\,X_n)<X_n$ for all $n=0,1,2,3,\ldots$

We expect stock prices to be *sub*-martingales, not martingales, for two separate and different reasons:

1. All assets, risky or not, have to provide a reward for time and waiting. This reward is the risk-free rate.

2. Risky assets have to also reward investors for non-diversifiable risks.

15.4.1 The Equivalent Martingale Representation of Stock Prices

Not all hope is lost for the martingale representation of stock prices under risk neutrality. We start with defining a bond price process in discrete time, which in this context is a *numeraire*. (This concept will be discussed in Chapter 16, section 16.4.)

Time starts at time $t=0$. The bond is just like a bank account paying interest at the rate r'. The initial price of the bond is $B(0)=\$1$. It then grows at the rate r' to generate a value of $B(1)=\$1(1+r')$ at the end of period 1. This formulation is just like the one in continuous time where $B(t)=e^{r\tau}$.

We now define what is known as the '*discounted stock price process*', S'_i, for $i=0,1$.

$$S'_1(\omega) = \frac{S_1(\omega)}{B(1)}$$

$$= \frac{S_1(\omega)}{1+r'}$$

and,

$$S'_0(\omega) = \frac{S_0(\omega)}{B(0)}$$

$$= \frac{S_0(\omega)}{1+r'}$$

EQUIVALENT MARTINGALE MEASURES 525

Taking the expectation of $S_1'(\omega)$ we obtain from $E*(S_1(\omega)\,|\,S_0)=(1+r')S_0$ after dividing both sides by $(1+r')$ that,

$$E'\left(\frac{(S_1(\omega)\,|\,S_0)}{1+r'}\bigg|\frac{S_0}{1.0}\right) = E'(S_1'(\omega)\,|\,S_0')$$
$$= S_0'$$

The last equality is the martingale condition.

■ CONCEPT CHECK 4

a. Starting from $E'(S_1(\omega)\,|\,S_0)=(1+r')S_0$, go through the steps to make sure you get the result, $E'(S_1'(\omega)\,|\,S_0')=S_0'$.

This shows that the *discounted stock price* process is a martingale. We know that this works in continuous time from Chapter 4, where it was shown that multiplying a process with drift rdt by e^{-rt} (equivalently, dividing it by e^{rt}) removes the drift. In continuous time, the bond's price at time t is $B(t)=e^{rt}$ assuming $B(0)=1$. A martingale is a driftless process. It neither increases nor decreases on average.

Basically, by discounting the price process by the riskless bond, we embed the drift, $-rdt$, in the undiscounted process, so that the resulting process has zero drift. If we take the original, undiscounted price process to be risk neutral (that is, with drift rdt), as we have done, then the discounted price process becomes an *equivalent* martingale.

Equivalent is a technical term meaning, in the case of the BOPM, $N=1$, that events with positive probability under the original, physical probability measure $(p, 1-p)$—which we have hardly ever talked about except when we consider risk averse investors valuing options—also have positive probability under the risk-neutralized probability measure $(p',1-p')$.

This is pretty obvious here because $p>0$ is the probability of an upward move in the original, not risk-neutralized stock price process and is positive. It is also a positive probability even under the risk-neutralized probability p' simply because $p'>0$. So $p'>0$ if and only if $p>0$.

That the discounted, risk-neutralized stock price process has zero drift, a necessary condition for it be a martingale, can be seen as follows. The drift in $S_1'(\omega)$ is given by its expected return,

526 **OPTIONS**

$$E'\left(\frac{(S_1'(\omega)\,|\,S_0')}{S_0'}\right) = E'\left(\frac{(S_1(\omega)\,|\,S_0')}{(1+r')S_0'}\right) \text{ because } S_1'(\omega) = \frac{S_1(\omega)}{1+r'}$$

$$= E'\left(\frac{(S_1(\omega)\,|\,S_0)}{(1+r')S_0}\right) \text{ because } S_0'(\omega) = \frac{S_0}{1.0} = S_0$$

Then the numerator of E' equals the denominator. That is, $E'(S_1(\omega)\,|\,S_0) = (1+r')S_0$, because E' represents expectation under the risk-neutral measure (the measure under which the undiscounted process $S_1(\omega)$ has drift r).

Therefore,

$$E'\left(\frac{(S_1(\omega)\,|\,S_0)}{(1+r')S_0'}\right) = E'(1)$$

$$= 1+0$$

which means that the implied drift in $S_1'(\omega)$ is the zero in 1+0. That is, the discounted, risk-neutralized price process is a zero-drift process. We also verified that $S_1'(\omega)$ is a martingale under E' just above (see concept check 4).

15.5 THE EQUIVALENT MARTINGALE REPRESENTATION OF OPTION PRICES

What we just did for the risk-neutralized price process, we should also be able to do for the option price because it would also be risk-neutralized from the point of view of a risk-neutral investor. Even from the point of view of a risk-averse investor, we know that if the stock is assumed to be risk neutral then the option must also be risk neutral, because different risks cannot co-exist in the riskless hedge portfolio (see Chapter 17).

If they did, there would be no way to cancel them out, as they must in order to generate a riskless hedge. By risk is meant relative risk, which is also called the '*Sharpe ratio*'.

Once again, what do we know? We know that the no-arbitrage, replicable option price, C_0, is given under the risk-neutralized stock price measure $(p',1-p')$. That is,

$$\frac{E'(C_1(\omega)\,|\,C_0)}{C_0} = 1+r'$$

Evaluating $E^r(C_1(\omega)\,|\,C_0)$ we obtain,

$$E^r(C_1(\omega)\,|\,C_0) = p'C_u + (1-p')C_d$$

Therefore,

$$\frac{E^r(C_1(\omega)\,|\,C_0)}{C_0} = \frac{p'C_u + (1-p')C_d}{C_0}$$

$$= 1 + r'$$

or, since $p'=p'$,

$$C_0 = \frac{p'}{1+r'} * C_u + \frac{1-p'}{1+r'} * C_d$$

We can also get the same result using the state price representation of C_0 as,

$$C_0 = P_0\big(AD_u(\omega)\big) * C_u + P_0\big(AD_d(\omega)\big) * C_d$$

$$= \frac{p^r}{1+r'} * C_u + \frac{1-p^r}{1+r'} * C_d$$

This says that the current no-arbitrage option price is the weighted sum of its payoffs times the no-arbitrage prices of the primitive AD securities.

Once again, it's pretty clear that $(C_0, C_1(\omega))$ is a sub-martingale, even under risk neutrality. Just as before for $E^r(S_1(\omega)\,|\,S_0)$, the (percentage) expected return of the option is the risk-free rate r', and $E^r(C_1(\omega)\,|\,C_0)=(1+r')C_0 > C_0$ unless $r'=0$.

15.5.1 Discounted Option Prices

But we can use the same technique to obtain the 'discounted option price process', from which the martingale property for the discounted option price process will easily follow. It's exactly the same argument as for $E^r(S_1(\omega)\,|\,S_0)$.

We now define what is known as the 'discounted option price process', C'_i, for $i=0,1$. We divide by the appropriate riskless bond price $B(0)$ or $B(1)$, which in this context is a numeraire,

$$C'_1(\omega) = \frac{C_1(\omega)}{B(1)}$$

$$= \frac{C_1(\omega)}{1+r'}$$

528 **OPTIONS**

$$C_0' = \frac{C_0}{B(0)}$$

$$= \frac{C_0}{1.0}$$

From $E^r(C_1(\omega) \mid C_0) = (1+r')C_0$, after dividing both sides by $(1+r')$ we find that,

$$E^r(C_1'(\omega) \mid C_0') = E^r\left(\frac{C_1(\omega)}{1+r'} \bigg| \frac{C_0}{1.0}\right)$$

$$= C_0$$

$$= C_0'$$

This says that the discounted option price process $(C_1'(\omega), C_0')$ is a martingale under the risk-neutral measure, $E^r(C_1'(\omega) \mid C_0') = C_0'$.

15.5.2 Summary of the EMM Approach

The EMM approach is useful because,

1. It reduces the search for no-arbitrage contingent claim prices to the search for equivalent martingale measures. The first fundamental theorem of asset pricing (FTAP$_1$) tells us that, as long as there is no-arbitrage, there must be *at least one* such EMM measure. The problem is that there may be many.

2. When is there one and only one EMM for a given contingent claim? To summarize what we have already learned in Chapter 13, section 13.5.2, this is where the second fundamental theorem of asset pricing (FTAP$_2$) enters the picture.

As long as the contingent claim is replicable by a replicating portfolio of traded instruments, then there will be one and only one EMM. Thus the EMM is unique on replicable claims. (If *all* contingent claims are replicable, then there is a unique EMM that prices all contingent claims, and the market is said to be *complete*).

Note that we have rephrased the fundamental theorems of asset pricing in terms of the EMMs. These kinds of statements are part of the *modern* way of looking at contingent claim pricing. As can be seen, they rely heavily on the martingale concept. We discussed the fundamental theorems as tools in Chapter 13. A brief discussion of the *computation* of EMMs may be helpful here.

The EMM approach is a fairly abstract approach to pricing contingent claims. In fact, the first fundamental theorem of asset pricing ($FTAP_1$) is a *non-constructive existence theorem* for EMMs.

The question remains as to how to actually compute EMMs. First, you have to determine whether uniqueness (replicability) holds or not. On replicable claims, EMMs are indeed unique. In this case, you then construct a replicating portfolio and its price must be equal to that of the contingent claim. In other words, as discussed in Chapter 13, replicability is the *practical* route to computing no-arbitrage contingent claim prices, or what is the same, the unique EMM.

Note that this is precisely what we did for the BOPM, (N=1). Once we found only one replicating portfolio (because two independent equations in two unknowns have exactly one solution), then we know it is the only EMM. That is, the BOPM, (N=1) model is complete.

In Chapter 16, we will indicate another practical route for actually calculating EMMs, in terms of *risk-neutral transition density functions*.

15.6 THE EFFICIENT MARKET HYPOTHESIS (EMH), A GUIDE TO MODELING PRICES

In this section, we look at a little of the history of investments. This will help us to understand why certain processes are used in pricing options in continuous time finance, the topic of Chapter 16. Ultimately, we want to choose tractable processes that represent the empirical behavior of asset prices, like the stocks, foreign currencies, and other assets that underlie derivatives. There is also the modern theory of asset pricing to contend with. Let's look at that for a moment.

To review what we know. The no-arbitrage condition *must* hold because, without the no-arbitrage condition, we have no hope of consistently pricing derivatives, let alone uniquely doing so.

In fact, without the no-arbitrage condition, we have little hope of pricing even the instruments underlying derivatives, because the first $FTAP_1$ tells us that there is no linear, positive pricing mechanism (EMM) when the market permits arbitrage. There would not even be state prices! No-arbitrage is certainly the basis for pricing financial instruments, and arbitrage is not consistent with the existence of a well-behaved pricing mechanism (EMM).

530 OPTIONS

One thing to keep in mind here is the difference between derivatives pricing and looking for the *best* process to describe the underlying stock price process. All that matters for derivatives pricing is that there exist an *equivalent* martingale measure under which the *discounted* underlying price process, while not necessarily already a martingale, becomes a martingale.

Derivatives pricing *does not require* that the discounted underlying stock price process actually be a martingale under the physical probability measure. The *physical probability measure* is the measure that defines *actual* prices, not *risk neutral* prices. The question that naturally arises is, which discounted underlying price processes admit at least one EMM? What do these processes look like?

One seemingly easy way to answer this question is simply to hypothesize that original, actual discounted underlying price processes are already martingales under the *physical probability measure*! This is a very nice trick, because in this case we would already have an EMM. (Provided we can describe its probability structure, which may still be quite a challenge, we could implement it.) If the above was literally true, then the no-arbitrage condition would also automatically hold.

If discounted prices were already martingales under the *physical* probability measure, then an EMM already exists and therefore there can be no-arbitrage, due to $FTAP_1$.

We could use that EMM to price contingent claims as well. The only question that would remain is uniqueness of the EMM or, what is equivalent, market completeness.

What this all amounts to in the context of the BOPM, $N \geqslant 1$ is that $p'=p$, which may be a fairly remote possibility. The BOPM also assumes that stock prices are well described by a Binomial process.

Turning to the empirical side, the early empirical literature focused on something very close to this hypothesis, which we will call *the martingale hypothesis for the physical probability measure*. It wasn't exactly this hypothesis because actual prices were not discounted. However, for the short intervals of time over which price changes were measured, this would make little difference since the discount factor is small.

Commodity prices and stock prices have been intensively studied for a very long time. Many of the early empirical studies found little or no significant correlation between *past changes* in stock prices and *subsequent price changes*. This finding was also confirmed for futures prices. This suggested that empirical stock price processes meet the condition of '*independent increments*'.

The first model of prices consistent with the empirical findings was the *random walk model* or what we will call, in continuous time, the *arithmetic*

EQUIVALENT MARTINGALE MEASURES 531

Brownian motion model (ABM). We will be discussing this model in detail in Chapter 16.

Later, it was found that independence was too strong a condition, because the results of the empirical tests seemed only to establish the weaker *uncorrelated increments* property (see the Appendix, section 15.7, for this distinction).

This is when martingales entered the picture, because Samuelson (1965) produced his theoretical paper explaining the empirical findings that many researchers had observed up to that time.

As established in the Appendix, section 15.7, if the underlying martingale process has finite first and second moments, then martingales will have uncorrelated increments. Therefore, martingales with finite first and second moments are consistent with the empirical evidence.

After this initial research, a vast amount of further research formulated and tested the *efficient market hypothesis (EMH)*. There are several variations of this model, namely *weak*, *semi-strong*, and *strong* form efficiency.

The EMH relates the expectations of future prices to information sets. Let I_N denote the information available at time N for $N=0,1,2,\ldots$, and note that I_N is an *evolving* information set in the sense that, $I_0 \subseteq I_1 \subseteq I_2 \subseteq I_3 \subseteq \ldots$.

This just means that as time evolves, the currently available information set—which includes all previous information—gets bigger, or at least it doesn't get smaller. Previously available information is also currently available.

Now we can state the EMH in its three forms in terms of martingales. We are standing at time $t=N$ and trying to predict the random stock price one period ahead, at time $t=N+1$. We have available the information set at time $t=N$, I_N. What can we say?

According to the EMH, the *best predictor* of *future* stock prices is the current price S_N. The EMH is just the martingale hypothesis, where the conditioning variable is information itself. The EMH says that the sequence of prices is a *martingale with respect to I_N*. That is,

$$E(S_{N+1}(\omega) \mid I_N)=S_N \text{ for all } N=0,1,2,3,\ldots$$

The currently available information set, I_N, can be in at least one of three forms:

1. *Weak-Form EMH*, $I_N=\{$all historical stock prices $S_0, S_1, S_2,\ldots S_N\}$.

2. *Semi-Strong Form EMH*, $I_N=\{$all historical stock prices and other publicly available information, such as accounting statements as of time $t=N\}$.

OPTIONS

3. *Strong-Form EMH*, I_N={all publicly available information and also all private information, for example, information held by insiders}.

There are a number of interesting features of the EMH. First, it ties price formation in with information and information flows. By analyzing the nature of information flows, one can say quite a bit about the structure of equilibrium prices. For example, are price paths continuous, or do they have predictable or unpredictable jumps?

Second, we know that square-integrable martingales have increments that are uncorrelated (see section 15.7). This means that *past* information I_N is useless in predicting future prices or even subsequent price changes.

That's why martingales predict using the current value, S_N. That's also why martingales can do no better in predicting than the current market price. There are no trends in prices, martingales are driftless. Any kind of trend or correlation could be used to forecast prices and could lead to arbitrage opportunities. Thus the martingale formulation is one that is consistent with no-arbitrage.

All forms of the EMH conclude that it is effectively impossible to predict future price changes from past information. The different forms of the EMH specify what information one has access to in attempting to predict.

It is pretty clear that if a market is *informationally efficient* in any reasonable sense, then there exists a positive, linear pricing mechanism (this would be implied by efficiency). Then, the no-arbitrage condition must hold by the $FTAP_1$. That is, there can be no-arbitrage opportunities in an informationally efficient market.

Another interesting aspect of the EMH is that it says that one need not look far and wide for at least one EMM. If actual prices form a martingale, and discounting has minimal effect on the actual prices, then the most obvious example of an EMM is the actual price process! The actual price process is equivalent to itself. Of course, this can only happen if there is no-arbitrage.

What could stand in the way of the actual price process being an EMM? The risk-free rate $r>0$ is one candidate. Discounting prices by the numeraire eliminates that part of drift caused by the risk-free rate and thereby makes the *discounted* price process (but not the *actual* price process) a martingale.

If there is an empirically measurable *risk premium* in stock prices, then actual prices would form a *sub-martingale*, not a martingale. A risk premium in stock prices would not create arbitrage, but rather is a reward for taking on non-diversifiable risk(s). If these are the only two factors contributing to positive

EQUIVALENT MARTINGALE MEASURES   533

drift, which is not consistent with martingale behavior, then by de-trending the price series, one should be left with a martingale.

Even if actual (de-trended) prices do not form a martingale, the EMH suggests a very interesting hypothesis. That hypothesis is that the actual price process cannot be very far from being a martingale, as long as no-arbitrage holds. Because, if there is no-arbitrage, we know that there is at least one EMM for the discounted price process.

So the question is, if no-arbitrage holds, then do actual price processes (while not necessarily martingales themselves) have a martingale *component*?

This takes us into the research literature. Instead of going that route, we will examine some actual continuous time price processes that *are* consistent with the EMH, and for which we can price options and therefore, for which there is at least one EMM for the discounted price process (FTAP$_1$). We will also look for martingale components in the actual price processes. Chapter 16 begins this program.

15.7 APPENDIX: ESSENTIAL MARTINGALE PROPERTIES

Here we collect a few of the many properties of martingales that are used in proving results that make martingales useful in applied finance. We restrict attention to discrete-time martingales and sometimes even choose $N=2$. No attempt at mathematical rigor is claimed. The intuition behind these results is the primary concern.

We start with a discrete-time stochastic process $(X_n(\omega)_{n=0,1,2,3,...}$ with finite first and second moments $E(X_n)<\infty$ and $E(X_n^2)<\infty$ for all $n=0,1,2,3,...$ and the *martingale property*,

$$E(X_{n+1}(\omega)\,|\,X_n)=X_n \text{ for all } n=0,1,2,3,... \tag{MP1}$$

1. Tower Property (TP)

$$E(X_2\,|\,X_0)=E\{E(X_2\,|\,X_1)\,|\,X_0\} \tag{TP}$$

This is a general property of conditional expectations and doesn't require a martingale. The Tower Property says that, whenever we condition a martingale process by an event earlier than the immediately preceding one, like X_0, we can break this down into a two-step process. First, condition by the immediately preceding event. Then condition that conditional expectation by the earlier one.

One implication of TP is that the martingale property MP also holds for all *earlier* events. Let's see. Suppose $(X_n(\omega))_{n=0,1,2}$ is a martingale.

$$E(X_2 \mid X_0)=E\{E(X_2 \mid X_1) \mid X_0\}$$
$$=E\{X_1 \mid X_0\}$$
$$=X_0.$$

Here we used the martingale property twice. First, $E(X_2 \mid X_1)=X_1$. Second, $E(X_1 \mid X_0)=X_0$. The TP allows us to rephrase the martingale property as,

$$E(X_{n+1}(\omega) \mid X_m)=X_m \text{ for all } m \leqslant n=0,1,2,3,\ldots \tag{MP2}$$

Sometimes you will see the (MP1) property stated as (MP2). By the tower property, (MP2) follows from (MP1).

2. Double Expectations (DE)

This is another general property of conditional and unconditional expectations, with important applications to martingales,

$$E\{E(X_2 \mid X_0)\}=E(X_2) \tag{DE}$$

This says that we first calculate the conditional expectation of a random variable, say X_2, with respect to another random variable, say X_0. If we *integrate out* the conditioning variable, X_0, then we obtain the unconditional expectation $E(X_2)$.

One immediate application of *DE* is to show that the *means of a martingale process are constant*. Start with a martingale process $(X_n(\omega))$, $n=0,1,2$.

$$E\{E(X_2 \mid X_1)\}=E(X_2) \quad \text{by (DE)}$$

$$E(X_2 \mid X_1)=X_1 \quad\quad\quad \text{by (MP1)}$$

Therefore,

$$E\{E(X_2 \mid X_1)\}=E(X_1).$$

So we conclude that $E(X_2)=E(X_1)$.

EQUIVALENT MARTINGALE MEASURES 535

This justifies the statement that a martingale process neither increases nor decreases on average. The same statement is that the means of a martingale process are constant.

3. Uncorrelated Martingale Increments (UCMI)

This is probably the most important property of martingales from the point of view of finance. Recall that we assume that our martingales have finite means and variances. Then the result is that *the changes of a square-integrable martingale process, while not necessarily independent, are uncorrelated.*

Consider the two martingale increments (changes) X_2-X_1 and X_1-X_0. First note that $E(X_2-X_1)=E(X_2)-E(X_1)=0$ because of the constant means property. For the same reason, $E(X_1-X_0)=E(X_1)-E(X_0)=0$.

The definition of the covariance between two random variables X and Y is $\mathrm{Cov}(X,Y)=E\{(X-E(X))(Y-E(Y))\}$. In our case $X=X_2-X_1$ and $Y=X_1-X_0$ so, for our case, $\mathrm{Cov}(X,Y)=E\{XY\}$ because $E(X)=E(Y)=0$.

Then,

$$\mathrm{Cov}(X_2-X_1,X_1-X_0)=E\{(X_2-X_1)(X_1-X_0)\}$$
$$=E\{X_2-X_1)X_1\}-E\{(X_2-X_1)X_0\}.$$

We will consider each term separately. For the first term, $E\{(X_2-X_1)X_1\}$,

$$\begin{aligned}
E\{(X_2-X_1)X_1\}&=E\{E\{(X_2-X_1)X_1\,|\,X_1\}\}\text{ by (DE)},\\
&=E\{E\{(X_2X_1-X_1^2)\,|\,X_1\}\}\text{ by expanding all terms},\\
&=E\{E(X_2X_1\,|\,X_1)-E(X_1^2\,|\,X_1)\}\text{ by linearity of}\\
&\qquad\qquad\qquad\qquad\qquad\text{conditional expectation},\\
&=E\{X_1E(X_2\,|\,X_1)-X_1^2\}\text{ by factoring out the constant}\\
&\qquad\qquad\qquad X_1\text{ in }E(X_2\,|\,X_1)\text{, and noting that}\\
&\qquad\qquad\qquad E(X_1^2\,|\,X_1)=X_1^2,\\
&=E\{X_1X_1-X_1^2\}\text{ by (MP1)}\\
&=E\{X_1^2-X_1^2\}\\
&=0.
\end{aligned}$$

Next we consider the second term $E\{(X_2-X_1)X_0\}$,

$$\begin{aligned}
E\{(X_2-X_1)X_0\}&=E\{E\{(X_2-X_1)X_0\,|\,X_0\}\}\text{ again by (DE)},\\
&=E\{E\{(X_2X_0-X_1X_0)\,|\,X_0\}\}\text{ by expanding all terms},
\end{aligned}$$

$$=E\{E(X_2X_0\,|\,X_0)-E(X_1X_0\,|\,X_0)\} \text{ by linearity of}$$
$$\text{conditional expectations,}$$
$$=E\{X_0E(X_2\,|\,X_0)-X_0\,E(X_1\,|\,X_0)\} \text{ by factoring out the}$$
$$\text{constant } X_0 \text{ in } E(X_1\,|\,X_0),$$
$$=E\{X_0X_0-X_0X_0\} \text{ by (MP2)}$$
$$=E\{X_0{}^2-X_0{}^2\}$$
$$=0.$$

Combining both terms, we have proved that $\mathrm{Cov}(X_2-X_1,X_1-X_0)=0$, so that the martingale increments X_2-X_1 and X_1-X_0 are uncorrelated.

4. Degrees of 'Independence': Independent, Uncorrelated, and Orthogonal Random Variables

Understanding the EMH requires an intimate knowledge of the types of correlation between random variables that can occur. So we collect the three basic notions here.

A. Two random variables $X(\omega)$ and $Y(\omega)$ are said to be *independent* if

$$E[X(\omega)*Y(\omega)]=E[X(\omega)]*E[Y(\omega)].$$

B. Two random variables $X(\omega)$ and $Y(\omega)$ are said to be *orthogonal* if

$$E[X(\omega)*Y(\omega)]=0.$$

C. Two random variables $X(\omega)$ and $Y(\omega)$ are said to be *uncorrelated* if

$$\mathrm{COV}(X(\omega),Y(\omega))=E[(X(\omega)-E(X(\omega))(Y(\omega)-E(Y(\omega))]=0.$$

This means that, after subtracting their means, $X'(\omega)=X(\omega)-E(X(\omega))$ and $Y'(\omega)=Y(\omega)-E(Y(\omega))$ are orthogonal.

The strongest form of unrelatedness is independence. Then comes orthogonality. Finally, there is uncorrelatedness. Thus, martingales enjoy a weak form of unrelatedness between their increments. Weaker than independence of increments, which some processes exhibit.

EQUIVALENT MARTINGALE MEASURES 537

■ KEY CONCEPTS

1. Primitive Arrow–Debreu Securities and Option Pricing.
2. Exercise 1, Pricing $B(0,1)$.
3. Exercise 2, Pricing $AD_u(\omega)$ and $AD_d(\omega)$.
4. Pricing a European Call Option.
5. Pricing any Contingent Claim.
6. Equivalent Martingale Measures (EMMs).
7. Introduction and Examples.
8. Definition of a Discrete-Time Martingale.
9. Martingales and Stock Prices.
10. The Equivalent Martingale Representation of Stock Prices.
11. The Equivalent Martingale Representation of Option Prices.
12. Discounted Option Prices.
13. Summary of the EMM Approach.
14. The Efficient Market Hypothesis (EMH), A Guide to Modeling Prices.
15. Essential Martingale Properties.

■ END OF CHAPTER EXERCISES FOR CHAPTER 15

1. (*Pricing AD securities in a Binomial model*)

   Make the usual assumptions of the BOPM, $N=1$. Suppose that $u'=8\%$, $r'=5\%$ and that $d'=-3\%$. The current stock price is $S_0=\$100$. Assume that the term to expiration is one year, so everything is already annualized.

   a. Calculate $P_0(AD_u(\omega))$.
   b. Calculate $P_0(AD_d(\omega))$.

2. Assume the same scenario as in exercise 1 with the same parameters.

   a. Price an *at-the-money* European call option.
   b. Price an *at-the-money* European put option.

3. Write out the single–period, discrete version of European Put-Call Parity and confirm that the results of your calculations conform to it.

4. Consider a generalized option with payoff function $\text{MAX}[S_T^2-K, 0]$. Use AD securities to price it in the usual Binomial framework.

538 OPTIONS

■ SELECTED CONCEPT CHECK SOLUTIONS

Concept Check 3

$$
\begin{aligned}
E(W_1 \mid W_0) &= E(W_0 + X_1(\omega) \mid W_0) \\
&= E(W_0 \mid W_0) + E(X_1(\omega) \mid W_0) \\
&= W_0 + E(X_1(\omega) \mid W_0) \\
&= W_0 + E(X_1(\omega)) \\
&= W_0 + 0 \\
&= W_0.
\end{aligned}
$$

We used the fact that $X_1(\omega)$ is independent of W_0 in the fourth equality. Our conclusion is that the property $E(W_1(\omega) \mid W_0) = W_0$ holds.

CHAPTER 16

OPTION PRICING IN CONTINUOUS TIME

16.1	Arithmetic Brownian Motion (ABM)	540
16.2	Shifted Arithmetic Brownian Motion	541
16.3	Pricing European Options under Shifted Arithmetic Brownian Motion with No Drift (Bachelier)	542
	16.3.1 Theory (FTAP_1 and FTAP_2)	542
	16.3.2 Transition Density Functions	543
	16.3.3 Deriving the Bachelier Option Pricing Formula	547
16.4	Defining and Pricing a Standard Numeraire	551
16.5	Geometric Brownian Motion (GBM)	553
	16.5.1 GBM (Discrete Version)	553
	16.5.2 Geometric Brownian Motion (GBM), Continuous Version	559
16.6	Itô's Lemma	562
16.7	Black–Scholes Option Pricing	566
	16.7.1 Reducing GBM to an ABM with Drift	567
	16.7.2 Preliminaries on Generating Unknown Risk-Neutral Transition Density Functions from Known Ones	570
	16.7.3 Black–Scholes Options Pricing from Bachelier	571
	16.7.4 Volatility Estimation in the Black–Scholes Model	582
16.8	Non-Constant Volatility Models	585
	16.8.1 Empirical Features of Volatility	585
	16.8.2 Economic Reasons for why Volatility is not Constant, the Leverage Effect	586

16.8.3	Modeling Changing Volatility, the Deterministic Volatility Model	586
16.8.4	Modeling Changing Volatility, Stochastic Volatility Models	587
16.9	Why Black–Scholes Is Still Important	588

In this chapter we are going to give an introduction to continuous-time finance. This can be a daunting and rather technical subject but we will try to cut through all of that and stress the intuition. At the same time, we want to work through some important examples to get the flavor of the continuous-time framework.

Many of the same ideas from the discrete-time framework we have been discussing carry over to the continuous-time case. Risk-neutral valuation carries over, and dynamic hedging which we discussed in the BOPM, $N>1$ is the very essence of continuous-time trading and hedging.

Equivalent martingales measures (EMMs) form the foundation for the modern approach to pricing derivatives, as we have discussed in Chapter 15. The fundamental theorems of asset pricing, $FTAP_1$ and $FTAP_2$, apply in this continuous-time context as well.

We will begin with the prototype of all continuous time models, and that is arithmetic Brownian motion (ABM). ABM is the most basic and important stochastic process in continuous time and continuous space, and it has many desirable properties including the strong Markov property, the martingale property, independent increments, normality, and continuous sample paths.

Of course, here we want to focus on options pricing rather than the pure mathematical theory. The idea here is to partially prepare you for courses in mathematical finance. The details we have to leave out are usually covered in such courses.

16.1 ARITHMETIC BROWNIAN MOTION (ABM)

ABM is a stochastic process $\{W_t(\omega)\}_{t \geqslant 0}$ defined on a sample space $(\Omega, \Im^W, \wp^W)$.

We won't go into all the details as to exactly what $(\Omega, \Im^W, \wp^W)$ represents but you can think of the probability measure, $\wp^W$, which is called *Wiener measure*, to be defined in terms of the transition density function $p(T, y; t, x)$ for $\tau = T - t$,

OPTION PRICING IN CONTINUOUS TIME 541

$$p(T,y;t,x) = p(\tau,x,y)$$

$$= \left(\frac{1}{\sqrt{2\pi\tau}}\right)e^{-(y-x)^2/2\tau}$$

Norbert Wiener gave the first rigorous mathematical construction (existence proof) for ABM and, because of this, it is sometimes called the Wiener process. It has the following properties,

1. $W_0 = 0$ (*starts at 0*).

2. For every set of times $t_0 = 0 < t_1 < t_2 < \ldots t_{n-1} < t_n$ the increments (changes) $W_{t_1} - W_{t_0}, W_{t_2} - W_{t_1}, \ldots, W_{t_n} - W_{t_{n-1}}$ are independent (*independent increments*).

3. For any times s and t with $0 \leq s < t$, the random variable $W_t(\omega) - W_s(\omega)$ is normally distributed with mean $E(W_t(\omega) - W_s(\omega)) = 0$ and variance $\mathrm{Var}(W_t(\omega) - W_s(\omega)) = t - s$ (*normally distributed increments*).

4. Almost all the sample paths of $\{W_t(\omega)\}_{t \geq 0}$ are continuous (*continuous sample paths*).

From the perspective of modeling limited liability assets like common stocks, ABM can go negative, which doesn't make much economic sense. Once a firm reaches bankruptcy, its stock price $S_t = 0$. After that, its stock price cannot continue to decline in value below zero, because the stock price has effectively ceased to exist. In other words, zero is an *absorbing boundary*.

However, ABM is still the most basic stochastic process of its kind, so not too much should initially be made of this defect. In particular, it is possible to generate an option pricing formula (Black–Scholes) for an underlying process that makes sense (GBM), from the option pricing formula (Bachelier) for an underlying process that has some flaws (ABM). Showing this connection is one of the main purposes of this chapter.

16.2 SHIFTED ARITHMETIC BROWNIAN MOTION

The first step in pricing options is to get a *reasonable* process for the underlying stock where the obvious, removable flaws have been removed. Denote arithmetic Brownian motion, $\{W_t(\omega)\}_{t \geq 0}$, by (W_t).

We *shift* the ABM process, (W_t), by adding to it the current stock price $S_0 > 0$. It doesn't make sense to start the process at 0, which would happen if we didn't shift, because property 1 says that $W_0=0$. In that case, the company would start out already being bankrupt.

This is an easy fix. Our shifted process is $X_t(\omega)=S_0+W_t(\omega)$, for $t\geq0$. We do *not* add a drift term μt. Also note that while ABM is defined over the infinite time interval, $t\geq0$, we only need it defined up until the expiration date of the option, time T.

Note that $X_0=S_0+W_0=S_0$ because $W_0=0$. Further, $X_t(\omega)$ is a martingale process because, for any $t\geq0$,

$$E(X_t(\omega)\,|\,X_0)=E(S_0+W_t(\omega\,|\,X_0)$$
$$=E(S_0\,|\,X_0)+E(W_t(\omega)\,|\,X_0).$$

But $X_0=S_0$, therefore the first term on the right-hand side is, $E(S_0\,|\,S_0)=S_0$. The second term, $E(W_t(\omega)\,|\,X_0)=E(W_t(\omega)\,|\,S_0+W_0)$ doesn't depend on S_0.

Therefore,

$$E(W_t(\omega)\,|\,S_0+W_0)=E(W_t(\omega)\,|\,W_0)$$
$$=W_0,$$

since $W_t(\omega)$ is a martingale. The net result is that,

$$E(X_t(\omega)\,|\,X_0)=S_0+W_0=X_0,$$

which is the martingale requirement for $X_t(\omega)$.

16.3 PRICING EUROPEAN OPTIONS UNDER SHIFTED ARITHMETIC BROWNIAN MOTION WITH NO DRIFT (BACHELIER)

16.3.1 Theory (FTAP$_1$ and FTAP$_2$)

To price a European option on a shifted ABM, we will use the modern EMM representation from FTAP$_1$. In order to implement this, we have to calculate an EMM for the 'discounted price process'. In this case, the risk-free rate $r=0$, so there is no need to discount $X_t(\omega)$ by the bond price e^{rt} at time t.

This numeraire process, which in general is needed, is discussed in section 16.4. Further, $X_t(\omega)$ is already a martingale, so it is clearly equivalent (has the same null sets) to itself. It is proven in the research literature that this is the

OPTION PRICING IN CONTINUOUS TIME | **543**

only EMM, so the ABM model is complete by FTAP$_2$. It is also arbitrage-free, even though it can go negative, because if it were not, then an EMM would not exist (FTAP$_1$). We will come back to this point.

Denote the unique EMM by E^*, and the physical (actual) measure of the shifted ABM process itself by E. Then $E^*=E$. Therefore, the arbitrage-free current price of a European call option with exercise price K and time to expiration T is,

$$C(X_0, T;K)=E^*\{\text{MAX}[X_T(\omega)-K, 0] \mid X_0\}$$

(EMM Option Price Representation)

But $E^*\{\text{MAX}[X_T(\omega)-K, 0] \mid X_0\}=E\{\text{MAX}[X_T(\omega)-K, 0] \mid X_0\}$ because $E^*=E$. $E(\cdot \mid X_0)$ is the conditional expectation with respect to X_0 and is the (physical, actual) probability measure defining the process $X_t(\omega)$, $t \geq 0$.

This representation is called the EMM (arbitrage-free, 'risk–neutral') option price representation. We discussed how to determine EMMs in Chapter 15 via replication. However, in continuous time, dynamic replication can be quite complicated.

Here is a more practical approach to calculating EMMs. In order to calculate an EMM, we need the (risk-neutral) probability distribution of $X_T(\omega)$ conditional upon the process starting at X_0 at $t=0$. This requires the risk-neutral transition density function of $X_T(\omega)$, given X_0.

16.3.2 Transition Density Functions

In general, the transition density function describes the probabilistic evolution of a stochastic process from a known position $x=X_0$ assumed at time t to random positions $y=y_T(\omega)=X_T(\omega)$ assumed at time T. Let τ denote the time difference $T-t=T$ assuming $t=0$.

The *(risk-neutral) transition density function* (RNTDF) is the key to pricing options, and it is relatively easy to derive in our case since $X_T(\omega)$ is Gaussian. Therefore its transition density function is completely described in terms of two parameters; its conditional mean and its conditional variance. This means that all we have to do is derive the mean and the variance of $X_T(\omega)$ conditional upon X_0.

These are easily calculated as follows. As we have just seen, $E(X_T(\omega) \mid X_0)=X_0$, by the martingale property of $X_T(\omega)$, which simply calculates the conditional mean as the conditioning variable. The conditional variance of $X_T(\omega)$ given X_0 is,

544 OPTIONS

$$\mathrm{Var}(X_T(\omega)\,|\,X_0) = \mathrm{Var}(S_0 + W_T(\omega)\,|\,X_0)$$
$$= \mathrm{Var}(W_T(\omega)\,|\,X_0)$$

since adding a constant, S_0 in this case, to a random variable doesn't affect its variance (conditional or unconditional). Therefore,

$$\mathrm{Var}(S_0 + W_T(\omega)\,|\,X_0) = \mathrm{Var}(W_T(\omega)\,|\,S_0 + W_0)$$
$$= \mathrm{Var}(W_T(\omega)\,|\,S_0) \text{ since } W_0 = 0.$$

But $\mathrm{Var}(W_T(\omega)\,|\,S_0) = \mathrm{Var}(W_T(\omega))$, since $W_T(\omega)$ doesn't depend on S_0, and $\mathrm{Var}(W_T(\omega)) = T$.

We conclude that,

$$\mathrm{Var}(X_T(\omega)\,|\,X_0) = T.$$

■ CONCEPT CHECK 1

a. Show that $\mathrm{Var}(W_t(\omega)) = t$ for any t with $0 \le t \le T$ using the properties of ABM.

The next step is to get the risk–neutral transition density function of the process $(X_t(\omega))$. To do this, we start with the probability density function (pdf), $f(y)$, for a standard normalized normal random variable which is usually denoted by $N(0,1)$,

$$f(y) = \left(\frac{1}{\sqrt{2\pi}}\right) e^{-y^2/2} \qquad \textbf{(Probability Density Function of } N(0,1)\textbf{)}$$

The *cumulative* normal distribution function $N(.)$ is just the integral of the pdf $f(y)$ up to a given value z (called the z-value) and is denoted by $N(z)$,

$$N(z) = \int_{-\infty}^{z} f(y)\,dy \qquad \textbf{(Cumulative Distribution Function}$$
$$= \frac{1}{\sqrt{2\pi}} \int_{-\infty}^{z} e^{-y^2/2}\,dy \qquad \textbf{of } N(0,1)\textbf{)}$$

OPTION PRICING IN CONTINUOUS TIME 545

A normal random variable with mean 0 and variance (or standard deviation) equal to 1.0 is denoted by $N(0,1)$. If we have a *non-standard* normal random variable, y, with mean μ and standard deviation σ, denoted by $N(\mu,\sigma)$, we can always *normalize* it by subtracting the mean and dividing by the standard deviation to obtain,

$$y' = \frac{y - \mu}{\sigma}$$

Then,

$$E(y') = E\left(\frac{y - \mu}{\sigma}\right)$$

$$= \frac{1}{\sigma} E\left(y - \mu\right)$$

$$= \frac{1}{\sigma}\left(E(y) - \mu\right)$$

$$= \frac{0}{\sigma}$$

$$= 0$$

and, $\mathrm{Var}(y') = 1.0$.

■ CONCEPT CHECK 2

a. Show that $\mathrm{Var}(y')=1.0$ using the rules for calculating variances we derived in Chapter 6, section 6.3.1.

This shows that the normalization works in generating an $N(0,1)$ random variable.

In order to derive the transition density function for shifted arithmetic Brownian motion, we just have to normalize the terminal (at time T) stock price distribution by subtracting the conditional mean and dividing by the conditional standard deviation. These were calculated as,

$$E(X_T(\omega) \mid X_0) = X_0 \text{ and,}$$

546 **OPTIONS**

$$\sqrt{\operatorname{Var}\left(X_T(\omega)\,|\,X_0\right)} = \sqrt{T}$$

Thus

$$\gamma' = \frac{\gamma - \mu}{\sigma}$$

$$= \frac{\gamma - X_0}{\sqrt{T}}$$

is now an $N(0,1)$ random variable. By γ we mean $X_T(\omega)$.

When we integrate something like the payoff to a European call option with respect to the density $f(\gamma)$ of an $N(0,1)$ random variable, we have to multiply by the $d\gamma$ term and integrate an integral involving $f(\gamma)d\gamma$. This means that when we make a *change of variables* γ', the new density becomes $f(\gamma')d\gamma'$. Note that for the change of variables γ' above $d\gamma'=d\gamma/\sqrt{T}$.

We can make this slightly neater by summarizing it by the risk-neutral transition density function, which we will denote by $p(T,\gamma;t,x)$. The notation indicates that the process is at x at time t, it *will be* at some random point γ at time T, and the transition is random but defined by a specific terminal (time T) probability distribution $p(T,\gamma;t,x)$.

In our case, the terminal probability distribution, $\gamma(\omega)=X_T(\omega)$, is Gaussian with conditional mean $x=X_0$ and conditional standard deviation, $\sqrt{T}$, as we have just derived. Remember that $t=0$ and $T=T$.

In this case, the terminal density is $f(\gamma')d\gamma'$ where

$$f(\gamma) = \left(\frac{1}{\sqrt{2\pi}}\right)e^{-\gamma^2/2} \text{ and } \gamma' = \frac{\gamma - X_0}{\sqrt{T}}$$

Substituting γ' into $f(\gamma)$ and calculating $f(\gamma')d\gamma'$ produces,

$$f(\gamma')d\gamma' = \frac{1}{\sqrt{2\pi}}e^{-\gamma'^2/2}\frac{d\gamma}{\sqrt{T}}$$

$$= \frac{1}{\sqrt{2\pi T}}e^{-\gamma'/2}d\gamma$$

$$= \left(\frac{1}{\sqrt{2\pi T}}\right)e^{-(\gamma-X_0)^2/2T}d\gamma$$

$$= p(T,\gamma;0,x)d\gamma$$

Therefore, the risk-neutral transition density function (RNTDF) of shifted ABM is,

$$p(T,y;\,0,X_0) = \left(\frac{1}{\sqrt{2\pi T}}\right)e^{-(y-X_0)^2/2T}dy \qquad \textbf{(RNTDF for Shifted ABM)}$$

Sometimes, such as in our case, the (risk-neutral) transition density function depends only on $\tau = T-t$. It is then said to be a *stationary* transition density function, and is customarily abbreviated as $p(\tau,x,y)$ and written as,

$$p(\tau,x,y) = p(T,y;t,x) = \left(\frac{1}{\sqrt{2\pi\tau}}\right)e^{-(y-x)^2/2\tau}$$

16.3.3 Deriving the Bachelier Option Pricing Formula

We are now in a position, as was Bachelier for the first time in 1900, to derive the arbitrage-free price of a European call option for an asset $(X_t)_{0\leqslant t\leqslant T}$ following a shifted arithmetic Brownian motion. K is the exercise price of the option, $t=0$, and the option expires at time T.

Given all the work we have already done in setting up the problem, we are in the fortunate position of being required to solve an integration problem using ordinary (non-stochastic) calculus. It's nice to know what results in Derivatives require stochastic calculus and what results require ordinary (non-stochastic) calculus.

Using the (EMM Option Price Representation), in section 15.5.1, we find that,

$$C(X_0,T;K) = E\left\{\mathrm{MAX}[X_T(\omega) - K, 0]\,|\,X_0\right\} \qquad \textbf{(ABM 1)}$$

$$= \int_{y>K}(y-K)p(T,y;\,0,X_0)dy \qquad \textbf{(ABM 2)}$$

$$= \int_{y>K}(y-K)\left(\frac{1}{\sqrt{2\pi T}}\right)e^{-(y-X_0)^2/2T}dy \qquad \textbf{(ABM 3)}$$

Now, we make the change of variables

$$y' = \frac{y - X_0}{\sqrt{T}} \qquad \textbf{(ABM 4)}$$

548 OPTIONS

Then

$$y = \left(\sqrt{T}\right)y' + X_0 \tag{ABM 5}$$

and

$$dy' = \frac{dy}{\sqrt{T}} \tag{ABM 6}$$

Making these substitutions into the integral we obtain that (ABM 3),

$$\int_{y'>(K-X_0)/\sqrt{T}} \left(\left(\sqrt{T}\right)y' + X_0 - K\right)\left(\frac{1}{\sqrt{2\pi}}\right)e^{-y'^2/2}dy' \tag{ABM 7}$$

$$= \int_{y'>(K-X_0)/\sqrt{T}} \left(\left(\sqrt{T}\right)y'\right)\left(\frac{1}{\sqrt{2\pi}}\right)e^{-y'^2/2}dy' \tag{ABM 8a}$$

$$+ \int_{y'>(K-X_0)/\sqrt{T}} \left(X_0 - K\right)\left(\frac{1}{\sqrt{2\pi}}\right)e^{-y'^2/2}dy' \tag{ABM 8b}$$

The second integral, (ABM 8b), is easy to evaluate so we will do it first,

$$\int_{y'>(K-X_0)/\sqrt{T}} \left(X_0 - K\right)\left(\frac{1}{\sqrt{2\pi}}\right)e^{-y'^2/2}dy' \tag{ABM 9}$$

$$= \left(X_0 - K\right)\int_{y'>(K-X_0)/\sqrt{T}} \left(\frac{1}{\sqrt{2\pi}}\right)e^{-y'^2/2}dy' \tag{ABM 10}$$

since X_0-K is known at time $t=0$.

The integral in (ABM 10) represents the cumulative probability that an $N(0,1)$ random variable lies above $z=(K-X_0)/\sqrt{T}$. In other words, it is the *right tail* probability above z. Because the Gaussian $N(0,1)$ is a symmetric random variable centered at 0, the quantity $1-N(z)$ is also equal to the corresponding tail probability below $-z$. That is, $N(-z)=1-N(z)$ for a symmetric distribution around 0 like an $N(0,1)$.

■ CONCEPT CHECK 3

a. Draw a picture of, and verify that, $N(-z)=1-N(z)$ for any z.

Therefore the entire second integral,

$$\left(X_0 - K\right) \int_{y' > (K - X_0)/\sqrt{T}} \left(\frac{1}{\sqrt{2\pi}}\right) e^{-y'^2/2} dy'$$

in (ABM10), is equal to,

$$= \left(X_0 - K\right) N(-z) \text{ where } -z = \frac{X_0 - K}{\sqrt{T}} \qquad \text{(ABM 11)}$$

$$= \left(X_0 - K\right) N\left(\frac{X_0 - K}{\sqrt{T}}\right) \qquad \text{(ABM 12)}$$

This leaves the first integral (ABM 8a),

$$\int_{y' > (K - X_0)/\sqrt{T}} \left((\sqrt{T})y'\right) \left(\frac{1}{\sqrt{2\pi}}\right) e^{-y'^2/2} dy'$$

to evaluate,

$$= \sqrt{T} \int_{y' > (K - X_0)/\sqrt{T}} (y') \left(\frac{1}{\sqrt{2\pi}}\right) e^{-y'^2/2} dy' \qquad \text{(ABM 13)}$$

$$= \sqrt{T} \int_{y' > (K - X_0)/\sqrt{T}} \left(\frac{1}{\sqrt{2\pi}}\right) e^{-y'^2/2} (y') dy' \qquad \text{(ABM 14)}$$

Note that

$$f(y') = \frac{1}{\sqrt{2\pi}} e^{-y'^2/2}$$

Therefore, the first derivative of $f(y')$, which we can denote by $f'(y')$, is given by,

$$f'(y') = \frac{1}{\sqrt{2\pi}} e^{-y'^2/2} \left(\frac{-2y'}{2}\right) \qquad \text{(ABM 15)}$$

$$= -\frac{1}{\sqrt{2\pi}} e^{-y'^2/2} y'$$

If we look at the integral in (ABM 14),

$$\sqrt{T} \int_{y' > (K - X_0)/\sqrt{T}} \left(\frac{1}{\sqrt{2\pi}}\right) e^{-y'^2/2} (y') dy'$$

550 OPTIONS

we now see that it is equal to (ABM 16),

$$= \sqrt{T} \int_{y' > (K-X_0)/\sqrt{T}} \left(-f'(y') \right) dy'$$

$$= -\sqrt{T} \int_{y' > (K-X_0)/\sqrt{T}} f'(y') dy'$$

$$= -\sqrt{T} \left[f(\infty) - f\left(\frac{K - X_0}{\sqrt{T}} \right) \right]$$

$$= -\sqrt{T} \left[-f\left(\frac{K - X_0}{\sqrt{T}} \right) \right]$$

$$= \sqrt{T} f\left(\frac{K - X_0}{\sqrt{T}} \right) \qquad\qquad\qquad \textbf{(ABM 16)}$$

We used the fundamental theorem of calculus to evaluate the integral,

$$\int_{y' > (K-X_0)/\sqrt{T}} f'(y') dy' = f(\infty) - f\left(\frac{K - X_0}{\sqrt{T}} \right)$$

Since $f(\infty)=0$, (ABM 16) is equal to

$$-\sqrt{T} \left[f(\infty) - f\left(\frac{K - X_0}{\sqrt{T}} \right) \right] = \sqrt{T} f\left(\frac{K - X_0}{\sqrt{T}} \right)$$

But $f((K-X_0)/\sqrt{T})$ can also be written as $N'(z(K))$, where $N(\cdot)$ is the cumulative distribution function,

$$N\left(z(K) \right) = \int_{-\infty}^{z(K)} f(y) dy$$

$$= \frac{1}{\sqrt{2\pi}} \int_{-\infty}^{z(K)} e^{-y^2/2} dy$$

and $N'(z(K))$ is the first derivative of $N(z(K))$ evaluated at $z(K)=(K-X_0)/\sqrt{T}$

■ CONCEPT CHECK 4

a. Show that

$$f\left(\frac{K - X_0}{\sqrt{T}} \right) = N'\left(\frac{K - X_0}{\sqrt{T}} \right)$$

OPTION PRICING IN CONTINUOUS TIME **551**

Adding up (ABM 16) and (ABM 12), we obtain Bachelier's option pricing formula,

$$C(X_0, T; K) = \sqrt{T}\; N'\!\left(\frac{K - X_0}{\sqrt{T}}\right) + \left(X_0 - K\right) N\!\left(\frac{X_0 - K}{\sqrt{T}}\right)$$

Since $X_0 = S_0$, the current stock price, Bachelier's option pricing can be rewritten as,

$$C(S_0, T; K) = \sqrt{T}\; N'\!\left(\frac{K - S_0}{\sqrt{T}}\right) + \left(S_0 - K\right) N\!\left(\frac{S_0 - K}{\sqrt{T}}\right) \qquad \textbf{(Bachelier)}$$

This is Bachelier's famous option pricing formula, derived in 1900. It was basically rediscovered around 1965. At that point, it was dismissed for three reasons by Samuelson, who presented three objections to Bachelier.

First, shifted arithmetic Brownian motion violates the limited liability property of stock prices, because the process can go negative. This can be resolved by absorbing the ABM at zero, when it first hits zero.

This also takes care of the second objection which is that, as the time to expiration $\tau = T$ of the option increases, the call value becomes larger than any given current value of the underlying asset.

This actually is *not* a contradiction and it does not represent an arbitrage opportunity. We know that the Bachelier model is arbitrage-free because there exists an EMM. This phenomenon happens only when the stock price goes negative, in which case the option (with any exercise price $K \geqslant 0$) should be, and is, worth more than the stock, namely zero, since the stock price is negative!

Finally, the process is consistent with only one form of risk-neutrality, $r=0$, since its drift is zero. However, one can add a drift term, μt, to ABM that is proportional to time.

Samuelson's well-known resolution of these issues was to replace shifted arithmetic Brownian motion with geometric Brownian motion (GBM), also called the usual log-normal diffusion process. However, as indicated, it is relatively easy to resolve Samuelson's three objections within the context of shifted arithmetic Brownian motion.

16.4 DEFINING AND PRICING A STANDARD NUMERAIRE

In Chapter 4, section 4.2.1, we discussed how to price a zero-coupon bond with a face value of $1 at maturity. Here we will price a zero-coupon bond that *starts off* at $t=0$ with a value of \$1. We want to see what it pays off at any time $t>0$.

This is important, because it is used in martingale pricing to first 'discount' the asset price underlying contingent claims as discussed in Chapter 15. The contingent claim's price is then based on this *'discounted price process'*, and constitutes a martingale under an EMM. This also proves the absence of arbitrage.

This particular price process is the standard *numeraire* (unit of account) and X_t is its time t price which is easy to determine.

$$\frac{dX_t}{X_t} = rdt \qquad \textbf{(Bond equation)}$$

(Bond equation) says that the *instantaneous* percentage rate of return on the bond, the change in the bond price over a very small interval of time, dX_t, divided by what you currently have to pay for the bond, X_t, is the instantaneous risk-free rate and is equal to rdt. r is an *annualized* rate as we discussed in Chapter 4.

We can solve (Bond equation), the result of which is to get $X_t = e^{rt}$. We will work with the natural log function of the bond price, $\ln(X_t)$, and use the 'chain rule' of calculus once again,

$$\frac{d \ln(X_t)}{dt} = \frac{d \ln(X_t)}{dX_t} * \frac{dX_t}{dt}$$

$$= \frac{1}{X_t} * \frac{dX_t}{dt}$$

$$= \frac{dX_t / X_t}{dt}$$

$$= r$$

Or, from (Bond equation),

$$d \ln(X_t) = rdt \qquad \textbf{(Log Bond equation)}$$

This new (Log Bond equation) can be integrated using basic calculus.

The definite integral of the left-hand side of (Log Bond equation) is,

$$\int_0^t \frac{d\,\ln(X_t)}{dv}dv = \ln(X_t) - \ln(X_0)$$

$$= \ln\left(\frac{X_t}{X_0}\right)$$

The definite integral on the right-hand side of (Log Bond equation) is,

$$\int_0^t rdv = r*t - r*0$$

$$= r*t$$

Note that the current (time 0) price of the zero-coupon bond is now assumed to be X_0=\$1.0, which is *not* what we assumed in Chapter 4. There, we assumed that the *face value* at time T, X_T=\$1.0.

Equating the definite integral of the left-hand side of (Log Bond equation) to the definite integral of the right-hand side of (Log Bond equation) we find that,

$$\ln\left(\frac{X_t}{1.0}\right) = r*t$$

Applying the exponential function, exp(.), to both sides of this equation we get exp $(\ln(X_t))$=e^{rt}. Or, because the exp function and the ln function are inverse to each other, X_t=e^{rt}.

This shows that the numeraire's price at time t is simply X_t=e^{rt}. This is used, in general, to discount the underlying price process in order to obtain an EMM with which to price the financial derivative.

16.5 GEOMETRIC BROWNIAN MOTION (GBM)

16.5.1 GBM (Discrete Version)

In order to price European options on GBM, which is considered the workhorse for underlying processes used to price options, we have to first understand how the GBM process behaves. Also, it doesn't hurt to know where it comes from.

This involves ideas from *stochastic differential equations* (SDEs). In particular, *Itô's lemma (stochastic chain rule)* is a key component. Fortunately, an intuitive description of the GBM process is possible, and we give it now.

554 OPTIONS

We start with what we know which is how to model returns for a riskless, zero-coupon bond paying off $1.0 *at expiration* (not a numeraire). We did this in detail in Chapter 4, section 4.2.1, where we found it as the solution to (Bond equation), where we imposed the boundary condition on it that *it pays $1.0 at maturity*, X_T=$1.0.

We slightly modified this in this chapter to obtain a *numeraire*, where its starting boundary condition is X_0=$1.0. That's because a numeraire is the unit of account. Everything else can be expressed in units of the numeraire. It's like, but doesn't have to be, a monetary unit such as $1. As we indicated, it could be a zero-coupon bond maturing at time T, starting out at time t=0 at the given value of $1.

$$\frac{dX_t}{X_t} = rdt \qquad\qquad \textbf{(Bond equation)}$$

The solution is $X_0=e^{-rt}$, assuming that we start at 0, T=t, and X_T=1.0.

Note that our time interval here is $[0,t]$. In Chapter 4, the time interval was $[t,T]$, then we used $\tau=T-t$, and our solution was $X_{t,T}=B(t,T)=e^{-r\tau}$.

(Bond equation) is a purely deterministic equation in the sense that it incorporates no risk. That's why its solution is a risk-free bond. When we turn to stocks, and other risky assets, the first thing we notice is price volatility which is another name for risk. We also hope that risky assets, such as common stocks, promise a *higher* expected return than risk-free bonds. Otherwise, why take on the extra risk and invest in them? The amount higher is called the *risk premium* as briefly discussed in the Appendix to Chapter 4, section 4.8.

Let's call μ the expected *return* of the stock. The *risk premium* is then the *excess* (above r) expected return and, it is equal to μ-r. We can easily incorporate this into (Bond equation) by just changing r to μ in (Bond equation),

$$\frac{dX_t}{X_t} = \mu dt \qquad\qquad \textbf{(\mu \ equation)}$$

Unfortunately, this would still represent a riskless bond, and if μ>r, then there would also be a riskless arbitrage opportunity.

■ CONCEPT CHECK 5

a. Suppose that r=5% annually and that the expected return on some equally riskless bond were μ=6% annually. Construct an arbitrage opportunity.

OPTION PRICING IN CONTINUOUS TIME   555

So, we have to do more to (Bond equation) to get it to meaningfully incorporate risk and (expected) return. The solution to (equation μ depends on the time interval, say $[t,T]$, and the boundary condition.

Since it doesn't make a lot of economic sense to constrain a stock to grow to \$1 at a specific point in time, we start with a given value of the asset, X_t, and let it grow unconstrained (except by (equation μ) to its time T value.

Then the value of the solution to (equation μ) at time T is $X_T = e^{\mu\tau}X_t$. This says that if you put \$1 into an asset that is expected to grow by its continuously compounded growth rate, μ, over a period $[t,T]$, then its future value will be $e^{\mu\tau}*\$1$ where $\tau = T - t$.

Now, we have to add risk into (equation μ). We start with a discrete version of (equation μ) by replacing dX_t by $\Delta X_t = X_{t+\Delta t} - X_t$, which is simply the change in X_t over a small interval of time Δt. Then we would re-write the discrete version of (equation μ) as,

$$\frac{\Delta X_t}{X_t} = \mu\Delta t \qquad\qquad (\mu \text{ equation discrete})$$

The simplest way to model risk and uncertainty in asset prices is to add to (equation μ discrete) the scaled increment of an ABM process, $\sigma*(W_t(\omega))_{t\geq 0}$. That is, we add to (equation μ discrete) the increment $W_{t+\Delta t}(\omega) - W_t$ random variable, scaled by the constant σ. The notation $\Delta W_t(\omega)$ is just a short form for the *increment*,

$$\sigma*\Delta W_t(\omega) = \sigma*(W_{t+\Delta t}(\omega) - W_t) \qquad\qquad \textbf{(scaled-by-}\sigma\textbf{ Increment of an}$$
$$\textbf{ABM process)}$$

where σ is a constant volatility parameter.

Our discrete risk-adjusted equation is now (equation μ discrete, risk-adjusted) where now we emphasize randomness and its source which is the 'driving' scaled, increment of an ABM, $\sigma*(W_{t+\Delta t}(\omega) - W_t)$.

$$\frac{\Delta X_t(\omega)}{X_t} = \mu\Delta t + \sigma*\Delta W_t(\omega) \qquad\qquad (\mu \text{ equation discrete, risk-}$$
$$\text{adjusted)}$$

This equation says that the *percentage rate of return* of the risky asset over a small time interval of length Δt consists of two components,

556 OPTIONS

1. The reward-for-risk factor, $\mu\Delta t$, in the form of the risk-adjusted expected return, which is also adjusted for the time that one holds the risky asset, Δt.

2. A risk-factor, $\sigma * \Delta W_t(\omega)$, which means that there is no guarantee of actually earning $\mu\Delta t$ over the time interval, since this factor makes the *actual* return deviate from the expected return. In other words, the *actual* return on the risky asset is random and depends on the driving, scaled increment of an ABM.

To see how this plays out we calculate the conditional mean and conditional variance of the process in (μ equation discrete, risk-adjusted),

$$E\left(\frac{\Delta X_t(\omega)}{X_t}\Big| X_t\right)$$

$$=E(\mu\Delta t+\sigma * \Delta W_t(\omega)\,|\,X_t)$$

$$=\mu E(\Delta t\,|\,X_t)+\sigma E(\Delta W_t(\omega)\,|\,X_t) \text{ by linearity of } E(\cdot\,|\,X_t),$$

$$=\mu\Delta t+\sigma E(\Delta W_t(\omega)\,|\,X_t) \text{ since } \Delta t \text{ is a constant that does not depend}$$
$$\text{on } X_t,$$

$$=\mu\Delta t+\sigma E(W_{t+\Delta t}(\omega)-W_t\,|\,X_t) \text{ by plugging in the definition of } \Delta W_t(\omega),$$

$$=\mu\Delta t+\sigma E(W_{t+\Delta t}(\omega)\,|\,X_t)-\sigma E(W_t\,|\,X_t) \text{ by linearity of } E(\cdot\,|\,X_t),$$

$$=\mu\Delta t+\sigma E(W_{t+\Delta t}(\omega)\,|\,W_t)-\sigma E(W_t\,|\,W_t) \text{ since } W_t \text{ is the only source of}$$
$$\text{uncertainty,}$$

$$=\mu\Delta t+\sigma W_t-\sigma W_t \text{ since } (W_t(\omega))_{t\geqslant 0} \text{ is a martingale and } E(W_t\,|\,W_t)=W_t,$$

$$=\mu\Delta t$$

Next,

$$\text{Var}\left(\frac{\Delta X_t(\omega)}{X_t}\Big| X_t\right)$$

$$=\text{Var}(\mu\Delta t+\sigma * \Delta W_t(\omega)\,|\,X_t) \text{ by plugging in (equation } \mu \text{ discrete, risk-}$$
$$\text{adjusted),}$$

$$=\text{Var}(\mu\Delta t+\sigma * \Delta W_t(\omega)) \text{ since } \mu\Delta t+\sigma * \Delta W_t(\omega) \text{ does not depend on } X_t,$$

$$=\text{Var}(\mu\Delta t)+\text{Var}(\sigma * \Delta W_t(\omega)) \text{ because } \text{cov}(\mu\Delta t,\sigma * \Delta W_t(\omega))=0,$$

$$=0+\text{Var}(\sigma * \Delta W_t(\omega))$$

$$=\sigma^2\text{Var}(\Delta W_t(\omega)) \text{ by a standard property of Var,}$$

$$=\sigma^2\Delta t \text{ by property 3 of ABM}$$

We conclude that $\Delta X_t(\omega)/X_t$ is a Gaussian distribution with conditional mean $\mu\Delta t$ and (conditional) variance $\sigma^2\Delta t$, because $\mu\Delta t + \sigma * \Delta W_t(\omega)$ is a constant plus the increment of a scaled Brownian motion, which by assumption is Gaussian (see property 3 in the definition of an ABM).

Note that all of these calculations are in discrete time. When we move to continuous time, things get more complicated and we will need Itô's lemma, which provides a stochastic calculus for the continuous version of equations driven by scaled ABMs, such as (equation μ discrete, risk-adjusted).

The other characteristic we want to look at is the correlation between successive values of $\Delta X_t(\omega)/X_t$ such as $\Delta X_s(\omega)/X_s$ and $\Delta X_t(\omega)/X_t$ where $s>t$.

We know that $t<t+\Delta t$ and that $s<s+\Delta s$ and will assume that $t+\Delta t \leq s$. So this gives us times $t<t+\Delta t \leq s<s+\Delta s$. Then,

$$\text{Covariance}\left(\frac{\Delta X_t(\omega)}{X_t}, \frac{\Delta X_s(\omega)}{X_s}\right)$$

$$=\text{Cov}(\mu\Delta t + \sigma * \Delta W_t(\omega), \mu\Delta s + \sigma * \Delta W_s(\omega))$$

$$=\text{Cov}(\mu\Delta t, \mu\Delta s) + \text{Cov}(\mu\Delta t, \sigma * \Delta W_s(\omega)) + \text{Cov}(\sigma * \Delta W_t(\omega), \mu\Delta s)$$
$$\quad + \text{Cov}(\sigma * \Delta W_t(\omega), \sigma * \Delta W_s(\omega))$$

$$=\text{Cov}(\sigma * \Delta W_t(\omega), \sigma * \Delta W_s(\omega)).$$

The only term left standing is the last term, because $\mu\Delta t$ and $\mu\Delta s$ are non-stochastic, which means that they do not move and therefore must be uncorrelated (since correlation is a measure of the co-movement between random variables). For the same reason, the next two terms are also zero, the correlation between a random variable and a constant such as $\mu\Delta t$ or $\mu\Delta s$ is zero. Let's look at the remaining term,

$$\text{Cov}(\sigma * \Delta W_t(\omega), \sigma * \Delta W_s(\omega))$$
$$=\text{Cov}(\sigma * (W_{t+\Delta t}(\omega) - W_t), \sigma * (W_{s+\Delta s}(\omega) - W_s))$$
$$=\sigma^2\text{Cov}(W_{t+\Delta t}(\omega) - W_t, W_{s+\Delta s}(\omega) - W_s) \text{ by linearity of Cov }(\cdot,\cdot)$$
$$=0.$$

By property 2 of the definition of ABM, $(W_t(\omega))_{t \geq 0}$ has independent increments which implies that this correlation is zero. In particular, successive increments are independent.

This fact is what accounts for the tremendous appeal of processes driven by ABM. They are consistent with the *efficient market hypothesis* (EMH) (Chapter 15, section 15.6), which implies zero correlation in asset returns. To be more precise, one should add the qualifier '*after adjusting for drift*'. EMH processes can earn a risk premium, but their returns are otherwise unpredictable from period to period.

Now we run up against a characteristic feature of processes defined by equation (equation μ discrete, risk-adjusted). We just showed that the correlation (covariance) between returns $\Delta X_t(\omega)/X_t$ and $\Delta X_s(\omega)/X_s$ calculated over non-overlapping time intervals $[t, t+\Delta t]$ and $[s, s+\Delta s]$ where $t < t+\Delta t \leq s < s+\Delta s$ *unadjusted for risk* is zero.

And yet the process in (equation μ discrete, risk-adjusted) clearly has a risk premium in the term $\mu \Delta t$ where $\mu > r$. How can this be? One would think that a positive drift term $\mu > r > 0$ would induce correlation in stock returns. But we just showed that it doesn't, in our case.

Suppose that we have a stock whose price at time $t_0 = 0$ is \$100. We'll assume that $\mu = .10$ on an annualized basis. Let us make it simple and assume that $\Delta t = 1$ year. At the end of the first year, we expect the stock price to be $\$110 = (1+\mu) * \$100$.

Now we will go ahead and calculate the expected returns over years 1, 2, 3, and 4.

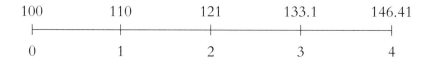

The expected return over year 1 is $(110-100)/100 = .10$, over year 2 it is $(121-110)/110 = .10$, over year 3 it is $(133.1-121)/121 = .10$, and over year 4 it is $(146.41-133.1)/133.1 = .10$.

In each case, the expected return stays at the constant level of $\mu = .10$. That is what (equation μ discrete, risk-adjusted) says. The price level is clearly increasing; it *has to* in order to earn 10% on a percentage basis. Therefore, stock *prices* are clearly positively correlated. However, *percentage expected returns remain constant*.

A constant has zero correlation with itself, because it doesn't move at all. Therefore, the drift μ induces no correlation whatsoever. In fact, the model in (μ equation discrete, risk-adjusted) constrains the expected price level to move up in such a manner that μ remains constant. In section 16.5.2, we will see that this is the defining characteristic of the continuous analogue of the discrete-time GBM process in (μ equation discrete, risk-adjusted). That process is called the *log-normal* process or *geometric Brownian motion* (GBM).

The reason for calling it *geometric,* as opposed to *arithmetic* Brownian motion is that it expresses the idea of *geometric growth*, otherwise known as continuous compounding. Over any period of length $\mu\Delta t$, the GBM process grows by a *fixed percentage* amount, $\mu\Delta t$, relative to its current value. In the ABM process one is looking at *absolute* dollar changes in the asset's value—as opposed to percentage changes.

16.5.2 Geometric Brownian Motion (GBM), Continuous Version

Take (equation μ discrete, risk-adjusted) and wherever you see Δ, replace it by the letter d,

$$\frac{dX_t(\omega)}{X_t} = \mu dt + \sigma dW_t(\omega) \qquad \textbf{(GBM equation)}$$

Now drop the ω and multiply through by X_t. You will obtain the usual *stochastic differential equation* (SDE) for the log-normal (GBM) process as,

$$dX_t = \mu X_t dt + \sigma X_t dW_t \qquad \textbf{(GBM SDE)}$$

Integrating along a path ω, the (GBM SDE) would appear to lead to its solution, given an initial value of the process X_0,

$$X_T(\omega) = X_0 + \int_0^T \mu X_s(\omega)ds + \int_0^T \sigma X_s(\omega)dW_s(\omega) \qquad \textbf{(GBM SIE)}$$

This is actually the meaning of (GBM SDE), which is written in differential equation format. So that when you see a stochastic differential equation (SDE) like (GBM SDE), its meaning is strictly in terms of the corresponding *stochastic integral equation* (SIE).

Of course, both equivalent formulations, as an (SDE) or as an (SIE) are just notation and don't fit into the framework of ordinary non-stochastic calculus.

The first integral in (GBM SIE) can be given a meaning path by path ω. However, the second integral is far more problematic, even path by path ω. To see this suppose that, instead of dW_s in the second integral, we have some smooth function $g(s)$ that we are integrating with respect to, so the term is $dg(s)$. If $g(s)$ is differentiable, then $dg(s)=g'(s)ds$ and we can integrate with respect to it. The integral is

$$\int_0^T \sigma X_s(\omega)dg(s) = \int_0^T \sigma X_s(\omega)g'(s)ds$$

which can be integrated path by path.

In the case of (GBM SIE), there are several serious issues. First, the integrals are *stochastic* integrals, because they depend on randomness as represented by the 'state of the world', ω. This wouldn't stop us from evaluating the integrals path by path as just discussed and then providing a meaning to the integrals across paths, by averaging, for example.

However, integration with respect to dW_s requires that W_s has sufficiently 'nice' paths, which means differentiable paths. One of the main features of the Brownian motion paths $(W_s(\omega))$ is that, while they are almost surely continuous, they are almost surely *nowhere differentiable*. We can't prove that here but we can give an economic rationale for it in terms of the EMH.

FIGURE 16.1 Non Smoothness of Brownian Motion Paths

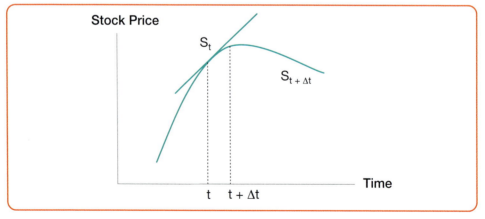

If a Brownian motion path happened to be differentiable at some stock price and the derivative was positive, for example, then it would be *locally riskless*. This means that, near the stock price at which the derivative is positive, the price path is like a straight line, as indicated in Figure 16.1.

OPTION PRICING IN CONTINUOUS TIME 561

In Figure 16.1, the stock price is increasing *near* the stock price S_t. Investment in the stock would earn the risk-free rate, $r\Delta t$, over a small interval of time of length Δt, as indicated. This would imply *predictability* of the stock price near S_t, which contradicts the EMH. It also conflicts with the notion that stocks, unlike bonds, are risky everywhere.

Because almost all the sample paths of ABM are nowhere differentiable, it becomes quite difficult to define the integral

$$\int_0^T \sigma X_s(\omega)dW_s(\omega)$$

as an ordinary integral. Fortunately, K. Itô developed a definition now known as the *Itô integral*, and his definition is consistent with the EMH. This means that the Itô integral is a martingale.

Equations such as

$$X_T(\omega) = X_0 + \int_0^T \mu X_s(\omega)ds + \int_0^T \sigma X_s(\omega)dW_s(\omega) \qquad \textbf{(GBM SIE)}$$

then say that the random value $X_T(\omega)$ is its current value plus a drift term

$$\int_0^T \mu X_s(\omega)ds$$

which incorporates the risk premium of the asset.

Finally, volatility is incorporated as unpredictable volatility in the form of a martingale Itô integral,

$$\int_0^T \sigma X_s(\omega)dW_s(\omega)$$

The increments of a square integrable martingale are uncorrelated (see the Appendix to Chapter 15, section 15.7) and enough conditions are usually imposed so that the Itô integral is square integrable.

For the case of GBM, *both* the drift coefficient and the diffusion coefficient are linear in the underlying process $\mu(X_s)=\mu X_s$ and $\sigma(X_s)=\sigma X_s$. Linearity of the drift coefficient $\mu(X_s)$, and of the diffusion coefficient $\sigma(X_s)$, are the *defining* features of the log-normal diffusion process defined in (GBM SIE). In more general scenarios, of course, we could have both $\mu(X_s)$ and $\sigma(X_s)$ non-linear in X_s and they could also be time dependent $\mu(X_s,s)$ and $\sigma(X_s,s)$.

The mathematical theory of stochastic integration is highly developed and is important in mathematical finance. For our purposes, we need only one more ingredient. Then we can actually solve (GBM SIE) and then derive Black–Scholes using *ordinary* calculus. This ingredient is stochastic calculus in the form of Itô's lemma.

16.6 ITÔ'S LEMMA

We start with ordinary calculus which says that if we have a smooth function of x, $f(x)$, then its derivative, $f'(x)$, can be written as $df(x)/dx = f'(x)$. This leads to a formula for the *total differential* of $f(x)$,

$$df(x) = \frac{df(x)}{dx}dx$$
$$= f'(x)dx$$

Suppose now that $f(x)$ also depends upon time, so that $f = f(x,t)$. If we want to take the total differential of $f(x,t)$, we have to also incorporate its time dimension,

$$df(x,t) = \frac{\partial f(x,t)}{\partial x}dx + \frac{\partial f(x,t)}{\partial t}dt$$
$$= f_x(x,t)dx + f_x(x,t)dt$$

where $f_x(x,t) = \dfrac{\partial f(x,t)}{\partial x}$,

which is the partial derivative of $f(x,t)$ with respect to x and,

$$f_t(x,t) = \frac{\partial f(x,t)}{\partial t},$$

which is the partial derivative of $f(x,t)$ with respect to t. So far so good.

Now for a huge jump. How do we take derivatives of smooth functions of stochastic processes, say $F(X_t,t)$, such as (GBM SDE) where the process is the solution of a stochastic differential equation $dX_t = \mu X_t dt + \sigma X_t dW_t$ with initial value X_0?

We start with the observation that we can expect to end up with another stochastic process that is also the solution to another stochastic differential equation. This new stochastic differential equation for the total differential of $F(X_t,t)$ will have a new set of drift and diffusion coefficients. The question is what exactly are the drift and diffusion coefficients of $dF(X_t,t)$? This is one of the problems that K. Itô solved in his famous formula called Itô's lemma.

To understand Itô's lemma, keep in mind that there are two stochastic processes involved. The first is the underlying process (think of it as the stock). The second process is the derived process, which is a sufficiently smooth function of the underlying process (think of it as the derivative security). Our underlying process will be described as the solution to the following SDE, where we no longer assume linearity of $\mu(X_t)$ and $\sigma(X_t)$,

$$dX_t = \mu(X_t)dt + \sigma(X_t)dW_t \qquad \textbf{(SDE)}$$

$F(X_t,t)$ is a smooth function of X_t and time t with partial derivatives $\partial F(x,t)/\partial x$, $\partial F(x,t)/\partial t$ and $\partial^2 F(x,t)/\partial x^2$. Note that $x=X_t$ is the short form used here.

Then *Itô's lemma* says that,

$$dF(x,t) = \frac{\partial F(x,t)}{\partial x}dX_t + \frac{\partial F(x,t)}{\partial t}dt + \frac{\sigma^2(X_t)}{2}\frac{\partial^2 F(x,t)}{\partial x^2}dt \qquad \textbf{(Itô's lemma)}$$

This is just like the ordinary calculus formula, except for the inclusion of the last term,

$$\frac{\sigma^2(X_t)}{2}\frac{\partial^2 F(x,t)}{\partial x^2}dt$$

We won't attempt to prove Itô's lemma here. Rather, we will apply it immediately to the problem of solving (GBM SDE).

Take (GBM SDE) and let's just divide it by X_t (assuming it is not zero, which we will see is true) to go from (GBM SDE) to (LOG GBM SDE),

$$dX_t = \mu X_t dt + \sigma X_t dW_t \qquad \textbf{(GBM SDE)}$$

$$\frac{dX_t}{X_t} = \mu dt + \sigma dW_t \qquad \textbf{(LOG GBM SDE)}$$

We have played around with the deterministic form of this equation dX_t/X_t $=rdt$ long enough to recognize that it involves the log (or ln) function, and that this is because $d\ln(X_t)/dX_t=1/X_t$. This is all deterministic, but it strongly suggests for the stochastic case (GBM SDE) that we try to apply Itô's lemma to the function $F(X_t)=\ln(X_t)$. Note that $\ln(\cdot)$ is the natural log function, which is the inverse of the exponential function.

This turns out to be a really good idea because it quickly leads to a solution to (GBM SDE). All we need to do is to calculate the partial derivatives and plug into Itô's lemma,

$$\frac{\partial F(x,t)}{\partial x} = \frac{d\ln(x)}{dx} = \frac{1}{x} \text{ and,}$$

$$\frac{\partial^2 F(x,t)}{\partial x^2} = \frac{d^2\ln(x)}{dx^2} = -\frac{1}{x^2}$$

There is no $\partial F(x,t)/\partial t$. We don't have to worry about the partial derivative operator, ∂, here since it is the same as the ordinary derivative operator, d, in this one variable case. Plugging into Itô's lemma, we obtain,

$$d \ln(X_t) = \frac{d \ln(x)}{dx} dX_t + \frac{\sigma^2(X_t)}{2} \frac{d^2 F(x,t)}{dx^2} dt$$

$$= \frac{1}{x} dX_t + \frac{\sigma^2 X_t^2}{2} \left(-\frac{1}{x^2} \right) dt$$

Remember that x is short form for X_t so we obtain,

$$d \ln(X_t) = \frac{1}{X_t} dX_t + \frac{\sigma^2 X_t^2}{2} \left(-\frac{1}{X_t^2} \right) dt$$

$$= \mu dt + \sigma dW_t - \frac{\sigma^2}{2} dt$$

$$= \left(\mu - \frac{\sigma^2}{2} \right) dt + \sigma dW_t$$

So we have obtained the (SDE),

$$d \ln(X_t) = \left(\mu - \frac{\sigma^2}{2} \right) dt + \sigma dW_t$$

which is short form for the (GBM-SIE)

$$\ln(X_T(\omega)) - \ln(X_0) = \int_0^T \left(\mu - \frac{\sigma^2}{2} \right) ds + \int_0^T \sigma dW_s(\omega) \qquad \textbf{(GBM-SIE)}$$

Since

$$\ln(X_T(\omega)) - \ln(X_0) = \ln\left(\frac{X_T(\omega)}{X_0} \right)$$

a little more manipulation of (GBM-SIE) results in,

$$\ln\left(\frac{X_T(\omega)}{X_0} \right) = \int_0^T \left(\mu - \frac{\sigma^2}{2} \right) ds + \int_0^T \sigma dW_s(\omega) \qquad \textbf{(GBM-SIE)}$$

$$= \left(\mu - \frac{\sigma^2}{2} \right) T + \sigma \left(W_T(\omega) - W_0 \right)$$

OPTION PRICING IN CONTINUOUS TIME 565

Because $(\mu - \sigma^2/2)T$ is a constant, the first integral is an ordinary (non-stochastic) integral. Further, the second stochastic integral is easily evaluated as,

$$\int_0^T \sigma dW_s(\omega) = \sigma \int_0^T dW_s(\omega)$$
$$= \sigma \left(W_T(\omega) - W_0 \right)$$
$$= \sigma W_T(\omega) \text{ because } W_0 = 0$$

The interval of time is $[0, T]$ and $X_0 = S_0$ is the initial stock price, which is currently known. Therefore, we do not need an ω to describe it.

We can easily solve (GBM-SIE) but before we do, we pause to see what we have done. Since $W_0 = 0$, the (SIE) we have obtained is,

$$\ln\left(\frac{X_T(\omega)}{X_0} \right) = \left(\mu - \frac{\sigma^2}{2} \right) T + \sigma W_T(\omega) \qquad \textbf{(GBM-SIE)}$$

Note that this is a shifted ABM process *with drift* (think Bachelier), which tells us that the function,

$$F\left(X_T(\omega) \right) = \ln\left(\frac{X_T(\omega)}{X_0} \right)$$
$$= \ln\left(X_T(\omega) \right) - \ln\left(X_0 \right)$$

reduces the GBM process, normalized by its initial value X_0, to a Gaussian process with drift.

We will use this very helpful fact to systematically derive the Black–Scholes formula for a European call option on GBM in section 16.7. Thereby, we tie together Bachelier and Black–Scholes and we see that they are not very far apart at all. This is an interesting connection that links up two points in time, 1900 (Bachelier) and 1973 (Black–Scholes).

Solving (GBM-SIE) is simple. Just exponentiate both sides to obtain,

$$\exp\left[\ln\left(\frac{X_T(\omega)}{X_0} \right) \right] = \frac{X_T(\omega)}{X_0}$$
$$= \exp\left[\left(\mu - \frac{\sigma^2}{2} \right) T + \sigma W_T(\omega) \right]$$

The first equality holds because exp(.) and ln(.) are the inverse functions of each other. Thus the solution to (GBM-SIE) is,

$$X_T(\omega) = X_0 \exp\left[\left(\mu - \frac{\sigma^2}{2}\right)T + \sigma W_T(\omega)\right] \qquad \textbf{(Solution to GBM-SIE)}$$

This is our log-normal diffusion process, and we just saw why it is log-normal. The reason is that the ln function reduces it to a normal with drift.

One other important thing to note here is that, while the drift defining percentage rates of return dX_t/X_t is μ (see (LOG GBM SDE)), the drift of $d\ln(X_T)$ is $(\mu - \sigma^2/2)T$.

This is interesting in that in ordinary (non-stochastic) calculus the two would be equal because $d\ln(x)/dx = 1/x$. Therefore, taking some liberties with differentials, $d\ln(x) = dx/x$ *when x is non-stochastic*. When $x = X_T(\omega)$ is stochastic, Itô's lemma tells us that,

$$d\ln(X_t(\omega)) \neq \frac{dX_t(\omega)}{X_t(\omega)}$$

In fact,

$$d\ln(X_t(\omega)) = \frac{dX_t(\omega)}{X_t(\omega)} + \frac{\sigma^2 X_t^2(\omega)}{2}\left(-\frac{1}{X_t^2(\omega)}\right)dt$$

$$= \frac{dX_t(\omega)}{X_t(\omega)} - \frac{\sigma^2}{2}dt$$

Itô's lemma tells us that the stochastic term $\sigma W_T(\omega)$ contributes the quantity $-(\sigma^2/2)dt$ to the drift of the $\ln(X_t(\omega))$ process. For the GBM process this results in a *reduced total* drift of $(\mu - \sigma^2/2)dt$.

16.7 BLACK–SCHOLES OPTION PRICING

There are many derivations of the Black–Scholes model. We want to derive it in a way that is consistent with the material we have developed in this chapter. Our components are:

1. ABM (with and without drift) and Bachelier.
2. SDEs and SIEs.
3. GBM and Itô's lemma.

16.7.1 Reducing GBM to an ABM with Drift

The first step is to reduce a GBM to an ABM with drift. The starting point is the reduction of GBM to ABM with drift as shown in (GBM-SIE) which we repeat here.

$$\ln\left(\frac{X_T(\omega)}{X_0}\right) = \left(\mu - \frac{\sigma^2}{2}\right)T + \sigma W_T(\omega) \qquad \textbf{(GBM-SIE)}$$

We first need to describe the *risk neutral* GBM process corresponding to,

$$dX_t = \mu X_t dt + \sigma X_t dW_t \qquad \textbf{(GBM SDE)}$$

This is just (GBM SDE) with μ replaced by the risk-free rate r. It's not as easy as just substituting r for μ in (GBM SDE), although the net result looks roughly the same. In order to reduce (GBM SDE) to (Risk-Neutralized GBM SDE), one has to change the Brownian motion measure using Girsanov's theorem, W_t, to get an *equivalent* Brownian motion process, $\widetilde{W}_t$.

The economics of this important mathematical procedure is that it removes the risk premium in μ by transferring it to $\widetilde{W}_t$, thereby *risk-neutralizing* the original (actual) process in (GBM SDE). The result is,

$$dX_t = rX_t dt + \sigma X_t d\widetilde{W}_t \qquad \textbf{(Risk-Neutralized GBM SDE)}$$

We will change the notation slightly here to avoid confusion, and call the Risk-Neutralized GBM Y_t, and we will drop the $\sim$, remembering that the Brownian motion process is $\widetilde{W}_t$. The SDE for it is simply (Risk-Neutralized GBM SDE),

$$dY_t = rY_t dt + \sigma Y_t dW_t \qquad \textbf{(Risk-Neutralized GBM SDE)}$$

Then Y_t is called the *risk-neutral GBM* and the unique solution to (Risk-Neutralized GBM SDE), given an initial value $Y_0 = S_0$, on the interval $[0, T]$ is,

$$\ln\left(\frac{Y_T(\omega)}{Y_0}\right) = \left(r - \frac{\sigma^2}{2}\right)T + \sigma W_T(\omega) \qquad \textbf{(Risk-Neutralized GBM-SIE)}$$

This shows that the function,

$$G\big(Y_T(\omega)\big) = \ln\left(\frac{Y_T(\omega)}{Y_0}\right)$$

reduces the normalized process $Y_T(\omega)/Y_0$ to the ABM with drift on the right side of the equation,

$$dG\left(Y_t(\omega)\right) = \left(r - \frac{\sigma^2}{2}\right)dt + \sigma W_t(\omega)$$

or dropping the ω and replacing T by t,

$$dG\left(Y_t\right) = \left(r - \frac{\sigma^2}{2}\right)dt + \sigma W_t \qquad \textbf{(Risk-Neutralized GBM-Reduced Process SDE)}$$

The *Risk-Neutralized GBM-Reduced Process* is the ABM process to which the normalized risk-neutral GBM process can be reduced using the reducing function,

$$G\left(Y_T(\omega)\right) = \ln\left(\frac{Y_T(\omega)}{Y_0}\right)$$

The net result of this reduction process, and its main benefit, is that we can get from it the risk-neutral transition density function of the $G(Y_T)$ process, which is an ABM process with drift parameter $r-(\sigma^2/2)$ and diffusion coefficient σ. To do so, all we need are the conditional mean and the conditional variance of the ABM process, $G(Y_T)$, given $G(Y_0)$. We did this earlier, but you can do it directly as a concept check by solving (Risk-Neutralized GBM-Reduced Process SDE).

■ CONCEPT CHECK 6

(Solving (Risk-Neutralized GBM-Reduced Process SDE))

a. Calculate $G(Y_0)$.
b. Calculate $E(G(Y_T) | G(Y_0))$.
c. Calculate $\text{Var}(G(Y_T) | G(Y_0))$.

The risk-neutral transition density function of the $G(Y_T)$ reduced ABM process is almost identical to what we derived earlier for shifted ABM except now we have to adjust for σ (corresponding to the σW_t process) and for the conditional mean $(r-\sigma^2/2)T$, which we will have to subtract. These are the only two adjustments needed.

OPTION PRICING IN CONTINUOUS TIME · 569

We repeat the risk-neutral transition density function for shifted ABM without drift, but adjusted for sigma, except we add the notation ABM,

$$P_{\text{ABM}}(T,y;0,X_0) = \left(\frac{1}{\sqrt{2\pi\sigma^2 T}}\right)\exp\left(\frac{-(y-X_0)^2}{2\sigma^2 T}\right)dy \qquad \textbf{(RNTDF for shifted ABM adjusted for } \boldsymbol{\sigma}\textbf{)}$$

Now it is our normalized ABM $G(Y.)$ that fits this model with $T=T$, $y=G(Y_T)$, $t=0$, $X_0=G(Y_0)=0$, and we now have the generally non-zero conditional mean $(r-\sigma^2/2)T$.

Subtracting it, according to the usual normalization procedure, results in the risk-neutral transition density function to which the GBM is reducible,

$$P_{\text{ABM}}\left(T,G(Y_T);0,G(Y_0)\right)$$

$$= \left(\frac{1}{\sqrt{2\pi\sigma^2 T}}\right)\exp\left(-\frac{\left(G(Y_T)-G(Y_0)-\left(r-\dfrac{\sigma^2}{2}\right)T\right)^2}{2\sigma^2 T}\right)$$

$$= \left(\frac{1}{\sqrt{2\pi\sigma^2 T}}\right)\exp\left(-\frac{\left(\ln\left(\dfrac{Y_T}{Y_0}\right)-0-\left(r-\dfrac{\sigma^2}{2}\right)T\right)^2}{2\sigma^2 T}\right)$$

$$= \left(\frac{1}{\sqrt{2\pi\sigma^2 T}}\right)\exp\left(-\frac{\left(\ln\left(\dfrac{Y_T}{Y_0}\right)-\left(r-\dfrac{\sigma^2}{2}\right)T\right)^2}{2\sigma^2 T}\right) \qquad \textbf{(RNTDF for the ABM process to which GBM is reducible)}$$

■ CONCEPT CHECK 7

a. Show that $p_{\text{ABM}}(T,G(Y_T);0,G(Y_0))$ is the same as $p_{\text{ABM}}(T,y;0,X_0)$ with the subtraction of the conditional mean, and adjusted for sigma. The parameters are given above.

With one more step, we will be in the very fortunate position of being able to simply repeat the European call option calculations we did for shifted ABM without drift, in order to generate the European call option formula for GBM, another name for which is the Black–Scholes formula.

This approach unifies the Bachelier model with the Black–Scholes model. This unity shouldn't be too surprising because GBM is a scaled, exponentiated ABM and, therefore, the ultimate driver of uncertainty in the Black–Scholes model is the ABM.

16.7.2 Preliminaries on Generating Unknown Risk-Neutral Transition Density Functions from Known Ones

The derivation is a general result, and is significantly easier if we write down the relationship between the risk-neutral transition density function of the risk-neutralized GBM process and the the risk-neutral transition density function of the shifted ABM to which it is reducible,

$$dY_t = rY_t dt + \sigma Y_t dW_t \qquad \textbf{(Risk-Neutralized GBM SDE)}$$

$$dG(Y_t) = \left(r - \frac{\sigma^2}{2}\right)dt + \sigma dW_t \qquad \textbf{(Shifted ABM Reduced Process)}$$

where the 'reducing function' is

$$G\left(Y_T(\omega)\right) = \ln\left(\frac{Y_T(\omega)}{Y_0}\right)$$

The risk-neutral transition density function for the shifted ABM reduced process is,

$$p_{ABM}\left(T, G(Y_T); 0, G(Y_0)\right)$$

$$= \left(\frac{1}{\sqrt{2\pi\sigma^2 T}}\right)\exp\left(-\frac{\left(\ln\left(\frac{Y_T}{Y_0}\right) - 0 - \left(r - \frac{\sigma^2}{2}\right)T\right)^2}{2\sigma^2 T}\right)$$

(RNTDF for the ABM process to which GBM is reducible)

The risk-neutral transition density function for the risk-neutralized GBM process will be denoted by $p_Y(T, y; 0, Y_0)$, because Y_t is the risk-neutralized GBM, where of course y is short form for $Y_T(\omega)$, the random outcome of the Y_T process at time T.

OPTION PRICING IN CONTINUOUS TIME 571

If we are valuing (at time $t=0$) a contingent claim, such as a European call option with maturity T and exercise price K over the time interval $[0,T]$, then the relevant transition density function is $p_Y(T,y;0,Y_0)$. We could derive it from scratch, but it is much easier to derive it from its relationship to the risk-neutral transition density function of the ABM-reduced process, $p(T,G(Y_T);0,G(Y_0))$ which we now know.

This relationship can be derived in general and it is,

$$p_Y\left(T,y;0,Y_0\right)$$
$$= p_{ABM}\left(T,G(Y_T);\, 0,G(Y_0)\right)G_y'(Y_T)$$

(Risk-Neutralized Transition Density Function of GBM)

where $G_y'(Y_T)$ is the derivative of the reducing function $G(Y_T)$ evaluated at Y_T and is the new component here.

16.7.3 Black–Scholes Options Pricing from Bachelier

In this section, we will simply replicate the Bachelier proof step by step. In doing so, we will see when it works and when it has to be modified. This will highlight the relationship between the GBM of Black–Scholes and the ABM of Bachelier and will provide support for the premise that these two models, while different, are very close to each other.

Line 1 of Bachelier is (ABM 1).

$$C(X_0,T;K) = E\left\{\text{MAX}[X_T(\omega) - K, 0] \mid X_0\right\}$$
(ABM 1)

Recall that the risk-free rate $r=0$ in the Bachelier model, while here in the GBM model, r, is the r from the (risk neutralized GBM SDE), $dY_t=rY_t dt + \sigma Y_t dW_t$. Thus, for the GBM, we are going to have to discount the expectation by the price of a unit discount bond which is what we called $B(t,T)=e^{-r\tau}$ where $\tau=T-t$.

With this slightly simplified notation, $t=0$ and $T=T$ so $\tau=T$ and $B(t,T)=B(0,T)=e^{-r't}$. Thus the first line of GBM becomes (GBM 1),

$$C(Y_0,T;K)=B(0,T)E\{\text{MAX}[Y_T(\omega)-K, 0] \mid Y_0\}$$
(GBM 1)

There is nothing much new here. Note that we could have taken the *'discounted-by-the-numeraire-price process'*, which is a martingale and applied the usual EMM approach. Note that the risk-neutralized GBM SDE *does not*

572 OPTIONS

describe a martingale, because it has a positive, proportional drift $rY_t dt$ and martingales have zero drift.

However, it is easily reduced to a martingale by dividing Y_t by the numeraire $e^{r\tau}$ as discussed earlier (here $\tau = T$). Note that dividing through by the numeraire, $e^{r\tau}$, is equivalent to discounting by $e^{-r\tau}$. Also note, from Chapter 4, that this is the classic way of removing a component, such as the risk-free return component from a stock's return. Multiply the current stock price, Y_t, by $e^{-r\tau}$. This explains the rationale behind the numeraire approach using the discounted price process.

We prefer to work with the *intermediate* process $dY_t = rY_t dt + \sigma Y_t dW_t$, which is intermediate between drift coefficient $0 * Y_t dt$ (the equivalent martingale process) and drift coefficient $\mu * Y_t dt$ (the actual process or the physical measure).

Next, we express the conditional expectation in (GBM 1) by the corresponding integral in (GBM 2).

$$E\left\{ \text{MAX}\left[Y_T(\omega) - K, 0 \right] \big| Y_0 \right\} = \int_{Y > K} (y - K) p_y (T, y; 0, Y_0) \qquad \begin{matrix} \textbf{(GBM 2)=} \\ \textbf{(ABM 2)} \end{matrix}$$

The only difference between (ABM 2) and (GBM 2) is a change of notation in that we call $X_0 = Y_0$.

Line 3 of ABM is that the expectation in (ABM 2) is,

$$\int_{y > K} (y - K) \left(\frac{1}{\sqrt{2\pi T}} \right) \exp\left(\frac{-(y - X_0)^2}{2T} \right) dy \qquad \textbf{(ABM 3)}$$

Here we encounter a difference between (ABM 3) and (GBM 3), which is that we had to work a lot harder to get the risk-neutral transition density function for the risk-neutralized GBM. Not that hard mind you, because according to the risk-neutralized transition density function of GBM, it is simply a transformed, risk-neutralized transition density function of shifted ABM given by $p_Y(T, y; 0, Y_0) = p_{ABM}(T, G(Y_T); 0, G(Y_0))G'_y(Y_T)$. This is the relationship between the risk-neutralized transition density function of GBM and the risk-neutralized transition density function of shifted ABM, as we know.

We simply 'plug' this relationship into (GBM 2) to obtain (GBM 3),

$$\int_{y > K} (y - K) p_{ABM} (T, G(Y_T); 0, G(Y_0)) G'_y(Y_T) dy \qquad \textbf{(GBM 3)}$$

We note here that, as already calculated,

$$p_{ABM}\left(T,G(Y_T);0,G(Y_0)\right)$$

$$=\left(\frac{1}{\sqrt{2\pi\sigma^2 T}}\right)\exp\left(-\frac{\left(G(Y_T-G(Y_0)-\left(r-\frac{\sigma^2}{2}\right)T\right)^2}{2\sigma^2 T}\right)$$

$$=\left(\frac{1}{\sqrt{2\pi\sigma^2 T}}\right)\exp\left(-\frac{\left(\ln\left(\frac{Y_T}{Y_0}\right)-\left(r-\frac{\sigma^2}{2}\right)T\right)^2}{2\sigma^2 T}\right)$$

We substitute this into (GBM 3),

$$\int_{y>K}(y-K)\left(\frac{1}{\sqrt{2\pi\sigma^2 T}}\right)\exp\left(-\frac{\left(\ln\left(\frac{Y_T}{Y_0}\right)-\left(r-\frac{\sigma^2}{2}\right)T\right)^2}{2\sigma^2 T}\right)G_y'(Y_T)dy$$

$$=\int_{y>K}(y-K)\left(\frac{1}{\sqrt{2\pi\sigma^2 T}}\right)*$$

$$\exp\left(-\frac{\left(G(Y_T)-G(Y_0)-\left(r-\frac{\sigma^2}{2}\right)T\right)^2}{2\sigma^2 T}\right)G_y'(Y_T)dy$$

Recall that

$$G\left(Y_T(\omega)\right)=\ln\left(\frac{Y_T(\omega)}{Y_0}\right)$$

and therefore $G(Y_0)=0$.

Next, we make the obvious change of variables which is the equivalent of the change of variables $y'=(y-X_0)/\sqrt{T}$ in (ABM 4),

$$z = \frac{\ln\left(\dfrac{Y_T}{Y_0}\right) - \left(r - \dfrac{\sigma^2}{2}\right)T}{\sqrt{\sigma^2 T}} \qquad\qquad \textbf{(GBM 4)}$$

$$= \frac{G(Y_T) - \left(r - \dfrac{\sigma^2}{2}\right)T}{\sqrt{\sigma^2 T}}$$

and hence that,

$$dz = \frac{G'_y(Y_T)}{\sqrt{\sigma^2 T}}\,dy \qquad\qquad \textbf{(GBM 6)}$$

The notation $G'_y(Y_T)$ emphasizes that the derivative of G is with respect to y and that it is evaluated at $y=Y_T$. (GBM 5) is derived below.

Now everything lines up perfectly since,

$$\int_{y>K}(y-K)\left(\frac{1}{\sqrt{2\pi\sigma^2 T}}\right)\exp\left(-\frac{\left(G(Y_T - G(Y_0)) - \left(r - \dfrac{\sigma^2}{2}\right)T\right)^2}{2\sigma^2 T}\right)G'_y(Y_T)\,dy$$

$$= \int_{y>K}(y-K)\left[\frac{1}{\sqrt{2\pi}}\exp\left(-\frac{z^2}{2}\right)\right]\frac{G'_y(Y_T)}{\sqrt{\sigma^2 T}}\,dy$$

$$= \int_{y>K}(y-K)\left[\frac{1}{\sqrt{2\pi}}\exp\left(-\frac{z^2}{2}\right)\right]dz \qquad \textbf{(Intermediate GBM)}$$

This is an intermediate result. In it, we used the fact that

$$dz = \frac{G'_y(Y_T)}{\sqrt{\sigma^2 T}}\,dy$$

OPTION PRICING IN CONTINUOUS TIME 575

What is nice about (Intermediate GBM) is that you can see the density function of an $N(0,1)$,

$$\frac{1}{\sqrt{2\pi}}\exp\left(-\frac{z^2}{2}\right)$$

embedded in it. However, it is not in a plausible form.

We have to do some more work in order to get this into a plausible form: namely change the variable of integration $y>K$ to the equivalent involving z and figure out how to get rid of the y in $y-K$. Notice that we are integrating with respect to the density of a standardized normal random variable $z=N(0,1)$ with pdf.

$$f(z) = \frac{1}{\sqrt{2\pi}}\exp\left(-\frac{z^2}{2}\right)$$

For the first task, $y=Y_T>K$ if and only if

$$z > \frac{\ln\left(\dfrac{K}{Y_0}\right)-\left(r-\dfrac{\sigma^2}{2}\right)T}{\sqrt{\sigma^2 T}}$$

For the second task, in the case of (ABM 5), it was easy to solve $y'=(y-X_0)/\sqrt{T}$ (ABM 4) for $y=(\sqrt{T})y'+X_0$ (ABM 5) as a function of y' because of this linear relationship. This resulted in (ABM 7),

$$\int_{y'>(K-X_0)/\sqrt{T}}\left((\sqrt{T})y' + X_0 - K\right)\left(\frac{1}{\sqrt{2\pi}}\right)e^{-y'^2/2}dy' \qquad \textbf{(ABM 7)}$$

The same idea of solving

$$z = \frac{\ln\left(\dfrac{Y_T}{Y_0}\right)-\left(r-\dfrac{\sigma^2}{2}\right)T}{\sqrt{\sigma^2 T}}$$

for Y_T as a function of z applies here, except that this equation is non-linear. However, we can still 'invert' it because $\ln(Y_T/Y_0)$ is a monotonic function of Y_T. Here are the solution steps.

$$z = \frac{\ln\left(\dfrac{Y_T}{Y_0}\right) - \left(r - \dfrac{\sigma^2}{2}\right)T}{\sqrt{\sigma^2 T}}$$

$$\ln\left(\frac{Y_T}{Y_0}\right) = z\sqrt{\sigma^2 T} + \left(r - \frac{\sigma^2}{2}\right)T$$

$$\frac{Y_T}{Y_0} = \exp\left(z\sqrt{\sigma^2 T} + \left(r - \frac{\sigma^2}{2}\right)T\right)$$

$$Y_T = Y_0 \exp\left(z\sqrt{\sigma^2 T} + \left(r - \frac{\sigma^2}{2}\right)T\right) \tag{GBM 5}$$

So (GBM 4) inverts to (GBM 5) which when plugged into (Intermediate GBM), results in the analogue of (ABM 7), which is (GBM 7),

$$\int_{z>z(K)}^{\infty} \left[Y_0\exp\left(z\sqrt{\sigma^2 T} + \left(r - \frac{\sigma^2}{2}\right)T\right) - K\right]\left[\frac{1}{\sqrt{2\pi}}\exp\left(-\frac{z^2}{2}\right)\right]dz$$

$$\text{where } z(K) = \left[\ln\left(\frac{K}{Y_0}\right) - \left(r - \frac{\sigma^2}{2}\right)T\right]\Big/\sqrt{\sigma^2 T} \tag{GBM 7}$$

Now we can write this as two separate integrals, as in (ABM 8a-b), easily evaluate the second one, and then '*complete the square*' for the first integral, unlike the way we did it for the ABM.

Note that in (ABM 8a), we were able to use the derivative trick based on the appearance of

$$\exp\left(-\frac{y'^2}{2}\right)(y')dy'$$

in

$$\sqrt{T}\int_{y'>(K-X_0)/\sqrt{T}}\left(\frac{1}{\sqrt{2\pi}}\right)\exp\left(-\frac{y'^2}{2}\right)(y')dy' \tag{ABM 8a}$$

Here, for GBM, no analogous quantity appears, so we have to use the other technique of 'completing the square'. First, we split up the integral in (GBM 7) into two integrals to obtain (GBM 8a–b),

$$\int_{z>z(K)}^{\infty} \left[Y_0 \exp\left(z\sqrt{\sigma^2 T} + \left(r - \frac{\sigma^2}{2} \right)T \right) - K \right] \left[\frac{1}{\sqrt{2\pi}} \exp\left(-\frac{z^2}{2} \right) \right] dz$$

$$= \int_{z>z(K)}^{\infty} \left[Y_0 \exp\left(z\sqrt{\sigma^2 T} + \left(r - \frac{\sigma^2}{2} \right)T \right) \right] \left[\frac{1}{\sqrt{2\pi}} \exp\left(-\frac{z^2}{2} \right) \right] dz \quad \textbf{(GBM 8a)}$$

$$+ \int_{z>z(K)}^{\infty} [-K] \left[\frac{1}{\sqrt{2\pi}} \exp\left(-\frac{z^2}{2} \right) \right] dz \quad \textbf{(GBM 8b)}$$

$$\text{where } z(K) = \left[\ln\left(\frac{K}{Y_0} \right) - \left(r - \frac{\sigma^2}{2} \right)T \right] \bigg/ \sqrt{\sigma^2 T}$$

The second integral, (GBM 8b), is easy to evaluate so we will do it first. Since $-K$ is known at time $t=0$, it factors out and the integral in (GBM 8b) represents the cumulative probability that an $N(0,1)$ random variable lies above,

$$z(K) = \left[\ln\left(\frac{K}{Y_0} \right) - \left(r - \frac{\sigma^2}{2} \right)T \right] \bigg/ \sqrt{\sigma^2 T}$$

In other words, it is the *right tail* probability above $z(K)$.

Because the Gaussian is a symmetric random variable this quantity, which is $1-N(z(K))$, is equal to the corresponding left tail probability below $-z(K)$. That is $N(-z(K))=1-N(z(K))$.

Therefore, the entire second integral in (GBM 8b) is equal to,

$$-K \int_{z>z(K)}^{\infty} \left[\frac{1}{\sqrt{2\pi}} \exp\left(-\frac{z^2}{2} \right) \right] dz$$

$$= -K \int_{z<-z(K)}^{\infty} \left[\frac{1}{\sqrt{2\pi}} \exp\left(-\frac{z^2}{2} \right) \right] dz \quad \textbf{(GBM 9)}$$

$$\text{where } z(K) = \left[\ln\left(\frac{K}{Y_0} \right) - \left(r - \frac{\sigma^2}{2} \right)T \right] \bigg/ \sqrt{\sigma^2 T}$$

$$= -K N\left(-z(K) \right) \quad \textbf{(GBM 10)}$$

$$\text{where } -z(K) = -\left\{ \left[\ln\left(\frac{K}{Y_0} \right) - \left(r - \frac{\sigma^2}{2} \right)T \right] \bigg/ \sqrt{\sigma^2 T} \right\}$$

578 OPTIONS

We can further simplify (GBM 10) in a form that will lead to Black–Scholes, because,

$$= -KN\left\{-\left[\ln\left(\frac{K}{Y_0}\right)-\left(r-\frac{\sigma^2}{2}\right)T\right]\Big/\sqrt{\sigma^2 T}\right\}$$

$$= -KN\left\{\left[\ln\left(\frac{Y_0}{K}\right)+\left(r-\frac{\sigma^2}{2}\right)T\right]\Big/\sqrt{\sigma^2 T}\right\}$$

$$= -KN\left(d_2\right) \hspace{3cm} \textbf{(GBM 11)}$$

where $d_2 = \left[\ln\left(\frac{Y_0}{K}\right)+\left(r-\frac{\sigma^2}{2}\right)T\right]\Big/\sqrt{\sigma^2 T}$

We have used the fact in (GBM 11) that

$$-\ln\left(\frac{K}{Y_0}\right) = \ln\left(\frac{Y_0}{K}\right)$$

The quantity

$$\left[\ln\left(\frac{Y_0}{K}\right)-\left(r-\frac{\sigma^2}{2}\right)T\right]\Big/\sqrt{\sigma^2 T}$$

is known as d_2 in the world of Black–Scholes. $N(d_2)$ is the cumulative probability of an $N(0,1)$ random variable up to d_2. This fully takes care of the second integral in (GBM 8b).

Now we have to deal with the first integral (GBM 8a) which is,

$$\int_{z>z(K)}^{\infty}\left[Y_0\exp\left(z\sqrt{\sigma^2 T}+\left(r-\frac{\sigma^2}{2}\right)T\right)\right]\left[\frac{1}{\sqrt{2\pi}}\exp\left(-\frac{z^2}{2}\right)\right]dz \hspace{1cm} \textbf{(GBM 8a)}$$

where $z(K) = \left[\ln\left(\frac{K}{Y_0}\right)-\left(r-\frac{\sigma^2}{2}\right)T\right]\Big/\sqrt{\sigma^2 T}$

This expression is analogous to (ABM 13) but in place of y' we have,

$$Y_0\exp\left(z\sqrt{\sigma^2 T}+\left(r-\frac{\sigma^2}{2}\right)T\right)$$

and the limits of integration are in terms of z and $z(K)$, of course.

We collect the terms involving the exponentials involving z and z^2 to arrive at,

$$\int_{z>z(K)}^{\infty} \frac{Y_0}{\sqrt{2\pi}} \exp\left(-\frac{z^2}{2} + z\sigma\sqrt{T} + \left(r - \frac{\sigma^2}{2}\right)T\right)dz \qquad \textbf{(GBM 12)}$$

since $\sqrt{\sigma^2 T} = \sigma\sqrt{T}$

where $z(K) = \left[\ln\left(\frac{K}{Y_0}\right) - \left(r - \frac{\sigma^2}{2}\right)T\right]\bigg/\sqrt{\sigma^2 T}$

$$= \int_{z>z(K)}^{\infty} \frac{Y_0}{\sqrt{2\pi}} \exp\left(-\frac{z^2}{2} + z\sigma\sqrt{T}\right) \exp\left(\left[r - \frac{\sigma^2}{2}\right]T\right)dz \qquad \textbf{(GBM 13)}$$

since $e^x e^y = e^{x+y}$

where $z(K) = \left[\ln\left(\frac{K}{Y_0}\right) - \left(r - \frac{\sigma^2}{2}\right)T\right]\bigg/\sqrt{\sigma^2 T}$

As noted, this diverges from the ABM treatment in (ABM 14–16) , being only slightly more complicated. To complete the square in the expression,

$$\exp\left(-\frac{z^2}{2} + z\sigma\sqrt{T}\right)$$

we note that,

$$\left(-\frac{z^2}{2} + z\sigma\sqrt{T}\right) = -\frac{1}{2}\left(z^2 - 2z\sigma\sqrt{T}\right)$$

$$= -\frac{1}{2}\left(z - \sigma\sqrt{T}\right)^2 + \frac{\sigma^2}{2}T$$

Therefore,

$$\exp\left(-\frac{z^2}{2} + z\sigma\sqrt{T}\right) = \exp\left[-\frac{1}{2}\left(z - \sigma\sqrt{T}\right)^2 + \left(\frac{\sigma^2}{2}\right)T\right] \qquad \textbf{(GBM 14)}$$

$$= \exp\left[-\frac{1}{2}\left(z - \sigma\sqrt{T}\right)^2\right] \exp\left[\left(\frac{\sigma^2}{2}\right)T\right]$$

again using the fact that $e^x e^y = e^{x+y}$.

580 OPTIONS

Therefore,

$$\int_{z>z(K)}^{\infty} \frac{Y_0}{\sqrt{2\pi}} \exp\left[-\frac{z^2}{2} + z\sigma\sqrt{T}\right] \exp\left[r - \frac{\sigma^2}{2}\right] dz$$

where $z(K) = \left[\ln\left(\frac{K}{Y_0}\right) - \left(r - \frac{\sigma^2}{2}\right)T\right] \Big/ \sqrt{\sigma^2 T}$

$$= \int_{z>z(K)}^{\infty} \frac{Y_0}{\sqrt{2\pi}} \exp\left[-\frac{1}{2}\left(z - \sigma\sqrt{T}\right)^2\right] \exp\left[\frac{\sigma^2}{2}T\right] \exp\left[\left(r - \frac{\sigma^2}{2}\right)T\right] dz$$

$$= \int_{z>z(K)}^{\infty} \frac{Y_0}{\sqrt{2\pi}} \exp\left[-\frac{1}{2}\left(z - \sigma\sqrt{T}\right)^2\right] \exp\left[\frac{\sigma^2}{2}T + \left(r - \frac{\sigma^2}{2}\right)T\right] dz$$

$$= \int_{z>z(K)}^{\infty} \frac{Y_0}{\sqrt{2\pi}} \exp\left[-\frac{1}{2}\left(z - \sigma\sqrt{T}\right)^2\right] \exp\left[rT\right] dz$$

$$= \exp\left[rT\right] Y_0 \int_{z>z(K)}^{\infty} \frac{\exp\left[-\frac{1}{2}\left(z - \sigma\sqrt{T}\right)^2\right]}{\sqrt{2\pi}} dz \qquad \textbf{(GBM 15)}$$

Now we make another obvious change of variables $z'=z-\sigma\sqrt{T}$. Then $dz'=dz$ and

$$z > z(K) = \left[\ln\left(\frac{K}{Y_0}\right) - \left(r - \frac{\sigma^2}{2}\right)T\right] \Big/ \sqrt{\sigma^2 T} \text{ if and only if } z' > z(K) - \sigma\sqrt{T}$$

Now the last integral (GBM 15) is,

$$= e^{rT} Y_0 \int_{z>z(K)}^{\infty} \left\{ \exp\left[-\frac{1}{2}\left(z - \sigma\sqrt{T}\right)^2\right] \Big/ \sqrt{2\pi} \right\} dz \qquad \textbf{(GBM 16)}$$

$$= e^{rT} Y_0 \int_{z'>z(K)-\sigma\sqrt{T}}^{\infty} \left\{ \exp\left[-\frac{1}{2}\left(z'\right)^2\right] \Big/ \sqrt{2\pi} \right\} dz'$$

But (GBM 16) is just the *right tail* probability of an $N(0,1)$ random variable above $z(K)-\sigma\sqrt{T}$, which is the same as the *left tail* probability below $-(z(K)-\sigma\sqrt{T})$.

OPTION PRICING IN CONTINUOUS TIME 581

Therefore (GBM 16) is equal to,

$$e^{rT}Y_0\int_{z'<-(z(K)-\sigma\sqrt{T})}^{\infty}\frac{e^{-\frac{1}{2}(z')^2}}{\sqrt{2\pi}}dz'$$

$$= e^{rT}Y_0 N\left[-\left(z(K)-\sigma\sqrt{T}\right)\right] \qquad\qquad\textbf{(GBM 17)}$$

Now all we have to do is to calculate,

$$-\left(z(K)-\sigma\sqrt{T}\right) = -\frac{\left[\ln\left(\dfrac{K}{Y_0}\right)-\left(r-\dfrac{\sigma^2}{2}\right)T\right]}{\sqrt{\sigma^2 T}}+\sigma\sqrt{T}$$

$$= \frac{\left[\ln\left(\dfrac{Y_0}{K}\right)+\left(r-\dfrac{\sigma^2}{2}\right)T\right]}{\sigma\sqrt{T}}+\sigma\sqrt{T}$$

$$= \frac{\left[\ln\left(\dfrac{Y_0}{K}\right)+\left(r-\dfrac{\sigma^2}{2}\right)T+\sigma^2 T\right]}{\sigma\sqrt{T}}$$

$$= \frac{\left[\ln\left(\dfrac{Y_0}{K}\right)+\left(r+\dfrac{\sigma^2}{2}\right)T\right]}{\sigma\sqrt{T}}$$

$$\equiv d_1$$

This is the definition of d_1 in the Black–Scholes formula, where we again used the fact that,

$$-\ln\left(\frac{K}{Y_0}\right) = \ln\left(\frac{Y_0}{K}\right)$$

Hence,

$$e^{rT}Y_0\int_{z'<-(z(K)-\sigma\sqrt{T})}^{\infty}\left[\exp\left(-\frac{1}{2}(z')^2\right)\Big/\sqrt{2\pi}\right]dz' \qquad\qquad\textbf{(GBM 18)}$$

$$= e^{rT}Y_0 N\left(d_1\right)$$

This completes the derivation of the integral in GBM (8a).

582 **OPTIONS**

To get the full European call option price, we have to remember to discount by $B(0,T)$. When we do so, we obtain that our entire European call option formula reduces to,

$$C(Y_0,T;K) = e^{-rT}\left[e^{rT}Y_0N(d_1) - KN(d_2)\right]$$
$$= Y_0N(d_1) - e^{-rT}KN(d_2)$$

Therefore, the Black–Scholes formula is given by,

$$C(Y_0,T;K) = Y_0N(d_1) - e^{-rT}KN(d_2) \qquad \textbf{(Black–Scholes, } [0,T]\textbf{)}$$

$$d_1 = \frac{\left[\ln\left(\dfrac{Y_0}{K}\right) + \left(r + \dfrac{\sigma^2}{2}\right)T\right]}{\sigma\sqrt{T}} \quad \text{and,}$$

$$d_2 = d_1 - \sigma\sqrt{T}$$

$N(d_i)$ is the cumulative normal distribution up to d_i, $i=1,2$. Recall that $Y_0=S_0$, the initial ($t=0$) stock price.

In the usual Black–Scholes formula, the variable $\tau = T - t$ is involved and the formula is given by ($Y_t=S_t$, the initial (time t) stock price),

$$C(Y_t,\tau;K) = e^{-r\tau}\left[e^{r\tau}Y_tN(d_1) - KN(d_2)\right] \qquad \textbf{(Black–Scholes, } [t,T]\textbf{)}$$

$$= Y_tN(d_1) - e^{-r\tau}KN(d_2)$$

$$d_1 = \frac{\left[\ln\left(\dfrac{Y_t}{K}\right) + \left(r + \dfrac{\sigma^2}{2}\right)\tau\right]}{\sigma\sqrt{\tau}} \quad \text{and,}$$

$$d_2 = d_1 - \sigma\sqrt{\tau}$$

$N(d_i)$ is the cumulative normal distribution up to d_i, $i=1,2$. Recall that $Y_t=S_t$, the initial (time t) stock price.

■ CONCEPT CHECK 8

a. Confirm that d_2 defined as

$$\frac{\left[\ln\left(\dfrac{Y_0}{K}\right) + \left(r - \dfrac{\sigma^2}{2}\right)T\right]}{\sigma\sqrt{T}}$$

OPTION PRICING IN CONTINUOUS TIME 583

below (GBM 11) is equal to $d_1 - \sigma\sqrt{T}$ where

$$d_1 = \frac{\left[\ln\left(\dfrac{Y_0}{K}\right) + \left(r + \dfrac{\sigma^2}{2}\right)T\right]}{\sigma\sqrt{T}}$$

16.7.4 Volatility Estimation in the Black–Scholes Model

If we go back to the defining SDE for GBM, (GBM SDE), and let X_t be the stock price S_t, then we call μ the *drift coefficient* and σ is called the *diffusion coefficient* in (equation GBM).

$$\frac{dS_t}{S_t} = \mu dt + \sigma dW_t \qquad\qquad \textbf{(GBM equation)}$$

Both the drift and the diffusion coefficient are assumed to be constant. σ doesn't change when we move to the risk-neutral measure, but μ gets replaced by r.

The fact that σ doesn't change is often thought of as the Achilles heel of the Black–Scholes formula, but it is this constancy assumption that facilitates its estimation. It is much harder to estimate a moving target. There are several ways to estimate it. The first method will be called *the historical volatility estimator method*. It is described below,

A. The Historical Volatility Estimator Method

1. Collect historical data, say daily closing prices, for a given stock over a given historical period.

2. Calculate the *log price relatives* which are defined as $\ln(S_i/S_{i-1})$. This represents the continuously compounded rate of return of the stock over the period $[i-1,i]$.

3. Calculate the mean of these log price relatives in the ordinary manner as the sum of the log price relatives divided by the number of log price relatives. Call this quantity $E\{\ln(S_i/S_{i-1})\}$.

584 **OPTIONS**

4. The next step is to calculate the standard deviation of these log price relatives over the entire period, $\widehat{\sigma}_{daily}$. This is defined as,

$$\widehat{\sigma}_{daily} = \sqrt{\sum_{i=1}^{N}\left[\ln\left(\frac{S_i}{S_{i-1}}\right) - E\left\{\ln\left(\frac{S_i}{S_{i-1}}\right)\right\}\right]^2 \Big/ (N-1)}$$

where N is the number of log price relatives. This is the usual calculation of the sample standard deviation of a set of numbers. This number is called the *daily standard deviation*, or the *standard deviation of daily returns*.

5. The final step is to annualize $\widehat{\sigma}_{daily}$. This is usually done by multiplying $\widehat{\sigma}_{daily}$ by the square root of the number of *trading days* in the year, $\sqrt{252}$ or $\sqrt{250}$. The final estimate is,

$$\widehat{\sigma}_{annual} = \sqrt{252} * \widehat{\sigma}_{daily}$$

This estimator

$$\widehat{\sigma}_{annual} = \sqrt{252} * \widehat{\sigma}_{daily}$$

is called the *historical* (volatility) estimator.

There are many computer programs online that will perform these calculations. You can also do it in Microsoft Excel, which is a useful exercise in the End of Chapter Exercise 3.

There is another method which follows directly from Black–Scholes. It is called the *implied volatility method* and it generates the *implied volatility estimator*. The idea behind implied volatility is that the Black–Scholes formula embodies an implicit volatility estimator.

If we compare market option prices to Black–Scholes model option prices, we can extract the Black–Scholes implicit volatility estimator. Since option prices incorporate a wide variety of *forward* views of volatility, implied volatility could be a better estimator of unknown volatility than the historical estimator, which is a *backward* looking estimator.

B. The Implied Volatility Estimator Method

Volatility is one of the key parameters in the Black–Scholes formula, but it is unobservable. Why not let the model generate estimates of σ that are consistent with the assumption that the market prices options using the Black–Scholes formula? This is a good idea.

In order to implement it, all we have to do is plug all the parameters, except σ, into the Black–Scholes formula. Then, if we take the market's (not the model's) option price we can equate $C_{t,\text{Black–Scholes}}$ to $C_{t,\text{Market}}$, and obtain a non-linear equation in σ that can be iteratively solved for the implied volatility estimator, which we will denote by σ_{IV}.

The brief version of this procedure is, $C_{t,\text{Black–Scholes}} = C_{t,\text{Market}}$ *implies* σ_{IV}. End of Chapter Exercises 4 and 5 implement this procedure. The IV estimator turns out empirically to be a better estimator than the historical σ, which is probably not too surprising.

Unfortunately, whether we use the historical volatility estimator or the implied volatility estimator, we are still stuck with the constant σ assumption. If σ is constant, then it is also constant across options with *different* exercise prices and σ_{IV} should not depend upon which exercise price K is used to estimate it. This turns out *not* to be empirically true, at least since the market crash of 1987, and it generates a *volatility smile*, and its variations.

A vast literature has developed around explaining volatility smiles and its variations. We can't cover that here, but we can look at the *economic* reasons for expecting σ not to be a constant.

16.8 NON-CONSTANT VOLATILITY MODELS

16.8.1 Empirical Features of Volatility

Some of the general empirical features that imply some degree of volatility predictability are *clustering (persistence)*, which means that periods of high (low) volatility seem to persist, and *reversion to the mean*, which means that too high (too low) volatility seems to correct itself by moving back to the normal, long-run average level. Furthermore, individual stocks tend to contemporaneously exhibit similar volatilities because of common factors.

Note that, when it comes to forecasting volatility, *out-of-sample* prediction of volatility changes is the goal, and not simply getting the best *in-sample* fit to the data.

16.8.2 Economic Reasons for why Volatility is not Constant, the Leverage Effect

Why does volatility change and how? A related issue is volatility predictability. Black (1976) explored this issue in a paper. He wanted to know the form and causes of changing stock price volatility, and introduced one rationale for the dependence of volatility on the stock price, known as the '*leverage effect*', which has become part of option pricing folklore.

Black's starting point was the empirical observation that when stock prices are relatively 'high', volatility is relatively 'low' and vice versa. The prime example of this was during the Great Depression of the 1920s–1930s.

The leverage effect is based on the basic corporate finance result that, if the stock price of a given firm goes up (down), then the debt–equity ratio goes down (up). Therefore, stock prices and D/E=Debt/Equity are inversely related. The leverage effect states that,

$$\sigma_E = \sigma_A \left(1 + \frac{D}{E} \right)$$

where σ_E is the σ of the firm's equity and σ_A is the σ of the firm's assets.

This is interesting, because it is an *economic* rationale for level-dependent volatility, and not just a statistical, or purely mathematical generalization of constant σ.

16.8.3 Modeling Changing Volatility, the Deterministic Volatility Model

There are three initial ways to alter σ, the instantaneous volatility of percentage returns, that appears in the Black–Scholes formula.

1. $\sigma = \sigma(t) = \sigma_t$, meaning that σ is not constant but is a *deterministic* function of time. Black–Scholes can be easily modified to accommodate this case simply by averaging σ_t. A modification of the Black–Scholes formula holds even if the instantaneous variance of percentage returns, σ_t, depends on time. One obtains it by substituting

$$\int_t^T \sigma_s^2 ds \text{ for } \sigma^2 (T - t)$$

in the Black–Scholes formula.

Of course, this assumes that the functional dependence of σ on time is known, or can be estimated.

2. $\sigma = \sigma(S_t)$, meaning that σ depends upon the current stock price. Black–Scholes per se no longer holds, but in many cases one can derive an explicit option pricing formula.

3. $\sigma = \sigma(S_t, t)$, meaning the combination of 1. and 2. in that σ is *both* time-dependent and stock price level dependent.

In the literature case 3. is known as the *deterministic volatility Dupire* (DV) model. The main virtue of the DV approach in modeling varying volatility is that it generates option pricing models that are complete in the sense we described.

16.8.4 Modeling Changing Volatility, Stochastic Volatility Models

Stochastic volatility (SVOL) models are beyond the scope of this text. However, a few comments may indicate the flavor of this approach. In the deterministic volatility model, randomness in volatility is purely a result of randomness in the underlying stock price process. This is not an *independent* source of randomness, since it is induced by the stock price.

SVOL models introduce new source(s) of randomness into the volatility process. You can do this, and remain in a continuous (ABM style) framework, and/or you can introduce jumps. Both components can induce randomness in volatility.

One of the most popular models is the Heston (1993) model, which assumes that the stock price process S_t *resembles* a standard GBM, with the twist that σ_t is not only time-dependent, but is a stochastic process itself.

The risk-neutral form of the Heston model is,

$$dS_t = rS_t dt + \sigma_t S_t dW_t \qquad \textbf{(Heston 1)}$$

where the variance, σ_t^2, is itself a process defined by,

$$d\sigma_t^2 = \kappa\left(\theta - \sigma_t^2\right)dt + \sigma_{\sigma_t}\sqrt{\sigma_t^2}\,dZ_t \qquad \textbf{(Heston 2)}$$

Note that Z_t is a *new* ABM process, assumed to be correlated with W_t.

We won't go into all of the mathematical assumptions required to make the Heston model 'work'. The strange symbol σ_{σ_t} means the sigma of the sigma (*volatility of the volatility*).

588 OPTIONS

The Heston model attempts to incorporate some of the empirical features of the volatility process, such as the leverage effect and mean reversion in volatility, and it also introduces *skewness*. One unfortunate feature of the Heston model is that it is *not* complete, as it stands.

However, it can be easily completed. Note that generalizing volatility behavior takes us one step forward relative to Black–Scholes. But it also takes us one step backwards because completeness is lost, unless the necessary securities to complete the market are tradable.

16.9 WHY BLACK–SCHOLES IS STILL IMPORTANT

Black–Scholes is a parsimonious option pricing model because its implementation only involves the following inputs:

1. The current stock price $Y_t = S_t$;
2. the exercise price K;
3. the time to expiration, τ;
4. the annualized risk-free rate; and
5. the annualized volatility, assumed to be constant, of instantaneous returns on the underling stock.

Inputs 1.–4. are directly observable, while 5. is not. The option is priced under the unique EMM, so μ does not appear in it. Replicability then implies that the option and the stock have the same Sharpe ratio. Therefore, no risk premium for pricing the option is needed; a risk premium is built into the pricing of the underlying stock, S_t (see Chapter 17).

There is no immediate and completely adequate empirical fix for the constant σ assumption, except to throw out Black–Scholes' assumption of a stationary log-normal diffusion, and search for a viable (smile-consistent) underlying stochastic process among the vast set of alternatives, many of which will lead to incomplete markets.

Black–Scholes and its modifications, however, still have tremendous appeal, especially among traders, who use Black–Scholes calibrated to an *implied volatility surface*. Traders use ATM options to imply volatility, since these are the most liquid, and therefore most informative about future volatility.

Furthermore, there are exotic and American options for which the log-normal GBM remains the workhorse. This is for the simple reason that it is difficult (or so far impossible) to price these complex options for any processes other than a standard GBM. Black–Scholes usually appears as a *component* of the option prices for these option types; for example, for American options.

Should we abandon Black–Scholes (1973) as a hopelessly antiquated option pricing model or, should we keep it around as a useful tool in the financial engineer's toolbox? In answering this question, there is at first a logical problem.

It is logically possible that Black–Scholes is an inadequate *stand-alone* model and, at the same time, may be important as a potential *component* of more complex models. Indeed, this is what the research literature suggests.

For example, Black–Scholes constitutes a *lower bound* on option prices in some complex '*mixed diffusion*' models. Further, even in certain SVOL models—Hull and White (1987)—Black–Scholes reappears in some form. Heston's model also resembles Black–Scholes.

Black–Scholes (1973), which is a continuous time, continuous state space model even shows up in some jump option pricing models, such as Merton's (1976) jump model. Thus, Black–Scholes may indeed survive as a component of some option pricing models. We should probably keep it around for these reasons.

590 OPTIONS

■ KEY CONCEPTS

1. Arithmetic Brownian Motion (ABM).
2. Shifted Arithmetic Brownian Motion.
3. Pricing European Options under Shifted Arithmetic Brownian Motion (Bachelier).
4. Theory ($FTAP_1$ and $FTAP_2$).
5. Transition Density Functions.
6. Deriving the Bachelier Option Pricing Formula.
7. Defining and Pricing a Standard Numeraire.
8. Geometric Brownian Motion (GBM).
9. GBM (Discrete Version).
10. Geometric Brownian Motion (GBM), Continuous Version.
11. Itô's Lemma.
12. Black–Scholes Option Pricing.
13. Reducing GBM to an ABM with Drift.
14. Preliminaries on Risk-Neutral Transition Density Functions.
15. Black–Scholes Pricing from Bachelier.
16. Volatility Estimation in the Black–Scholes Model.
17. Non-Constant Volatility Models.
18. Why Volatility is not Constant.
19. Economic Reasons for why Volatility is not Constant, the Leverage Effect.
20. Modeling Changing Volatility, the Deterministic Volatility Model.
21. Modeling Changing Volatility, Stochastic Volatility Models.
22. Why Black–Scholes is Still Important.

■ END OF CHAPTER EXERCISES FOR CHAPTER 16

1. In this exercise, you will calculate the historical sigma based on 30 days of Google's stock price data. We went to nasdaq.com to download the price data for the period September 2–September 30, 2014.

    This was done through 'basic charting'. Copy the following data into Microsoft Excel. Note that you will have to first reverse it in time order to calculate $\ln(S_i/S_{i-1})$.

    a. Calculate the price relatives for the period, (S_i/S_{i-1}).

    b. Calculate the log price relatives for the period, $\ln(S_i/S_{i-1})$.

OPTION PRICING IN CONTINUOUS TIME **591**

c. Calculate the mean of the daily log price relatives, $E\{\ln(S_i/S_{i-1})\}$.

d. Calculate the standard deviation of the daily log price relatives, $\widehat{\sigma}_{daily}$.

e. Calculate the historical estimator, $\widehat{\sigma}_{annual}$.

TABLE 16.1 **Price Data for End of Chapter 16, Exercise 1**

Date	Close/Last	Volume
9/30/2014	577.36	1,617,320
9/29/2014	576.36	1,278,274
9/26/2014	577.1	1,439,687
9/25/2014	575.06	1,918,179
9/24/2014	587.99	1,723,438
9/23/2014	581.13	1,464,386
9/22/2014	587.37	1,684,861
9/19/2014	596.08	3,724,109
9/18/2014	589.27	1,438,201
9/17/2014	584.77	1,687,731
9/16/2014	579.95	1,475,668
9/15/2014	573.1	1,593,030
9/12/2014	575.62	1,594,177
9/11/2014	581.35	1,215,910
9/10/2014	583.1	972,057
9/9/2014	581.01	1,283,678
9/8/2014	589.72	1,426,597
9/5/2014	586.08	1,626,806
9/4/2014	581.98	1,454,229
9/3/2014	577.94	1,211,507
9/2/2014	577.33	1,574,096

592 OPTIONS

2. Let S_t=\$60, K=\$50, τ=3 months, annualized r=8%, and annualized σ=20%.

    a. Calculate the current (time=t) Black–Scholes European call option price, C_t.

    First calculate:

    d_1=_____

    $N(d_1)$=_____

    d_2=_____

    $N(d_2)$=_____

    $PV(K)$=_____

    C_t=_____

    b. State the put-call parity relationship for European options.

    c. Calculate the Black–Scholes European put option price using the put-call parity relationship for European options defined in b.

3. In this exercise, you will create a Black–Scholes calculator in Excel. The input list consists of the usual five inputs.

    a. List the *inputs*,

        1.=

        2.=

        3.=

        4.=

        5.=

    b. Code up the following *outputs* in Excel,

        1. d_1

        2. d_2

        3. $N(d_1)$

        4. $N(d_2)$

        5. C_t, the Black–Scholes call option price.

    c. Calculate the Black–Scholes call option price for the input data in exercise 2.

    d. Check your result in c. against an online Black–Scholes calculator. The one at http://www.hoadley.net/ is good. This site also produces the

OPTION PRICING IN CONTINUOUS TIME **593**

Black–Scholes greeks, or *partial sensitivities*, to the option parameters. These are helpful for managing an options portfolio, assuming Black–Scholes holds.

You now have three ways to calculate Black–Scholes: by hand, as in exercise 2; by your own Excel program, as in this exercise 3; and using online calculators.

4. Define what is meant by *implied volatility* and explain how Black–Scholes could be used to generate estimates of the market's volatility.

5. Once you have an Excel Black–Scholes calculator, it is easy to generate a mini-implied volatility calculator.

Step 1

In the Black–Scholes spreadsheet, enter the following values for the spot price, strike price, risk-free rate and time to maturity.

Input Parameters
Spot Price=490
Strike Price=470
Risk-Free Rate=.033
Volatility=0.2
Maturity=0.08

Also, enter an initial guess value for the volatility. This will give you an initial call price that is refined in the next step.

Use your Black–Scholes calculator to generate a European call option value for these parameters, which should be 24.5942, which say is in cell E5 in the spreadsheet.

a. Verify the call option price of around 24.5942.

Step 2

Go to Data>What If Analysis>Goal Seek. Set the Call value to 30 (say in cell $E5$ in the spreadsheet) by changing the volatility (say cell $B8$ in the spreadsheet). Goal seek will iterate until it finds the value of σ that is consistent with this call price of 30.

b. Verify the implied volatility which should be around 0.32094.

594 OPTIONS

■ SELECTED CONCEPT CHECK SOLUTIONS

Concept Check 2

a. $\text{Var}(y') = \text{Var}\left(\dfrac{y - \sigma}{\sigma}\right)$

$= \dfrac{1}{\sigma^2} \text{Var}(y - \mu)$

$= \dfrac{1}{\sigma^2} \text{Var}(y)$

$= \dfrac{1}{\sigma^2} \sigma^2$

$= 1.0$

Concept Check 6

a. $G(Y_0) = \ln\left(\dfrac{Y_0}{Y_0}\right)$

$= \ln(1.0)$

$= 0$

b. $E\left(G(Y_T) \mid G(Y_0) = 0\right) = \left(r - \dfrac{\sigma^2}{2}\right)T$

c. $\text{Var}\left(G(Y_T) \mid G(Y_0) = 0\right) = \sigma^2 T$

CHAPTER 17

RISK-NEUTRAL VALUATION, EMMS, THE BOPM, AND BLACK–SCHOLES

17.1	Introduction	596
	17.1.1 Preliminaries on $FTAP_1$ and $FTAP_2$ and Navigating the Terminology	596
	17.1.2 Pricing by Arbitrage and the $FTAP_2$	597
	17.1.3 Risk-Neutral Valuation without Consensus and with Consensus	598
	17.1.4 Risk-Neutral Valuation without Consensus, Pricing Contingent Claims with Unhedgeable Risks	599
	17.1.5 Black–Scholes' Contribution	601
17.2	Formal Risk-Neutral Valuation without Replication	601
	17.2.1 Constructing EMMs	601
	17.2.2 Interpreting Formal Risk-Neutral Probabilities	602
17.3	MPRs and EMMs, Another Version of $FTAP_2$	605
17.4	Complete Risk-Expected Return Analysis of the Riskless Hedge in the (BOPM, $N=1$)	607
	17.4.1 Volatility of the Hedge Portfolio	608
	17.4.2 Direct Calculation of σ_S	611
	17.4.3 Direct Calculation of σ_C	612
	17.4.4 Expected Return of the Hedge Portfolio	616
17.5	Analysis of the Relative Risks of the Hedge Portfolio's Return	618
	17.5.1 An Initial Look at Risk Neutrality in the Hedge Portfolio	620

	17.5.2	Role of the Risk Premia for a Risk-Averse Investor in the Hedge Portfolio	620
17.6		Option Valuation	624
	17.6.1	Some Manipulations	624
	17.6.2	Option Valuation Done Directly by a Risk-Averse Investor	626
	17.6.3	Option Valuation for the Risk-Neutral Investor	631

17.1 INTRODUCTION

17.1.1 Preliminaries on FTAP$_1$ and FTAP$_2$ and Navigating the Terminology

This chapter is a supplemental chapter that consolidates the topics listed above. It discusses the meaning and the underpinnings of '*risk-neutral valuation*', and it clarifies how EMMs capture the idea of 'risk-neutral valuation', and how they do not.

Interestingly, 'risk-neutral valuation' has at least two, not just one, different senses corresponding to the two fundamental theorems of asset pricing. Unfortunately, the notion of EMM tends to be a purely mathematical notion, while risk-neutral valuation is an economic concept. It is important to make these alternative approaches mutually consistent, and this is not always easily accomplished.

The beauty of the fundamental theorems of asset pricing, FTAP$_1$ and FTAP$_2$, is that they recast the economic notions of pricing in mathematical terms, thereby unleashing the full power of mathematical methods to analyze pricing. Specifically, the lessons we learn from the fundamental theorems of asset pricing are the relationships between no–arbitrage, the *existence* of a linear, positive pricing mechanism, and the *uniqueness* of the pricing mechanism. However, we have to be careful in applying these theorems, as there are numerous pitfalls in doing so.

We already know, from Chapter 15, that the existence of a linear, positive pricing mechanism that can be used to price all contingent claims (including the underlying asset), is equivalent to the existence of an EMM for the discounted, underlying price process. (Think of the contingent claim as having only one risky security in its replicating portfolio). No-arbitrage, in turn, is equivalent to the existence of a linear, positive pricing mechanism; the first fundamental theorem of asset pricing encapsulates the economic content of no-arbitrage in mathematical terms.

Furthermore, no claim of uniqueness can be made based solely upon the first fundamental theorem of asset pricing, without making further assumptions. Therefore, all that we can prove by using the no-arbitrage assumption *only,* is that there exists a linear, positive pricing mechanism that can be used to price all assets.

Or the existence of an EMM for the discounted underlying price process, which is the same thing. *We can't make any general statements about uniqueness based upon no-arbitrage alone.* That presumably is part of the content of $FTAP_2$.

17.1.2 Pricing by Arbitrage and the $FTAP_2$

An example of a statement that appears to contradict the above is the claim that a specific contingent claim (or that all claims) is (are) '*priced by arbitrage*'. A reader might easily interpret this as '*uniquely* priced by arbitrage', since most readers probably don't think in terms of non-uniqueness of the pricing mechanism in a world of no-arbitrage.

However, *no* claim is uniquely priced by arbitrage, unless it is replicable ($FTAP_2$). Of course, we can't do away with no-arbitrage, as discussed, because in that case we wouldn't be able to come up with a linear, positive pricing mechanism at all. Therefore, no-arbitrage enters into everything that we do. It is the standing assumption.

It would not make a lot of economic sense to replicate a contingent claim in the presence of arbitrage. In that case, we could not say that the price of the contingent claim is equal to the price of its replicating portfolio, which is a direct consequence of the assumption of no-arbitrage (or at least of the law of one price (LOP)). Knowing that the pricing mechanism is unique *if* it exists is nice but rather empty, except in a mathematical sense.

However, also as discussed, if we want to claim *unique* pricing of a contingent claim, then we have to assume that it is replicable. Otherwise, it is not uniquely priced. It makes sense to include the word 'replicable' somewhere in the description of the pricing method. So we might say, 'priced by replication' or 'priced by replication and no-arbitrage', or even '*given* replicability, priced by arbitrage'. The blank statement 'priced by arbitrage' is not fully correct, or at least ambiguous and a potential source of confusion.

OPTIONS

While we cannot do without no-arbitrage, in an exactly parallel manner we also cannot do without replicability (market completeness, in the case of all claims), *if* we want to claim uniqueness. Apparently, the importance of $FTAP_1$ is far better appreciated than the importance of $FTAP_2$. That, of course, doesn't make it any less important.

This is also why so many research papers and presentations often assume market completeness. Even in mathematics, existence *and* uniqueness are the sought-after goals of the analysis. From a practical perspective, running a numerical algorithm, without knowing that there is a single solution to the problem at hand, is fraught with potential error.

17.1.3 Risk-Neutral Valuation without Consensus and with Consensus

When we turn to attempting to understand risk-neutral valuation, there is another major potential pitfall. The EMM representation is often called a risk-neutral valuation representation. But it is only so in the sense of the first fundamental theorem of asset pricing, and not in the sense of the second fundamental theorem of asset pricing.

Since the risk-neutral valuation method is often illustrated in the context of the BOPM, a complete model, one obtains the bonus result that the BOPM is *preference-free*. This often leads people to believe that the existence of an EMM (which is implied by no-arbitrage) leads to a risk-neutral valuation that is also preference-free. Unfortunately, this is *not* true.

The fact is that what leads to *preference-free*, risk-neutral valuation is the additional assumption (beyond no-arbitrage) of replicability! This is actually the major contribution of Black–Scholes, which was to show that a European call (put) option could be dynamically hedged with the appropriate number of shares of the underlying stock and a risk-free bond.

That is, the risk associated with the long call option could be *neutralized* by an opposite, dynamically adjusted position in the appropriate number of shares of the underlying stock. In other words, the long European call option position could be replicated. Therefore, no additional risk premium would, or could, be demanded by risk-averse investors for investing in a European call (put) option.

This is another way to say that the risk-averse investor would value the option '*risk-neutrally*'; that is, in the same way that a risk-neutral investor would value the option. Valuing the option risk neutrally should mean not simply coming up with an EMM, but also not using subjective preferences for the trade-off between risk and expected return in valuing the option. This is what is, or should be, meant by preference-free, risk-neutral valuation.

It could be called *'risk-neutral valuation with consensus'*. The risk-neutral investor's valuation of a European call option would be *agreed to* by all risk-averse investors, because all risk-averse investors know that the risk(s) associated with the option could be diversified away (hedged out) in the hedge portfolio. We will illustrate this in the case of the BOPM, N=1.

This is similar to the situation in ordinary portfolio analysis, in which no risk premia are required for the *diversifiable* risks associated with the stocks in a portfolio. Since you can diversify away diversifiable risks, risk-averse investors would not require risk premia in order to compensate them for the diversifiable risks in risky securities such as the underlying stock, for example. They would only have to be compensated for the non-diversifiable risks. Note that, in the context of ordinary stock portfolios, the non-diversifiable risks would therefore have risk premia, and these would be priced into the stock portfolio's price.

17.1.4 Risk-Neutral Valuation without Consensus, Pricing Contingent Claims with Unhedgeable Risks

We can extrapolate from this understanding of portfolio analysis to speculate as to what would happen to the *non-hedgeable* risks in the option valuation scenario. The non-hedgeable risks are those that cannot be hedged away by attempting to replicate the European call option. These are perfectly analogous to the non-diversifiable risks on the underlier.

It is important to note here, that if a contingent claim (say, a European call option) is not replicable using a portfolio of the underlying(s) and a riskless bond, then that is because the claim involves risk(s) that cannot be neutralized by any replicating portfolio. The contingent claim's risk is not *spanned* by any replicating portfolio of underlying(s) and a riskless bond.

This could happen because there are fewer independent sources of risk than independent securities (see the rule of thumb in Chapter 13, section 13.5.2). In this case, just as in the portfolio case, these non-hedgeable risks would carry risk premia that *would* be priced in the contingent claim.

Risk premia involve risk aversion, which depends on risk preferences and therefore, even though there are EMMs, the resulting option pricing valuations would be *formally* risk-neutral (consistent with no-arbitrage), but *not* preference-free. Risk-averse investors need not agree with the risk-neutral investor's (no risk premia, therefore preference-free) valuation of the

600 OPTIONS

contingent claim. Nor would they even have to agree with *each other* as to the magnitudes of the risk premia, due to their varying degrees of risk aversion. This is why there are multiple EMMs for non-replicable contingent claims.

Note that the phenomenon that we are discussing above is not the same as the often-noted observation that a replicable, contingent claim's price does not have to include risk premia for the non-diversifiable risks of the underlier, because these would already be embodied in the underlying's price. (The underlier would *not* include risk premia for the diversifiable risks of the underlier because they could be diversified).Therefore, preferences can enter into 'preference-free', risk–neutrally valued replicable, contingent claim prices, but only *indirectly* through the prices of the underlier. No separate adjustment for such risk premia need be incorporated into replicable option prices. This is true, and general equilibrium models of option prices would address this issue.

The discussion above concerns the *extra, not spannable* risks of non-replicable, contingent claims. These are not hedgeable (spanned) by any portfolio of existing underliers and other marketed assets, such as a risk-free bond. There are simply not enough *independent* securities to span all of the risks associated with the contingent claim, which is why the claim is not replicable.

Examples of such risks could be 'jump' risk in a continuous state space model, or 'volatility' risk in a constant volatility model (see Chapter 16, section 16.8.4). The fact that these risks are not hedgeable means that there are no securities that reflect these risks.

Therefore, such extra contingent claim risks may *not* be priced in the underliers that do exist. Even if they are priced, there still have be as many *independent* securities as there are independent risks to hedge, according to our rule of thumb from Chapter 13, section 13.5.2. For example, suppose that the unhedgeable risks are 'jump' risk and 'volatility' risk. If one wanted to 'complete' the market, then independent securities or indexes that reflect these risks must be introduced.

What do we do with these risks? As discussed above, our extrapolated, basic portfolio analysis tells us that they would have to be priced in the contingent claim price, in order for risk-averse investors to be willing to invest in them. They are perfectly analogous to the non-diversifiable risks on the underlier(s).

Because the non–hedgeable risks are precisely those that *cannot* be diversified away (hedged out) by attempting to replicate the contingent claim, they would command risk premia in the contingent claim price. These would, of necessity, show up in arbitrage-free pricing formulas for the contingent claim. This also renders such contingent claim prices not preference-free.

We can summarize this as follows. In incomplete markets, non-replicable claims could be priced in a manner that is arbitrage-free (EMMs exist), and yet not preference-free. Furthermore, there would be multiple arbitrage-free, non-preference-free valuations of non-replicable claims. We know this is true, because $FTAP_2$ tells us that a claim is replicable if and only if there is a unique EMM for the discounted price process. We will also see this in another, more practical manner below.

17.1.5 Black–Scholes' Contribution

A few more observations about Black–Scholes are in order. First, Black–Scholes' contribution was not simply coming up with an EMM (arbitrage-free, formally risk-neutral) valuation formula for a European call option, in their dynamic context.

They showed that a standard European call option was replicable, hence it would have a unique arbitrage-free, *and* preference-free pricing formula. They further derived the exact unique formula (see Chapter 16, section 16.7.3), under their assumptions. Later work showed that the Black–Scholes scenario is *dynamically complete*, therefore *any* contingent claim can be uniquely priced within the Black–Scholes scenario.

17.2 FORMAL RISK-NEUTRAL VALUATION WITHOUT REPLICATION

17.2.1 Constructing EMMs

Once we have a linear, positive pricing mechanism, it is an easy exercise to determine 'risk-neutral probabilities' and an EMM. At this point, it is useful to revisit Chapter 15, section 15.1.2. In that section, we took the stock and a riskless bond as the primitive securities, and we used static replication to uniquely price the two AD securities.

Here, we start with *any* given set of positive state prices implied by no-arbitrage, our only assumption. *We do not assume replicability*. We then show that we can always obtain an equivalent 'formally risk-neutral' representation of such prices (an EMM). There will be as many EMMs (risk-neutral representations) as there are non-risk neutral pricing mechanisms implied by no-arbitrage.

Note that no-arbitrage (FTAP$_1$) does not say that the *only* way to price assets in an arbitrage-free market is with risk-neutral probabilities. It does say that once we do have a pricing mechanism, we can find an *equivalent* pricing mechanism using risk-neutral probabilities.

To see this, we will use a discrete model. So suppose that there are a finite number, S, of states $\{1,2,\ldots, S\}$ and let $q_i>0$ be one of the many current arbitrage-free prices of the i-th Arrow-Debreu security AD_i at time 0 (that is, of the state prices),

$$q_i=P_0(AD_i) \text{ for } i=1,\ldots S.$$

The sum security, $AD_{sum}\equiv\Sigma AD_i$ pays off exactly \$1 with certainty (in each and every state of the world), and is therefore a zero-coupon riskless bond. Next, by linearity of $P_0(\cdot)$ which *does* follow from the no-arbitrage assumption,

$$P_0(AD_{sum})=\Sigma P_0(AD_i)$$
$$=\Sigma q_i$$

Now, we simply *define* one of the many riskless rates r as the percentage rate of return over the period $[0,1]$ of the sum security,

$$r \equiv \frac{1-\Sigma q_i}{\Sigma q_i}$$

The solution for $P_0(AD_{sum})$ is then the usual present value formula,

$$P_0(AD_{sum})=\Sigma q_i$$
$$=(1+r)^{-1}$$

To obtain an EMM is easy. Just define $q_i^* \equiv q_i/\Sigma q_i$. Clearly, the q_i^* satisfy $q_i^*>0$ and $\Sigma q_i^*=1.0$, by construction, so they can be interpreted as probabilities. Moreover $q_i^*\times\Sigma q_i=q_i^*\times(1+r)^{-1}=q_i$. This says that the current price of the i-th AD security, q_i, has an equivalent risk-neutral representation in terms of the risk-neutral probabilities q_i^* (because these are discounted by $1+r$). That is,

$$P_0(AD_i) = q_i$$

$$= \frac{q_i^* \times \$1}{1+r}$$

Note that this final quantity is the expectation of the security's payoff (\$1 if and only if state i occurs at time 1 using the risk-neutral probability q_i^*, then discounted appropriately by the risk-free rate.

That is, it represents an EMM for the discounted price process. This argument shows that once you have any set of state prices, q_i (that are not necessarily priced using risk-neutral probabilities), then you can always obtain *equivalent*, risk-neutralized probabilities q_i^*, yielding the identical prices when discounted by $1+r$.

It doesn't follow that this construction represents the *only* way to derive an EMM from a given, positive linear pricing mechanism. There would be many EMMs for the state prices if they were not replicable in terms of some given (exogenous) assets.

17.2.2 Interpreting Formal Risk-Neutral Probabilities

We could call $(q_i^* \times \$1)/(1+r)$ the *certainty equivalent* (*CE*) state price corresponding to q_i. Note that the above construction is a mechanical process. We can also call $(q_i^* \times \$1)/(1+r)$ a 'risk-neutral' representation of state prices. But, since we cannot claim replicability and thereby uniqueness, we cannot claim that it is preference free.

We can also give an argument for exactly where risk preferences enter into $(q_i^* \times \$1)/(1+r)$, when uniqueness (replicability) does not hold. When replicability (therefore uniqueness) *does* hold, then risk preferences do *not* enter the pricing mechanism for contingent claims, because the risk(s) associated with such claims can be, and have been, hedged out in the hedge portfolio.

So why isn't $(q_i^* \times \$1)/(1+r)$ preference-free? It appears to be 'risk-neutral'. How exactly do preferences enter into $(q_i^* \times \$1)/(1+r)$? We will focus on q_i^*. The original *non-risk-neutral* representation of q_i can be written as,

$$q_i = \frac{p_i \times \$1}{r + RP_i}$$

where RP_i is a risk premium associated with investors' valuation of state-price Arrow–Debreu security i, AD_i.

p_i is the *physical* (actual) probability associated with the occurrence of state i. The occurrence of state i is not risk-free under this specification, and because we are using the *actual* probabilities p_i, according to basic finance we must discount the expected value $p_i \times \$1$ by a risk-adjusted discount rate RP_i.

Next, we want to move from the actual probabilities, p_i, to the risk-neutral probabilities q_i^*. This is what we are doing when we construct a certainty equivalent representation $(q_i^* \times \$1)/(1+r)$. In order to do so, we have to *risk-neutralize* the actual probability p_i.

How we risk neutralize it depends on how it was adjusted for risk in the first place. That, in turn, depends on how risk averse investors are. Two different risk-averse investors may require different adjustments in order to risk-neutralize the actual probability p_i.

Therefore, p_i may depend on who is evaluating the probability. In that case, it would be better represented by $p_{i,j}$, where j represents investor j. For that matter, the risk premia RP_i could also depend on the investor j and would then be better represented by $RP_{i,j}$!

Alternative degrees of risk aversion for the representative investor (if there is one, which there typically is not, unless the market is complete) will lead to different certainty equivalent (risk-neutral) probabilities, different state prices, and different EMMs for the discounted price process. This occurs only when the state prices are not replicable in terms of other even more basic assets (see Chapter 15, section 15.1.2).

There are many ways to explain why there are multiple linear, positive pricing mechanisms in a world of simple no-arbitrage, but non-replicability. First, the connection to risk-neutral probabilities is due to the fact that they are proportional to the state prices (see Chapter 15, section 15.1.2, exercise 2 on pricing $AD_u(\omega)$ and $AD_d(\omega)$). Thus, every set of state prices gives rise to a corresponding set of 'risk-neutral probabilities'. EMMs, in turn, are determined by these risk-neutral probabilities.

The connection of state prices ('risk-neutral' probabilities, EMMs) to risk aversion can be explained by the fact that state prices are also proportional to the *marginal rates of substitution* between current consumption and uncertain consumption in the alternative states in equilibrium. If you think about it, the economic effect of an Arrow–Debreu security is to transform an amount of certain present consumption, say $AD_i(\omega)$, into an uncertain dollar of consumption if and only if state i occurs.

Under uncertainty, investors value consumption claims to present and risky future consumption by means of utility functions that incorporate their alternative degrees of risk aversion. Therefore, how a given investor prices the states (the Arrow–Debreu securities) depends on, and incorporates his degree of risk aversion (however, see the next paragraph).

Only in the case in which markets are complete (or for replicable claims) will the state prices (marginal rates of substitution) be uniquely determined (FTAP$_2$). Thus, marginal rates of substitution for all agents, for each state, would have to be equal in equilibrium.

If markets are not complete, then we know that there are multiple sets of state prices. This means that the marginal rates of substitution (reflecting alternative degrees of risk aversion) of all agents are *not* all equal, for each state in equilibrium. Different agents will impose their different degrees of risk aversion in pricing the risk premia associated with non-replicable contingent claims. Therefore, such claims will not be preference-free.

There are even equilibrium models of the risk premia, in complete markets, that can be demanded on risky securities for which the risks are hedgeable. The most relevant model is the *consumption CAPM* (CCAPM). One of its conclusions is that the risk premia on risky securities in equilibrium is proportional to the covariance between its rate of return and the marginal rate of substitution (MRS) between current and future consumption (state prices, aggregate risk aversion).

These kinds of models involve *aggregation*, which is possible under complete markets. So the MRSs are for the *representative* investor. This leads to a final way of understanding the generation of EMMs in a world of nonreplicability.

17.3 MPRS AND EMMS, ANOTHER VERSION OF FTAP$_2$

We start with the condition for no-arbitrage. It is shown in mathematical finance that there are equivalent ways to ensure the existence of an EMM for the discounted underlying price process (no-arbitrage). One important necessary and sufficient condition is the existence of a '*Market Price of Risk*' (MPR), which is also called the *Sharpe Ratio*. We mentioned this important concept briefly as a relative risk measure in Chapter 15.

Under the appropriate technical assumptions, EMMs are in one-to-one correspondence with Sharpe ratios. This is because the market price of risk for security i, $(MPR_i)=(\mu_i-r)/\sigma_i$. is the generator of EMMs. In terms of risk-neutral probabilities and the actual probabilities, the mechanism of the transformation from p_i to q_i^* is *Girsanov's Theorem*, provided the assumptions underlying Girsanov actually hold. Note that q_i^* is also usually called p_i^*.

OPTIONS

Note that, in the case of non-replicability, the MPR_i could depend on the investor j because different investors could demand different risk premia on the same security i. That is,

$$MPR_i = MPR_{i,j}$$
$$= \frac{\mu_{i,j} - r}{\sigma_i}$$

In this case, there could be a different 'market' price of risk for each security i, for each investor j. But then, there would be a corresponding number of multiple, linear, positive pricing mechanisms.

Turning to completeness (replicability), it follows that uniqueness of the Sharpe ratio (MPR) implies uniqueness of the EMM for the discounted price process, and vice versa. Therefore, under completeness, all assets (including the underlier, see Chapter 13, section 13.5.2) must have the same market price of risk by $FTAP_2$.

Assume that risk is one dimensional. If a claim is replicable then it must have the same market price of risk as the risky asset in its replicating portfolio. Therefore the following is an equivalent version of $FTAP_2$:

1. *The market is complete if and only if all assets have the same market price of risk.*
2. *If a claim is replicable, then it has the same market price of risk as the risky asset in its replicating portfolio.*

The uniqueness of the market price of risk across all contingent claims (including the underliers) is often regarded as a consequence of simple no-arbitrage. If that were true, then there would *not* be multiple EMMs under no-arbitrage. But there are multiple EMMs for non-replicable claims under no-arbitrage. Therefore, identity of the market price of risk across all contingent claims, or across a subset of contingent claims, is a consequence of replicability.

If you examine the alleged no-arbitrage proofs of the identity of the market price of risk, you will see that they all invoke replicability. Thus replicability is the driver of the uniqueness of the market price of risk, as it must be.

So far this chapter has been very abstract. We will now change that by focusing on these ideas in the context of the BOPM, $N=1$.

17.4 COMPLETE RISK-EXPECTED RETURN ANALYSIS OF THE RISKLESS HEDGE IN THE (BOPM, *N*=1)

The riskless hedge is based on the idea of starting with the option's replication strategy, defined as Δ units of long stock and a dollar borrowing position in $\$B$ bonds. The implication of this strategy is the unique option pricing mechanism,

$$C_0 = \Delta * S_0 + B$$

where,

$$\Delta = \frac{C_u - C_d}{uS_0 - dS_0} \text{ and}$$

$$B = \frac{uC_d - dC_u}{r(u-d)}$$

Based on our previous costs-to-strategies technique from Chapter 11, section 11.5.3, we can easily replicate any component of the portfolio. That is, we could replicate the underlying stock itself or the dollar bond position by means of a replicating portfolio consisting of the other two instruments.

Replication is just another term for hedging, where hedging is given the usual interpretation of minimizing or even eliminating the risk associated to a position in a financial instrument, in this case the long call position. Suppose that we want to hedge the long call option position. All we need is a short position in Δ units of underlying stock.

To see this, all we have to do is re-arrange $C_0 = \Delta * S_0 + B$ to have B on the right-hand side, $C_0 - \Delta * S_0 = B$. This has the economic interpretation that a long position in one call option combined with a *short* position in Δ units of underlying stock is economically equivalent to a riskless borrowing position consisting of $\$B$ of issued bonds, using our technique from Chapter 11 of moving from current costs to underlying strategies. In other words, $C_0 - \Delta * S_0$ is riskless. This means that we have perfectly hedged out all of the risk associated with the uncertainty of up and down moves of the option, to C_u and C_d.

This is what is meant by the *riskless hedge*, the portfolio consisting of one long call position and a short position in Δ units of underlying stock. Note that this position is not costless. In fact its current cost is a current benefit equal to $C_0 - \Delta * S_0 = B < 0$. This is negative (you have to borrow $\$B$) because the short sale of Δ units of stock more than offsets the cost of one long call option.

If one wanted to synthesize a lending position, then one would short the call option and go long Δ units of stock. This is easily seen by multiplying $C_0-\Delta*S_0=B$ by -1.0 to obtain $-C_0+\Delta*S_0=\Delta*S_0-C_0=-B>0$. The risk of either portfolio is still zero; that is, riskless borrowing or riskless lending, respectively.

A good notation for the hedge in dollar terms is $H=C-\Delta*S$, where we suppress the time subscript. However, note that H can assume one of two values corresponding to $t=0$ or to $t=1$,

$H_0=C_0-\Delta*S_0$ is the hedge's value at time 0 while,

$H_1=C_1-\Delta*S_1$ is the hedge's value at time 1.

We are assured by replication (and no-arbitrage, of course) that,

$H_1=C_1-\Delta*S_1=rB$ and therefore,

$H_0=C_0-\Delta*S_0=B.$

17.4.1 Volatility of the Hedge Portfolio

We now want to look at the volatility of the hedged portfolio, H, in another way in terms of its components. We write it generically as $H=C-\Delta*S$ and calculate its variance using our rule from portfolio analysis that says,

$$\text{Var}(aX+bY)=a^2\text{Var}(X)+b^2\text{Var}(Y)+2*a*b*\text{Cov}(X,Y)$$
$$=a^2\text{Var}(X)+b^2\text{Var}(Y)+2*a*b*\rho_{X,Y}*\sigma_X*\sigma_Y$$

where $\sigma_X=\sqrt{\text{Var}(X)}$ and $\rho_{X,Y}$ is the correlation coefficient between X and Y defined by $\rho_{X,Y}\equiv\text{Cov}(X,Y)/(\sigma_X*\sigma_Y)$.

Applying this rule to our hedge portfolio H we obtain,

$$\text{Var}(H_1)=\text{Var}(C_1-\Delta*S_1)$$
$$=\text{Var}(C_1)+2\text{Cov}(C_1,-\Delta*S_1)+\text{Var}(-\Delta*S_1)$$
$$=\sigma_C^2-2\Delta*\rho_{C,S}*\sigma_C*\sigma_S+\Delta^2*\sigma_S^2 \qquad \textbf{(VAR}(H)\textbf{)}$$

The interpretation of σ_C^2 is the variance of the *dollar returns* on the option. Similarly, σ_S^2 is the variance of the dollar returns on the underlying stock.

Why dollar returns? We will demonstrate this shortly and also formulate the analysis in terms of *percentage* returns to the option, the stock, and the hedge.

We can simplify (VAR(H)) even more and get some further insight into why $-\Delta*S$ is able to hedge out all the risk of the option, C_1. A small result from statistics applied to our problem will be very helpful.

A Statistics Result on Perfect Positive Correlation

Two random variables X and Y are perfectly, positively correlated if and only if $Y=aX+b$ where a and b are constants and $a>0$.

Proof:

Suppose that $Y=aX+b$. Then

$$Cov(Y,X)=Cov(aX+b,X)$$
$$=Cov(aX,X)+Cov(b,X)$$

The second term drops out because b is a constant. Therefore, it does not co-vary with any (random) variable.

$$Cov(Y,X)=Cov(aX,X)$$
$$=aCov(X,X)$$
$$=aVar(X)$$
$$=a\sigma_X^2$$

Using the definition,

$$\rho_{X,Y}=Cov(X,Y)/(\sigma_X*\sigma_Y)$$
$$=Cov(Y,X)/(\sigma_X*\sigma_Y)$$
$$=a\sigma_X^2/(\sigma_X*\sigma_Y)$$
$$=a\sigma_X/\sigma_Y.$$

But since $Y=aX+b$ it follows that $\sigma_Y=|a|\sigma_X$ where $|a|$ denotes the absolute value of a. Since $a>0$, $|a|=a$. It follows that $\rho_{X,Y}=1.0$. The reverse implication is harder to prove, but we don't need it.

Now, consider the relationship between the option price and the underlying stock price. Once again, replication tells us the $C=\Delta S+B$ where $\Delta>0$ is a constant and $B<0$ is a constant. By our basic statistics result, it follows that C and S are *perfectly positively correlated*, $\rho_{C,S}=1.0$. This is an extremely important fact.

It explains why it is possible to *perfectly* hedge the risk of the option using Δ units of the stock alone. The reason is perfect, positive correlation, which means that every move in the option price can be perfectly matched, without residual error, by a corresponding move in the opposite direction of the shorted Δ units of the stock.

In effect, we have *synthesized* perfect, negative correlation between the long call option and the Δ units of the shorted stock. This is not surprising as the BOPM model was set up to guarantee this possibility. That is also one reason why the BOPM is a complete model; all risk can be hedged away within the model using the securities available.

The connection to portfolio theory is interesting. We know from portfolio theory, that when two assets are perfectly, negatively correlated, it is possible to synthesize a riskless Treasury bill, as we discussed in Chapter 6, section 6.1. This is exactly what we have accomplished with the hedge portfolio.

The difference between the world of underlying assets, such as stocks, and the world of derivatives is that, in the former, it may be quite difficult to find natural perfect, negative correlation. In the world of derivatives, it's easy. We just *synthesize* it.

We know that H is riskless by construction. Equating VAR$(H)=0$, we can give another equivalent expression for the hedge ratio Δ,

$$Var(H)=\sigma_C^2-2\Delta*\rho_{C,S}*\sigma_C*\sigma_S+\Delta^2*\sigma_S^2$$
$$=\sigma_C^2-2\Delta*\sigma_C*\sigma_S+\Delta^2*\sigma_S^2$$

This last expression is a 'perfect square'. This allows us to factor it,

$$\sigma_C^2-2\Delta*\sigma_C*\sigma_S+\Delta^2*\sigma_S^2=(\sigma_C-\Delta*\sigma_S)^2$$

Equating this to zero yields another expression for the risk-minimizing hedge ratio.

$$\sigma_C-\Delta*\sigma_S=0$$
$$\sigma_C-\Delta*\sigma_S=0$$
$$\Delta=\sigma_C/\sigma_S$$

In words, the risk-minimizing hedge ratio is the ratio of the standard deviation of the dollar returns to the option to the standard deviation of the dollar returns to the underlying stock. In terms of our beta analysis from Chapter 6, section 6.4.2 this is just the beta of the option with respect to the stock.

RISK-NEUTRAL VALUATION

This is due to the fact that $\rho_{C,S}=1.0$ which implies that,

$$\beta_{c,s} = \rho_{C,S} * (\sigma_C/\sigma_S)$$
$$= \sigma_C/\sigma_S$$
$$= \Delta.$$

Thus our theory of hedging options fits in nicely with the general theory of hedging, such as that discussed for futures in Chapter 6. In other words, we don't have to re-invent the wheel in order to hedge options.

Our previous expression for Δ was,

$$\Delta = \frac{C_u - C_d}{uS_0 - dS_0}$$

By what we just proved, Δ is also,

$$\Delta = \frac{\sigma_C}{\sigma_S}$$
$$= \frac{C_u - C_d}{uS_0 - dS_0}$$

However, one should *not* conclude that $\sigma_C = C_u - C_d$, nor that $\sigma_S = (u-d)*S_0$, because only *the ratios* are equal.

17.4.2 Direct Calculation of σ_S

Our now familiar graphic for the evolution of the underlying stock price is,

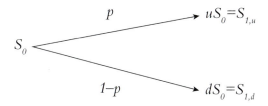

The useful notation $S_{1,u}$ means the stock price at the end of the period *if* it went up over the period and $S_{1,d}$ means the stock price at the end of the period *if* it went down over the period. Note that, as of time=0, both $S_{1,u}$ and $S_{1,d}$ are random, respectively occurring with probability p and $1-p$.

The definition of $\text{Var}(S_1)$ is $E(S_1-E(S_1))^2$ and this is easily calculated. When we calculate a variance we do use the real probabilities defining the evolution of the process, not the risk-neutral probabilities. This is an important point to remember in pricing options.

612 **OPTIONS**

1. $E(S_1)=p*S_{1,u}+(1-p)*S_{1,d}$
   $\quad\quad=p*uS_0+(1-p)*dS_0$

2. $uS_0-E(S_1)=uS_0-(p*uS_0+(1-p)*dS_0)$
   $\quad\quad\quad\quad=S_0*(u-pu-(1-p)d)$
   $\quad\quad\quad\quad=S_0*(u(1-p)-(1-p)d)$
   $\quad\quad\quad\quad=S_0*(1-p)*(u-d)$

3. $dS_0-E(S_1)=dS_0-(p*uS_0+(1-p)*dS_0)$
   $\quad\quad\quad\quad=S_0*(d-pu-(1-p)d)$
   $\quad\quad\quad\quad=S_0*(d-pu-(1-p)d)$
   $\quad\quad\quad\quad=S_0*p*(d-u)$

Therefore,

$$(uS_0-E(S_1))^2=(S_0*(1-p)*(u-d))^2$$
$$=S_0^2*(1-p)^2*(u-d)^2 \text{ and,} \quad\quad\quad\quad\textbf{(UP)}$$

$$(dS_0-E(S_1))^2=(S_0*p*(d-u))$$
$$=S_0^2*p^2*(d-u)^2 \quad\quad\quad\quad\textbf{(DOWN)}$$

Multiplying (UP) by p and (DOWN) by $1-p$ we obtain,

4. $\text{VAR}(S_1)=p*S_0^2*(1-p)^2*(u-d)^2+(1-p)*S_0^2*p^2*(d-u)^2$
   $\quad\quad\quad\quad=S_0^2*(u-d)^2*p*(1-p)*[(1-p)+p]$
   $\quad\quad\quad\quad=p*(1-p)*S_0^2*(u-d)^2$

Clearly $\text{VAR}(S_1)$ involves the real-world probability p.

In our previous notation,

$\sigma_S^2=p*(1-p)*S_0^2*(u-d)^2$ and therefore,
$\sigma_S=S_0*(u-d)*\sqrt{(p*(1-p))}$.

17.4.3 Direct Calculation of σ_C

The corresponding graphic for evolution of the option price is,

RISK-NEUTRAL VALUATION · 613

Note that the spread in C_1 is smaller than the spread in S_1 and we have purposely drawn it to reflect this. This is also why we need a hedge ratio Δ typically (but not always) <1.0. The hedge ratio is based on dollar move equivalency, which means that we have to match the dollar move in the option price by an equivalent dollar move in Δ units of the stock price.

The definition of $\text{Var}(C_1)$ is $E(C_1-E(C_1))^2$ and this is just as easily calculated as $\text{Var}(S_1)$. Again, when we calculate a variance we do use the real probabilities defining the evolution of the process, not the risk-neutral probabilities.

1. $E(C_1)=pC_{1,u}+(1-p)C_{1,d}$
$\qquad =pC_u+(1-p)C_d$

2. $C_u-E(C_1)=C_u-(pC_u+(1-p)C_d)$
$\qquad\qquad =(1-p)(C_u-C_d)$

3. $C_d-E(C_1)=C_d-(pC_u+(1-p)C_d)$
$\qquad\qquad =C_d-pC_u-(1-p)C_d$
$\qquad\qquad =p(C_d-C_u)$

Therefore,

$$(C_u-E(C_u))^2=(1-p)^2(C_u-C_d)^2 \quad \text{and,} \qquad\qquad \textbf{(UP)}$$

$$(C_d-E(C_1))^2=p^2(C_d-C_u)^2 \qquad\qquad\qquad \textbf{(DOWN)}$$

Multiplying (UP) by p and (DOWN) by $(1-p)$ we obtain,

4. $\text{VAR}(C_1)=p(1-p)^2(C_u-C_d)^2+(1-p)p^2(C_d-C_u)^2$
$\qquad\qquad =(C_u-C_d)^2(p(1-p)^2+(1-p)p^2)$
$\qquad\qquad =(C_u-C_d)^2p(1-p)$

Hence,

$\sigma_C^2=p(1-p)(C_u-C_d)^2$ and therefore,

$$\sigma_C=(C_u-C_d)*\sqrt{(p*(1-p))}$$

Thus, it appears that we have the *probability based* parameter $\sqrt{(p*(1-p))}$ to worry about. However, when we take the *ratio* of σ_C to σ_S the interesting fact is that it cancels out and so causes no worries,

$$\Delta = \frac{\sigma_C}{\sigma_S}$$

$$= \frac{\left(C_u - C_d\right) * \sqrt{\left(p*(1-p)\right)}}{S_0 * \left(u-d\right) * \sqrt{\left(p*(1-p)\right)}}$$

$$= \frac{C_u - C_d}{\left(u-d\right)S_0}$$

This result is what all methods for determining the hedge ratio end up calculating, due to completeness of the BOPM. So while p is important in determining σ_C and σ_S, terms involving it cancel out in the hedge ratio, which appears to be the main other entry point for p to enter the option pricing formula.

There are two other points at which p could enter the option price. This is evident from $C_0 = \Delta * S_0 + B$. B and S_0 are the other two candidates. We just showed that p does not enter Δ. If the expected return on the stock (more generally the stock market) $E(S_1) = puS_0 + (1-p)dS_0$ did not suit stock investors because p was too low, they could switch out to the riskless bond. This would have the effect of driving up bond prices and thereby lowering the riskless rate, r. So p could have an *indirect* effect on r and enter the formula that way. However, this takes us beyond the partial equilibrium scope of the BOPM where r is taken as given.

The most natural entry point at which p could enter the BOPM is, of course, through S_0. For example, if good news about the stock price were announced then S_0 could increase. An increase in S_0, other variables held constant, would increase the option price, C_0.

Thus, the actual probability can affect the current option price but, in the case of replicability, only in this indirect manner by first affecting S_0. This is to say, that p does not enter *directly* into the option pricing formula. The practical implication of this is that we do not have to make an adjustment to option prices for p. Rather, p affects S_0 and then S_0 *automatically* feeds into the option price.

We need to clarify the nature of option pricing models like the BOPM. In the language of economics, these kinds of models fit into the category of what are known as *partial equilibrium* (PE) models. In partial equilibrium models, we don't try to explain all the variables simultaneously. That is, some variables are taken as given. These variables are labeled *exogenous*. Other variables are explained by the exogenous variables. These are called the *endogenous* variables.

In the case of the BOPM, the exogenous variables are the underlying stock price, S_0, the risk-free rate r, the percentage up move in the stock u', the percentage down move in the stock d', and the number of periods. Given all this information, the option price C_0 is determined as a function of these exogenous variables.

The option pricing formula gives the *form* of the relationship between the current option price and the current values of the exogenous variables. No attempt is made to explain, or endogenize the exogenous variables. The meaning of the statement '*the actual probability p does not affect the current option price*' is that the *form* of the relationship relating the option price to the exogenous variables is not affected by p. If you look at the (BOPM, $N=1$), you will see that this is exactly correct.

Further, as we will discuss, a risk-averse investor, using the actual probability p and a risk-adjusted discount rate, would arrive at exactly the same pricing formula as the risk-neutral investor using the risk-neutral probability. Therefore, the risk preferences embedded in p do not enter into a *replicable* claim's price.

It is still true that, even for replicable claims, the actual probability p is buried mostly within the exogenous current stock price, S_0. Nor is the current stock price, S_0, the only exogenous variable within which the actual probability could be buried. It is embedded in the volatility parameter, σ, in more general option pricing models such as Black–Scholes. The partial equilibrium nature of such models is expressed in the assumption that σ is constant. This is why such models make these kinds of assumptions. The reason is that they cannot, nor do they wish to, explain the exogenous variables such as σ (see Chapter 16, section 16.8).

In *general equilibrium* (GE) models, an attempt is made to explain all of the variables. In other words, to endogenize all the exogenous variables. However, such models are rare for option prices.

It should be noted that GE models typically involve risk premia due to the problem that not all risks may be fully hedgeable (incomplete markets). If they aren't, we don't get the strong preference-free results of partial equilibrium models like the BOPM or Black–Scholes. These models are complete. The valuation problem they solve is much more tractable than when multiple, potentially uninsurable risks have to be considered.

616 OPTIONS

17.4.4 Expected Return of the Hedge Portfolio

In this section, we look at the (expected) return of the hedge portfolio. In particular, we examine whether a risk-averse investor would (could) demand a risk premium on the hedge portfolio *vis-à-vis* a risk-neutral investor who would not.

We must remember here that the (riskless) hedge portfolio implies nothing about the risk preferences of investors (see the End of Chapter Exercise 3). Such risk preferences are unconstrained by replication.

The Return to the Hedge Portfolio

In order to analyze the (expected) return of the hedge portfolio, we have to first define percentage returns for it and its components.

Using our previous notation,

$H_0 = C_0 - \Delta * S_0$ is the hedge's value at time 0 while,

$H_1 = C_1 - \Delta * S_1$ is the hedge's value at time 1.

Note that the hedge is a net borrowing position.

We define the *percentage* return to the option, using continuous-time notation, as,

$$R_C \equiv \frac{dC}{C}$$
$$= \frac{C_1 - C_0}{C_0}$$
$$= \frac{C_1}{C_0} - 1$$

Similarly the *percentage* return to the underlying stock is,

$$R_S \equiv \frac{dS}{S}$$
$$= \frac{S_1 - S_0}{S_0}$$
$$= \frac{S_1}{S_0} - 1$$

RISK-NEUTRAL VALUATION 617

Our hedge portfolio is defined by $H=C-\Delta*S$. Note that $H_0=B_0<0$ and that $H_1=B_1<0$. The correct way to define the return to the *normal* hedge (short the risk-free bond), R_H, in this scenario is as $R'_H=-R_H$ where R_H is defined in the normal way below. We simply do the calculations for R_H and multiply by -1.0 to get the portfolio weights for R'_H. Therefore, its percentage return is similarly defined as,

$$R_H \equiv \frac{dH}{H}$$

$$= \frac{H_1 - H_0}{H_0}$$

$$= \frac{H_1}{H_0} - 1$$

Now,

$$dH = d\left(C - \Delta * S\right)$$

$$= dC - \Delta * dS$$

Therefore,

$$R_H = \frac{dC - \Delta dS}{C_0 - \Delta S_0}$$

$$= \frac{dC}{C_0 - \Delta S_0} - \frac{\Delta dS}{C_0 - \Delta S_0}$$

$$= \frac{dC}{C_0} * \frac{C_0}{C_0 - \Delta S_0} - \Delta \frac{dS}{S_0} * \frac{S_0}{C_0 - \Delta S_0}$$

Noting that $C_0-\Delta*S_0=B_0$ we obtain a weighted-average expression for R_H,

$$R_H = \frac{dC}{C_0} * \frac{C_0}{B_0} - \Delta \frac{dS}{S_0} * \frac{S_0}{B_0}$$

$$= X_C * \frac{dC}{C_0} + X_S * \frac{dS}{S_0}$$

$$= X_C * R_C + X_S * R_S \qquad\qquad [R_H]$$

where $X_C=[C_0/B_0]<0$ and $X_S=-\Delta[S_0/B_0]>0$ because we are shorting the option in the reverse hedge.

618 OPTIONS

The portfolio weights add up to 1.0 as they should,

$$X_C + X_S = \frac{C_0}{B} - \Delta \frac{S_0}{B_0}$$

$$= \frac{C - \Delta * S_0}{B_0}$$

$$= 1.0$$

and so R_H represents the return to the reverse hedge (short the option and long Delta units of stock). It is the *reverse* hedge (long the risk-free bond) that *earns* the risk-free rate. The normal hedge (short the risk-free bond) *pays* the risk-free rate (*earns* negative the risk-free rate).

17.5 ANALYSIS OF THE RELATIVE RISKS OF THE HEDGE PORTFOLIO'S RETURN

17.5.1 An Initial Look at Risk Neutrality in the Hedge Portfolio

Now, in analyzing R_H there is no reason to believe, nor to assume, that either of its component returns R_C and R_S are riskless. This assumption, which would satisfy a risk-neutral investor only, would take the form,

$$\frac{dC}{C} = r'dt \qquad\qquad \textbf{(C riskless)}$$

$$\frac{dS}{S} = r'dt \qquad\qquad \textbf{(S riskless)}$$

However we can demonstrate Statement 6 (see End of Chapter Exercise 4) which says that *if* C is riskless then S must be riskless, and that *if* S is riskless then C must be riskless.

Since $C = \Delta S + B$ by the exact same weighted-average portfolio construction we just performed,

$$\frac{dC}{C} = \frac{d(\Delta S + B)}{C}$$

$$= \frac{\Delta S}{C} * \frac{dS}{S} + \frac{dB}{B} * \frac{B}{C}$$

The bond is clearly riskless so $[dB/B]=r'dt$. Now suppose that C is also riskless, $[dC/C]=r'dt$. Then,

$$r'dt = \frac{\Delta S}{C} * \frac{dS}{S} + r'dt * \frac{B}{C}$$

This implies that,

$$\frac{\Delta S}{C} * \frac{dS}{S} = r'dt - \left(r'dt * \frac{B}{C} \right)$$

$$= r'dt \left(1 - \frac{B}{C} \right)$$

Multiplying both sides by $[C/\Delta S]$ we obtain,

$$\frac{dS}{S} = r'dt \left(1 - \frac{B}{C} \right) * \left(\frac{C}{\Delta S} \right)$$

Expanding the term multiplying $r'dt$ we obtain,

$$\left(1 - \frac{B}{C} \right) * \left(\frac{C}{\Delta S} \right) = \left(\frac{C-B}{C} \right) * \left(\frac{C}{\Delta S} \right)$$

But $C-B=\Delta S$ so this term is,

$$\left(\frac{\Delta S}{C} \right) * \left(\frac{C}{\Delta S} \right) = 1.0$$

We have just shown that *if* C is riskless then, in the hedge portfolio, S must also be riskless. The economic reason is clear. *All risks must cancel out in the hedge portfolio* because it is riskless. If C were riskless and S were not, there would be no way to combine them into a portfolio so that their risks would cancel out.

Next, we will demonstrate the other half of Statement 6 (see End of Chapter Exercise 4). Suppose now that S is riskless.

Then,

$$\frac{dC}{C} = \frac{dC}{\Delta S + B}$$

$$= \frac{\Delta S}{C} * \frac{dS}{S} + \frac{dB}{B} * \frac{B}{C}$$

620 **OPTIONS**

$$= \frac{\Delta S}{C} * \left(r'dt \right) + \left(r'dt \right) * \frac{B}{C}$$

$$= \left(r'dt \right) * \left(\frac{\Delta S}{C} + \frac{B}{C} \right)$$

$$= \left(r'dt \right) * \left(\frac{\Delta S + B}{C} \right)$$

$$= r'dt$$

Thus C is riskless, *if* S is riskless. The same economic reason applies. If one of C or S were riskless but the other was not, then it would never be possible for their relative risks to cancel out to create a riskless overall result, the hedge portfolio.

17.5.2 Role of the Risk Premia for a Risk-Averse Investor in the Hedge Portfolio

Can *both* R_C and R_S be risky in the hedge portfolio? And can they command risk premia? The answers are clearly yes, if their risks cancel each other out in the hedge portfolio. They will even command different risk premia demanded by risk-averse investors.

However, a risk-averse investor would construct exactly the same riskless portfolio as a risk-neutral investor, namely the riskless hedge portfolio. Since it has no risk, risk-averse investors would have no reason to require anything other than the riskless rate of return, r', from that hedge portfolio.

This *suggests* (but does not prove) that risk-averse investors would construct the same *option price* as their cousins, the risk-neutral investors. *If* all investors, risk-neutral and risk-averse, come up with the same BOPM price, then this says that that unique price is independent of preferences. It is preference-free.

To verify the above, once again write out $[R_H]$, the return to the reverse hedge, and note that R_H is random because its randomness is induced by the randomness of R_C and R_S. Using our previous notation, ω denotes the random 'state of the world' which is either UP or DOWN in our model,

$$R_H(\omega) = X_C R_C(\omega) + X_S R_S(\omega) \qquad\qquad [R_H(\omega)]$$

RISK-NEUTRAL VALUATION 621

Now, take the expected value of both sides of $[R_H(\omega)]$ to obtain the familiar result from portfolio analysis that the expected return of a portfolio is the portfolio weighted-average of its components' expected returns,

$$E[R_H(\omega)] = X_C E[R_C(\omega)] + X_S E[R_S(\omega)] \qquad\qquad [E[R_H(\omega)]]$$

Assume now that a risk-averse investor evaluates $E[R_C(\omega)]$ and $E[R_S(\omega)]$ and establishes that, due to the non-diversifiable risks in $R_C(\omega)$ and $R_S(\omega)$, each must pay a risk premium above the riskless rate r',

$$E[R_C(\omega)] = r' + \delta_C \qquad\qquad [\delta_C]$$

where δ_C is the risk premium for $E[R_C(\omega)]$ and $\delta_C > 0$,

$$E[R_S(\omega)] = r' + \delta_S \qquad\qquad [\delta_S]$$

where δ_S is the risk premium for $E[R_S(\omega)]$ and $\delta_S > 0$,

There is no reason to assume that $\delta_C = \delta_S$, since the leveraged return to the option is certainly riskier than that of the stock on the upside. However, there must be a relationship between δ_C and δ_S, which we will now demonstrate.

Substitute $[\delta_C]$ and $[\delta_S]$ into $[E[R_H(\omega)]]$ to obtain,

$$
\begin{aligned}
E[R_H(\omega)] &= X_C E[R_C(\omega)] + X_S E[R_S(\omega)] \\
&= X_C[r' + \delta_C] + X_S[r' + \delta_S] \\
&= (X_C + X_S)[r'] + [X_C\delta_C + X_S\delta_S]r' \\
&= 1.0r' + [X_C\delta_C + X_S\delta_S]r'
\end{aligned}
$$

because $X_C + X_S = 1.0$. Note that the expected return to the normal hedge (short the riskless bond), R'_H, is $-r'$. But we continue to work with R_H (the reverse hedge, long the riskless bond).

Now, we have to think about this carefully. Even though $R_C(\omega)$ and $R_S(\omega)$ are risky, and would be evaluated as such by a risk-averse investor, $R_H(\omega)$ is not risky.

Previously, we showed only that the *dollar* risk of H is zero, but this easily transfers to the percentage risk of R_H as follows,

$$\sigma^2_{R_H} = \mathrm{Var}\left(R_H\right)$$

$$= \mathrm{Var}\left(\frac{dH}{H}\right)$$

$$= \mathrm{Var}\left(\frac{H_1 - H_0}{H_0}\right)$$

$$= \mathrm{Var}\left(\frac{H_1}{H_0} - 1\right)$$

$$= \mathrm{Var}\left(\frac{H_1}{H_0}\right)$$

$$= \left(\frac{1}{H_0^2}\right)\mathrm{Var}\left(H_1(\omega)\right)$$

$$= 0 \text{ if and only if } \mathrm{Var}\left(H_1(\omega)\right) = 0$$

That is, $\sigma^2_{R_H} = (1/H_0^2)\sigma^2_H$, which implies that $\sigma_{R_H} = \sigma_H/H_0$, so we can always get the standard deviation of percentage returns from the standard deviation of dollar returns. Then the result is that the variance of percentage returns on the hedge portfolio is equal to zero if and only if the variance of dollar returns is zero. Here $H_1(\omega)$ denotes the *dollar* returns to the hedge portfolio.

We showed earlier that all it takes is replication (the correct choice of Δ and of B) to *completely neutralize* the risk of H. But, if the hedge portfolio is rendered riskless, then it is riskless for all investors, risk-neutral and risk-averse alike. Replication has nothing to do with the risk preferences of investors.

Since $R_H(\omega)$ is riskless to risk-averse investors, they would not require a risk premium from it. Nor could they; an arbitrage-free market would not permit one. If it did, you could borrow at r', invest in the hedge portfolio, and expect to earn a riskless risk premium at no current cost.

Therefore,

$$E[R_H(\omega)] = R_H(\omega)$$
$$= r'$$

Going back to our risk-premium-adjusted equation for $E[R_H(\omega)]$,

$$E[R_H(\omega)] = 1.0 * r' + [X_C\delta_C + X_S\delta_S] * r'$$
$$= r'.$$

The only way that this can happen is when $X_C\delta_C + X_S\delta_S = 0$; the portfolio-weighted risk premia for $E[R_C(\omega)]$ and $E[R_S(\omega)]$ must be zero. Therefore, the risk premia, δ_C and δ_S, cancel each other out when weighted by X_C and X_S respectively in the hedge portfolio.

Recall that X_C and X_S have opposite signs, due to the longness of the option C and the shortness of ΔS in the hedge portfolio, $X_C = [C/B] < 0$ and $X_S = -\Delta[S/B] > 0$.

This is the vehicle for the cancellation of risks contributed by $R_C(\omega)$ and $R_S(\omega)$ to the non-risk of the hedge portfolio.

The *risk cancellation condition* is,

$$X_C\delta_C + X_S\delta_S = \left(\frac{C}{B}\right)\delta_C + \left[-\Delta\left(\frac{S}{B}\right)\right]\delta_S$$
$$= 0$$

or

$$\left(\frac{C}{B}\right)\delta_C - \Delta\left(\frac{S}{B}\right)\delta_S = 0$$

Multiplying both sides of this relationship by B we obtain,

$$C\delta_C - \Delta S\delta_S = 0$$

which translates into,

$$C\delta_C = \Delta S\delta_S \qquad \textbf{[Risk Premia Cancellation Condition, Dollars]}$$

This says that the *dollar risk-premium* contributed to the hedge portfolio by the long position in C is exactly equal, but opposite in sign, to the dollar risk-premium contributed to the hedge portfolio by the short position in ΔS.

Therefore they cancel out. They must cancel out, otherwise the hedge portfolio would not be riskless. We can further simplify the [Risk Premia Cancellation Condition] by substituting Δ into it,

$$C\delta_C = \Delta S\delta_S$$
$$= \left(\frac{\sigma_C}{\sigma_S}\right)S\delta_S$$

624 **OPTIONS**

which says, after a little algebra, that,

$$\frac{\delta_C}{\sigma_C/C} = \frac{\delta_S}{\sigma_S/S}$$

or,

$$\frac{\delta_C}{\sigma_{R_C}} = \frac{\delta_S}{\sigma_{R_S}} \qquad \textbf{[Risk Premia Cancellation Condition, Returns]}$$

Note that, just as $\sigma_{R_H} = \sigma_H/H_0$, by exactly the same argument, $\sigma_{R_C} = \sigma_C/C_0$ and $\sigma_{R_S} = \sigma_S/S_0$.

This equilibrium condition, [*Risk Premia Cancellation Condition, Returns*], between the risk premium on the option and the risk premium on the underlying stock says that, in order for the hedge portfolio to be riskless, the *Sharpe ratios* of the option and the stock must be equal. The Sharpe ratio is a standard portfolio risk measure defined as risk-premium to standard deviation and was introduced in Chapter 15. We have also called it the *Market Price of Risk* (MPR).

As we have just demonstrated, [Risk Premia Cancellation Condition, Returns] is a consequence of the fact that it is possible to replicate the call option in the (BOPM, $N=1$). If this condition is necessary and sufficient for replication of any contingent claim (which it is by the revised version of $FTAP_2$ in section 17.3), then this is just another way to say that the (BOPM, $N=1$) is complete.

We see that the equal MPRs condition follows from risklessness of the hedge portfolio, which is implied by replication, which is in turn implied by market completeness. So the fundamental driver of the Risk Premia Cancellation Condition is market completeness. Under market completeness, all contingent claims (including the underlier) have exactly the same MPR.

17.6 OPTION VALUATION

17.6.1 Some Manipulations

In this subsection, we take another look at how risk-averse investors would evaluate the option based on the explicit inclusion of their risk premia. We already effectively did this, but another demonstration will help us further understand how risks cancel out in the hedge portfolio.

RISK-NEUTRAL VALUATION 625

We are going to focus on particularly stubborn risk-averse investors who don't necessarily 'buy into' risk-neutral valuation. In the next section, we will focus on option valuation for risk-neutral investors. The net result, for both risk-averse investors and risk-neutral investors, is exactly the same risk-neutral option valuation result, given by the BOPM, $N=1$.

We start with $[E[R_H(\omega)]]$,

$$E[R_H(\omega)]=X_C E[R_C(\omega)]+X_S E[R_S(\omega)] \qquad\qquad [E[R_H(\omega)]]$$

where $X_C=[C/B]<0$ and $X_S=-\Delta[S/B]>0$.

Then we calculate the returns and expected returns of the underlying stock and of the call option,

$$R_C(\omega) = \frac{dC}{C}$$
$$= \frac{C_1(\omega)-C_0}{C_0}$$
$$= \left(\frac{C_1(\omega)}{C_0}\right)-1$$

and,

$$R_S(\omega) = \frac{dS}{S}$$
$$= \frac{S_1(\omega)-S_0}{S}$$
$$= \left(\frac{S_1(\omega)}{S_0}\right)-1$$

Then, taking expectations,

$$E\left(R_C(\omega)\right) = E\left(\frac{C_1(\omega)}{C_0}\right)-1$$

and,

$$E\left(R_S(\omega)\right) = E\left(\frac{S_1(\omega)}{S_0}\right)-1$$

626 OPTIONS

Substituting into $[E[R_H(\omega)]]$ we obtain,

$$E\left(R_H(\omega)\right) = \left(\frac{C_0}{B}\right)\left[\frac{E(C_1(\omega))}{C_0} - 1\right] - \Delta\left(\frac{S_0}{B}\right)\left[\frac{E(S_1(\omega))}{S_0} - 1\right]$$

$$= \left[\frac{E(C_1(\omega))}{B} - \frac{C_0}{B}\right] - \Delta\left[\left(\frac{E(S_1(\omega))}{S_0}\right) - \frac{S_0}{B}\right]$$

$$= \left[\frac{E(C_1(\omega))}{B}\right] - \Delta\left[\frac{E(S_1(\omega))}{S_0}\right] - \left[\left(\frac{C_0}{B}\right) - \Delta\left(\frac{S_0}{B}\right)\right]$$

$$= r'$$

Multiplying both sides by B we obtain,

$$E(C_1(\omega)) - \Delta E(S_1(\omega)) - (C_0 - \Delta S_0) = r'B$$

Note that $C_0 - \Delta S_0 = B$. Therefore,

$$E(C_1(\omega)) - \Delta E(S_1(\omega)) = r'B + B$$
$$= (r' + 1)B$$
$$= rB$$

This says just that the mean of $C_1(\omega) - \Delta S_1(\omega)$ replicates rB. Not quite what we mean by replication, but getting there.

17.6.2 Option Valuation Done Directly by a Risk-Averse Investor

Our risk-averse investor insists on valuing the option *directly*. To do so, he uses different risk-adjusted probabilities p_C and p_S to value $E(C_1(\omega))$ and $E(S_1(\omega))$ respectively. Further, discounting is done using the appropriate risk premia, δ_S for $E(S_1(\omega))$ and δ_C for $E(C_1(\omega))$.

Using this procedure, the risk-averse investor finds that,

$$E(C_1(\omega)) = p_C C_u + (1 - p_C) C_d$$

and,

$$E(S_1(\omega)) = p_S S_u + (1 - p_S) S_d$$
$$= p_S u S_0 + (1 - p_S) d S_0$$

From this we obtain the hedging relationship,

$$E(C_1(\omega)) - \Delta E(S_1(\omega)) = [p_C C_u + (1-p_C)C_d] - \Delta[p_S * uS_0 + (1-p_S)dS_0]$$
$$= rB$$

Evaluating the option component first we obtain,

$$C_0 = \frac{E(C_1(\omega))}{r + \delta_C}$$
$$= \frac{p_C C_u + (1 - p_C)C_d}{r + \delta_C}$$

Note that the risk-averse investor *could* value the option in what looks like a *non-risk-neutral* manner using this formula. Assuming that he had the correct p_C and the appropriate risk premium for discounting the option, δ_C. This is a lot of new information required to do so, but this *does* show that the option *could* be valued without using the risk-neutral formula.

However, as we are going to now show, the option price using this method would be identical to the risk-neutral one. So all the effort would be fruitless. Nothing new would arise from it.

Substituting the replicating portfolio conditions, we find that,

$$C_0 = \frac{p_C C_u + (1 - p_C)C_d}{r + \delta_C}$$
$$= \frac{\Delta\left[p_S uS_0 + (1 - p_S)dS_0\right] + rB}{r + \delta_C}$$

This, in turn, says that,

$$(r + \delta_C)C_0 = \Delta[p_S uS_0 + (1-p_S)dS_0] + rB.$$

The left-hand side of this expression is,

$$rC_0 + \delta_C C_0.$$

628 OPTIONS

But the riskless hedge does impose the [Risk Premia Cancellation Condition, Dollars], $C_0\delta_C = \Delta S_0\delta_S$, so we substitute this into the left-hand side to obtain,

$$(r+\delta_C)C_0 = rC_0 + \delta_C C_0$$
$$= rC_0 + \Delta S_0\delta_S$$

Moving the $\Delta S_0\delta_S$ term to the right-hand side we obtain that,

$$rC_0 = \Delta[p_S u S_0 + (1-p_S)dS_0] - \Delta S\delta_S + rB$$
$$= \Delta[p_S u S_0 + (1-p_S)dS_0 - S_0\delta_S] + rB. \qquad (rC_0)$$

Now, we will consider the first term in brackets on the right-hand side of this equation, $p_S u S_0 + (1-p_S)dS_0 - S_0\delta_S$. This term is $E(S_1(\omega))$ *as if it had no risk premium.*

To show this, we use the definition of the risk premium, δ_S, from $E[R_S(\omega)] = r' + \delta_S$ and we follow through a series of equations,

$$E[R_S(\omega)] = (E(S_1(\omega))/S_0) - 1$$
$$= r' + \delta_S$$

Therefore, since $r = 1 + r'$,

$$E(S_1(\omega))/S_0 = 1 + r' + \delta_S$$
$$= r + \delta_S$$

Isolating $E(S_1(\omega))$, we obtain,

$$E(S_1(\omega)) = S_0(r + \delta_S)$$

Therefore,

$$E(S_1(\omega)) = p_S u S_0 + (1-p_S)dS_0$$
$$= S_0(r + \delta_S)$$

Solving to obtain rS_0 on one side of this equation we obtain,

$$p_S u S_0 + (1-p_S)dS_0 - \delta_S S_0 = rS_0$$

This shows that $p_S u S_0 + (1-p_S)dS_0 - \delta_S S_0$ earns the risk-free rate on a percentage basis because it says that,

RISK-NEUTRAL VALUATION 629

$$\frac{\left[p_S u S_0 + \left(1 - p_S\right) d S_0 - \delta_S S_0\right]}{S_0} = r.$$

Now the stock price *without its risk premium* is simply the risk-neutral stock price. That is, the stock price valued by discounting at the risk-free rate.

The question is, what are the correct probabilities to determine $E(S_1(\omega))$? We could label them risk-neutral probabilities. Denote these risk-neutral probabilities by p^* and the corresponding expectation using these probabilities as E^*.

Then,

$$E^*\left(S_1(\omega)\right) = p^* u S_0 + \left(1 - p^*\right) d S_0$$

which would be discounted by $r = 1 + r'$ in valuing S_0,

$$S_0 = \frac{E^*\left(S_1(\omega)\right)}{r}$$

$$= \frac{\left[p^* u S_0 + \left(1 - p^*\right) d S_0\right]}{r}$$

Cancelling S_0 on both sides of this expression and multiplying through by r we obtain,

$$r = p^* u + (1 - p^*) d$$

Solving for p^* we obtain,

$$p^*(u - d) = r - d$$

and finally,

$$p^* = \frac{r - d}{u - d}$$

But these are just our old risk-neutral probabilities, p', from the BOPM, ($N=1$). We just showed that the probabilities under which the stock price would be valued as a security that has no risk premium, p^*, are exactly the same as the risk-neutral probabilities, p', used to price the call option in the BOPM, ($N=1$).

630 OPTIONS

We conclude that,

$$p_S\, uS_0 + (1-p_S)dS_0 - \delta_S S_0$$
$$= p'uS_0 + (1-p')dS_0$$

where $p' = p^* = (r-d)/(u-d)$ are the Binomial's $(N=1)$ risk-neutral probabilities.

Now we can go back and substitute this result into (rC_0), and see what we get for the risk-averse investor's valuation of rC_0,

$$rC_0 = \Delta[p_S uS_0 + (1-p_S)dS_0 - S_0\delta_S] + rB$$
$$= \Delta[p'uS_0 + (1-p')dS_0] + rB$$

Rearranging this,

$$C_0 = \frac{\Delta\left[p'uS_0 + \left(1-p'\right)dS_0\right]}{r} + \frac{rB}{r}$$

$$= \frac{\Delta\left[p'uS_0 + \left(1-p'\right)dS_0\right]}{r} + B$$

$$= \Delta S_0 \frac{\left[p'u + \left(1-p'\right)d\right]}{r} + B$$

Looking at the numerator of the bracketed term and using the definition of p',

$$\left[p'u + \left(1-p'\right)d\right] = \left(\frac{r-d}{u-d}\right)u + \left(1 - \frac{r-d}{u-d}\right)d$$

$$= u\left(\frac{r-d}{u-d}\right) + d\left(\frac{u-r}{u-d}\right)$$

$$= \frac{u\left(r-d\right) + d\left(u-r\right)}{u-d}$$

$$= \frac{ur - ud + du - dr}{u-d}$$

$$= \frac{r\left(u-d\right)}{u-d}$$

$$= r$$

RISK-NEUTRAL VALUATION **631**

Thus $\{[p'u+(1-p')d]/r\}=1.0$, since the numerator equals the denominator.

Therefore, the risk-averse investor's valuation of C_0 boils down to,

$$C_0 = \Delta S_0 \frac{\left[p'u+\left(1-p'\right)d\right]}{r} + B$$

$$= \Delta S_0 * 1.0 + B$$

We conclude that $C_0=\Delta S_0+B$, where Δ is the hedge ratio and B are defined exactly as in the risk-neutral valuation approach. The right-hand side is just the current value of the replicating portfolio, and we have shown that the current option price must be exactly equal to it. That is, we are back to the risk-neutral valuation approach discussed in Chapter 13, section 13.8.

This therefore demonstrates that an independent valuation of C_0 by a risk-averse investor *would* make economic sense if all the input data regarding preferences was available. But it wouldn't result in a new option pricing formula different from that produced by the replication approach under which risk preferences are not required! Indeed all the extra work is unnecessary. This isn't really surprising as it is an implication of replicability (FTAP$_2$) and no-arbitrage (FTAP$_1$).

Let's now close this chapter by contrasting the risk-averse investor's direct calculation of his option price with how a risk-neutral investor would value the option.

17.6.3 Option Valuation for the Risk-Neutral Investor

We know how *any* investor, risk averse or risk neutral, would or should value the option, which is through replication using the stock and riskless bond. The risk-averse investor knows that he can agree with the risk-neutral investor's valuation of the option for the simple reason that the risks of the option are hedgeable. That is, there is risk-neutral valuation with consensus. Another way to say this is that replication is independent of preferences. Risk preferences only enter the picture for claims that are not replicable.

Why not assume risk-neutral preferences and value the option under those? We know that we will get the correct result. In fact, one could value the option under *any* set of risk preferences, and be assured of getting the right answer. There is only one by FTAP$_2$.

We just did this for the risk-averse investor and, while it is a bit of work, it *does* work. All roads lead to the same option price, which is that based on replication. It is just considerably easier to value the option from a risk-neutral investor's point of view. This could be called risk-neutral valuation by *convenience*.

Through the eyes of a risk-neutral investor, all securities, risky and riskless, earn the risk-free rate and require no risk premia whatsoever. Risk is a matter of indifference to risk-neutral investors. Thus both the option and the underlying stock would earn the riskless rate. This is good because we know from Statement 6 that both have to be riskless together. Riskiness and risklessness cannot co-exist in the hedge portfolio because, if they did, they would not be able to neutralize each other to create a riskless hedge portfolio.

So, not only is the riskless hedge portfolio riskless to the risk-neutral investor, but the option and the stock are riskless as well. Keep in mind that the statement '*the option is riskless*' doesn't mean that the real world option is riskless. Indeed it is not. The statement that 'the stock is riskless' is another statement that is clearly not true in the real world.

The meaning of each statement becomes apparent when the necessary qualifier is added, '*only from a risk-neutral investor's point of view is everything riskless*'. However, the point of replication is that a risk-averse investor could act *as if* he was risk neutral in valuing the option. This is because he actually *is* risk neutral with regard to risks that can be hedged in the hedge portfolio. (Note that he doesn't have to, as seen above. He could value the option directly.)

We will continue to use our randomness notation even though we know there is no risk. The risk-neutral investor uses the risk-neutral probabilities $p*$ in evaluating *all* investments and the corresponding expectations operator, $E*$.

Then,

$$E^r\left(R_C(\omega)\right) = \frac{E^r\left(C_1(\omega)\right)}{C_0} - 1 \qquad\qquad (E^r(R_S(\omega)))$$

$$E^r\left(R_S(\omega)\right) = \frac{E^r\left(S_1(\omega)\right)}{S_0} - 1 \qquad\qquad (E^r(R_C(\omega)))$$

From $(E^r(R_C(\omega)))$, it follows, using the risk-neutral investor's expectation operator E^r that

$$\frac{E^r\left(C_1(\omega)\right)}{C_0} - 1 = r'$$

Therefore,

$$\frac{E^r\left(C_1(\omega)\right)}{C_0} = 1 + r'$$

$$= r$$

Therefore, substituting the expected value, we obtain,

$$C_0 = \frac{E^r\left(C_1(\omega)\right)}{r}$$

$$= \frac{p^r C_u + \left(1 - p^r\right)C_d}{r}$$

Note that the risk-neutral investor doesn't use the physical, risk-adjusted expectation operator, E, to value risky securities. Rather, he uses the risk-neutral expectation E^r, as indicated because he is risk neutral.

We know what the risk-neutral probabilities are. They are the probabilities under which all securities are riskless. In particular, S_0 is riskless. We just showed that these are $p'=((r-d)/(u-d))$. Thus, once again $p'=p'$.

The formula above for C_0 is just the usual risk-neutral valuation expressed in the BOPM, $(N=1)$. We have reached our goal which was to value the option for a risk-neutral investor. It's convenient, but not necessary, to value the option using the preferences of a risk-neutral investor.

To summarize, it's possible to act as a risk-neutral investor when valuing a contingent claim—if the claim is replicable. In that case and only in that case are any extra risks associated with the contingent claim diversifiable (hedgeable). It's the same as for a portfolio investor who diversifies away the diversifiable risks of his portfolio, and then essentially becomes risk neutral with regard to those irrelevant risks. The hedge mechanism is slightly different, of course. But the *net* result is the same.

You wouldn't buy flight insurance to take a train from Boston to New York. But you probably would recommend doing so to your flying friends.

634 OPTIONS

■ KEY CONCEPTS

1. Introduction.
2. Preliminaries on $FTAP_1$ and $FTAP_2$ and Navigating the Terminology.
3. Pricing by Arbitrage and $FTAP_2$.
4. Risk-Neutral Valuation with Consensus and without Consensus.
5. Risk-Neutral Valuation without Consensus, Pricing Contingent Claims with Unhedgeable Risks.
6. Black–Scholes' Contribution.
7. Formal Risk-Neutral Valuation without Replication.
8. Constructing EMMs.
9. Interpreting Formal Risk-Neutral Probabilities.
10. MPRs and EMMs, Another Version of $FTAP_2$.
11. Complete Risk-Expected Return Analysis of the Riskless Hedge in the (BOPM, $N=1$).
12. Volatility of the Hedge Portfolio.
13. Direct Calculation of σ_S.
14. Direct Calculation of σ_C.
15. Expected Return of the Hedge Portfolio.
16. Analysis of the Relative Risks of the Hedge Portfolio's Return.
17. A Beginning Look at Risk-Neutrality in the Hedge Portfolio.
18. Role of the Risk Premia for a Risk-Averse Investor in the Hedge Portfolio.
19. Option Valuation.
20. Some Manipulations.
21. Option Valuation Done Directly by a Risk-Averse Investor.
22. Option Valuation for the Risk-Neutral Investor.

■ END OF CHAPTER EXERCISES FOR CHAPTER 17

1. Consider the following two statements and determine whether they are true or false, with reasons.

Statement 1

'The only consistent (with no-arbitrage and complete markets) way to price the option is *risk-neutrally*.'

Statement 2

'The only risk preferences consistent with the resulting (BOPM, $N=1$) pricing formula are risk-neutral preferences.'

RISK-NEUTRAL VALUATION · 635

2. True or false? With reasons.

Statement 3

'While risk neutrally is the only way to consistently price the option, the resulting option pricing formula (BOPM, $N=1$) is consistent with *all* risk preferences. The reason is that the derivation of (BOPM, $N=1$) makes no assumptions limiting investor preferences. Therefore, the RNVR (BOPM, $N=1$) holds for all investors, regardless of their risk preferences.'

3. What is it about replication that sets risk neutrality as a valuation method in motion?

Evaluate Statement 4 and Statement 5, which constitute the usual implied explanation.

Statement 4

'The ability to replicate a European call option means that we can set up a riskless hedge between a long position in it and a short position in Δ units of the underlying stock. The hedge thereby formed is fully riskless. The option is then priced based upon this riskless hedge.'

Statement 5

'Since the hedge is riskless, *therefore* so must the option also be riskless. In fact, everything in sight must be riskless, including the underlying stock. This is why risk–neutral probabilities appear in the (BOPM, $N=1$).'

4. True or false? With reasons.

Statement 6

'Replication implies that *if* the option is riskless then the underlying stock is riskless, and *if* the underlying stock is riskless then the option is riskless. That is, the stock and option must be riskless together, if either one is riskless.'

INDEX

adjusted intrinsic value (AIV) 381, 396–7, 406; for European call, definition of 375–6

adjusted time premium (ATP) 396, 397

All-or-None (AON) orders 214, 215

American options 328

annualized dividend yields 88

anticipatory selling 339

anticipatory buying 339–40

arbitrage: arbitrage definitions 100–2; arbitrage opportunities 75, 77–8, 100–1, 103, 167, 172, 188, 192, 208, 260, 292, 450, 474; pricing by 464; risk-free arbitrage 100, 373; risky arbitrage 100–1

arithmetic Brownian motion (ABM) model of prices: equivalent martingale measures (EMMs) 530–1; option pricing in continuous time 540–1

back stub period 294

backwardation, contango and 198–9

Bank of International Settlements (BIS) 246

basic American call (put) option pricing model 332–4

basic European option pricing model, interpretation of 397–8

basic (naked) strategies 347–63

basis risk 223, 237, 238; cross hedging and 244; spot price risk and 178–82

bid-asked spread, trading within 133–4

bid prices 127, 134, 136, 161, 336

binomial option pricing model (BOPM) 436–48, 467–8, 475–6, 485–506; arbitrage, pricing by 464; binomial process (any N) 439; binomial process (N=1) 448; combination function C(N,j) 443–4; concept checks: algorithm for determination of B, verification of 485; binomial completeness, rule of thumb on 449; binomial model, time modeling in

438; calculation of combination function C(N,j) 444; hedge ratio interpretation 482; hedging a European call option in BOPM (N=2) 477; solution to 505; option price behavior (N=2) 477; solution to 505–6; path 2 contribution analysis 496; path 3 contribution analysis solution to 506; path structures of binomial process, working with 442; solution to 472; price paths for N-period binomial model 442; solution to 471–2; pricing terminal options 446; underlying stock price uncertainty modeling 438–40; valuation of option (time=0) using RNVR 490; verification of numerical example (N=2) numbers 489; verification of option values (N=2) in comparison with replicating portfolio method 493; European call option valuation at expiration 446; exercises for learning development of 501–5; fundamental theorem of asset pricing (FTAP$_2$) 490; hedging a European call option (N=2) 477–85; implementation (N=2) 485–90; joint probability of given path 444; key concepts 501; logic of BOPM (N=1) and its drivers 463; multi-period model (N >1), path integral approach 493–500; numerical example (N=2) 487–90; option price behavior (N=2) 476; option valuation for 445–8; path structure of binomial process 440–2, 442–4; paths, thinking of BOPM in terms of 493–9; price paths, total number of 440–2; price paths ending at specific terminal price, total number of 442–4; pricing option at expiration 445–6; pricing option currently (time t=0) 446–8; proof that the BOPM (N=1) is complete, three parts of 517; proof of model for general N 499–500; replication, no-arbitrage and 464; risk-neutral valuation, exogenous variables and 615; risk-neutral valuation relationship: derivation as 467–8; interpretation of 468; as risk-neutral valuation relationship (RNVR) formula (N > 1) 490–3; as set of BOPMs (N=1) 491; stock price behavior (N=2) 475–6; stock price evolution: for binomial process (N=2) 440; for N-period binomial process, summary of 444–5; stock price tree (N=2) 488; stock price uncertainty 439; time in discrete time framework, modeling of 437–8; trinomial model (three stock outcomes) 464

Black-Scholes option pricing model: option pricing in continuous time 566–85, 588–9; from Bachelier 571–83; historical volatility estimator method 583–4; implied volatility estimator method 585; importance of 588–9; parsimony of 588; potential for 589; reduction of GBM to ABM with drift 567–70; risk-neutral transition density functions, generation of unknown from knowns 570–1; volatility estimation in Black-Scholes model 583–5; risk-neutral valuation, contribution to 598, 601; valuation of forward contracts in continuous time (assets with a dividend yield) 88

block trade eligibility 214, 228
block trade minimum 214, 228
Bond Equation 552, 554–5
boundaries, absorption of 541
Brownian motion paths, non-smoothness of 560; *see also* arithmetic Brownian motion (ABM); geometric Brownian motion (GBM)
Buffett, Warren 252
buyers and sellers, matching of 125, 126–7
buying back stock 339
buying forward 7–8

calendar spreads 199
'calling away' of stock 422

capital asset pricing model (CAPM) 447, 605
capital gains: effect on stock prices 98–9; capital gains process 98–9, 111
carrying charge hedging 188–93; convergence, implications for 189; equilibrium (no-arbitrage) in full carrying charge market 190–3; overall profits on 189
cash and carry transactions 5
cash commodity prices 35
cash flows: for annual rate swap 302; in non-intermediated swaps 282–4
cash settlement *vs.* commodity settlement 157; implications from problem of 157
CBOE (Chicago Board Options Exchange) 324–5, 334; asked price entries 335, 336; bid entries 335, 336; equity option specifications 343; exchange-traded option contracts 325; last sale entries 335, 336; Merck call options and price quotes 334–7; mini equity option specifications 344; net entries 335, 336; open interest entries 335, 336; volume entries 335, 336
certainty equivalent (CE): certainty equivalent cash flow 397; risk-neutral valuation and 603, 604
Clearing Houses: counterparty risk 140; futures exchange and 140; guarantor of trades 140; intermediation by 14–15; membership 140; operations and functions 139–53
clearing of trades 126; process of, offsetting futures trades and 141–4
close of market 145
clustering (persistence), volatility and 585
combination function C(N,j) 443–4
combinations of positions 50
combining charts to *see* profits from hedged positions 54–5
commentary on financial futures contracts price quotes 216–17
commitment prices 41
commitment to buy 67

commodities, ways to buy and sell 5

commodity forward contracts: paying fixed and receiving floating in 276; as single period swaps 275–6

Commodity Futures Trading Commission (CFTC) 123, 124, 125, 140, 215, 229

Commodity Pool Operators (CPOs) 123

Commodity Trading Advisors (CTAs) 123

complete markets 449

complete risk-expected return analysis of riskless hedge (BOPM, N=1) 607–18; direct calculation of $?_c$ 612–15; direct calculation of $?_s$ 611–12; expected return of hedge portfolio 616–18; hedge portfolio, percentage returns for 616–18; perfect positive correlation, statistics result for 609–11; volatility of hedge portfolio 608–11

concept checks: binomial option pricing model (BOPM): algorithm for determination of B, verification of 485; binomial completeness, rule of thumb on 449; binomial model, time modeling in 438; calculation of combination function C(N,j) 444; hedge ratio interpretation 482; hedging a European call option in BOPM (N=2) 477; option price behavior (N=2) 477; solution to 505–6; path 2 contribution analysis 496; path 3 contribution analysis: solution to 506; path structure of binomial process, working with 442; solution to 472; price paths for N-period binomial model 442; solution to 471–2; pricing terminal options 446; underlying stock price uncertainty modeling 438; valuation of option (time=0) using RNVR 490; verification of numerical example (N=2) numbers 489; verification of option values (N=2) in comparison with replicating portfolio method 493; equivalent martingale measures (EMMs): contingent claim pricing, working with 514; martingale condition, calculation of 525; option pricing, working with 514; two period investment strategy under EMM, proof for (t=0) 521; solution to

538; financial futures contracts: backwardation and contango, markets in 224; bank borrowing in spot Eurodollar (ED) market 250; 'buying' and 'selling' Eurodollar (ED) futures 256; calculation of adjusted hedge ratios 245; solution to 269; calculation of optimal (risk-minimizing) hedge ratio 240; cash settlement and effective price on S&P 500 spot index units 234; solution to 269; exchange rate risk, currency positions and 218; solution to 268; foreign exchange (FX) risk and jet fuel market 219; solution to 268–9; underlying spot 3-month Eurodollar (ED) time deposit 261; solution to 270; forward market contracting: controlling for counterparty risk 12–13; exploration of forward rates in long-term mortgage market 9–10; exploration of spot rates in long-term mortgage market 11; solution to 29; intermediation by Clearing House 15–16; solution to 29–30; spot markets, dealing with price quotes in 6–7; futures market contracting: price quotes in futures markets 19; hedging a European call option in BOPM (N=2): value confirmation 485; hedging with forward contracts: charting payoff to long forward position 39; solution to 62; charting payoff to short forward position 42; solution to 62; charting profits to fully unhedged position 45; solution to 63; charting profits to long spot position sold forward 49; payoff per share to long forward position 39; solution to 61; payoff per share to short forward position 42; profits to fully naked (unhedged) short forward position 50; solution to 64; profits to long spot position sold forward 48–9; profits to naked long spot position 45; wheat price volatility, dealing with 36; hedging with futures contracts: bond equivalent yield (BEY) of actual T-bill 167; solution to 207–8; construction of risk-free arb if r > 0 with no dividends 173; solution to 208; effect of narrowing basis in traditional short hedge 178; solution to 208–9; effect of widening basis in traditional short hedge 176; failure of traditional hedging 184; solution to 209; profits in traditional short hedge and the basis 172; verification that arb is arb without non-interest carrying charges and is riskless 192–3; solution to 209; verification of no current cost in arb 190; verification of riskless arb 191; interest-rate swaps: calculation of implied forward rates (IFRs) 310; solution to 319; graphical representation of swap's cash flows 283; solution to 318; paying fixed in an interest rate derivative (IRD) 279; solution to 317–18; receiving variable in an interest rate derivative (IRD) 280; strip of forward contracts, short's position in 278; solution to 317; swapping fixed for floating payments 276; solution to 317; market organization for futures contracts: Globex LOB trading, practicalities in 135–6; solution to 160–1; limit order execution 132; market order with protection, processing with CME Globex 128–9; solution to 160; market price best bids below sell market orders with and without protection, results? 130; solution to 160; trading crude oil futures 147; solution to 161; option pricing in continuous time: arbitrage opportunity construction 554; Bachelier option pricing formula, derivation of 550; Black-Scholes options pricing from Bachelier 582–3; risk-neutral transition density function (RNTDF) 544; risk-neutral transition density function (RNTDF) for ABM process to which GBM is reducible 569; solving risk-neutralized GBM-reduced process SDE 568; solution to 594; transition density function variance calculation 545; solution to 594; verification of $N(-z) = 1 - N(z)$ for any z in Bachelier calculation 548; option trading strategies: covered

call strategies, choice of 426; solution to 434; covered call write, upside potential of 422; solution to 433; cushioning calls 422; In-the-Money covered call writes 421; solution to 433; market for call options, dealing with profit potential and 354; solution to 367; payout present value on longing zero-coupon riskless bond 362; solution to 367; positions taken, definition of risk relative to 427; profit diagram for long call option, working on 418; rationalization of profits, short call positions 357; stock price fluctuations, dealing with 353; solution to 366–7; upside volatility in short positions, dealing with 359; options markets: individual equity options, product specifications for 326; solution to 342; mini equity options, product specifications for 326; solution to 342; MRK OV-E price quote 337; option positions 331; option sales 332; solution to 342; option's rights 331; payoff diagram construction 338; put option positions 332; rational option pricing (ROP): adjusted intrinsic value (AIV) for calls, calculation of 413; solution to 413; adjusted intrinsic value (AIV) for puts, calculation of 381; solution to 413; directional trades and relative trades, difference between 372; dominance principle and value of European call option 376; solution to 413; exercise price of options, working with 391; forward contracts, overpaying on 403; generalized forward contracts, current value on 404; rational option pricing (ROP) or model-based option pricing (MBOP) 407; short stock position, risk management of 399; solution to 413–14; working from strategies to current costs and back 393; solution to 413; spot, forward, and futures contracting: drawing conclusions from spot price charts 22–3; solution to 32; foreign currencies, forward prices on 25; foreign currencies, futures prices on 26; solution

INDEX **641**

to 32; past as guide to future price behavior 21; spot market contracting: exploration of spot rates in long-term mortgage market 11; solution to 29; present and future spot prices 21; solution to 32; price quotes in spot markets 6–7; solution to 29; valuation of forward contracts (assets with dividend yield): arbitrage opportunities, working with 101–2; solution 118–19; calculation of total stock price return minus dividend yield 99; solution 118; direct and indirect costs 89; solution 117–18; modeling continuous dividend yields for stocks 94; modeling continuous dividend yields for stocks: solution 118; modeling zero-coupon bond yields 92; pricing currency forwards 105; solution 119; pricing foreign exchange contracts 106; stock price, effect of dividend payments on 97; valuation of forward contracts (assets without dividend yield): annualized, continuously compounded 3%, worth after 2 months? 71; annualized, continuously compounded 6%, worth after 12 months? 71; solution to 85; annualized, continuously compounded 10%, worth after 3 months? 71; calculation of equilibrium forward prices 78; solution 86; pricing zero-coupon bond with face value equal to current forward price of underlying commodity 73; solution to 86; pricing zero-coupon bonds 72; solution to 86; settling a forward commitment 72; zero-coupon bond, pricing on basis of forward contract at compounded risk-free rate 73

consensus in risk-neutral valuation 598–9; with consensus 599; without consensus 599–601

consumption capital asset pricing model (CCAPM) 605

contango and backwardation 198–9

context in study of options markets 326–7

contingent claim pricing 514–17

continuation region 385

continuous compounding and discounting 69–71

continuous dividends from stocks, modeling yields from 93–4

continuous yields, modeling of 90–4

contract life, payments over 88

contract month listings 214, 215, 228

contract offerings 227–8

contract size 19, 214, 215, 227, 228

contract specifications 17, 18–19

contracts offered 257–8

convenience, risk-neutral valuation by 631–2

convenience yield 89

convergence of futures to cash price at expiration 189

convexity of option price 406

correlation effect 165–6

cost-of-carry 89; model of, spread and price of storage for 195

counterparty risk 11, 12–13, 140

covered call hedging strategy 419–27; economic interpretation of 426–7; protective put strategies, covered calls and 419; writes, types of 420–6

credit spreads 298–9

cumulative distribution function 544

currency futures 213–17; contract specifications 213–15; forward positions *vs.* futures positions 220; pricing *vs.* currency forward pricing 225; quote mechanism, future price quotes 216–17; risk management strategies using 217–24

currency spot and currency forwards 103–9

currency swaps, notional value of 274

current costs: of generating alternative payoffs 78; payoffs and 66; related strategies and, technique of going back and forth between 393

current price as predictor of future stock prices 531

daily price limits 228, 229

daily settlement process 144–51, 153; financial futures contracts and 216, 260

INDEX

dealer intermediated plain vanilla swaps 284–93; arbitraging swaps market 292–3; asked side in 286; bid side in 285; dealer's spread 286; example of 284–6; hedging strategy: implications of 291–2; outline of 288–90; plain vanilla swaps as hedge vehicles 286–92

dealer's problem, finding other side to swap 294–8; asked side in 295; bid side in 295; credit spreads in spot market (AA-type firms) 296; dealer swap schedule (AA-type firms) 295; selling a swap 296; swap cash flows 298; synthetic floating-rate financing (AA-type firms) 297; transformation from fixed-rate to floating rate borrowing 297–8

decision-making: option concept in 324; process of, protection of potential value in 36–7

default in forward market contracting 11–12

deferred spot transactions 78–9

delayed exercise premium 331, 337

delivery dates 19

demutualization 139–40

derivative prices: co-movements between spot prices and 26; underlying securities and 66

directional trades 371–2

discounted option prices 527–8

discounted stock price process 524–5, 527–8, 530

discrete-time martingale, definition of 521

diversifiable risk 225

diversification, maximum effect of 419–20

dividend-adjusted geometric mean (for S&P 500) 227

dividend payments, effect on stock prices 94–8

dividend payout process 97, 111; connection between capital gains process and 111–13

dollar equivalency 227, 234, 239–40

dollar returns, percentage rates of 366

domestic economy (DE) 103–4, 105

dominance principle 372, 373; implications of 374–88

double expectations (DE) 534–5

duration for interest-rate swaps 300

dynamic hedging 473–506; BOPM as risk-neutral valuation relationship (RNVR) formula (N > 1) 490–3; hedging a European call option (N=2) 477–85; implementation of binomial option pricing model for (N=2) 485–90; multi-period BOPM model (N=3) 494; multi-period BOPM model (N > 1), path integral approach 493–500; numerical example of binomial option pricing model (N=2) 487–90; option price behavior (N=2) 476; path structure for multi-period BOPM model (N=3) 497; stock price behavior (N=2) 475–6; stock price evolution (N-period binomial process), summary of 499; value contributions for multi-period BOPM model (N=3) 498; see also binomial option pricing model (BOPM)

economy-wide factors, risk and 225–6

effective date 293

effective payoff 220, 233

effective price, invoice price on delivery and 153–6

efficient market hypotheses (EMH) 517; features of 532; guide to modeling prices 529–33; option pricing in continuous time 558, 560, 561; semi-strong form of 531; strong form of 531, 532; weak form of 531

EFP eligibility 214

embedded leverage 79–80

endogenous variables 614–15

equilibrium forward prices 402; comparison with equilibrium futures prices 193–5; valuation of forward contracts (assets without dividend yield) 78

equilibrium (no-arbitrage) in full carrying charge market 190–3; classical short selling a commodity 192; Exchange Traded Funds (ETF) 191–2; formal arbitrage opportunity 192; non-interest carrying changes, arb without 192–3; setting up arb 190; unwinding arb 190–2

equity in customer's account 145, 148
equivalent annual rate (EAR) 70
equivalent martingale measures (EMMs)
507–38; arithmetic Brownian motion
(ABM) model of prices 530–1;
computation of EMMs 529; concept
checks: contingent claim pricing,
working with 514; martingale condition,
calculation of 525; option pricing,
working with 514; two period
investment strategy under EMM, proof
for (t=0) 521; solution to 538;
contingent claim pricing 514–17;
concept check: interpretation of pricing
a European call option 514; pricing a
European call option 514–15; pricing
any contingent claim 515–17; current
price as predictor of future stock prices
531; discounted option prices 527–8;
discounted stock price process 524–5,
527–8, 530; discrete-time martingale,
definition of 521; double expectations
(DE) 534–5; efficient market hypotheses
(EMH) basis for modeling 517; features
of 532; guide to modeling prices 529–33;
semi-strong form of 531; strong form of
531, 532; weak form of 531; equivalent
martingale representation of stock prices
524–6; examples of EMMs 517–21;
exercises for learning development of
537; fair game, notion of 518–19;
fundamental theorem of asset pricing
(FTAP_1) 509, 511–12, 517, 528–9,
530, 532, 533; 'independence,' degrees
of 536; investment strategy under, two-
period example 519–21; key concepts
537; martingale properties 533–6; non-
constructive existence theorem for 529;
numeraire, concept of 524; option
prices, equivalent martingale
representation of 526–8; option pricing
in continuous time 540; option price
representation 543; physical probability
measure, martingale hypothesis for 530;
pricing states 509; primitive Arrow-
Debreu (AD) securities, option pricing
and 508–14; concept check: pricing

$AD_u(\omega)$ and $AD_d(\omega)$ 514; exercise 1,
pricing B(0,1) 510; exercise 2, pricing
$AD_u(\omega)$ and $AD_d(\omega)$ 511–14; random
variables 536; random walk model of
prices 530–1; risk-averse investment 522;
risk-neutral investment 521–2, 523; risk-
neutral valuation 596–7; construction of
601–3; risk premiums in stock prices and
532–3; riskless bonds 509; Sharpe ratio
526; state-contingent financial securities
508; 'state prices' 509; stock prices and
martingales 521–6; sub (super)
martingale, definition of 524; summary
of EMM approach 528–9; tower
property (TP) 533–4; uncorrelated
martingale increments (UCMI) 531,
535–6; wealth change, fair game
expectation 520
Eurodollar (ED) deposit creation 253
Eurodollar (ED) futures 220–1, 245, 246,
249, 250, 252–64; 'buying' and 'selling'
futures 256; cash settlement, forced
convergence and 258–61; contract
specifications for 254–5; forced
conversion of 260; interest-rate swaps
278; strips of 280–1; lending (offering)
249–50; liabilities and 246; open
positions, calculation of profits and losses
on 262–4; placing 248–9; quote
mechanism 256–8; spot Eurodollar
market 245–54; taking 249; timing in
257
European call options: synthesis of: model-
based option pricing (MBOP) 453–64;
hedge ratio and dollar bond position,
definition of (step 2) 455; implications of
replication (step 4) 462–4;
parameterization (step 1) 454; replicating
portfolio, construction of 456–62;
replication, pricing by 463; valuation at
expiration 446; *see also* hedging a
European call option in BOPM (N=2)
European options 328, 333, 342, 357, 375,
398, 445, 553
European Put-Call Parity 416, 417, 418,
419, 426, 429; financial innovation with
401–5; implications of 394–400;

American option pricing model, analogue for European options 396–8; European call option 394–6; European option pricing model, interpretation of 397–8; European put option 398–9; synthesis of forward contracts from puts and calls 399–400

exchange membership 139–40

exchange rate risks and currency futures positions 217–20; Lufthansa example 217–20

exchange rates, New York closing snapshot (April 7, 2014) 104

exchange rule in financial futures contracts 214, 228

exchange-traded funds (ETFs) 191–2, 226

exercise of options 328

exercise price 328, 336

exercises for learning development: binomial option pricing model (BOPM) 501–5; equivalent martingale measures (EMMs) 537; financial futures contracts 266–8; hedging with forward contracts 56–61; hedging with futures contracts 205–7; interest-rate swaps 315–16; market organization for futures contracts 158–9; model-based option pricing (MBOP) 469–71; option pricing in continuous time 590–3; option trading strategies 364–6, 431–3; options markets 341–2; rational option pricing (ROP) 409–12; risk-neutral valuation 634–5; spot, forward, and futures contracting 27–9; valuation of forward contracts (assets with dividend yield) 116–17; valuation of forward contracts (assets without dividend yield) 83–5

exit mechanism in forward market contracting 15–16

exogenous variables in risk-neutral valuation 614–15

expiration date in options markets 336

expiration month code 336

fair game, notion of 518–19

fancy forward prices 19, 25

Fed Funds Rate (FFR) 251

Federal Funds (FF) 249–50, 251, 252

Federal Reserve system (US) 249

financial engineering techniques 337–8

financial futures contracts 211–70; all-or-None (AON) orders 215; Bank of International Settlements (BIS) 246; basis risk 223, 237, 238; cross hedging and 244; block trade eligibility 214, 228; block trade minimum 214, 228; commentary 216–17; concept checks: backwardation and contango, markets in? 224; bank borrowing in spot Eurodollar (ED) market 250; 'buying' and 'selling' Eurodollar (ED) futures 256; calculation of adjusted hedge ratios 245; solution to 269; calculation of optimal (risk-minimizing) hedge ratio 240; cash settlement and effective price on S&P 500 spot index units 234; solution to 269; exchange rate risk, currency positions and 218; solution to 268; foreign exchange (FX) risk and jet fuel market 219; solution to 268–9; underlying spot 3-month Eurodollar (ED) time deposit 261; solution to 270; contract month listings 214, 215, 228; contract offerings 227–8; contract size 214, 215, 227, 228; contracts offered 257–8; currency forward positions vs. currency futures positions 220; currency futures 213–17; contract specifications 213–15; pricing vs. currency forward pricing 225; quote mechanism, future price quotes 216–17; risk management strategies using 217–24; daily price limits 228, 229; daily settlements 216, 260; diversifiable risk 225; dividend-adjusted geometric mean (for S&P 500) 227; dollar equivalency 227, 234, 239–40; economy-wide factors, risk and 225–6; effective payoff 220, 233; EFP eligibility 214; Eurodollar (ED) deposit creation 253; Eurodollar (ED) futures 220–1, 245, 246, 249, 250, 252–64; cash settlement, forced convergence and 258–61; contract specifications 254–5; forced convergence, cash settlement and

258–61; open positions, calculation of profits and losses on 262–4; quote mechanism 256–8; exchange rate risks and currency futures positions 217–20; Lufthansa example 217–20; exchange rule 214, 228; exchange-traded funds (ETFs) 226; exercises for learning development 266–8; Fed Funds Rate (FFR) 251; Federal Funds (FF) 249–50, 251, 252; Federal Reserve system (US) 249; financial futures contracts, selection of 213; FLIBOR (Futures LIBOR) 256, 257, 262, 263, 264, 267–8; forced conversion of Eurodollar (ED) futures 260; foreign exchange (FX) reserves, currency composition of 247–8; forward price change, present value of 242; hedging 224–5; hedging a cross hedge 244; issues in 224–5; quantity uncertainty 224–5; holding period rate of return 237; idiosyncratic risk 225; index points 226; interest rate derivatives (IRDs) 254; International Monetary Fund (IMF) 246; JPY/USD futures 213–15; key concepts 265–6; last trade date/time view calendar 214, 228; lending (offering) Eurodollars (EDs) 249–50; liabilities, Eurodollars (EDs) and 246; LIBID (London Interbank Bid Rate) 249–50, 252; LIBOR (London Interbank Offered Rate) 249, 250–4, 262, 263–4; Federal Funds (FF) *vs.* 251–2; liquidity and 220, 222, 231, 237, 252, 258; lock-in characteristics 220, 233; market risk 225–6; minimum price increment 214, 215; naive hedge ratio (NHR) 234, 240–1, 243; open interest 258; placing Eurodollars (EDs) 248–9; position accountability 214, 215, 228, 229; raw price change, present value of 243; realized daily cash flows, creation of 243; risk management strategies using currency futures 217–24; risk management using stock index futures 231–45; cross-hedging 243–5; monetizing S&P 500 Spot Index 231–4; naive hedge ratio, adjustment for risk-

minimizing hedge ratio 239–41; non S&P 500 portfolios, adjustment of hedge for 243–5; pricing and hedging preliminaries 231; profits from traditional hedge 235–6; risk, return analysis of traditional hedge 236–8; risk minimizing hedge using forward *vs.* futures contracts 241–3; risk-minimizing hedging 238–9; rolling hedge strategy: efficient market hypothesis (EMH) 223; interpretations of profits from rolling hedge 221–3; Metallgesellschaft example 223; numerical example of 223–4; rule book chapter 228; settlement procedure 214, 228, 229, 258–9; S&P 500 Fact Sheet 226; S&P 500 Futures 228; spot commodities, S&P 500 futures contracts as 233–4; spot Eurodollar market 245–54; Eurodollar time deposits, creation of 252–4; spot 3-month Eurodollar time deposits 246–8; spot trading terminology 248–50; *Stigum's Money Market* (Stigum, M.) 252; stock index futures 225–30; commentary 230; S&P 500 futures quotes, quote mechanism for 230; S&P 500 Spot Index 225–7; S&P 500 Spot Index, effective payoff on monetization of 233; S&P 500 Spot Index, monetization of 231–4; S&P 500 Stock Index Futures Contract Specifications 227–9; tailing the hedge 241–2; taking Eurodollars (EDs) 249; ticker symbol 214, 215, 228, 229, 261; timing in Eurodollar (ED) futures 257; tick size 228, 229; trading hours 214, 228; traditional hedge, risk and return analysis on 236–8; basis risk 238; holding period rate 237; intermediate execution, basis risk and 237–8; liquidity advantage in execution 237; unallocated foreign exchange (FX) reserves 248

financial innovation using European Put-Call Parity 401–5; American Put-Call Parity (no dividends) 403–5; generalized forward contracts 401–3

financial institutions and use of swaps 299–301

finite-maturity financial instruments,
options as 20, 354
fixed leg in interest-rate swaps 293
fixed payments in interest-rate swaps 278–9
fixed-rate mortgages 7
FLIBOR (Futures LIBOR): financial
futures contracts 256, 257, 262, 263,
264, 267–8; interest-rate swaps 278, 287
floating leg in interest-rate swaps 293
floating payments in interest-rate swaps
279–80
floating-rate bond implicit in swap 306
floating-rate payments as expected cash
flows 306
floor-brokers 140
floor-traders 140
foreign currencies: forward prices on 24–5;
futures prices on 25–6; *see also* currency
futures
foreign economy (FE) 103–4
foreign exchange (FX) forward contracts:
example of pricing 107–9; pricing using
no-arbitrage 106–7
foreign exchange (FX) markets, price
quotes in 103–5
foreign exchange (FX) rates (New York,
March 11, 2014) 30–1
foreign exchange (FX) reserves, currency
composition of 247–8
foreign exchange (FX) risk 3–5
forward contracts: differences between
futures contracts and 122; on dividend-
paying stocks, pricing with no-arbitrage
100–3; hedging with 37, 43–5; on stocks
with dividend yield, pricing with net
interest model 99–100; swaps as strips of
274–8; valuation of (assets without
dividend yield): default on 76;
interpretation via synthetic contracts
78–82; leverage and 80–2; no up-front
payments on 75; payment on maturity,
expectation of 81; price *vs.* value for 73;
valuing at expiration 74–5; valuing at
initiation 75–8
forward market contracting: buying forward
7–8; Clearing House intermediation
14–15; concept checks: controlling for

counterparty risk 12–13; exploration of
forward rates in long-term mortgage
market 9–10; exploration of spot rates in
long-term mortgage market 11; solution
29; intermediation by Clearing House
15–16; solution 29–30; spot markets,
dealing with price quotes in 6–7;
counterparty risk 11; default 11–12; exit
mechanism 15–16; features of 8; fixed-
rate mortgages 7; forward agreement,
terms of 8; forward contracts, differences
between futures contracts and 122;
forward market 8; forward prices 9,
24–5; forward transactions 8; historical
data, checking on 9–10; interest-rate risk
management 9–10; intermediation
13–14, 14–15; liquidity, enablement of
16; locked-in prices 12; market levels 11;
market organization, importance of 13,
14; obligations, transfer of 16; offsetting
trades 15–16; overnight averages 11;
price quotes in forward markets 9–11;
problems with forward markets 11–13;
'reversing' of trades 15–16; short
positions 7; SouthWest Airlines, case
example 12–13; spot, forward, and
futures contracting 7–13; standardization
14; transfer of obligations 16; *see also*
hedging with forward contracts;
valuation of forward contracts
forward prices 9, 24–5; change in, present
value of 242; no-arbitrage, forward
pricing with 102–3
front stub period 294
fundamental theorem of asset pricing
number one (FTAP$_1$): equivalent
martingale measures (EMMs) 509,
511–12, 517, 528–9, 530, 532, 533;
model-based option pricing (MBOP)
450, 451, 452; option pricing in
continuous time 540; risk-neutral
valuation 596–7, 601–2, 605, 606, 624,
631
fundamental theorem of asset pricing
number two (FTAP$_2$): binomial option
pricing model (BOPM) 490; model-
based option pricing (MBOP) 452;

option pricing in continuous time 540;
risk-neutral valuation 596–7, 601–2, 605,
606, 624, 631; risk-neutral valuation and
another version of 606
future value (FV) 69–70, 382, 386, 390,
395
Futures Commission Merchant (FCM) 122,
123, 124, 125, 137, 140
futures contracts: futures market contracting
17; market organization for: 'buying' and
'selling' of 126–7; daily value of 146;
differences between forward contracts
and 122; futures price and 127; market
participants 122–5
futures market contracting 17–26; concept
check, price quotes in futures markets
19; contract size 19; contract
specifications 17, 18–19; delivery dates
19; fancy forward prices 19, 25; futures
contract 17; futures market 17; futures
prices 17, 25–6; futures transaction 17;
key definition, futures contract 17;
mapping out spot, forward, and futures
prices 20–6; 'Open Outcry Futures' 19;
price quotes in futures markets 17–19;
seller's options 17; as solution to forward
market problems 13–16; volatility
(uncertainty) 22; *see also* hedging with
futures contracts; market organization for
futures contracts
futures trading: hedging with forward
contracts 35; market organization for
futures contracts: cash flow implications
of 144; daily settlement, perspectives on
144; delivery obligations 142; offsetting
trades 142–4; phases of 125–6

gap management problem, solutions for
300–1
Gaussian distributions 543, 546, 548, 557,
565, 577
general equilibrium (GE) 453; models of,
risk-neutral valuation and 615
generalized forward price 402
geometric Brownian motion (GBM)
553–61; continuous version 559–61;
discrete version 553–9

Girsanov's theorem 605
Globex and Globex LOB 134–6
Globex trades, rule for recording of 135
Gold pricing on London Bullion Market
20–3
guaranteeing futures obligations 139–41

hedge ratio: dollar bond position and 478;
model-based option pricing (MBOP)
and 455
hedging: financial futures contracts 224–5;
hedging a cross hedge 244; issues in
224–5; quantity uncertainty 224–5;
hedged position profits, graphical
method for finding 55; hedgers 37;
hedging definitions 168; minimum
variance hedging 185–8; estimation of
risk minimization hedge ratio 187–8;
OLS regression 187–8; risk minimization
hedge ratio, derivation of 186–7;
motivation for hedging with forward
contracts 33–7; objective of 167–8; as
portfolio theory 165–8; reverse hedge
618, 620, 621; riskless hedge 607, 616,
620, 628, 632; rolling hedge strategy:
efficient market hypothesis (EMH) 223;
interpretations of profits from rolling
hedge 221–3; Metallgesellschaft example
223; numerical example of 223–4; short
hedge 168; synthesis of negative
correlation, hedging as 165–7
hedging a European call option in BOPM
(N=2) 477–85; complete hedging
program (for BOPM, N=2) 484–5;
concept check, value confirmation 485;
hedge ratio and dollar bond position,
definition of (step 2) 478;
parameterization (step 1) 477–8;
replicating portfolio, construction of
(step 3) 478–84; concept check:
interpretation of hedge ratio 482; down
state, replication in 481; hedge ratio,
interpretation of 482–3; replication over
period 2 (under scenario 1) 479–82;
replication under scenario 2 (over period
2) 484; scenarios 478–9; solving
equations for ? and B 481; solving for

INDEX

dollar position in bonds under scenario 1 (over period 2) 483; up state, replication in 480

hedging with forward contracts 33–64; cash commodity prices 35; combinations of positions 50; combining charts to *see* profits from hedged positions 54–5; commitment prices 41; concept checks: charting payoff to long forward position 39; solution to 62; charting payoff to short forward position 42; solution to 62; charting profits to fully unhedged position 45; solution to 63; charting profits to long spot position sold forward 49; payoff per share to long forward position 39; solution to 61; payoff per share to short forward position 42; profits to fully naked (unhedged) short forward position 50; solution to 64; profits to long spot position sold forward 48–9; profits to naked long spot position 45; wheat price volatility, dealing with 36; decision-making process, protection of potential value 36–7; exercises for learning development of 56–61; forward contracts 37; hedging with 43–5; fully hedged current long spot position, profits to 47–9; fully hedged position, adding profit tables to determine profits from 50–4; futures trading 35; hedged position profits, graphical method for finding 55; hedgers 37; individual stock forwards: long position 38–9; short position 41–3; key concepts 56; long forward position, payoff to 37–9; motivation for 33–7; naked (unhedged) forward contracts 41; naked (unhedged) long spot position, profits to 45–6; payoff position 37; payoff to long forward position in IBM 40; payoff to short forward position in IBM 43; profit from fully hedged spot position in wheat 53; profits from fully naked (unhedged) spot position in wheat 51; profits from short forward position in wheat 52; profits to long spot position sold forward 49; profits to naked (unhedged) long spot position 46;

risk aversion 37; scenarios: adding profit tables to determine profits from fully hedged position 52–4; hedging with forward contracts 44–5; long position contracts 38–9; short position contracts 42; selling a forward contract 40–1, 47–8; settlement price 35; short forward position, payoff to 39–43; spot prices 34–5; uncertainty (volatility), unhedged positions and 45; wheat price uncertainties, dealing with 33–7

hedging with futures contracts 163–209; backwardation, contango and 198–9; basis risk *vs.* spot price risk 178–82; calendar spreads 199; carrying charge hedging 188–93; convergence, implications for 189; equilibrium (no-arbitrage) in full carrying charge market 190–3; overall profits on 189; concept checks: bond equivalent yield (BEY) of actual T-bill 167; solution to 207–8; construction of risk-free arb if r > 0 with no dividends 173; solution to 208; effect of narrowing basis in traditional short hedge 178; solution to 208–9; effect of widening basis in traditional short hedge 176; failure of traditional hedging 184; solution to 209; profits in traditional short hedge and the basis 172; verification arb is arb without non-interest carrying charges and is riskless 192–3; solution to 209; verification of no current cost in arb 190; verification of riskless arb 191; contango and backwardation 198–9; convergence of futures to cash price at expiration 189; correlation effect 165–6; cost-of-carry model, spread and price of storage for 195; equilibrium forward pricing, comparison with equilibrium futures pricing 193–5; equilibrium (no-arbitrage) in full carrying charge market 190–3; classical short selling a commodity 192; Exchange Traded Funds (ETF) 191–2; formal arbitrage opportunity 192; non-interest carrying changes, arb without 192–3; setting up arb 190; unwinding arb 190–2; exercises for learning development of 205–7; hedging as portfolio theory 165–8; hedging definitions 168; informational effects 181–2; inter-commodity spreads 199; inter-market spreads 199; interest-adjusted marginal carrying costs 196; key concepts 204; long *vs.* short positions 164; marginal carrying charges 188; minimum variance hedging 185–8; estimation of risk minimization hedge ratio 187–8; OLS regression 187–8; risk minimization hedge ratio, derivation of 186–7; non-traditional (λ-for-one) hedging theory 182–8; objective of hedging 167–8; OLS regression 181–2, 187–8; one-for-one theory with basis risk 174–8; non-constant basis example with basis narrowing 177; non-constant basis example with basis widening 175–6; one-for-one theory with no basis risk 168–71; basis, concept of 170–1; consistency with no-arbitrage 172–4; constant basis example 168–71; with dividends, r > 0 and r=p, case of 173–4; no dividends and r=0, case of 172–3; speculation on the basis 171; perfectly negatively correlated asset returns 166; portfolio theory, hedging as 165–8; portfolio variance, calculation of 179–81; profits in one-for-one short hedge and basis 171–2; risk reduction with (λ-for-one) hedging 183–5; risk reduction with traditional hedging 179–82; informational effect 181–2; OLS regression 181–2; portfolio variance calculation 179–81; selling hedge 168; short hedge 168; spread basis, definition of 200–1; spreads as speculative investment 199–203; stock index futures contracts, introduction of 167; storage and price (cost) of 195–7; subsequent inventory sale price, locking in of 195; synthesis of negative correlation, hedging as 165–7; synthetic risk, diversifying away of 167; synthetic treasury bill *vs.* actual bill 165; systematic, market risk

after diversification, protection against 168; transportation across time, storage as 195; treasury bill synthesis 166–7
Heston volatility model 587–8
historical data, checking on 9–10
holding period rate of return 237

idiosyncratic risk 225
immediate exercise value 330
implicit bonds 303, 304; implicit floating-rate bond, valuation of 308
implicit short positions 340
In-the-Money calls 337
In-the-Money covered call writes 421–4
incomplete markets 450–1
independent securities and risks 600
index points 226
individual stock forwards: long position 38–9; short position 41–3
infinitesimal intervals 93
informational effects 181–2
instantaneous yields 90–2, 93–4
insurance features, options and 327
inter-commodity spreads 199
inter-market spreads 199
interest-adjusted marginal carrying costs 196
interest rate derivatives (IRDs): financial futures contracts 254; interest-rate swaps 278–80; paying fixed in 278–9; receiving variable in 279–80
interest-rate risk management 9–10
interest-rate swaps 273–319; back stub period 294; cash flows for annual rate swap 302; cash flows in non-intermediated swaps 282–4; commodity forward contracts: paying fixed and receiving floating in 276; as single period swaps 275–6; concept checks: calculation of implied forward rates (IFRs) 310; solution to 319; graphical representation of swap's cash flows 283; solution to 318; paying fixed in an interest rate derivative (IRD) 279; solution to 317–18; receiving variable in an interest rate derivative (IRD) 280; strip of forward contracts, short's position in

278; solution to 317; swapping fixed for floating payments 276; solution to 317; credit spreads 298–9; currency swaps, notional value of 274; dealer intermediated plain vanilla swaps 284–93; arbitraging swaps market 292–3; asked side in 286; bid side in 285; dealer's spread 286; example of 284–6; hedging strategy: implications of 291–2; outline of 288–90; plain vanilla swaps as hedge vehicles 286–92; dealer's problem, finding other side to swap 294–8; asked side in 295; bid side in 295; credit spreads in spot market (AA-type firms) 296; dealer swap schedule (AA-type firms) 295; selling a swap 296; swap cash flows 298; synthetic floating-rate financing (AA-type firms) 297; transformation from fixed-rate to floating rate borrowing 297–8; duration 300; effective date 293; Eurodollar (ED) futures 278; strips of 280–1; exercises for learning development of 315–16; financial institutions and use of swaps 299–301; fixed leg 293; fixed payments 278–9; FLIBOR (Futures LIBOR) 278, 287; floating leg 293; floating payments 279–80; floating-rate bond implicit in swap 306; floating-rate payments as expected cash flows 306; forward contracts, swaps as strips of 274–8; front stub period 294; gap management problem, solutions for 300–1; generic example, five-year swap 294; implicit bonds 303, 304; implicit floating-rate bond, valuation of 308; interest rate derivatives (IRDs) 278–80; paying fixed in 278–9; receiving variable in 279–80; key concepts 315; LIBOR (London Interbank Offered Rate) 274–5, 278, 282, 293, 297, 303, 304, 306, 307, 309–10, 311–13; yield curve (spot rates) 304; matching principle 300; mortgage bonds 279; non-dealer intermediated plain vanilla swaps 281–4; notional value of 274; over-the-counter (OTC) bilateral agreements 278; par swap rate 294, 301;

paying fixed 293; in interest rate derivatives (IRDs) 278–9; and receiving floating in commodity forward contracts 276; plain vanilla interest-rate swaps 274; dealer intermediated swaps 284–93; non-dealer intermediated swaps 281–4; pricing a swap 294; quality spreads 299; receiving floating 293; receiving variable in interest rate derivatives (IRDs) 279–80; reset date 293; resetting floating rate 293; selling short 293; single period swaps, commodity forward contracts as 275–6; strip cash flows, generation of 277; strips of forward contracts 277–8; swap cash flows: decomposition into implicit bonds 303; graphical representation of 318; swap spread 294; swapping fixed for floating payments 276; swaps as strips of forward contracts 274–8; swaps pricing 301–14; example of 301–3; fixed-rate bond, valuation of 303–5; floating-rate bond, valuation of 305–8; implied forward rates (IFRs) 309–11; par swap rate 301; interpretations of 311–14; swap at initiation, valuation of 308–9; synthetic fixed-rate bond 291–2; synthetic fixed-rate financing 290; tenor of swap 293; terminology for 278–81, 293–4; trade date 293; valuation of floating-rate bonds prior to maturity 306–7; zero sum game, swaps as? 298–9

intermediate settlement prices 154
intermediation 13–14, 14–15
International Monetary Fund (IMF) 246
intrinsic value 326, 330, 333, 337
Introducing Broker (IB) 123
investor's accounts, tracking equity in 151–3
invoice price on delivery 153–6
Itô's Lemma 562–6

joint probability of given path 444
JPY/USD futures 213–15

key concepts: binomial option pricing model (BOPM) 501; equivalent martingale measures (EMMs) 537; financial futures contracts 265–6; hedging with forward contracts 56; hedging with futures contracts 204; interest-rate swaps 315; market organization for futures contracts 158; model-based option pricing (MBOP) 466; option pricing in continuous time 590; option trading strategies 364, 431; options markets 341; rational option pricing (ROP) 408–9; risk-neutral valuation 634; spot, forward, and futures contracting 27; valuation of forward contracts (assets with dividend yield) 116; valuation of forward contracts (assets without dividend yield) 83

last trade date/time view calendar 214, 228

law of one price (LOP): model-based option pricing (MBOP) 452; risk-neutral valuation 597; valuation of forward contracts (assets without dividend yield) 77

LBAC (lower bound for American call option on underlying, no dividends) 374–5

LBACD (lower bound for American call option on underlying, continuous dividends) 383–5; call on underlier with continuous, proportional dividends over life of option 384–5; call on underlier with no dividends over life of option 384

LBAP (lower bound for American put option on underlying, no dividends) 378–80; intrinsic value lower bound for American put, example of 379–80

LBAPD (lower bound for American put option on underlying, continuous dividends) 387–8

LBEC (lower bound for European call option on underlying, no dividends) 375–8; implications of 377–8

LBECD (lower bound for European call option on underlying, continuous dividends) 382–3

LBEP (lower bound for European put option on underlying, no dividends) 380–1; adjusted intrinsic value (AIV) for European put, definition of 380–1

LBEPD (lower bound for European put option on underlying, continuous dividends) 386–7

learning about options, framework for 326–7

leverage, options and 327

LIBID (London Interbank Bid Rate) 249–50, 252

LIBOR (London Interbank Offered Rate) 249, 250–4, 262, 263–4; Federal Funds (FF) vs. 251–2; interest-rate swaps 274–5, 278, 282, 293, 297, 303, 304, 306, 307, 309–10, 311–13; yield curve (spot rates) 304

Limit Bid (LBid) 129

Limit Offer (LOff) 129

limit order book (LOB) 130–1; depth in 131–4; Globex LOB trading, practicalities in 135–6

limit orders 129–30

liquidity: enablement of 16; financial futures contracts and 220, 222, 231, 237, 252, 258; liquidity options 333

lock-in characteristics 220, 233

locked-in prices 12

Log Bond equation: option pricing in continuous time 552–3; valuation of forward contracts (assets with dividend yield) 96

long a European call option on the underlying 351–5; economic characteristics 353

long a European put option on the underlying 348, 357–9; economic characteristics 358

long a zero-coupon riskless bond and hold to maturity 348, 360–2; economic characteristic 361

long and short positions, identification of 339–40

long call positions, difference between long underlying positions and 354

long forward positions, payoff to 37–9

652 INDEX

long positions in options markets 339–40
long spot and long forward positions, difference between payoffs to 76–7
long the underlying 347–9; economic characteristics 349
long *vs.* short positions: hedging with futures contracts 164; options markets 339–40
Lufthansa 217–20

mapping out prices, spot, forward, and futures contracting 20–6
margin calls 145, 147–8, 152
marginal carrying charges 188
marginal rate of substitution (MRS) 604, 605
margins (performance bonds) 144–5, 148; initial margin 145; maintenance margin 145
market completeness 598
market levels 11
market orders 127–9
market organization for futures contracts 121–61; bid-asked spread, trading within 133–4; bid prices 127; buyers and sellers, matching of 125, 126–7; cash settlement *vs.* commodity settlement 157; implications from problem of 157; Clearing Houses: counterparty risk 140; futures exchange and 140; guarantor of trades 140; membership 140; operations and functions 139–53; clearing of trades 126; clearing process, offsetting futures trades and 141–4; close of market 145; Commodity Futures Trading Commission (CFTC) 123, 124, 125, 140, 215, 229; Commodity Pool Operators (CPOs) 123; Commodity Trading Advisors (CTAs) 123; concept checks: Globex LOB trading, practicalities in 135–6; solution to 160–1; limit order execution 132; market order with protection, processing with CME Globex 128–9; solution to 160; market price best bids below sell market orders with and without protection, results? 130; solution to 160; trading crude oil

futures 147; solution to 161; convergence, forcing of 157; daily settlement process 144–51, 153; demutualization 139–40; depth in limit order book (LOB) 131–4; effective price and invoice price on delivery 153–6; equity in customer's account 145, 148; exchange membership 139–40; exercises for learning development of 158–9; floor-brokers 140; floor-traders 140; Futures Commission Merchant (FCM) 122, 123, 124, 125, 137, 140; futures contracts: 'buying' and 'selling' of 126–7; daily value of 146; differences between forward contracts and 122; futures price and 127; market participants 122–5; futures trading: cash flow implications of 144; daily settlement, perspectives on 144; delivery obligations 142; offsetting trades 142–4; phases of 125–6; Globex and Globex LOB 134–6; Globex trades, rule for recording of 135; guaranteeing futures obligations 139–41; intermediate settlement prices 154; Introducing Broker (IB) 123; investor's accounts, tracking equity in 151–3; invoice price on delivery 153–6; key concepts 158; Limit Bid (LBid) 129; Limit Offer (LOff) 129; limit order book (LOB) 130–1; depth in 131–4; limit orders 129–30; margin calls 145, 147–8, 152; margins (performance bonds) 144–5, 148; initial margin 145; maintenance margin 145; market orders 127–9; market with protection market orders (CME Group) 128; marking to market 144–51; daily unrealized gains and losses, adjustments for 146; matching trades 139–41; National Futures Association (NFA) 123; offset *vs.* delivery 155–6; long offsets futures position just prior to expiration 156; long trader takes delivery of underlying commodity 155–6; offsetting futures trades 141–4; open access trading 140; open contract 145; open interest 145; open outcry pit trades: CME Clearing House requirements for 137–9;

trades entry into clearing system 138–9; trading cards, submission of 139; order execution 125–6; futures contract definition and 126; order submission 125–6; orders, types of 127–34; overall profits (and losses) 144, 150, 151, 153, 156, 157; participants in futures market 122–5; performance bonds (margins) 144–5, 148; pit trading, order flow process and 136–9; protection, market orders with 127–9; realization of daily value 149; recontracting futures positions 149, 151; Registered Commodity Representatives (RCRs) 122–3; segregated consumer funds 123–5; settlement prices 145–6, 151; settlement variation 146; short positions, assumption of 147–8; tracking equity in investor's account 151–3; trading futures contracts, questions on organizational structures for 141

market price of risk (MPR): equivalent martingale measures (EMMs) and 605–6; risk-neutral valuation and 624

market risk 225–6

market with protection market orders (CME Group) 128

marking to market 144–51; daily unrealized gains and losses, adjustments for 146

martingale properties 533–6

matching principle 300

matching trades 139–41

mathematical modeling 596–7

maturity dates 328

Merck stock price fluctuations 346–7

minimum price increment 214, 215

minimum variance hedging 185–8; estimation of risk minimization hedge ratio 187–8; OLS regression 187–8; risk minimization hedge ratio, derivation of 186–7

model-based option pricing (MBOP) 398, 406, 455; alternative option pricing techniques 464–5; complete markets 449; European call option, synthesis of 453–64; hedge ratio and dollar bond position, definition of (step 2) 455;

implications of replication (step 4) 462–4; parameterization (step 1) 454; replicating portfolio, construction of (step 3) 456–62; down-state, replication in 457; hedge ratio, magnitude of 461–2; sign of B 459–60; solving equations for ? and B 458–9; up-state, replication in 457; replication, pricing by 463; exercises for learning development of 469–71; fundamental theorem of asset pricing one (FTAP$_1$) 450, 451, 452; fundamental theorem of asset pricing two (FTAP$_2$) 452; general equilibrium (GE) 453; hedge ratio 455; incomplete markets 450–1; key concepts 466; law of one price (LOP) 452; model-independent $vs.$ MBOP 370–1; no-arbitrage, principle of 448; objective of 437; option price dynamics 457; partial equilibrium (PE) 453; portfolio price dynamics, replication of 457; pricing options, tools for 448–53; relationships between tools 450–3; rational option pricing (ROP) 371, 398; replication: dynamic and static 450; hedging and 453; replicability and 449; rule of thumb 449; see $also$ binomial option pricing model (BOPM)

model-independent $vs.$ model-based option pricing 370–1

model risk 372

moneyness 329

mortgage bonds 279

multi-grade spot commodities, determination of standards for pricing 23

multi-period BOPM model see dynamic hedging

naive hedge ratio (NHR) 234, 240–1, 243

naked (unhedged) forward contracts 41

naked (unhedged) long spot and forward positions, comparison of payoffs from 66–9

naked (unhedged) long spot position, profits to 45–6

naked (unhedged) positions 327

National Futures Association (NFA) 123

natural and synthetic strategies 416

natural stock, economic equivalence with synthetic stock 418

net interest model 99–100

no-arbitrage: assumption of, risk–neutral valuation and 596–7, 598, 602, 604, 605, 606, 608; no-arbitrage in equilibrium (NAIE) 372, 405–6; principle of: model-based option pricing (MBOP) and 448; valuation of forward contracts (assets without dividend yield) 77

non-constant volatility models 585–8; changing volatility modeling 586–7, 587–8; deterministic volatility model 586–7; economic reasons for inconsistency of volatility 586; empirical features of volatility 585; leverage effect 586; stochastic volatility (SVOL) models 586–7

non-dealer intermediated plain vanilla swaps 281–4

non-hedgeable risks 599–601

non-replicability: contingent claims, extra risks and 600; risk-neutral valuation and 599–601, 603, 604, 605, 606

non-simultaneous price quote problem 334–6

non-stochastic differential equations 90–4

non-traditional (λ-for-one) hedging theory 182–8

notional value of interest-rate swaps 274

numeraire 554; concept of 524; definition and pricing a standard 551–3

obligations, transfer of 16

offset *vs.* delivery 155–6; long offsets futures position just prior to expiration 156; long trader takes delivery of underlying commodity 155–6

offsetting forward trades 15–16

offsetting futures trades 141–4

OLS regression 181–2, 187–8

one-for-one theory with basis risk 174–8; non-constant basis example with basis narrowing 177; non-constant basis example with basis widening 175–6

one-for-one theory with no basis risk 168–71; basis, concept of 170–1; consistency with no-arbitrage 172–4; constant basis example 168–71; with dividends, r > 0 and r=p, case of 173–4; no dividends and r=0, case of 172–3; speculation on the basis 171

open access trading 140

open contract 145

open interest: financial futures contracts 258; market organization for futures contracts 145

'Open Outcry Futures' 19

open outcry pit trades: CME Clearing House requirements for 137–9; trades entry into clearing system 138–9; trading cards, submission of 139

option buyers 328

option pricing in continuous time: absorbing boundaries 541; arithmetic Brownian motion (ABM) model of prices 540–1; Black-Scholes option pricing 566–85, 588–9; from Bachelier 571–83; historical volatility estimator method 583–4; implied volatility estimator method 585; importance of 588–9; parsimony of model 588; potential for 589; reduction of GBM to ABM with drift 567–70; risk-neutral transition density functions, generation of unknown from knowns 570–1; volatility estimation in Black-Scholes model 583–5; Bond Equation 552, 554–5; Brownian motion paths, non-smoothness of 560; clustering (persistence), volatility and 585; concept checks: arbitrage opportunity construction 554; Bachelier option pricing formula, derivation of 550; Black-Scholes options pricing from Bachelier 582–3; risk-neutral transition density function (RNTDF) 544; risk-neutral transition density function (RNTDF) for ABM process to which GBM is reducible 569; solving risk-neutralized GBM-reduced process SDE 568; solution to 594; tradition density function variance calculation 545; solution to 594; verification of N(-z)=1-N(z) for any z in Bachelier calculation 548; cumulative distribution function 544; efficient market hypothesis (EMH) 558, 560, 561; equation μ 554; equation μ discrete 555; equation μ discrete, risk-adjusted 555, 556–7, 558–9; equivalent martingale measures (EMMs) 540; option price representation 543; exercises for learning development of 590–3; fundamental theorems of asset pricing (FTAP$_1$ and FTAP$_2$) 540; Gaussian distributions 543, 546, 548, 557, 565, 577; geometric Brownian motion (GBM) 553–61; continuous version 559–61; discrete version 553–9; Heston volatility model 587–8; Itô's Lemma 562–6; key concepts 590; Log Bond Equation 552–3; non-constant volatility models 585–8; changing volatility modeling 586–7, 587–8; deterministic volatility model 586–7; economic reasons for inconsistency of volatility 586; empirical features of volatility 585; leverage effect 586; stochastic volatility (SVOL) models 586–7; numeraire 554; definition and pricing a standard 551–3; pricing European options under shifted arithmetic Brownian motion (ABM) with no drift 542–51; Bachelier option pricing formula, derivation of 547–51; fundamental theorems of asset pricing (FTAP) 542–3; transition density functions 543–7; probability density function 544; rate of return of risky asset over small time interval, components of 555–6; replicability 588; risk-neutral transition density function (RNTDF) 543–4, 547, 569, 570, 571; for ABM process to which GBM is reducible 569, 570; of GBM 571; risk-neutralized GBM-reduced process SDE 568; risk-neutralized GBM SDE 567, 570; risk premia 554, 558, 561, 567, 588; scaled-by-? increment of ABM process 555; shifted arithmetic Brownian motion

(ABM) model of prices 541–2; reduced process 570; stochastic differential equations (SDEs) 553, 559, 562–3, 564, 566, 567–8, 570, 571, 583; stochastic integral equations (SIEs) 559, 560, 561, 564, 565–6, 567; stochastic processes 540–1, 543, 562, 587, 588; transition density function for shifted arithmetic Brownian motion 545–6; Wiener measure (and process) 540–1

option sellers 328

option trading strategies 345–67, 415–34; basic (naked) strategies 347–63; 'calling away' of stock 422; concept checks: covered call strategies, choice of 426; solution to 434; covered call write, upside potential of 422; solution to 433; cushioning calls 422; In-the-Money covered call writes 421; solution to 433; market for call options, dealing with profit potential and 354; solution to 367; payout present value on longing zero-coupon riskless bond 362; solution to 367; positions taken, definition of risk relative to 427; profit diagram for long call option, working on 418; rationalization of profits, short call positions 357; stock price fluctuations, dealing with 353; solution to 366–7; upside volatility in short positions, dealing with 359; covered call hedging strategy 419–27; economic interpretation of 426–7; covered call writes, types of 420–6; covered calls and protective put strategies 419; diversification, maximum effect of 419–20; Dollar Returns, percentage rates of 366; economic characteristics 358; European Put-Call Parity 416, 417, 418, 419, 426, 429; exercises for learning development of 364–6, 431–3; finite-maturity financial instruments, options as 354; generation of synthetic option strategies from European Put-Call Parity 416–18; In-the-Money covered call writes 421–4; key concepts 364, 431; long a European call option on the underlying 351–5;

economic characteristics 353; long a European put option on the underlying 348, 357–9; economic characteristics 358; long a zero-coupon riskless bond and hold to maturity 348, 360–2; economic characteristic 361; long call positions, difference between long underlying positions and 354; long the underlying 347–9; economic characteristics 349; Merck stock price fluctuations 346–7; natural and synthetic strategies 416; natural stock, economic equivalence with synthetic stock 418; Out-of-the-Money covered call writes 424–6; potential price paths 346–7; profit diagrams 346–7; protective put hedging strategy 427–30; economic interpretation of 429–30; insurance, puts as 427–9; puts as insurance 427–9; short a European call option on the underlying 348, 355–7; economic characteristics 357; short a European put option on the underlying 348, 359–60; economic characteristics 360; short a zero-coupon riskless bond and hold to maturity 348, 362–3; economic characteristic 363; short the underlying 348, 349–51; economic characteristics 351; synthetic equivalents on basic (naked) strategies 416–18; synthetic strategies, natural strategies and 416

option valuation: binomial option pricing model (BOPM) 445–8; risk-neutral valuation 624–33; direct valuation by risk-averse investor 626–31; manipulations 624–6; for risk-neutral investors 631–3

options and options scenarios 323–6

Options Clearing Corporation (OCC) 328

options markets 323–44; American options 328; anticipation of selling 339; anticipatory buying 339–40; basic American call (put) option pricing model 332–4; buying back stock 339; CBOE (Chicago Board Options Exchange) 324–5, 334; asked price entries 335, 336; bid entries 335, 336; equity option

specifications 343; exchange-traded option contracts 325; last sale entries 335, 336; Merck call options and price quotes 334–7; mini equity option specifications 344; net entries 335, 336; open interest entries 335, 336; volume entries 335, 336; concept checks: individual equity options, product specifications for 326; solution to 342; mini equity options, product specifications for 326; solution to 342; MRK OV-E price quote 337; option positions 331; option sales 332; solution to 342; option's rights 331; payoff diagram construction 338; put option positions 332; context in study of 326–7; decision-making, option concept in 324; delayed exercise premium 331, 337; European options 328; exercise price 328, 336; exercises for learning development of 341–2; exercising options 328; expiration date 336; expiration month code 336; financial engineering techniques 337–8; immediate exercise value 330; implicit short positions 340; importance of options 323–4; In-the-Money calls 337; insurance features, options and 327; intrinsic value 326, 330, 333, 337; key concepts 341; learning options, framework for 326–7; leverage, options and 327; liquidity option 333; long and short positions, identification of 339–40; long positions 339–40; long vs. short positions 339–40; maturity dates 328; moneyness 329; naked (unhedged) positions 327; non-simultaneous price quote problem 334–6; option buyers 328; option market premiums 328; option sellers 328; options and options scenarios 323–6; Options Clearing Corporation (OCC) 328; options embedded in ordinary securities 324; options in corporate finance 324; payoff and profit diagrams 326, 338; plain vanilla put and call options, definitions and terminology for 327–32; put and call

options 323–5, 327, 328, 329, 338; puts and calls, infrastructure for understanding about 337–8; reading option price quotes 334–7; real asset options 324; short positions 339–40; short sales, covering of 339; speculation on option prices 327; standard equity option 336; standard stock option 334; strategic, option-like scenarios 324; strike price 328; strike price code 336; time premium 326, 330–1, 333, 337; underlying assets or scenarios 327, 334; identification of long and short positions in 339–40; *see also* binomial option pricing model (BOPM); equivalent martingale measures (EMMs); model-based option pricing (MBOP) in real time; rational option pricing (ROP)
order execution 125–6; futures contract definition and 126
order submission 125–6
orders, types of 127–34
Out-of-the-Money covered call writes 424–6
over the counter (OTC): markets 12–13, 14, 17
over-the-counter (OTC): bilateral agreements 278
overall profits (and losses) 144, 150, 151, 153, 156, 157
overnight averages 11

par swap rate 294, 301
parameterization 454, 477–8, 502
partial equilibrium (PE) 453; models of, risk-neutral valuation and 614
participants in futures market 122–5
path structures: in binomial process 440–2, 442–4; multi-period BOPM model (N=3) 497; thinking of BOPM in terms of paths 493–9
paying fixed 293, in interest rate derivatives (IRDs) 278–9; and receiving floating in commodity forward contracts 276
payoff and profit: diagrams of 326, 338; difference between 66
payoff position with forward contracts 37
payoff to long forward position in IBM 40

payoff to short forward position in IBM 43
payoffs per share: to naked long forward contract 68–9; to naked long spot position 67, 68–9
perfect negative correlation 166
perfect positive correlation 609–11
performance bonds (margins) 144–5, 148
physical probability: measure of, martingale hypothesis for 530; risk-neutralization of 604
pit trading, order flow process and 136–9
plain vanilla interest-rate swaps 274; dealer intermediated swaps 284–93; non-dealer intermediated swaps 281–4
plain vanilla put and call options, definitions and terminology for 327–32
portfolio price dynamics, replication of 457
portfolio theory, hedging as 165–8
portfolio variance, calculation of 179–81
position accountability 214, 215, 228, 229
preference-free risk-neutral valuation 598, 600
present and future spot prices 20–3
present value (PV): valuation of forward contracts (assets with dividend yield) 94; valuation of forward contracts (assets without dividend yield) 69, 75
price contingent claims with unhedgeable risks 599–601
price paths: ending at specific terminal price, numbers of 442–4; numbers of 440–2
price quotes: in forward markets 9–11; in futures markets 17–19; in spot markets 6–7
pricing a swap 294
pricing by arbitrage and FTAP$_2$ 597–8
pricing currency forwards 105
pricing European options under shifted arithmetic Brownian motion (ABM) with no drift 542–51; Bachelier option pricing formula, derivation of 547–51; fundamental theorems of asset pricing (FTAP) 542–3; transition density functions 543–7

INDEX

pricing foreign exchange forward contracts using no-arbitrage 106–7

pricing mechanism, risk-neutral valuation and 596

pricing options: at expiration (BOPM) 445–6; at time t=0 (BOPM) 446–8; tools for (MBOP) 448–53; relationships between tools 450–3

pricing states 509

pricing zero-coupon, unit discount bonds in continuous time 69–73

primitive Arrow-Debreu (AD) securities, option pricing and 508–14; concept check, pricing $AD_u(\omega)$ and $AD_d(\omega)$ 514; exercise 1, pricing B(0,1) 510; exercise 2, pricing $AD_u(\omega)$ and $AD_d(\omega)$ 511–14

probability density function 544

profit diagrams 346–7

protection, market orders with 127–9

protective put hedging strategy 427–30; economic interpretation of 429–30; insurance, puts as 427–9

put and call options 323–5, 327, 328, 329, 338; infrastructure for understanding about 337–8

puts as insurance 427–9

quality spreads 299

random variables 536

random walk model of prices 530–1

randomness, state of nature and 23

rate of return of risky asset over small time interval, components of 555–6

rational option pricing (ROP) 369–414; adjusted intrinsic value (AIV) for a European call, definition of 375–6; adjusted time premium (ATP) 397; basic European option pricing model, interpretation of 397–8; certainty equivalent (CE) cash flow 397; concept checks: adjusted intrinsic value (AIV) for calls, calculation of 413; solution to 413; adjusted intrinsic value (AIV) for puts, calculation of 381; solution to 413; directional trades and relative trades, difference between 372; dominance

principle and value of European call option 376; solution to 413; exercise price of options, working with 391; forward contracts, overpaying on 403; generalized forward contracts, current value on 404; rational option pricing (ROP) or model-based option pricing (MBOP) 407; short stock position, risk management of 399; solution to 413–14; working from strategies to current costs and back 393; solution to 413; continuation region 385; convexity of option price 406; current costs and related strategies, technique of going back and forth between 393; directional trades 371–2; dominance principle 372, 373; implications of 374–88; equilibrium forward price 402; European Put-Call Parity, financial innovation with 401–5; European Put-Call Parity, implications of 394–400; American option pricing model, analogue for European options 396–8; European call option 394–6; European option pricing model, interpretation of 397–8; European put option 398–9; synthesis of forward contracts from puts and calls 399–400; exercises for learning development of 409–12; financial innovation using European Put-Call Parity 401–5; American Put-Call Parity (no dividends) 403–5; generalized forward contracts 401–3; full replication of European call option (embedded insurance contract) 391–2; generalized forward price 402; key concepts 408–9; LBAC (lower bound for American call option on underlying, no dividends) 374–5; LBACD (lower bound for American call option on underlying, continuous dividends) 383–5; call on underlier with continuous, proportional dividends over life of option 384–5; call on underlier with no dividends over life of option 384; LBAP (lower bound for American put option on underlying, no dividends) 378–80; intrinsic value lower bound for American put, example of 379–80; LBAPD (lower bound for American put option on underlying, continuous dividends) 387–8; LBEC (lower bound for European call option on underlying, no dividends) 375–8; implications of 377–8; LBECD (lower bound for European call option on underlying, continuous dividends) 382–3; LBEP (lower bound for European put option on underlying, no dividends) 380–1; adjusted intrinsic value (AIV) for European put, definition of 380–1; LBEPD (lower bound for European put option on underlying, continuous dividends) 386–7; model-based option pricing (MBOP) 371, 398; model-independent *vs.* model-based option pricing 370–1; model risk 372; No-Arbitrage in Equilibrium (NAIE) 372, 405–6; partial replication of European call option (embedded forward contract) 388–91; postscript on 405–7; relative pricing trades *vs.* directional trades 371–2; risk-free arbitrage 373; static replication, principle of 393–4; static replication and European Put-Call Parity (no dividends) 388–94; current costs and related strategies, technique of going back and forth between 393; fully replicating European call option (embedded insurance contract) 391–2; partially replicating European call option (embedded forward contract) 388–91; working backwards from payoffs to costs to derive European Put-Call Parity 393–4; sub-replication 404; super-replication 404; working backwards from payoffs to costs to derive European Put-Call Parity 393–4

raw price change, present value of 243
reading option price quotes 334–7
real asset options 324
realization of daily value 149

realized daily cash flows, creation of 243
receiving floating 293
receiving variable in interest rate derivatives (IRDs) 279–80
recontracting future positions 149, 151
Registered Commodity Representatives (RCRs) 122–3
relative pricing 65–6
relative pricing trades *vs.* directional trades 371–2
relative risks of hedge portfolio's return, analysis of 618–24; risk-averse investor in hedge portfolio, role of risk premia for 620–4; risk neutrality in hedge portfolio, initial look at 618–20
replicability: option pricing in continuous time 588; risk-neutral valuation 597–8, 600, 601, 603, 605, 606, 614, 615, 631, 633
replicating portfolio, construction of 478–84; concept check, interpretation of hedge ratio 482; down state, replication in 481; hedge ratio, interpretation of 482–3; replication over period 2 (under scenario 1) 479–82; replication under scenario 2 (over period 2) 484; scenarios 478–9; solving equations for ? and B 481; solving for dollar position in bonds under scenario 1 (over period 2) 483; up state, replication in 480
replication: model-based option pricing (MBOP): dynamic and static 450; hedging and 453; replicability and 449; no-arbitrage and (BOPM) 464; partial replication of European call option (embedded forward contract) 388–91; super-replication 404; valuation of forward contracts (assets without dividend yield) 77, 80; *see also* replicability; static replication
reset date 293
resetting floating rates 293
reverse hedge 618, 620, 621
'reversing' of trades 15–16
risk-adjusted discount rate (RADR) 447; valuation of forward contracts (assets with dividend yield) 94; valuation of

forward contracts (assets without dividend yield) 75

risk associated with long call options, neutralization of 598–9

risk aversion: hedging with forward contracts 37; risk-averse investment 522

risk cancellation condition 623

risk-free arbitrage 100, 373

risk management strategies using currency futures 217–24

risk management using stock index futures 231–45; cross-hedging 243–5; monetizing S&P 500 Spot Index 231–4; naive hedge ratio, adjustment for risk-minimizing hedge ratio 239–41; non S&P 500 portfolios, adjustment of hedge for 243–5; pricing and hedging preliminaries 231; profits from traditional hedge 235–6; risk, return analysis of traditional hedge 236–8; risk-minimizing hedge using forward *vs.* futures contracts 241–3; risk-minimizing hedging 238–9

risk-neutral investment 521–2, 523

risk-neutral transition density function (RNTDF) 543–4, 547, 569, 570, 571; for ABM process to which GBM is reducible 569, 570; of GBM 571

risk-neutral valuation 595–635; Black-Scholes' contribution 598, 601; BOPM, exogenous variables and 615; certainty equivalent (CE) 603, 604; complete risk-expected return analysis of riskless hedge (BOPM, N=1) 607–18; direct calculation of λ_c 612–15; direct calculation of λ_s 611–12; expected return of hedge portfolio 616–18; hedge portfolio, percentage returns for 616–18; perfect positive correlation, statistics result of 609–11; volatility of hedge portfolio 608–11; with consensus 599; consensus and (with and without) 598–9; consumption capital asset pricing model (CCAPM) 605; convenience, risk-neutral valuation by 631–2; endogenous variables 614–15; equivalent martingale measures (EMMs) 596–7; construction

of 601–3; exercises for learning development of 634–5; exogenous variables 614–615; formal risk-neutral probabilities, interpretation of 603–5; formal valuation without replication 601–5; fundamental theorem of asset pricing (FTAP$_2$), another version of 606; fundamental theorems of asset pricing (FTAP$_1$ and FTAP$_2$) 596–7, 601–2, 605, 606, 624, 631; general equilibrium (GE) models 615; Girsanov's theorem 605; independent securities and risks 600; key concepts 634; law of one price (LOP) 597; marginal rate of substitution (MRS) 604, 605; market completeness 598; market price of risk (MPR) 624; equivalent martingale measures (EMMs) and 605–6; mathematical modeling 596–7; no-arbitrage assumption 596–7, 598, 602, 604, 605, 606, 608; non-hedgeable risks 599–601; non-replicability 599–601, 603, 604, 605, 606; non-replicable contingent claims, extra risks of 600; option valuation 624–33; direct valuation by risk-averse investor 626–31; manipulations 624–6; for risk-neutral investors 631–3; partial equilibrium (PE) models 614; perfect positive correlation 609–11; physical probability, risk-neutralization of 604; preference-free risk-neutral valuation 598, 600; price contingent claims with unhedgeable risks 599–601; pricing by arbitrage and FTAP$_2$ 597–8; pricing mechanism 596; relative risks of hedge portfolio's return, analysis of 618–24; risk-averse investor in hedge portfolio, role of risk premia for 620–4; risk neutrality in hedge portfolio, initial look at 618–20; replicability 597–8, 598, 600, 601, 603, 605, 606, 614, 615, 631, 633; reverse hedge 618, 620, 621; risk associated with long call options, neutralization of 598–9; risk cancellation condition 623; risk-neutral valuation relationship (BOPM): derivation as 467–8; interpretation of 468; risk premia

598, 603, 616, 621–2, 627, 629; risk premia, diversifiable risks and 599; risk premia cancellation condition 623–4, 628; riskless hedge 607, 616, 620, 628, 632; senses of 596; Sharpe ratio 624; equivalent martingale measures (EMMs) and 605–6; terminological navigation 596–7; unique pricing of a contingent claim 597–8; volatility risk 600; without consensus 599–601

risk premia: diversifiable risks and 599; option pricing in continuous time 554, 558, 561, 567, 588; risk-neutral valuation 598, 603, 616, 621–2, 627, 629; risk premia cancellation condition 623–4, 628; in stock prices, equivalent martingale measures (EMMs) and 532–3

risk reduction: with (λ-for-one) hedging 183–5; with traditional hedging 179–82; informational effect 181–2; OLS regression 181–2; portfolio variance calculation 179–81

riskless bonds 509

riskless hedge 607, 616, 620, 628, 632

rolling hedge strategy: efficient market hypothesis (EMH) 223; interpretations of profits from rolling hedge 221–3; Metallgesellschaft example 223; numerical example of 223–4

rule book chapters 228

rule of thumb 449

scenarios, hedging with forward contracts: adding profit tables to determine profits from fully hedges position 52–4; hedging with forward contracts 44–5; long position contracts 38–9; short position contracts 42

segregated consumer funds 123–5

seller's options 17

selling forward contracts 40–1, 47–8

selling hedges 168

selling short 293

settlement prices: hedging with forward contracts 35; market organization for futures contracts 145–6, 151

settlement procedure 214, 228, 229, 258–9

settlement variation 146

Sharpe ratio: equivalent martingale measures (EMMs) and 526, 605–6; risk-neutral valuation and 624

shifted arithmetic Brownian motion (ABM) model of prices 541–2; reduced process 570

short a European call option on the underlying 348, 355–7; economic characteristics 357

short a European put option on the underlying 348, 359–60; economic characteristics 360

short a zero-coupon riskless bond and hold to maturity 348, 362–3; economic characteristic 363

short forward position, payoff to 39–43

short hedge 168

short positions: assumption of 147–8; forward market contracting 7; options markets 339–40

short sales, covering of 339

short the underlying 348, 349–51; economic characteristics 351

single period swaps, commodity forward contracts as 275–6

SouthWest Airlines 12–13

S&P 500 Fact Sheet 226

S&P 500 Futures 228

S&P 500 Index 88

speculation on option prices 327

spot, forward, and futures contracting 3–32; commodities, ways to buy and sell 5; concept checks: drawing conclusions from spot price charts 22–3; solution to 32; foreign currencies, forward prices on 25; foreign currencies, futures prices on 26; solution to 32; past as guide to future price behavior 21; exercises for learning development 27–9; finite-lived instruments 20; foreign currencies: forward prices on 24–5; futures prices on 25–6; foreign exchange risk 3–5; forward market contracting 7–13; futures market contracting 13–19; Gold pricing on London Bullion Market 20–3; key concepts 27; mapping out prices 20–6; multi-grade spot commodities, determination of standards for pricing 23; over the counter (OTC) markets 12–13, 14, 17; randomness, state of nature and 23; spot market contracting 5–7; time lines 20, 23

spot commodities, S&P 500 futures contracts as 233–4

spot Eurodollar market 245–54; Eurodollar time deposits, creation of 252–4; spot 3-month Eurodollar time deposits 246–8; spot trading terminology 248–50

spot market contracting: cash and carry transactions 5; concept checks: exploration of spot rates in long-term mortgage market 11; solution to 29; present and future spot prices 21; solution to 32; price quotes in spot markets 6–7; solution to 29; present and future spot prices 20–3; price quotes in spot markets 6–7; spot, forward, and futures contracting 5–7; spot agreements (and terms of) 5–6; spot (cash), features of 5; spot market 6; spot mortgage market 11; spot price 6; spot transactions 6

spot prices, forward contracts and 34–5

spread basis, definition of 200–1

spreads as speculative investment 199–203

standard equity option 336

standard stock option 334

standardization, forward markets and 14

state-contingent financial securities 508

static replication: European Put-Call Parity (no dividends) and 388–94; current costs and related strategies, technique of going back and forth between 393; fully replicating European call option (embedded insurance contract) 391–2; partially replicating European call option (embedded forward contract) 388–91; working backwards from payoffs to costs to derive European Put-Call Parity 393–4; principle of 393–4

Stigum's Money Market (Stigum, M.) 252

stochastic differential equations (SDEs) 553, 559, 562–3, 564, 566, 567–8, 570, 571, 583

stochastic integral equations (SIEs) 559, 560, 561, 564, 565–6, 567

stochastic processes 540–1, 543, 562, 587, 588

stock forwards when stock pays dividends 88–90

stock index futures 225–30; commentary 230; futures contracts, introduction of 167; S&P 500 futures quotes, quote mechanism for 230; S&P 500 Spot Index 225–7; effective payoff on monetization of 233; monetization of 231–4; S&P 500 Stock Index Futures Contract Specifications 227–9

stock price evolution (BOPM): for binomial process (N=2) 440; for N-period binomial process, summary of 444–5, 499; number of price paths 441; number of price paths ending at specific prices 443

stock price tree 488

stock prices: affect of capital gains on 98–9; affect of dividend payments on 94–8; martingales and 521–6

stock returns, modeling with and without dividends 109–15

storage and price (cost) of 195–7

strategic, option-like scenarios 324

strike price 328

strike price code 336

strip cash flows, generation of 277

strips of forward contracts 277–8

sub-replication 404

sub (super) martingale, definition of 524

subsequent inventory sale price, locking in of 195

super-replication 404

swap cash flows: decomposition into implicit bonds 303; graphical representation of 318

swap spread 294

swapping fixed for floating payments 276

swaps as strips of forward contracts 274–8

swaps pricing 301–14; example of 301–3; fixed-rate bond, valuation of 303–5; floating-rate bond, valuation of 305–8; implied forward rates (IFRs) 309–11; par swap rate 301; interpretations of 311–14; swap at initiation, valuation of 308–9

synthesis of negative correlation, hedging as 165–7

synthetic equivalents on basic (naked) strategies 416–18

synthetic fixed-rate bonds 291–2

synthetic fixed-rate financing 290

synthetic risk, diversifying away of 167

synthetic strategies, natural strategies and 416

synthetic treasury bill vs. actual bill 165

systematic, market risk after diversification, protection against 168

tailing the hedge 241–2

tenor of swap 293

terminological navigation 596–7; interest-rate swaps 278–81, 293–4

tick size 228, 229

ticker symbol 214, 215, 228, 229, 261

time in discrete time framework, modeling of 437–8

time lines 20, 23

time premia 326, 330–1, 333, 337

total stock process with dividends (before dividends are paid) 110

total stock return process 98–9

tower property (TP) 533–4

tracking equity in investor's accounts 151–3

trade date 293

trading futures contracts, questions on organizational structures for 141

trading hours 214, 228

traditional; hedge, risk and return analysis on 236–8; basis risk 238, holding period rate 237; intermediate execution, basis risk and 237–8; liquidity advantage in execution 237

transfer of obligations 16

transition density function for shifted arithmetic Brownian motion 545–6

transportation across time, storage as 195

treasury bill synthesis 166–7

trinomial model (three stock outcomes) 464

turning points 22

unallocated foreign exchange (FX) reserves 248

uncertainty (volatility): naked (unhedged) positions and 45; see also volatility (uncertainty) 45

uncorrelated martingale increments (UCMI) 531, 535–6

underlying assets or scenarios 327, 334; identification of long and short positions in 339–40

underlying stock price uncertainty, modeling of 438–40

unique pricing of a contingent claim 597–8

valuation of floating-rate bonds prior to maturity 306–7

valuation of forward contracts (assets with dividend yield) 87–119; annualized dividend yields 88; arbitrage definitions 100–2; Black-Scholes option pricing model 88; capital gains, affect on stock prices 98–9; capital gains process 98–9, 111; concept checks: arbitrage opportunities, working with 101–2; solution 118–19; calculation of total stock price return minus dividend yield 99; solution 118; direct and indirect costs 89; solution 117–18; modeling continuous dividend yields for stocks 94; modeling continuous dividend yields for stocks: solution 118; modeling zero-coupon bond yields 92; pricing currencies forwards 105; solution 119; pricing foreign exchange contracts 106; stock price, effect of dividend payments on 97; continuous dividends from stocks, modeling yields from 93–4; continuous yields, modeling of 90–4; contract life, payments over 88; convenience yield 89; cost of carry 89; currency spot and currency forwards 103–9; dividend payments, affect on stock prices 94–8; dividend payout process 97; connection between capital gains process and 111–13; domestic economy (DE) 103–4, 105; exchange rates, New York closing snapshot (April 7, 2014) 104; exercises for learning development of 116–17; foreign economy (FE) 103–4; foreign exchange (FX) forward contracts: example of pricing 107–9; pricing using no-arbitrage 106–7; foreign exchange (FX) markets, price quotes in 103–5; forward contracts on dividend-paying stocks, pricing with no-arbitrage 100–3; forward contracts on stocks with dividend yield, pricing with net interest model 99–100; forward pricing using no-arbitrage 102–3; infinitesimal intervals 93; instantaneous yields 90–2, 93–4; key concepts 116; Log Bond equation 96; net interest model 99–100; non-stochastic differential equations 90–4; present value (PV) 94; pricing currency forwards 105; pricing foreign exchange forward contracts using no-arbitrage 106–7; risk-adjusted discount rate (RADR) 94; S&P 500 Index 88; stock forwards when stock pays dividends 88–90; stock prices: affect of capital gains on 98–9; affect of dividend payments on 94–8; stock returns, modeling with and without dividends 109–15; total stock process with dividends (before dividends are paid) 110; total stock return process 98–9; zero-coupon bonds, modeling yields from 90–2

valuation of forward contracts (assets without dividend yield) 65–86; arbitrage opportunities 75; commitment to buy 67; concept checks: annualized, continuously compounded 3%, worth after 2 months? 71; annualized, continuously compounded 6%, worth after 12 months? 71; solution to 85; annualized, continuously compounded

10%, worth after 3 months? 71; calculation of equilibrium forward prices 78; solution 86; pricing zero-coupon bond with face value equal to current forward price of underlying commodity 73; solution to 86; pricing zero-coupon bonds 72; solution to 86; settling a forward commitment 72; zero-coupon bond, pricing on basis of forward contract at compounded risk-free rate 73; continuous compounding and discounting 69–71; current costs: of generating alternative payoffs 78; payoffs and 66; deferred spot transactions 78–9; derivative prices, underlying securities and 66; embedded leverage 79–80; equilibrium forward prices 78; equivalent annual rate (EAR) 70; exercises for learning development of 83–5; forward contracts: default on 76; interpretation via synthetic contracts 78–82; leverage and 80–2; no up-front payments on 75; payment on maturity, expectation of 81; price *vs.* value for 73; valuing at expiration 74–5; valuing at initiation 75–8; future value (FV) 69–70; key concepts 83; law of one price 77; long spot and long forward positions, difference between payoffs to 76–7; naked long spot and forward positions, comparison of payoffs from 66–9; no-arbitrage principle 77; payoff and profit, difference between 66; payoffs per share: to naked long spot and naked long forward positions 68–9; to naked long spot position 67; payoffs (=profits) per share to naked long forward contract 68; potential values, negativity and positivity in 75–6; present value (PV) 69, 75; pricing zero-coupon, unit discount bonds in continuous time 69–73; profits per share to naked long spot position 67; relative pricing 65–6; replication 77, 80; risk-adjusted discount rate (RADR) 75; values, realization and reconciliation of 73; zero-coupon bonds 77, 78, 79–80, 81, 82; pricing of 71–3 values: adjusted intrinsic value (AIV) 381, 396–7, 406; for European call, definition of 375–6; currency swaps, notional value of 274; decision-making process, protection of potential value in 36–7; forward price change, present value of 242; future value (FV) 69–70, 382, 386, 390, 395; immediate exercise value 330; intrinsic value in options markets 326, 330, 333, 337; potential values, negativity and positivity in 75–6; raw price change, present value of 243; realization and reconciliation of 73; realization of daily value 149; valuation of (assets without dividend yield), price *vs.* value for 73; value contributions for multi-period BOPM model (N=3) 498

volatility (uncertainty): clustering (persistence), volatility and 585; deterministic volatility model 586–7; economic reasons for inconsistency of 586; empirical features of 585; futures market contracting 22; Heston volatility model 587–8; historical volatility estimator method 583–4; implied volatility estimator method 585; risk in risk-neutral valuation of 600; stochastic volatility (SVOL) models 586–7; volatility estimation in Black-Scholes model 583–5; *see also* non-constant volatility models

Wall Street Journal 6, 165, 334
wealth change, fair game expectation 520
wheat price uncertainties, dealing with 33–7
Wiener measure (and process) 540–1
working backwards (from payoffs to costs), European Put-Call Parity and 393–4

zero-coupon bonds: modeling yields from 90–2; valuation of forward contracts (assets without dividend yield) 77, 78, 79–80, 81, 82; pricing of 71–3
zero sum game, swaps as? 298–9

Taylor & Francis eBooks

Helping you to choose the right eBooks for your Library

Add Routledge titles to your library's digital collection today. Taylor and Francis ebooks contains over 50,000 titles in the Humanities, Social Sciences, Behavioural Sciences, Built Environment and Law.

Choose from a range of subject packages or create your own!

Benefits for you
- Free MARC records
- COUNTER-compliant usage statistics
- Flexible purchase and pricing options
- All titles DRM-free.

Benefits for your user
- Off-site, anytime access via Athens or referring URL
- Print or copy pages or chapters
- Full content search
- Bookmark, highlight and annotate text
- Access to thousands of pages of quality research at the click of a button.

REQUEST YOUR FREE INSTITUTIONAL TRIAL TODAY

Free Trials Available
We offer free trials to qualifying academic, corporate and government customers.

eCollections – Choose from over 30 subject eCollections, including:

Archaeology	Language Learning
Architecture	Law
Asian Studies	Literature
Business & Management	Media & Communication
Classical Studies	Middle East Studies
Construction	Music
Creative & Media Arts	Philosophy
Criminology & Criminal Justice	Planning
Economics	Politics
Education	Psychology & Mental Health
Energy	Religion
Engineering	Security
English Language & Linguistics	Social Work
Environment & Sustainability	Sociology
Geography	Sport
Health Studies	Theatre & Performance
History	Tourism, Hospitality & Events

For more information, pricing enquiries or to order a free trial, please contact your local sales team:
www.tandfebooks.com/page/sales

 Routledge
Taylor & Francis Group

The home of Routledge books

www.tandfebooks.com